PART THREE
The Multimodal Writer

PART FOUR
The Writer as Researcher

Appendixes

"How to Read" sections guide
you through the process of
reading critically.

Writing assignments include
expanded instruction and at least
one new multimodal project.

Why Do You Need This New Edition?

If you're wondering why you should buy this new edition of *Writing*, here are 8 good reasons!

Learning to write well is the most important skill you will learn in college, no matter what your major.

1. Do you need some help finding good topics for your papers and projects? In Part 2, you'll find 25 **new readings on engaging, current topics** intended to spark ideas for your own writing, such as how gossip is good for you, Twitter, and the values of eating local food. Also, **new "Exploring Ideas and Issues" questions** to accompany each reading are designed to help you connect the ideas in the readings to the outside world and generate ideas for your writing projects.

2. Could you use help with navigating the challenging readings you encounter in college? Successful writers are also smart, effective readers. So, every chapter in Part 2 now features a **two-page "How to Read" guide** that will help you be a more critical, effective reader.

3. Would you benefit from seeing examples of students working through all the messy, creative steps of the writing process? New **student "Writer at Work" sections** in Part 1 highlight one student's work as she moves from planning to drafting to revising. Also, in each Part 2 chapter, you will find student Writers at Work showing every stage of their work, from understanding the assignment to producing the final paper.

4. Do you learn from reading student model papers? This edition has **more student writing samples than ever**, including a new literary analysis paper, a new annotated bibliography, and three all-new argument papers.

5. Would you like to link easily to videos and animations that support the content you are studying? A dynamic, online version of *Writing: A Guide for College and Beyond* is available in MyCompLab.com and gives you an enhanced, interactive learning experience. By using the eText and MyCompLab, you will have access to multimedia tutorials, an integrated writing space, online tutoring, and exercises for writing, grammar, and research to help you complete your writing assignments.

6. Are you encouraged to do more thorough revision of your college papers? A **new Chapter 5** focuses exclusively on the process of revision, offering ideas for evaluating your own and others' drafts, a handy checklist of questions to ask when revising any paper, and also advice for understanding an instructor's comments on your work.

7. Would it be helpful to have a clear and simple overview of the key steps to follow when writing a research project? See the **new research process map** that appears at the very beginning of Part 4.

8. Are you taking online courses? Are you being asked to develop visual and multimedia texts in your courses? You will find help with both of these topics. First, a new Chapter 17 on **writing for online** courses provides helpful guidance for your online courses. Second, the "Projects" at the end the Part 2 chapters feature at least one **new multimodal assignment**, giving you opportunities to try your hand at creating a Web site or an audio podcast.

PEARSON

WRITING

A Guide for College and Beyond

BRIEF THIRD EDITION

WRITING

A Guide for College and Beyond
BRIEF THIRD EDITION

LESTER FAIGLEY
University of Texas at Austin

PEARSON

Boston   Columbus   Indianapolis   New York   San Francisco   Upper Saddle River   Amsterdam
Cape Town   Dubai   London   Madrid   Milan   Munich   Paris   Montréal   Toronto   Delhi   Mexico City
São Paulo   Sydney   Hong Kong   Seoul   Singapore   Taipei   Tokyo

Senior Acquisitions Editor: Lauren A Finn
Senior Development Editor: Katharine Glynn
Senior Marketing Manager: Sandra McGuire
Senior Supplements Editor: Donna Campion
Senior Media Producer: Stefanie Liebman
Digital Project Manager: Janell Lantana
Production Manager: Bob Ginsberg
Project Coordination: PreMediaGlobal USA Inc.
Cover Design Manager: Wendy Ann Fredericks
Cover Photos: (lower left) © F1 Online/
    SuperStock; (lower right) © StockbrokerXtra/
    Alamy; all other photos: © Lester Faigley
Senior Manufacturing Buyer: Dennis J. Para
Printer/Binder: Quad Graphics/Taunton
Cover Printer: Lehigh-Phoenix Color

Dorling Kindersley Education
Text design and page layout by
    Stuart Jackman
Design: Ann Cannings
Cover design by Stuart Jackman

Credits and acknowledgments borrowed from other sources and reproduced, with permission, in this textbook appear on the appropriate page within text [or on pages 665–666].

Library of Congress Cataloging-in-Publication Data
Faigley, Lester, (date)
  Writing: a guide for college and beyond/Lester Faigley.—3rd ed.
      p. cm.
  Includes bibliographical references and index.
  ISBN 978-0-205-22331-2 (full book: alk. paper)—ISBN 978-0-205-22329-9 (brief book: alk. paper)
  1. English language—Rhetoric. 2. English language—Grammar. 3. Academic writing. 4. Critical thinking.
I. Title.
  PE1408.F255 2012
  808'.042—dc23

                        2011038684

Copyright © 2012, 2010, 2007 by Pearson Education, Inc.

All rights reserved. Manufactured in the United States of America. This publication is protected by Copyright, and permission should be obtained from the publisher prior to any prohibited reproduction, storage in a retrieval system, or transmission in any form or by any means, electronic, mechanical, photocopying, recording, or likewise. To obtain permission(s) to use material from this work, please submit a written request to Pearson Education, Inc., Permissions Department, One Lake Street, Upper Saddle River, New Jersey 07458, or you may fax your request to 201-236-3290.

10 9 8 7 6 5 4 3 2 1—QGT—14 13 12 11

Student Edition
ISBN-10: 0-205-22329-X
ISBN-13: 978-0-205-22329-9

A la carte edition
ISBN-10: 0-205-85137-1
ISBN-13: 978-0-205-85137-9

PART 1
The Writer as Explorer

PART 2
The Writer as Guide

Writing to Reflect

Writing to Inform

Writing to Analyze

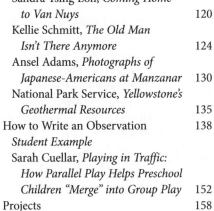

Writing Arguments

12. Position Arguments

13 Proposal Arguments

PART 3
The Multimodal Writer

15 Designing Documents

16 Delivering Presentations

17 Writing for Online Courses

18 Working as a Team

PART 4
The Writer as Researcher

22 Exploring in the Field

23 Writing the Research Project

24 MLA Documentation

25 APA Documentation

Appendixes

Preface

The title of this book, *Writing: A Guide for College and Beyond,* emphasizes the often-overlooked fact that writing courses make students better writers not just for other college courses, but for writing situations throughout their lives. Students who learn to negotiate particular subject matters, audiences, purposes, and genres in particular contexts go on to achieve success in their educational, professional, and public lives.

I am pleased and grateful for the enthusiastic response of many instructors and students to the previous editions of *Writing: A Guide for College and Beyond.* When writing the first edition of this book, I started with the question: How do students learn best? That question continues to guide my work on this third edition, and I have developed this edition with the following principles in mind:

Students learn best when a guide to writing is easy to use and well designed	No matter where you open the book, the content on a particular page and the place of that content in the overall organization should be evident. Textbooks don't have to be dull.
Students learn best when a guide to writing shows what readers and writers actually do	Students learn best from examples of what readers and writers do not by reading only discussions of what they do.
Students learn best when they can see examples of what works and what doesn't work	Putting effective and ineffective examples side-by-side allows students to see strategies to employ and pitfalls to avoid.

The third edition also supports the broad goals for a first-year college writing course are those identified in the Outcomes Statement from the Council of Writing Program Administrators.

1. Rhetorical knowledge	Students should respond to different situations and the needs of different audiences, understand how genres shape reading and writing, and write in several genres.
2. Critical thinking, reading, and writing	Students should find, evaluate, analyze, and synthesize sources and integrate their ideas with those of others.
3. Processes	Students should develop flexible strategies for generating, revising, editing, and proofreading, and should understand how to collaborate effectively with others.
4. Knowledge of conventions	Students should learn the common formats for different kinds of texts, practice appropriate documentation, and control surface features of grammar, mechanics, and spelling.
5. Composing in electronic environments	Students should use electronic environments for drafting, reviewing, revising, editing, and sharing texts as well as to locate, evaluate, organize, and use research material collected from electronic sources.

What's new in this edition of
Writing: A Guide for College and Beyond

More help with the fundamentals of the writing process

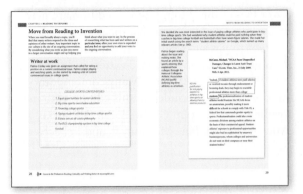

Part 1 now offers more detailed instruction on the planning, drafting, and revising stages of the writing process, including a new stand-alone chapter on revision (Chapter 5), and new discussion of how to move from reading to writing in Chapter 2. Also, a new student "Writer at Work" example extends through the chapters in Part 1, following a student through the writing process, from planning to revising.

New and expanded guides for reading

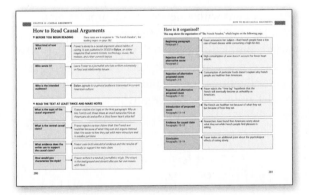

Chapters in Part 2 feature expanded, two-page "How to Read" guides that give a list of thoughtful questions students can ask before and during reading, and also walk students through the process of mapping the organization of a text as one important part of the reading process. These guides use the first reading in each chapter as their example.

New examples of student work

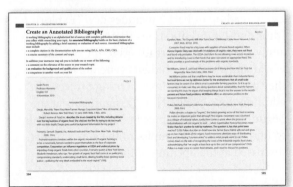

This edition features many new examples of student work, such as the new student literary analysis in Chapter 9, a new annotated bibliography in Chapter 21, and entirely new "Writer at Work" sections in the Causal Arguments, Evaluation Arguments, and Position Arguments chapters (Chapters 10, 11, and 12).

What's new in this edition of
Writing: A Guide for College and Beyond

New engaging readings

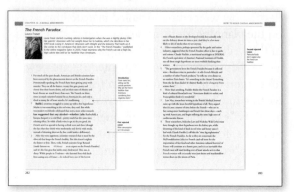

Over half of the readings in this edition are new, including new selections that focus on engaging, current topics such as the immigration experience, how gossip is good for you, Twitter, and the values of eating local food. Many contemporary authors are also included in this edition with new readings by Malcolm Gladwell, P.J. O'Rourke, Michael Pollan, Jane McGonigal, and Rebecca Solnit.

Updated instruction on research

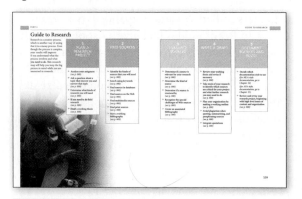

Part 4 opens with a new research process map that lays out for students the key steps to follow when completing a research project. This Part also features new separate chapters on finding sources and evaluating sources, and it includes a new model annotated bibliography in Chapter 21.

More ideas for writing

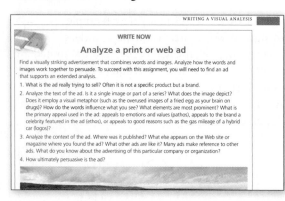

Every reading in Part 2 includes new "Exploring Ideas and Issues" questions that help students apply the ideas in the readings to the outside world and also help students generate ideas that they can use for their main writing projects. In addition, new "Write Now" assignments at the beginning of each chapter in Part 2 ask students to find real world examples of the aim or genres discussed at the opening of the chapter.

Expanded and new major "Project" assignments

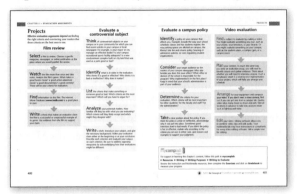

The Projects at the end of each chapter in Part 2 feature at least one new multimodal assignment per chapter, and also expanded instruction on all other assignments. For example, in Chapter 8, one of the new assignments asks students to create an audio podcast, and in Chapter 10, a new project asks students to create a Web site.

New multimodal and online coverage

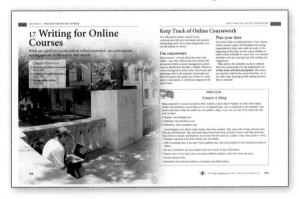

Chapters on design, collaboration, and oral presentations have been moved to a new Part Three, "The Multimodal Writer," integrating these topics with a new Chapter 17 on writing for online courses that offers advice on using courseware, participating in online discussions, and keeping track of online coursework.

What's new in this edition of
Writing: A Guide for College and Beyond

New Media Enhancements

The dynamic, online version of *Writing: A Guide for College and Beyond* links students to videos, animations, interactive documents, podcasts, and activities in MyCompLab to create a rich, interactive learning experience for writing students. These resources support and extend *Writing's* instructional content, help students with different learning styles understand key concepts, and let students access additional help as needed. The icons below indicate throughout the book where additional content can be found, and in the Pearson eText, link directly to the content.

Watch the Animation presents abstract concepts (such as the rhetorical situation or logical fallacies) or processes (such as synthesis or evaluating sources) using visually animated text with audio narrative to extend and expand discussions in the book.

Watch the Video uses student/teacher conferences or student / student collaboration to illustrate processes such as narrowing a topic, revising, or citing sources.

Analyze the Interactive Document provides additional sample texts with annotations or commentary to help students think critically about the decisions writers make. Concepts highlighted include audience, design, use of graphs and charts, and more.

Listen to the Podcast offers brief audio lessons especially useful to students who benefit from reinforcement. Topics include key steps in the writing process as well as help with grammar.

Apply the Concept suggests additional activities and writing prompts that give students the chance to practice content they have learned such as evaluating arguments and document design. .

Study the Topic provides audio commentary from Lester Faigley that gives more guidance on important topics covered in the text including writing a rhetorical analysis and writing a position argument.

Resources for teachers and students

Instructor's Resource Manual

The Instructor's Resource Manual, prepared by Rick Iadonisi of Grand Valley State University, offers detailed chapter-by-chapter suggestions to help both new and experienced instructors. For every chapter in the student text, this manual includes chapter goals and chapter challenges, suggestions for different ways to use the assignments and boxed tips in the chapter, additional activities and resources, and more. It also features an overall discussion of teaching a writing class, including discussion of the Writing Program Administrators Outcomes for first-year composition. Finally, the manual offers suggested syllabi and ideas for teaching students with different learning styles.

MyCompLab

By integrating a writing environment with proven resources for grammar, writing, and research, MyCompLab gives students help at their fingertips as they draft and revise. Teachers can recommend MyCompLab to students for self-study, set up courses to track student progress, and leverage the power of administrative features to be more effective and save time. Assessment tools including text and audio commenting capabilities, diagnostics and study plans, and an e-portfolio. Created after years of research and in partnership with faculty and students, MyCompLab offers a seamless and flexible teaching and learning environment. Visit www.mycomplab.com to learn more.

An Interactive Pearson eText in My CompLab

A dynamic, online version of *Writing: A Guide for College and Beyond* is available in MyCompLab; this eText brings together the many resources of MyCompLab, the content of this successful writing guide, and multimedia tutorials to create an enhanced, interactive learning experience for students.

CourseSmart eTextbook

Writing: A Guide for College and Beyond is also available as a CourseSmart eTextbook at www.coursesmart.com. Students can subscribe to and search the text, make notes online, print out reading assignments and incorporate lecture notes, and bookmark important passages.

Acknowledgments

I am quite fortunate to work with the same team of co-creators in London, New York, New Jersey, Massachusetts, Maine, and Texas that contributed to the success of the first two editions. Executive editor Lynn Huddon and I have collaborated on over thirty previous books and editions, and I much appreciate the vision she has brought to each project along with her talents as an editor and manager. She has well earned her reputation as one of the best in her profession. My development editor, Katharine Glynn, has also brought a wealth of knowledge to the book. Even more appreciated is the calmness she inspires in the often stressful process of publishing a book. Joseph Opiela, editorial director, and Mary Ellen Curley, director of development for English, have also been close to the project and have made many insightful suggestions.

Others at Longman who contributed their wisdom and experience include Roth Wilkofsky, president; Megan Galvin-Fak, director of marketing; Sandra McGuire, senior marketing manager; Lauren Finn, senior acquisitions editor; Donna Campion, senior supplements editor; Wendy Ann Fredericks, cover design manager; Rona Tuccillo, visual researcher; Bob Ginsberg, production manager; and Rebecca Gilpin, assistant editor. At PreMediaGlobal, two other excellent people whom I have enjoyed working with in the past guided the book into print: Lindsay Bethoney, project manager, and copy editor Elsa van Bergen.

The experience of working across the Atlantic with Stuart Jackman, design director of DK Education in London, again has been a great pleasure. Stuart continues to teach me a great deal about using effective design for learning.

I also thank those collaborators who helped with this edition, especially Linda Stern, who assisted in assembling the work of student writers and updating some parts of the grammar and documentation chapters; Kristin Bowen also reviewed student work in this edition. Linda and

Kate Goodfellow helped me develop some of the headnotes and questions that accompany the readings in the book. I cannot say enough about how much I have learned over the years from colleagues and students at the University of Texas, a few of whom are represented by their writing here.

I have benefited enormously from the advice of colleagues across the country who contributed many splendid ideas in reviews. I am especially grateful to these colleagues who reviewed this and previous editions:

Susan Achziger, *Community College of Aurora*

Devon Adams, *Mesa Community College*

Matthew Allen, *Wright College*

Resa Crane Bizzaro, *Indiana University of Pennsylvania*

Joel R. Brouwer, *Montcalm Community College*

Gina Burkart, *University of Northern Iowa*

Dan Butcher, *University of Alabama at Birmingham*

M. L. Byrd, *Virginia State University*

Mechel Camp, *Jackson State Community College*

Chandra Speight Cerutti, *East Carolina University*

Ron Christiansen, *Salt Lake Community College*

Ruth L. Copp, *Saginaw Valley State University*

Virginia Crank, *University of Wisconsin-La Crosse*

Cherie Dargan, *Hawkeye Community College*

Cathy Decker, *Chaffey College*

Navdeep Singh Dhillon, *Hudson County Community College*

Rocco Ditello, *Broward College*

Gary Dop, *North Central University*

Stacey Donohue, *Central Oregon Community College*

Stephanie L. Dowdle, *Salt Lake Community College*

Sarah Duerden, *Arizona State University*

H. M. (Mickey) Gentry, *College of the Mainland*

Annette M. Formella, *Baker College of Clinton Township*

Mary Val Gerstle, *University of Cincinnati*

Angelina Gonzales, *California State University, Northridge*

Maya Greene, *Columbia Greene Community College*

Susan Grimland, *Collin County Community College*

Jacqueline Harris, *Utah State University*

Brigitte Harvey, *Broome Community College*

Judy Hauser, *Des Moines Area Community College*

Mark Heimermann, *Saint Cloud State University*

Richard A. Iadonisi, *Grand Valley State University*

Kristen Isabelle, *Columbia-Greene Community College*

Michael Jackman, *Indiana University Southeast*

Linda S. Jacobs, *Jackson Community College*

Mary Ann Jacobs, *Northern Kentucky University*

John Jones, *West Virginia University*

Kent Kaiser, *University of Minnesota*

Nadene Keene, *Indiana University Kokomo*

Catherine Keohane, *Bergen Community College*

Janet Knepper, *Clarion University*

Sally Lahmon, *Sinclair Community College*

Fran L. Lassiter, *University of the District of Columbia*

Sara Lewis, *Pine Manor College*

Seeta Mangra, *Des Moines Area Community College*

Julia McGregor, *Inver Hills Community College*

Janice McIntire-Strasburg, *Saint Louis University*

Rexann A. McKinley, *Kankakee Community College*

Tim Miank, *Lansing Community College*

Rhonda Morris, *Santa Fe College*

Lynanne Page, *Eastern Illinois University*

Martha J. Payne, *Ball State University*

Eden F. Pearson, *Des Moines Area Community College*

Mack Perry, *Jackson State Community College*

Timothy Ray, *West Chester University of Pennsylvania*

Charlotte Teresa Reynolds, *Indiana University Southeast*

Tammy Robinson, *Los Angeles City College*

Nina Sabolik, *Arizona State University*

Jack Shear, *Binghamton University*

Betty H. Stack, *Rowan Cabarrus Community College*

Karla Farmer Stouse, *Indiana University Kokomo*

Theresa Stowell, *Jackson Community College*

Jane Stubbs, *University of New Orleans*

Diane Tetreault, *Bentley College*

Michelle Trim, *Elon University*

Sherri L.VandenAkker, *Springfield College*

Suzanne Van Wert, *Northern Essex Community College*

Nancy Wallin, *St. Cloud State University*

Leslie Kreiner Wilson, *Pepperdine University*

Carole Yee, *Los Angeles Valley College*

Finally, without my wife Linda's deep reserves of patience in putting up with a husband who becomes distracted and grumpy when he is writing, the book would never have been written.

Part 1

The Writer as Explorer

1 Thinking as a Writer

Learning to write is the most valuable part of your college education.

Chapter Overview

Explore Through Writing

From the earliest times in human history to the present, people have always wanted to know more, from finding out what was on the other side of the hill to finding out if life exists beyond our solar system. The effort to find new knowledge is an act of discovery. One of the best ways to discover is by writing.

PREPARING

Exploration begins with an impulse. Sometimes it's curiosity about a place. Sometime it's a hunch. The curiosity or the hunch takes the form of a question. To answer that question, we set out to explore.

As a writer in college you prepare by being open to the possibility of learning new things and revising your ideas as your writing develops.

EXPLORING

Ancient explorers were highly skilled navigators, but in order to find new lands and new peoples, they had to enter unknown regions.

College writers seldom create anything worth reading if everything is common knowledge at the outset. If you can connect what's new to what you know, however, entering the unknown can be a creative time for a writer.

RETURNING

Explorers are successful only if they return or send word back about what they discovered. They must make a difference in the minds of the people they left behind.

Through your writing, you can make a difference to others and enlarge the worlds of your readers.

Understand the Process of Writing

People today write constantly in text messages, e-mail, social networking sites, chat rooms, and message boards, just to name a few. Most of this writing is composed quickly, read quickly, and discarded quickly.

In college, in the workplace, and in public life, however, you will often engage in writing that is composed slowly, read carefully, and stored for future reference. This more engaged kind of writing is similar to exploring in many ways. Indeed, Ralph Waldo Emerson observed that "the writer is an explorer. Every step is an advance into a new land."

Like explorers, writers prepare by assembling materials and establishing goals, they plan and organize, they explore by reading and writing, and they offer what they have learned to others.

But unlike explorers who travel to distant lands and have distinct stages in the process, writers intermingle different activities during writing. The process of writing may seem linear when described, but in practice, a diagram of how a writer actually works would look more like a plate of spaghetti. This messiness, however, often generates new ideas.

PREPARE

Analyze the assignment and take stock.

See the rest of this chapter.

EXPLORE BY READING

Read to broaden your knowledge of your topic and to help you identify different views.

See Chapter 2

PLAN AND ORGANIZE

Narrow your topic, darft a working thesis, and create a working outline.

See Chapter 3

DRAFT

Use your working outline to draft paragraphs and to explore your topic further through writing.

See Chapter 4

REVIEW AND REVISE

Switch from writer to reader to review your draft and identify goals for revising.

See Chapter 5

Be prepared to go back and forth

Revising will often take you back to exploring and organizing.

Understand the Rhetorical Situation

Successful writers understand that all acts of writing and speaking include three essential elements that interact with each other: the **writer** or speaker, the **subject**, and the **audience**. Every piece of writing is a negotiation among these three elements, even if we are jotting down a grocery list for our own use.

Every instance of writing, which we will define as **text**, is also of a particular category, called a **genre**, or a mixture of genres. Each text is delivered using a particular **medium**, or a combination of media. For example, Twitter messages (tweets) are a well-defined genre. They have to be text only and are limited to no more than 140 characters. The medium is digital.

The rhetorical triangle

These elements—writer, audience, subject, and text—are often represented as a triangle

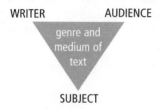

The rhetorical triangle can be used to determine a writer's **purpose** or **aim**. Writers who focus on their own personal experience have a primarily **reflective** aim. Those who are most concerned with explaining a subject have an **informative** aim. Writers who want their audiences to hold certain beliefs or take certain actions have a **persuasive** aim.

The larger context

Communication does not take place in a vacuum. Writers and readers both have knowledge, beliefs, and attitudes about particular subjects. What is happening in the larger world has a great deal to do with how we understand a text.

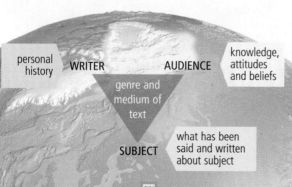

Take, for example, the first two paragraphs of a press release from the World Bank issued in February 2011.

> **WASHINGTON, February 15, 2011** – Rising food prices have driven an estimated 44 million people into poverty in developing countries since last June as food costs continue to rise to near 2008 levels, according to new World Bank Group numbers released ahead of the G20 Meeting of Finance Ministers and Central Bank Governors in Paris.
>
> "Global food prices are rising to dangerous levels and threaten tens of millions of poor people around the world," said World Bank Group President Robert B. Zoellick. "The price hike is already pushing millions of people into poverty, and putting stress on the most vulnerable, who spend more than half of their income on food."

This press release came from the public relations department of the World Bank and was published on the Bank's Web site.

The World Bank is an international financial institution that was established by wealthy countries to assist developing countries and to reduce poverty. It's not surprising that the World Bank is concerned with rising food prices in developing countries because, according to the Bank's statistics, over 20% of the world's population lives on less than $1.25 a day.

The press release is informative in giving statistics, but it is also making a persuasive case that the Bank's mission of reducing poverty will become more difficult if food prices continue to rise.

Analyze Your Assignment

When your instructor gives you a writing assignment, look closely at what you are being asked to do. Circle the information about the required length, the due dates, the format, and other requirements. You can attend to these details later.

Make notes on the assignment sheet. You can find examples of eight different kinds of assignments listed on the facing page.

WHAT'S YOUR PURPOSE?

Does your assignment contain words like *reflect, describe, explain, analyze, evaluate, argue,* and *propose* that signal your purpose?

See next page.

WHAT'S YOUR TOPIC?

Do you have some freedom in choosing a topic? What interests you? What can you explore in depth in the length assigned?

See page 12.

WHAT'S YOUR GENRE AND MEDIUM?

Are you being asked to write an essay, another kind of written text, or a media project?

See page 10.

WHO IS YOUR AUDIENCE?

Does your assignment specify an audience? If so, what will they likely expect?

See page 14.

HOW DO YOU GAIN CREDIBILITY?

What can you do to make your readers trust you and believe that you know what you're talking about?

See page 16.

AIM	FOCUS	EXAMPLE GENRES
WRITING TO REFLECT	**Reflections:** Narrating personal experience and personal insights for a public audience *(Example assignment on page 94)*	Journals, personal letters, blogs, memoirs, essays
WRITING TO INFORM	**Observations:** Describing accurately and vividly *(Example assignment on page 140)*	Ethnographies, travel accounts, case studies, photo essays
	Informative essays: Communicating information clearly *(Example assignment on page 196)*	Newspaper and magazine articles, academic articles, reports, profiles, essays
WRITING TO ANALYZE	**Rhetorical and literary analysis:** Analyzing what makes a text successful and why the author made particular choices *(Example assignment on page 260)*	Rhetorical analysis, short story analysis, visual analysis, essays
WRITING TO PERSUADE	**Causal arguments:** Exploring why an event, phenomenon, or trend happened *(Example assignment on page 330)*	History, accident analysis, financial analysis, essays
	Evaluation arguments: Assessing whether something is good or bad according to particular criteria *(Example assignment on page 380)*	Reviews, essays, performance evaluations, product evaluations
	Position arguments: Convincing others through reasoned argument to accept or reject a position *(Example assignment on page 444)*	Speeches, letters to the editor, op-ed columns, editorials, essays
	Proposal arguments: Convincing others through reasoned argument to take action *(Example assignment on page 506)*	Speeches, business proposals, grant proposals, essays, advocacy Web sites

Think About Your Genre and Medium

Be aware of genre and medium

The word *genre* may be unfamiliar, but the idea isn't. Netflix and other online movie services classify movies as action and adventure, children and family, classics, comedy, documentary, drama, horror, musical, sci-fi and fantasy, thriller, and so on. The music industry classifies music as alternative, blues, classical, country, electronic, folk, gospel, hip hop/rap, jazz, Latino, reggae, rock, world, and so on. These are all genres. Of course, there are many sub-genres within these broad genres.

Most of the time we recognize writing genres immediately. We know, for example, that junk mail is trying to sell us something and we're suspicious of anything offered for free. Likewise,

we're accustomed to using different media. We read newspapers, magazines, and books online and on paper. We read written blogs on the Web and watch video blogs on YouTube.

But while we often don't think consciously about genre and medium when we are reading, listening, and viewing, when we write we often have to make conscious decisions according to genre and medium we choose.

Be aware of how genre and medium influence

The genre you select has a strong influence on the style you use. Compare the first paragraphs of a research report, a news article, and a blog on beach erosion.

Research report

Coastal management as a distinct practice emerged just a few decades ago, when ideas and information were exchanged through mostly conventional means. Scientists and coastal planners gave talks and presented posters at conferences and workshops, as they still do. Field trips and tours organized as part of these events highlighted problems and success stories. Agency experts prepared and distributed reports and guidelines. Academics researched problems and systematically evaluated methods to address them, reporting their results in new periodicals like the *Coastal Zone Management Journal*. Face-to-face meetings, telephone conversations, the U.S. Postal Service, and later the fax machine played key roles in the development of ideas and movement of information to address coastal problems. Working with these communication tools, professionals and concerned citizens alike drew from their personal experience, new state and federal legislative mandates, and a palpable sense of urgency to create a new practice called coastal zone management. At the time, the demand was great for scientific data and information about coastal resources and use, for tools to interpret this information, and for strategies and processes to apply it for problem solving. And the information flowed freely, albeit by slower and less sophisticated means than today.

Innovation by Design: Improving Learning Networks in Coastal Management. Washington, D.C., The Heinz Center, 2004. Print.

Watch the Animation on **Genres and the Rhetorical Situation** at mycomplab.com

News article

When scientists consider the possible effects of global warming, there is a lot they don't know. But they can say one thing for sure: sea levels will rise.

Dean, Cornelia. "New Victim of Global Warming: The Beaches." *New York Times.* New York Times. 20 June 2006. Web. 6 Oct. 2011.

Blog

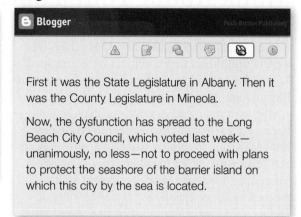

First it was the State Legislature in Albany. Then it was the County Legislature in Mineola.

Now, the dysfunction has spread to the Long Beach City Council, which voted last week—unanimously, no less—not to proceed with plans to protect the seashore of the barrier island on which this city by the sea is located.

"Legislative Dysfunction Under the Boardwalk." *Community Alliance Blog.* N.p. 8 May 2006. Web. 14 Nov. 2011.

Even though each writer is writing about the same subject, notice what is different.

Sentence length	• The report has much longer sentences than the newspaper article or the blog.
Paragraph length	• The report has long paragraphs compared to the short paragraphs of the newspaper article and the blog.
Word choice	• The report uses much more formal language than the blog. The newspaper language is neutral.
Relationship with the reader	• The report and newspaper writers are distant and objective. The blog writer is passionately involved with the issue.

WRITE NOW

Compare styles across genres and media

Find a newspaper article on a current social, economic, political, or scientific issue. Then find a scholarly article on the same subject using scholar.google.com or one of the databases on your library's Web site. Next, search blogs for the same subject using blogsearch.google.com.

Compare the styles of the scholarly article, the newspaper article, and the blog using the following criteria: overall length, paragraph length, sentence length, word choice, relationship with the reader, and use of graphics and images. Write a summary of your analysis.

Think About Your Topic

Writers begin by exploring. When they start writing, exploration doesn't stop. Once they start, writers find things they could not have imagined. Where writers end up is often far away from where they thought they were going.

Most writing in college concerns exploration because academic disciplines seek to create new knowledge and to rethink what is known. Colleges and universities bring together people who ask interesting questions: How does recent archaeological evidence change our understanding of Homer's *Iliad* and *Odyssey*? Why does eyesight deteriorate with age? How do volcanoes affect the world climate? How do chameleons regenerate lost body parts? How do Rousseau's ideas about nature continue to shape notions about wilderness? How do electric eels generate voltage and not get shocked in the process? How can a poll of a thousand people represent over 300 million Americans with only a 3% margin of error?

Writers in colleges and universities respond to these questions and many others. They challenge old answers and contribute new answers. Readers of college writing expect to learn something when they read—new knowledge, a fresh interpretation, another point of view that they had not considered.

At first glance the expectations of college writing seem impossible. How can you as an undergraduate student expect to contribute new knowledge? But just as there is a great deal that maps do not show, you can find many uncertainties, controversies, and unresolved problems in any field of study. You just have to ask the right questions.

Ask interesting questions

Good questions can take you to places that will interest you and your readers alike.

- Focus on an area you don't know and want to know more about.

- Find out where experts disagree. What exactly is the source of the disagreement? Why do they come to different conclusions using the same evidence?

- Analyze explanations of current trends and events. What possible causes might be left out?

- Examine proposals to solve problems. Does the solution fix the problem? Will people support the solution if it costs them effort or money?

- Compare what people claim and the reality. Often people (especially politicians) represent things and their role in making things much better than they actually are.

Local questions are often more interesting than broad, general questions. For example, should historic neighborhoods be preserved, or should they give way to urban renewal and gentrification, as has happened to Chinatown in Washington, D.C.?

Use strategies for finding a topic

Sometimes your instructor will assign a topic, but more often you will have to come up with your own topic. Look first at material from your course. You might find a topic to explore in the readings or from class discussion.

Start with what interests you. It's hard to write about topics that you care little about. If your assignment gives you a range of options, make more than one list.

PERSONAL
1. History of Anime in Japan
2. Cave exploration and conservation
3. Learning to windsurf

CAMPUS
1. Pros and cons of computer fees
2. Excessive litter on campus
3. Fellowships for study-abroad programs

COMMUNITY
1. Safe bicycle commuting
2. Bilingual education programs
3. Better public transportation

NATION/WORLD
1. Advertising aimed at preschool children
2. Censorship of the Internet
3. Genetically altered crops

WRITE NOW

Mapping your campus

Your campus likely has an information desk for students and visitors. Information centers typically will have several brochures with maps. Visit the information desk and collect everything that includes a map. Then compare the maps. Make a checklist for what the maps show and don't show (building names, streets, shuttle bus routes, bicycle routes, parking, landmarks, hotels, and more).

Create a map for new students on your campus that contains insider knowledge that would not appear on the maps your school produces. For example, where can you find the best burger on or close to campus? The best cup of coffee or cookies? A quiet place to study? A great place to meet friends?

Make a list of places that need to be included on your map. Then draw the map. Google Maps is an excellent tool for making maps of campuses and neighborhoods.

Think About Your Audience

When you talk with someone face-to-face, you receive constant feedback from that person, even when you're doing all the talking. Your listener may nod in agreement, frown, act bored, and give you a variety of other signals.

Imagine your readers

When you write, you rarely receive immediate response from readers. Most of the time you don't know exactly how readers will react to what you write. You have to think consciously about your readers and anticipate how they might respond.

Readers of college writing

Readers of college writing expect more than what they can find out from a Google search or an online encyclopedia. Facts are easy to obtain from databases and print sources. Readers want to know how these facts are connected.

Good college writing involves an element of surprise. If readers can predict exactly where a writer is going, even if they fully agree, they will either skim to the end or stop reading. Readers expect you to tell them something that they don't already know.

Writing in college . . .	Writers are expected to . . .
States explicit claims	Make a claim that isn't obvious. The claim is often called a thesis statement.
Develops an argument	Support their claims with facts, evidence, reasons, and testimony from experts.
Analyzes with insight	Analyze in depth what they read and view.
Investigates complexity	Explore the complexity of a subject, challenging their readers by asking "Have you thought about this?" or "What if you discard the usual way of thinking about a subject and take the opposite point of view?"
Organizes with a hierarchical structure	Make the major parts evident to readers and indicate which parts are subordinate to others.
Signals with transitions	Indicate logical relationships clearly so readers can follow a pathway without getting lost.
Documents sources carefully	Provide the sources of information so readers can consult the same sources the writer used.

Know what college readers expect

Readers expect to be challenged.
Simple answers that can be easily looked up are not adequate.

OFF TRACK
The United States entered World War II when the Japanese attacked Pearl Harbor on December 7, 1941. (This fact is well known and not informative for college readers.)

ON TRACK
The war with Japan actually began on July 25, 1941, when President Franklin Roosevelt froze Japanese assets and declared an oil embargo, leaving the Japanese with the choices of abandoning the war with China or neutralizing the United States Navy in order to secure oil resources in Indonesia.

Readers expect claims to be backed up with reasons and evidence.
Simple explanations without support are not adequate.

OFF TRACK
New York City is an exciting place to live, but I wouldn't want to move there because of the crime. (Is crime really that much higher in New York City?)

ON TRACK
Many people don't know that New York City is the safest large city in the United States according to FBI crime statistics. It even ranks in the top 20 safest cities among the 210 cities with populations over 100,000.

Readers expect complex answers for complex problems.
Simple solutions for complex problems are not adequate.

OFF TRACK
We need posters urging students not to litter so much on campus. *(Are posters alone likely to solve the problem?)*

ON TRACK
Most of the litter on our campus is paper, bottles, and cans—all recyclable—yet there are almost no recycle containers on campus. Putting recycle containers in high-litter locations along with a "don't litter" campaign could go a long way toward making our campus cleaner.

Readers expect writers to be engaged.
Readers expect writers to be curious and genuinely concerned about their subjects.

OFF TRACK
Older people have to deal with too much bureaucracy to obtain health care. *(The statement rings true but doesn't motivate readers.)*

ON TRACK
After spending a day with my 78-year-old aunt sorting through stacks of booklets and forms and waiting on a help line that never answered, I became convinced that the Medicare prescription drug program is an aging American's worst nightmare.

Think About Your Credibility

Some writers begin with credibility because of who they are. If you wonder what foods compose a balanced meal for your dog, you probably would listen carefully to the advice of a veterinarian. Most writers, however, have to convince their readers to keep reading by demonstrating knowledge of their subject and concern with their readers' needs.

Think about how you want your readers to see you

To get your readers to take you seriously, you must convince them that they can trust you. You need to get them to see you as

Concerned
Readers want you to be committed to what you are writing about. They also expect you to be concerned with them as readers. After all, if you don't care about them, why should they read what you write?

Well informed
Many people ramble on about any subject without knowing anything about it. If they are family members, you have to suffer their opinions, but it is not enjoyable. College writing requires that you do your homework on a subject.

Fair
Many writers look at only one side of an issue. Readers respect objectivity and an unbiased approach.

Ethical
Many writers use only the facts that support their positions and often distort facts and sources. Critical readers often notice what is being left out. Don't try to conceal what doesn't support your position.

Considerate
Writers who don't bother to create new paragraphs when they move to new idea or fail to signal that they are making a transition to a new topic force readers to make extra effort. Readers can become annoyed in a hurry.

Aware of writing in a discipline
Different disciplines use different vocabularies, formats, and evidence to make and support claims.

Careful
No one likes to read sloppy, error-filled writing. Readers appreciate writers who take extra time to get the little things right.

Visually fluent
Digital technologies have made it easy to insert images and graphics in your writing and to publish on the Web. But these technologies don't tell you if, when, and how images and graphics should be used.

STAYING ON TRACK

Build your credibility

Know what's at stake

What you are writing about should matter to your readers.
If its importance is not evident, it's your job to explain why your readers should consider it important.

OFF TRACK

We should be concerned about two-thirds of Central and South America's 110 brightly colored harlequin frog species becoming extinct in the last twenty years. (The loss of any species is unfortunate, but the writer gives us no other reason for concern.)

ON TRACK

The rapid decline of amphibians worldwide due to global warming may be the advance warning of the loss of cold-weather species such as polar bears, penguins, and reindeer.

Have your readers in mind

If you are writing about a specialized subject that your readers don't know much about, take the time to explain key concepts.

OFF TRACK

Reduction in the value of a debt security, especially a bond, results from a rise in interest rates. Conversely, a decline in interest rates results in an increase in the value of a debt security, especially bonds. *(The basic idea is here, but it is not expressed clearly, especially if the reader is not familiar with investing.)*

ON TRACK

Bond prices move inversely to interest rates. When interest rates go up, bond prices go down, and when interest rates go down, bond prices go up.

Think about alternative solutions and points of view

Readers appreciate a writer's ability to see a subject from multiple perspectives.

OFF TRACK

We will reduce greenhouse gas and global warming only if we greatly increase wind-generated electricity. *(Wind power is an alternative energy source, but it is expensive and many people don't want windmills in scenic areas. The writer also doesn't mention using energy more efficiently.)*

ON TRACK

If the world is serious about limiting carbon emissions to reduce global warming, then along with increasing efficient energy use, all non-carbon-emitting energy sources must be considered, including nuclear power. Nuclear power now produces about 20% of U.S. electricity with no emissions—the equivalent of taking 58 million passenger cars off the road.

2 Reading to Explore

Along with learning to write well, learning to think critically is essential in a college education.

Chapter Overview

Become a Critical Reader

Critical thinking begins with critical reading. For most of what you read, one time through is enough. When you start asking questions about what you are reading, you are engaging in critical reading. Critical reading is a four-part process. First, begin by asking where a piece of writing came from and why it was written. Second, read the text carefully to find the author's central claim or thesis and the major points. Third, decide if you can trust the author. Fourth, read the text again to understand how it works.

1. Where did it come from? • Who wrote this material? • Where did it first appear? In a book, newspaper, magazine, or online? • What else has been written about the topic or issue? • What do you expect after reading the title?	**2. What does it say?** • What is the topic or issue? • What is the writer's thesis or central idea? • What reasons or evidence does the writer offer? • Who are the intended readers? What does the writer assume the readers know and believe?
3. Can you trust the writer? • Does the writer have the necessary knowledge and experience to write on this subject? • Do you detect a bias in the writer's position? • Are the facts relevant to the writer's claims? • Can you trust the writer's facts? Where did the facts come from? • Does the writer acknowledge opposing views and unfavorable evidence? Does the writer deal fairly with opposing views?	**4. How does it work?** • How is the piece of writing organized? How are the major points arranged? • How does the writer conclude? Does the conclusion follow from the evidence the writer offers? • How would you characterize the style? Describe the language that the writer uses. • How does the writer represent herself or himself?

WRITE NOW

Analyze information for students on your campus

No doubt your school sent you a great deal of information when you were admitted. Schools continue to distribute information to students when they get to campus. You can find informative brochures and flyers at your school's student services building and informative pages on your school's Web site. Pick one of the brochures or Web pages to analyze. Remember that you are the intended audience.

Write a one-page evaluation about why the brochure or Web page is effective or ineffective for an audience of college students. If it is ineffective, what changes need to be made to make it effective? If it works, what does it do well?

Look with a Critical Eye

Critical viewing, like critical reading, requires thinking about where the image or visual came from. Begin by asking the following.

- What kind of an image or visual is it?
- Who created this image (movie, advertisement, television program, and so on)?
- What is it about? What is portrayed in the image?
- Where did it first appear? Where do you usually find images like this one?
- When did it appear?

The Pharaoh Menkaure (Mycerinus) and his queen, Giza, Old Kingdom, 2548–2530 BCE. One of the finest statues from ancient Egypt depicts a royal couple. Compare the statue to formal portraits of couples today. Why does the queen have one arm around his waist and the other touching the king's arm? Do you think it depicts how they looked in real life? Or how they might have wanted to look in the afterlife? How do you think people in ancient Egypt might have viewed this statue?

The following questions are primarily for still images. For animations, movies, and television, you also have to ask questions about how the story is being told.

- What attracts your eye first? If there is an attention-grabbing element, how does it connect with the rest of the image?
- What impression of the subject does the image create?
- How does the image appeal to the values of the audience? (For example, politicians love to be photographed with children.)
- How does the image relate to what surrounds it?
- Was it intended to serve purposes besides art and entertainment?

Watch the Animation on Elements of Visuals at mycomplab.com

Arthur Rothstein made this photograph of black clouds of dust rising over the Texas Panhandle in March 1936. Look closely at the photo. What attracts your eye first? Snapshots usually put the horizon line in the center. Why did Rothstein put the horizon at the bottom? What impression does this photo convey to you?

WRITE NOW

Analyze political cartoons

Political cartoons make comments on politics in drawings combined with words. Bring a political cartoon to class. You can find many political cartoons on the Web in addition to ones in newspapers and magazines.

Answer these questions.

1. What is the point of the cartoon?

2. What do you need to know to understand the cartoon? Political cartoons usually make reference to current events, television shows, and popular culture.

3. Political cartoons often exaggerate physical attributes. Is anything exaggerated?

4. Political cartoons are often ironic—pointing to the difference between the way things really are and what they are expected to be. Is the cartoon ironic?

5. Why is the cartoon funny or not funny?

Organize in groups of three or four students. Exchange your cartoons and answer the same questions for your classmates' cartoons.

When everyone finishes, compare your answers for each cartoon. Where there is disagreement, stop to discuss why you came up with different answers.

Read Actively

If you own what you are reading (or are able to make yourself a photocopy of borrowed materials), read with a pencil in hand. Pens and highlighters don't erase, and often you don't remember why you highlighted a particular sentence.

Annotate what you read

Using annotating strategies will make your effort more rewarding.

Mark major points and key concepts	Sometimes major points are indicated by headings, but often you will need to locate them.
Connect passages	Notice how ideas connect to each other. Draw lines and arrows. If an idea connects to something a few pages before, write a note in the margin with the page number.
Ask questions	Note anything that puzzles you, including words to look up.

Annotate difficult readings

Much of what you read in college will deal with unfamiliar concepts, which are often defined by other concepts. Annotating a difficult reading will help you understand the relationship of concepts, and the annotations will be valuable in remembering key points when you come back to the reading later. In this passage from John Heskett's *Toothpicks and Logos, Design in Everyday Life*, the author defines function in terms of two other concepts.

A more inclusive definition of function is needed, which can be opened up by breaking the concept of function into a twofold division: the key concepts of utility and significance.

definition of function—utility and significance

Utility can be defined as the quality of appropriateness in use. This means it is concerned with how things work, of the degree to which designs serve practical purposes and provide affordances or capabilities. A simple example is a professional kitchen knife used to prepare food: its primary utility value is as a cutting tool. In order for it to work effectively, the blade needs to possess material qualities enabling a sharp edge to be maintained and for it to remain stable in use.

definition of utility

example— kitchen knife

? *affordances? odd word—author is British*

Significance, as a concept in design, explains how forms assume meaning in the ways they are used, or the roles and meaning assigned them, often becoming powerful symbols or icons in patterns of habit and ritual.

definition of significance

● Watch the Animation on Highlighting and Annotating at mycomplab.com

other examples:
computer keyboard,
pencil,
traffic light

examples of
designs for
significance

In contrast to the emphasis on efficiency, significance has more to do with expression and meaning.

It is possible to find designs of many kinds defined solely in terms of utility or significance. Many examples of the former are products related to the performance of professional services, tools with highly specific purposes, such as a handsaw or a lathe, or medical equipment, such as an ultrasound machine. Where information has to perform a highly specific task, as in a railway timetable, the layout and type forms should be clean, simple, and directed wholly to imparting essential facts. A primary condition of utilitarian design is that it must effectively execute or support certain tasks. In contrast, a piece of jewelry, a porcelain figurine, or a frame for a family photograph has no such specific purpose—instead their purpose can be described in terms of contemplative pleasure or adornment.

examples of
designs for
utility

Map what you read

Drawing a map of a text can help you to identify key points and understand the relationships of concepts.

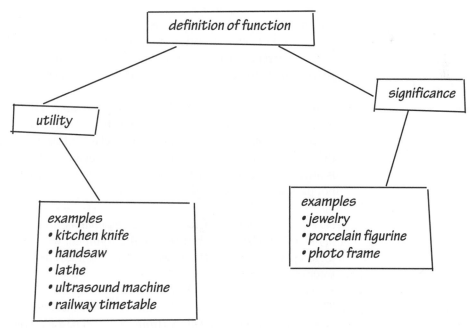

Recognize Fallacies

Writers of arguments make claims based on reasons and evidence (see Chapters 10–13). When you read critically, you stay alert for flaws in reasoning and evidence. The kinds of faulty reasoning called logical fallacies reflect a failure to provide sufficient evidence for a claim that is being made.

Fallacies of logic

Begging the question	*Politicians are inherently dishonest because no honest person would run for public office.* The fallacy of begging the question occurs when the claim is restated and passed off as evidence.
Either-or	*Either we eliminate the regulation of businesses or else profits will suffer.* The either-or fallacy suggests that there are only two choices in a complex situation. Rarely, if ever, is this the case. (In this example, the writer ignores the fact that Enron was unregulated and went bankrupt.)
False analogies	*Japan quit fighting in 1945 when we dropped nuclear bombs on them. We should use nuclear weapons against other countries.* Analogies always depend on the degree of resemblance of one situation to another. In this case, the analogy fails to recognize that circumstances today are very different from those in 1945; many countries now possess nuclear weapons, and we know their use could harm the entire world.
Hasty generalization	*We have been in a drought for three years; that's a sure sign of climate change.* A hasty generalization is a broad claim made on the basis of a few occurrences. Climate cycles occur regularly over spans of a few years; climate trends must be observed over centuries.
Non sequitur	*A university that can raise a billion dollars from alumni should not have to raise tuition.* A *non sequitur* (which is a Latin term meaning "it does not follow") ties together two unrelated ideas. In this case, the argument fails to recognize that the money for capital campaigns is often donated for special purposes such as athletic facilities and is not part of a university's general revenue.
Oversimplification	*No one would run stop signs if we had a mandatory death penalty for doing it.* This claim may be true, but the argument would be unacceptable to most citizens. More complex, if less definitive, solutions are called for.
Post hoc fallacy	*The stock market goes down when the AFC wins the Super Bowl in even years.* The *post hoc* fallacy (from the Latin *post hoc ergo hoc,*

which means "after this, therefore this") assumes that things that follow in time have a causal relationship.

Rationalization

I could have finished my paper on time if my printer was working. People frequently come up with excuses and weak explanations for their own and others' behavior that often avoid actual causes.

Slippery slope

We shouldn't grant citizenship to illegal immigrants now living in the United States because no one will want to obey our laws. The slippery slope fallacy maintains that one thing inevitably will cause something else to happen.

Fallacies of emotion and language

Bandwagon appeals

It doesn't matter if I copy a paper off the Web because everyone else does. This argument suggests that everyone is doing it, so why shouldn't you? But on close examination, it may be that everyone really isn't doing it—and in any case, it may not be the right thing to do.

Name calling

Name calling is frequent in politics and among competing groups (*radical, tax-and-spend liberal, racist, fascist, right-wing ideologue*). Unless these terms are carefully defined, they are meaningless.

Polarization

Feminists are all man-haters. Polarization, like name-calling, exaggerates positions and groups by representing them as extreme and divisive.

Straw man

Environmentalists won't be satisfied until not a single human being is allowed to enter a national park. A straw man argument is a diversionary tactic that sets up another's position in a way that can be easily rejected. In fact, only a small percentage of environmentalists would make an argument even close to this one.

WRITE NOW

Analyze opinion writing

Examine writing that expresses opinions: blogs, discussion boards, editorials, advocacy Web sites, the letters to the editor on the editorial pages of your campus or local newspaper. Read with a pencil in hand, and mark where you think there may be fallacies.

Select the example that has the clearest fallacy. Explain in a paragraph the cause of the fallacy.

Respond as a Reader

Engage in a dialogue with what you read. Talk back to the author. If you are having trouble understanding a difficult section, read it aloud and listen to the author's voice. Hearing something read will sometimes help you to imagine being in a conversation with the author.

Make notes

As you read, write down your thoughts.

- Imagine that the author is with you. What points does the writer make that you would respond to in person?
- What questions would you have of the author? These indicate what you might need to look up.
- What ideas do you find that you might develop or interpret differently?

Write summaries

When you summarize, you state the major ideas of an entire source or part of a source in your own words. Short summaries can an important strategy in critical reading. Longer, formal summaries are sometimes assigned as stand-alone writing projects. The keys to writing a good summary are identifying the main points and then putting those points into your own words. If you use words from the source, you have to put those words in quotation marks.

> *John Heskett argues that the concept of function in design should be understood in terms of "utility" and "significance." He defines utility as the degree a design accomplishes its purpose, such as how well a knife cuts. Significance is defined as the degree to which an object is designed to give pleasure or create meaning. A piece of art is an example of something designed exclusively for significance.*

Build on what you read

Keeping a reading journal is a good practice for a writer. You'll have a record of your thinking as you read that you can return to later. Record your first impressions, note any ideas you find stimulating or useful, explore relationships, and write down questions. Often you can connect different ideas from different readings. A reading journal is a great place to test ideas that you can later develop for a writing assignment.

Heskett says, "It is possible to find designs of many kinds defined solely in terms of utility and significance." I'll grant the distinction, but his examples suggest that most things have elements of both.

He uses tools as objects designed strictly for utility, but look at a tool catalog and you'll see lots of bright colors and handsome cases. He uses a photograph frame as an example of significance. True enough that frames are often decorative, but a frame also has to fit the picture. The frame should use non-glare glass to reduce reflected light. A frame has to do more than just look good.

But a bigger point is that anything can have significance for a particular person. I have my grandfather's hammer. It is nearly worthless because the handle is so old and worn that it would snap if you swung it hard against a nail. I took the hammer to work one day to hang a picture, and it shortly disappeared. I searched and couldn't find it. I forgot about it, but then I noticed it in a storeroom months later and recovered it.

WRITE NOW

Respond to what you read

Select a reading in one of the chapters in Part 2 that interests you. Write a one-paragraph summary of either the entire reading or of a part that contains a stimulating idea.

Write a second paragraph that develops one or more of the ideas in the reading. Think of some way of expanding or extending one of the author's ideas, either by relating it to your own experience or to something else you have read.

Move from Reading to Invention

When you read broadly about a topic, you'll find that many writers respond to the ideas and opinions of other writers. Any important topic in our culture is the site of an ongoing conversation. By considering what you write as just one move in a larger conversation might end up helping you think about what you want to say. In the process of researching what has been said and written on a particular issue, often your own view is expanded and you find an opportunity to add your voice to the ongoing conversation.

Writer at work

Patrice Conley was given an assignment that called for taking a position on a current controversial issue. Patrice enjoys playing and watching sports, so she started by making a list of current controversial issues in college sports.

COLLEGE SPORTS CONTROVERSIES

1. Equal opportunities for women athletes

2. Big-time sports overshadow education

3. Financing college sports

4. Paying student-athletes in big-time college sports

5. Ethics: win-at-all-costs philosophy

6. The BCS championship system in big-time college

football

She decided she was most interested in the issue of paying college athletes who participate in big-time college sports. She had wondered why student-athletes could be paid nothing when their coaches in big-time college football and basketball often have seven-figure salaries. She made her initial search using the search terms "student athlete salaries" on Google, which turned up many relevant articles.

Patrice began reading about the issue and making notes. She found an article by a sports attorney that explained how colleges through the National Collegiate Athletic Association (NCAA) justify defining big-time athletes as amateurs.

NCAA's justification for not paying salaries to athletes in big-time sports or allowing them to endorse products

McCann, Michael. "NCAA Faces Unspecified Damages, Changes in Latest Anti-Trust Case." *SI.com*. Time, Inc., 21 July 2009. Web. 6 Apr. 2011.

"Indeed, if student-athletes were paid salaries or received income through endorsement or licensing deals, they may begin to resemble professional athletes more than college students. The professionalization of student-athletes would frustrate the NCAA's focus on amateurism, possibly making it more difficult for schools to comply with Title IX, a federal law that commands gender equity in sports. Professionalization could also create economic divisions among student-athletes on the basis of their commercial appeal. Student-athletes' exposure to professional opportunities might also lead to exploitation by unsavory businesspersons, whom colleges and universities do not want on their campuses or near their student bodies."

She did another search to find out how much money is generated by big-time college sports and learned that top college coaches are paid salaries similar to those of their professional counterparts.

Van Riper, Thomas. "The Highest-Paid College Basketball Coaches." *Forbes.com.* Forbes, 8 Mar. 2010. Web. 6 Apr. 2011.

Take Kentucky's John Calipari. . . . Calipari (who left his two prior college programs—Massachusetts and Memphis—in hot water with the NCAA for alleged violations) pulls down 10% or so of the $35 million to $40 million that his program generates for the university (the entire athletic department generates $72 million a year, the school says). The corporate equivalent for Calipari's pay package would be Microsoft handing Steve Ballmer $6 billion a year. The average NBA coach, who works twice as many games as his college counterpart, makes $4 million a year, about 3.5% of an average club's revenue.

Some college coaches make as much as NBA coaches and receive a higher precentage of total revenue.

Then she accessed her library's Web site and found a book that gave her valuable background information.

Zimbalist, Andrew. *Unpaid Professionals: Commercialism and Conflict in Big-Time College Sports.* Princeton UP, 2001. Print.

The line between professionalism and amateurism in big-time sports was blurry from the beginning

Already in the 1880s Yale had a $100,000 slush fund to aid football. Teams regularly used graduate students and paid ringers to play. In 1896 Lafayette College enrolled tackle Fielding Yost, a student at West Virginia University, in time to play in the game against the football powerhouse of the University of Pennsylvania, which had won thirty-six consecutive games. With Yost's assistance, Lafayette beat Penn, 6 to 4; then Yost was sent back to West Virginia. A few years later, Yale lured tackle James Hogan by offering him free meals and tuition, a suite in Vanderbilt Hall, a trip to Cuba, a monopoly on the sale of game scorecards, and a job as cigarette agent for the American Tobacco Company.

After reading several articles and a book, Patrice began to identify specific issues in the debate over paying college athletes. She imagined the writers being in a conversation about these issues.

"The NCAA draws a clear line between professionalism and amateur sports"

"But that line seems to be for the players alone in big-time college sports. The coaches, networks, and schools make millions."

"Too few college athletes graduate or go on to lucrative professional careers."

"Colleges argue that scholarships are adequate payment for big-time college athletes."

"The NCAA should return to an older definition of amateur, which comes from Latin meaning "lover of." If students are lucky enough to be paid for doing what they love, so be it."

Imagining different positions as turns in a conversation helped her to think about what she might contribute.

WRITE NOW

Imagine a conversation about a controversial issue

Think of a controversial issue that you know something about. It could be a local issue such as the overpopulation of deer in a neighborhood or the creation of bicycle lanes on busy streets. Or it could be a national or global issue such as Internet privacy or nuclear energy.

Think about the positions as turns in a conversation. What can you add to what's been said? Use the template below.

Some people claim that ....

Other people respond that ....

Still others claim that ....

I agree with X's and Y's points, but I maintain that ....

because ....

3 Planning

Developing a plan for writing is the key to success.

Chapter Overview

► **Move from a general topic to a writing plan**
(see p. 33)

► **Narrow your topic**
(see p. 34)

► **Write a thesis**
(see p. 36)

► **Make a plan**
(see p. 38)

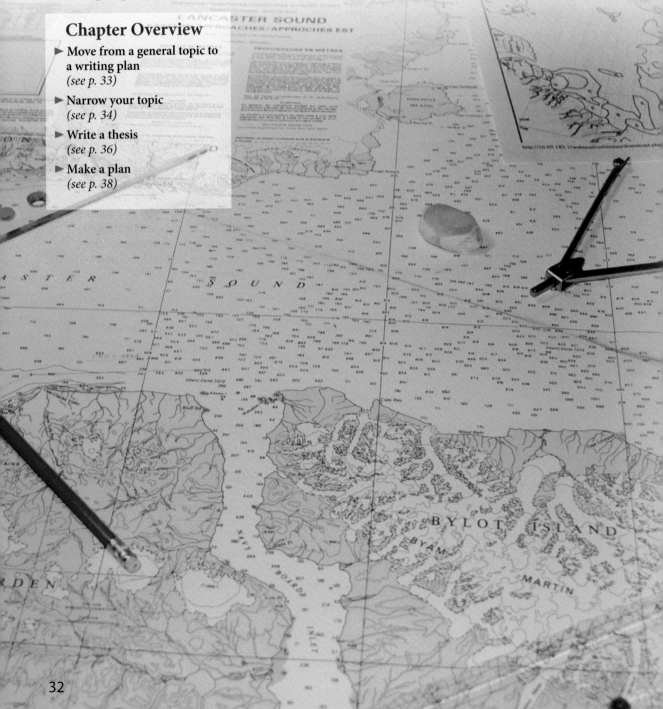

Move from a General Topic to a Writing Plan

After you have found a topic (see Chapter 1) and likely have read about the topic (see Chapter 2), you need to formulate a plan for writing. Planning in advance will make your time more productive and lead to better results.

IDENTIFY YOUR PURPOSE	Often your assignment will direct your purpose. Look for words like these.
	Reflect: Think about an event or a concept in terms of your own experience. → **See Chapter 6**
	Describe: Observe carefully, make notes, and report what you saw, heard, and experienced. → **See Chapter 7**
	Inform: Report information or explain a concept or idea. → **See Chapter 8**
	Analyze: Interpret a text or event to find connections and reach conclusions. → **See Chapter 9**
	Analyze causes: Identify probable causes of a trend, event, or phenomenon. → **See Chapter 10**
	Evaluate: Determine whether something is good or bad according to criteria that you identify. → **See Chapter 11**
	Argue: Take a position on an issue or propose a course of action. → **See Chapters 12 and 13**
NARROW YOUR TOPIC	If your topic is too broad, you will find too much information and will not be able to cover the topic adequately. → **See page 34**
WRITE A WORKING THESIS	Avoid sentences that begin "I'm going to write about computer games and children," or "My topic is computer games and children." Write a complete sentence that states your main idea and makes an assertion about that main idea. (For example, "Computer games are valuable because they improve children's visual attention skills and literacy skills.") → **See page 36**
EVALUATE YOUR THESIS	Your working thesis should progress to a statement that is of increasing interest to your readers. → **See page 37**
MAKE A VISUAL PLAN OR A WORKING OUTLINE	A visual plan or a working outline will list the major sections and sketch the overall development. → **See page 38**

Narrow Your Topic

Until you can focus a broad topic, you will not be able to organize your project and treat your subject in enough depth.

Take, for example, the broad topic of whether genetically modified foods (GM foods) are safe for consumers. The topic is much too large to cover adequately in a course project. Ask questions and brainstorm (see page 12).

- Who is involved in the issue? Governments? corporations? farmers? consumers?
- Which crops are genetically modified?
- What time period is involved?
- What countries are involved?
- Why are GM foods controversial?

You may need to do research to find out more about your topic in order to narrow it (see Chapter 20). Your readers will stay better focused if you have a specific topic, and you will be better equipped to cover your topic thoroughly.

Broad topic
Are GM foods safe for consumers?

Narrower topic
What is the European Union's policy on selling and labeling GM foods?

Specific topic
Why did France and other European countries ban Monsanto's MON0810 corn and similar genetically modified crops in 2007?

Map your topic

Mapping is another method of narrowing your topic. Mapping can also help you to create a working outline if you connect the ideas you set out. See the facing page for how Patrice Conley used mapping to narrow her topic.

To create a map you can use either pen and paper or mapping software available on the Internet. Google Docs has a free drawing program that can make diagrams.

Watch the Video on *Narrowing a Subject* at mycomplab.com

Writer at work

Patrice Conley decided to make a map in order to find a center for her broad topic of whether student athletes in big-time college sports should be paid.

She started with her general topic, stating it in a few words and drawing a box around it.

Next Patrice asked additional questions:
- What is the current situation?
- Who is involved?
- How long has it been going on?
- What else is like it?
- What exactly is the problem?
- What possible solutions are there for the problem?

She thought of some general categories for her topic in response to those questions and drew boxes for each.

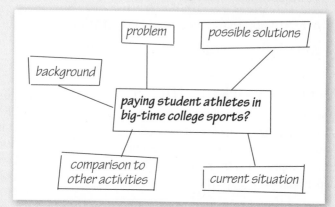

She then looked at her notes from what she had read. She began to generate ideas for each of the subcategories and put them on her map.

When she finished she took stock of her map. She picked up a marker and drew a box around a possible central idea for her project.

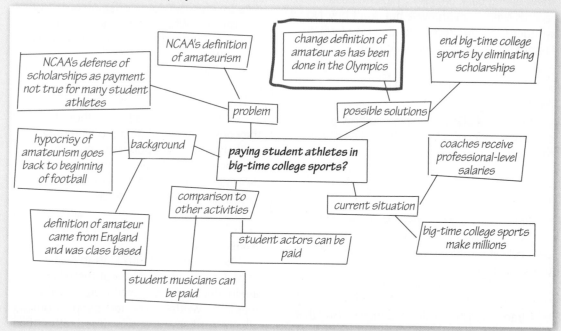

She succeeded in narrowing her general topic to the more specific topic of changing the definition of amateur as it applies to student athletes.

Write a Thesis

The thesis announces your topic and states what point or points you want to make about that topic. A thesis is a statement, not a question. A thesis has a subject and an assertion.

Subject | **Assertion** |
▼   ▼

Advertisers use Facebook's list of friends to determine where you live and what you buy in order to send you targeted ads.

Write a working thesis

Your working thesis should follow the direction your assignment calls for. These examples show how the broad subject of databases and privacy can be approached from different directions, depending on your purpose.

Describe

WORKING THESIS: My Amazon.com account has a list of every book I have purchased from them dating back ten years, plus Amazon records every item I browse but don't buy. No wonder Amazon's recommendations of what I might like are so uncannily accurate!

Analyze

WORKING THESIS: Understanding how the concept of privacy is legally defined is critical for strengthening privacy laws.

Inform

WORKING THESIS: Imagine a government that compels its citizens to reveal vast amounts of personal data, including your physical description, your phone number, your political party, your parents' and spouse's names, where you work, where you live, what property you own, and every legal transaction in your life, and then making that data available to anyone on the Web—which is exactly what federal, state, and local governments are doing today in the United States.

Argue

WORKING THESIS: Unlike the government, companies have almost no restrictions on what information they collect or what they do with it. Laws should be passed that make companies responsible for the misuse of personal information and allow people to have greater participation in how that information is used.

Evaluate

WORKING THESIS: Using personal consumer data to refuse service or offer inferior service to customers who likely will not spend much money is an example of the misuse of personal information.

Reflect

WORKING THESIS: I had never thought about the consequences of data profiling until I read about Netflix's policy of "throttling" frequent users, which explained why deliveries of movies I had requested from Netflix grew slower and slower.

Analyze causes

WORKING THESIS: Many laws to protect privacy are on the books, but these laws are ineffective for the digital era because they were written to protect people from government spying and intrusion rather than from the collection and selling of personal information by companies.

◉ Watch the Animation on Writing Thesis Statements at mycomplab.com

Evaluate your working thesis

Ask yourself these questions about your working thesis.

1. Is it specific?
2. Is it manageable in terms of the assigned length and the amount of time you have?
3. Is it interesting to your intended readers?

Example 1

WORKING THESIS: Steroids are a problem in Major League Baseball.

- Specific? The thesis is too broad. What exactly is the problem? Is the problem the same now as it was a few years ago?

- Manageable? Because the thesis is not limited, it cannot be discussed adequately.

- Interesting? The topic is potentially interesting, but many people are aware that baseball players used steroids. How can you lead readers to think about the topic in a new way?

Example 1 revised

THESIS: Home run records from 1993 through 2004 should be placed in a special category because of the high use of steroids in Major League Baseball before testing began in 2004.

Example 2

WORKING THESIS: "Nanotechnology" refers to any technology that deals with particles measured in units of a nanometer, which is one billionth (10^{-9}) of a meter.

- **Specific?** The thesis is specific, but it is too narrow. It offers only a definition of nanotechnology.

- **Manageable?** The thesis states a fact.

- **Interesting?** Nanotechnology could be interesting if some of its potential effects are included.

Example 2 revised

THESIS: Nanotechnology may soon change concepts of social identity by making it possible for individuals to alter their physical appearances either through cosmetic surgery performed by nanorobots or changes in genetic sequences on chromosomes.

WRITE NOW

Write a bold thesis

Too much of what we read says what we've all heard before. Instead of serving up what readers likely know, try challenging readers. For example, in *Everything Bad Is Good for You*, Steven Johnson argues that video games are not a total waste of time but teach children valuable problem-solving skills.

Think of something that many people accept as common sense or general wisdom—that junk food is bad for you, reality television is garbage, or graffiti is vandalism—and argue the opposite. Or that something thought of as boring might be really interesting: bird watching, classical Indian music, or ancient Greek drama. Write a thesis that stands common wisdom on its head.

Then write a paragraph about how you might argue for your controversial thesis. What evidence might you supply?

Make a Plan

Get out your notes and all the information you have collected. You may find it helpful to write major points on sticky notes so you can move them around. If your topic is the effects of nanotechnology on the body, you might produce an organization plan similar to this one.

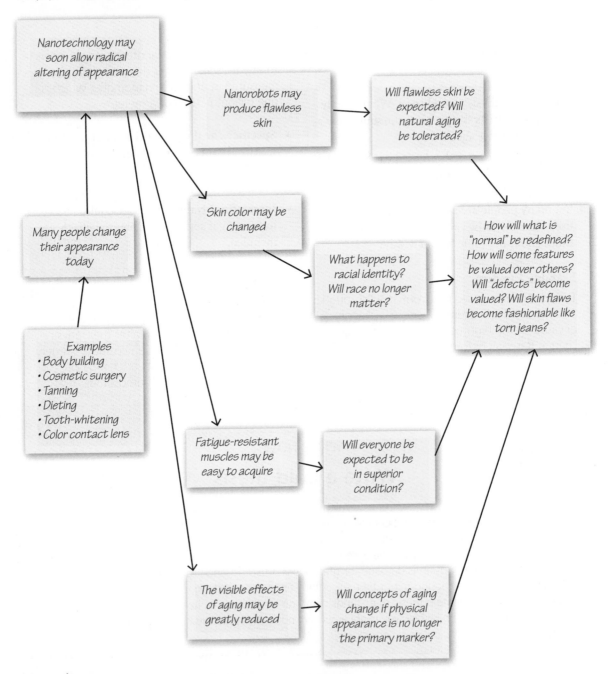

Listen to the Podcast on **Organizing** at mycomplab.com

Writing plans often take the form of outlines, either formal outlines or working outlines.

A **formal outline** typically begins with the working thesis, which anchors the entire outline.

A **working outline** is a sketch of how you will arrange the major sections.

WORKING THESIS: Nanotechnology may soon allow radical altering of the human body, which will have major social consequences.

I. Altering the appearance of the body has become common.

   A. Cosmetic surgery is now routine.

   B. Body building is popular.

   C. Most people are aware of diet and many attempt to control their weight.

   D. Tanning, changing eye color, and tooth-whitening are frequent.

II. Nanotechnology may soon radically accelerate these trends.

   A. Nanorobots may produce flawless skin.

   B. Skin color may be changed.

   C. Wrinkles and other signs of aging may be eliminated or reduced.

   D. Muscle tissue may be enhanced.

Effects of nanotechnology on the body

SECTION 1: *Begin with how people change the appearance of their bodies today.*

SECTION 2: *Discuss how nanotechnology will accelerate these trends, giving people the potential for perfect skin, changing their skin color, and reducing aging.*

SECTION 3: *Move to the questions these technologies raise, such as how aging will be perceived and how race will be understood.*

SECTION 4: *Raise the issue of how "normal" will be defined if people can choose how they look.*

SECTION 5: *Expand the idea of "normal" to who will control what is desirable and how social hierarchies might be changed or reinforced.*

SECTION 6: *End by connecting body issues to larger issues such as who gets to live for how long.*

WRITE NOW

Compare planning methods

First, write a working thesis. Ask the questions on page 37.

• Is the thesis specific? • Is it manageable? • Is it interesting?

Revise your thesis if necessary.

   Then use two of the three methods—a visual organization plan, a formal outline, or a working outline—to develop a plan for writing a paper based on the thesis. When you finish, compare the plans. Which will be easier to use for writing your paper?

4 Drafting

Drafting is easier when you think ahead with strategies in mind for writing.

Chapter Overview

► **Draft with strategies in mind**
(see p. 41)

► **Write a zero draft**
(see p. 42)

► **Draft from a working outline**
(see p. 44)

► **Start fast with an engaging title and opening paragraph**
(see p. 46)

► **Develop paragraphs**
(see p. 47)

► **Conclude with strength**
(see p. 48)

► **Link within and across paragraphs**
(see p. 49)

Draft with Strategies in Mind

People who write frequently on the job or who make their living as writers have many different strategies for producing a successful piece of writing. Some plan extensively in advance, specifying what will go in each section.

Other writers find that putting ideas into words often changes the ideas and generates new ones. These writers start with what is sometimes called a zero draft or discovery draft, which resembles a sculptor's untouched clay to be molded later into the finished project.

FIND A DRAFTING STRATEGY THAT WORKS FOR YOU	Think about how you will write your project. **Write a zero draft:** If you do not have a plan, you may want to write a zero draft, then determine your plan. → **See page 42** **Write from an outline:** If you have a formal or working outline, you can use the outline to write individual paragraphs. → **See page 44**
WRITE AN ENGAGING TITLE AND INTRODUCTION	Get off to a fast start. Make your readers interested in your topic. → **See page 46**
DEVELOP YOUR BODY PARAGRAPHS	Paragraphs, like essays, have a beginning, middle, and end organized around a central idea. → **See page 47**
WRITE A STRONG CONCLUSION	Conclusions that offer only a summary bore readers. Effective conclusions are interesting and provocative, leaving readers with something to think about. → **See page 48**
CHECK YOUR LINKS WITHIN AND BETWEEN PARAGRAPHS	Writing that flows is coherent, which means that readers understand how sentences and paragraphs fit together. Repeating key words and phrases and signaling transitions builds coherence. → **See page 49**

Watch the Video on Drafting at mycomplab.com   41

Write a Zero Draft

One method of drafting is to start writing before you know where you are headed. A zero draft or discovery draft is similar to freewriting, where you write quickly for a set time, often five to ten minutes.

The idea of a zero draft is to get as much down as you can and not worry about producing a finished product. Don't worry about grammar, spelling, or gaps in logic. If you start writing about side issues, don't worry about that either; it might eventually turn into the focus of your project.

Writer at work

For assigned writing in her classes, Patrice Conley prefers writing first and then determining her organization. She knows in advance that nearly all of what she writes will not make it into the final draft she submits to her instructor. Nevertheless, she finds writing as fast as she can frees up her thinking and gives her words to start with rather than a blank page.

Patrice later goes back to her zero draft to identify key ideas, which she underlines.

PATRICE'S ZERO DRAFT

I can't believe how much colleges and universities that play big-time football and basketball are making off the student athletes. It's ridiculous. The schools are making a fortune, the networks that televise the games are making a fortune, and the coaches are making a fortune. Everybody is getting filthy rich except the stars of the show, the players, who get nothing out of it. They can't even be paid after they graduate if their school uses their names and images to make money. I know the NCAA—that's the organization that runs college sports—claims that student athletes are paid with scholarships. But that assumes that they will graduate, and a lot of them will drop out. They spend so much time on athletics that once their eligibility is gone, they are way behind and don't have the athletics' tutors to help them. I know this has been going on for years, but it just isn't right. Why don't the players sue? Other students can get paid for working as professionals. Our music school has a service for helping talented musicians to find jobs. I know other students who have had bit parts in movies. How can students who aren't athletes work professionally in their specialty and get paid when athletes can't. The reason colleges get by with treating athletes unfairly is because they define them as amateurs. The Olympics used to do this too, but they have dropped this distinction. Professional athletes compete in the Olympics in every sport except boxing. The definition needs to be changed.

When Patrice finished her zero draft, she let it sit for a day and then took stock of the key points that she had underlined. She rearranged these key points into a working outline.

PATRICE CREATES A WORKING OUTLINE FROM HER ZERO DRAFT

WORKING TITLE: *Should Student Athletes in Big-Time College Sports Be Paid?*

SECTION 1: *Student athletes in college sign away their rights for payment.*

SECTION 2: *College athletics are big business, and top coaches receive multimillion-dollar salaries.*

SECTION 3: *NCAA defends classifying student athletes as amateurs to protect them from exploitation.*

SECTION 4: *The history of amateurism arose in 19th c. Britain when middle- and upper-class sportsmen didn't want to play against working-class teams. The Olympics abandoned the distinction in 1988.*

SECTION 5: *Student musicians and student actors get paid when they perform professionally.*

SECTION 6: *Student athletes cannot be paid for use of their names and images even after they graduate.*

SECTION 7: *Defenders of the current system claim that student athletes are paid with scholarships, but in big-time sports many do not graduate.*

SECTION 8: *NCAA should adopt a different definition of amateur that allows those lucky enough to be paid for what they earn for their schools.*

WRITE NOW

Your drafting strategies

Think about two or three pieces of writing you have done for school or work recently. What method did you use? Did you make an outline or a visual plan or did you start writing?

Write a paragraph for each piece of writing about your writing process. What was easy for you? What was most difficult?

Draft from a Working Outline

Writers who like to lay out sections in advance of writing use formal or working outlines. These advance planners want to know where they are headed when they start typing sentences.

One issue to consider is where to place the thesis for the project. You may have been told at some point that your thesis should be the last sentence in the first paragraph. In some kinds of writing, especially arguments, the organization builds toward a thesis, which may come as late as the conclusion. Nonetheless, the opening paragraph should clearly indicate your topic and where you are headed.

This working outline on the risks of nanotechnology describes potential risks before presenting the thesis in the final paragraph.

TITLE: Managing the Risks of Nanotechnology While Reaping the Rewards

SECTION 1: Begin by defining nanotechnology—manipulating particles between 1 and 100 nanometers (nanometer is a billionth of a meter). Describe the rapid spread of nanotechnology in consumer products including clothing, food, sports equipment, medicines, electronics, and cars. State projection of 15% of global manufactured goods containing nanotechnology in 2014: But is it safe?

SECTION 2: Most Americans know nothing about nanotechnology. Companies have stopped advertising that their products contain nanotechnology because of fear of potential lawsuits. Asbestos, once thought safe, now is known to be toxic and has cost companies $250 billion in lawsuits in the United States alone.

SECTION 3: Relatively little research has been done on the safety of nanotechnology. No testing is required for new products because the materials are common, but materials behave differently at nano-scale (example—aluminum normally inert but combustible at nano-scale).

SECTION 4: Nanoparticles are highly mobile and can cross the blood-brain barrier and through the placenta. They are toxic in brains of fish and may collect in lungs.

SECTION 5: Urge that the federal government develop a master plan for identifying and reducing potential risks of nanotechnology and provide sufficient funding to carry out the plan. The federal government needs to create a master plan for risk research and to increase spending at least tenfold to ensure sufficient funding to carry out the plan.

The working thesis is stated as the conclusion.

Use your working outline to write paragraphs

Using a working outline to guide a writing project requires you to decide how you convert sections into paragraphs. Some sections might translate into a single paragraph; other sections might require two or more paragraphs.

For example, the first section of the working outline on the opposite page might be the first paragraph.

Construct effective paragraphs

For each paragraph you will need either to identify the main idea or write a topic sentence. Paragraphs are organized much like essays with an introduction, a body, and a conclusion. The topic sentence often is the first sentence and serves as the introduction. The body expands the main idea of the paragraph. The conclusion either reinforces the main point or it provides a bridge to what follows in the next paragraph and beyond.

Opening paragraphs need to do more than provide information about the topic. They need either to include the thesis statement or else they need to cue the reader to where the project is headed. In this case, the writer poses a question. This opening paragraph develops section 1 of the working outline.

Managing the Risks of Nanotechnology While Reaping the Rewards

Topic sentence →
The revolutionary potential of nanotechnology for medicine, energy production, and communication is now at the research and development stage, but the future has arrived in consumer products. Nanotechnology has given us products we hardly could have imagined just a few years ago: socks that never smell; pants that repel water yet keep you cool; eyeglasses that won't scratch; "smart" foods that add nutrition and reduce cholesterol; DVDs that are incredibly lifelike; bandages that speed healing; tennis balls that last longer; golf balls that fly straighter;

Details build the paragraph →
pharmaceuticals that selectively deliver drugs; various digital devices like palm pilots, digital cameras, and cell phones that have longer battery lives and more vivid displays; and cars that are lighter, stronger, and more fuel efficient. These miracle products are now possible because scientists have learned how to manipulate nano-scale particles from 1–100 nanometers (a nanometer is a billionth of a meter; a human hair is about 100,000 nanometers in width). Experts estimate that 15% of all consumer products will contain nanotechnology by 2014.

A question indicates the direction for the rest of the paper →
In the rush to create new consumer products, however, one question has not been asked: Is nanotechnology safe for those who use the products and the workers who are exposed to nanoparticles daily?

45

Start Fast with an Engaging Title and Opening Paragraph

Often you have but a few seconds to convince a reader to keep reading what you've written. Make those few seconds count.

Titles

Vague titles give no motivation to read on.

VAGUE

Good and Bad Fats

Specific titles are like a tasty appetizer; if you like the appetizer, you'll probably like the main course.

SPECIFIC

The Secret Killer: Hydrogenated Fats

Cut out empty phrases and sentences

Writers often start a draft with empty phrases and sentences, much as speakers clear their throats before starting.

~~Americans have seen many new digital technologies in just a few years. These technologies are capable of delivering massive amounts of information almost instantly.~~ Unlike the past two centuries, where each new communication technology was celebrated as the means to a glorious future, few now claim that more information will lead to better lives. The glut of information that is readily accessible has not led to broader global understanding but instead in the view of many observers has led to increased fragmentation, confusion, and exhaustion.

Don't apologize

Readers dismiss writers who begin by making excuses. Do your homework as a writer and you can offer an informed perspective.

WEAK

I'm not an economics major, and I don't know much about financial issues, but it costs a lot to fill up my car each week.

STRONGER

Could small changes in behavior lead to big economic changes in the lives of Americans? I tested that question for a week by walking, biking, and taking public transportation to avoid driving and by eating healthy foods bought in bulk or from the farmers' market rather than more expensive packaged foods.

● Watch the Animation on Introductions at mycomplab.com

Develop Paragraphs

Readers expect paragraphs in essays to be developed.

This paragraph gives the main ideas but with no examples. The writing is abstract and limp.

THIN

> We now live in a global economy where all countries are connected. When something happens to the economy in one country, it affects others. Many factories have moved to developing nations, and the economic activity in advanced nations focuses more on concept development and marketing.

Developed paragraphs often include examples that illustrate main points. Key ideas are emphasized in vivid sentences.

DEVELOPED

> We now live in a global economy, where more than a trillion dollars is exchanged in currency markets daily and where a burp in Malaysia can tumble stock exchanges in the West. The creation of wealth has moved from production in fortress-like factories to global networks of management and distribution, so that, when you buy a product at your local Walmart or Costco, the purchase data are sent not only to a corporation but also to the manufacturer of that product. Tomorrow's production in distant developing nations is determined by what is purchased today in the United States and other affluent nations. In the fast and light capitalism of the new economy, how and where goods are produced has become relatively unimportant compared to creating new concepts and marketing those concepts.

Pay attention to paragraphs when you revise

In revising, focus on each paragraph—one at a time. For each one, ask yourself what your reader will notice and remember.

- Is the main point fully developed?
- Does the paragraph include examples?
- Are key ideas emphasized in vivid sentences?

 Watch the Animation on Paragraph Development at mycomplab.com

Conclude with Strength

The challenge in ending paragraphs is to leave the reader with something provocative, something beyond pure summary of the previous paragraphs.

Issue a call to action	Although ecological problems in Russia seem distant, students like you and me can help protect the snow leopard by joining the World Wildlife Fund campaign.
Make a recommendation	Russia's creditors would be wise to sign on to the World Wildlife Fund's proposal to relieve some of the country's debt in order to protect snow leopard habitat. After all, if Russia is going to be economically viable, it needs to be ecologically healthy.
Give an example that illustrates a key point	Poachers are so uncowed by authorities that they even tried to sell a leopard skin to a reporter researching a story on endangered species.
Speculate about the future	Unless Nepali and Chinese officials devote more resources to snow leopard preservation, these beautiful animals will be gone in a few years.
Ask rhetorical questions	In general the larger and more majestic (or better yet, cute) an endangered animal is, the better its chances of being saved. Bumper stickers don't implore us to save blind cave insects; they ask us to save the whales, elephants, and tigers. But snow leopards aren't cave bugs; they are beautiful, impressive animals that should be the easiest of all to protect. If we can't save them, do any endangered species stand a chance?

Link Within and Across Paragraphs

Transitions at the beginnings and ends of paragraphs guide readers. They explain why a paragraph follows from the previous one. They offer writers the opportunity to highlight the turns in their thinking.

Build coherence

The first paragraph introduces the metaphor of the "Information Superhighway" and connects the metaphor to the American myth of the frontier. The words in bold are repeated verbatim or with synonyms in the next paragraph.

The metaphor of the "Information Superhighway," popularized by Al Gore in the 1990s, sprang from a long-standing American myth about the freedom of **the open road**. Throughout the twentieth century the automobile represented freedom of action—not just the pleasures of driving around aimlessly for recreation but the possibility of exploring new territories and reaching **the frontier**. When talking about the Internet, both Republicans and Democrats in the 1990s invoked the idealized highway in the American imagination—**the highway** that leads to **the frontier.**

The second paragraph begins with the frontier and examines how roads are also tied to ideas of a free-market economy.

Exploration of the **frontier** is linked to democracy in this rhetoric. From Thomas Jefferson onward, American leaders have maintained that **good roads** are a prerequisite to democracy. With **good roads** farmers could transport their crops directly to local markets and competitive railheads.

WRITE NOW

What makes a paragraph good or bad?

Find examples of well-written paragraphs and poorly written paragraphs in print or on the Web using the criteria covered in this chapter. Look for examples of opening and concluding paragraphs as well as body paragraphs. What exactly makes the good examples well written? Likewise, what makes the bad examples poorly written?

Revise one of the bad examples to improve it.

5 Revising

In order to revise effectively, you must "re-see" what you have written, which, after all, is what revision means.

Chapter Overview

▶ **Revising and editing**
 (see p. 51)

▶ **Evaluate your draft**
 (see p. 52)

▶ **Respond to others**
 (see p. 54)

▶ **Pay attention to details last**
 (see p. 55)

▶ **Revise using your instructor's comments**
 (see p. 56)

Revising and Editing

Revision is a two-step process that involves both revising and editing. The revising step can involve a major overhaul of your paper or media project. You may have to rewrite entire sections. The editing step deals with local concerns: making sentences read better, inserting transitions between sentences and paragraphs, checking for correct format, and eliminating errors in grammar, punctuation, and spelling.

Experienced writers know that both steps are critical for success. Even the best writers have to revise several times to get the result they want. Inexperienced writers too often skip the revising step and go straight to the issues of copyediting and proofreading. They are unwilling to make major changes.

To be able to revise effectively, you have to plan your time. You cannot revise a paper or a media project effectively if you wait until the last minute to begin working. Allow at least a day between the time you finish your draft and when you begin revising to let what you write cool off.

A good method to begin your revision is to read your paper out loud to someone else. Ask that person to give you a quick response. Is the organization clear? Is anything confusing? Is there anything that the listener wants to know more about? You'll likely also notice rough spots in your writing because these places will be difficult to read. What you are after is an overall sense of how well you have accomplished what you set out to do.

EVALUATE YOUR DRAFT	Start with the big picture. Does your project meet the assignment? Does it have a clear focus? Are the main points adequately developed? Is the organization effective? ➜ **See page 52**
RESPOND TO OTHERS	Responding to the writing of others is one of the most practical skills you learn in a writing class. College-educated people write frequently in their jobs and professions—often as a team—and they are regularly asked to review what coworkers have written. ➜ **See page 54**
PAY ATTENTION TO DETAILS LAST	Your sentences should be clearly written and free of errors in grammar and punctuation. ➜ **See page 55**
REVISE USING YOUR INSTRUCTOR'S COMMENTS	Your instructor's comments give you the benefit of advice from an expert reader. ➜ **See page 56**

Evaluate Your Draft

Use these questions to evaluate your draft. Note any places where you might make improvements.

Does your paper or project meet the assignment?	• Look again at your assignment and especially at the key words such as *analyze, define, evaluate*, and *propose*. Does your paper or project do what the assignment asks for? If not, how can you change it?
	• Look again at the assignment for specific guidelines including length, format, and amount of research. Does your work meet these guidelines? If not, how can you change it?
Do you have a clear focus?	• Underline your thesis. Think how you might make your thesis more precise.
	• Underline the main idea of each paragraph. Check how each paragraph connects to your thesis. Think about how you can strengthen the connections.
Are your main points adequately developed?	• Put brackets around the reasons and evidence that support your main points.
	• Can you find places to add more examples and details that would help to explain your main points?
Is your organization effective?	• Make a quick outline of your draft if you have not done so already.
	• Mark the places where you find abrupt shifts or gaps.
	• Think about how you might rearrange sections or paragraphs to make your draft more effective.
Do you consider your potential readers' knowledge and points of view?	• Where do you give background if your readers are unfamiliar with your subject?
	• Where do you acknowledge any opposing views your readers might have?
Do you represent yourself effectively?	• To the extent you can, forget for a moment that you wrote what you are reading. What impression do you have of you, the writer?
	• Does the writer have an appropriate tone?
	• Is the writer visually effective? Is the type easy to read? Does the writer use headings and illustrations where they are helpful?

When you finish, make a list of your goals in the revision. You may have to scrap the draft and start over, but you will have a better sense of your subject and your goals.

Strategies for rewriting

Now it's time to go through your draft in detail. You should work on the goals you identify in your review. Also, look for other opportunities using this checklist.

1.
KEEP YOUR AUDIENCE IN MIND

Reread each of your paragraphs' opening sentences and ask yourself whether they are engaging enough to keep your readers interested.

2.
SHARPEN YOUR FOCUS WHEREVER POSSIBLE

You may have started out with a large topic but most of what you wrote concerns only one aspect. You may need to revise your thesis and supporting paragraphs.

3.
CHECK IF KEY TERMS ARE ADEQUATELY DEFINED

What are your key terms? Are they defined precisely enough to be meaningful?

4.
DEVELOP YOUR IDEAS WHERE NECESSARY

Key points and claims may need more explanation and supporting evidence. Look for opportunities to add support without becoming redundant.

5.
CHECK LINKS BETWEEN PARAGRAPHS

Look for any places where you make abrupt shifts and make the transitions better. Check if you signal the relationship from one paragraph to the next.

6.
CONSIDER YOUR TITLE

Many writers don't think much about titles, but they are very important. A good title makes the reader want to see what you have to say. Be as specific as you can in your title, and if possible, suggest your stance.

7.
CONSIDER YOUR INTRODUCTION

In the introduction you want to get off to a fast start and convince your reader to keep reading. Cut to the chase.

8.
CONSIDER YOUR CONCLUSION

Restating your thesis usually isn't the best way to finish; conclusions that offer only summary bore readers. The worst endings say something like "in my paper I've said this." Effective conclusions are interesting and provocative, leaving readers with something to think about.

9.
IMPROVE THE VISUAL ASPECTS OF YOUR TEXT

Does the font you selected look attractive using your printer? Would headings and subheadings help to identify key sections? If you include statistical data, would charts be effective? Would illustrations help to establish key points?

Respond to Others

Your instructor may ask you to respond to the drafts of your classmates. Responding to other people's writing requires the same careful attention you give to your own draft.

First reading:
Read at your normal rate the first time through without stopping. When you finish you should have a clear sense of what the writer is trying to accomplish.

- **Main idea:** Write a sentence that summarizes what you think is the writer's main idea in the draft.
- **Purpose:** Write a sentence that summarizes what you think the writer was trying to accomplish in the draft.

Second reading:
In your second reading, you should be most concerned with the content, organization, and completeness of the draft. Make notes as you read.

- **Introduction:** Does the writer's first paragraph effectively introduce the topic and engage your interest?
- **Thesis:** Where exactly is the writer's thesis? Note in the margin where you think the thesis is located.
- **Focus:** Does the writer maintain focus on the thesis? Note any places where the writer seems to wander off to another topic.
- **Organization:** Are the ideas presented in effective order? Can you suggest a better order for the paragraphs?
- **Completeness:** Are there sections and paragraphs that lack adequate development? Where do you want to know more?
- **Sources:** If the draft uses outside sources, are they cited accurately? If there are quotations, are they used correctly and worked into the fabric of the draft?

Third reading:
In your third reading, turn your attention to matters of audience, style, and tone.

- **Audience:** Who is the writer's intended audience? What does the writer assume the audience knows and believes?
- **Style:** Is the writer's style engaging? How would you describe the writer's voice?
- **Tone:** Is the tone appropriate for the writer's purpose and audience? Is the tone consistent throughout the draft? Are there places where another word or phrase might work better?

When you have finished the third reading, write a short paragraph on each bulleted item above—audience, style, and tone—referring to specific paragraphs in the draft by number. Then end by answering these two questions:

1. What does the writer do especially well in the draft?

2. What one or two things would most improve the draft in a revision?

  Watch the Animation on Responding to Others' Writing at mycomplab.com

Pay Attention to Details Last

When you finish revising, you are ready for one final careful reading, keeping the goals of improving your style and eliminating errors in mind.

Edit different elements in turn

1. Check the connections between sentences.	Notice how your sentences are connected. If you need to signal the relationship from one sentence to the next, use a transition word or phrase.
2. Check your sentences.	If you notice that a sentence doesn't sound right, think about how you might rephrase it. Often you will pick up problems by reading aloud. If a sentence seems too long, then you might break it into two or more sentences. If you notice a string of short sentences that sound choppy, then you might combine them.
3. Eliminate wordiness.	Writers tend to introduce wordiness in drafts. Look for long expressions that can easily be shortened ("at this point in time" –> "now") and for unnecessary repetition. Remove unnecessary words like *very, really*, and *totally*. See how many words you can take out without losing the meaning.
4. Use active verbs.	Anytime you can use a verb besides a form of be (*is, are, was, were*) or a verb ending in *–ing*, take advantage of the opportunity to make your style more lively. Sentences that begin with "There is (are)" and "It is" often have better alternatives.

Proofread carefully

In your final pass through your text, eliminate as many errors as you can. To become an effective proofreader, you have to learn to slow down. Some writers find that moving from word to word with a pencil slows them down enough to find errors. Others read backwards to force concentration on each word.

1. Know what your spelling checker can and can't do.	Spelling checkers are the greatest invention since peanut butter. They turn up many typos and misspellings that are hard to catch. But spelling checkers do not catch wrong words (e.g., "to much" should be "too much"), where you leave off endings ("three dog"), and other similar errors.
2. Check for grammar and punctuation.	Nothing hurts your credibility more than leaving many errors in what you write. Many job application letters get tossed in the reject pile because an applicant made a single, glaring error. Readers probably shouldn't make such harsh judgments when they find errors, but in real life they do.

Watch the Animation on Spelling and Grammar Checkers at **mycomplab.com**   **55**

Revise Using Your Instructor's Comments

After you have put in a great deal of work writing a paper, sometimes you may find it discouraging to get your paper back with numerous comments from your instructor. Revising with your instructor's comments, however, is the best way to learn how to become a better writer.

Here are a few points to keep in mind.

- **Think of your instructor as a coach whose goal is to make you the best writer you can be.**
  When your coach tells you that your writing can improve, it's not the same thing as telling you that you are a bad writer. Don't take your instructor's advice personally.

- **Read the comments carefully.**
  Often what your instructor is asking you to do is not difficult.

- **Talk with your instructor if you do not understand a comment.**
  Your instructor can explain the comment, and both you and your instructor will benefit from the conversation.

- **Go to your writing center.**
  The consultants at your writing center will help you to interpret your instructor's comments and to plan strategies for using the comments.

Identify your instructor's local and global comments

Your instructor likely will make local and global comments, and it's important to distinguish them. Start with the global comments. These may be comments in the margins like "I can't follow your logic here" and "This section appears out of place." Or they may be in a final comment like "Your organization would be more effective if you presented other proposed solutions first and held your solution until the end." Address these big issues first.

Local comments may be circled or underlined works and punctuation and short comments. Understand that your instructor is not editing the paper for you and will not mark every error. Your instructor wants you to recognize categories of errors; for example, if you have one problem with using commas, you likely have others.

Don't limit your revisions to addressing your instructor's comments. Many times revising a paper will bring new ideas. Realize too that it's your responsibility to make sure that your paper is error-free when you submit the final draft.

WRITE NOW
Make a reverse outline

Find a paper that you wrote for another course. Number the paragraphs in the paper. On a separate sheet of paper, write the main point of the first paragraph. Then, write the main point of the second paragraph. Go through the entire paper this way. When you have gone through the whole paper, you will have a reverse outline, an outline done after writing the paper.

Look at your reverse outline. Does the outline fulfill what you promise in the introduction? Can any ideas be deleted without losing content? Can any ideas be moved? Can you revise the outline to better organize your paper?

Watch the Video on Revising at mycomplab.com

Writer at work

Patrice Conley received both global and local comments from her instructor. Patrice first dealt with her instructor's global comments.

RETURNED DRAFT WITH COMMENTS

> College athletics are big business. The most visible college sports—big-time men's football and basketball—generate staggering sums of money. Even more money comes in from video games, clothing, and similar licenses.

Your major claims need to be supported with evidence. Give specific examples.

Patrice did additional research to find examples to support her claim.

PATRICE'S REVISION

Make no mistake: college athletics are big business. The most visible college sports—big-time men's football and basketball—generate staggering sums of money. For example, the twelve universities in the Southeastern Conference receive $205 million each year from CBS and ESPN for the right to broadcast its football games (Smith and Ourand). Even more money comes in from video games, clothing, and similar licenses. In 2010, the *New York Times* reported, "the NCAA's licensing deals are estimated at more than $4 billion" per year (Thamel). While the staggering executive pay at big corporations has brought public outrage, coaches' salaries are even more outlandish. Kentucky basketball coach John Calipari is paid over $4 million a year for a basketball program that makes about $35-40 million a year, more than 10% of the entire revenue.

Then she moved on to her instructor's local comments. Her instructor noted a transition is needed between two paragraphs, and Patrice added a sentence, highlighted in yellow below.

PATRICE'S REVISION

The college sports empire in the United States run by the NCAA is the last bastion of amateurism for sports that draw audiences large enough to be televised. Colleges might be able to defend the policy of amateurism if they extended this definition to all students. A fair policy is one that treats all students the same. A fair policy doesn't result in some students getting paid for professional work, while other students do not.

You can read Patrice's completed paper on pages 452–457.

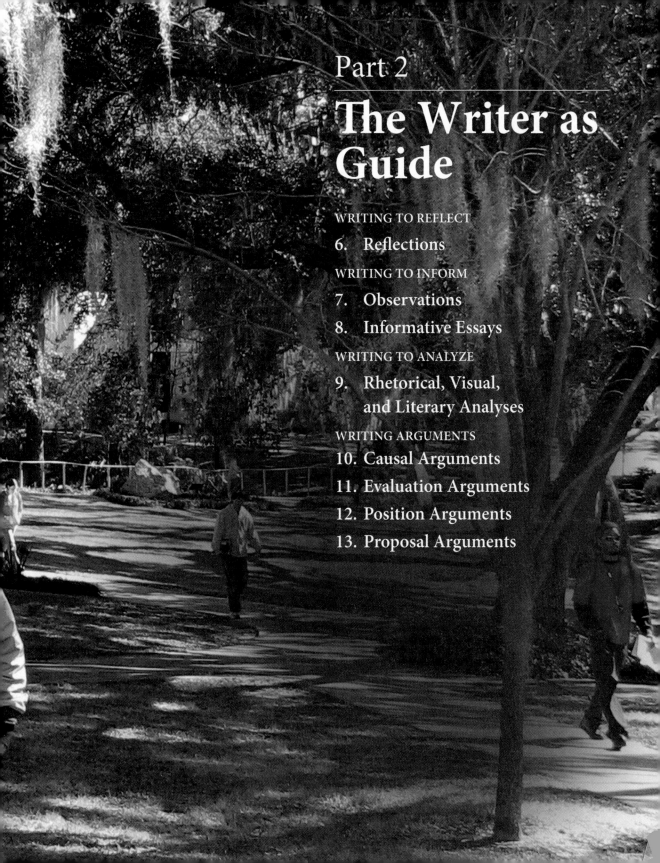

Part 2
The Writer as Guide

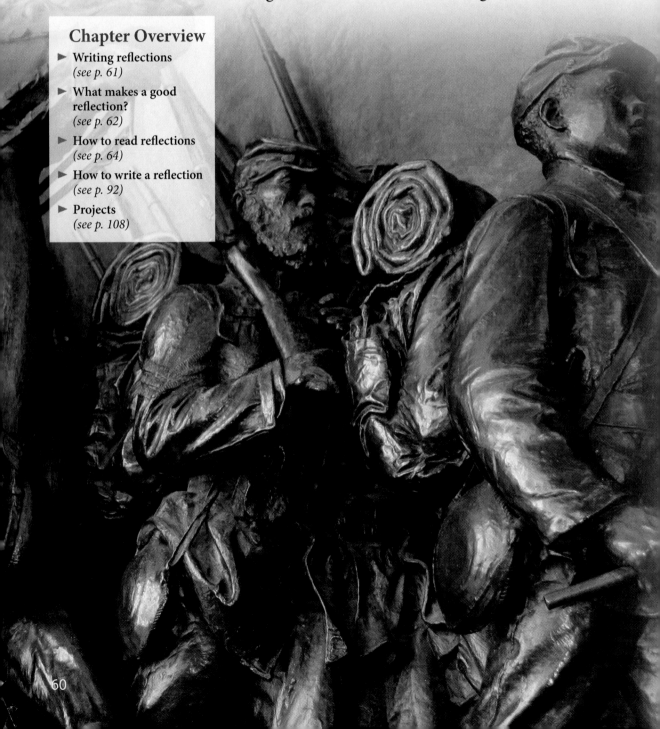

6 Reflections

A successful reflection challenges readers to learn something about themselves.

Chapter Overview

Writing Reflections

When we reflect, we consider an idea or experience in order to come to a greater understanding of its significance. Reflecting is a way of understanding ourselves. By connecting memories of the past with our knowledge of the present, we learn about who we were and who we have become.

Reflections can explore deeply emotional issues like family relationships, personal failings, and dramatic crises. The goal of a reflection, however, should not be simply to vent pent-up emotions or to expose secrets (although when done well, these techniques can be effective). Instead, a reflection should allow readers to share with the writer a discovery of significance.

Keys to reflections

TELL A GOOD STORY	Readers have to be interested in your story to gain its insights. Often reflections keep readers' interest by presenting a conflict or a difficult decision that must be resolved.
LET THE DETAILS CONVEY THE SIGNIFICANCE	Select details carefully to communicate meaning. Identify people by more than how they look. Think about mannerisms, gestures, and habits to suggest their character.
BE HONEST	Telling the truth about your thoughts and actions can build a strong connection with your readers.
FOCUS ON THE LITTLE THINGS	A reflection doesn't have to teach big lessons about life. Small moments such as what makes you happy can be as rewarding for readers as great events.

Informative writing in the world

Memoirs reflect on personal memories and life experiences. People write memoirs for many reasons, but successful memoirs explore questions about personal experience and invite readers also to reflect on those experiences and probe their deeper significance. Recent memoirs that combine self-discovery and travel, such as Elizabeth Gilbert's *Eat, Pray, Love* and Frances Mayes's *Under the Tuscan Sun,* have stayed at the top of best-seller lists for many months.

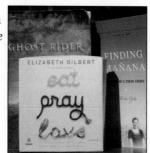

Other genres of informative writing

- **Narratives** tell stories about other people as well as the writer's life and offer unique perspectives.
- **Personal statements** are required for many scholarship applications and for admission to graduate and professional schools.
- **Blogs** reflect on events of the day, books, films, music, and popular culture.

Watch the Animation on Writing Memoirs at mycomplab.com

What Makes a Good Reflection?

1

What makes a good reflection?
Listing is one method to identify possible topics for reflections. You might list people, events, places, and objects that have been important in your life. When you finish, look back over your list and check the items that seem especially vivid to you.

Think about how interesting your topic will be to your potential readers. Your greatest moment in sports or the time you met your current partner may be peak experiences for you, but how engrossing with they be for your readers?

2

Engage readers at the beginning
Get your readers' attention with your title and first sentences.

OPEN DOOR

Leave the door open for the unknown, the door into the dark. That's where the most important things come from, where you yourself came from, and where you will go.
—Rebecca Solnit (see page 76)

3

Write with a personal voice
Reflections should not sound like they were written by a committee. Your reflection should convey your personality.

Poor Tiffany. She'd do just about anything in return for a little affection. All you had to do was call her Tiff and whatever you wanted was yours: her allowance money, her dinner, the contents of her Easter basket.
—David Sedaris (see page 70)

4

Introduce a complication
A conflict or a tension usually motivates a reflection. While the complication is often between people, it can involve objects and ideas.

5

Provide concrete details
Details make reflections come alive. Don't limit details to what you can see. Include sounds, smells, textures, physical actions, and tastes where possible.

Stacy and I pushed through hundreds of leg lifts on her bedroom floor, an open *Seventeen* magazine as a tiny table for our lemon water, and the sound of cicadas grinding away in the tree outside.
—Alisa Valdes-Rodriguez (see page 73)

6

Use dialogue when possible
People come to life when you let them talk.

We were talking about the price of new and used furniture and I heard myself saying this: "Not waste money that way."
—Amy Tan (see page 84)

7

Identify a central theme
Sometimes a central theme is at the heart of a reflection such as Rebecca Solnit's reflection on why "getting lost" can be valuable. In other cases the theme is implied but still provides a center for the reflection.

This was how things went. One moment she was locking out of our own house and the next we were rooting around in the snow, looking for her left shoe.
—David Sedaris (see page 70)

8

Come to a new understanding
Effective conclusions invite readers to reflect further. Ending by inviting readers to think about what they have just read is usually better than trying to sum up with a moral lesson.

Watch the Animation on Writing to Reflect at mycomplab.com

Reflections about visuals

The Kodak Brownie, introduced in 1900, popularized snapshot photography and allowed families to construct their own histories in the family album. Kodak urged consumers to "celebrate moments of your life." Photographs indeed freeze moments in the past, documenting that the camera was present at a precisely datable time.

But photographs also take on lives of their own much like our memories of the past, where seemingly insignificant conversations and events from years ago keep popping into our heads. Photographs show us people we have known as adults when they were children and remind us that they too were once young. We imagine people, including ourselves, at times in the past by reflecting on photographs.

Two girls in a park near Union Station, Washington, D.C. (1943).

WRITE NOW

Reflecting on photographs

1. Look at personal photographs on *Flickr, Photobucket, Picasa, Yahoo! Photos,* or another Web hosting service and find a set of images that stick with you.

2. Select three or four photographs of people by one photographer that appear to be taken within an hour or a few hours. Make a list of people in each photograph. What can you infer about them by the way they are dressed and what they are doing? Where were the photographs taken? What do you associate with the place?

3. Write a narrative about what you think was going on when the pictures were taken. What was the relationship of the people in the photographs with the photographer? What might they have been thinking at the time? Why were they in this particular place? Why were the photographs taken?

How to Read Reflections

▼ **BEFORE YOU BEGIN READING**

These notes are in response to "Some Lines for a Younger Brother . . ."; the reading begins on page 66.

What kind of text is it?	⋯⋯▶	The text is a reflective essay that appeared first in *Gidra*, a magazine published in Los Angeles from 1969 to 1974.

Who wrote it?	⋯⋯▶	Sue Kunitonomi Embry became a spokesperson for thousands of Japanese Americans who were imprisoned during the anti-Japanese hysteria at the beginning of World War II.

Who is the intended audience?	⋯⋯▶	*Gidra* was a newsmagazine aimed at the Asian American community in southern California.

▼ **READ THE TEXT AT LEAST TWICE AND MAKE NOTES**

What is the focus of the reflection?	⋯⋯▶	"The title and first paragraph announce that the focus of the reflection is Embrey's younger brother Tets.

What did the writer learn or understand differently from the reflection?	⋯⋯▶	Embrey came to terms with painful memories of being interned in the Manzanar concentration camp and losing her brother after the war.

Where does the writer include details and dialogue?	⋯⋯▶	Details and dialogue show the evolving relationship between Embrey and her younger brother.

How would you characterize the style?	⋯⋯▶	The style is informal and personal. The writer conveys her feelings about the loss of her brother.

How is it organized?

This map shows the organization of "Some Lines for a Younger Brother . . .", which begins on the following page.

Introductory paragraphs Paragraphs 1–3	Embrey sets the scene by describing the day her younger brother was born. She describes her family of eight children and her father's occupation, ending the section with his early death.
Complication Paragraphs 4–6	After the Japanese attack on Pearl Harbor in December 1941, the family lost their business and possessions and were sent to the Manzanar Relocation Camp.
Effects Paragraphs 7–17	Growing up in a concentration camp disillusioned Embrey's younger brother Tets. The family was scattered during the war. When the family was partially reunited after the war, Tets could not readjust. He joined the Army to escape.
Resolution Paragraphs 18–19	The resolution is tragic. Tets came home from the Korean War in a coffin.
Conclusion Paragraphs 20–22	Embrey returns the Manzanar Relocation Camp in 1969. The visit brings back memories of Tets as a 12-year-old and brings a sense of closure.

Some Lines for a Younger Brother . . .
Sue Kunitonomi Embrey

Sue Kunitonomi Embrey (1923–2006) was born in Los Angeles. Instead of starting college in 1942, she was forced to move to the Manzanar Relocation Center in Inyo County, California, with other Japanese Americans. She spent the years during World War II in the concentration camp. After the war most of the people who were interned did not want to talk about the experience, but Embrey became an activist and made a pilgrimage in 1969 to remember what happened at Manzanar. She eventually was successful in getting Manzanar declared a national historic site. "Some Lines for a Younger Brother . . ." was published in *Gidra* in 1970.

Some Lines for a Younger Brother . . .

1   I still remember the day he was born. It was early April and Papa came into the kitchen with a smile on his face. He said we had a baby brother. In the months to follow, we were busy carrying and cuddling the brother who was many years younger than the rest of us. When he cried from hunger and Mama was busy, one of us would run into the bedroom and rock the bed or pick him up and quiet him.

Introduction: Embrey begins with her earliest memory of her brother, making it clear that he will be the focus of her reflection.

2   We were a family of five sons and three daughters. Money was scarce. My father ran a moving and transfer business in L'il Tokyo, the Japanese community in the shadow of City Hall in Los Angeles, but people had little money to pay him. He came home with boxes of books bartered for his services, and we spent many hours curled up in a corner reading some popular fiction story.

3   Tets, as we called him, was eight years old when Papa was killed in an automobile accident a week before Christmas. Tets cried because he could not give his dad the present he had made at school. The bullies would beat him up now that he had no father, he said.

Complication: Outside events are fitted into the family's personal chronology. Embrey shows vividly the impact of the decision to intern Japanese Americans.

4   Pearl Harbor was attacked by the Japanese when Tets was in elementary school. Rumors of sabotage couldn't be separated from the facts. Soon there was a clamor on the West Coast for wholesale

evacuation of all Japanese into inland camps. The democratic process was lost in hysteria. The grocery store which we had purchased only a year before was sold at a loss. All the furniture we couldn't sell, the plants my mother had tenderly cared for, our small personal treasures went to a neighborhood junk dealer. Tears came when we saw the truck being loaded.

5   On the first Sunday in May, 1942, Manzanar Relocation Center became our war-time home. Before breakfast, we walked around the dry, dusty land, to get acquainted with the landscape. The sun sparkled against the Sierra Nevada mountains to the west. The brown Inyo hills were high-rising barriers, more formidable than the barbed wire which was soon to enclose us. As we wondered how the pioneers had crossed over the Sierras, someone asked, "How long do we have to stay here?" and someone quoted from the military instructions, "For the duration of the war, and six months thereafter." Six months are forever, and forever is a long, long time.

> **Details:**
> Details about the relocation camp reinforce the sense of isolation and hopelessness it evokes.

6   Some order became evident within a few months after the fear, confusion and shock of transplantation from the big city to the arid land of Manzanar. Catholic nuns, who had joined the evacuees, found empty barracks and started a school. The War Relocation Authority recruited teachers from the "outside." Many of them were Quakers with a real desire to serve their fellow man.

7   When I asked Tets what he was studying, he shrugged his shoulders. There were no chairs, no desks, no supplies, he said. "What's the use of studying American history when we're behind barbed wires?" he asked. I tried to tell him that it would matter some day, but I was not sure any more. "Someday," I said, "the government would realize it had made a mistake and would try to correct it." His eyes were narrow against the noon sun, his whole body positioned badly to the right as he looked at me and said, "You 'da kind'? I lose fight." The colloquial speech was everywhere among the second generation. "Da kind" categorically placed me among those who argued for and defended American democracy. The second expression was used constantly, but it meant different things to different people.

> **Dialogue:**
> Embrey uses dialogue to recount a significant conversation she had with her brother, one that she has remembered for many years.

8   "Try walking out that gate," he added. "See if they don't shoot you in the back." With that, he walked away.

9   The rest of us managed to get out of confinement—to Chicago, to Madison, Wisconsin. Three brothers entered the United States Army. Tets was left with his aging mother and he was to spend almost three years behind barbed wires.

10   By 1948 when the family was partially reunited and settled in Los Angeles, Tets was in high school, or we thought he was. One day a school counselor came to the door. He reported that Tets had not been in school for several weeks and that he had been missing school sporadically for several months. He saw the shock on our faces. We had been too busy working to be suspicious.

11   "I'm looking for a job," Tets said, when confronted.

12   "But you can't find a job without a high school diploma," ◄───── I protested.

13   "So I found out," he answered. "Learning to say 'isn't' instead of 'ain't' doesn't get you a job. They want us to have experience to land a job, but how can we get experience if we can't get a job?"

14   I asked him what he was going to do.

15   "I'm going to join the Army," was his reply.

16   Day in and day out, this was his argument. "I'm going to join the Army when I'm eighteen. You won't have me around to bother you and I'll be doing some traveling. I'm tired of holding up the buildings in L'il Tokyo. There's nothing to do and no place to go where I can be with my friends."

17   He was sure that wars were over for a while and there would be no danger. He signed up one day and was gone the next. He came home on furlough, husky and tanned, a lot taller and more confident than when he had left. He had been in training camp in Louisiana and had seen much of the country. Before he left, he broke the news to us that he had signed up for another three years so he wouldn't have to serve in the reserves. He was transferred to the West Coast and we saw him often when he hitch-hiked home on weekends. One day he phoned collect from San Jose. He was being shipped out to Japan and it would probably be a year before he would be back.

Effects:
Again, Embrey uses dialogue to show viewers a turning point in her brother's life. As in the internment camp, this argument centers on whether he should go to school, but it is clear there are deeper issues at play for Embrey and for Tets.

18   His hitch was almost over when the Korean War broke out. Soon after his 22nd birthday, he wrote that he hoped to be home for Christmas. He explained that he had not been sleeping well lately since some veterans had been brought into his barracks. They had nightmares and they screamed in the night. The stories of war they told could not be shut out of his mind. There was a rumor going around that his company might be going over to replace the first groups. He hoped his timetable for discharge would not change. He was worried and that was why he had not written.

19   Tets came home before Christmas. He came home in a flag-draped coffin, with one of his buddies as a military escort. The funeral at the Koyasan Buddhist Church was impressive. There was a change of guards every few minutes. Their soft-spoken order mixed with the solemn chants. The curling incense smoke made hazy halos of the young faces who came mourning a dead friend.

Resolution: Embrey uses vivid detail to re-create her dead brother's funeral.

20   On December 27, 1969, I joined several hundred young people who made a day-long pilgrimage to the Manzanar cemetery. While I helped clean out the sagebrush and manzanilla, pulled tumbleweeds out of my boots, I was interrupted many times to recall facts and figures for the NBC and CBS television crews who were there to record the event.

21   Mt. Williamson's peak crested somewhere in the grey clouds that drew menacingly closer as the hours passed. Soon there was no sun. No seven-mile shadow lay across Owens Valley.

22   Dedication services ended that freezing, windswept and emotional day. I looked beyond the crowd and the monument. Out of the painful memories my mind dusted out of the past, I saw again the blurred impressions of the barbed-wire fence, the sentry towers and the tar-papered barracks. For a moment I saw again the 12-year-old boy with his head cocked, his shoulders sagging, his eyes fighting to keep open in the sun, while the long and lonely desert stretched out behind him.

Conclusion: Embrey ends with an almost wistful recollection of her brother.

Let It Snow
David Sedaris

David Sedaris is a writer, playwright, and radio commentator whose work often has an autobiographical focus. He became famous for *The Santaland Diaries,* a play about his job as a Christmas elf in Macy's department store. In this essay, from his collection *Dress Your Family in Corduroy and Denim,* he recalls a single day from his childhood in North Carolina.

Return to these questions after you have finished reading.

Analyzing the Reading

1. On the surface, this story centers around a snowstorm and children playing in it. Underlying these events are the much darker issues of the narrator's mother, her drinking, and her treatment of her children. How exactly does the snowstorm focus Sedaris's investigation of his family's past?

2. The narrator, as a fifth-grader, thinks that having his sister get hit by a car would be "the perfect solution" to their problem. What do you believe the adult narrator thinks of this "solution"? Are there any other clues that the narrator feels differently now?

3. The humor turns a potentially sad story into a ridiculous one. Think about how this essay might have been written without the humor. Could it be as effective?

4. Although this story deals with intensely personal issues, the tone is quite ironic and detached. Given the tone, what do you make of the story's ending, with the children surrounding their mother "tightly on all sides," finally going back to their house?

Exploring Ideas and Issues

In the essay, Sedaris shows how his mother's alcoholism affected his family. However, episodes in the life of a family can also be positive. Whether they are negative or positive, vivid memories can present a snapshot, a moment in time that can be representative of larger patterns in a family and its relationships.

1. In the essay, the author comes up with a plan to teach his parents a lesson. Most children probably have the wish, at one time or another, to punish their parents. Recall a time you thought your parents treated you unjustly. Did you feel angry, sad, confused, or ashamed? Describe the incident and your response at the time. Then reflect on whether or not your feelings have remained the same. Explain why.

2. Think of a snapshot moment in your life that could reflect a larger pattern or situation. The experience could concern your family life, work, school, or friendships. Describe the incident and explain how it represents a larger reality. For example, you might show how the cutting remark made by a coworker was typical of the atmosphere at your first job.

3. Think of a relationship—for example, with a sibling, teacher, or grandparent—that you particularly treasure. In a two-page essay, describe two or three experiences you've had that demonstrate why you value this relationship. Be sure to express how you felt about these incidents or what you learned from them.

Let It Snow

In Binghamton, New York, winter meant snow, and though I was young when we left, I was able to recall great heaps of it, and use that memory as evidence that North Carolina was, at best, a third-rate institution. What little snow there was would usually melt an hour or two after hitting the ground, and there you'd be in your windbreaker and unconvincing mittens, forming a lumpy figure made mostly of mud. Snow Negroes, we called them.

The winter I was in the fifth grade we got lucky. Snow fell, and for the first time in years, it accumulated. School was canceled and two days later we got lucky again. There were eight inches on the ground, and rather than melting, it froze. On the fifth day of our vacation my mother had a little breakdown. Our presence had disrupted the secret life she led while we were at school, and when she could no longer take it she threw us out. It wasn't a gentle request, but something closer to an eviction. "Get the hell out of my house," she said.

We reminded her that it was our house, too, and she opened the front door and shoved us into the carport. "And stay out!" she shouted.

My sisters and I went down the hill and sledded with other children from the neighborhood. A few hours later we returned home, surprised to find that the door was still locked. "Oh, come on," we said. I rang the bell and when no one answered we went to the window and saw our mother in the kitchen, watching television. Normally she waited until five o'clock to have a drink, but for the past few days she'd been making an exception. Drinking didn't count if you followed a glass of wine with a cup of coffee, and so she had both a goblet and a mug positioned before her on the countertop.

"Hey!" we yelled. "Open the door. It's us." We knocked on the pane, and without looking in our direction, she refilled her goblet and left the room.

"That bitch," my sister Lisa said. We pounded again and again, and when our mother failed to answer we went around back and threw snowballs at her bedroom window. "You are going to be in so much trouble when Dad gets home!" we shouted, and in response my mother pulled the drapes. Dusk approached, and as it grew colder it occurred to us that we could possibly die. It happened, surely. Selfish mothers wanted the house to themselves, and their children were discovered years later, frozen like mastodons in blocks of ice.

My sister Gretchen suggested that we call our father, but none of us knew his number, and he probably wouldn't have done anything anyway. He'd gone to work specifically to escape our mother, and between the weather and her mood, it could be hours or even days before he returned home.

"One of us should get hit by a car," I said. "That would teach the both of them." I pictured Gretchen, her life hanging by a thread as my parents paced the halls of Rex Hospital, wishing they had been more attentive. It was really the perfect solution. With her out of the way, the rest of us would be more valuable and have a bit more room to spread out. "Gretchen, go lie in the street."

"Make Amy do it," she said.

Amy, in turn, pushed it off onto Tiffany, who was the youngest and had no concept of death. "It's like sleeping," we told her. "Only you get a canopy bed."

Poor Tiffany. She'd do just about anything in return for a little affection. All you had to do was call her Tiff and whatever you wanted was yours: her allowance money, her dinner, the contents of her Easter basket. Her eagerness to please was absolute and naked. When we asked her to lie in the middle of the street, her only question was "Where?"

We chose a quiet dip between two hills, a spot where drivers were almost required to skid out of control. She took her place, this six-year-old in a butter-colored coat, and we gathered on the curb to watch. The first car to happen by belonged to a neighbor, a fellow Yankee who had outfitted his tires with chains and stopped a few feet from our sister's body. "Is that a person?" he asked.

"Well, sort of," Lisa said. She explained that we'd been locked out of our house and though the man appeared to accept it as a reasonable explanation, I'm pretty sure it was him who told on us. Another car passed and then we saw our mother, this puffy figure awkwardly negotiating the crest of the hill. She did not own a pair of pants, and her legs were buried to the calves in snow. We wanted to send her home, to kick her out of nature just as she had kicked us out of the house, but it was hard to stay angry at someone that pitiful-looking.

"Are you wearing your loafers?" Lisa asked, and in response our mother raised her bare foot. "I was wearing loafers," she said. "I mean, really, it was there a second ago."

This was how things went. One moment she was locking us out of our own house and the next we were rooting around in the snow, looking for her left shoe. "Oh, forget about it," she said. "It'll turn up in a few days." Gretchen fitted her cap over my mother's foot. Lisa secured it with her scarf, and surrounding her tightly on all sides, we made our way back home.

My Hips, My Caderas
Alisa Valdes-Rodriguez

 Alisa Valdes-Rodriguez is the author of several books, including *The Dirty Girls Social Club* (2003), *Playing With Boys* (2004), and *The Three Kings* (2010). Valdez-Rodriquez is the daughter of Nelson Valdes, a retired sociology professor who emigrated from Cuba, and Maxine Conant, a poet and novelist of Irish descent. This essay appeared on MSN's *Underwire*, in April 2000.

Return to these questions after you have finished reading.

Analyzing the Reading

1. Valdes-Rodriguez observes that in cultures where more "traditional" roles for women are observed, such as on her Cuban side of the family, big hips and rounded curves are considered beautiful. What accounts for this preference? What beauty traits are valued in cultures where women have less traditional roles?

2. How does the author feel about her hips and her body? About the different opinions people have of her shape? Identify areas in her essay where she clearly reveals her view.

3. How does Valdes-Rodriguez describe her mother's side of the family? Her father's? Which does she prefer?

4. The author describes different phases in her life when she tried to change her body to please others or meet a cultural ideal. Can you think of a time in your own life in which you tried to change something about yourself to please others or to fit in? Explain.

Exploring Ideas and Issues

In April 2010, Gad Saad blogged in *Psychology Today* that while social constructivists argue that there are no universal metrics of beauty, studies indicate that our appreciation of beauty is hard-wired universally into our brains and that we innately prefer the symmetry of phi—also called the "golden ratio." He observes, "You can visit Bedouins in the Middle East, the Yanomamo in the Amazon, and Inuits in the Canadian north, and they will all agree as to who is or is not beautiful. . . . Rotund Rubanesque women, heavier women preferred in Central Africa, and catwalk thin models, while varying greatly in terms of their weight, all tend to have hourglass figures that correspond roughly to a waist-to-hip ratio of 0.70."

1. Images of female bodies are everywhere, selling everything from food to cars. Models and women actors have become younger, taller, and thinner. Articles in women's magazines proclaim that if women can just lose those last twenty pounds, they'll have a happy life at home and at work.

Media critics argue that unnatural and often altered images of thin female bodies cause women and girls to lose self-esteem, become depressed, and develop unhealthy eating habits. Write an essay in which you argue either that the media have a powerful influence on our notion of female beauty or you argue that, in reality, the media have little influence.

2. Write a personal narrative in which you recount a moment when your self-esteem was influenced by what others thought about your physical appearance.

3. Research the "golden ratio," phi. Then view popular celebrities from several cultures, such as India, Mexico, Germany, and Japan. Contrast the differences, if any, you see in physical attributes, including faces, hair, and body types. What do your observations reveal about the social and innate influences of beauty?

MY HIPS, MY CADERAS

MY FATHER IS CUBAN, with dark hair, a cleft in his chin, and feet that can dance the Guaguanco.

My mother is white and American, as blue-eyed as they come.

My voluptuous/big hips are both Cuban and American. And neither. Just like me. As I shift different halves of my soul daily to match whichever cultural backdrop I happen to face, I also carefully prepare myself for how differently my womanly/fat hips will be treated in my two realities.

It all started 15 years ago, when my hips bloomed in Albuquerque, New Mexico, where I was born. I went from being a track club twig—mistaken more than once for a boy—to being a splendidly curving thing that Chicano men with their bandanas down low whistled at as they drove by in their low-riders. White boys in my middle school thought I suddenly had a fat ass, and had no problem saying so.

But the cholos loved me. San Mateo Boulevard . . . remember it well. Jack in the Box on one corner, me on a splintered wooden bench with a Three Musketeers bar, tight shorts, a hot summer sun, and those catcalls and woof-woofs like slaps. I was 12.

My best friend Stacy and I set out dieting right away that summer, to lose our new hips so boys from the heights, like the nearly albino Tom Fairfield with the orange soccer socks, would like us. In those days, I was too naïve to know that dismissing the Chicano guys from the valley and taking French instead of Spanish in middle school were leftovers of colonialism. Taking Spanish still had the stigma of shame, like it would make you a dirty wetback. So Stacy and I pushed through hundreds of leg lifts on her bedroom floor, an open *Seventeen* magazine as a tiny table for our lemon water, and the sound of cicadas grinding away in the tree outside.

In Spanish, the word for hip is *caderas*—a broad term used to denote everything a real woman carries from her waist to her thighs, all the way around. Belly, butt, it's all part of your caderas. And caderas are a magical sphere of womanhood. In the lyrics of Merengue and Salsa, caderas are to be shaken, caressed, admired and exalted. The bigger, the better. In Spanish, you eat your rice and beans and sometimes your *chicharrones* because you fear your caderas will disappear.

In my work as a Latin music critic for a Boston newspaper, I frequent nightclubs with wood-paneled walls and Christmas lights flashing all year long. I wear short rubber skirts and tall shoes. There, I swing my round hips like a metronome. I become fierce. I strut. In the red disco lights, my hips absolutely torture men. I can see it on their faces.

"Mujeron!" they exclaim as I shimmy past. Much woman. They click their tongues, buy me drinks. They ask me to dance, and I often say "no," because I can. And these men suffer. Ironically, this makes the feminist in me very happy. In these places, my mujeron's hips get more nods than they might at a pony farm.

In English, your hips are those pesky things on the sides of your hipbones. They don't *"menear,"* as they do in Spanish; they "jiggle." In English, hips are something women try to be rid of. Hips are why women bruise themselves in the name of lipsuction.

My mother's people hate my hips. They diet. My aunt smokes so she won't eat. And in the gym where I teach step aerobics—a habit I took up in the days when I identified more with my mother's than my father's people—I sometimes hear the suburban anorexics whisper in the front row: "My God, would you look at those hips." Sometimes they walk out of the room even before I have begun teaching, as if hips were contagious. In these situations, I am sad. I drive home and examine my hips in the mirror, hit them for being so imprudent, and like great big ears on the side of my body. Sometimes I fast for days. Sometimes I make myself puke up rice and beans. Usually I get over it, but it always comes back.

Sociologists will tell you that in cultures where women are valued for traditional roles of mother and caregiver, hips are in, and that in cultures where those roles have been broken down and women try to be like men were in traditional societies—i.e, have jobs—hips are out.

So when I want to be loved for my body, I am a Latina. But most Latino men will not love my mind as they do my body, because I am an Americanized professional. Indeed, they will feel threatened, and will soon lose interest in hips that want to "andar por la calle come un hombre" (carry themselves like a man).

When I want to be loved for my mind, I flock to liberal intellectuals, usually whites. They listen to my writings and nod . . . and then suggest I use skim milk instead of cream. These men love my fire and passion—words they always use to describe a Latina—but they are embarrassed by my hips. They want me to wear looser pants.

In some ways I am lucky to be able to move between two worlds. At least my hips get acknowledged as beautiful. I can't say the same for a lot of my bulimic friends, who don't have a second set of standards to turn to. But still, I dream of the day when bicultural Latinas will set the standards for beauty and success, when our voluptuous caderas won't bar us from getting through those narrow American doors.

Open Door

Rebecca Solnit

 Rebecca Solnit, a journalist and environmental activist, is the author of thirteen books on topics as diverse as art, public and collective life, politics, landscape, ecology, hope, and memory. In addition to antinuclear and antiwar issues, she has worked on climate change, Native American land rights, and human rights. Her most recent book, *Infinite City: A San Francisco Atlas,* is about her native city. The following selection is excerpted from the first chapter of *A Field Guide to Getting Lost,* published in 2006.

Return to these questions after you have finished reading.

Analyzing the Reading

1. The author starts off with a question from the philosopher Meno and a question of her own. What is the importance of those questions to Solnit? Why does she think it's valuable "to lose oneself"?

2. In seven of fourteen paragraphs, the author talks about the wilderness, relating her experiences with the outdoors as well as anecdotes she has heard. Why does she devote so much space to this subject? What is its connection to the question she asks at the end of the first paragraph?

3. In addition to Meno, the author cites J. Robert Oppenheimer, Edgar Allan Poe, John Keats, and Walter Benjamin. What is the effect of these references? Do they help support and clarify the author's ideas, or not?

4. Why, in the author's view, are children better at getting lost? What distinction does the author make between "losing things" and "getting lost"? Does the author offer any advice about "getting lost"? If so, what is it?

Exploring Ideas and Issues

Getting lost in the wilderness is an enduring literary theme, from fairy tales such as Hansel and Gretel, to modern-day stories such as the true-life tale depicted in the movie *127 Hours*. Why does this theme hold such fascination for us?

1. Think of a time when you were lost or you lost track of someone. Maybe you momentarily stepped away from your friends in a crowd and then couldn't spot them. Or perhaps you lost your way driving in an unfamiliar place. What were your thoughts and feelings at the time? What reflections, if any, did you have after the event? Write an essay in which you describe your experience and your conclusions about it.

2. Solnit expresses some concern about the limits to exploration that society places on children. What experiences did you have with exploration and adventure as a child? For example, do you remember the first time you were permitted to go bicycling with friends unaccompanied by an adult? Write an essay on the pros and cons of unsupervised adventures for children, concluding either that the benefits outweigh the risks, or vice versa. Use examples from your own experiences and the experiences of people you know to make your points.

3. Select a story, movie, or other work that uses the theme of getting lost in the wilderness. Some choices are movies like *The Emerald Forest* (1985), stories like *Beauty and the Beast*, and novels like *Robinson Crusoe*. Why do the main characters get lost? What, if anything, do they discover about themselves? Write an essay in which you give your ideas about the use of this theme. Include at least three examples from the work to support your conclusions.

OPEN DOOR

Leave the door open for the unknown, the door into the dark. That's where the most important things come from, where you yourself came from, where you will go. Three years ago I was giving a workshop in the Rockies. A student came in bearing a quote from what she said was the pre-Socratic philosopher Meno. It read, "How will you go about finding that thing the nature of which is totally unknown to you?" I copied it down, and it has stayed with me since. The student made big transparent photographs of swimmers underwater and hung them, so that to walk among them was to have the shadows of swimmers travel across your body in a space that itself came to seem aquatic and mysterious. The question she carried struck me as the basic question in life. The things we want are transformative, and we don't know or only think we know what is on the other side of that transformation. Love, wisdom, grace, inspiration—how do you go about finding these things that are in some ways about extending the boundaries of the self into unknown territory, about becoming someone else?

Certainly for artists of all stripes, the unknown, the idea or the form or the tale that has not yet arrived, is what must be found. It is the job of artists to open doors and invite in prophesies, the unknown, the unfamiliar; it's where their work comes from, although its arrival signals the beginning of the long disciplined process of making it their own. Scientists too, as J. Robert Oppenheimer once remarked, "live always at the 'edge of mystery'—the boundary of the unknown." But they transform the unknown into the known, haul it in like fisherman; artists get you out into that dark sea.

Edgar Allan Poe declared, "All experience, in matters of philosophical discovery, teaches us that, in such discovery, it is the unforeseen upon which we must calculate most largely." Poe is consciously juxtaposing the word "calculate," which implies a cold counting up of the facts or measurements, with "the unforeseen," that which cannot be measured or counted, only anticipated. How do you calculate upon the unforeseen? It seems to be an art of recognizing the role of the unforeseen, of keeping your balance amid surprises, of collaborating with chance, of recognizing that there are some essential mysteries in the world and thereby a limit to calculation, to plan, to control. To calculate on the unforeseen is perhaps exactly the paradoxical operation that life most requires of us.

On a celebrated midwinter's night in 1817 the poet John Keats walked home talking with some friends "and several things dove-tailed in my mind, and at once it struck me what quality went to form a Man of Achievement, especially in Literature . . . I mean Negative Capability, that is, when a man is capable of being in uncertainties, mysteries, doubts, without any irritable reaching after fact and reason." One way or another this notion occurs over and over again, like the spots labeled "terra incognita" on old maps.

"Not to find one's way in a city may well be uninteresting and banal. It requites ignorance—nothing more," says the twentieth-century philosopher-essayist Walter Benjamin. "But to lose oneself in a city—as one loses oneself in a forest—that calls for quite a different schooling." To lose yourself: a voluptuous surrender, lost in your arms, lost to the worlds, utterly immersed in what is present so that its surroundings fade away. In Benjamin's terms, to be lost is to be fully present, and to be fully present is to be capable of being in uncertainty and mystery. And one does not get lost but loses oneself, with the implication that it is a conscious choice, a chosen surrender, a psychic state achievable through geography.

That thing the nature of which is totally unknown to you is usually what you need to find, and finding it is a matter of getting lost. The word "lost" comes from the Old Norse *los*, meaning the disbanding of an army, and the origin suggests soldiers falling out of formation to go home, a truce with the wide world. I worry now that many people never disband their armies, never go beyond what they know. Advertising, alarmist news, technology, incessant busyness, and the design of public and private space conspire to make it so. A recent article about the return of wildlife to suburbia described snow-covered yards in which the footprints of animals are abundant and those of children are entirely absent. As far as the animals are concerned, the suburbs are an abandoned landscape, and so they roam with confidence. Children seldom roam, even in the safest places. Because of their parents' fear of the monstrous things that might happen (and do happen, but rarely), the wonderful things that happen as a matter of course are stripped away from them. For me, childhood roaming was what developed self-reliance, a sense of direction and adventure, imagination, a will to explore, to be able to get a little lost and then figure out the way back. I wonder what will come of placing this generation under house arrest.

That summer in the Rockies when I heard Meno's question, I went on a walk with the students into a landscape I'd never seen before. Between the white columns of aspens, delicate green plants grew knee-deep, sporting leaves like green fans and lozenges and scallops, and the stems waved white and violet flowers in the breeze. The path led down to a river dear to bears. When we got back, a strong brown-skinned woman was waiting at the trailhead, a woman I'd met briefly a decade earlier. That she recognized me and I recalled her was surprising; that we became friends after this second meeting was my good fortune. Sallie had long been a member of the Mountain Search and Rescue team, and that day at the trailhead she was on a routine mission—one of those quests for lost hikers in which, she said, they usually reappear somewhere near where they vanished. She was monitoring her radio and watching to see who came up that trail, one of the trails the straying party was likely to appear on, and so she found me. The Rockies thereabouts are like crumbled fabric, a steep landscape of ridges and valleys running in all directions, easy to get lost in and not so hard to walk out of, down to the roads that run through the bottom of a lot of the valleys. For the search-and-rescue volunteers themselves, every rescue is a trip into the unknown. They may find a grateful person or a corpse, may find quickly or after weeks of intensive fieldwork, or never find the mission or solve their mystery at all.

Three years later I went back to visit Sallie and her mountains and ask her about getting lost. One day of that visit we walked along the Continental Divide on a path that rose from twelve thousand feet along ridge-lines, across the alpine tundra carpeting the landscape above tree line. As we proceeded uphill, the view opened up in all directions until our trail seemed like the center seam of a world hemmed all around the horizon in rows of jagged blue mountains. Calling this place the Continental Divide made you picture water flowing toward both oceans, the spine of mountains running most of the length of the continent, made you imagine the cardinal directions radiating from it, gave you a sense of where you were in the most metaphysical if not the most practical sense. I would have walked forever into those heights, but thunder in the massed clouds and a long bolt of lightning made Sallie turn around. On the way down, I asked her about the rescues that stood out for her. One was about rescuing a man killed by lightning, not an uncommon way to die up there, which is why we were heading downhill from that glorious crest.

Then, she told me about a lost eleven-year-old, a deaf boy who was also losing his eyesight as part of a degenerative disease that would eventually cut short his life. He had been at a camp where the counselors took the kids on an excursion and then led them in a game of hide-and-seek. He must have hidden too well, for they could not find him when the day was done, and he did not find his way back. Search and Rescue was called out in the dark, and Sallie went into the swampy area with dread, expecting that in the nearly freezing night they could find nothing but a body. They blanketed the area, and just as the sun came over the horizon, she heard a whistle and ran toward it. It was the boy, shivering and blowing a whistle, and she hugged him and then stripped off most of her clothing to put it on him. He had done everything right—his whistle had not been loud enough for the counselors to hear above the running water, but he had whistled until nightfall, then curled up between two fallen trees, and begun whistling again as soon as it was light. He was radiant at being found, and she was in tears at finding him.

Search-and-rescue teams have made an art of finding and a science of how people get lost, though as many or more of their forays are rescues for people who are injured or stranded. The simplest answer nowadays for literal getting lost is that a lot of the people who get lost aren't paying attention when they do so, don't know what to do when they realize they don't know how to return, or don't admit they don't know. There's an art of attending to weather, to the route you take, to the landmarks along the way, to how if you turn around you can see how different the journey back looks from the journey out, to reading the sun and moon and stars to orient yourself, to the direction of running water, to the thousand things that make the wild a text that can be read by the literate. The lost are often illiterate in this language that is the language of the earth itself, or don't stop to read it. And there's another art of being at home in the unknown, so that being in its midst isn't cause for panic or suffering, of being at home with being lost. That ability may not be so far astray from Keats's capability "of being in uncertainties, mysteries, doubts." (Cell phones and GPS have become substitutes for this ability as more and more people use them to order their own rescues like pizza, though there are still many places without phone signals.)

Hunters get lost a lot in this stretch of the Rockies, Sallie's friend Landon told me, sitting at her desk surrounded by photographs of family and animals on the ranch she ran with her husband, because they routinely go off trail in pursuit of game. She told me about a deer hunter who glanced around on a plateau where the peaks in opposite directions look identical. Where he stood, one of those sets of peaks was obscured by trees, so he later traveled in exactly the wrong direction. Convinced that arrival was just over the next ridge or the next, he walked all day and night, exhausting himself and getting chilled and then, with the delusion of severe hypothermia, he began to feel hot and to shed his clothes. Leaving a trail of garments they tracked him by for the last few miles. Children, Landon said, are good at getting lost, because "the key in survival is knowing you're lost": they don't stray far, they curl up in some sheltered place at night, they know they need help.

Landon talked about the old skills and instincts that people need in the wild and about her husband's uncanny intuition, which she saw as much one of those abilities as all the concrete arts of navigating, tracking, and surviving she studied. He had driven a snowmobile right up to the feet of a doctor lost when a warm winter walk turned into a whiteout, knowing by some immeasurable instinct where the freezing man was, off the trail and across a snowed-over meadow. A ranch hand had commented on how strange another rescue had been because they had gone out into the snowy night silently, instead of calling. The rancher didn't call because he knew where he was headed, and he stopped on the brink of the ledge below which the skier was stuck. The lost skier had tried to follow the stream out, usually a good technique for navigating, but this stream narrowed and deepened until it was a series of waterfalls and precipitous drops. The skier had gotten stranded down a drop, huddled up with his sweater over his knees. The wet sweater was so frozen they'd almost had to chip him out of it.

I was trained by an outdoorsman who insisted you should always carry rain gear, water and other supplies on the least excursion, that you should be prepared to be out for any amount of time, since plans go astray and the one certain thing about weather is that it changes. My skills are not notable, but I never seem to do more than flirt with getting lost on streets and trails and highways and sometimes cross country, touching the edge of the unknown that sharpens the senses. I love going out of my way, beyond what I know, and finding my way back a few extra miles, by another trail, with a compass that argues with a map, with strangers' contrary anecdotal directions. Nights alone in motels in remote western towns where I know no one and no one I know knows where I am, nights with strange paintings and floral spreads and cable television that furnish a reprieve from my own biography, when in Benjamin's terms I have lost myself though I know where I am. Moments when I say to myself as feet or car clear a crest or round a bend, I have never seen this place before. Times when some architectural detail or vista that has escaped me these many years says to me that I never did know where I was, even when I was home. Stories that make the familiar strange again, like those that revealed the lost landscapes, lost cemeteries, lost spaces around my home. Conversations that make everything around them disappear. Dreams that I forget until I realize they have colored everything I felt and did that day. Getting lost like that seems like the beginning of finding your way or finding another way, though there are other ways of being lost.

Lost really has two disparate meanings. Losing things is about the familiar falling away, getting lost is about the unfamiliar appearing. These are objects and people that disappear from your sight or knowledge or possession; you lose a bracelet, a friend, the key. You still know where you are. Everything is familiar except that there is one item less, one missing element. Or you get lost, in which case the world has become larger than your knowledge of it. Either way, there is a loss of control. Imagine yourself streaming through time shedding gloves, umbrellas, wrenches, books, friends, homes, names. This is what the view looks like if you take a rear-facing seat on the train. Looking forward you constantly acquire moments of arrival, moments of realization, moments of discovery. The wind blows your hair back and you are greeted by what you have never seen before. The material falls away in onrushing experience. It peels off like skin from a molting snake. Of course to forget the past is to lose the sense of loss that is also memory of an absent richness and a set of clues to navigate the present by; the art is not one of forgetting but letting go. And when everything else is gone, you can be rich in loss.

Mother Tongue

Amy Tan

Amy Tan is well known for novels that concern the bonds between Chinese American mothers and daughters. She has introduced a rich world of Chinese myth and history to a global audience, but her themes of love and forgiveness are universal. Tan began writing fiction along with playing the piano to curb her workaholic tendencies, but with the publication of *The Joy Luck Club* in 1989, her talent as a writer became widely celebrated. She reflects on her career in this essay.

Return to these questions after you have finished reading.

Analyzing the Reading

1. How did Tan's attitude toward her mother's use of language change over the years? Use evidence from the text to support your statements.

2. Tan writes about value judgments based on language. How does Tan account for these judgments?

3. Why was Tan's awareness of different Englishes important to her development as a writer?

4. Tan says that an insight she had as a beginning writer was to imagine a reader. Why was imagining a reader so important?

Exploring Ideas and Issues

Linguists describe going back and forth between different languages, or between varieties of one language, as *code switching*. Tan tells how she goes back and forth between standard English and her home dialect in her own speaking and writing. Code-switching used to be considered nonstandard usage, but more recently linguists consider code switching a natural product of language use. Just as we dress differently for more formal and less formal occasions, so too we adjust our language depending on the situation.

Indeed, we all code switch constantly. New digital technologies have led to new forms of code switching, especially in media such as Twitter, that force extreme brevity. Without giving it much conscious thought, we adjust our language to the medium we're using as well as to who will be reading our message and what we are trying to accomplish.

1. Tan says, "Recently I was made aware of all of the different Englishes I do use." What different Englishes, or other languages, do you use? List each and explain the different contexts and relationships in which you use them. Write an essay in which you compare two different "languages" (either styles of English or English and another language) that you use. Give examples of when, where, and how you use them.

2. You may have grown up in an ethnically diverse neighborhood or a neighborhood with little diversity. Either way, you were aware of prevailing attitudes and beliefs about race and ethnicity as you grew older. Write an essay describing one positive and one negative belief you encountered and the reasons people had for holding these beliefs. Include examples from the experiences of people you know.

3. Do you think being a "good" American depends on speaking English? Can people have an American identity without being able to speak English? Write a short essay in which you answer yes or no to these questions. Include examples of specific people you have known to support your view.

MOTHER TONGUE

I am not a scholar of English or literature. I cannot give you much more than personal opinions on the English language and its variations in this country or others. I am a writer. And by that definition, I am someone who has always loved language. I am fascinated by language in daily life. I spend a great deal of my time thinking about the power of language—the way it can evoke an emotion, a visual image, a complex idea, or a simple truth. Language is the tool of my trade. And I use them all—all the Englishes I grew up with.

Recently, I was made keenly aware of the different Englishes I do use. I was giving a talk to a large group of people, the same talk I had already given to half a dozen other groups. The nature of the talk was about my writing, my life, and my book, *The Joy Luck Club*. The talk was going along well enough, until I remembered one major difference that made the whole talk sound wrong. My mother was in the room. And it was perhaps the first time she had heard me give a lengthy speech, using the kind of English I have never used with her. I was saying things like, "The intersection of memory upon imagination" and "There is an aspect of my fiction that relates to thus-and-thus"—a speech filled with carefully wrought grammatical phrases, burdened, it suddenly seemed to me, with nominalized forms, past perfect tenses, conditional phrases, all the forms of standard English that I had learned in school and through books, the forms of English I did not use at home with my mother.

Just last week, I was walking down the street with my mother, and I again found myself conscious of the English I was using, the English I do use with her. We were talking about the price of new and used furniture and I heard myself saying this: "Not waste money that way."

My husband was with us as well, and he didn't notice any switch in my English. And then I realized why. It's because over the twenty years we've been together I've often used that same kind of English with him, and sometimes he even uses it with me. It has become our language of intimacy, a different sort of English that relates to family talk, the language I grew up with.

So you'll have some idea of what this family talk I heard sounds like, I'll quote what my mother said during a recent conversation which I videotaped and then transcribed. During this conversation, my mother was talking about a political gangster in Shanghai who had the same last name as her family's, Du, and how the gangster in his early years wanted to be adopted by her family, which was rich by comparison. Later, the gangster became more powerful, far richer than my mother's family, and one day showed up at my mother's wedding to pay his respects. Here's what she said in part:

Du-Yusong having business like fruit stand. Like off the street kind. He is Du like Du Zong—but not Tsung-ming Island people. The local people call putong, the river east side, he belong to that side local people. That man want to ask Du Zong father take him in like become own family. Du Zong father wasn't look down on him, but didn't take seriously, until that man big like become a mafia. Now important person, very hard to inviting him. Chinese way, came only to show respect, don't stay for dinner. Respect for making big celebration, he shows up. Mean gives lots of respect. Chinese custom. Chinese social life that way. If too important won't have to stay too long. He come to my wedding. I didn't see, I heard it. I gone to boy's side, they have YMCA dinner. Chinese age I was nineteen.

You should know that my mother's expressive command of English belies how much she actually understands. She reads the *Forbes* report, listens to *Wall Street Week*, converses daily with her stockbroker, reads all of Shirley MacLaine's books with ease—all kinds of things I can't begin to understand. Yet some of my friends tell me they understand 50 percent of what my mother says. Some say they understand 80 to 90 percent. Some say they understand none of it, as if she were speaking pure Chinese. But to me, my mother's English is perfectly clear, perfectly natural. It's my mother tongue. Her language, as I hear it, is vivid, direct, full of observation and imagery. That was the language that helped shape the way I saw things, expressed things, made sense of the world.

Lately, I've been giving more thought to the kind of English my mother speaks. Like others, I have described it to people as "broken" or "fractured" English. But I wince when I say that. It has always bothered me that I can think of no way to describe it other than "broken," as if it were damaged and needed to be fixed, as if it lacked a certain wholeness and soundness. I've heard other terms used, "limited English," for example. But they seem just as bad, as if everything is limited, including people's perceptions of the limited English speaker.

I know this for a fact, because when I was growing up, my mother's "limited" English limited my perception of her. I was ashamed of her English. I believed that her English reflected the quality of what she had to say. That is, because she expressed them imperfectly her thoughts were imperfect. And I had plenty of empirical evidence to support me: the fact that people in department stores, at banks, and at restaurants did not take her seriously, did not give her good service, pretended not to understand her, or even acted as if they did not hear her.

My mother had long realized the limitations of her English as well. When I was fifteen, she used to have me call people on the phone to pretend I was she. In this guise, I was forced to ask for information or even to complain and yell at people who had been rude to her. One time it was a call to her stockbroker in New York. She had cashed out her small portfolio and it just so happened we were going to go to New York the next week, our very first trip outside California. I had to get on the phone and say in an adolescent voice that was not very convincing, "This is Mrs. Tan."

And my mother was standing in the back whispering loudly, "Why he don't send me check, already two weeks late. So mad he lie to me, losing me money."

And then I said in perfect English, "Yes, I'm getting rather concerned. You had agreed to send the check two weeks ago, but it hasn't arrived."

Then she began to talk more loudly. "What he want, I come to New York tell him front of his boss, you cheating me?" And I was trying to calm her down, make her be quiet, while telling the stockbroker, "I can't tolerate any more excuses. If I don't receive the check immediately, I am going to have to speak to your manager when I'm in New York next week." And sure enough, the following week there we were in front of this astonished stockbroker, and I was sitting there red-faced and quiet, and my mother, the real Mrs. Tan, was shouting at his boss in her impeccable broken English.

We used a similar routine just five days ago, for a situation that was far less humorous. My mother had gone to the hospital for an appointment, to find out about a benign brain tumor a CAT scan had revealed a month ago. She said she had spoken very good English, her best English, no mistakes. Still, she said, the hospital did not apologize when they said they had lost the CAT scan and she had come for nothing. She said they did not seem to have any sympathy when she told them she was anxious to know the exact diagnosis, since her husband and son had both died of brain tumors. She said they would not give her any more information until the next time and she would have to make another appointment for that. So she said she would not leave until the doctor called her daughter. She wouldn't budge. And when the doctor finally called her daughter, me, who spoke in perfect English—lo and behold—we had assurances the CAT scan would be found, promises that a conference call on Monday would be held, and apologies for any suffering my mother had gone through for a most regrettable mistake.

I think my mother's English almost had an effect on limiting my possibilities in life as well. Sociologists and linguists probably will tell you that a person's developing language skills are more influenced by peers. But I do think that the language spoken in the family, especially in immigrant families which are more insular, plays a large role in shaping the language of the child. And I believe that it affected my results on achievement tests, IQ tests, and the SAT. While my English skills were never judged as poor, compared to math, English could not be considered my strong suit. In grade school I did moderately well, getting perhaps B's, sometimes B-pluses, in English and scoring perhaps in the sixtieth or seventieth percentile on achievement tests. But those scores were not good enough to override the opinion that my true abilities lay in math and science, because in those areas I achieved A's and scored in the ninetieth percentile or higher.

This was understandable. Math is precise; there is only one correct answer. Whereas, for me at least, the answers on English tests were always a judgment call, a matter of opinion and personal experience. Those tests were constructed around items like fill-in-the-blank sentence completion, such as, "Even though Tom was _____, Mary thought he was _____." And the correct answer always seemed to be the most bland combinations of thoughts, for example, "Even though Tom was shy, Mary thought he was charming," with the grammatical structure "even though" limiting the correct answer to some sort of semantic opposites, so you wouldn't get answers like, "Even though Tom was foolish, Mary thought he was ridiculous." Well, according to my mother, there were very few limitations as to what Tom could have been and what Mary might have thought of him. So I never did well on tests like that.

The same was true with word analogies, pairs of words in which you were supposed to find some sort of logical, semantic relationship—for example, "*Sunset is to nightfall* as _____ is to _____." And here you would be presented with a list of four possible pairs, one of which showed the same kind of relationship: *red* is to *stoplight*, *bus* is to *arrival*, *chills is to fever*, *yawn* is to *boring*. Well, I could never think that way. I knew what the tests were asking, but I could not block out of my mind the images already created by the first pair, "*sunset* is to *nightfall*"—and I would see a burst of colors against a darkening sky, the moon rising, the lowering of a curtain of stars. And all the other pairs of words—red, bus, stoplight, boring—just threw up a mass of confusing images, making it impossible for me to sort out something as logical as saying: "A sunset precedes nightfall" is the same as "a chill precedes a fever." The only way I would have gotten that answer right would have been to imagine an associative situation, for example, my being disobedient and staying out past sunset, catching a chill at night, which turns into feverish pneumonia as punishment, which indeed did happen to me.

I have been thinking about all this lately, about my mother's English, about achievement tests. Because lately I've been asked, as a writer, why there are not more Asian Americans represented in American literature. Why are there few Asian Americans enrolled in creative writing programs? Why do so many Chinese students go into engineering? Well, these are broad sociological questions I can't begin to answer. But I have noticed in surveys—in fact, just last week—that Asian students, as a whole, always do significantly better on math achievement tests than in English. And this makes me think that there are other Asian-American students whose English spoken in the home might also be described as "broken" or "limited." And perhaps they also have teachers who are steering them away from writing and into math and science, which is what happened to me.

Fortunately, I happen to be rebellious in nature and enjoy the challenge of disproving assumptions made about me. I became an English major my first year in college, after being enrolled as pre-med. I started writing nonfiction as a freelancer the week after I was told by my former boss that writing was my worst skill and I should hone my talents toward account management.

But it wasn't until 1985 that I finally began to write fiction. And at first I wrote using what I thought to be wittily crafted sentences, sentences that would finally prove I had mastery over the English language. Here's an example from the first draft of a story that later made its way into *The Joy Luck Club*, but without this line: "That was my mental quandary in its nascent state." A terrible line, which I can barely pronounce.

Fortunately, for reasons I won't get into today, I later decided I should envision a reader for the stories I would write. And the reader I decided upon was my mother, because these were stories about mothers. So with this reader in mind—and in fact she did read my early drafts—I began to write stories using all the Englishes I grew up with: the English I spoke to my mother, which for lack of a better term might be described as "simple"; the English she used with me, which for lack of a better term might be described as "broken"; my translation of her Chinese, which could certainly be described as "watered down"; and what I imagined to be her translation of her Chinese if she could speak in perfect English, her internal language, and for that I sought to preserve the essence, but neither an English nor a Chinese structure. I wanted to capture what language ability tests can never reveal: her intent, her passion, her imagery, the rhythms of her speech and the nature of her thoughts.

Apart from what any critic had to say about my writing, I knew I had succeeded where it counted when my mother finished reading my book and gave me her verdict: "So easy to read."

How to Write a Reflection

These steps for the process of writing a reflection may not progress as neatly as this chart might suggest. Writing is not an assembly-line process. Writing about a remembered event, place, or person is, in itself, a powerful way to reflect. Be open to uncovering insights and understanding more broadly the significance.

1 CHOOSE A SUBJECT

- Analyze the assignment.
- Explore possible topics. Make lists of memories connected with your family, work, school, friends, and travels.
- Examine your lists for what might interest readers.
- Consider why this person, place, event, or object is significant to you.

2 IDEAS AND TEXT

- Describe the scene in as much detail as you can remember with visual details, sounds, smells, tastes, and tactile feelings.
- Tell the story of what happened, capturing actions with active verbs.
- Make people come alive. Recreate conversations that reveal character. Record gestures and other details that make people unique.
- Think about the context. What was happening at the time for you and the larger community?
- Relate your experience to the experiences of others.

✓ Study the Reflection Essay at **mycomplab.com**

3
WRITE A DRAFT

- Plan your organization, either chronologically or conceptually.

- Write an engaging title that suggest the direction or the significance of your reflection.

- Draft a strong beginning that establishes a focus and makes your readers want to continue.

- Introduce a tension between people or a problem early on that motivates your reflection.

- Select vivid details and dialogue that let readers experience what you experienced.

- Describe how the tension or problem was resolved.

- Leave your readers with something to think about. Your conclusion should invite readers to reflect on what you've written.

4
REVISE, REVISE, REVISE

- Check that your paper or project fulfills the assignment.

- Make sure that the subject is focused.

- Add details, description, or dialogue.

- Make sure your voice and tone will engage readers.

- Examine your organization and think of possible better ways to organize.

- Review the visual presentation.

- Proofread carefully.

5
SUBMITTED VERSION

- Make sure your finished writing meets all formatting requirements.

1: Choose a Subject

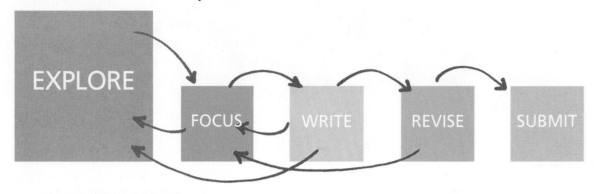

Analyze the assignment

Read your assignment slowly and carefully. Look for key words like *reflection*, *memoir*, or *personal narrative*, which signal a reflective essay. Identify any information about the length specified, date due, formatting, and other requirements. You can attend to this information later. At this point you want to give your attention to your topic and the focus of your reflection.

Explore possible topics

The challenge is to find a topic that will be interesting to your readers, presents a complication that must be resolved, and offers you the opportunity to reflect on the person, event, or experience.

Start by making lists.

- Your childhood: What do you remember most vividly from your childhood? What scared you as a child? When were the happiest times you can remember?

- Your family: What memories stand out about your parents? your brothers and sisters? your grandparents and other relatives? family vacations and other family experiences? How has your perspective on your family changed over time?

- Your work experience: What was your first job? Did you ever have a great boss or a horrible boss? What important learning experiences did you have while working?

- Your school experience: What school memories stand out? Did a particular teacher have a strong influence on you?

- Your friends and social relationships: What stands out among memories of your friends? about people you have dated? about your experiences on social networks?

Remember places and objects

Is a particular place important to you? Why is it critical? For example how did you gain an understanding of your mother's attitudes when you visited the place where she grew up? Is a particular object important to you, such as something that belonged to your great-grandmother and was passed down to you?

Consider the importance in your life

Ask yourself: Why is this person, event, place, or object significant to me? Think about why the person, place, event, or object seems more important today than it did in your initial experience. Think about how the person, place, event, or object changed you as a person.

Analyze your potential readers

What do your readers likely know about your subject? What might your readers gain from reading your reflection? What might you need to tell your readers about the background? For example, Amy Tan (see page 84) provides more background about her Chinese American mother than David Sedaris (see page 70) does about his mother. Tan examines how her mother's use of language became important to Tan as a writer whereas Sedaris' focus is on how he and his sisters resolved the problem of their mother locking them out of the house.

WRITE NOW

Explore memories

- Select one of the items that you have checked on your lists.

- Write nonstop for five minutes to explore the event, situation, place, or object.
  What was your initial reaction? Who else was there? Did you share your reaction at the time?

- Write nonstop for five minutes to explore your current perspective. How did an experience change you? Why do you remember this person, event, place, or object so well? Looking back, what do you see now that you didn't recognize at the time?

- Stop and read what you have written. Do you see possibilities for writing at length about this person, event, or situation? If you do, then begin generating more content. If the idea seems limited, try writing nonstop about another person, event, place, or object.

Writer at work

Janine Carter received the following assignment in her Introduction to Archeology class. She made notes on her assignment sheet as the class discussed the assignment.

Archeology 201
Reflection on an Artifact

We have read about and discussed *artifacts* at great length in this unit—how and where they are found, what they indicate about human cultures, and what they mean to archeologists. But not all artifacts are found in museums. Almost any human-made object can be considered an artifact, because it contains information about its makers. Archeologists study artifacts because they teach us about people we do not know, and because they teach us things about ourselves.

For your first paper, I would like you to find an artifact in your daily life. This might be a family heirloom with a great deal of personal meaning, or it might be something you have no emotional attachment to at all, like a soda can or a discarded newspaper. Write a 4–6 page essay reflecting upon your artifact. Describe it in as much detail as you can. Consider what its construction tells you about its maker. Why was it made? When? By whom? What clues does the artifact contain about its own history?   *"Think like a detective"*

Use lots of detail

Spend some time considering what the artifact means to you. What is your relationship to the person who created the artifact? What can you construct about the culture and conditions in which it was created? What sorts of things can you not figure out about it?

Writing Process
Bring in a good draft of your essay on October 3rd. We will discuss them in class so you can revise carefully before you turn your essay in on October 10.   *Two weeks for first draft*
One week for revision

Grading
I will look for the following qualities in your essay: detailed description, logical deduction, and an interesting account of the artifact's significance or meaning.

Then Janine made a list of possible objects to write about.

<u>HEIRLOOMS/EMOTIONAL CONNECTION</u>
- Aunt Marie's tulip quilt—shows my connection to a long line of quilters
- ~~Sea shells from Girl Scout camp~~–NOT MAN-MADE
- Bracelet from graduation
- Terry's photo
- Stuffed elephant–shows how much I have grown up. Where was it made?

✓ - Garage sale quilt—don't know much about this; could guess a lot though.
- Diploma

<u>LESS IMPORTANT OBJECTS</u>
- Cereal box—ingredients show lack of nutrition. Pictures show how kids are bombarded with cartoons and colorful images. Expiration date and other clues to where it was made.
- Desk in dorm room—Must have been used by dozens of people like me (?)
- Old calendar
- Old cookbook
- Old cell phone—Could talk about how fast technology is changing. Do I have one?

2: Develop Ideas and Text

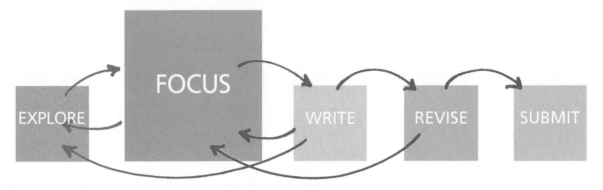

Writing a draft will be much easier if you generate ideas and text in advance. Having some material to work from will help you to plan your organization.

Set the scene

Describe the setting of your reflection in as much detail as you can remember. Write down all the sights, sounds, smells, tastes, and tactile feelings you associate with your topic. If the subject of your reflection is a photograph or an object, write a detailed description of it.

Describe what happened

Tell the story of what happened in as much detail as you can remember. Capture the action with active verbs (*giggled, whistled, devoured, sauntered, witnessed*).

Make people come alive

Use dialogue to let readers hear people talk, which reveals much about character. Recreate a conversation between key people in your reflection. Also, record the little mannerisms, gestures, clothing, and personal habits that distinguish people. Don't forget to make yourself come alive. If you are reflecting on an incident from your childhood, how old were you? What do you remember about yourself at that age?

Consider the larger context

Write about what else was going on at the time, both with the immediate people involved and in the larger culture. How does your memory compare with similar experiences you have read or heard about from others? Does your memory connect to larger trends going on at the time?

Think about the significance

Write about the meaning the person, place, event, or object has for you today. The fact that you find the topic memorable means there is something you can share with others. What do you notice, as you reflect, that other people might not notice? This is the "added value" that will make your reflection more than a mere description or memory.

Writer at work

Janine Carter sat down with her garage-sale quilt and a pen and paper. She observed it carefully and made a list of detailed observations about its physical appearance. Then, she added her conclusions and guesses about the quilt, its history, and its maker, based on these clues.

Janine thought about her relationship to the quilt. She jotted down, in no particular order, what she remembered about buying the quilt, conversations she had had with her grandmother about quilting, and ideas that occurred to her.

- Unbleached muslin, pink calico, coral calico
- Most stitching is white thread and quilting is pink thread
  - All these materials are very cheap

- Nine-patch plus a 5-patch alternating throughout; binding is plain muslin
  - I do not know the name of this pattern. Looks a little like Churn Dash.

- Batting is coming through in many areas
- Lots of stains, even some paint
  - Has been used a lot and has been used for unintended purposes—discarded?

- Large muslin patches are cut on bias
  - Means the person knew what she was doing and planned ahead

- Quilting is in nested L-blocks. Is there a name for that?

- 1372 patches (approx.) Small squares are 1-1/2 inches

- Quilting is about 5 stitches/inch on average, 1" apart. Over 100 yards total.

- The two colors clash and are not mixed together; one runs out and the other starts. Why?

  - New quilter? Poor planning? To make it bigger? Unforeseen accident?
  - Grandma would have had a fit if I ever made a quilt this ugly. So why did I buy it?

3: Write a Draft

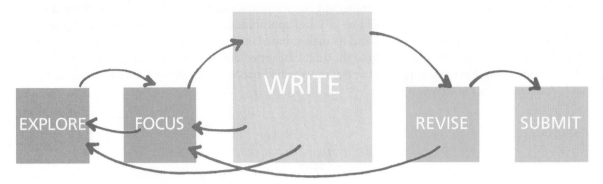

Plan your organization

Consider how to tell your story. Embrey (see page 66), Sedaris (see page 70), and Valdez-Rodriguez (see page 73) narrate events in chronological order. Solnit (see page 76) and Tan (see page 84) focus on a central idea and organize according to different aspects of that idea.

Write an engaging title

Your title should suggest the direction or the significance of your reflection.

Draft a strong beginning

You might start by describing the setting of your reflection. You might narrate the central event, which you will expand and reflect on later. Or you might give critical background.

Introduce a complication early on

The complication is a tension or problem that motivates the reflection. Embrey's family is relocated to a concentration camp. Sedaris and his sisters are locked out of their house by their drunken mother. Both writers describe the immediate reactions of the people involved.

Select vivid details and dialogue

Let your readers experience what you experienced. Small details can say a great deal. Likewise, dialogue reveals the character of people in your reflection.

Describe how the complication was resolved

How did the people involved resolve the complication? Sometimes the resolution is the solution to a practical problem like getting locked out, and in other cases the resolution is coming to terms with an idea.

Leave your readers with something to think about

Your conclusion should invite readers to reflect on what you've written. Solnit introduces a paradox, writing that getting lost is the "beginning of finding your way." Tan ends with her mother's appreciation of her writing. Valdes-Rodriguez expands her reflection to challenge prevailing ideals of female beauty.

Watch the Animation on Titles at mycomplab.com

Writer at work

Janine Carter tried several organizational patterns for her essay. Because she knew so little about the quilt's history, she did not feel chronological organization would be a good strategy. However, as she worked through her draft she realized that readers would appreciate a firsthand account of her purchase of the quilt. She decided to include this story near the beginning of her essay, after describing the quilt. She organized the rest of her essay around the questions that occurred to her as she considered the quilt's appearance. As she worked, she referred back to her assignment frequently to make sure she was fulfilling all its terms. She decided to cut one section, about the names of various quilt patterns, because it was too general and distracted from the main focus of her essay. Here is the original outline Janine began working from, along with revisions she made.

I.   Intro—describe quilt with detail

> *< tell story of "Miracle" salesman*

II. Cheap material and clashing colors–poor person, or some other reason?

III. Bias-cut material indicates experienced quilter

IV. ~~Names and meanings of quilt patterns.~~

V.   Number of patches, stitching: this information means more to quilters than to average people. Explain.

VI. Quilting's meaning for women (cultural use). Tell Grandma's story about the work on the farm.

VII. My relationship with the quilt

> *< contrast w/how much I know about quilts in our family*
>
> *< add more detail here, and talk about quilt's probable history*

4: Revise, Revise, Revise

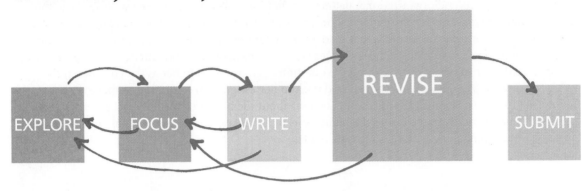

Skilled writers know that the secret to writing well is rewriting. Even the best writers often have to revise several times to get the result they want. You also must have effective strategies for revising if you're going to be successful. The biggest trap you can fall into is starting off with correcting errors. Leave the small stuff for last.

Does your paper or project meet the assignment?	• Look again at the assignment for specific guidelines, including length, format, and amount of research. Does your work meet these guidelines?
Is the subject focused?	• Will readers find your subject early on? • Is the significance evident?
Can you add dialogue, description, and other details?	• Can you make events and memories from the past more concrete?
Is your tone engaging?	• Will readers sympathize and identify with you, or will they find your tone too negative, angry, or intensely personal? • Does your tone fit your topic? Some intensely personal topics may not be suited to humorous treatment.
Is your organization effective?	• Are links between concepts and ideas clear? • Are there any places where you find abrupt shifts or gaps? • Are there sections or paragraphs that could be rearranged to make your draft more effective?
Is the writing project visually effective?	• Is the font attractive and readable? • Are the headings and visuals effective? • If you have included an image associated with your reflection, where should it be placed for maximum impact?
Save the editing for last.	• When you have finished revising, edit and proofread carefully.

A peer review guide is on page 54.

Writer at work

Janine Carter was not satisfied with her opening paragraph, or her title. After talking to a consultant at her campus writing center, she worked on ending her opening paragraph with a surprising twist that would engage readers. She also realized that she could draw out the concept of "miracles" from within her essay to tie together the beginning and end. Here are the first drafts of Janine's opening and concluding paragraphs, with her notes.

My Mystery Quilt   *This is so boring!*

[introduction]   *Too obvious. That's sort of the point of the assignment, looking for clues.*

The quilt folded at the foot of my bed is a mystery. It is made of cotton: plain muslin and two patterns of calico, with a cotton batt inside, sewn by hand with careful stitches. Some of its thread is white and some is pink. It is frayed around the edges, so someone has obviously used it. But unlike quilts in my own family, this quilt was not handed down as a cherished heirloom. I rescued it from a garage sale and have tried to "piece together" its history.

Consultant says puns are usually a bad idea—especially in opening.

[conclusion]

When I am cold at night I pull the quilt up over my knees and think about the stranger who made it, wondering who she was, who her loved ones were, whether she was happy. Her quilt gives me warmth, and I give her thanks. There is a bond between us because of this quilt.

This is boring/obvious. Can I make it more special?

5: Submitted Version

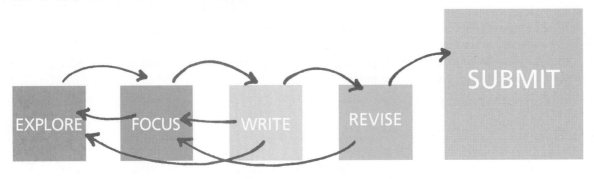

Carter 1

Janine Carter
Dr. Shapiro
Archeology 201
10 October 2011

The Miracle Quilt

The quilt folded at the foot of my bed has a long history. It is made of cotton: plain muslin and two patterns of calico, with a cotton batt inside, sewn by hand with careful stitches. Some of its thread is white and some is pink. It is frayed around the edges and has obviously lived a long, useful life. It is steeped in memories. Unfortunately, I don't know what any of them are.

I found the quilt at a city-wide garage sale. At the end of the auditorium, taking up half of the bleachers, was a vendor's booth called "Miracles by the Pound." The gentleman who ran the booth went around buying up vintage fabrics in bad condition. He would dump huge piles of them on the bleachers for people to pick through. When you had found what you wanted, he would weigh it on a scale and tell you how much it cost. Everything was five dollars per pound. As he weighed your purchase, he would call out the price so everyone at the garage sale could hear what a good deal you were getting. My quilt weighed three pounds. "Fifteen dollar miracle!" the vendor sang out as I opened my purse.

My quilt had already been dug out of the pile and discarded by another woman at the garage sale, who had two or three other vintage quilts in her arms. She told me

Fig. 1. Detail of the miracle quilt.

she bought old, damaged quilts and cut them up to make sofa pillows. My quilt didn't interest her because it wasn't in very good shape, and the blocks were the wrong size for the pillow forms she used. I come from a family of quilters, so when I saw the quilt I felt it needed a good home. I didn't like the idea of someone using it to wrap around furniture in a moving van, or even cutting it up for pillows. I took it home and washed it, and put it on my bed, and took a good look at it.

The quilt was probably made by someone poor, or at least very frugal, I decided. The muslin, which provides the background, is the cheapest unbleached kind. Even the binding around the edges, which in most quilts is a bright, contrasting color, is plain muslin. Whoever pieced the quilt—and it was almost certainly a woman, because quilting has always been women's work—started out using a coral-toned calico. But before she finished, she ran out and had to switch to a rose-colored calico. The effect is jarring, as the colors do not complement each other. The coral marches two-thirds of the way across the quilt, and then stumbles into rose. I do not know why the quiltmaker did not work the two colors evenly throughout the quilt; this is what my own grandmother taught me to do when I didn't have enough of one color.

Perhaps she was inexperienced; perhaps this was her first quilt, or perhaps she hadn't intended to make the quilt as large as it is. The coral would have been sufficient to cover a single bed; maybe, I think to myself, someone proposed to her while she was making it, and she ended up enlarging it to fit a double bed after she got married.

But there are other clues that suggest experience and planning. The octagon-shaped patches of muslin that center the five-patch blocks are cut so that the lines of quilting cross them on the bias—that is, diagonally across the up-and-down and side-to-side warp and woof threads of the fabric. Fabric is more flexible on the bias (this, my grandmother once explained to me, is why clothing cut on the bias fits and looks better, and is more expensive). A needle slips in and out between the threads more easily, so a quilter is wise to arrange pieces so as to maximize bias quilting. The quilting itself (that is the stitching through all the layers of the quilt) is respectable enough, about five stitches per inch. No fancy 12-stitch-per-inch quilting like you would see in a showpiece quilt, but quite firm and straight, in neat pink rows spaced an inch apart. The quilting pattern is in L-shaped blocks, which I have never seen before. There must be over one hundred yards of quilting all together; the length of a football field, taken one stitch at a time.

The quilt's pattern looks like a variation of wagon tracks, but it uses an octagonal block like a "churn-dash" pattern that sets it apart from a more straightforward Irish chain. Nine-patch and five-patch blocks alternate across it. By my count it contains 1,372 separate pieces, all cut, sewn, and quilted by hand. The nine-patch blocks use 1-1/2-inch patches. These may seem like insignificant details to most people, but to quilters they are important. They tell you how much work went into the quilt. The first nine-patch quilt I made with my grandmother contained a grand total of 675 patches, and I thought it would take forever to sew it (even using a sewing machine!). I remember asking my grandmother how she ever made her more complicated quilts: the flower garden with its thousands of tiny hexagons; the Dutchman's puzzle that was so mesmerizing you could hardly stop your eyes from running over it, trying to pick out the "real" pattern. "Doesn't quilting drive you crazy sometimes?" I asked her. She thought that was pretty funny. "Quilting was how we used to keep from going crazy," she told me.

When she first married my grandfather and moved to a farm in the Brazos River bottom over sixty years ago, there was no television and no neighbors for miles.

In the spring, rain would turn the roads to thick clay mud and no one could get off their property for days at a time. Quilting was the way women dealt with the isolation. "That is what the pioneer women did too," she told me. Stuck out alone on the prairies and in the mountains, they kept their sanity by cutting and arranging hundreds of pieces of cloth in different patterns, methodically assembling quilts to bring some order into their own bleak lives.

"It looks like hard work to you now," my grandmother explained, "but for us it was like a vacation. So much of women's work was never done, but you could sit down after dinner in the evening and finish a quilt block and feel like you had done something that would last. You might have spent the whole day dirtying and washing the same set of dishes three times, feeding the same chickens and milking the same cows twice, and you knew you'd have to get up in the morning and do the same things all over again, from top to bottom. But quilt blocks added up to something. Nobody was going to take your finished quilt block and sit down at the breakfast table and pick it apart, and expect you to sew it back together again before lunch. It was done, and it stayed done. There wasn't much else you could say that about, on a farm."

In my family, quilts are heirlooms and are handed down with stories about who made them, who owned them, what they were used for, and what events they had been part of. Some were wedding presents, others were made for relatives when they were first born. I don't know the stories that go with my miracle quilt. It has had a hard life; that is easy to see. Most of the binding has frayed off and there are some spots where the quilt has holes worn straight through it—top, batting, and backing. There are stains that suggest coffee or tea or perhaps medicines from a sickbed spilled on it. There are some spots of dried paint. Evidently at some point it was used as a drop-cloth. But at least, I tell myself, it has found a home with someone who appreciates the work that went into it, and can guess at some of its history.

When I am cold at night I pull the quilt up over my knees and think about the stranger who made it, wondering who she was, who her loved ones were, whether she was happy. Her quilt gives me warmth, and I give her thanks. Though we will never meet, or even know each other's identity, there is a bond between us because of this quilt. And so it seems that the man who sold me this quilt was right: it is a sort of miracle.

Projects

Reflections focus on people, places, events, and things—past and present—that have significance in the writer's life.

Reflection on the past

List people, events, or places that have been significant in your life or in some way changed you. Many reflections focus on a conflict of some kind and how it was resolved. Look back over your list and check the items that seem especially vivid to you.

Family photograph

Family photographs and cherished objects can be subjects for reflection. Try carefully observing (or picturing in your mind) an object or photograph that has special meaning for you. Write down all the details you can. What memories does each observation evoke? Do you find that different aspects of the photograph make you feel different ways?

Take a few minutes to write first about the person, event, or place as you remember it, and then write about how you regard it today. What was your initial reaction? Did your initial reaction change over time? Why do you feel differently now?

Choose as a topic something that is significant to you, and which you can recall with a reasonable amount of detail. But also consider how interesting this topic will be to others. Will an audience want to share in your experience?

Think about the significance of the person, event, or place in your life. What details best convey that significance? If conversations were involved, remember what was said and create dialogue.

Organize your essay around the focus. Start fast to engage your readers. If there is a conflict in your reflection, get it up front.

Write a reflective essay about that photograph. What does the photograph convey that other similar snapshots do not? What does it hide or not show? What does it say about your family?

Show the significance through describing, vivid details, and dialogue. Make the characters and the places come to life.

For support in learning this chapter's content, follow this path in mycomplab:

▶ **Resources** ▶ **Writing** ▶ **The Writing Process** ▶ **Planning**

Review the Instruction and Multimedia resources, then complete the Exercises and click on Gradebook to measure your progress.

Literacy narrative

Think about a childhood memory of reading or writing that remains especially vivid. The memory may be of a particular book you read, of something you wrote, or a teacher who was important in teaching you to read or write. Or think of a more recent experience of reading and writing. What have you written lately that was especially difficult? Or especially rewarding? List as many possibilities as you can think of.

Look over the items on the list and pick one that remains significant to you. Begin writing by describing the experience in as much detail as you can remember. Describe who was involved and recall what was said. Describe the setting of the experience: where exactly were you and what difference did it make? Remember key passages from what you either read or wrote. How did you understand the experience at the time? How do you understand it now? What makes it special?

Review what you have written and consider how to shape your raw material into an engaging essay. You may want to narrate the experience in the order it happened; you may want to start in the middle of the experience and give the background later; or you may want to start in the present as you look back. Above all, start fast. Somewhere along the way, you will need to convey why the experience was significant for you, but avoid the temptation to end with a moral. Don't forget to include a title that makes your readers want to read your literacy narrative.

Personal blog

Read blogs on sites such as blogger.com (click on the BLOGS OF NOTE link). You'll find that personal blogs take on a wide range of subject matter from thoughts about life in general to reflections on specific subjects like art, films, fashion, education, music, and family. Many blogs are multimedia including vlogs (video blogs), sketchblogs (portfolios of sketches), and photoblogs (photographic records of daily life).

Decide on a general subject matter for your blog. The most interesting blogs come from writers who spend much time thinking about that subject, perhaps to the point of obsession. Write about what you love. If you have strong dedication to a particular subject, likely you can get others interested.

Write your blog with your readers in mind. Write with a personal voice that engages your readers. Make your blog fun to read. Use paragraphs and pay attention to the little things. Error-filled writing is not enjoyable to read, no matter how fresh the content.

Encourage your readers to respond. Web hosting sites allow you to have a comment section so that readers can interact with you.

Publish your blog on a Web hosting site or a site at your school. Commit to a schedule of posting blog entries with regular frequency such as once a week.

 Apply the Concept of Writing to Reflect at mycomplab.com **109**

7 Observations

Effective observations capture readers' attention through details that may be unfamiliar or surprising but always fresh and vivid.

Chapter Overview

Writing Observations

Observing is often the first step to understanding. In fields such as anthropology, sociology, and psychology, scientists observe people and processes and use their observations to answer questions like these: How is death regarded in Navajo societies? What groups of people are most likely to visit an urban parkland? How do primates interact?

In everyday life, we use our observational skills to learn more about people and places we encounter. We learn how our neighbors feel about certain political issues by observing the signs they put up on their lawn. Businesses and governments also use observation to learn more about the people they serve. City officials might observe children playing on a public playground to see what kinds of equipment are used.

Observations begin with thorough research. Your firsthand impressions must be carefully recorded in as much detail as possible. These observations, often called field notes, provide your raw material. When you write as an observer, you place yourself in the background, and give readers the clearest, most detailed view you can of your subject.

Keys to reflections

BUILD A STRONG SENSE OF PLACE	Help readers locate themselves along with you as you describe your observations. Tell them the date, time, and exact location of your observations, if possible. Give the names of the objects present.
SHOW, NOT TELL	Concrete imagery and descriptions of what you see, hear, smell, taste, and feel during your observation will ground your writing, helping readers "see" as if through your eyes.
PROVIDE VIVID, WELL-CHOSEN DETAILS	Select details to create an overall impression that grows out of the details. Think about which details are critical for that impression.
KNOW WHEN YOU ARE EXPECTED TO BE OBJECTIVE	Field observations in the sciences and social sciences keep the writer in the background, focusing instead on the subject. But essays often allow for personal reflection. Ask your instructor what is expected.

Observations in the world

Descriptive essays use sensory detail to give a vivid experience of a a place, an animal, an or an object.

Other genres of observations

- **Documentaries** are a broad category of films and photographic essays, sometimes combined with written text, that intend to represent accurately some part of reality.

- **Ethnographies** collect data from observation, interviews, and daily participation to describe human societies and culture in rich detail.

- **Case studies** are used in a wide range of fields such as nursing, psychology, business, and anthropology to create detailed portraits.

What Makes a Good Observation?

1

Identify your subject

Be specific about who or what you are observing. If it is a certain group of people, what sets them apart as a group? Do they share a common interest? If it is a place, what makes it special?

Nowhere else in the world can we find the array or number of geysers, hot springs, mud pots, and fumaroles found in Yellowstone.
   —National Park Service (see page 135)

2

Provide background on the subject

Readers need some idea of why your observations are significant. Is there a question that could be answered by your observations? Give readers the context they need to appreciate the picture you are about to present and to understand your motivation for observing.

As an American, I was raised to believe that the simple act of passing one's soles across a nubbly plastic map sporting a cute saying will somehow magically dislodge an accumulated eight hours of filth, muck, and germs. . . . The Japanese remove their shoes at the door.
   —Sandra Tsing Loh (see page 120)

3

Assemble your observations

You may approach your observations chrono-logically, leading readers through your day-to-day or hour-by-hour experience as an observer. Or you may find other ways to organize that work better for your purposes: perhaps starting with the most surprising discovery you made while observing.

4

Provide vivid sensory details

Build your observation with concrete details. For example, think about the sounds of food as well as how it looks and tastes.

Three more dollars earned you a trip to the salad bar—featuring Lady Lee peas, which the cook poured expressionlessly from the can. They made a gentle splattering sound as they slid into the copious salad-bar vat.
   —Mary Roach (see page 116)

5

Place your observations in a larger context

Firsthand observation is a powerful tool for understanding, but it has its limits. What questions are left unanswered by your observations? How might your observations be atypical? Give your readers a framework within which to understand your observations.

I realized that I had unknowingly committed the most egregious of cultural misunderstandings. Forget the glaring red bouquet, my self-conscious sobs, or my battle with the chicken feet; I have absolutely no idea whose funeral I attended.
   —Kellie Schmitt (see page 124)

6

Know when you are expected to be objective.

Field observations in the sciences and social sciences keep the writer in the background, focusing instead on the subject. In contrast, descriptive essays often make the writer the central character, and we see through the writer's eyes. Ask your instructor what is expected.

7

Provide visuals if needed

Photographs and other images can work in combination with words to enhance observations. Close attention to details is critical for both descriptive writing and descriptive visual.

Visual observations

Photographs and other images can work in combination with words to enhance observations. Close attention to details is critical for both descriptive writing and descriptive visuals.

Photographs are valuable for providing concrete examples. For instance, Frank Lloyd Wright's attention to detail is evident in his 1905 design for the lobby of the Rookery Building in Chicago.

WRITE NOW

Visit a place or event

In small groups of three or four students, visit the same place or event, such as a museum, a parade or festival, or a political rally. Each group member should make notes about what he or she observes and write a short synopsis of the visit (one to two pages). Then, as a group, read each other's synopses. How different was each person's experience? What, if anything, did they have in common?

Working together, draft a short introduction that summarizes the different perspectives your observations provide. What can an audience learn by reading multiple accounts of the same experience?

How to Read Observations

▼ BEFORE YOU BEGIN READING

These notes are in response to "Monster in a Ryokan"; the reading begins on page 116.

| What kind of text is it? | ·······▶ | Roach's essay is a travel account. It was published in Travelers' Tales Japan, a collection of experiences of people who have traveled in Japan. |

| Who wrote it? | ·······▶ | Mary Roach is a journalist and a popular science writer. |

| Who is the intended audience? | ·······▶ | The Travelers' Tales series is aimed at people who want to read about journeys to foreign places. |

▼ READ THE TEXT AT LEAST TWICE AND MAKE NOTES

| What is the subject of the observation? | ·······▶ | The immediate subject is the Japanese ryokan, a traditional inn, but the larger subject is the cultural differences between Japan and the United States. |

| What is the overall impression? | ·······▶ | We see Roach as large, clumsy, and rude in the ryokan; however, her self-effacing humor suggests she is simply unaware of Japanese customs and more sensitive to cultural differences than she lets on. |

| What kinds of details are included? | ·······▶ | Roach gives many details about what is expected in a ryokan, including wearing special hallway slippers and special toilet slippers. |

| How would you characterize the style? | ·······▶ | The style is informal and humorous. Roach employs metaphors to describe herself (Godzilla and King Kong) and to compare American hotel rooms (which have "prairies and vistas") with small Japanese hotel rooms ("like living inside a Dixie Cup"). |

How is it organized?

This map shows the organization of "Monster in a Ryokan," which begins on the following page.

Introduction Paragraphs 1–3	Roach announces that size is a relative concept and then identifies the site where she will explore that concept—a Japanese *ryokan*.
Arrival at ryokan Paragraphs 4–7	Roach begins to portray herself as clumsy, "crashing" into bicycles as she approaches the *ryokan*.
Details about Japanese customs Paragraphs 8–11	The Japanese care in wearing special slippers inside a hotel and in the toilet illustrates a major cultural difference with American customs.
Godzilla in the ryokan Paragraphs 12–16	Roach describes herself as a large reptile stumbling over the tiny furniture and soaping up in a tub meant for relaxing only in clean water.
Conclusion Paragraphs 17–19	Roach tries to regain her composure when the hotel proprietor brings her a tray of tea, but she realizes she has made every mistake possible in violating customs.

Monster in a Ryokan

Mary Roach

Mary Roach grew up in New Hampshire, moved to San Francisco, and began writing irreverent and witty articles for newspapers and magazines about offbeat topics. Her three most recent books—*Stiff: The Curious Lives of Human Cadavers* (2003); *Spook: Science Tackles the Afterlife* (2005); and *Bonk: The Curious Coupling of Science and Sex* (2008)—have earned her praise as the funniest science writer on the planet. In this essay, she describes her awkward experiences in a *ryokan*, a traditional Japanese hotel.

Monster in a Ryokan

A monster is a relative thing. In Godzilla's hometown, everyone was fifty feet tall and scaly. The sidewalks were wide enough that no one had to trample parked cars and knock over buildings. Only in Tokyo did Godzilla become a monster.

Likewise myself. In my own country, I am not thought of as brutish and rude—or anyway, no more so than the next slob. But in Japan, I am suddenly huge and clueless. I sprout extra limbs and make loud, unintelligible noises. In Japan, I am a monster.

Introduction: Roach represents herself as an oversized monster in Japan in the setting of a *ryokan*.

I came to this conclusion following a recent stay at a ryokan, a traditional Japanese inn. It was raining the night I flew in to Tokyo, and the cab had dropped me at the wrong place. Having walked the remaining distance, stopping every few blocks to perform the quaint flailing pantomime of the lost foreigner, I was drenched and disheveled by the time I arrived at the right place.

I lumbered down the foot-path, crashing into bicycles and trampling tiny ornamental trees. As I opened the door, several of the staff could be seen fleeing from the room. Others crouched behind traditional Japanese furnishings, which, though pleasing to the eye, offer little in the way of protective cover.

Organization: The basic organization is chronological, beginning with Roach's arrival, but she offers mini-essays particular topics along the way

"HRRARGGHH ARGGHH HAARGH RARRRRHSCHRV-RANN." (Hello, I have a reservation.)

I lurched forward and stepped up to the reception window. The woman's face crumbled in distress. A large portion of this appeared to be directed at my feet. She pointed to a shelf of shoes and then she pointed to mine. The shoes on the shelf were dainty and immaculate. The shoes on my feet were wet and battered and huge.

I apologized for the size and condition of my footwear. This was not the problem. The problem was that I was wearing them inside the ryokan.

As an American, I was raised to believe that the simple act of passing one's soles across a nubbly plastic mat sporting a cute saying will somehow magically dislodge an accumulated eight hours of filth, muck, and germs. The Japanese do not share our faith in doormats. The Japanese remove their shoes at the door.

Details:
Roach makes the first direct comparison of Japanese and American customs.

As a ryokan guest, you are expected to do the same. Inside the front door is a bench for you to sit on and take off your shoes. This is normally located directly across from the reception window, enabling the staff to tell at a glance that your socks a) don't match, b) need washing, and c) have little threadbare patches at the heels. You are then provided with a pair of Japanese slippers, which are open in the back so that the staff, over the course of your visit, can see that, indeed, all of your socks have threadbare heels.

The slippers, you soon learn, are special hallway slippers, not to be worn inside the rooms. In the rooms you wear only socks. That is, unless you are in the toilet room, in which case you exchange your special hallway slippers for special toilet slippers, which are never, under penalty of shame and humiliation, to be worn anywhere but the toilet.

I do not mean to imply that Japanese people are needlessly fastidious. I mean to imply that Americans are needlessly squalid—especially in hotels. In American hotels, the whole idea is to create as much of a mess as possible, as someone else will be cleaning it up. Do unto others as you figure they'd do unto you if you had a job cleaning hotel rooms.

Properly shod, I was shown to my room. It was approximately nine feet square and contained three or four pieces of traditional ankle-high furniture. To someone accustomed to the vast prairies and vistas of the American hotel room, this takes getting used to. In America, a single-occupancy room must contain a bed—heck, make it two!—large enough to accommodate lumberjacks and NBA centers lying spread-eagle in any direction. Though guests will be leaving their belongings strewn about the bed and floor, there must be a dresser, a desk, and a closet the size of Maine. There must be six bars of soap and a telephone in the bathroom. A ryokan room, on the other hand, serves the simple purpose for which it was designed: that is, to provide a neat, comfortable place to sleep for a few nights.

Style:
Roach exaggerates for humorous effect.

Though I appreciated the rational scale and modest aesthetics of my accommodations, I was nonetheless hopelessly disoriented. I kept running into walls and stumbling over traditional ankle-high furniture. Someone had spread bedding out all over the floor, which caused me to trip and smash headlong into a low-hanging lantern. Tea cups were capsized. Miniature dressers toppled and rolled. Soon the Japanese national guard would arrive with rifles and tranquilizer darts.

I tried to get a grip on myself. Thrashing violently in a small Japanese room is a dangerous proposition, as the walls are fashioned not from plaster, but from delicate sheets of waxy rice paper. It's like living inside a Dixie Cup. One false step and you come crashing through to the adjoining room, which in this case

Style:
Metaphors and similes add to the humor.

happened to be a carp pond, and god only knows what sort of slippers are required for that.

I decided to go soak in the tub. Like other large reptiles, I am plodding and ungainly on land, but surprisingly graceful underwater. I asked the staff for a robe and entered the steamy, tiled sanctum. To my great relief, the bath was already drawn and everything seemed self-explanatory.

Later, back in my room, I noticed a small booklet on the table. It was called Information on How to Enjoy a Ryokan—a "guide book" to "living, eating, and sleeping as the Japanese do." According to a section titled "Tips for Taking a Bath," I had committed no less than three ablutionary offenses. For starters, the bathtub is not for bathing, but for relaxing. To soap and rinse yourself inside the tub is an unthinkable act, akin to peeing in the pool or drinking milk straight from the carton. The cute plastic baskets are not floating soap dishes; they are for storing your clothes. The traditional Japanese robe closes left side over right, not right over left, and is called a yukata, not— as I had called it—a yakuza. (Yakuza are Japanese mafiosi, the guys who chop off their pinkies for dishonorable behavior, such as cowardice or soaping oneself in the tub.)

While I contemplated my sins, there was a knock (rustle? thwap?) on the wax paper. It was the proprietress, bearing a tray of tea. She seemed displeased. "I'm sorry about the soap," I blurted. "I didn't see the instruction book."

She smiled—the sort of bemused, resigned smile Fay Wray used to give King Kong after he tipped over the garage or stepped on the house pets. Without a word, she set down the tray and left.

Shortly thereafter, I noticed the toilet slippers on my feet. It was almost a relief. Every wrong thing that could be done had been done. I could only go uphill from here. I rested my huge wet head on my little prehensile arms and went to sleep.

Style:
Roach continues to make fun of herself as a large reptile.

Conclusion:
Roach ends her first day in the *ryokan* having done everything wrong.

Coming Home to Van Nuys
Sandra Tsing Loh

Sandra Tsing Loh is a performance artist, radio personality, and author whose writings have appeared in a number of publications, including *The Atlantic*. While her college degree is in physics, Loh writes on a range of subjects, including pop culture. "Coming Home to Van Nuys" is taken from her book *Depth Takes a Holiday: Essays from Lesser Los Angeles*, published in 1996.

Return to these questions after you have finished reading.

Analyzing the Reading

1. What is the main point that Loh is making in her essay? Why does she write that "The notion of 'ethnic charm' is a hoary Americanism from the seventies"?

2. Loh focuses on one aspect of life in Van Nuys— "ethnic" food restaurants. Why does she choose this focus? What do you think she hopes to achieve with it?

3. How would you characterize Loh's tone? What words or passages are most effective in conveying her tone?

4. Is it important for Loh's audience to be very familiar with Van Nuys? Why or why not?

Exploring Ideas and Issues

Kevin Roderick, a journalist in Los Angeles, has called the San Fernando Valley, in which Van Nuys is situated, "America's Suburb." Recently, a grassroots movement, claiming in part that the Valley is culturally distinct from Los Angeles and would benefit from having its own government, advocated for secession, and in November 2002 a vote was held on whether or not to allow the Valley to secede from the city. The vote failed.

1. Loh gives many examples of restaurants to support her ideas about Van Nuys. Select a single feature—important or trivial—that you feel says something important about where you live. Write a short essay in which you explore this feature and its meaning. Include several examples as illustration of your ideas.

2. The San Fernando Valley has been the subject or setting of many well-known movies, including *Chinatown* (1974) and *Fast Times at Ridgemont High* (1982). View a movie set in the Valley or in another place, preferably a location you are unfamiliar with. In a short essay, describe how the place is portrayed in the film. What is your impression of the setting? Does the portrayal seem reasonable? Give at least three examples from the film to support your conclusions.

3. For immigrants to America, the tension between holding on to an ethnic identity and assimilating into mainstream American culture has always been deeply felt. Write an essay on the struggle to find just the right degree of assimilation. How important is it for people to hold on to traditional foods, a native language, and traditional customs and rituals? Use examples from your own experience and from your observations of others' experience.

Coming Home to Van Nuys

It can be hard, sometimes, to come home to Van Nuys.

Especially via LAX, when you've just gotten off the plane from New Mexico or Minnesota or some other faraway place where pale green cornfields shiver under a cobalt sky. . . .

So unlike Airport Parking Lot C, really, where Burger King debris sucks up around your ankles and rows and rows of battered automobiles sulk beneath an oil sun. You step over a smashed Michelob bottle and suddenly you remember your life: you're poor, you're anonymous, and you drive a shitty car.

You think about the scenic drive ahead, deep into the Grid of the sweltering Valley, home of a hundred King Bear Auto Centers, a thousand Yoshinoya Beef Bowls, and ten thousand yard sales, some consisting of no more than a couple of "Disco Lady" T-shirts flung out on a scabrous lawn like some kind of SOS. You want to close your eyes and say, "There's no place like home." But in fact, you *are* home.

On my last return to L.A., the mantra I put to myself as I wandered the grim expanse of Parking Lot C, looking for my 1973 VW with its bad clutch, was: "What do I love about Van Nuys? What do I love about Van Nuys?" Twenty minutes later, when I found the car (in section Ss), I had an epithany.

What's great about living in Van Nuys is that we, uh . . . we have a pretty good variety of take-out. Maybe that doesn't sound like much, but it's something they sure don't have in Minnesota.

And besides, we're talking a whole world of take-out possibilities. My kitchen drawer is bursting with menus that must have been hurled onto my front porch in the dead of night. Within five minutes of my house I can get at least a dozen different kinds of "ethnic" food—including 100 percent authentic soul food, Thai, Chinese, Salvadoran, East Indian, Northern Italian, Spanish (the chef is from Barcelona, not Mexico), Israeli, Cajun, German, and Japanese.

Ah, yes. You're imagining the vivid cadences of exotic languages. The bustle of wonderful bazaars and open-air markets full of kiosks, and street cars, and flapping geese, and bicycle bells. French guys with fresh baguettes roller-skating in Gene Kelly pants, matiachi music, an honest cobbler from Istanbul, and a very wise man from Tibet who can tell you everything about yaks.

The problem, of course, is that this is joyous melting pot doesn't describe Van Nuys at all. Walt Disney never made it over here to redecorate. The notion of "ethnic charm" is a hoary old Americanism from the seventies. There are few vibrant ethnic enclaves in the Valley; what I didn't tell you is that for each nationality I've named, there is exactly one restaurant. One. Marooned by itself in a tiny strip mall, generally sandwiched between an X-rated video store and a Sally for Nails salon. Not all of them do very well.

The take-out places that do flourish here are ones that dispense terrific food at terrific speed. At one of my favorites, Golan Restaurant, the employees wear perpetual scowls as they hurl peppers and falafel into paper bags with deadly urgency. And the folks at Thai Koon Café, another find, do a mean delivery— clocking in at something like twelve minutes from their door to mine—no doubt having knocked down a few Domino's delivery guys on the way.

More common are the ethnic restaurants that are slowly dying on the vine. They have a certain lost quality I can identify with. NO one seems to understand what they're doing here. It is the way of the Grid.

One example. About three years ago a Egyptian restaurant opened in a strip mall not far from here. And I don't mean your generic Middle Easternish Pita Hut chain. I mean *Egyptians*. I'm not sure if this place ever had a name. The location's previous take-out tenant was a Chicken Delight franchise, and the sign, featuring a startled yellow bird, remained up for a while even though the Egyptians didn't sell chicken. Nor was there much cause for delight; the place was always empty. You could see the young cook through the window, sitting by himself in an orange plastic chair, smoking cigarettes, reading the paper.

About two months later, suddenly a crudely lettered sign that simply read KABOB went up. Still nothing. Soon after, the management decided to abandon the idea of using English at all; KABOB came down, and energetic banners in Arabic flew up around the windows.

It was at this point that I really became interested. (I'm the worst kind of consumer: small and exacting standards. You have to do a lot to get my attention,

because when I let go of twelve dollars, I don't do it lightly.) Aha! I thought.
They're only communicating with their own people. Something really fabulous
must be going on.

But still masses failed to flock. Why wasn't the Egyptian community (wherever
it was) catching on to this? An eager visit to the restaurant revealed the answer.
The authentic Egyptian-food experience turned out to be an overpriced (paper)
plate of stringy beef, instant rice, and runny tomatoes. Three more dollars earned
you a trip to the salad bar—featuring Lady Lee peas, which the cook poured
expressionlessly from the can. They made a gentle splattering sound as they slid
into the copious salad-bar vat.

What inspires some folks to relocate halfway around the world to the San
Fernando Valley in order to feed bad food on paper plates to their own people?
Perhaps the chef really did not want to be in the food industry at all. Perhaps his
family pushed him into it, like my own Chinese father pushed me to be an
aeronautical engineer. (He believed I was destined to shine in the Advanced
Tactical Weapons Division at Hughes Aircraft Company. He was wrong.)

But the take-out place that makes me feel the worst is the one in the strip mall
on my corner—the home of Royal India. I've come to know the owner; his name is
Shah. Unfortunately, I've also come to know his troubles. Like many Indian
restaurants languishing in the Valley, the food is incredible: there's rich vindaloo,
tikka masala like red paint, lamb sag delicately aromatic in its gleaming metal
dish. The interior, too, is embarrassingly classy for a place flanked by an "All-Nite"
liquor store. There are white tablecloths, napkins stuffed in wineglasses like
bouquets, and two bow-tied waiters who speak in perfectly modulated British
accents. And it's going out of business. It kills me. I want to write the owner a note:

Dear Shah, I can't afford to spend twenty-five dollars on dinner every night,
but I want to keep you in my neighborhood. You are a culinary genius. I wish
I could help!

But I don't. Instead, I slide another frozen dinner into the microwave. One
block away, Shah peers out of Royal India's red curtains, watching for invisible
customers on what is called Victory Boulevard. Up above him, a neon COIN
LAUNDRY sign blinks on and off.

The Old Man Isn't There Anymore
Kellie Schmitt

During the two years she spent in China, the journalist Kellie Schmitt was a frequent contributor to CNNgo, a travel and lifestyle Web site. Her articles have also appeared in the *Wall Street Journal, Marie Claire, Afar Magazine,* and *The Economist's Business China.*

Return to these questions after you have finished reading.

Analyzing the Reading

1. What is Schmitt's purpose is in writing this travel narrative? What kind of audience is she writing for, and what might the audience be interested in learning?

2. The author borrows techniques from fiction to tell a story about living in China. Is her use of storytelling useful in illustrating her main ideas? Identify two or more examples of narrative techniques that Schmitt uses.

3. At least a quarter of the paragraphs are devoted to describing the funeral and cremation. Why does Schmitt dedicate so much space to this description? How effective is the description?

4. Although this story is about a death, Schmitt's tone is not somber. What tone does Schmitt use? How does her tone reflect her attitude toward her Chinese neighbors?

Exploring Ideas and Issues

Cultures have deeply entrenched ways of dealing with the profound reality of death. In addition to rituals for disposing of the body, many societies have distinctive ways to observe or facilitate mourning. Schmitt says that she "felt uneasy" witnessing the cremation. Perhaps she is simply reacting to an unfamiliar ritual, or perhaps one purpose of this or any such ritual is to force a confrontation with and acknowledgment of the person's death.

1. Most of us have probably found ourselves, at least once, in a culturally unfamiliar situation. We might attend a wedding held in a religious tradition different from our own, for example. Think of a time when you had such an experience. What happened? What were your thoughts and feelings? Do you wish you had acted differently? Why or why not? Write a short essay in which you explain your observations. Remember to use specific details to engage your reader.

2. Schmitt is eager to become friends, or at least acquaintances, with her Chinese neighbors. But "friendship" has different meanings in different cultures. What does friendship mean to you? Write an essay in which you either categorize your friendships by type (work friend, best friend, and so on) or explain what qualities make for a good friend. Support your ideas with examples from your own and others' experiences.

3. That the dead should be treated with dignity and mourners with compassion is a belief most of us probably share. In what ways do a culture's funeral practices illustrate this belief? Write an essay in which you describe the traditions in your own or another culture or religion. What benefits, or drawbacks, do you think these traditions have for mourners? Include examples from your own observations or from research you have conducted.

The Old Man Isn't There Anymore

I found myself in a Chinese funeral parlor because of a phone call I made to my cleaning lady.

The previous evening, my husband Gregg had seen our neighbors crying in the hallway. We'd wondered if the old grandpa, the one with the buzz-cut hair, had died. Gregg had suggested we shouldn't interfere, but curiosity had gotten the best of me. I'd called the all-knowing cleaning lady.

"Do you know why the neighbors," I paused. I knew the word in Mandarin for "crying" but not hallway.

"Do you know why the neighbors are very sad?" I asked.

"The old man isn't there anymore," she replied, which I guessed was her baby Chinese way of telling me he died.

"Ah, the old man who lives on the second floor?" I asked.

Even though we had lived in this old three-story house in Shanghai for more than a year, I couldn't map out the neighbors and where they resided. While we lived in a spacious apartment on the renovated top floor, the other two floors remained as they had been during the height of Communism: cheap, basic and subdivided. As a result, we shared the house with many neighbors. They'd pop out of doorways, hallways, and hidden bathrooms, often wearing just slippers and underwear. There were at least a dozen, all local Shanghainese.

When we had first seen the apartment, I had created stories in my head of the relationships we'd establish with our cohabitants. I'd wander into their kitchens in the late afternoon and we'd sit around sipping green tea and chatting in Chinese about our lives. That fairy-tale ended when we moved in: Nobody would even say hello to us.

I grilled our Chinese teacher for an explanation. Am I saying *ni hao* wrong? Was there some moving-in etiquette that I'd forgotten? In China, do people not speak to those who walk around in their underwear under the same roof? My teacher said she wasn't sure.

Still, I was persistent. I would repeatedly try to engage them, saying hello at every encounter. Sometimes, I'd offer a comment on the weather, or tell the grandpa with the buzz cut: "We're off to America for two weeks! See you when we get back!"

Around month three, I got a disgruntled nod from one of the underwear men. One day, the second-floor dad, who was always cooking in the communal kitchen, told me his family's white cat liked me. And, miraculously, when I returned from Christmas vacation with two heavy suitcases, the burly second-floor mom helped me lug them up the steep wooden stairs. We had turned a corner.

I was so grateful that I wanted to show my appreciation. I dashed down the stairs and offered the mom and grandpa a plate of fresh brownies. Grandpa didn't say anything, just looked at me with a bemused smile. I shoved one onto his plate, blushing as it occurred to me that Chinese traditionally don't like excessively sweet Western desserts.

From there, I progressed to exchanging pleasantries, mostly commenting on the lazy white cat who liked to sleep all day in the nook beneath the banister.

When I hung up the phone with the cleaning lady, I made the bold decision to buy sympathy flowers. After all, grandpa and I had often exchanged hellos. He would stand in his undershirt in the doorway, a stout man with full cheeks and an easy smile. His face had few wrinkles though it was patterned with age spots, and I had imagined he was in his 70s. He always looked perplexed by our presence and I'd sometimes wonder what the China of his youth was like, when the country was closed to the West. What a contrast to be spending his final days living a floor away from two Americans.

With my basket of roses in hand, I knocked on the family's door. The dad, dressed in loose white fabric, opened it with a surprised smile. In Chinese, he said, over and over, that I was too polite. For the first time, he beckoned me into their one-room space, now covered in white floral arrangements. The sweet scent of lilies perfumed the air.

My local florist didn't do funeral-specific arrangements so I'd asked her to create an appropriate alternative. Apparently something got lost in the translation. Nobody had mentioned I should have requested white, the color associated with death in China.

The mom wrote my Chinese name, 可莉, on a long paper scroll and hung it across my scarlet-colored flowers like a beauty pageant sash. Great, I thought. Now everyone will know who got the wrong color.

Their rarely-seen, 25-year-old daughter, Lili, spoke up in English. She explained that her grandfather had died from cancer, and while they were very sad, it was considered a good omen for the family that he had a long life.

"We would be very honored if you'd attend the funeral on Saturday," she said. "Since he died at 91, it's a joyous occasion and we want you to be there."

I deflected the offer, using the words I had learned for "don't want to bother you." I was aware that the Chinese often extended invites just to be polite. It was my job to refuse. Still, they insisted and insisted, which made me wonder if they were seriously asking me to attend grandpa's funeral. When they mentioned that it would mean a lot to the deceased, I wavered. And when they told me that everyone who attends will also live a long life, I finally agreed.

As soon as our coach arrived at the funeral home that Saturday, Lili began translating the remarks of the passersby: Wow a foreigner is here! What is a foreigner doing here? We've never seen a foreigner here.

As we silently filed into the room, trumpets and saxophones sounded, a little off-key, punctuated with a clash of symbols. We all wore black fabric swatches pinned to our arms to acknowledge we were part of the grieving party. Inside, there were about 30 people, mostly family and some old friends. I urged Lili to join her family in the front while I shuffled to the back of the room.

The emcee orchestrated the order of events with short commentaries. Soon, the microphone was given to the mom's older sister. I was able to follow her speech for about two sentences, up to the point where she said she'd be representing her siblings. She quickly lost me, but I still understood the parts where she cried, "Baba," or daddy, then sobbed. She wailed, her voice broke, and then she repeated it, "Baba, Baba." In the front row, her three sisters joined the chorus.

There was something about the sister's impassioned cry to her daddy that stirred my own emotions. Suddenly the grandpa was my own father, or my mother's father, who'd died young, years before I was born. Tears filled my eyes, and before long, I was turning my face toward the lilies to hide my sobs. Now I wasn't just the foreigner, I was the foreigner drawing attention to herself by crying at her old neighbor's funeral, a neighbor with whom she had only exchanged ni haos.

I watched Lili in the front row, leaning slightly against her father, and I was filled with longing for my own family. They were thousands of miles away in Baltimore, and I hadn't seen them in months.

After the speeches, we filed around the coffin in a circle. I could see my red flowers positioned on the mantle directly in front of the casket. I snuck a glimpse at the grandfather. He was mostly obscured under mounds of flowers, but his bruised face looked much older than I remembered, his hair grayer. I focused on the actions of the people going before me—a ritual sequence of pauses and bows. I sighed with relief when I passed the casket and entered the receiving line of grieving family members.

The ceremony ended at the crematorium. We walked down a hallway past orange plastic chairs and crammed, elbow to elbow, into a small room. The casket, now closed, sat in an elevator shaft of sorts with a row of buttons. This was the last chance to say goodbye before plunging grandpa into the depths.

Lili whispered: "We paid extra so he'd go to the fire alone." Apparently, there had been some problems with getting the wrong ashes if you went economy style, and had your loved one cremated alongside other people.

Perhaps Chinese are more comfortable with the inner workings of cremation since, in crowded cities like Shanghai, the rate of cremation approaches 100 percent. I felt uneasy though as I watched the staff send grandpa into the fire.

Afterward, we did a final walk around the place, this time tossing the black fabric patches we had worn on our arms into an outdoor fireplace. Then we each took one leaping step forward—away from the fire—to help the deceased transcend the gap between life and death. Before boarding the bus, we all sipped sugar water, a symbol of heavenly bliss that came in the form of iced tea juice boxes.

As we headed back on the bus, I tried to justify my presence at grandpa's funeral.

"Once, I brought him a freshly-made extra chocolate brownie," I told Lily, brightly. "I am not sure if he ate it, but he was sitting there smiling in the kitchen."

"Really?" she said, looking at me a bit strangely. I figured she didn't know the English for brownie so she wasn't quite sure what I had offered him. We didn't have much more to chat about, so we sat in silence and watched the skyscrapers emerge again.

Back downtown, at the post-ceremony lunch, I struggled to eat a helping of chicken feet as the entire table watched. Apart from that, though, it seemed as if I had made it through my first Chinese funeral with minimal social missteps. Maybe I was finally getting into the swing of life in China.

Then one day I breezed down the stairs and saw a familiar silhouette in the second-floor kitchen. I grasped the banister and stared. If I believed in ghosts, I might have fainted in fear. It was the old grandfather, the same buzz-cut hair, the thin white undershirt, even that same bemused look he always gave me.

This elderly man, I realized, must have been just another of the numerous neighbors, without any familial relation to mom, dad and Lili. But, if it wasn't the buzz-cut man in the coffin, who was it? And had I ever even met him?

I realized that I had unknowingly committed the most egregious of cultural misunderstandings. Forget the glaring red bouquet, my self-conscious sobs, or my battle with the chicken feet; I have absolutely no idea whose funeral I attended.

I kept that information to myself, though, and focused on getting to know the family downstairs. Since the funeral, our relationship achieved a new level of familiarity.

The dad offered to teach me how to cook Kung Pao chicken. Lili invited me for tea, and asked for advice on her latest love interest. The mom insisted on carrying my luggage down the stairs, even if it was only a duffel bag. And, without fail, every single time we passed in the hallway, they gave me a friendly ni hao.

Photographs of Japanese-Americans at Manzanar
Ansel Adams

 Ansel Adams (1902–1984) was an American photographer known for his black-and-white photographs capturing the splendor of the American West. His photographs are acclaimed for their clarity and depth, and are featured in many museums, including the Museum of Modern Art. During World War II, Adams requested permission to photograph the Manzanar War Relocation Center, a Japanese internment camp, in Owens Valley in California. His resulting photo-essay first appeared in a Museum of Modern Art exhibit and was later published in *Born Free and Equal: The Story of Loyal Japanese-Americans.*

Return to these questions after you have finished reading.

Analyzing the Reading

1. Read Kunitomi Embrey's account of life in Manzanar on pages 66–69. What do we learn about Manzanar from Embery's account that we do not learn from Adams' photographs? Conversely, what do the photographs tell us that her narrative does not?

2. Adams was known for his skill in photographing landscapes and the natural environment. Look at the landscape in these images. How does Adams capture the relationship of the people at Manzarar with their environment?

3. What details caught Adams' eye? Why do you think these details were important?

4. The people in these photographs were posed. What directions do you think Adams gave his subjects, and why?

Exploring Ideas and Issues

Ansel Adams's Manzanar photographic collection is a departure from the landscape photography for which he is best known. Although a majority of the photographs are portraits, his images also include carefully composed scene of daily life at the camp. When he gave the collection to the Library of Congress in 1965, Adams wrote, "The purpose of my work was to show how these people, suffering under a great injustice, and loss of property, businesses and professions, had overcome the sense of defeat and despair by building for themselves a vital community in an arid (but magnificent) environment . . . All in all, I think this Manzanar Collection is an important historical document, and I trust it can be put to good use."

1. View the Adams exhibit at the Library of Congress at http://international.loc.gov/ammem/collections/anseladams. How is the Library using the photographs? Do you think that Adams would agree that the collection has indeed been "put to good use"?

2. When viewed as a collection, what "story" does Adams' photography tell? Write an essay exploring the message(s) conveyed by this collection, as a group or as individual works of art.

3. Adams chose to use his camera to record and expose a great injustice. Write an essay exploring the ways photography can raise awareness of social and political injustice. Connect your points to a current issue locally or globally.

MANZANAR FROM GUARD TOWER, VIEW WEST

DRESSMAKING CLASS: MRS. RYIE YOSHIZAWA, INSTRUCTOR

CATHOLIC CHURCH

YONEHISA YAMAGAMI, ELECTRICIAN

JOYCE YUKI NAKAMURA, ELDEST DAUGHTER

FARM WORKERS, MT. WILLIAMSON IN BACKGROUND

RICHARD KOBAYASHI, FARMER WITH CABBAGES

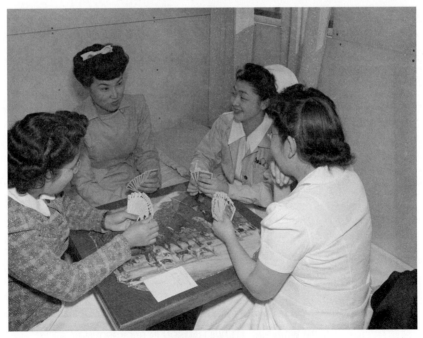

BRIDGE GAME

Yellowstone's Geothermal Resources
National Park Service

Yellowstone National Park, which is located primarily in Wyoming but also includes parts of Idaho and Montana, is home to almost half of the Earth's geothermal resources. Geothermal features include hot springs, geysers, mudpots (pools of hot bubbling mud), and fumaroles (openings in the Earth's crust that emit steam and gases). In fact, its more than 300 geysers make up two thirds of all those found on Earth. Yellowstone's vast collection of thermal features attest to the park's volcanic past. Geothermal resources invite us to consider ways to use the Earth's interior as an energy source.

Return to these questions after you have finished reading.

Analyzing the Reading

1. Yellowstone National Park is the largest ecosystem in the northern temperate zone that is still largely intact. Why is its preservation important?

2. The Yellowstone Caldera, where Yellowstone Lake is located today, is the largest volcanic system in North America. It has been called a "super volcano" because the caldera was formed by a series of massive explosive eruptions. Each year there are many minor earthquakes, and the possibility of major future seismic activity is high. Should the National Park Service give greater emphasis to the dangers of visiting Yellowstone?

3. Acts of vandalism have harmed Yellowstone's geothermal resources. Why do you think people vandalize these features?

Exploring Ideas and Issues

In a 2009 article on the human impact on geyser basins, Alethea Steingisser and W. Andrew Marcus noted that "many of the world's geysers have already been altered or completely extinguished by geothermal energy development and tourism. Yellowstone National Park was set aside as the world's first national park due primarily to its multiple geyser basins, an act that set the stage for protecting lands deemed unique in the world. The park has lost a relatively small number of geysers to tourism-related activities, but there is potential for greater damage if geothermal development occurs outside the park."

1. Write about the geologic processes at work in one of Yellowstone's natural wonders—a geyser, hot spring, mudhole, or fumerole.

2. Alethea Steingisser and W. Andrew Marcus are concerned about geothermal development. Write an essay describing what geothermal development is. What are the pros and cons of this type of development?

3. In your opinion, if harnessing the energy Old Faithful (or other geothermal resources) could help power a city but destroy the landmarks in the process, would it be worth it? Why or why not?

Yellowstone's Geothermal Resources

Nowhere else in the world can we find the array or number of geysers, hot springs, mudpots, and fumaroles found in Yellowstone. More than 75% of the world's geysers, including the world's largest, are here in 7 major basins. Steamboat, the world's tallest active geyser, is in the Norris Geyser Basin. Old Faithful, Grand, Castle, Giantess, Beehive, and Lion geysers may be frequently observed in the Upper Geyser Basin. Old Faithful Geyser has never been either the largest or most regular of geysers, yet it has been the most regular and frequent geyser that erupts to a height of more than 100 feet; the average time between eruptions ranges between about 60 and 110 minutes, although occasionally visitors must wait two hours between eruptions of Old Faithful. For other major geysers in the Old Faithful and Norris geyser basins, eruption frequencies, durations, and heights change fairly often, especially in response to seismic activity.

The park's thermal features lie in the only essentially undisturbed geyser basins left worldwide. In Iceland and New Zealand, geothermal drill holes and wells have reduced geyser activity and hot spring discharge. Despite the proximity of roads and trails in the largest basins, few park features have ever been diverted for human use (such as bathing pools or energy). YNP offers visitors and scientists an opportunity to appreciate thermal features in their natural, changing state. For example, research on thermophilic bacteria, algae mats, predators, and their environments is applied elsewhere to energy fuel production and extraction, bio-mining, control and removal of toxic wastes, development of new surfactants and fermentation processes, and other fields.

Park features have always been subject to some influence from human vandalism. In the park's early years it was common for visitors to use thermal features as "wishing wells," and this practice continues to some degree today. Coins, rocks, trash, logs or stumps, and other paraphernalia are found in the narrow vents of geysers and hot springs. Features have been plugged up, and little can be done to repair the damage. Radical attempts to siphon surface water and induce eruptions have occasionally been tried on famous features such as Morning Glory Pool, with varying degrees of success. Damage also occurs when people leave walkways and climb on features, or occasionally break pieces of sinter or travertine off for souvenirs.

Features can also be affected by nearby ground-disturbing activities. The presence of water, sewer, and other utility systems adjacent to thermal areas has likely affected features in the past. Since many major features are located near roads and developed areas, major maintenance and construction activities must be carefully designed and monitored so as not to alter thermal features.

Volcanic and seismic processes are very active in the park. A network of seismic monitoring stations in the park provides data to help understand overall seismicity in the region and gauge the magnitude of earth tremors. Thermal features and basins respond violently to volcanic and seismic activity, which creates both a serious hazard to humans and an opportunity to study and possibly predict major geologic hazards. Thus, maintenance of a long-term geothermal database also helps us manage visitor use to increase public safety in a naturally hazardous environment.

How to Write an Observation

These steps for the process of writing an observation may not progress as neatly as this chart might suggest. Writing is not an assembly-line process. As you write, you are constantly reading what you have written and rethinking.

Writing may help you to remember details about what you have observed.

1 CHOOSE A SUBJECT

- Analyze the assignment.
- Identify your goals.
- Choose a person or people.
- Choose a place.
- Plan your observations.
- Analyze your genre. Observations in the sciences and social sciences aim for objectivity and minimize personal reactions.

2 OBSERVE & ANALYZE

- Make observations. Carefully record details of what you see, hear, smell, touch, and taste.
- Record the exact names of people, places, and things.
- Observe more than one time and note what changes.
- Analyze the observations by organizing them into categories.
- Analyze patterns and draw implications.
- Be a "participant observer." You often can learn a great deal by talking to people.

3
WRITE A DRAFT

4
REVISE, REVISE, REVISE

5
SUBMITTED VERSION

- Determine your point of view. If you are writing an "objective" description, your point of view is the fly on the wall, describing everything you observe.

- If you are writing a more personal description, think about the ideas and impressions you want to convey.

- Determine an organizational strategy.

- Select details. Give the names of places, people, and things. Give sensory details of sight, sound, smell, touch, and taste.

- "Objective" descriptions in the social sciences and sciences conclude with summarizing your observations in light of your goals.

- Personal descriptions do not have to summarize, but you do want to leave readers with something to think about.

- Check that your paper or project fulfills the assignment.

- Make sure that you have a focused thesis or a clear overall impression

- Revise your introduction, if needed, to draw readers in.

- Examine the organization.

- Add details to make the description more concrete.

- Check that the conclusion gives a sense of the significance of the observations.

- Review the visual presentation.

- Proofread carefully.

- Make sure your finished writing meets all formatting requirements.

1: Choose a Subject

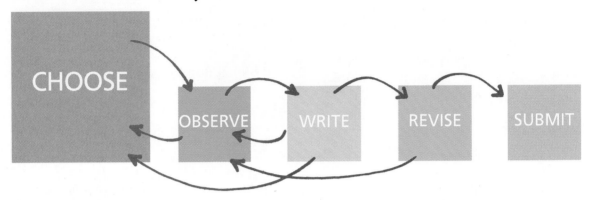

Analyze the assignment

Read your assignment slowly and carefully. Look for words like *observe, field research,* or *field observation,* which tell you that you are writing about your firsthand observations. Identify any information about the length specified, date due, formatting, and other requirements. You can attend to this information later. At this point you want to give your attention to your subject and your goals.

Identify your genre and goals

Different kinds of observing have different goals. What exactly would make an observation effective for your assignment? If your assignment to observe is in the sciences, social sciences, and education, your readers will expect you to be objective and not to emphasize your personal reactions.

Choose a person or people

If your assignment asks you to observe a person or people, think about whom you might observe—a front-desk person, an athlete on and off the field, players of video games and other games, people building something, people exercising, and so on. Consider how each person interacts with others or how a group maintains its identity.

Choose a place

If your assignment asks you to observe a place or object, think about where or what you might observe—a park, a downtown street, a market, a factory, a bowling alley, and so on. Consider what recurring activities that you can observe at this place.

Choose an event

If your assignment asks you to observe an event, look at the event calendars on your school's Web site and in your local newspaper. You'll find many possibilities. Observe what goes on besides the main event. For example, if you attend a sports event, observe the concession stands, the first-aid station, the ticket staff, and other people besides the players.

Be aware of ethical considerations

Be open and honest about what you are doing. Observing should not involve becoming a spy. If you need permission to visit a site, obtain it in advance.

Plan your observations

Determine what times you will need to visit and what will be going on. Plan to spend a long time observing. The longer you observe, the more likely you will encounter something out of the ordinary that will give your description a special insight.

WRITE NOW

Find a place

Think about possible places that might work for your assignment. Divide a sheet of paper into four columns and label them place, people, activities, and times. List your places in the first column. Then list the people who go there, their behavior, and the times they are present.

PLACE	PEOPLE	ACTIVITIES	TIMES
Television room in student union.	Some of the same people every day.	They view particular programs but also talk.	Most busy around lunch time.

When you have at least five possible places, select the one you feel will work best.

Writer at work

Sarah Cuellar was asked to conduct observations for her Early Childhood Development class, and write a report about them. She made notes on and highlighted important parts of her assignment sheet.

Early Childhood Development 324
Observation Assignment

For this assignment you will observe preschool children during normal school activities. You will analyze the behavior you observe within the context of a behavioral theory we have studied in class. To start this project, you will need to

- Choose the age of student and type of behavior you want to observe.
- Review the readings and your class notes covering theories about that behavior.
- Schedule at least three observation periods of thirty to sixty minutes each, about three to five days apart. Our class will observe students at the Babiya Montessori school at 1700 Crown Ave.
- Fill out the informed consent form for your observation and have it signed by one of the instructors at Babiya Montessori.

Make sure you do the following in your paper: *EXPLAIN the theory*

1) Introduce the behavior you are studying, <u>summarize the theory</u> or theories you are working with, and explain why you want to study it. *DESCRIBE*
2) Provide substantial <u>detailed observations</u> from your field journal, *what you* with context and explanations. *saw*
3) Relate the behaviors you observe to the theories about behavior we are studying.
4) Conclude by noting how your observations <u>did or did not align</u> with a given theory, OR suggesting how your observations may indicate a need for further research to clarify or test the theory, OR explaining *Did observing* how the behaviors you observed may support a new theory. *help you*
5) Use APA-style documentation. You do not need to include a *understand* title page or abstract. *the theory any better?*

Due dates:
March 17: Informed consent forms and observation schedules due
April 14: Draft due
April 28: Final version due

After she felt she understood the assignment, Sarah listed several theories discussed in class that interested her. For each theory, she wrote down questions that occurred to her about the behavior. Then she considered which of these questions she might be able to learn more about by observing preschool children.

POSSIBLE BEHAVIORS TO OBSERVE:

Make-believe/imaginative play—How much variation in ages when it begins?

Oppositional behavior—Do students "talk back" more to some teachers than others?

Solitary/parallel/group play—What is the progression and how do children learn group play skills?

Object play—Are there differences between boys and girls (frequency, purpose, and so on)?

Because she planned to teach preschool, Sarah decided to observe children's solitary, parallel, and group play patterns. She felt that learning more about how children's play skills progressed might help her discover whether teachers could help students develop their social play skills.

Sarah then reviewed her notes from class and from her readings. She summarized the readings that addressed types of play.

Parten, M. (1932). Social participation among preschool children. *Journal of Abnormal and Social Psychology, 27,* 242–269.

> Classic study of preschool behavior. Parten's scale of solitary and group play assumes each "step up" requires better social skills.

> 1) unoccupied play   2) solitary play
> 3) onlooker play   4) parallel play
> 5) associative play 6) cooperative play

Smith, P. K. (1978). A longitudinal study of social participation in preschool children: solitary and parallel play reexamined. *Developmental Psychology, 14,* 517–523.

> Data did not prove that children progress "through" parallel play as a stage, so posited that it is "optional," and that some kids do while others don't.

Bakeman, R., & Brownlee, J. R. (1980). The strategic use of parallel play: A sequential analysis. *Child Development, 51,* 873–878.

> Parallel play does not ever become the dominant play style. Children use it a lot but they do not go through a stage where they use primarily parallel play. "Parallel play often functions in the stream of activities as a bridge to group play."

2: Make Observations and Analyze Them

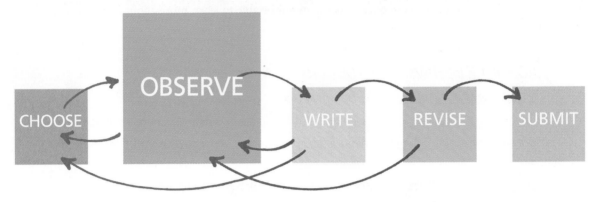

Make observations

Take notes that record what you use in detail, using either pen and paper notebook or a tablet computer or mobile device. If you use pen and paper, leave space for comments after your observations are complete. Pay attention to all your senses—smell, taste, touch, and hearing as well as sight. Take photos if possible.

Be a "participant observer"

Talk to the people you observe. Ask them questions about their activities, opinions, and feelings. If you are polite and unobtrusive, you will learn a great deal more than if you keep silent. Keep your own language distinct, in your notes, from the language of your subjects.

Record times, places, and names of people

Always note exactly where you were, when you were there, and the people you talked with.

Assemble your observations

Gather your notes and read then carefully. You may want to do an initial sorting by putting them in chronological order or else categorizing them by major theme.

Analyze the observations

How many different activities were going on during your observations? Which activities were particular to this place? Were there significant differences among the subjects you observed? Were these differences behavioral or of some other type? Did anything unusual happen? Why were the subjects there?

Analyze patterns and draw implications

What patterns can you identify? What implications can you draw from these patterns?

Writer at work

After observing, Sarah went back over her notes and made comments on them in order to analyze what she had observed.

3/24/11

10:15 a.m.

Sadie is playing with blocks. Lilly is putting away some books nearby. The teacher shows Lilly another bin of blocks and asks if she would like to build something, "like Sadie." Lilly looks at Sadie and Sadie's blocks and then says "yes." Both girls play separately for about two minutes. They watch each other work but do not speak. Then Lilly knocks down her blocks and laughs. She looks at Sadie who also laughs. Sadie pushes over her own blocks and then they both laugh again.

Encouragement from teacher

Laughing is the first real communication between the two girls. Lilly is looking at Sadie when she laughs. Sadie copies Lilly's action and response. She seems to be saying, "I like to do what you like to do."

Lilly: "Now we have to clean up."

Both girls put some blocks back in their bins.

Sadie: "I made a tower all of orange bricks."

Cooperative activity.

Lilly: "One time I made a big, big house, so big."

Sadie: "You can have green blocks."

The girls begin to sort the blocks into colors, sharing blocks. The teacher comes by and says "Are you making a house together?"

The teachers have been talking about sharing a lot. The girls do not use the word "share" but they are mimicking the behavior the teachers have modeled.

Lilly: "Yes, and I made the green blocks."

Sadie: "I like orange because orange is my best color."

Teacher: "It's a pretty house. You are both working very hard! I like to see you sharing."

Verbal reinforcement.

3: Write a Draft

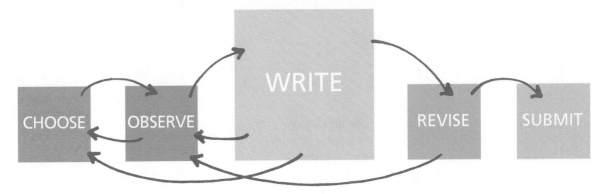

Determine your thesis or the overall impression you want to convey

If your assignment asks you to observe for a particular purpose, likely you will need to provide a clear, significant thesis early on. If you are writing a travel account or describing a place, you many not have an explicit thesis, but you will want to convey an overall impression through the details you select.

Determine your point of view

If you are observing for a science or social science class, focus on when and what you observed. If you are writing a travel account or describing a place, you may want to foreground yourself as a participant—why you went there and how you responded to the place and people.

Determine an organization

You might organize by chronology or by special location. You may need to classify your observations into subtopics and organize accordingly.

Select details

Give accurate, specific information about the place and, if present, the people. Include short quotations if you record conversations and attribute them accurately.

Grab readers at the beginning and leave them with something to think about

Choose an appropriate title that will immediately get readers' attention. Conclude by leaving your readers with a sense of why your observations matter. Press beyond the superficial.

STAYING ON TRACK

STAYING ON TRACK
Work for precise description

Show, not tell

OFF TRACK
It is very difficult to hike cross-country in the Arctic National Wildlife Refuge.

ON TRACK
Every inch of ground challenges human walking: meadows of waist-high muskeg brush, quicksand beside the streams and slick rocks in them, loose shale on the hillsides, and uneven tundra hillocks on flat sections that offer no good way to negotiate—plant your foot on them and they collapse sideways, step between them and you sink to your calf.

Provide exact details

OFF TRACK
Grizzly bears and black bears look different.

ON TRACK
Rely on body shape rather than size and color to distinguish grizzly bears from black bears. Grizzlies have a hump above their front shoulders; black bears lack this hump. In profile, grizzlies have a depression between their eyes and nose, while black bears have a "Roman" profile with a straight line between the forehead and nose.

Give names where possible

OFF TRACK
The courthouse stands in the center of the town square, bordered by streets named for Civil War generals.

ON TRACK
The courthouse stands in the center of the town square, bordered by streets named for Confederate heroes: Lee, Jackson, Stuart, and Davis.

Writer at work

Sarah needed to synthesize her observations with the behavioral theories discussed in her class. She went back to her notes on parallel play and looked for specific concepts that helped explain the behaviors she had observed. She made an outline of the points she thought she should cover in her paper. This outline also helped her make certain she was fulfilling all the requirements of her assignment.

From Bakeman & Brownlee:

"Those who play beside others may indeed desire their company and use parallel play as a strategy (albeit not necessarily in a conscious sense) that often brings them into group play" (877).

Sometimes the kids send pretty obvious signals that they would like to be playing with the child next to them. Ellen pretty clearly wanted to play with Lilly and set up her own doll so she could suggest a shared activity. Keyshawn often will put down a toy he is playing with and change to the type of toy another child has. Does this imitation send a "cue" to the other child that he would like to play?

"Parallel play among preschoolers may be important then, not as a type of play which dominates or characterizes a given developmental stage but as a type of play which frequently initiates or leads into group play" (877).

I didn't see any child who used primarily parallel play. Generally the kids represented a pretty wide range of developmental levels, so if parallel play was associated with one stage it should have been evident in certain kids. However, it was really common for group play to come about after a period of parallel play.

"It may be that parallel play often serves as a brief interlude during which preschoolers have both an increased opportunity to socialize as well as a chance to 'size up' those to whom they are proximal. In fact, such a pause for evaluation and initial coordination of one's actions to those of another might be one of the more important functions of parallel play" (877).

There were many times kids did not move into group play from parallel play. Was this because they decided it would be a "bad fit"?

Playing in Traffic: How Parallel Play Helps Preschool Children "Merge" into Group Play

I. Theories of parallel play
   A. Parten theorized developmental play stages in 1932.
   B. Smith proposed that parallel play is an "optional stage" in 1978.
   C. Bakeman and Brownlee viewed parallel play as a transition.

II. My observations
   A. I observed a class of 11 children, 32 to 50 months of age, at Babiya Montessori preschool.
   B. My observations were not a formal study.

IV. Thesis
   A. I did not observe parallel play as a stage.
   B. I did not observe parallel play as social adaptation.
   C. "Merge lane" might be a better metaphor than "bridge."

V. Detailed observations
   A. Lilly and Sadie play with blocks.
      1. Lilly and Sadie use parallel play to "size up," as Bakeman and Brownlee describe.
      2. Sharing has been modeled by teachers.
   B. Ellen and Lilly play with dolls.
      1. Ellen uses parallel play to "size up" Lilly.
      2. She uses parallel play again with Sadie later.

VI. Teachers' involvement shifts to group play
   A. The playroom set up to encourage parallel play.
   B. Teachers sometimes facilitate group play, but they allow the children to decide.

VII. Different rates of parallel play related to social comfort
   A. Keyshawn uses more parallel play than other children.
   B. He is developmentally equal with other kids his age.

VIII. Conclusion
   A. Even the most mature children frequently played alone.
   B. Children use different kinds of play at different times for different purposes.

4: Revise, Revise, Revise

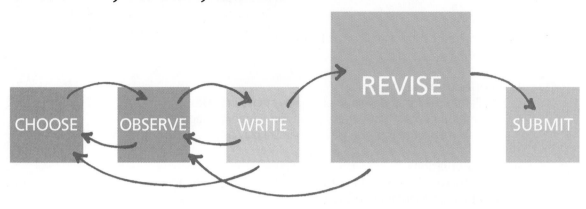

Skilled writers know that the secret to writing well is rewriting. Even the best writers often have to revise several times to get the result they want. You also must have effective strategies for revising if you're going to be successful. The biggest trap you can fall into is starting off with the little stuff first. Leave the small stuff for last.

Does your paper or project meet the assignment?	• Look again at the assignment for specific guidelines, including length, format, and amount of research. Does your work meet these guidelines?
Do you have a focused thesis or a clear overall impression?	• Is it clear to readers what is most important about your observations?
Is your introduction effective?	• Will your title grab people's attention? • Does your introduction draw readers in?
Is your organization effective?	• Is the order the best for your purpose? Possibly you may need to shift the order of some of your paragraphs.
Do you provide vivid, well-chosen details?	• Can you add details to increase interest and paint a clearer picture?
Is your conclusion effective?	• Do you place your observations in a larger overall context? • Do you leave readers with the feeling that they have learned something valuable?
Is the writing project visually effective?	• Is the font attractive and readable? • Are the headings and visuals effective?
Save the editing for last.	• When you have finished revising, edit and proofread carefully.

A peer review guide is on page 54.

Writer at work

Sarah took a draft of her paper to her instructor's office hours and discussed it with him. She made notes during their conversation and used his comments to guide her revisions. Her completed revision of the entire paper begins on the next page.

Add date after Brownlee

Bakeman and Brownlee theorized that parallel play, instead of being a developmental stage children go through, is actually a social adaptation that allows them to move from solitary play into group play in specific situations. In their study, parallel play often preceded group play, indicating that children used it to transition into group play. "[T]hose who play beside others may indeed desire their company and use parallel play as a strategy (albeit not necessarily in a conscious sense) that often brings them into group play" (p. 877).

Incorporate this quote more smoothly

Focus should not be on what I believe, but on what the evidence shows. Also nothing has been "proven"; B&B say more research is called for

After observing a group of eight preschool children, ages 38–50 months, at Babiya Montessori preschool, I believe that Bakeman and Brownlee were right. Parallel play is a social adaptation rather than a developmental stage. I observed many instances in which children used parallel play to move into group play, or to try to do so. But while Bakeman and Brownlee conclude that parallel play is a "bridge to group play" (p. 873), I think a better analogy is that parallel play works like the merge lane on a highway. It allows kids to get "up to speed" and find the right way to work themselves into a specific group play situation. For example, if one kid did not want to participate in group play, his preference was often made evident during parallel play. He might move away from the other child near him, or provide a verbal or physical clue that he wanted to remain solitary.

Change "kids" to "children"– more formal tone is needed for this paper

5: Submitted Version

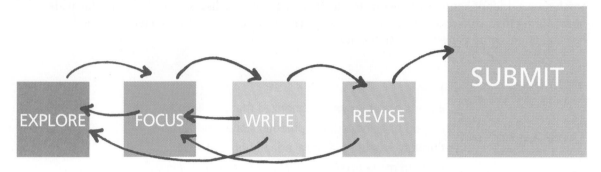

PLAYING IN TRAFFIC   1

Sarah Cuellar

Professor Barone

Early Childhood Development 324

28 April 2011

Playing in Traffic: How Parallel Play Helps Preschool Children

"Merge" into Group Play

The term parallel play was invented by Mildred Parten (1932) to describe the
way preschool age children will play next to each other, doing the same things, but
without interacting. Parten thought that parallel play was a developmental stage
between solitary play and group play. However, later research showed that most
children do not develop along a simple track from solitary play to parallel play and
then to group play. Parallel play is very common in almost all children, but children do
not go through a stage where it dominates their play. It is more mixed along their
developmental path.

Smith (1978) proposed that parallel play may be an "optional" stage that only some
children go through, which could explain why it doesn't show up as a definite
developmental phase in large studies. However, other researchers make the case that
parallel play isn't a developmental stage at all. Bakeman and Brownlee (1980) theorized
that parallel play, instead of being a developmental stage children go through, is
actually a social adaptation that allows them to move from solitary play into group play
in specific situations. In their study, parallel play often preceded group play, meaning

that children used it to transition into group play. Bakeman and Brownlee posit that "those who play beside others may indeed desire their company and use parallel play as a strategy (albeit not necessarily in a conscious sense) that often brings them into group play" (p. 877). Group play requires complex social skills that children develop gradually, like sharing, patience, and communication. It also requires multiple focuses of attention. Children playing in a group have to focus on toys and on playmates. Parallel play may be a way for children to coordinate all these skills and get them all working at the same time so that they can play successfully with others.

My reading about types of play has left me with many questions. How accurately does play activity reflect a child's developmental level? How can I as a teacher encourage play that promotes development? How much conflict during play is normal and healthy? How can a teacher identify and minimize play behavior that impedes development? I had all these questions in mind when I began my observations.

I observed a class of 11 children, 32 to 50 months of age, at Babiya Montessori preschool over a two-week period. Six were girls and five were boys. They came from a variety of backgrounds but none of them could really be described as disadvantaged, according to the teachers at the school. I did not conduct a formal study like Parten, Smith, or Bakeman and Brownlee; thus my observations cannot be directly compared to their findings. Those researchers recorded children's play and divided time up into small increments for analysis. I simply observed and made notes. But what I observed did seem to align more closely with Bakeman and Brownlee's theories than with those of Parten or Smith.

My observations tend to support Bakeman and Brownlee's theory that parallel play is a social adaptation rather than a developmental stage. In my observations, age was not a good predictor of which children used parallel play most. If parallel play were a developmental stage, I would expect to see more use of it in younger children, and less use by older children who had matured and moved away from the solitary play stage, into the group play stage. However, I did observe many instances in which children of all ages used parallel play to move into group play, or to try to do so.

While Bakeman and Brownlee describe parallel play as a "bridge to group play" (p. 873), I think a better analogy is that parallel play works like the merge lane on a highway. Parallel play allows children to get "up to speed" and find the right way to move into a specific group play situation. For example, I observed that if a child wanted to play with another child near him, he could signal his intentions by talking, touching, or some other means of expressing his interest in group play. If a child did not want to participate in group play, his preference was often made evident during parallel play. He might move away from the other child near him, or provide a verbal or physical clue that he wanted to remain solitary.

Here is a typical shift from parallel to group play as I observed it:

3/24/08

10:15 a.m.

Sadie is playing with blocks. Lilly is putting away some books nearby. The teacher shows Lilly another bin of blocks and asks if she would like to build something, "like Sadie." Lilly looks at Sadie and Sadie's blocks and then says "yes." Both girls play separately for about two minutes. They watch each other work but do not speak. Then Lilly knocks down her blocks and laughs. She looks at Sadie who also laughs. Sadie pushes over her own blocks and then they both laugh again.

Lilly: "Now we have to clean up."

Both girls put some blocks back in their bins.

Sadie: "I made a tower all of orange bricks."

Lilly: "One time I made a big, big house, so big."

Sadie: "You can have green blocks."

The girls begin to sort the blocks into colors, sharing blocks. The teacher comes by and says "Are you making a house together?"

Lilly: "Yes, and I made the green blocks."

Sadie: "I like orange because orange is my best color."

Teacher: "It's a pretty house. You are both working very hard! I like to see you sharing."

Here we see Lilly and Sadie using parallel play the way Bakeman and Brownlee describe it, as "a chance to 'size up' those to whom they are proximal" p. (877). Lilly knocks down her blocks in part to see if she can get a reaction from Sadie. When Sadie notices her, Lilly laughs. She looks at Sadie while she is laughing, which encourages Sadie to laugh too. When Sadie laughs with her, and then knocks over her own blocks, imitating Lilly, Lilly knows that Sadie has accepted her "invitation" to play. At that point they are willing to work together. When Lilly orders "We have to clean up," Sadie goes along with her and puts the blocks away. They verbally share information with each other about things they like or that they have done. They also make a joint decision to share the blocks by dividing them into the colors each girl likes best. This decision making is a complicated process and requires some cooperation by each girl, who must be willing to "give up" some blocks to her friend.

PLAYING IN TRAFFIC   4

I noticed that the teachers had been talking often about sharing during the time I was there, and I concluded Lilly and Sadie were actually mimicking some behaviors the teachers had modeled for them already. Doing so helped them play together successfully. This observation leads me to believe that there are many strategies that children use to learn social interaction, and that some of them, like the concept of sharing, can be taught. Others, like parallel play, may be more developmental in character.

Many times I observed parallel play that did not lead to group play. Often neither child really made an effort to join the other perhaps because children use parallel play when they see someone doing something interesting and want to try it themselves, not because they have the explicit goal of wanting to play with another child. This type of parallel play can lead into group play, but the children often seemed just as happy staying in parallel play. In fact, it seemed to me that parallel play is in some ways easier for the teacher, because then the children don't fight with each other.

Sometimes one child tried to move from parallel to group play and was rejected. Here is the way one attempted shift ended.

3/26/08

1:30 p.m.

Lilly is dressing a doll. Ellen comes in from the playground and finds another doll. She dresses her doll and then puts it on the floor and covers it with a towel.

Ellen (pointing at her doll): "Nap!"

Ellen tugs on Lilly's dress and points to her doll. Lilly looks at Ellen and makes a face.

Ellen: "Lilly! Naptime!"

Lilly: "No!"

Lilly turns her back.

By demonstrating a play activity and indicating that Lilly should share or imitate it, Ellen has used her "turn signal" to let Lilly know she would like to merge into Lilly's "lane" on the "play highway." By shouting "No!" and making a face, Lilly is honking her horn to tell Ellen she is not interested in sharing her lane. Instead of playing with Lilly, Ellen took her doll to another area of the classroom and played alone. After a few minutes she and Sadie took the doll "on a ride" in the toy shopping cart Sadie was pushing. So Ellen managed to transition successfully into group play, but only after finding a child who (unlike Lilly) was interested in playing with her. Parallel play allowed her to determine who would welcome her as a playmate.

After my observations were concluded, I talked to the teachers about the shift from parallel to group play. I wanted to see if they ever intervened to move children from one state to another, or if such shifts were entirely up to the children. They said the classroom was set up in part to encourage parallel play, with similar toys grouped in certain areas (the doll corner, the block wall, and so on). They also said they will sometimes facilitate parallel play by providing similar toys for children. If the children do start playing together, the teachers will encourage them by praising them and by intervening if there are arguments, reminding them to share. But they let the children figure out if they are ready to play together.

As noted earlier, I did not observe children using parallel play more at one age than at another. However, I did notice that children who were newer to the group did use parallel pay more than those who already had friends in the school. This observation supports Bakeman and Brownlee's claim that parallel play is a tool that the children use to help them function socially. For example, Keyshawn, the newest child at the school, used parallel play the most, and often stayed in parallel play for long periods. This behavior may have been because he was trying to get to know the other children better and to figure out who was likely to play well with him. Keyshawn was almost four years old, and all of his other behaviors that I observed (like vocabulary, drawing skills, motor coordination) were equal to those of the older children. Keyshawn's greater use of parallel play does not seem to be tied to his developmental level. I predict that as Keyshawn becomes more comfortable at the school, he will spend less time in parallel play and more time in group play.

My observations suggest that Parten's concept of "development" of play skills distorts what really happens when children play. Even the most mature children in the group played alone frequently. The teachers said this time alone is necessary because social play is hard work for children, and they need "down time." Just like adults, children need some time without the stimulus of others. Thinking of group play as a goal, with solitary play as a basic skill that should be left behind during normal development, is a mistake. Instead, it is better to see types of play as different tools children use to develop their mental, physical, and social skills. Different children will use different tools in different situations, and it is the teacher's job to make sure students have all the tools they need and to suggest using certain ones when the time seems right. Tools like parallel play and sharing skills let children merge onto the highway of social play successfully, with as few fender benders as possible.

References

Bakeman, R. & Brownlee, J. R. (1980). The strategic use of parallel play: A sequential analysis. *Child Development, 51,* 873-878.

Parten, M. (1932). Social participation among preschool children. *Journal of Abnormal and Social Psychology, 27,* 242-269.

Smith, P. K. (1978). A longitudinal study of social participation in preschool children: Solitary and parallel play reexamined. *Developmental Psychology, 14,* 517-523.

Projects

Observations span a wide range of writing, from objective scientific reports to highly personal descriptions of places. Accurate, detailed description is valued in all kinds of observations.

Description of a place

Write an essay describing a place. Select one of these options:

Visit an urban neighborhood that is not familiar to you. Pay close attention to what distinguishes this neighborhood from other neighborhoods in the city.

or

Visit a small town near you, preferably one that is not on a major highway. Likely you will find that many of the businesses that once thrived on Main Street or on the courthouse square are gone. Pay close attention to signs and other things that give indications to what goes on in the town.

Visit some stores, a local coffee shop, and other places where you can talk to people. Ask them about their neighborhood or their town. Then reconstruct conversations in your notebook.

Natural observation

Find a setting in which you can observe animals or natural phenomena such as tides, weather patterns, or erosion. In a large city, you might watch pigeons interacting with people in a park, observe feeding time at a zoo, or watch how insects behave during a rainstorm.

Use your observations to generate a list of questions that would help you fill in any gaps in what you observed. Can you explain the behavior of any animals you observed? If not, how could you determine the causes of their behavior? Can your localized observation of a spring-fed pool uncover the causes of the heavy algae growth there, or do you need to look further to find an explanation?

Analyze your observations by placing them in categories. Note any patterns. Think about what generalizations you can make from the patterns.

Write a brief description about what you observed, including the questions your observation raised, and any answers you found.

For support in learning this chapter's content, follow this path in **mycomplab:**

▶ **Resources** ▶ **Writing** ▶ **Writing Purposes** ▶ **Writing to Observe**

Review the Instruction and Multimedia resources, then complete the **Exercises** and click on **Gradebook** to measure your progress.

Field observation

Observe people in a public setting you frequent, such as your student union, a library, a coffee shop, a dormitory lounge, a gym, a basketball court, or bus route. Think of one or more questions that field observation might answer. For example, students who use your campus library go there for multiple reasons: to study, to find books, to find journal articles, to use a computer, to watch movies on DVD, to meet their friends, and others.

Collect field notes by observing. Take a tablet computer or a paper notebook and write only on the right-hand pages. Use the left-hand pages later to analyze your data. Plan to spend at least three hours a week at your site for two weeks. You should gather at least ten pages of notes per week. Listen carefully to conversations and record direct quotations. After you leave the site, make comments on your notes on the left-hand page.

Analyze your notes after two weeks of observations. What constitutes abnormal behavior? How do people learn the normal behavior for that setting? What happens when the norm is violated by someone?

Write a detailed field observation that includes concrete details and quotations from people at your site. Make your paper interesting to readers by showing them something about the setting they didn't already know or had never noticed.

Photo essay of a place

Select a place that potentially is an interesting subject for a photo essay. Places that have people and activities are often more interesting than places without people. Check if it is possible to take photographs. Many malls, stores, and other private spaces do not allow to you take photos. Public spaces are unrestricted.

Think about the focus and purpose of your photo essay. If, for example, you decide to photograph an animal shelter, will your focus be on the work volunteers do or on the animals?

Visit the place several times. Don't take photographs at the outset but instead get a sense of the place first at different times of the day. Record the dates of your visits and what was going on. Note the lighting conditions

Take photographs that give an overall sense of the place and take others that show key details.

Select and edit photographs with a photo editor. Arrange them so they tell a story and add captions. You can show your photo essay with presentation software like PowerPoint or upload your photos to a Web site like Flickr.

8 Informative Essays

Successful informative writing begins with what the reader needs to know.

Chapter Overview

Reporting Information

Whether reading the news, following a recipe, hooking up a new computer, deciding which course to take, or engaging in a multitude of other events in our daily lives, we depend on reliable and clear information. Reporting information takes many forms, ranging from newspaper articles and reports of experimental research to tables, charts, and simple lists of information.

In one sense, most kinds of writing, including writing to reflect and writing to persuade, also report information. The main difference is that the focus of a report and other informative kinds of writing is on the subject, not on the writer's reflections or on changing readers' minds or on getting them to take action.

Keys to informative writing

FIND INFORMATION	Knowing where to find information and knowing how much you need is critical for writing reports and other kinds of informative writing.
INTERPRET INFORMATION	The Internet gives access to billions of pages of information. The value in informative writing lies in filtering this glut of information.
EXPLAIN INFORMATION	Often what you know well is difficult to explain to others. For example, explaining a process requires that you break down the process into steps.
EXPLORE QUESTIONS AND PROBLEMS	Not all topics can be brought to closure. Often college writing involves issues or problems that perplex us and for which we cannot come to a definitive conclusion.

Informative writing in the world

Reports present information to specific audiences. They are a frequent genre in government, business, nonprofits, science, education, and other fields. They often have a summary or abstract at the beginning that gives the content in a nutshell. Most reports require some analysis of data, which informs readers who make decisions based on the data.

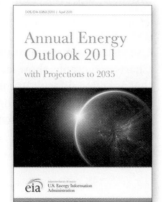

Other genres of informative writing

- **News articles and features** inform us about events around the world and in our neighborhoods.
- **Scholarly articles** report original research.
- **Instructions** help readers to accomplish a task quickly and efficiently.
- **Web sites** are often the first place people go to for answers.
- **Podcasts** are streaming or downloadable digital media files.

161

What Makes Good Informative Writing?

1

Focus on a central idea

The key to success is limiting your topic to one you can cover adequately.

UNFOCUSED

Madagascar has many strange plants and wildlife found nowhere else on earth.

FOCUSED

Among the many animals found only in Madagascar is the Golden Bamboo Lemur, which consumes enough cyanide each day to kill twelve humans.

2

Stay objective

Writers whose purpose is to inform usually stay in the background, taking the stance of an impartial, objective observer. Absence from bias helps readers to believe that you are trustworthy.

3

Do the necessary research and document your sources

If you use sources in a college assignment, you will be expected to document those sources. Lakshmi Kotra's essay at the end of this chapter (see pages 212–219) follows an academic format for citing sources.

4

Start fast

Your title and introduction should entice readers to want to read the rest. Readers become bored quickly if they have heard it all before. Once you have made your readers curious to know more, don't disappoint them.

5

Define key terms

Define any key terms and concepts that might be unfamiliar

For the ancient Greeks, *areté*, which is most frequently associated with bravery in battle, actually meant something closer to be the best you can be and could describe knowledge and eloquence as well as athletic prowess and courage.

6

Present information clearly with relevant examples

Organize for the benefit of readers, establishing your major points early on. Define any key terms and concepts that might be unfamiliar. The examples and details make or break informative writing, whether it is a news article, a profile, or even a cookbook.

For a century advertising has had a powerful influence on popular culture. Many credit Coca-Cola's winter advertising campaign in the 1930s for inventing the modern image of Santa Claus in a red suit, but the modern Santa was used twenty years earlier to sell mineral water.

7

Conclude with strength

Leave your readers something to think about—a memorable example, a key point, an anecdote, implications of the information you have provided, or a projection into the future.

8

Use visuals where appropriate

Charts and graphs show facts and relationships that are often difficult to communicate with words alone. Maps, drawings, and photographs can provide concrete evidence for what is being described in words.

Using informative visuals

Effective informative visuals can communicate complex ideas and phenomena at a glance. NASA frequently uses computer-enhanced imagery for examining objects and events in space and on earth.

A 9.0-magnitude earthquake off the coast of Japan on March 11, 2011, triggered tsunami waves up to 33 feet that devastated coastal areas. The city of Ishinomaki was one of the hardest hit. On March 14, 2011, three days after the tsunami, the Advanced Spaceborne Thermal Emission and Reflection Radiometer (ASTER) on NASA's Terra satellite acquired the right-hand image with water

still inundating the city. The left-hand image, from August 8, 2008, shows water levels under normal circumstances.

NASA uses false color to interpret these images. Water is dark blue, plant-covered land is red, exposed earth is tan, and the city is silver. Water is standing in the flat, open places that were once fields.

WRITE NOW

Examine informative media

1. Popular articles versus scholarly articles: Find an article in a newspaper or an online popular magazine like *Time* or *Newsweek* that reports a scientific discovery or experiment. Select key words from the article that you can use to find a scholarly article in a database. Use a database like *Google Scholar* or *Academic Search Complete*, which allows you to limit the search to scholarly journals. Read both articles and make a list of the differences between them. Notice differences in the language used, the overall length, the format, and the listing of sources.

2. Profiles: On your school's Web site or in the school newspaper, find several written profiles of people at your school. Likely you can find profiles

of the president, deans, coaches, athletes, some professors, and award-winning students. Read the profiles and note what kinds of information are included about each person and what information is left out. Are the profiles written for different audiences? If so, how does the information included depend on the audience?

3. Instructional videos: *YouTube, MyVideo, Vimeo,* and other video hosts have thousands of instructional videos. Think of something you would like to learn how to do, and combine the name of this activity or skill with "instruction" in a search on *YouTube* or another video host. Watch the two videos. Which one is more effective? Why?

How to Read Informative Writing

▼ **BEFORE YOU BEGIN READING**

These notes are in response to *"Affairs of the Lips"*; the reading begins on page 166.

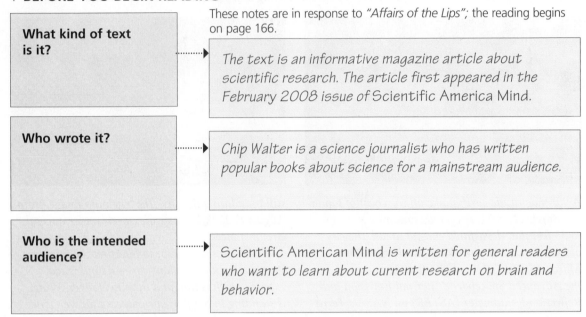

| What kind of text is it? | ┈┈┈▶ | The text is an informative magazine article about scientific research. The article first appeared in the February 2008 issue of Scientific America Mind. |

| Who wrote it? | ┈┈┈▶ | Chip Walter is a science journalist who has written popular books about science for a mainstream audience. |

| Who is the intended audience? | ┈┈┈▶ | Scientific American Mind *is written for general readers who want to learn about current research on brain and behavior.* |

▼ **READ THE TEXT AT LEAST TWICE AND MAKE NOTES**

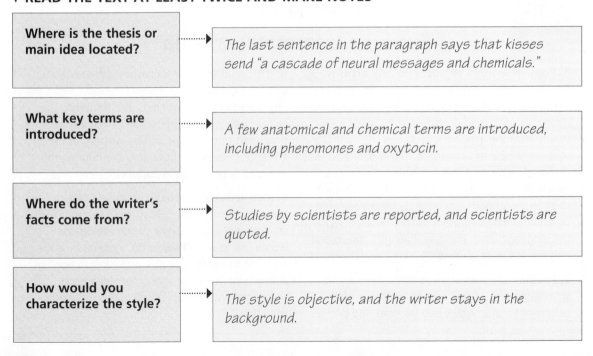

| Where is the thesis or main idea located? | ┈┈┈▶ | The last sentence in the paragraph says that kisses send "a cascade of neural messages and chemicals." |

| What key terms are introduced? | ┈┈┈▶ | A few anatomical and chemical terms are introduced, including pheromones and oxytocin. |

| Where do the writer's facts come from? | ┈┈┈▶ | Studies by scientists are reported, and scientists are quoted. |

| How would you characterize the style? | ┈┈┈▶ | The style is objective, and the writer stays in the background. |

How is it organized?

This map shows the organization of "Affairs of the Lips," which begins on the following page.

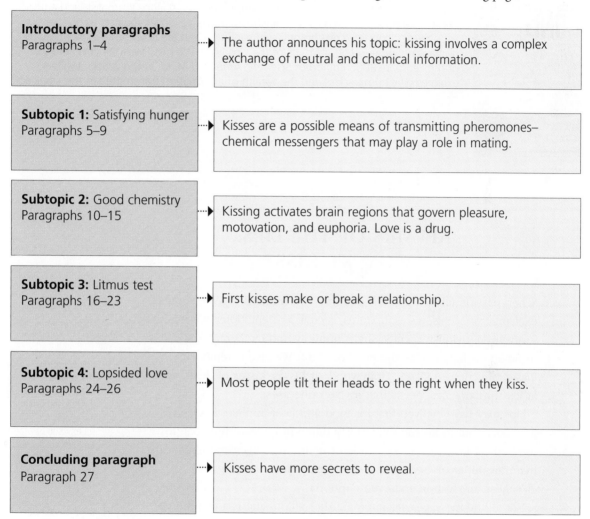

Introductory paragraphs
Paragraphs 1–4

┈▶ The author announces his topic: kissing involves a complex exchange of neutral and chemical information.

Subtopic 1: Satisfying hunger
Paragraphs 5–9

┈▶ Kisses are a possible means of transmitting pheromones–chemical messengers that may play a role in mating.

Subtopic 2: Good chemistry
Paragraphs 10–15

┈▶ Kissing activates brain regions that govern pleasure, motovation, and euphoria. Love is a drug.

Subtopic 3: Litmus test
Paragraphs 16–23

┈▶ First kisses make or break a relationship.

Subtopic 4: Lopsided love
Paragraphs 24–26

┈▶ Most people tilt their heads to the right when they kiss.

Concluding paragraph
Paragraph 27

┈▶ Kisses have more secrets to reveal.

Affairs of the Lips: Why We Kiss

Chip Walter

Chip Walter is a former CNN bureau chief, filmmaker, science journalist, and author. His science books, written for a mainstream audience, cover subjects as diverse as astrophysics, cognitive psychology, and evolution and are devoted to exploring why humans do what we do. "Affairs of the Lips: Why We Kiss" was the cover story of the February 2008 edition of *Scientific American Mind*. In this article, Walters explores why humans kiss and the wealth of information transmitted in this small act.

AFFAIRS OF THE LIPS: WHY WE KISS

1   When passion takes a grip, a kiss locks two humans together in an exchange of scents, tastes, textures, secrets and emotions. We kiss furtively, lasciviously, gently, shyly, hungrily and exuberantly. We kiss in broad daylight and in the dead of night. We give ceremonial kisses, affectionate kisses, Hollywood air kisses, kisses of death and, at least in fairytales, pecks that revive princesses.

2   Lips may have evolved first for food and later applied themselves to speech, but in kissing they satisfy different kinds of hungers. In the body, a kiss triggers a cascade of neural messages and chemicals that transmit tactile sensations, sexual excitement, feelings of closeness, motivation and even euphoria.

3   Not all the messages are internal. After all, kissing is a communal affair. The fusion of two bodies dispatches communiqués to your partner as powerful as the data you stream to yourself. Kisses can convey important information about the status and future of a relationship. So much, in fact, that, according to recent research, if a first kiss goes bad, it can stop an otherwise promising relationship dead in its tracks.

4   Some scientists believe that the fusing of lips evolved because it

Introduction:
The topic is announced in the title and first paragraph. The subtopics to be explored are set out in paragraphs 2–4.
Introduction:
The topic is announced in the title and first paragraph. The subtopics to be explored are set out in paragraphs 2–4.

facilitates mate selection. "Kissing," said evolutionary psychologist Gordon G. Gallup of the University at Albany, State University of New York, last September in an interview with the BBC, "involves a very complicated exchange of information—olfactory information, tactile information and postural types of adjustments that may tap into underlying evolved and unconscious mechanisms that enable people to make determinations . . . about the degree to which they are genetically incompatible." Kissing may even reveal the extent to which a partner is willing to commit to raising children, a central issue in long-term relationships and crucial to the survival of our species.

Source of information: A quotation from a scientist establishes the scientific perspective about what is at stake in studying kissing.

SATISFYING HUNGER

5 Whatever else is going on when we kiss, our evolutionary history is embedded within this tender, tempestuous act. In the 1960s British zoologist and author Desmond Morris first proposed that kissing might have evolved from the practice in which primate mothers chewed food for their young and then fed them mouth-to-mouth, lips puckered. Chimpanzees feed in this manner, so our hominid ancestors probably did, too. Pressing outturned lips against lips may have then later developed as a way to comfort hungry children when food was scarce and, in time, to express love and affection in general. The human species might eventually have taken these proto-parental kisses down other roads until we came up with the more passionate varieties we have today.

6 Silent chemical messengers called pheromones could have sped the evolution of the intimate kiss. Many animals and plants use pheromones to communicate with other members of the same species. Insects, in particular, are known to emit pheromones to signal alarm, for example, the presence of a food trail, or sexual attraction.

Organization: The first subtopic considers kissing as a possible chemical transmitter. Key terms, including pheromes, are introduced.

7 Whether humans sense pheromones is controversial. Unlike rats and pigs, people are not known to have a specialized pheromone detector, or vomeronasal organ, between their nose and mouth [see "Sex and the Secret Nerve," by R. Douglas Fields; *Scientific American Mind*, February/March 2007]. Nevertheless, biologist Sarah Woodley of

Duquesne University suggests that we might be able to sense pheromones with our nose. And chemical communication could explain such curious findings as a tendency of the menstrual cycles of female dormitory mates to synchronize or the attraction of women to the scents of T-shirts worn by men whose immune systems are genetically compatible with theirs. Human pheromones could include androstenol, a chemical component of male sweat that may boost sexual arousal in women, and female vaginal hormones called copulins that some researchers have found raise testosterone levels and increase sexual appetite in men.

8   If pheromones do play a role in human courtship and procreation, then kissing would be an extremely effective way to pass them from one person to another. The behavior may have evolved because it helps humans find a suitable mate—making love, or at least attraction, quite literally blind.

9   We might also have inherited the intimate kiss from our primate ancestors. Bonobos, which are genetically very similar to us (although we are not their direct descendants), are a particularly passionate bunch, for example. Emory University primatologist Frans B. M. de Waal recalls a zookeeper who accepted what he thought would be a friendly kiss from one of the bonobos, until he felt the ape's tongue in his mouth!

GOOD CHEMISTRY

Design:
Headings signal the major subtopics.

10   Since kissing evolved, the act seems to have become addictive. Human lips enjoy the slimmest layer of skin on the human body, and the lips are among the most densely populated with sensory neurons of any body region. When we kiss, these neurons, along with those in the tongue and mouth, rocket messages to the brain and body, setting off delightful sensations, intense emotions and physical reactions.

11   Of the 12 or 13 cranial nerves that affect cerebral function, five are at work when we kiss, shuttling messages from our lips, tongue, cheeks and nose to a brain that snatches information about the

Second subtopic:
Kissing prompts complex chemical effects on the brain.

temperature, taste, smell and movements of the entire affair. Some of that information arrives in the somatosensory cortex, a swath of tissue on the surface of the brain that represents tactile information in a map of the body. In that map, the lips loom large because the size of each represented body region is proportional to the density of its nerve endings.

12   Kissing unleashes a cocktail of chemicals that govern human stress, motivation, social bonding and sexual stimulation. In a new study, psychologist Wendy L. Hill and her student Carey A. Wilson of Lafayette College compared the levels of two key hormones in 15 college male-female couples before and after they kissed and before and after they talked to each other while holding hands. One hormone, oxytocin, is involved in social bonding, and the other, cortisol, plays a role in stress. Hill and Wilson predicted that kissing would boost levels of oxytocin, which also influences social recognition, male and female orgasm, and childbirth. They expected this effect to be particularly pronounced in the study's females, who reported higher levels of intimacy in their relationships. They also forecast a dip in cortisol, because kissing is presumably a stress reliever.

13   But the researchers were surprised to find that oxytocin levels rose only in the males, whereas it decreased in the females, after either kissing or talking while holding hands. They concluded that females must require more than a kiss to feel emotionally connected or sexually excited during physical contact. Females might, for example, need a more romantic atmosphere than the experimental setting provided, the authors speculate. The study, which Hill and Wilson reported in November 2007 at the annual meeting of the Society for Neuroscience, revealed that cortisol levels dropped for both sexes no matter the form of intimacy, a hint that kissing does in fact reduce stress.

14   To the extent that kissing is linked to love, the act may similarly boost brain chemicals associated with pleasure, euphoria and a motivation to connect with a certain someone. In 2005 anthropologist Helen Fisher of Rutgers University and her colleagues

reported scanning the brains of 17 individuals as they gazed at pictures of people with whom they were deeply in love. The researchers found an unusual flurry of activity in two brain regions that govern pleasure, motivation and reward: the right ventral tegmental area and the right caudate nucleus. Addictive drugs such as cocaine similarly stimulate these reward centers, through the release of the neurotransmitter dopamine. Love, it seems, is a kind of drug for us humans.

15   Kissing has other primal effects on us as well. Visceral marching orders boost pulse and blood pressure. The pupils dilate, breathing deepens and rational thought retreats, as desire suppresses both prudence and self-consciousness. For their part, the participants are probably too enthralled to care. As poet e. e. cummings once observed: "Kisses are a better fate / than wisdom."

LITMUS TEST

16   Although a kiss may not be wise, it can be pivotal to a relationship. "One dance," Alex "Hitch" Hitchens says to his client and friend in the 2005 movie *Hitch*, "one look, one kiss, that's all we get . . . one shot, to make the difference between 'happily ever after' and, 'Oh? He's just some guy I went to some thing with once.' "

17   Can a kiss be that powerful? Some research indicates it can be. In a recent survey Gallup and his colleagues found that 59 percent of 58 men and 66 percent of 122 women admitted there had been times when they were attracted to someone only to find that their interest evaporated after their first kiss. The "bad" kisses had no particular flaws; they simply did not feel right—and they ended the romantic relationship then and there—a kiss of death for that coupling.

Third subtopic: The first kiss can make or break a relationship.

18   The reason a kiss carries such weight, Gallup theorizes, is that it conveys subconscious information about the genetic compatibility of a prospective mate. His hypothesis is consistent with the idea that kissing evolved as a courtship strategy because it helps us rate potential partners.

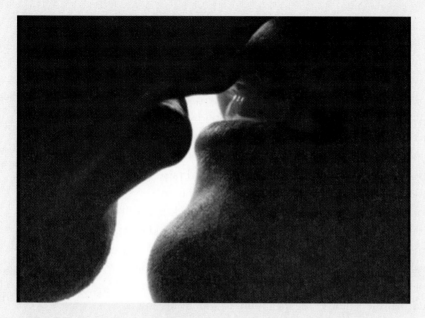

19   From a Darwinian perspective, sexual selection is the key to passing on your genes. For us humans, mate choice often involves falling in love. Fisher wrote in her 2005 paper that this "attraction mechanism" in humans "evolved to enable individuals to focus their mating energy on specific others, thereby conserving energy and facilitating mate choice—a primary aspect of reproduction."

20   According to Gallup's new findings, kissing may play a crucial role in the progression of a partnership but one that differs between men and women. In a study published in September 2007 Gallup and his colleagues surveyed 1,041 college undergraduates of both sexes about kissing. For most of the men, a deep kiss was largely a way of advancing to the next level sexually. But women were generally looking to take the relationship to the next stage emotionally, assessing not simply whether the other person would make a first-rate source of DNA but also whether he would be a good long-term partner.

21   "Females use [kissing] . . . to provide information about the level of commitment if they happen to be in a continuing relationship,"

Gallup told the BBC in September. The locking of lips is thus a kind of emotional barometer: the more enthusiastic it is, the healthier the relationship.

22   Because women need to invest more energy in producing children and have a shorter biological window in which to reproduce, they need to be pickier about whom they choose for a partner—and they cannot afford to get it wrong. So, at least for women, a passionate kiss may help them choose a mate who is not only good at fathering children but also committed enough to stick around and raise them.

Organization at the micro level: Author compares the different meanings kissing has for men and women.

23   That said, kissing is probably not strictly necessary from an evolutionary point of view. Most other animals do not neck and still manage to produce plenty of offspring. Not even all humans kiss. At the turn of the 20th century Danish scientist Kristoffer Nyrop described Finnish tribes whose members bathed together but considered kissing indecent. In 1897 French anthropologist Paul d'Enjoy reported that the Chinese regard mouth-to-mouth kissing to be as horrifying as many people deem cannibalism to be. In Mongolia some fathers do not kiss their sons. (They smell their heads instead.)

Style: The author introduces counterevidence, which makes him appear objective.

24   In fact, up to 10 percent of humanity does not touch lips, according to human ethology pioneer Irenäus Eibl-Eibesfeldt, now head of the Max-Planck-Society Film Archive of Human Ethology in Andechs, Germany, writing in his 1970 book, *Love and Hate: The Natural History of Behavior Patterns*. Fisher published a similar figure in 1992. Their findings suggest that some 650 million members of the human species have not mastered the art of osculation, the scientific term for kissing; that is more than the population of any nation on earth except for China and India.

LOPSIDED LOVE

25   For those cultures that do kiss, however, osculation conveys additional hidden messages. Psychologist Onur Güntürkün of the Ruhr-University of Bochum in Germany recently surveyed 124 couples kissing in public places in the U.S., Germany and Turkey

and found that they tilted their heads to the right twice as often as to the left before their lips touched. Right-handedness cannot explain this tendency, because being right-handed is four times more common than is the act of kissing on the right. Instead Güntürkün suspects that right-tilted kissing results from a general preference that develops at the end of gestation and in infancy. This "behavioral asymmetry" is related to the lateralization of brain functions such as speech and spatial awareness.

Fourth subtopic: Most people tilt their heads to the right when the kiss.

26   Nurture may also influence our tendency to tilt to the right. Studies show that as many as 80 percent of mothers, whether right-handed or left-handed, cradle their infants on their left side. Infants cradled, face up, on the left must turn to the right to nurse or nuzzle. As a result, most of us may have learned to associate warmth and security with turning to the right.

27   Some scientists have proposed that those who tilt their heads to the left when they kiss may be showing less warmth and love than those who tilt to the right. In one theory, tilting right exposes the left cheek, which is controlled by the right, more emotional half of the brain. But a 2006 study by naturalist Julian Greenwood and his colleagues at Stranmillis University College in Belfast, Northern Ireland, counters this notion. The researchers found that 77 percent of 240 undergraduate students leaned right when kissing a doll on the cheek or lips. Tilting to the right with the doll, an impassive act, was nearly as prevalent among subjects as it was among 125 couples observed osculating in Belfast; they tilted right 80 percent of the time. The conclusion: right-kissing probably results from a motor preference, as Güntürkün hypothesized, rather than an emotional one.

Conclusion: The brief concluding paragraph notes that there is much left to learn about kissing.

28   Despite all these observations, a kiss continues to resist complete scientific dissection. Close scrutiny of couples has illuminated new complexities woven throughout this simplest and most natural of acts—and the quest to unmask the secrets of passion and love is not likely to end soon. But romance gives up its mysteries grudgingly. And in some ways, we like it like that.

Understanding China's Middle Class

Kheehong Song and Allison Cui

Kheehong Song is a partner of Monitor Group, a marketing consultation firm. He is also the head of M2C (Monitor's marketing practice) Asia and managing director of Monitor's Shanghai office. Allison Cui, who is based in Shanghai, is a senior consultant for Monitor Group. Monitor consultants Angela Wang, Moon Heo Koo, Min Tian, James Bian, and Wendy Yu also contributed to this article, which was published in the March 2008 issue of *China Entrepreneur*.

Return to these questions after you have finished reading.

Analyzing the Reading

1. Who do you think is the audience for this reading? What is the reading's purpose?

2. Much of the selection is focused on defining the Chinese middle class and its purchasing habits. What criteria, in addition to income, do the authors say are important to understanding the consumer habits of middle-class Chinese?

3. What kinds of evidence do the authors use to support their points? Give at least two examples. How persuasive is their choice of evidence?

4. The authors divide the Chinese middle class into subsegments. How many subsegments do they identify? Do the descriptions of these groups seem useful? In what ways? What is the purpose of giving names to these subsegments?

Exploring Ideas and Issues

Identifying consumers' needs is a vital step in successful marketing. Companies like the Monitor Group specialize in systematically and objectively gathering and analyzing marketing information for producers. Though marketing research uses many of the tools of statistical analysis, it also depends to a great extent on the expertise of knowledgeable people in the field for interpretation of results.

1. The authors looked at the buying habits of middle-class Chinese. Think of three specific people you know in terms of their buying habits. Maybe one is an impulse buyer and another buys only high-status items, for example. How typical are these habits? Write an essay in which you generalize from your observations about these people to create three consumer "types."

2. Think of a widely known company—for example, Coca-Cola or Jeep. How does the company reach different U.S. population segments? Do some research, including observing TV commercials, print ads, and Internet marketing, on the company's products. What information do the ads convey? Which consumers do you think the company is trying to reach? Why? Write an essay in which you describe your research and give your conclusions.

3. With its rapidly growing middles class—340 million by 2016, according to Song and Cui—China has become a very desirable market for many companies worldwide. Do some research on marketing to China or another country with a growing economy, such as Brazil or India. Identify a marketing trend. Then write a short report to an imaginary U.S. company suggesting how the company can take advantage of that trend. You may use "Understanding China's Middle Class" as an information source for your essay.

Understanding China's Middle Class

Targeting key segments of China's diverse and rapidly emerging middle class will be crucial as household incomes rise

Gone are the days when companies looked at China as a monolithic land of 1 billion potential customers. Companies are now focusing on how to capture small segments of China's giant market, and none of these segments is as attractive or as full of potential as the country's rapidly growing—and multifaceted—middle class. As China's economy continues to grow, more people will migrate to China's booming metropolises to find better-paying jobs. These working consumers, once among the country's poorest, will steadily climb the income ladder and join the new middle class. Companies that can effectively understand the composition and needs of this diverse group will be positioned to reap massive rewards.

WHY THE MIDDLE CLASS?

Though many foreign companies have remarked on the importance of China's middle class as a consumer segment, few realize just how dramatic its ascendance is. From 1995 to 2005, the population of China's middle class—defined here as households with annual incomes ranging from $6,000 to $25,000—grew from close to zero in 1995 to an estimated 87 million in 2005, according to MasterCard Worldwide, Asia Pacific. China's middle class will jump to 340 million by 2016. The purchasing power—disposable income minus savings—of China's middle class is also growing. In 2006, around 39 percent of urban households were middle class. By 2016, that percentage will likely rise to 60 percent. At present, the middle class accounts for 27 percent of China's total urban disposable income. By 2015, that percentage is expected to rise to more than 40 percent (see Figure 1). Considering

its swelling numbers, purchasing power, and trajectory, China's middle class presents marketing opportunities that companies cannot afford to miss.

WHAT DOES IT MEAN TO BE MIDDLE CLASS?

Different types of companies have different concepts of exactly what it means to be middle class in China. For example, HSBC Holdings plc and Deutsche Bank AG have used income to differentiate the middle class from the affluent and laboring classes in China. From an investment bank's perspective, using income level as the defining criterion makes sense. But simply judging a group by income is far from sufficient for marketers of consumer goods. Such marketers trying to reach the middle class have to know more than their salaries: They must know what makes middle class consumers tick.

Income plays a powerful role in most purchasing decisions for any consumer segment, but other elements play a role that is sometimes greater than income. When products are relatively inexpensive, income has little influence on a consumer's decisionmaking process. Deciding to buy chocolate, for example, depends significantly more on consumers' emotion and shopping experience—a store's ambience, for example—than it does on how much money they make. Using income as the only indicator of spending habits allows much information to slip through the cracks. In addition, income is a difficult variable to act upon, in part because the data on income in China tends to be either unavailable or unreliable. Thus, companies must find meaningful alternatives to predict what consumers can afford and what they are willing to pay for certain goods and services. Studies by the Monitor Group indicate that scores of non-income-related hooks—including age, the stage in a consumer's career, and location of purchase—influence purchase decisions.

The Chinese badminton industry is a good example. Most Chinese school kids who play badminton do so in an outdoor playground with a group of friends, wear non-professional badminton sportswear, and purchase a relatively inexpensive racket in a sports stadium or shop near school. Professionals and businesspeople, however, usually play badminton in indoor badminton clubs, gyms, or stadiums. One of the major reasons they play badminton is to make friends or develop business relationships. They are aware of racket brands and wear professional sportswear to display social status.

The differences between school kids and professionals are mainly due to their disparate life stages and buying power. If a sports equipment and apparel company understands the differences between these two segments, it will use varying products and prices to target them through different channels. Nonetheless, even within the professional segments, consumers exhibit distinct buying behavior based on their occupation and level of career development. For example, engineers usually exhibit different buying behavior from marketing professionals, and senior managers may not care as much about brands as junior managers, who tend to buy famous brands to show their emerging social status.

PURCHASING POWER AND HOW THE MIDDLE CLASS BUYS

Of all the challenges that the middle class presents to marketers, understanding the specific

> ## Quick Glance
>
> ■ China's middle class, defined here as those earning $6,000 to $25,000, will increase from 87 million in 2005 to 340 million in 2016.
>
> ■ Several non-income-related hooks, such as age, the stage in a consumer's career, and location of purchase, influence purchase decisions for China's middle-class consumers.
>
> ■ Monitor identified six subsegments within China's middle class, each with its own unique needs and consumption patterns.

needs and purchasing power of the group is of utmost importance. Though middle-class consumers have rising purchasing power and are increasingly willing to pay more for higher quality, brand names, and differentiated features, they are still price sensitive. Recognizing differences in behavior within middle-class segments is essential to success in the Chinese marketplace.

When Inter IKEA Systems B.V. first entered China in 1998, its strategy was to offer stylish furniture at premium prices. The strategy was a flop. Middle-class customers filled IKEA's stores to look around but bought less than expected.

In the last few years, however, IKEA has repositioned itself as a brand targeting segments with annual household incomes above ¥40,000 ($5,857). Thanks to achievements in localization, the company has been able to cut prices by an average of 54 percent in more than 1,000 categories since 2005. IKEA broke the bottleneck and succeeded in China because it recognized that middle-class consumers wanted and would pay for high-quality products, but not at the same premiums as the affluent class.

MEET THE MIDDLE CLASS

China's relatively new middle class consists of a rapidly shifting, diverse population. At present, China's lower middle class accounts for 44 percent of the total middle class. As the middle class matures, however, the number of people in the upper middle class—households that earn $12,000 to $25,000—will spike dramatically. Companies must prepare for the different shopping behaviors of each sub-segment within the middle class. Lower-middle-class shoppers, for example, tend to buy top-tier products that can display their wealth and status. These middle-class consumers sometimes spend a large portion of their income on expensive goods. By contrast, upper-middle-class shoppers, who are more experienced with different types of brands, will seek out relatively high-quality products without paying as much attention to brands or will pick out products that merely reflect personal tastes.

To differentiate customer segments, Monitor Group has used "action segmentation," a market analysis strategy that draws on statistical data from a customer survey with several thousand samples and wide coverage. This methodology identifies multiple consumer segments to help companies address core organizational issues, achieve a well-designed marketing mix, reach growth targets, and more effectively engage their market. In the case of China's middle class, Monitor focused on purchasing behavior and demographic features, rather than income, as the key measures for understanding the middle class.

In one case, Monitor examined the correlation between consumer occupation and purchasing decisions within the tourism industry, the results of which allowed companies to customize their tourist packages more effectively. Monitor found three distinct segments of Chinese tourists: business, leisure, and backpacking travelers. Business travelers have fairly stable travel schedules throughout the year. They are reimbursed for some expenses and tend to spend more than leisure travelers. Leisure travelers enjoy sightseeing and recreational activities and tend to be more cost-conscious and self-organized. Chinese backpackers are willing to spend more and care most about uniqueness and experience. They want more personalized services, such as global positioning systems and specially trained tour guides. Unlike US backpackers, they have money and time and backpack mainly to be fashionable and gain new experiences.

In another case, an examination of the different levels of daily exercise among men and women revealed that although men tend to exercise at a more or less constant rate throughout their lives, women exercise less after marriage and still less after having children.

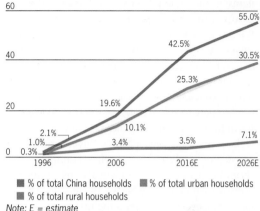

■ % of total China households   ■ % of total urban households
■ % of total rural households

Note: E = estimate
Sources: Global Demographics, DRC, and Monitor

Figure 1: Middle-class Consumer Households as a Percentage of Total Households, 1996–2026

This information helped sportswear companies identify which demographic segments were most profitable to target.

Applying the action segmentation methodology to the Chinese middle class, Monitor identified six sub-segments within the group, each with its own unique needs and consumption patterns. These include Early Heavy Buyers, the Smarts, the Quality-Oriented, Trend Followers, Driven Businesspeople, and Value Seekers.

To serve the specific needs of China's diverse middle class, companies must understand the desires of these six sub-segments and learn how to reach them. Early Heavy Buyers are energetic consumers, consisting primarily of professionals in tertiary industries and junior managers at multinational corporations. They tend to be young and well-educated, with an interest in and exposure to the world outside China. As consumers, they are early adopters of the latest products and aggressively seek out fashion that can help them stand out from their peers. Because they serve as trendsetters, members of this group actively search for information online and share that information with peers. They predominantly make purchases online or by mail order and have a high willingness to spend, especially on discretionary goods such as fashion items and lifestyle products and services. This group of trendsetters stands out from Trend Followers, who attempt to emulate Early Heavy Buyers in certain ways but approach purchasing decisions differently. Trend Followers tend to be junior white-collar workers and civil servants who have some leisure time and a stable salary but are new to the middle class and have less room for discretionary spending. They are less wellinformed than Early Heavy Buyers and consequently place more emphasis on the shopping experience. They are also more price sensitive. Though Early Heavy Buyers may be more concerned with being the first to get a new product, Trend Followers will wait for discounts and tend to take advantage of promotions.

Like Trend Followers, Value Seekers are usually junior white collar office workers or government employees. As their incomes rise, they increasingly demand better quality and service, but remain sensitive to price. Though they purchase some goods from relatively inexpensive luxury brands to help show their status, they remain more concerned about value than other middle-class segments. Trend Followers may choose products that are in fashion, while Value Seekers tend to look for the best quality-to-price ratio regardless of how popular the item may be at the time.

The final three—the Smarts, the Quality-Oriented, and Driven Businesspeople—tend to be older and to have been in the middle class longer. The Smarts are usually more sophisticated shoppers who prefer to buy from specialty stores and boutiques instead of major outlets. They regularly order business and fashion magazines to stay on top of trends but also rely on word of mouth.

Like the Smarts, Driven Businesspeople are willing to pay premiums for convenience. Driven Businesspeople are relatively wealthy and lead extremely busy lives. They do not have much time to gather information and compare different brands or clothes, but they have higher purchasing power. They usually trust friends'

recommendations, develop brand preferences before they buy, and are not price sensitive. They are experienced consumers with high degrees of brand loyalty, especially in fashion. For this group, product and service quality are much more important than price. The Quality-Oriented share much in common with the Smarts and Driven Businesspeople but tend to have more leisure time. More than either of those groups, family is a priority for the Quality-Oriented and has a strong influence on their purchasing decisions. For example, large markets and department stores that carry a range of products important to a family are the major purchasing channels for the Quality-Oriented, and television is their dominant information resource for new products.

Monitor helped a sportswear client target two of the six middle class segments—Driven Businesspeople and Value Seekers—by understanding different buying habits. To better target Driven Businesspeople, Monitor recommended that its client market products in mid-range to high-end gyms and fitness clubs, where many businesspeople usually go, to develop brand awareness and attract customers. Monitor also recommended that its client place mid-to-high-end products in department stores and flagship shops, where Driven Businesspeople usually go to buy sportswear. By contrast, to target Value Seekers, Monitor recommended that the client become more aware of Value Seekers' tendency to spend time comparing products, shopping at hypermarkets, and buying less expensive products.

WHAT IT MEANS FOR YOUR BUSINESS

There is no denying the enormous benefit that companies can gain from a better understanding of China's emerging middle class. Marketing effectively to any group of middle-class consumers requires an understanding of the needs of specific segments and the recognition of which segments provide the greatest potential profitability for a particular product.

Why Gossip Is Good for You

Robin Dunbar

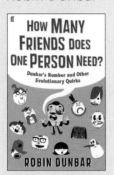

An anthropologist and evolutionary psychologist specializing in primate behavior, Robin Dunbar is a professor at Oxford University. Dunbar is perhaps best known for postulating Dunbar's number, the maximum number of people—approximately 150—with whom any one individual can have stable and meaningful relationships. The following selection is a chapter in his book *How Many Friends Does One Person Need? Dunbar's Number and Other Evolutionary Quirks* (2010).

Return to these questions after you have finished reading.

Analyzing the Reading

1. What is the main idea of the chapter? How do the chapter's title and four subheadings advance the main idea?

2. What distinctions does the author make between men's speech and women's speech? What evidence does he give for his assertions about the importance of "motherese"? Is his evidence convincing? Why or why not?

3. What is the role of gossip? How is it related to storytelling?

4. What does the author's language tell us about the intended audience? What do the phrases "nineteen to the dozen" and "that silly mid-on dropped the catch" and spellings like "categorise," "favours," and "defence" tell us about the author's identity?

Exploring Ideas and Issues

Theories about the origins of language and the structure of human society continue to fascinate us—not the least because they are impossible to prove. Comparing human behavior to that of animals, especially other primates, as the author does, is one way to look for answers. Another way is to closely observe the behavior of our own species.

1. Dunbar discusses what he sees as differences between men's speech and women's speech. Do his ideas match your observations and experiences? Why or why not? Write a short essay in which you agree or disagree with Dunbar. Include examples from your own experiences as evidence for your claims.

2. Dunbar says, "Classifications and social conventions allow us to broaden the network of social relationships by making networks of networks, and this in turn allows us to create very large groups indeed." Think of the communities you belong to—college, church, clubs, and so on. What are their characteristics and purposes? What impact do you think social networking applications, such as Facebook and Twitter, have on the concept of community? Write an essay in which you explore the idea of community, including why they succeed or fail. Use your own experiences and the experiences of people you know as examples.

3. Dunbar mentions the pleasures of music and storytelling. Think of your interactions with different forms of art. Do you think that making and experiencing art are valuable human activities? Why or why not? Write a short essay in which you give three reasons for your position. Include examples from your own experiences or from research you conduct as evidence.

Why Gossip Is Good for You

Why is it that we are so fascinated by what others get up to? Why should we find tittle-tattle about the private lives of minor celebrities, royalty, politicians and even each other of such overwhelming interest that it can drive the starving children of Darfur or the war-ravaged cities of Somalia and Iraq off the front pages of even the most sedate of newspapers? The reason is very simple: gossip makes the world go round.

Men Talk, Women Gossip...

So how much time did you waste yesterday wittering away nineteen to the dozen? I'll wager it was getting on for a quarter of your entire day. And what came of it all? Probably not a lot, you might say. But it wasn't totally frivolous. It's an odd thing, this language business: we find it intensely embarrassing to remain silent in company. We cast around desperately for something to say, however meaningless. Um . . . do you come here often?

So why do we do it?

One answer is that language is just a form of grooming. For monkeys and apes, grooming is less a matter of hygiene and more an expression of commitment. Its sense is more that of: "I'd rather be here grooming with you than over there with Jennifer." We still do a great deal of mutual mauling of this kind, of course. It is an essential feature of all intimate relationships. Parents and offspring, lovers, friends—all are willing to spend hours stroking, touching, leafing through hair. Physical contact, in short, is an essential part of the rhythm of social life.

To this, we humans add language. It's a kind of grooming at a distance and, in many ways, serves much the same kind of purpose. It allows us to make that all-important statement about commitment: "I find you interesting enough to waste time talking to." Forget all that highfalutin' nonsense about Shakespeare and Goethe. Real conversations in the everyday world are simply plain honest grooming.

Of course, language allows us to go one step beyond mere signals of commitment. It allows us to exchange information. Monkeys and apes are restricted to direct observation when it comes to learning about who might make a good friend and who is unreliable, or who is going out with whom. But we can learn about these things at second and third hand, and that greatly extends our circle of social knowledge.

Take a listen to the conversation next to you. It will soon become clear that most of our conversations are concerned with social doings. Sometimes our own, sometimes other people's. It's the Harry-met-Sally-met-Susan syndrome.

But nothing comes for free in evolution. Being able to exchange information on who-is-doing-what-with-whom inevitably allows us to use language for more nefarious purposes. In short, advertising should probably be accorded the title of the oldest profession. We are past masters of it. If you don't believe me, listen more closely to that conversation.

There is, however, a curious asymmetry in the conversations of men and women. Harry, it seems, likes to talk about Harry, but Sally talks about Susan. Ah, you say, everyone's stereotypes confirmed. Well, yes and no. There's no smoke without fire, of course. But the really interesting question is why it should be like this.

Men and women's preferred conversation topics are often radically different because they are playing rather different games. Listen carefully to what they actually say, and you soon realise that women's conversations are primarily geared to servicing their social networks, building and maintaining a complex web of relationships in a social world that is forever in flux. Keeping up to date on everyone's doings is as important as the implicit suggestion that you are enough a member of the in-group to be worth talking to. This is not tittle-tattle. It's the very hub of the social merry-go-round, the foundation on which society itself is built.

In contrast, men's conversations seem to be geared as much to advertising as anything else. They talk about themselves or they talk about things they claim to know a lot about. It's a kind of vocal form of the peacock's tail. Male peacocks hang about on their mating territories and display their brilliant tails whenever a female hoves into view. The peahens wander from one male to another, choosing among the males on the basis of their trains.

Humans, it seems, do all this vocally. Like the peacocks that suddenly raise their tails when a peahen is near, men switch into advertising mode when women are present. Have a listen to the same man when he is talking only to other men and compare it with what he talks about when women are present. When there are women present, his conversational style changes dramatically. It becomes more showy, more designed to stimulate laughter as a response. But, in addition, you'll find that technical topics and other forms of "knowledge" become more intrusive. It's competitive and it's a manifesto. Politics is the name of the game. Language is indeed a many-splendoured thing.

Motherese Has So Much to Answer For

The American anthropologist Dean Falk has suggested that language might have come about through mothers singing to their babies. That peculiar form of speech known as *motherese* which women (in particular) seem to use so naturally when talking to infants has many of the hallmarks of music—a simple rhythmicity, a strikingly exaggerated sing-song intonation that can rise and fall two whole octaves, and a pitch that is significantly higher than normal speech. Next time you hear a mother talking to her baby, listen closely. You'll be listening to distant echoes of the past. Oh, and don't forget to watch the baby. This unique form of music is very calming for it, and babies seem to find it very attractive and soothing. It stimulates smiling. It's the magic of endorphins again, and their role in bonding.

But motherese has much more important effects than just calming baby. It can dramatically affect the speed with which a baby reaches its developmental milestones. Marilee Monnot, then a postgraduate student in biological anthropology at Cambridge University, observed fifty-two mothers and their newborn babies during the first year of the baby's life. She found that those mothers who used more motherese had babies that grew faster and reached developmental milestones (like smiling) more quickly than those who used less. That's quite scary.

Monkey and ape mothers do not croon to their babies. They don't even rock them. It seems to be something that is peculiar to humans. Nonetheless, it's not hard to see how motherese might have got going, though exactly when that might have happened is a tad more difficult to say. If humming soothes baby, and a less fractious baby is more healthy, then there is likely to have been very considerable selection pressure on mothers to do this kind of thing. But why us humans, and not, say, our great ape cousins? The answer surely has something to do with the fact that human babies are born around a whole year premature compared to what we would expect for an ape of monkey of our brain size (I'll have more to say on this later). By comparison, ape babies can pretty much look after themselves. Human babies need an awful lot more attention, and don't really get to the same stage of development as a newborn chimpanzee baby until they reach their first birthday. Since a whole lot more work has to be done by the human baby's long-suffering parent, a mechanism that quietens and soothes a fractious baby must have been all the more necessary in our lineage.

If so, then perhaps this gives us a clue as to when it might have evolved. If it was a response to the radical change in birthing pattern that resulted from the last big upward shift in brain size, then we can perhaps point to the appearance of archaic humans around a half a million years ago. This might well have coincided with the origins of music. Motherese might have been the precursor of music, or it might have been the stepping stone between music and language.

Motherese isn't really language. Although it often does consist of words, it doesn't have to. Often, it is just nonsense syllables. It shares much with nursery-rhymes—rhythm, rhyme and alliteration. *Hickory, dickory, dock* . . . That in itself suggests that it long predates the evolution of language. It is also much more like wordless singing, or humming—pure music. In this, it shares a great deal with sea shanties. And it also shares a great deal in common with that most extraordinary and unique form of vocal music, the waulking songs (*Úrain luaidh* in Gaelic) of the women of the Outer Hebrides. Part just nonsense syllables, part witty—often raunchy—reflections on lives coloured by poverty and hard work, and not infrequently by tragedy, these extraordinary songs have been sung for centuries by the women as they stretch and soften the newly woven tweed round a kitchen table. Passed down by word of mouth from one generation to the next, they are a remarkable and unique tradition. I wonder if they don't represent the very first kinds of situations when language was used—by women around the campfire, or out foraging for fruits and tubers. There is something about synchronised singing that seems especially good at triggering the release of endorphins: many voices make light work.

The Importance of a Good Gossip

In the end, of course, language evolved to allow us to integrate a large number of social relationships. And the way it does this is by allowing us to exchange information about other individuals who are not present. In other words, by talking to one person, we can find out a great deal about how other individuals are likely to behave, how we should react to them when we actually meet them and what kinds of relationships they have with third parties. All these things allow us to co-ordinate our social relationships within a group more effectively. And this is likely to be especially important in the large, dispersed groups that are characteristic of modern humans.

This would explain our fascination for social gossip in the newspapers, and why gossip about relationships accounts for an overwhelming proportion of human conversations. Even conversations in such august places as university coffee rooms tends to swing back and forth between academic issues and gossip about individuals. To get some idea of how important gossip is, we monitored conversations in a university refectory, scoring the topic at thirty-second intervals. Social relationships and personal experiences accounted for about seventy per cent of conversation time. About half of this was devoted to the relationships or experiences of third parties (people not present).

But since males tend to talk more about their own relationships and experiences, whereas females tend to talk most about other people's, this might suggest that language evolved in the context of social bonding between females. Most anthropologists have assumed that it evolved in the context of male-male relationships, during hunting for example. The suggestion that female-female bonding, based on knowledge of the relationships of individuals, was more important fits much better with views about the structure of nonhuman primate societies where relationships between females are all-important.

That conversations allow us to exchange information about people who are not present is vitally important. It allows us to teach others how to relate to individuals they have never seen before, or to handle difficult situations before they have to face them. Combined with the fact that language also makes it easy to categorize people into types, we can learn how to relate to classes of individuals as primates are when grooming. We can agree to give types of individuals special markers, such as dog collars, white lab coats or large blue helmets, which allow us to behave appropriately towards them even though we have never met before. Without that knowledge, it would take us days to work out the basis of a relationship.

Classifications and social conventions allow us to broaden the network of social relationships by making networks of networks, and this in turn allows us to create very large groups indeed. Of course, the level of the relationship is necessarily rather crude but at least it allows us to avoid major social faux pas at the more superficial levels of interaction when we first meet someone we don't know personally. Significantly, when it comes to really intense relationships that are especially important to us, we invariably abandon language and revert to that old fashioned primate form of direct interaction—mutual mauling.

What we seem to have here, then, is a theory for the evolution of language that also seems to account for a number of other facets of human behaviour. It explains why gossip about other people is so fascinating; it explains why human societies are so often hierarchical; it predicts the small size of conversation groups; it meshes well with our general understanding of why primates have larger brains than other mammals; and it agrees with the general view that language only evolved with the appearance of modern humans, *Homo sapiens*.

What it does not explain, of course, is why our ancestors should have needed to live in groups of about 150. It is unlikely that this has anything to do with defense against predators (the main reason why most nonhuman primates live in groups) because human groups far exceed the sizes of all other primate groups. But it might have something to do with the management or defence of resources, particularly dispersed resources such as water holes that nomadic hunter–gatherers might have had to depend on at certain times of the year.

Now Tell Me Another Story

Language is also crucial for one of our most peculiar activities—story-telling. It is something that humans all around the world do and love, and surely have done ever since time immemorial. It is not just a bit of old gossip, for stories told around the campfire are imbued with ritual and often have a very formal structure. Many are incredibly old, such as the great Hindu epic the Mahabharata, written around two thousand years ago, or the stories contained in the books of the Old Testament or the Bhagavadgita that were composed some five hundred years earlier, just a few centuries after Homer's great epic poems the *Iliad* and the *Odyssey*. Some of the stories told by Australian Aboriginals living along the south coast of the continent appear to be even more ancient: they are said to contain surprisingly accurate descriptions of the landscape on the sea floor of the Bass Strait that separates Tasmania from the Australian mainland—a land surface that was last exposed as dry land during the Ice Age that ended twelve thousand years ago.

So why should we be so fond of stories?

Well, for one thing, many such stories are origins stories—they tell us where we came from, and how we came to be the way we are. They tell us about community, they create a sense of belonging for us.

Shared knowledge itself is a good marker of community membership. That you know immediately what I mean when I observe that silly mid-on dropped the catch inexorably marks us out as belonging to the same community, the community of those who play or follow cricket. By virtue of that simple fact, we can be sure that we share enough in common to be willing to exchange favours should that ever be necessary. We have a common world view, and by implication subscribe to a common set of rules of how one should behave. It probably reflects the fact that, in our deep past, people who shared such knowledge lived together, and were almost certainly related to each other. So, discovering that we share esoteric knowledge still seems to create an instant bond between us, sets us apart from the rest of the common herd. That may be one reason why we are so fond of creating technical jargon—it sets us apart as special, a shadowy secret cabal that knows the innermost secrets of the universe. There's nothing like a good secret.

But while there is something deeply engrossing about a good story well told, there is perhaps nothing quite so captivating as a story told around the campfire at night. We seem to be especially fond of story-telling at night, and there can hardly be a culture around the world in which this is not true. But why should darkness make stories seem so much more vivid?

It's not enough to say that the evening round the campfire is the only time you have for relaxation—the day's work is done, there is nothing more to do, so idle chatter can fill the time before bed. That's not really a convincing explanation because, if there really was nothing useful to do, we could just easily go to sleep as soon as it gets dark just like all the other sensible monkeys and apes. But we don't: we stay up to chatter. What's more, it's a peculiarly social time, the time when we prefer to invite guests for dinner—even at the weekend when the days are presumably uncluttered by work and we could easily have invited them for breakfast, lunch or tea, it's still dinner that we prefer. Of course, we can—and sometimes do—sit around the campfire of an evening doing useful chores like making or repairing clothing or hunting equipment. Yet we still tell stories while we do these things.

Perhaps it has more to do with psychology and the ambience. Perhaps story-tellers find it easier to play with our emotions in the dark, and we rise to that precisely because we get more of a kick out of it. Perhaps it is because many such stories are about mythical creatures, and daylight casts too much of a cold dose of reality on them to make them believable. Such stories may need the uncertainty of the dark, when we feel vulnerable because danger—whether natural predators or human muggers—can too easily get within our "escape distance" (the distance at which we can still evade a predator once we have detected it). Perhaps it is just easier for a skilled story-teller to work on the audience's emotions at night.

Measuring Human Demand: Ecological Footprint

World Wildlife Fund

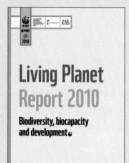

The WWF (also known as the World Wildlife Fund and the World Wide Fund for Nature) is a nonprofit conservation organization founded in 1961. Its mission, stated on its Web site (http://wwf.panda.org), is "To stop the degradation of the planet's natural environment and to build a future in which humans live in harmony with nature, by conserving the world's biological diversity, ensuring that the use of renewable natural resources is sustainable, [and] promoting the reduction of pollution and wasteful consumption." The following selection is taken from Chapter 1, "The State of the Planet," of the organization's *Living Planet Report 2010: Biodiversity, Biocapacity and Development*.

Return to these questions after you have finished reading.

Analyzing the Reading

1. Who is the audience for this report? How much does a reader have to know about ecology to understand the report? How is technical language used?

2. What is the report's definition of "Ecological Footprint"? What point is the report making about this Footprint?

3. Do the figures provide convincing evidence for the report's main point? Why or why not? What metaphor (or comparison) does the report use to clarify the meaning of "overshoot"?

4. Is the report successful in conveying important information? Does it aim to convince readers to act? If so, is it effectively persuasive?

Exploring Ideas and Issues

Though we all generally agree that we need to take care of the environment, we don't all necessarily agree on how to do that. Politicians, economists, businesspeople, conservationists, and even scientists interpret information in different ways and have a range of priorities.

1. A person who agrees with the report's assessment might be persuaded to take action in response. Think of the actions such a person could take both personally (for example, driving a hybrid car) and politically (for example, donating to conservation groups). Write a short essay in which you explain steps people could take to lower the Ecological Footprint.

2. You may have observed changes in the natural environment caused by human activity; for example, the commercial development of a rural area. List the positive and negative consequences you have seen or you anticipate from that change. Write a short essay in which you describe the situation and argue that the positive impact outweighs the negative, or vice versa.

3. While some organizations advocate for government involvement in protecting the environment, others maintain that economic forces, left to themselves, will eventually correct any environmental imbalances. Do some research on different approaches that groups have to keeping Earth's environment viable. Write an essay in which you compare not only the ideas but also the proposed actions of these groups.

MEASURING HUMAN DEMAND: ECOLOGICAL FOOTPRINT

The Ecological Footprint is an accounting framework that tracks humanity's competing demands on the biosphere by comparing human demand against the regenerative capacity of the planet. It does this by adding together the areas required to provide renewable resources people use, the areas occupied by infrastructure, and the areas required for absorbing waste. In the current National Footprint Accounts, the resource inputs tracked include crops and fish for food as well as other uses, timber, and grass used to feed livestock. CO_2 is the only waste product currently included. Since people consume resources from all over the world, the Ecological Footprint of consumption, the measure reported here, adds together these areas regardless of where they are located on the planet.

To determine whether human demand for renewable resources and CO_2 uptake can be maintained, the Ecological Footprint is compared to the regenerative capacity (or 'biocapacity') of the planet. Biocapacity is the total regenerative capacity available to serve the demand represented by the Footprint. Both the Ecological Footprint (which represents demand for resources) and biocapacity (which represents the availability of resources) are expressed in units called global hectares (gha), with 1gha representing the productive capacity of 1ha of land at world average productivity.

1.5 YRS
TO REGENERATE THE RENEWABLE RESOURCES USED IN 2007

187

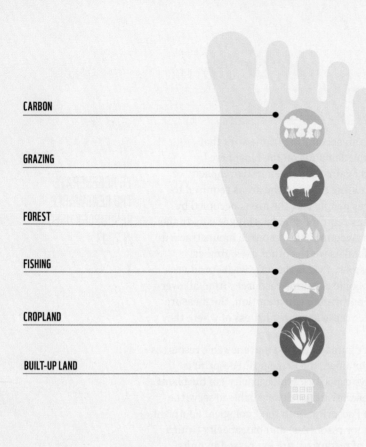

CARBON

GRAZING

FOREST

FISHING

CROPLAND

BUILT-UP LAND

Figure 15: Every human activity uses biologically productive land and/or fishing grounds

The Ecological Footprint is the sum of this area, regardless of where it is located on the planet

Footprint component definitions

CARBON UPTAKE FOOTPRINT:	Calculated as the amount of forest land required to absorb CO2 emissions from burning fossil fuels, land-use change and chemical processes, other than the portion absorbed by oceans
GRAZING LAND FOOTPRINT:	Calculated from the area used to raise livestock for meat, dairy, hide and wool products
FOREST FOOTPRINT:	Calculated from the amount of lumber, pulp, timber products and fuel wood consumed by a country each year
FISHING GROUNDS FOOTPRINT:	Calculated from the estimated primary production required to support the fish and seafood caught, based on catch data for 1,439 different marine species and more than 268 freshwater species
CROPLAND FOOTPRINT:	Calculated from the area used to produce food and fibre for human consumption, feed for livestock, oil crops and rubber
BUILT-UP-LAND FOOTPRINT:	Calculated from the area of land covered by human infrastructure, including transportation, housing, industrial structures, and reservoirs for hydropower

Ecological overshoot is growing

During the 1970s, humanity as a whole passed the point at which the annual Ecological Footprint matched the Earth's annual biocapacity — that is, the Earth's human population began consuming renewable resources faster than ecosystems can regenerate them and releasing more CO_2 than ecosystems can absorb. This situation is called "ecological overshoot", and has continued since then.

The latest Ecological Footprint shows this trend is unabated (Figure 16). In 2007, humanity's Footprint was 18 billion gha, or 2.7gha per person. However, the Earth's biocapacity was only 11.9 billion gha, or 1.8gha per person (Figure 17 and GFN, 2010a). This represents an ecological overshoot of 50 per cent. This means it would take 1.5 years for the Earth to regenerate the renewable resources that people used in 2007 and absorb CO_2 waste. Put another way, people used the equivalent of 1.5 planets in 2007 to support their activities (see Box: What does overshoot really mean?).

Figure 16: Ecological Footprint by component, 1961–2007
The Footprint is shown as number of planets. Total biocapacity, represented by the dashed line, always equals one planet Earth, although the biological productivity of the planet changes each year. Hydropower is included in built-up land and fuel wood in the forest component (Global Footprint Network, 2010)

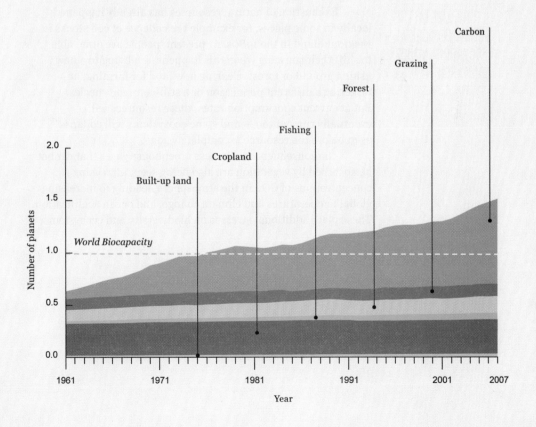

189

x2

THE SIZE OF THE
GLOBAL ECOLOGICAL
FOOTPRINT IN 2007
COMPARED TO 1966

What does overshoot really mean?

How can humanity be using the capacity of 1.5 Earths, when there is only one? Just as it is easy to withdraw more money from a bank account than the interest this money generates, it is possible to harvest renewable resources faster than they are being generated. More wood can be taken from a forest each year than re-grows, and more fish can be harvested than are replenished each year. But doing so is only possible for a limited time, as the resource will eventually be depleted.

Similarly, CO_2 emissions can exceed the rate at which forests and other ecosystems are able to absorb them, meaning additional Earths would be required to fully sequester these emissions.

Exhaustion of natural resources has already happened locally in some places, for example the collapse of cod stocks in Newfoundland in the 1980s. At present, people are often able to shift their sourcing when this happens — moving to a new fishing ground or forest, clearing new land for farming, or targeting a different population or a still-common species. But at current consumption rates, these resources will eventually run out too — and some ecosystems will collapse even before the resource is completely gone.

The consequences of excess greenhouse gases that cannot be absorbed by vegetation are also being seen: increasing concentrations of CO_2 in the atmosphere, leading to increasing global temperatures and climate change, and ocean acidification. These place additional stresses on biodiversity and ecosystems.

The Heart Disease Test

David McCandless

David McCandless is a London-based graphic designer and author specializing in the visual presentation of information and ideas. His work has appeared in numerous publications, such as *The Guardian*, a British newspaper. McCandless has also published several books, including *Information Is Beautiful* (2010), as well as other materials. His blog is available at www.informationisbeautiful.net. The following graphic redesign was commissioned by *Wired* magazine and appeared in the article "The Blood Test Gets a Makeover" by Steven Leckart in the November 29, 2010, issue of *Wired*.

Return to these questions after you have finished reading.

Analyzing the Reading

1. Compare the original and the redesigned reports. Who is the audience for the original design? Who is the audience for the redesign? What is the goal of the redesign?

2. The original report is annotated with four comments meant to guide the redesign. How effectively did the designer address the issues raised in these four comments? Explain your answer.

3. What typographic elements does McCandless use? In what ways do these elements contribute, or not contribute, to the redesign's effectiveness?

4. How much general education would a patient need to interpret the redesigned report? What pros and cons do you see to using the redesigned form?

Exploring Ideas and Issues

We see graphic presentations of information all around us—on traffic signs, restroom doors, elevator buttons, consumer electronics, and so on. Though many of these may seem simple to interpret, some graphic presentations can be quite sophisticated and reading them can take some practice.

1. Think of at least three situations in which you personally would prefer information in a graphic rather than written form, or vice versa. For example, are you more comfortable with written, step-by-step travel instructions, or do you find a map easier to follow? Write a short essay in which you describe why you prefer one method over the other, or explain why you think one approach is more effective.

2. Choose a document that you are familiar with but that others might find confusing; for example, a college transcript. Analyze the readability of the document, and write comments about how it could be improved. Now redesign the document in a more graphic format, taking care to incorporate your clarifications. If you cannot use computer design tools, sketch your redesign by hand.

3. McCandless's redesign reflects two important principles of medical ethics: patients have the right to make their own medical decisions, and patients must have sufficient information about the pros and cons of a procedure to give "informed consent." Do some research on at least two other tenets of medical ethics. Write an essay in which you list and explain these four principles. Give at least one example of how each principle works.

The Heart Disease Test

Alongside cholesterol tests and high-blood-pressure monitoring, the c-reactive protein, or CRP, test is widely used to spot people at risk for heart disease, the leading cause of death in the US.

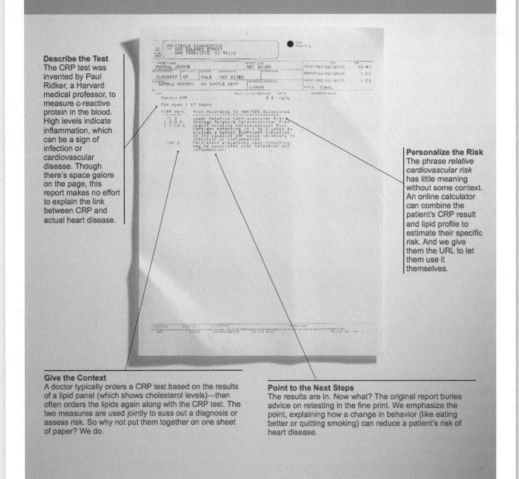

Describe the Test
The CRP test was invented by Paul Ridker, a Harvard medical professor, to measure c-reactive protein in the blood. High levels indicate inflammation, which can be a sign of infection or cardiovascular disease. Though there's space galore on the page, this report makes no effort to explain the link between CRP and actual heart disease.

Personalize the Risk
The phrase *relative cardiovascular risk* has little meaning without some context. An online calculator can combine the patient's CRP result and lipid profile to estimate their specific risk. And we give them the URL to let them use it themselves.

Give the Context
A doctor typically orders a CRP test based on the results of a lipid panel (which shows cholesterol levels)—then often orders the lipids again along with the CRP test. The two measures are used jointly to suss out a diagnosis or assess risk. So why not put them together on one sheet of paper? We do.

Point to the Next Steps
The results are in. Now what? The original report buries advice on retesting in the fine print. We emphasize the point, explaining how a change in behavior (like eating better or quitting smoking) can reduce a patient's risk of heart disease.

...Madeover

Click on the document below to view a larger image of the makeover of the heart disease test.

Results redesign: David McCandless

Blood Work Cardiology Result

BACTA MEDICAL CENTRE

ORDERED BY: Dr. Francis Pulaski
Bacta Medical Centre
pulaski.f@bactamed.edu
(603) 555-9564 x1523

Patient

NAME: **Jerome Morrow**

GENDER: **M**   AGE: **49**   DOB: **01/10/1961**

COLLECTED: 11/02/2010, 10:40 a.m.
RECEIVED: 11/02/2010, 1:03 p.m.

---

1 About this test

This report evaluates your potential risk of heart disease, heart attack, and stroke.

---

2 Your results

CRP level test

Your level of c-reactive protein in the blood. High levels are linked to inflammation of the blood vessels, which has been associated with an increased risk of heart disease.

3.3

mg/L

| Low risk | Average risk (1) | High risk of cardiovascular disease (3) | 10+ |

Total cholesterol level

265

mg/dL

| Desirable | Borderline (200) | High (240) | 280+ |

LDL ("bad" cholesterol)

233

mg/dL

| Optimal | Near optimal (100) | Borderline high (130) | High (160) | Very high (190) | 260+ |

HDL ("good" cholesterol)

32

mg/dL

| Low | Borderline (40) | Optimal (60) | 100+ |

---

3 Your risk You show an elevated risk of cardiovascular disease.

If you're a smoker with blood pressure of 130 mm/Hg but a family history of heart attack before age 60 (in one or both parents), your risk over the next 10 years is:

15%

Your risk would be lowered to:

12% if your blood pressure were 120 mm/Hg.
10% if you quit smoking.
6% if you reduced your cholesterol to 160 mg/DL.

Use your CRP results and cholesterol level to calculate your 10-year risk of a cardiovascular event at **www.reynoldsrisksscore.org**.

---

4 What now?

Diet and exercise can improve your cholesterol levels.

Avoid drinking alcohol, except in moderation: one to two drinks per day.

Ask your doctor about statins or other medications that can lower cholesterol.

Consider retesting in one to two weeks, in case your CRP level was caused by infection.

193

How to Write to Inform

These steps for the process of informative writing may not progress as neatly as this chart might suggest. Writing is not an assembly-line process. As you write, you are constantly reading what you have written and rethinking.

Keep your readers in mind while you are writing, and if you don't know who your readers might be, imagine someone. What questions might that person have? Where would they appreciate a more detailed explanation?

1
EXPLORE THE WRITING TASK

- Read the assignment, carefully noting key words.

- Determine what kind of writing is required. Who are the potential readers?

- Find the limits of your topic. What do you not need to cover? How far do you need to go in breaking down your explanations?

- Review class notes and textbooks; talk to instructor and peers.

- Search for topic ideas in Web subject directories and your library's online catalog.

2
FOCUS YOUR TOPIC AND WRITE A THESIS

- Within the scope of the assignment, explore what interests you.

- Ask yourself, "Who else will be interested in this topic?"

- Make a list of issues, questions, or problems associated with the topic area.

- Make idea maps about possible topics.

- Discuss possible choices with your peers, coworkers, or instructor.

- Ask questions:
  What happened? What do people need to know?
  Who is my audience?
  How can I connect with them on this topic?

- Narrow your topic. When you learn more about your topic, you should be able to identify one aspect or concept that you can cover thoroughly.

- Write a working thesis that describes what you plan to report or explain.

- If you are unsure if you can follow through with your thesis, do additional research and revise your thesis.

3
WRITE A DRAFT

- Write your revised thesis and main points.
- Think about how you will organize your main points.
- Make a working outline that lists the sections of your essay.
- Draft an introduction that will make readers interested in your subject.
- Build the organization by identifying the topic of each paragraph.
- Draft a conclusion that does more than summarize.
- Write an engaging title.
- If you have statistical information to present, consider using charts or graphs.

4
REVISE, REVISE, REVISE

- Reorganize your ideas for clarity.
- Add detail or further explanation where needed.
- Cut material that distracts from your thesis.
- Check that all key terms are defined.
- Frame your report with an introduction that interests readers and a conclusion that makes a point or raises an interesting question.
- Check that any sources are appropriately quoted or summarized and that they are documented correctly.
- Revise the title to be more accurate and to make readers more interested.
- Review the visual presentation of your report for readability and maximum impact.

5
SUBMITTED VERSION

- Make sure your finished writing meets all formatting requirements.

1: Explore the Writing Task

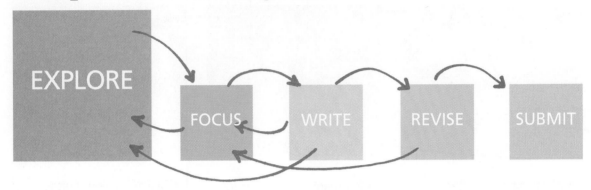

Analyze the assignment

Read your assignment slowly and carefully. Mark off any information about the length specified, date due, formatting, and other requirements. You can attend to this information later. At this point you want to zero in on the subject you will write about and how you will approach that subject.

What kind of informative writing is required?

Look for key words such as *analyze, compare and contrast,* or *explain.* Often these key words will help you in determining what direction to take.

- **Analyze:** Find connections among a set of facts, events, or things, and make them meaningful.

- **Compare and contrast:** Examine how two or more things are alike and how they differ.

- **Explain:** Go into detail about how something works or make an unfamiliar subject comprehensible.

Is the audience specified?

If the audience is mentioned in the assignment, how much will they know about your subject? How much background will you need to provide? What terms will you need to define?

Is the topic assigned?

If the topic is assigned, how much do you know about it? Think about which aspects might interest you. What angle or perspective might you take to make the topic interesting?

Are you able to choose a topic?

Think first about what is most interesting to you. Do you have any special knowledge about a hobby, job, or sport that you want to share with others? A good first step is to make an inventory of what you know. Make a list of possible ideas. After you write down as many ideas as you can, go back through the list and place a star beside the ideas that seem most promising.

- **What ideas can you find in your course notes, class discussions, and your textbooks?** Think about subjects raised in lectures, in class discussions, or in your textbooks for potential ideas.

- **What can you find in a database or online library catalog?**

- Subject directories on databases and your library's online catalog can be valuable sources of potential topics. See Chapter 20.

- **What might you find on the Web?** Google searches and other search engines often turn up promising ideas to pursue. Yahoo has a subject directory that breaks down large topics into subtopics. See Chapter 20.

- **What might you find doing field research?** Sometimes the information you need cannot be found in libraries or on the Web, and you have to collect the information firsthand through interviews, surveys, or observations. See Chapter 22.

WRITE NOW

Make a mind map

A good way to explore a topic is to make a mind map. You can create a mind map by using pen and paper or presentation software including Google Docs, which is a free service that allows you to collaborate with others.

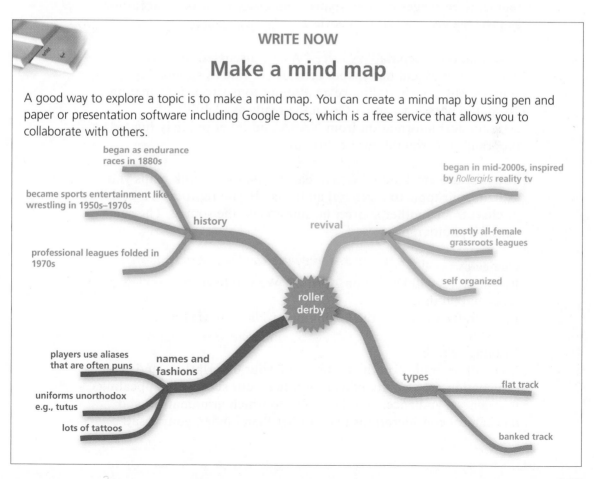

Writer at work

Astronomy 101
Writing Assignment #2

*Use examples
(Show, don't just tell)
Galaxy 999 shows
this process at work*

Explain an astronomical ⟨process,⟩ and the current ⟨theory⟩ that accounts for it, to a general audience. Use examples of specific phenomena to illustrate the process. Be sure to discuss observations or data that aren't well understood or don't fit the theory. Your paper should seek to make an astronomical process accessible and interesting to an average adult.

Do not "dumb down" your topic. Though you may choose to leave out more dry and complex aspects of a process, such as precise temperature ranges or time spans, your essay must be as accurate as possible given existing theories. *Keep it simple but be accurate. Interest*

You should use reputable sources. As we discussed in class, newsmagazines and newspaper articles are fine as supporting sources, but you should make an attempt to get your information "from the horse's mouth." Given the ready availability of astronomical information from NASA and other publicly funded programs, this should not be difficult.
Check NASA

You may use any kind of visual features that you think helps you explain your topic to a general audience. If you reproduce a graph or chart from another source, be sure to cite the source. The same goes for photographs.

Due dates *Have two weeks for research and writing rough draft*
Rough drafts will be due on April 22. We will have peer review in class on that day.
Final drafts are due at the beginning of class on May 6.
Two more weeks to revise

Grading criteria
You will be graded on the accuracy of your descriptions and explanations, the clarity of your writing, your success in appealing to a general audience, and the extent to which grammatical and mechanical considerations help, rather than hinder, your essay.

Assess the assignment

Lakshmi Kotra wrote a report in response to this assignment in her Introduction to Astronomy course. She made the following notes and observations to help determine what her essay needed to accomplish, and to explore how she might find a good topic.

Highlight key words

Lakshmi began by highlighting the words in the assignment that gave her specific information about the writing tasks she was to perform.

Identify goals

Then, she made notes on the assignment sheet to specify what she needed to do.

Note time frame

She also made notes about the time frame she has to work in.

Plan strategy

Lakshmi made notes about possible sources for her paper. Then she sketched out a brief time line to follow.

SOURCES

- Go back over lecture notes—Unit 3 was easiest for me to understand so may be best for a general audience?
- Review theories—what makes an idea a theory; who decides what is the accepted theory?
- See book also, esp. Table of contents, for topic ideas.
- Library subject index
- Online subject index
- Check NASA archives online for good pictures. Maybe categories there would help too.
- Ask Dr. Jenson if we can do something we haven't covered in class yet.

***Get to the library by Friday so topic is ready over the weekend. See if Karen wants to go too. Check reference librarian hours first, just in case.

- Outline over the weekend so I have next week to ask Dr. Jenson for help with the rough draft, if I need it.
- Visuals will help make the essay interesting and appealing to a general audience, and also can help explain. So maybe pick two or three topics and then look at NASA images and other visuals to see what is available. This should help narrow down my choices.

2: Focus Your Topic and Write a Thesis

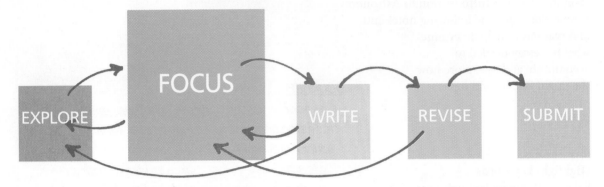

Choose a topic you will enjoy writing about

After you have done preliminary research and collected ideas, it's time to list possible topics and begin making connections. Circle the most interesting possibilities. Writing is fun when you discover new things along the way. If your topic isn't interesting for you, it likely won't be for your readers either.

Choose a topic that your readers will enjoy reading about

Readers may ask, "Why are you telling me this?" Your subject should be interesting to your readers. If the subject isn't one that is immediately interesting, think about ways you can make it so.

Choose a topic that either you know something about or for which you can find the information you need

A central difficulty with writing to inform is determining where to stop. The key to success is to limit the topic. Choose a topic for which you can find the information you need and which you can cover thoroughly in the space you have. If you choose an unfamiliar topic, you must be strongly committed to learning much about it in a short time.

Focus your topic and write a thesis

Look for ways of dividing large topics into smaller categories, and select one that is promising.

1. What is your topic exactly? (Try to state your answer in specific terms.)

   The grassroots revival and rapid spread of roller derby in the 2000s.

2. What points do you want to make about your topic?

   The revival of roller derby changed the character of roller derby from the staged sports entertainment of the 1950s–1970s period to a grassroots, women-organized, participatory sport that emphasizes athleticism.

3. What exactly is your purpose in this project? To analyze? compare? explain?

   Most people don't know about the revival of roller derby, so I will have to introduce the sport and explain who is involved, how it spread, and why it happened.

4. Develop a working thesis that draws on your answers to questions 1 and 2 and that reflects the purpose you described in your answer to question 3.

   The grassroots, women-organized revival and spread of roller derby in the 2000s reflects a new image of women as athletic and empowered.

Evaluate your thesis

Your thesis should fulfill the assignment

If your assignment is informative, your purpose is not to argue something is good or bad (see Chapter 11), not to argue for a position (see Chapter 12), and not to argue for change (see Chapter 13).

OFF TRACK

The electoral college is an antiquated system that results in unfair election results.
(evaluates rather than informs)

ON TRACK

Considering the huge impact the electoral college system has on American presidential elections, it is surprising that few people understand how it actually works.

Your thesis should be interesting

If your readers already know everything that you have to say, you will bore them. Likewise, your thesis should be significant. Readers will care little about what you have to say if they find your subject trivial.

OFF TRACK

There are many steps involved before a bill becomes a law.
(vague, bland)

ON TRACK

Only a tiny fraction of the bills proposed in Congress will ever become laws, and of those, most will accrue so many bizarre amendments and riders that they will barely resemble the original document.

Your thesis should be focused

You cannot tell the story of the Cold War in five pages. Narrow your thesis to a topic you can treat in depth.

OFF TRACK

Many new products were developed in the 1950s to support the boom in housing construction.
(possibly interesting if particular products are described)

ON TRACK

The rush to create new housing for returning WWII veterans in the 1950s resulted in many houses that are now extremely hazardous to live in.

Watch the Animation on Thesis Statements at mycomplab.com **201**

Writer at work

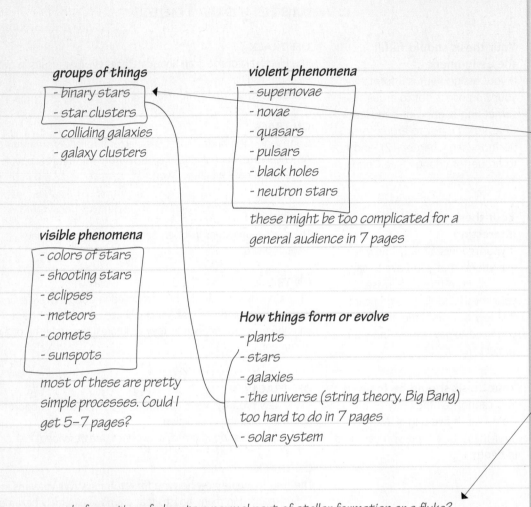

groups of things
- binary stars
- star clusters
- colliding galaxies
- galaxy clusters

violent phenomena
- supernovae
- novae
- quasars
- pulsars
- black holes
- neutron stars

these might be too complicated for a
general audience in 7 pages

visible phenomena
- colors of stars
- shooting stars
- eclipses
- meteors
- comets
- sunspots

most of these are pretty
simple processes. Could I
get 5–7 pages?

How things form or evolve
- plants
- stars
- galaxies
- the universe (string theory, Big Bang)
too hard to do in 7 pages
- solar system

Is formation of planets a normal part of stellar formation or a fluke?
Can binary star systems have planets?
How common are supernovae? Or black holes?
What will happen to the Sun when it runs out of hydrogen?
How do sunspots fit in with atomic processes in stars?
Why do stars start forming in the first place?

Map possible topics

Lakshmi Kotra began by reviewing her class notes and her textbooks. She also looked in the library's online catalog subject index and an online subject index. She listed all the possible topics she came across in these sources. Then she made an idea map of the topics that appealed to her, clustering types of theories, and adding new ones as they occurred to her. She made a few notes on some of her topic areas, describing how well they would meet the needs of her assignment. And she jotted down questions she had about some topics as well.

Narrow the search

Lakshmi narrowed her search by considering how complicated a topic she wanted to take on. Since she had to explain the theory to a general audience, she ruled out topics like black holes and string theory. She noticed that stellar processes showed up several times in her lists of interesting topics.

Identify the topic

Lakshmi settled on stellar formation as a theory that interested her and which she felt confident she could explain in layman's terms. Her preliminary research also indicated there was a wealth of observational data and photos that she could use in her report.

Find images and get source information

Lakshmi wanted to include photographs of star formation, and on NASA's Web site she located images that she could use legally. She carefully recorded all the information she would need to find the images again and to document the images in her paper.

AUTHOR: U.S. National Aeronautics and Space Administration

DATE: April 1, 1995

PAGE TITLE: The Eagle nebula.

SITE TITLE: Great Images in NASA

DATE OF RETRIEVAL: April 5, 2011

URL: http://grin.hq.nasa.gov/ABSTRACTS/ GPN-000987.html

3: Write a Draft

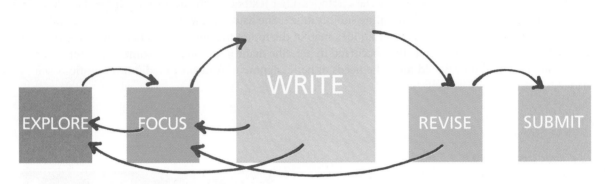

EXPLORE FOCUS WRITE REVISE SUBMIT

Organize your information

Gather your notes and other materials. Think about how you want to convey the information to your readers.

- If your subject matter occurs over time, you might want to use a chronological order.

- If you need to discuss several aspects, identify key concepts and think about how they relate to each other.

- If you are comparing two or more things, think about how these things are similar and how they are different.

Make a working outline

A working outline is a tool that you can use as you write your first draft. The more detailed it is, the better. List the sections in the order that you expect them to appear.

Working thesis: The grassroots, women-organized revival and spread of roller derby in the 2000s reflects a new image of women as athletic and empowered.

1. *Introduction: Give description of bout—loud rock music, noisy crowd, teams of five armored women*

2. *Brief history: began as endurance racing 1880s–1930s. Theatrical sports entertainment like wrestling in 1950s–1970s*

3. *Contemporary revival: Began in 2002 in Austin, Texas—grassroots, strictly amateur, open to women only with emphasis on athleticism*

4. *New image of women: aggressive attitudes, derby names often sexual puns, punk and "bad girl" costumes, lots of tattoos*

5. *Sudden growth in 2006: Reality TV show Rollergirls gave the sport exposure. Many new leagues and spread outside the U.S.*

6. *Move toward mainstream sports: In 2009 players in some leagues start using their real names.*

7. *Conclusion: Will roller derby remain popular or die like it did in the 1970s?*

Think of an effective title

An effective title motivates your readers to want to read what you have written.

DULL:

The Revival of Roller Derby in the 2000s

BETTER:

Tatts, Tutus, and Fishnets: The Grassroots Roller Derby Revival

Stay objective

You may have a strong opinion about your subject, but if your purpose is to inform rather than convince readers of your opinion, stay in the background. Readers appreciate a balanced, objective presentation.

Use quality sources

Unless you are writing about a subject well known to you, likely you will need to library and online research. A well-written report is useless if the information is suspect. See Chapters 20 and 21 for how to find and evaluate sources.

Think about design

Headings are frequent in informative writing, especially in long essays and reports. A list of items usually reads better in numbered or bulleted points. Charts and graphs help readers to understand data, maps help them to understand locations, and photographs let them see what you are talking about.

STAYING ON TRACK

Write an effective introduction and conclusion

Write an effective introduction
Get off to a fast start. Cut to the chase: no empty sentences or big generalizations at the beginning.

OFF TRACK
Because we all live such busy, hectic lives in these modern times, everyone wants to know why we must wait for hours and hours at the airport before boarding a flight.
(boring, predictable beginning—a signal that the paper will be dull)

ON TRACK
It's a traveler's worst nightmare: the long line of people at the security gate, snaking back and forth across the waiting area. What exactly goes on in an airport screening area, and how does it help to keep us safe?

Write an effective conclusion
Remember that a summary of what you have just written is the weakest way to conclude. Think of something interesting for your reader to take away such as an unexpected implication or a provocative example.

OFF TRACK
In conclusion, we have seen how peer-to-peer file sharing works.
(ineffective; says only that the paper is finished)

ON TRACK
The peer-to-peer file sharing process is relatively simple. Unfortunately, in many cases it is also illegal. It is ironic that a technology intended to help people has resulted in turning many of them into *de facto* criminals.
(ends with a significant point, which helps readers remember the paper)

Watch the Animation on Openings to Avoid at mycomplab.com   205

Writer at work

Lakshmi Kotra began with the following rough outline of the process she planned to write about.

Introduction—connect with audience and make them interested
(explain what the clouds are first—composed of what elements?)

I. molecular clouds—collapse begins

will need to explain HOW that happens. No one seems sure so this is a good place to "discuss things that don't fit the theory." Maybe start with one possibility and then describe an alternate explanation in the next paragraph, then go back to process.

II. protostar stage

describe cocoon nebulae—good image

III. fusion begins

will need to explain fusion process

IV. equilibrium

Before getting to equilibrium stage, describe how nebula is blown away and planetary disk forms (for some stars). Mention Earth's origin to interest readers again.

V. death
- ### white dwarfs
- ### supernova

End with supernova to connect back up with interstellar matter/ cycle of star formation.

Conclusion can highlight "cycle," and that can be built in at beginning too.

Think about organization

Lakshmi recognized that the process she was describing naturally lent itself to chronological, or time-order, organization, because one thing has to happen after another for a star to form. However, she found that she had to "break out" from the simple time line of stellar formation at some points, to explain in more detail or to trace multiple possibilities.

> *Stars have a complex and fascinating life cycle. Saying it's fascinating doesn't make it fascinating to readers.*

Make notes on how to develop the subject

She made notes on her outline indicating where she would step away from the chronological pattern to do this explaining. As she considered how she wanted to end her essay, she realized the idea of a "life cycle" for stars could point back toward the essay's beginning. This strategy helped her focus her thesis.

> *Have you ever looked up at the stars at night and wondered why they are there? Vague. Kind of sounds like I'm going to talk about religious or spiritual issues.*

> *Astronomers have spent many years studying the life cycle of stars. So? Anyway, I just want to talk about what they've found, not how long it took them.*

> *If "sunshine on your shoulders" makes you happy, you will be even happier to know that the sun will keep shining for at least another 8 billion years. Too corny. Does anyone even remember that song? Anyway, "happy" isn't the way I want readers to feel. But using a familiar phrase might be good.*

Connect with readers

Lakshmi realized that stellar formation would probably seem like a distant and forbidding topic to a general audience, so she thought carefully about making a connection with her readers. She began by trying out some different ways to introduce her essay. Here are some of her initial attempts and the comments she made on them. Lakshmi decided to work with the last of these openings and see how well she could integrate it with the rest of her essay.

> *"Twinkle, twinkle little star. How I wonder what you are." Good—more personal than "Have you ever looked up at the stars and wondered . . ." Astronomers wonder too. That could be the connection between them and scientists' work. More familiar song, also.*

4: Revise, Revise, Revise

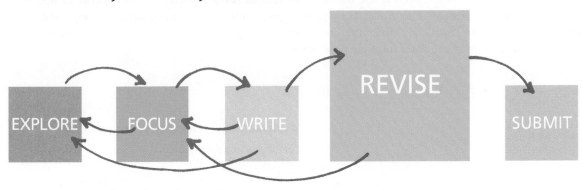

Skilled writers know that the secret to writing well is rewriting. Even the best writers often have to revise several times to get the result they want. You also must have effective strategies for revising if you're going to be successful. The biggest trap you can fall into is starting off with the little stuff first. Leave the small stuff for last.

Does your paper or project meet the assignment?	• Look again at your assignment. Does your paper or project do what the assignment asks? • Look again at the assignment for specific guidelines, including length, format, and amount of research. Does your work meet these guidelines?
Is your title specific?	• Vague titles suggest dull treatment of the topic. Can you make your title more accurate?
Does your writing have a clear focus?	• Does your project have an explicitly stated thesis? If not, is your thesis clearly implied? • Is each paragraph related to your thesis? • Do you get off the track at any point by introducing other topics? • Have you defined all terms that might be unfamiliar to your readers? • Can you add more examples and details that would help to explain your main points?
Is your organization effective?	• Is the order of your main points clear to your reader? • Are there any places where you find abrupt shifts or gaps? • Are there sections or paragraphs that could be rearranged to make your draft more effective?

Is your introduction effective?

- Do you have any general statements that you might cut to get off to a faster start?
- Can you think of a vivid example that might draw in readers?
- Can you use a striking fact to get readers interested?
- Does your introduction make clear where you are headed?

Is your conclusion effective?

- Conclusions that only summarize tend to bore readers. Does your conclusion add anything new to what you've said already?
- Can you use the conclusion to discuss further implications?
- Have you left your audience with a final provocative idea that might invite further discussion?

Do you represent yourself effectively?

- To the extent you can, forget for a moment that you wrote what you are reading. What impression do you have of you, the writer?
- Does "the writer" create an appropriate tone?
- Has "the writer" done his or her homework?

Is the writing project visually effective?

- Is the font attractive and readable?
- Are the headings and visuals effective?

Save the editing for last

- When you have finished revising, edit and proofread carefully.

STAYING ON TRACK

Reviewing your draft

Give yourself plenty of time for reviewing your draft. For detailed information on how to participate in a peer review; how to review it yourself; and how to respond to comments from your classmates, your instructor, or a campus writing consultant, see pages 52–56.

Some good questions to ask yourself when reviewing informative writing

- Are the explanations in the essay easy to follow?
- Are there gaps or places where you feel you need more information?
- Are any unusual or discipline-specific words defined for readers?
- Can the reader construct a clear picture of what the essay describes?
- Is the essay interesting enough to catch readers' attention and keep them reading?

Writer at work

Density increases much faster at the cloud's <u>center</u>

Once a section of a dust cloud starts to collapse, gravity relentlessly pulls the material together into a much smaller area. Gradually, <u>the cloud becomes denser</u> and less cloudlike. At this stage, astronomers refer to the object as a "protostar." For a star the size of our sun, the journey from cloud to protostar may take about 100,000 years (Chaisson and McMillan 429). <u>Bigger clouds of gas will develop faster—but they will also have shorter lives. The larger the star, the faster it uses up its "fuel." But first the fuel must start burning.</u> As the atoms of gas crowd into a smaller and smaller space, they bounce off one another faster and faster, and the protostar heats up. However, it is not a true star yet. That comes later, when nuclear fusion begins. <u>If a cloud segment is less than .08 solar masses, it won't get hot enough, and it will never become a star.</u>

When the protostar is dense enough, its nuclear heart finally starts to beat. This happens when hydrogen atoms are pushed close enough together to fuse into helium. This requires a total of six hydrogen atoms, which must combine in a specific sequence: hydrogen—deuterium—helium 3—helium + hydrogen. Every time fusion takes place, a small amount of energy is released.

You bring up a number of concepts here that don"t quite fit with the main idea of the paragraph. It might make sense to move the information about mass and lifespan to later in the paper

The "sequence" isn't clear. Can you break this down into simpler steps?

Read carefully your instructor's comments

Lakshmi Kotra gave a copy of her first draft to her instructor for feedback. She used his comments to guide her revision of the essay.

Determine a plan for revision in light of your instructor's comments

Based on her instructor's comments, Lakshmi decided to shift some information on the rates at which stars burn nuclear fuel from an earlier section of the paper to her later discussion of the fates of stars with different masses. This strategy also allowed her to flesh out the description of "brown dwarfs"—starlike objects that do not develop into stars.

Act on specific comments

She also took her instructor's advice about simplifying her explanation of hydrogen fusion.

Read your paper aloud to catch mistakes and awkward phrasing

Lakshmi also read her essay aloud to help identify spelling errors and missing or poorly chosen words.

Visit your writing center

Finally, Lakshmi visited her school's writing center. She asked for specific help in making the paper accessible for an audience without a scientific background. Working with a consultant, she recognized the need to define scientific terms, like *nebulae, protostar,* and *equilibrium,* that might not be familiar to a general audience.

5: Submitted Version

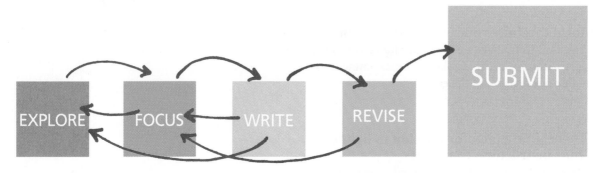

Kotra 1

Lakshmi Kotra

Professor Jenson

Astronomy 101

6 May 2011

The Life Cycle of Stars

"Twinkle, twinkle, little star; how I wonder what you are." This old nursery rhyme may not seem profound, but it echoes some of the biggest questions astronomers puzzle over: What are stars made of? How do they form? How are they born and how do they die? Current theories of star formation answer some of these questions, but not all of them. We do know that, even though stars are separated from one another by vast amounts of space, their life cycles are intertwined.

Twinkling stars are born in dark, cold clouds of dust and gas called nebulae. These clouds consist mainly of hydrogen, and may be as cold as 10 degrees Kelvin (Chaisson and McMillan 427). Nebulae are very dense compared to the near-vacuum of interstellar space. But something must concentrate this dust and gas even more if a star is to form. This first part of the star-forming process is not fully understood. Some force has to cause a portion of the nebula to begin collapsing. Magnetism and rotation are two forces already at work in most clouds, but astronomers have long thought that these forces are more likely to counteract the collapsing force of gravity (Chaisson and McMillan 427). However, new research may have found a solution to this problem. In some clouds, magnetic fields may cancel out some or all of the rotational force. This reorganization would allow gravity to begin collapsing the star (Farivar).

Another theory is that a shock wave from some outside event or object might trigger the collapse of a cloud. The Eagle Nebula provides a good illustration of this theory. Ultraviolet radiation from super-hot stars in the nebula has been observed bombarding the surrounding dust and gas. The radiation has stripped away a lot of dust but left dense columns of cloud where stars are believed to be forming. The impact of this "stellar wind" may have also triggered the star formation. Smaller clumps of denser gas are contracting within the columns, taking their first step on the journey to stardom (see fig. 1).

Once a section of a dust cloud starts to collapse, gravity relentlessly pulls the material together into a much smaller area. Gradually, the center of the cloud becomes denser and less cloudlike. At this stage, astronomers refer to the object as a "protostar." For a star the size of our sun, the journey from cloud to protostar may take about 100,000 years (Chaisson and McMillan 429). As the atoms of gas crowd into a smaller and smaller space, they bounce off one another faster and faster, and the protostar heats up. However, it is not a true star yet. That comes later, when nuclear fusion begins. For now,

Fig. 1. Eagle Nebula
The columns of interstellar gas in the Eagle Nebula are incubators for new stars (US, NASA, "Eagle").

the developing protostar is still surrounded by a shroud of dust that hides it from view. This dust mantle is called a cocoon nebula. Some protostars can be detected by the infrared glow of their cocoon nebulae (Chaisson and McMillan 435–36).

Over millions of years, the protostar continues to grow and change, like a butterfly in its cocoon. Gravity keeps compacting it, making it smaller in size and denser. When the protostar is dense enough, its nuclear heart finally starts to beat. This happens when hydrogen atoms are pushed close enough together to fuse into helium. The fusion process involves several steps. First, two hydrogen atoms will fuse to form an atom of deuterium, or heavy hydrogen. When a third hydrogen atom joins the deuterium atom, an isotope called helium 3 results.

Finally, when two helium 3 atoms fuse together, an atom of regular helium plus two of hydrogen are created. But the crucial part of this process is that, every time fusion takes place, a small amount of energy is released. The radiation emitted from the fusion of hydrogen into helium is what makes the majority of stars shine. Fusion radiation from the Sun lights our planet in the daytime, makes the moon shine at night—and gives you sunburn.

Hydrogen atoms must be moving at extremely high speeds in order to fuse. Another way to say this is that the temperature in the core of a protostar must be very high for fusion to take place: at least 10 million degrees Kelvin (Chaisson and McMillan 431). Now nuclear forces, not just gravity's grip, are controlling the star's development. In fact, these two forces will compete throughout the star's life. Gravity tries to collapse the star, while the pressure of its fast-moving, superheated atoms pushes it outward. As long as the two forces balance each other, the star will remain stable. Astronomers call this state "equilibrium."

During the intense heating at the end of the protostar stage, and when hydrogen fusion is beginning, intense radiation streams off the young star. The dust and gas that have surrounded the protostar are swept away by this energy bombardment, and the star emerges from its cocoon. This phenomenon can be observed visually in NGC 4214. Young stars in this nebula are pouring out radiation that has created "bubbles" in the surrounding gas. Brighter and older stars have pushed away more of the dust and gas. The bubbles around these stars are bigger than those around younger or cooler stars in the nebula (see fig. 2).

Sometimes, not all of a protostar's dust cocoon blows away. According to one theory, you can look around our own solar system and see the remnants of the dust that once surrounded our Sun. In fact, you are standing on some of it. The Earth and the rest of the planets in our solar system are believed to have formed from a disk of dust and gas left over after the sun formed. The reasons this happens are not entirely clear, but astronomers now think that many stellar systems have planetary disks around them. The Orion Nebula provides some confirmation of this theory. There, astronomers have observed many glowing disks of dust, called "proplyds." They think these disks are actually young stars surrounded by material that will eventually form a system of orbiting planets (see fig. 3).

Fig. 2. Star Formation
Clusters of new stars form from interstellar gas and dust in galaxy
NGC 4214 (US, NASA, "Star").

Kotra 6

The size of the original dust cloud a star is born from will also determine how it dies. Some protostars don't quite have what it takes to become a star. Clumps of dust and gas that are smaller than .08 solar masses never get hot enough to begin fusing hydrogen (Chaisson and McMillan 433). These "brown dwarfs" produce infrared radiation, but they never shine visibly.

True stars burn through their nuclear fuel at different rates. The larger the star, the faster its fuel is fused. Smaller stars, like our Sun, are called "dwarf stars." If they began life with less than eight times the mass of our Sun, they will quietly burn hydrogen for perhaps ten billion years. Toward the end of their lives, as they begin to run out of

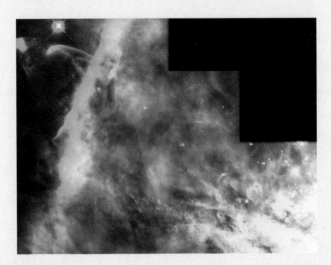

Fig. 3. Orion Nebula

This composite photo of the Orion nebula assembled from images taken by the Hubble Space Telescope shows the beginnings of new solar systems surrounding young stars (US, NASA, "Orion").

fuel, they will swell briefly into red giant stars, fusing their helium into carbon, and cooling substantially. Finally, they will subside into "white dwarf" stars, about the size of the planet Earth. Provided they do not have nearby neighboring stars that might interact with them, white dwarfs gradually dim and cool, until they go dark altogether (Chaisson and McMillan 459). This cooling process is what astronomers predict will some day happen to our Sun.

A star of more than about eight solar masses has a shorter but much more spectacular life. It will fuse all its available fuel in well under one billion years—perhaps in as little as one million years. When a giant star has run through all its available nuclear fuel, it develops a core of iron atoms, which cannot be fused into anything else. When this core has grown to about 1.4 solar masses, the star will explode in a supernova. All that will be left of the original star is a dark neutron star or black hole (Chaisson and McMillan 475). But the shock wave from the supernova may go on to trigger new star formation in dust clouds nearby. In this way, dying stars contribute to the birth of new ones, and the life cycle of stars continues.

Kotra 8

Works Cited

Chaisson, Eric, and Steve McMillan. *Astronomy Today*. 6th ed. Upper
Saddle River: Prentice, 2008. Print.

Farivar, Cyrus. "Galactic Map Aids Stellar Formation Theory." *Daily
Californian*. Daily Californian, 23 Jan. 2002. Web. 8 Apr. 2011.

United States. National Aeronautics and Space Adm. "The Eagle
Nebula." Photograph. *Great Images in NASA*. 1. Apr. 1995. Web. 8
Apr. 2011.

---. ---. "Fireworks of Star Formation Light Up a Galaxy." Photograph.
Great Images in NASA. 6 Jan. 2000. Web. 8 Apr. 2011.

---. ---. "The Orion Nebula." Photograph. *Great Images in NASA*. 20
Nov. 1995. Web. 8 Apr. 2011.

Projects

No matter how diverse its forms, successful informative writing begins with the basics.

- What do readers already know about a subject?
- What do readers need to know about a subject?
- What kind of writing is best suited for particular readers?

Instructions

Be aware that instructions are much harder to write than most people expect. They usually require a lot of detail, yet if they are too complex, people will be confused or intimidated.

Think of a fairly simple device you have learned to use, like an smart phone or an app.

Write a one- or two-page set of instructions explaining how to perform a simple task, such as creating a play list on your smart phone, using your school's Web-based e-mail service, or changing the toner cartridge in your printer. When you are finished, have a friend volunteer to try out your instructions. How easy is it to follow them? Do they work?

Profile of an individual

Choose a person to profile. The more interesting the person, the more interesting your profile will be. Make a list of possible people. Think about people who are known in your community such as politicians, business leaders, athletes, musicians, and other entertainers. Also think of people who have unusual occupations or unusual hobbies, complex life histories, or who have overcome challenges.

Arrange to interview the person at a time and place comfortable for the person. Ask if you can bring a digital recorder and a camera.

Find out as much as you can about the person before the interview. See if the person shows up on a Google search. If the person is in the public eye, use the LexisNexis database or other databases for newspapers (see pages 570–571) to learn what has been written about the person.

Prepare questions in advance (see page 587). Take brief notes during the interview. If you record the interview, transcribe the parts that you find important.

Decide what is most interesting about the person and make that the focus of your profile. Choose the details and quotations that are the most vivid. Then think about how you will organize your profile. Will you give the person's background first or will you start with your interview and work in the background later?

Apply the Concept of Writing to Inform at mycomplab.com

Report

Think of a subject you know a great deal about but most other people, especially those who are your intended readers, do not.

Your subject might come from your life experience

- What's it like to grow up on a family farm?
- What's it like to be an immigrant to the United States?

Your hobbies

- What's the best way to train for a marathon?
- How can you avoid injuries in sports by stretching?

Your personal interests

- Why everyone over age 20 should pay attention to cholesterol

A place that you have found fascinating, or a subject you have studied in college

- The misunderstood nature of conceptual art
- Breakthroughs in nanotechnology in the near future.

Consider what will likely be most interesting about your subject to your readers.

Engage your readers with a provocative title and a thesis that will challenge them to think about your subject in new ways.

Aim for a report of 700–1000 words or about 3–4 double-spaced pages.

Informative audio podcast

Listen to a few informative audio podcasts such as *This American Life* on Public Radio International. Pay attention to how they are organized and how narrators use their voices to signal key points, transitions, and conclusions.

Make a list of possible topics for your podcast. Think about possibilities on your campus, such as the history of a building or the research of a professor whom you could interview. Think about possibilities in your community such as an interesting nonprofit organization or hobby. Then think about the rhetorical situation. Who would be the likely audience?

Conduct research on the topic of your podcast. You may need to interview people in addition to library and online research. Make a working outline for the major segments of your podcast (see page 39).

Learn to use an audio editor. You may have one such as GarageBand installed already on your computer or you may download an open-source editor.

Write and record your podcast. If you have clips from interviews, insert them into your audio file. Next, listen to your podcast and revise.

For support in learning this chapter's content, follow this path in mycomplab:

▶ **Resources** ▶ **Writing** ▶ **Writing Purposes** ▶ **Writing to Inform**

Review the Instruction and Multimedia resources, then complete the **Exercises** and click on **Gradebook** to measure your progress

9 Rhetorical, Visual, and Literary Analyses

Every piece of writing, every painting, every building, every movie, every new product, every advertisement is a response to what came before it.

Chapter Overview

Writing an Analysis

Critical reading and viewing are essential skills for all kinds of writing. Analysis is a more specific aim where those critical reading and viewing skills are applied to particular subjects. Analysis involves dividing a whole into parts that can be studied both as individual entities and as parts of the whole.

Rhetorical analysis is a kind of analysis that divides a whole into parts to understand how an act of speaking or writing conveys meaning. *Visual analysis* is closely related to rhetorical analysis. The tools of rhetorical analysis have been applied to understanding how other human creations make meaning. The goal of *literary analysis* is to interpret a literary text and support that interpretation with evidence or, more simply, to make a discovery about a text that you share with your readers.

A rhetorical, visual, or literary analysis may be concerned with either text or context, but often it examines both. Textual analysis focuses on the features of a text. Contextual analysis reconstructs the cultural environment, or context.

Keys to analyses

ANALYZE THE TEXT	• What is the subject? • What are the main ideas? • What is the genre? a newspaper article? a short story? a documentary film? • What appeals are used? What facts or evidence does the author present? • How is the text organized? • What style does the author use?
ANALYZE THE CONTEXT	• Who is the author? What else has the author written or said on this subject? What motivated the author to address this issue? • Who is the audience? What is the occasion and forum? • What is the larger conversation? When did the text appear? Why did it appear at that particular moment? Who or what might this text be responding to?

Analyses in the world

Analyses are basic tools for all academic disciplines, which seek to break down complex subjects into smaller parts in order to gain a better understanding. Methods of analysis vary widely across disciplines.

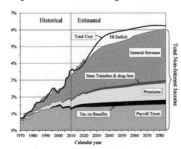

Other genres of analyses
• **Intelligence analyses** are used by business, law enforcement, and the military to inform planners.
• **Engineering analyses** employ scientific principles to understand how components interact in a system.
• **Business analyses** identify problems and opportunities.

223

Writing a Rhetorical Analysis

People often use the term *rhetoric* to describe empty language. "The governor's speech was just a bunch of rhetoric," you might say, meaning that the governor offered noble-sounding words but no real ideas. But rhetoric originated with a much more positive meaning. According to Aristotle, rhetoric is "the art of finding in any given case the available means of persuasion." Rhetoric is concerned with producing effective pieces of communication.

Keys to rhetorical analysis

IDENTIFY THE PURPOSE	• Some texts have an obvious purpose; for example, an ad wants you to buy something. • But texts can have more than one purpose. • The most effective texts are ones that are tailored specifically for an audience.
EXAMINE THE AUDIENCE	• What can you determine about the actual audience's values, attitudes, and beliefs?
EXAMINE THE AUTHOR	• How did the author come to this subject? • Is the author an expert or an outsider?
EXAMINE THE LARGER CONTEXT	• What else has been said or written on this topic? • What was going on at the time that influenced this text?
ANALYZE THE RHETORICAL APPEALS	• Aristotle set out three primary tactics of argument: appeals based on the trustworthiness of the speaker (ethos), appeals to good reasons (Logos), and appeals to the emotions and deepest held values of the audience (pathos).
EXAMINE THE LANGUAGE AND STYLE	• Is the style formal? informal? academic? • Does the writer or speaker use humor or satire? • What metaphors are used?

What makes a good rhetorical analysis?

1

Find an interesting text

Select a text that will be interesting both to you (perhaps because of the subject) and to your readers (perhaps because the text does something unusual with words and images).

2

Write a descriptive title and precise thesis

The title of your essay should indicate the focus of your analysis. Make sure your thesis is sensible and realistic as well as being supported by evidence and examples in the text.

3

Analyze the immediate context

- Who is the author? Learn all you can about the author. Has the author written anything similar? What was the author's purpose?

- Who is the audience? Learn all you can about the original publication or the occasion for your text.

- What are the medium and genre? What expectations would the audience have about this genre?

4

Analyze the larger context

Through research, find out what else was being said about the subject of your text. What other pieces of "cultural conversation" (e.g., TV shows, speeches, editorials, films) does your text reference or respond to?

5

Analyze the appeals used

- Analyze the ethos. How does the writer represent herself or himself? Do you trust the writer?

- Analyze the Logos. Where do you find facts and evidence in the argument? What kinds of facts and evidence are presented?

- Analyze the pathos. Does the writer attempt to invoke an emotional response? Where do you find appeals to shared values?

6

Analyze the language and style

Is the style formal, informal, satirical, or something else? Are any metaphors used?

WRITE NOW

Analyze a public speech

You can locate public speeches on several Web sites, including www.americanrhetoric.com. After answering the questions below, formulate a thesis for a rhetorical analysis.

1. What is the rhetorical purpose?
2. Who is the audience?
3. How does the speaker gain (or not gain) credibility?
4. What is the background of the speech?
5. What appeals does the speaker use?
6. How formal or informal is the style?
7. What metaphors does the speaker use?

 Study a Rhetorical Analysis at mycomplab.com

Writing a Visual Analysis

We are bombarded by images on a daily basis. They compete for our attention, urge us to buy things, and guide us on our way home from work. These visual texts frequently attempt to persuade us, to make us think, feel, or act a certain way. Yet we rarely stop to consider how they do their work.

Visual texts leave room for the audience to interpret to a greater degree than many verbal texts, which make them particularly rich subjects for analysis.

Keys to visual analysis

CHOOSE A VISUAL TEXT THAT YOU CARE ABOUT	If an image or other visual text means something to you, you will find it easier to analyze.
PAY CLOSE ATTENTION TO DETAILS	Identify the key details that keep the viewer's attention and convey meaning. Also, examine the point of view—the viewer's perspective of the subject.
PROVIDE A FRAME FOR UNDERSTANDING	Provide a context for understanding a visual text, giving a sense of how it is a response to events and trends going on at the time and how it was initially understood.
GO BEYOND THE OBVIOUS	A successful visual analysis gets readers to make connections and see aspects that they otherwise would not have noticed.

What makes a good visual analysis

1
Describe what you see
Is it a single image, part of a series, a sign, a building, or something else? What are the conventions for this kind of visual?

2
Analyze the composition
What elements are most prominent? Which are repeated? Which are balanced or in contrast to each other? Which details are important?

3
Examine the context
Who created the image? When and where did it first appear? Can you determine why it was created?

4
Look for connections
What is the genre? What kind of visual is it? What elements have you seen before? Which remind you of other visuals?

WRITE NOW

Analyze a print or web ad

Find a visually striking advertisement that combines words and images. Analyze how the words and images work together to persuade. To succeed with this assignment, you will need to find an ad that supports an extended analysis.

1. What is the ad really trying to sell? Often it is not a specific product but a brand.

2. Analyze the text of the ad. Is it a single image or part of a series? What does the image depict? Does it employ a visual metaphor (such as the overused images of a fried egg as your brain on drugs)? How do the words influence what you see? What elements are most prominent? What is the primary appeal used in the ad: appeals to emotions and values (pathos), appeals to the brand a celebrity featured in the ad (ethos), or appeals to good reasons such as the gas mileage of a hybrid car (logos)?

3. Analyze the context of the ad. Where was it published? What else appears on the Web site or magazine where you found the ad? What other ads are like it? Many ads make reference to other ads. What do you know about the advertising of this particular company or organization?

4. How ultimately persuasive is the ad?

This WWF ad uses the visual metaphor of a forest as lungs. Cutting trees decays our lungs. The words "Before it's too late" reinforce the message.

Writing a Literary Analysis

A literary analysis takes different forms. One form is to analyze patterns, such as how the repetition of particular images and even words contributes to the meaning. Another form is to pose a problem, such as why a particular character behaves in an odd way or why the narrator leaves out key information. Another approach is to use comparison and contrast to provide an analysis of two characters, two works of literature, or any pairs that help readers gain insight into a work. Finally, you can use one or more critical strategies as your approach. By using biographical criticism, for example, you might show how the life and times of the author shaped the literary work you are studying.

For an example of literary analysis, see pages 256–257.

Keys to a literary analysis

DEVELOP AN INTERPRETATION	Interpretations come from an in-depth examination of a literary work. Your thesis states your main interpretive claim about the work.
PROVIDE AS MUCH RELEVANT EVIDENCE AS POSSIBLE	You must show that your thesis and interpretation are supported by evidence from the text. Cite precise passages from the work and refer to specific details.
USE LITERARY CONCEPTS	Take into account literary concepts such as character, setting, theme, motif, symbol, point of view, and imagery to express your ideas. Your analysis will likely answer such questions as: who are the characters, what is the setting and what role does it play, what are themes or motifs in the text, from what point of view is the work told, what language choices are made, and what is the significance of the title?
AVOID PLOT SUMMARIES	Do not give plot summaries unless the summary relates directly to your thesis. Remember a plot summary is not an interpretation nor is it an arguable thesis.

What makes a good literary analysis?

1

Start with a close reading

Examine carefully the plot of your short story or novel, the characters, the setting, patterns of language, imagery, and metaphors. If you are analyzing a poem, study how the individual words and images connect to shape your interpretation.

2

Evaluate and revise your thesis

Make sure your thesis is specific and significant. If you identify a pattern but say nothing about why it is important, your reader will ask "So what?" What does the pattern contribute to an overall interpretation?

3

Select your evidence and examples with an eye on your thesis

Make sure your evidence and examples are relevant to your thesis. Explain the significance of the evidence for your thesis.

4

Integrate quotations from your text into your project

Quotations are critical to support your analysis, but they must be connected to your ideas and not dropped in (see pages 599–601).

5

Use the present tense

In writing about literature, refer to events in the present tense.

5

Document carefully

You will be quoting from the literary text and perhaps using secondary sources as well. Be sure to document your sources carefully using the MLA format.

WRITE NOW

Analyze characters in a literary work

A character analysis is assigned frequently in courses that examine literature. To begin a character analysis, make notes on the following:

1. Identify the main characters. Key characters are the protagonist—the main character—and the antagonist—the character who struggles against the main character.

2. Describe elements of the characters.
   Appearance: How does the character look?
   Personality: How does the character act?
   Motives: What does the character seek?
   Background: What in the character's past might explain current motives?
   Conflicts: What conflicts does the character have? internal conflicts? conflicts with other people? conflicts with nature?
   Choices: Does the character make good or bad choices?
   Change: How does the character change or does the character remain static?

Watch the Animation on Using Quotations at mycomplab.com

How to Read Analyses

▼ BEFORE YOU BEGIN READING

These notes are in response to "Straight from the Heart"; the reading begins on page 232

What kind of text is it?	*Collins's essay is a rhetorical analysis of a speech. It was published in 2005 in* The Guardian, *a leading British newspaper that is read widely around the world.*
Who wrote it?	*Tim Collins served as a colonel in the British Army, and in 2003 he gave a moving speech to his soldiers in Iraq before they entered battle that earned international acclaim.*
Who is the intended audience?	The Guardian *appeals to a general audience interested in current events.*

▼ READ THE TEXT AT LEAST TWICE AND MAKE NOTES

What is the focus of the analysis?	*Collins announces in the first paragraph that his focus is Marie Fatayi-Williams's extemporaneous speech on losing her son to a terrorist's bomb.*
What is the significance of the analysis?	*Collins asserts that Fatayi-Williams gives voice to the pain suffered by the people of Britain in the 2005 terrorist attack. Collins also examines how people can give eloquent speeches spontaneously in times of crisis.*
How does the writer represent himself or herself?	*Collins represents himself as deeply involved through his personal history of serving as a commanding officer in war.*
How would you characterize the style?	*Collins's style is both analytical and personal—the latter because he connects his own experience of speaking to soldiers on the eve of the Iraq war to Marie Fatayi-Williams's outcry over the loss of her son.*

How is it organized?

This map shows the organization of "Straight from the Heart," which begins on the following page.

Beginning paragraph
Paragraph 1

> Collins identifies Marie Fatayi-Williams' speech as the subject of his analysis.

Background
Paragraph 2

> Collins reports the tragic circumstances of Fatayi-Williams' speech.

Genre
Paragraph 3

> The genre is speech delivered on a momentous occasion that is intended to inspire others to action.

Analysis of rhetorical techniques
Paragraph 4

> Collins analyzes the form and language of Fatayi-Williams' speech. Allusions to the Bible and the Koran connect the speech to a long tradition.

Analysis of the occasion
Paragraph 5

> Collins brings in his own experience of speaking from the heart in a time of crisis, which gives him credibility.

Analysis of ethos
Paragraph 6

> Collins analyzes why Fatayi-Williams is convincing.

Analysis of the significance
Paragraph 7-9

> Collins finds the speech to be of lasting importance for giving comfort to the victims and challenging the goals of terrorism.

Mary Fatayi-Williams' speech
Paragraph 10ff

> Fatayi-Williams asks what terrorism accomplishes and concludes with a plea to end hatred.

Straight from the Heart
Tim Collins

On July 11, 2005, Marie Fatayi-Williams made an immensely moving speech in London at the site where her son Anthony had been killed in a terrorist bombing four days earlier. Her speech was reported in numerous media outlets. The *Guardian*, a British newspaper, printed Fatayi-Williams's speech on July 13, with an analysis and commentary by Tim Collins. Collins considers the factors that make Fatayi-Williams's speech so powerful, and places it in a larger context of responses to terrorism.

1   Caught in the spotlight of history, set on the stage of a very public event, Marie Fatayi-Williams, the mother of Anthony Fatayi-Williams, 26 and missing since Thursday, appeals for news of her son. Her words are a mixture of stirring rhetoric, heartfelt appeal and a stateswoman-like vision, and so speak on many levels to the nation and the world. Her appeal is a simple one—where is my son? If he has been killed, then why? Who has gained?

> **Introduction:**
> The subject is announced in the first sentence.

> **Analysis of rhetorical appeals:**
> Collins points out the appeal to pathos—the beliefs and values of the audience—that lies at the heart of Fatayi-Williams's speech.

2   Marie has found herself, as I did on the eve of the invasion of Iraq, an unwitting voice, speaking amid momentous events. Her appeal, delivered on Monday not far from Tavistock Square, where she fears her son died in the bomb attack on the number 30 bus, gives a verbal form to the whirlpool of emotions that have engulfed society as the result of last week's bombings. I suspect Marie, like myself, had no idea that her words would find such wide recognition, have fed such an acute hunger for explanation, have slaked such a thirst for expression of the sheer horror of Thursday's events.

3   This kind of speech is normally the preserve of the great orators, statesmen and playwrights, of Shakespeare, Churchill or Lincoln. It is often a single speech, a soliloquy or address from the steps of the gallows, that explains, inspires, exhorts and challenges. But always such addresses are crafted for effect and consciously intended to sway and influence, and often, as in the case of Shakespeare's Henry V, they are set in the mouth of a long dead hero or delivered by wordsmiths who are masters of their craft. It is rare in history that such oratory is the genuine article, springing from the

> **Genre:**
> Collins identifies the genre of the speech, which is usually crafted for a specific occasion. Marie's speech is remarkable because it is spontaneous.

heart and bursting forth to an unwitting audience. In Marie's case, her speech gains its power as a vehicle of grief and loss, and of the angst of a mother who yearns for her beloved son. In my case it was the opposite emotion from which I drew inspiration—an appeal to understand, to empathize, to give courage and purpose. I was motivated by a need to warn and teach as well as to encourage. Marie's motivation is a reflection on loss and that most powerful of all emotions, a mother's love.

4 The form the address takes is as poignant as the language used. There is an initial explanation of the extraordinary circumstances of the loss, a cri de coeur for the innocent blood lost, a rejection of the act by its comparison to the great liberators, and the assertion that her loss is all our loss in the family of humanity. It ends with her personal grief for her flesh and blood, her hopes and pride. The language echoes verses of the Bible as well as from the Koran. It has raw passion as well as heart-rending pathos.

Style:
Several rhetorical techniques used in the speech connect it to a larger historical tradition.

5 With only a photograph of her son and a sheet of paper as a prompt, Marie's words burst out with as much emotion as anger. Her speech stands in stark contrast to the pronouncements of politicians, prepared by aides and delivered from copious notes. It is indeed the raw originality and authentic angst that give the delivery such impact, the plea such effect. No knighted veteran of the Royal Shakespeare Company could deliver such an address without hours or even days of rehearsal. I know from my own experience that only momentous events can provoke such a moment, only raw emotion can inspire such a spontaneous plea. I am often asked how long it took me to write my speech, delivered to my regiment, the Royal Irish, on the eve of the invasion of Iraq on March 19, 2003, at Fort Blair Mayne camp in the Kuwaiti desert. My answer is simple— not one moment. There was no plan; I spoke without notes. For me there was only the looming specter of actual warfare and the certainty of loss and killing, and I was speaking to myself as well as to my men. I suspect for Marie there was only the yawning black void of loss, the cavern left behind in her life caused by the loss of a son who can never be replaced.

Personal connection:
Collins's own experience informs his understanding of what Fatayi-Williams might have been feeling. This helps assure his audience that he is qualified to comment on the meaning of her speech.

6 What, then, can we take from this? Marie's appeal is as important as it is momentous. Her words are as free from hatred as they are free from self-interest; it is clear that no man can give her her heart's desire—her son. I was also struck by the quiet dignity of her words, the clarity of her view and the weight of her convictions. She does not condemn, she appeals; her words act as an indictment of all war and violence, not just acts of terror but also the unnecessary aggression of nation states. Her message is simple: here is a human who only wanted to give, to succeed and to make his mother proud. Where is the victory in his death? Where is the progress in his destruction? In her own words: "What inspiration can senseless slaughter provide?"

> **Analysis of rhetorical appeals:** Collins examines how Marie creates her ethos, which convinces her audience of her sincerity and lack of malice.

7 I am certain that Marie's appeal will go down as one of the great speeches of our new century. It will give comfort to the families and friends of the dead and injured, both of this act and no doubt, regrettably, of events still to come. It should act as a caution to statesmen and leaders, a focus for public grief and, ultimately, as a challenge to, as well as a condemnation of, the perpetrators.

> **Style:** Collins sees Fatayi-Williams's directness as perhaps the most important aspect of her speech. She responds to historic events in a way that personalizes them and shows their human cost.

8 Marie is already an icon of the loss of Thursday July 7. Having travelled from Africa to find a better life, Anthony Fatayi-Williams carried the hopes and pride of his family. Now, as his mother has traveled to London, arguably one of the most cosmopolitan and integrated cities in the world, and standing nearby a wrecked icon of that city, a red double-decker bus, she has made an appeal which is as haunting as it is relevant, as poignant as it is appealing. It is a fact that such oratory as both Marie and I produced is born of momentous events, and inspired by hope and fears in equal measure.

9 But Marie's appeal is also important on another level. I have long urged soldiers in conflict zones to keep communicating with the population in order to be seen as people—it is easier to kill uniforms than it is to kill people. On July 7 the suicide bombers attacked icons of a society that they hated more than they loved life, the red London bus and the tube. Marie's speech has stressed the real victims' identities. They are all of us.

Marie's speech

10 This is Anthony, Anthony Fatayi-Williams, 26 years old, he's missing and we fear that he was in the bus explosion ... on Thursday. We don't know. We do know from the witnesses that he left the Northern line in Euston. We know he made a call to his office at Amec at 9.41 from the NW1 area to say he could not make [it] by the tube but he would find alternative means to work.

Marie Fatayi-Williams

Marie Fatayi-Williams' speech: She begins with the fact that her son is missing. She asks poignantly what terrorism accomplishes, and she concludes with a plea to end hatred.

11 Since then he has not made any contact with any single person. Not New York, not Madrid, not London. There has been widespread slaughter of innocent people. There have been streams of tears, innocent tears. There have been rivers of blood, innocent blood. Death in the morning, people going to find their livelihood, death in the noontime on the highways and streets.

12 They are not warriors. Which cause has been served? Certainly not the cause of God, not the cause of Allah because God Almighty only gives life and is full of mercy. Anyone who has been misled, or is being misled to believe that by killing innocent people he or she is serving God should think again because it's not true. Terrorism is not the way, terrorism is not the way. It doesn't beget peace. We can't deliver peace by terrorism, never can we deliver peace by killing people. Throughout history, those people who have changed the world have done so without violence, they have won people to their cause through peaceful protest. Nelson Mandela, Martin Luther King, Mahatma Gandhi, their discipline, their self-sacrifice, their conviction made people turn towards them, to follow them. What inspiration can senseless slaughter provide? Death and destruction of young people in their prime as well as old and helpless can never be the foundations for building society.

13 My son Anthony is my first son, my only son, the head of my family. In African society, we hold on to sons. He has dreams and hopes and I, his mother, must fight to protect them. This is now the fifth day, five days on, and we are waiting to know what happened

to him and I, his mother, I need to know what happened to Anthony. His young sisters need to know what happened, his uncles and aunties need to know what happened to Anthony, his father needs to know what happened to Anthony. Millions of my friends back home in Nigeria need to know what happened to Anthony. His friends surrounding me here, who have put this together, need to know what has happened to Anthony. I need to know, I want to protect him. I'm his mother, I will fight till I die to protect him. To protect his values and to protect his memory.

14 Innocent blood will always cry to God Almighty for reparation. How much blood must be spilled? How many tears shall we cry? How many mothers' hearts must be maimed? My heart is maimed. I pray I will see my son, Anthony. Why? I need to know, Anthony needs to know, Anthony needs to know, so do many other unaccounted for innocent victims, they need to know.

15 It's time to stop and think. We cannot live in fear because we are surrounded by hatred. Look around us today. Anthony is a Nigerian, born in London, worked in London, he is a world citizen. Here today we have Christians, Muslims, Jews, Sikhs, Hindus, all of us united in love for Anthony. Hatred begets only hatred. It is time to stop this vicious cycle of killing. We must all stand together, for our common humanity. I need to know what happened to my Anthony. He's the love of my life. My first son, my first son, 26. He tells me one day, "Mummy, I don't want to die, I don't want to die. I want to live, I want to take care of you, I will do great things for you, I will look after you, you will see what I will achieve for you. I will make you happy." And he was making me happy. I am proud of him, I am still very proud of him but I need to now where he is, I need to know what happened to him. I grieve, I am sad, I am distraught, I am destroyed.

16 He didn't do anything to anybody, he loved everybody so much. If what I hear is true, even when he came out of the underground he was directing people to take buses, to be sure that they were OK. Then he called his office at the same time to tell them he was running late. He was a multi-purpose person, trying to save people, trying to call his office, trying to meet his appointments. What did he then do to deserve this? Where is he, someone tell me, where is he?

The Collapse of Big Media: The Young and the Restless
David T. Z. Mindich

David T. Z. Mindich, a former assignment editor at CNN, holds a Ph.D. in American studies from New York University. In addition, he is chair of the journalism and mass communication department at St. Michael's College in Colchester, Vermont, and the author of *Tuned Out: Why Americans under 40 Don't Follow the News* (2005). "The Collapse of Big Media: The Young and the Restless" was published in the *Wilson Quarterly* in spring 2005.

Return to these questions after you have finished reading.

Analyzing the Reading

1. What is Mindich's thesis? What kind of evidence does he provide to support the points he makes? Is his evidence persuasive?

2. What does the author say are the causes of the situation he writes about? What evidence does he give to support his analysis of causes? Is the evidence persuasive?

3. At the end of the essay, the author makes some recommendations? What are these? Do these recommendations seem valuable?

4. What are the author's credentials? Do the author and the publication seem to be reliable sources of information and analysis?

Exploring Ideas and Issues

The Founding Fathers of the United States thought so highly of the role of a free press in a democracy that they enshrined that right in the First Amendment to the Constitution. Over the centuries, the press has changed in a number of ways—not the least of which is technologically—but its role as a "watchdog" has remained throughout.

Possibilities for Writing

1. Make a log for one entire day on all the news you read, watch, or listen to: newspapers, radio, television news broadcasts, comedy reporting of news like *The Daily Show,* comic monologues commenting on events, news flashes at the bottom of other television programs, news on the Web, blogs, and personal news sources such as e-mail. Make notes about what the news contained and keep track of the time you spent reading, viewing, or listening. On the next day total the time for each category. Write a short analysis of your data. Bring your analysis to class to compare with other students' totals. Do the results for the entire class surprise you in any way?

2. Do you agree with Mindich that young people display a "detachment" from political issues? Why or why not? Write a short essay explaining your reasons. Include examples from your own and your friends' personal experience of recent political events, such as the election of President Obama, the debate on health care legislation, and the wars in Afghanistan and Iraq.

3. Mindich, writing in 2007, says that "the theory that younger people are more reliant on the Internet for news than their elders doesn't hold up." However, the 2011 *State of the Media* study conducted by the Pew Research Center's Project for Excellence in Journalism notes, in its section "Mobile News and Paying Online," that 47 percent of 18-to-29-year-olds say they get information or news about their local community on their mobile devices. Do some additional research on the state of Internet news. Do you agree with Mindich's assessment, or do you think he has not sufficiently credited the online delivery of news for young adults? Write an essay in which you analyze your research and reach a conclusion.

The Collapse of Big Media:
The Young and the Restless

When news executives look at the decline over the past few decades in the number of people who read or watch the news, they're scared silly. But then they reassure themselves that the kids will come around. Conventional wisdom runs that as young men and women gain the trappings of adulthood—a job, a spouse, children, and a house—they tend to pick up the news habit, too. As CBS News president Andrew Heyward declared in 2002, "Time is on our side in that as you get older, you tend to get more interested in the world around you." Unfortunately for Heyward and other news executives, the evidence suggests that young people are not picking up the news habit—not in their teens, not in their twenties, not even in their thirties.

When they aren't reassuring themselves, editors and publishers are lying awake at night thinking about the dismaying trends of recent decades. In 1972, nearly half of 18-to-22-year-olds read a newspaper every day, according to research conducted by Wolfram Peiser, a scholar who studies newspaper readership. Today, less than a quarter do. That younger people are less likely to read than their elders is of grave concern, but perhaps not surprising. In fact, the baby boomers who came of age in the 1970s are less avid news consumers than their parents were. More ominous for the future of the news media, however, is Peiser's research showing that a particular age cohort's reading habits do not change much with time; in other words, as people age, they continue the news habits of their younger days. Thus, the real danger, Peiser says, is that cohort replacement builds in a general decline in newspaper reading. The deleterious effects of this phenomenon are clearly evident: In 1972, nearly three-quarters of the 34-to-37 age group read a paper daily. Those thirtysomethings have been replaced by successive crops of thirtysomethings, each reading less than its predecessor. Today, only about a third of this group reads a newspaper every day. This means that fewer parents are bringing home a newspaper or discussing current events over dinner. And fewer kids are growing up in households in which newspapers matter.

A similar decline is evident in television news viewership. In the past decade, the median age of network television news viewers has crept up from about 50 to about 60. Tune in to any network news show or CNN, and note the products hawked in the commercials: The pitches for Viagra, Metamucil, Depends, and Fixodent are not aimed at teenyboppers. Compounding the problem of a graying news audience is the proliferation of televisions within the typical household, which diminishes adult influence over what's watched. In 1970, six percent of all sixth graders had TVs in their bedrooms; today that number is an astonishing

77 percent. If you are in sixth grade and sitting alone in your room, you're probably not watching Peter Jennings.

One of the clearest signs of the sea change in news viewing habits was the uproar following the appearance last fall by Jon Stewart, host of *The Daily Show*, a parody of a news program, on CNN's *Crossfire*, a real one. With a median age of 34, *The Daily Show*'s audience is the envy of CNN, so when Stewart told *Crossfire*'s hosts that their show's predictable left/right approach to debates of current issues was "hurting America," one could have guessed that CNN bigwigs would pay attention. But who could have foreseen that CNN president Jonathan Klein would cancel *Crossfire*? "I agree wholeheartedly with Jon Stewart's overall premise," he told the *New York Times*. News executives are so desperate to get to consumers before the AARP does that they're willing to heed the advice of a comedian.

If the young (and not so young) are not reading newspapers or watching network television news, many assume that they are getting news online. Not so. Only 18 percent of Americans listed the Internet as a "primary news source" in a survey released earlier this year by the Pew Internet and American Life Project and the Pew Research Center for the People and the Press. And the theory that younger people are more reliant on the Internet for news than their elders doesn't hold up. Certainly an engaged minority of young people use the Net to get a lot of news, but studies show that most use it primarily for e-mailing,

instant messaging, games, and other diversions. You only need to wander into a computer lab at your local college or high school and see what the students have on their screens for the dismal confirmation of these choices.

If the youth audience is tuned out of newspaper, television, and Internet news, what, exactly, is it tuning in to? To answer this question, I traveled the country in 2002 speaking with groups of young people about their news habits. My research confirmed what many people already suspect: that most young people tune in to situation comedies and "reality" TV to the exclusion of news. I was surprised, though, by the scope of the trend: Most of the young people I interviewed had almost no measurable interest in political news. At Brandeis University in Massachusetts, one student explained that watching the situation comedy *Friends* creates a "sense of emotional investment" and "instant gratification." This engagement contrasts with the "detachment" young people feel from public issues such as campaign finance reform and news sources such as CNN and Peter Jennings. And when the news and its purveyors are seen simply as alternative forms of entertainment, they can't compete with the likes of *CSI*, *Las Vegas*, *American Idol*, and *Fear Factor*.

The entertainment options competing with the news for the attention of the youth audience have multiplied exponentially. In the 1960s, there were only a handful of television stations in any given market. When Walter Cronkite shook the nation by declaring in a February 1968 report on the Vietnam War that the

United States was "mired in stalemate," he spoke to a captive audience. New York City, for example, had only seven broadcast stations. At 10:30 p.m. on the night of Cronkite's remarks, channels 4 and 11 ran movies, channels 5 and 9 had discussion shows, and channel 7 was showing *N. Y. P. D.*, a cop show. In this media universe of limited competition, nearly 80 percent of all television viewers watched the nightly news, and from the late 1960s on, Cronkite won the lion's share of the total news audience. Today, young people can choose from hundreds of stations, less than a tenth of which are devoted to news. And that's not to mention the many competing diversions that weren't available in 1968, from video games to iPods. Amid this entertainment cornucopia, the combined network news viewership has shrunk significantly—from some 50 million nightly in the 1960s to about 25 million today. (In comparison, CNN's audience is minuscule, typically no more than a million or so viewers, while public television's *NewsHour with Jim Lehrer* generally reaches fewer than three million viewers.)

The effects of this diet are evident in how little Americans know about current events. True, Americans have been extremely uninformed for a long time. Most follow public affairs only in a vague way, and many don't bother to engage at all. In the 1950s and 1960s, at the height of the Cold War, a poll revealed that only 55 percent of Americans knew that East Germany was a communist country, and less than half knew that the Soviet Union was not part of NATO, report political scientists Michael X. Delli Carpini and Scott Keeter in *What Americans Know about Politics and Why It Matters* (1996). In short, there was never a golden age of informed citizenry. But in recent decades, Americans' ignorance has reached truly stupefying levels, particularly among young adults. A series of reports published over the past two decades by the Pew Research Center for the People and the Press (and its predecessor, the Times Mirror Center) suggest that young adults were once nearly as informed as their elders on a range of political issues. From 1944 to 1968, the interest of younger people in the news as reported in opinion surveys was less than five percent below that of the population at large. Political debates and elections in the 1940s, the Army-McCarthy hearings of the 1950s, and the Vietnam War in the 1960s generated as much interest among the young as among older people. But Watergate in the 1970s was the last in this series of defining events to draw general public attention. (Decades later, in 2001, the bombing of the World Trade Center towers revived general public engagement, at least for a few weeks.) Soon after Watergate, surveys began to show flagging interest in current affairs among younger people.

There is no single explanation for this sudden break. Many of the young people I spoke with in doing my research were disaffected with the political process and believed that it was completely insulated from public pressure. Why, in that case, keep up with public affairs? The blurring line between entertainment and journalism, along with corporate consolidation of big media companies, has also bred in some minds a deep skepticism about the news media's offerings. At bottom, however, the sense of community has declined as Americans are able to live increasingly isolated lives, spending long hours commuting to work and holing up in suburban homes cocooned from the rest of the world.

The extent of this withdrawal from civic involvement is evident in a poll conducted during the height of the 2004 Democratic presidential primaries. In response to the question, "Do you happen to know which of the presidential candidates served as an army general?" about 42 percent of the over-50 crowd could name Wesley Clark. Only 13 percent of those under 30 could. While these results reveal a general lack of political knowledge across ages, they also underscore the growing gap between ages.

The shrinking audience for news is undermining the health of many major news media outlets. The most recent symptom was the revelation last year that a number of major newspapers, notably the *Chicago Sun-Times* and New York's *Newsday*, had cooked their books, inflating circulation figures in order to mask declines and keep advertising revenues from falling. More insidious—and less widely decried—is the industry-wide practice of bolstering profits by reducing news content. In newspapers, this is done by cutting back on the number of reporters covering state government, Washington, and foreign affairs, and by shrinking the space in the paper devoted to news. The news media are, in a very real sense,

making our world smaller. On the broadcast networks, this shrinkage is easily measurable: In 1981, a 30-minute nightly newscast on CBS, minus commercials, was 23 minutes and 20 seconds, according to Leonard Downie, Jr., and Robert G. Kaiser's *The News about the News: American Journalism in Peril* (2002). In 2000, the same newscast was down to 18 minutes and 20 seconds. That's a lot of missing news.

The failing health of the nation's news media is not only a symptom of Americans' low levels of engagement in political life. It is a threat to political life itself. "The role of the press," writes news media critic James W. Carey, "is simply to make sure that in the short run we don't get screwed." Independent, fair, and accurate reporting is what gives "We the People" our check on power. Reporters dig up corruption and confront power; they focus the public's attention on government policies and actions that are unwise, unjust, or simply ineffective. It was the news media that exposed the Watergate burglary and cover-up engineered by Richard Nixon, sparked the investigation of the Iran-Contra affair during the watch of Ronald Reagan and George H. W. Bush, ferreted out Bill Clinton's Whitewater dealings, and turned a searchlight on George W. Bush's extrajudicial arrests of American citizens suspected of terrorism.

A shrinking audience impairs the news media's ability to carry out their watchdog role. It also permits the powers that be to undermine journalism's legitimate functions. Where was the public outrage when it was revealed that the current Bush administration had secretly paid journalists to carry its water, or when the White House denied a press pass to a real journalist, Maureen Dowd of the *New York Times*, and gave one to a political hack who wrote for purely partisan outlets using a fake identity? The whole notion of the news media as the public's watchdog, once an unquestioned article of the American civic faith, is now in jeopardy. A recent study commissioned by the John S. and James L. Knight Foundation showed that more than a third of high school students feel that newspaper articles should be vetted by the federal government before publication.

If we are entering a post-journalism age—in which the majority of Americans, young and old, have little interaction with mainstream news media—the most valuable thing we are losing is the marketplace of ideas that newspapers and news broadcasts uniquely provide, that place where views clash and the full range of democratic choices is debated. You usually don't get that on a blog. You don't get that in the left-leaning *Nation* or on right-wing talk shows. But any newspaper worth its salt, and there are plenty, presents a variety of views, including ones antithetical to its editorial page positions. These papers are hardly immune from criticism—they sometimes err, get sloppy, or succumb to partisan or ideological bias—but they do strive to be accurate and independent sources of fact and opinion, and more often than not they fulfill that indispensable public function.

America's newspapers and television news divisions aren't going to save themselves by competing with reality shows and soap operas. The appetite for news, and for engagement with civic life itself, must be nurtured and promoted, and it's very much in the public interest to undertake the task. It's not the impossible assignment it may seem. During the course of my research, I met a group of boys in New Orleans who were very unlikely consumers of news: They were saturated with television programs and video games, they were poor, and they were in eighth grade. Yet they were all reading the *New York Times* online. Why? Because one of their teachers had assigned the newspaper to them to read when they were in sixth grade, and the habit stuck. There's no reason why print and broadcast news shouldn't be a bigger part of the school curriculum, or why there shouldn't be a short civics/current affairs section on the SAT for college-bound students, or why all high school seniors shouldn't have to take a nonbinding version of the civics test given to immigrants who want to become U.S. citizens. And why shouldn't broadcasters be required to produce a certain amount of children's news programming in return for their access to the public airwaves? These are only the most obvious possibilities.

Reporters, editors, producers, and media business executives will all need to make their own adjustments to meet the demands of new times and new audiences, but only by reaching a collective judgment about the value and necessity of vigorous news media in American democracy can we hope to keep our public watchdogs on guard and in good health.

EXAMPLE FOR ANALYSIS

Volkswagen Beetle
Product Design

The Volkswagen Type 1, better known as the Beetle or Bug, is the most produced car in history. From 1938 until the last original Beetle came off an assembly line in Puebla, Mexico, more than twenty-one million were built. The Beetle began in Nazi Germany, when Adolf Hitler commissioned Ferdinand Porsche to produce a car for common people. Only a handful were produced before World War II started in 1939. Volkswagen was soon back in production after the war, and by 1954, the number of Beetles passed a million. Volkswagen began shipping cars to the United States at a time when American cars were big and boxy. The VW Beetle was just the opposite—small and rounded, inexpensive, and three times as fuel efficient. Beetles dominated the small-car market until Japanese imports showed up in large numbers in the mid-1970s.

More than the story of a car, however, the Beetle demonstrates how what we buy reflects cultural attitudes and values

Return to these questions after you have finished reading.

Analyzing the Reading

1. Volkswagen ads in the United States in the 1960s appealed to simplicity—simple shape, simple technology—which grew out of long-standing American values of honesty, economy, and lack of pretense. Look at automobile ads today, both in print and on television. What values do they appeal to?

2. Your campus may have a building that is better known by a nickname than its official name. Is the building liked or disliked by students? How does the nickname change the image of the building? For example, is it more friendly or less friendly?

3. Look up the word *bug* in the Oxford English Dictionary, which traces the histories of words. Your library has the print OED and may allow access through the library's Web site. How has the meaning of *bug* changed over time? Think about how *bug* is used today. For example, a common saying among computer programmers is "It's not a *bug*; it's a feature." Identify examples of other words such as *pimp* that have changed meanings in recent years.

4. Think of other products that we find cute and lovable. What makes them cute and lovable? Does advertising promote these associations?

Exploring Ideas and Issues

The Volkswagen Beetle has a complicated and dark history. Advertisements for the Beetle face the challenge of emphasizing the car's virtues while minimizing its historical associations.

1. Look closely at the ad with the heading "The Volkswagen Theory of Evolution" (page 244). In a short analysis, describe the visual component. What would you expect to see in an illustration of "evolution"? Would you say the heading is playful or serious? Why? What meaning does the advertiser want to convey?

2. Examine the ad with the heading "How much longer can we hand you this line?" (page 244). In a short essay, describe the visual component of the ad. What is the advertiser hoping to emphasize at a time when American cars are large and boxy?

What values from the car's conceptualization were carried over into the advertising you see here? What is the tone of the ad?

3. U.S. consumers who had lived through World War II might have been unsympathetic to Volkswagen and its associations with the Nazis. However, their children, who grew up in the postwar period, embraced the Beetle as a fuel-efficient and inexpensive alternative to American cars. Look at the Volkswagen ad on page 245. Write an analysis that compares the 1998 ad with the 1960s ads on the previous page. How are they similar and different? What is the tone of the newer ads? What values do the ads emphasize? What associations does the brand have now, and how do these associations relate (or not relate) to the car's history?

When Adolf Hitler became Chancellor of Germany in 1933, he declared that a centerpiece of Nazism would be the motorization of the country. He asked Ferdinand Porsche to design a car that would be affordable for everyone.

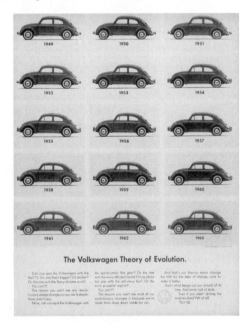

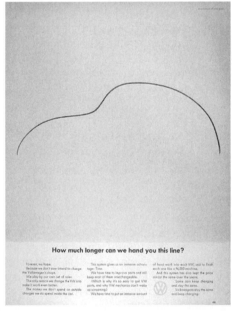

Clever advertising helped make the Beetle a hit in the 1960s. The American advertising firm Doyle Dane Bernbach (DDB) began a campaign in 1959 that emphasized the differences between the Beetle and bulky American cars that changed designs yearly.

In 1968, Walt Disney's *The Love Bug* created a new generation of Beetle fans and led to a series of Herbie sequels.

Beetles became part of the counterculture of the 1960s. Many were hand-painted and customized in various ways, even adding fins that mocked American cars.

Misery has enough company.
Dare to be happy.

In 1998 Volkswagen launched the New Beetle, which benefited from the lovable image of the original Beetle.

EXAMPLE FOR ANALYSIS
The Storm
Kate Chopin

Kate Chopin (1851–1904) was an American author of short stories and novels. Based upon the themes of many of her stories, Chopin is considered by some literary critics to be a forerunner of feminist authors of the twentieth century. "The Storm" was composed on July 19, 1898, and was first published in *The Complete Works of Kate Chopin* in 1969. The tale takes place sometime in the late nineteenth century at Friedheimer's store in Louisiana, and at the nearby house of Calixta and Bobinôt. The story is a sequel to another piece, "At the 'Cadian Ball," and features many of the same characters.

Return to these questions after you have finished reading.

Analyzing the Reading

1. Why does Bobinôt purchase of can of shrimps? Does it seem like a strange gift to buy for one's wife? Consider how he presents the can of shrimps to his wife at the end of the story.

2. Why does Chopin point out that Calixta has not seen Alcée very much, and "never alone" since her marriage to Bobinôt? Does this statement set up any expectations for the reader?

3. Think about who is relating the events, and how they are presented. Who is making the observations in the story? The narrator? Alcée? Does it matter? Why or why not?

4. Consider how the storm outside mirrors the growing storm inside the house. How does Chopin use the setting to reflect the feelings of her characters? Is there more than one storm in the story? Cite some examples from the text to support your response.

Exploring Ideas and Issues

In "At the 'Cadian Ball," the prequel to "The Storm," we learn that Alcee and Calixta have spent time together about a year before in Assumption Parish. At the Ball, Alcée catches Calixta alone.

"She was sitting upon a bench out in the shadow, with Alcée beside her. They were acting like fools. He had attempted to take a little gold ring from her finger; just for the fun of it, for there was nothing he could have done with the ring but replace it again. But she clinched her hand tight. He pretended that it was a very difficult matter to open it. Then he kept the hand in his. They seemed to forget about it. He played with her earring, a thin crescent of gold hanging from her small brown ear. He caught a wisp of the kinky hair that had escaped its fastening, and rubbed the ends of it against his shaven cheek."

Read "At the 'Cadian Ball" online. The incidents in "The Storm" happen five years after the events related in "At the 'Cadian Ball." How does "At the

'Cadian Ball" put the story of "The Storm" into context? Is it important to read both stories? Why or why not?

1. Analyze Calixta and Alcee's relationship. Based on what you have learned about them from the two stories, do you think their encounter will be an isolated incident? Explain.

2. What sort of moral judgment, if any, does Chopin make on the actions of Calixta and Alcée?

3. What parallels exist between "At the 'Cadian Ball" and "The Storm." How do these parallels they link the stories thematically?

The Storm

I

The leaves were so still that even Bibi thought it was going to rain. Bobinôt, who was accustomed to converse on terms of perfect equality with this little son, called the child's attention to certain somber clouds that were rolling with sinister intention from the west, accompanied by a sullen, threatening roar. They were at Friedheimer's store and decided to remain there till the storm had passed. They sat within the door on two empty kegs. Bibi was four years old and looked very wise.

"Mama'll be 'fraid, yes," he suggested with blinking eyes.

"She'll shut the house. Maybe she got Sylvie helpin' her this evenin'," Bobinôt responded reassuringly.

"No; she ent got Sylvie. Sylvie was helpin' her yistiday," piped Bibi.

Bobinôt arose and going across to the counter purchased a can of shrimps, of which Calixta was very fond. Then he returned to his perch on the keg and sat stolidly holding the can of shrimps while the storm burst. It shook the wooden store and seemed to be ripping great furrows in the distant field. Bibi laid his little hand on his father's knee and was not afraid.

II

Calixta, at home, felt no uneasiness for their safety. She sat at a side window sewing furiously on a sewing machine. She was greatly occupied and did not notice the approaching storm. But she felt very warm and often stopped to mop her face on which the perspiration gathered in beds. She unfastened her white sacque at the throat. It began to grow dark, and suddenly realizing the situation she got up hurriedly and went about closing windows and doors.

Out on the small front gallery she had hung Bobinôt's Sunday clothes to air and she hastened out to gather them before the rain fell. As she stepped outside Alcée Laballiére rode in at the gate. She had not seen him very often since her marriage, and never alone. She stood there with Bobinôt's coat in her hands, and the big rain drops began to fall. Alcée rode his horse under the shelter of a side projection where the chickens had huddled and there were plows and a harrow piled up in the corner.

May I come and wait in you gallery till the storm is over Calixta?" he asked.

"Come 'long in, M'sieur Alcée."

His voice and her own startled her as if from a trance, and she seized Bobinôt's vest. Alcée, mounting to the porch, grabbed the trousers and snatched Bibi's braided jacket that was about to be carried away by a sudden gust of wind. He expressed an intention to remain outside, but it was soon apparent that he might as well have been out in the open: the water beat in upon the boards in driving sheets, and he went inside, closing the door after him. It was even necessary to put something beneath the door to keep the water out.

"My! What a rain! It's a good two years sence it rain like that," exclaimed Calixta as she rolled up a piece of bagging and Alcée helped her to thrust it beneath the crack.

She was a little fuller of figure than five years before when she married; but she had lost nothing of her vivacity. Her blue eyes still retained their melting quality; and her yellow hair, disheveled by wind and rain, kinked more stubbornly than ever about her ears and temples.

The rain beat upon the low, shingled roof with a force and clatter that threatened to break an entrance and deluge them there. They were in the dining room—the sitting room—the general utility room. Adjoining was her bedroom, with Bibi's couch alongside her own. The door stood open, and the room with its white, monumental bed, its closed shutters, looked dim and mysterious.

Alcée flung himself in a rocker and Calixta nervously began to gather up from the floor the lengths of a cotton sheet which she had been sewing.

"If this keeps up, *Dieu sait* if the levees going to stan' it!" she exclaimed.

"What have you got to do with the levees?"

"I got enough to do! An' there's Bobinôt with Bibi out in that storm—if he only didn' left Friedheimer's!"

"Let us hope, Calixta, that Bobinôt got sense enough to come in out of a cyclone."

She went and stood at the window with a greatly disturbed look on her face. She wiped the frame that was clouded with moisture. It was stiflingly hot. Alcée got up and joined her at the window, looking over her shoulder. The rain was coming down in sheets obscuring the view of far-off cabins and enveloping the distant wood in a gray mist. The playing of the lightning was incessant. A bolt struck a tall chinaberry tree at the edge of the field. It filled all visible space with a blinding glare and the crash seemed to invade the very boards they stood upon.

Calixta put her hands to her eyes, and with a cry, staggered backward. Alcée's arm encircled her, and for an instant he drew her close and spasmodically to him.

"Bonté!" she cried, releasing herself from his encircling arm and retreating from the window, "the house'll go next! If I only knew w'ere Bibi was!" She would not compose herself; she would not be seated. Alcée clasped her shoulders and looked into her face. The contact of her warm palpitating body when he had unthinkingly drawn her into his arms, had aroused all the old-time infatuation and desire for her flesh.

"Calixta," he said, "don't be frightened. Nothing can happen. The house is too low to be struck, with so many tall trees standing about. There! aren't you going to be quiet? say, aren't you" He pushed her hair back from her face that was warm and steaming. Her lips were as red and moist as pomegranate seed. Her white neck and a glimpse of her full, firm bosom disturbed him powerfully. As she glanced up at him the fear in her liquid blue eyes had given place to a drowsy gleam that unconsciously betrayed a sensuous desire. He looked down into her eyes and there was nothing for him to do but gather her lips in a kiss. It reminding him of Assumption.

"Do you remember—in Assumption, Calixta?" he asked in a low voice broken with passion. Oh! she remembered; for in Assumption he had kissed her and kissed and kissed her; until his senses would well nigh fail, and to save her he would resort to a desperate flight. If she was not an immaculate dove in those days, she was still inviolate; a passionate creature whose very defenselessness had made her defense, against which his honor forbade him to prevail. Now—well, now—her lips seemed in a manner free to be tasted, as well as her round, white throat and her whiter breasts.

They did not heed the crashing torrents, and the roar of the elements made her laugh as she lay in his arms. She was a revelation in that dim, mysterious chamber; as white as the couch she lay upon. Her firm, elastic flesh that was knowing for the first time its birthright, was like a creamy lily that the sun invites to contribute its breath and perfume to the undying life of the world.

The generous abundance of her passion, without guile or trickery, was like a white flame which penetrated and found response in depths of his own sensuous nature that had never yet been reached.

When he touched her breasts they gave themselves up in quivering ecstasy, inviting his lips. Her mouth was a fountain of delight. And when he possessed her, they seemed to swoon together at the very borderland of life's mystery.

He stayed cushioned upon her, breathless, dazed, enervated, with his heart beating like a hammer upon her. With one hand she clasped his head, her lips lightly touching his forehead. The other hand stroked with a soothing rhythm his muscular shoulders.

The growl of the thunder was distant and passing away. The rain beat softly upon the singles, inviting them to drowsiness and sleep. But they dared not yield.

The rain was over; and the sun was turning the glistening green world into a palace of gems. Calixta, on the gallery, watched Alcée ride away. He turned and smiled at her with a beaming face; she lifted her pretty chin in the air and laughed aloud.

III

Bobinôt and Bibi, trudging home, stopped without at the cistern to make themselves presentable.

"My! Bibi, w'at will yo' mama say! You ought to be ashame'. You oughtn' put on those good pants. Look at' em! An' that mud on yo' collar! How you got that mud on yo' collar, Bibi? I never saw such a boy!" Bibi was a picture of pathetic resignation. Bobinôt was the embodiment of serious solicitude as he strove to remove from his own person and his son's the signs of their tramp over heavy roads and through wet fields. He scraped the mud off Bibi's bare legs and feet with a stick and carefully removed all traces from his heavy brogans. Then, prepared for the worst—the meeting with an over-scrupulous housewife, they entered cautiously at the back door.

Calixta was preparing supper. She had set the table and was dripping coffee at the hearth. She sprang up as they came in.

"Oh, Bobinôt! You back! My! but I was uneasy. W'ere you been during the rain? An' Bibi? he ain't wet? he ain't hurt?" She had clasped Bibi and was kissing him effusively. Bobinôt's explanations and apologies which he had bee composing all along the way, died on his lips as Calixta felt him to see if he were dry, and seemed to express nothing but satisfaction at their safe return.

"I bought you some shrimps, Calixta," offered Bobinôt, hauling the can from his ample side pocket and laying it on the table.

"Shrimps! Oh, Bobinôt! you too good fo' anything!" and she gave him a smacking kiss on the cheek that resounded. "J'vous résponds, we'll have a feas' tonight! umph-umph!"

Bobinôt and Bibi began to relax and enjoy themselves, and when the three seated themselves at table they laughed much and so loud that anyone might have heard them as far away as LaBalliére's.

IV

Alcée LaBalliére wrote to his wife, Clarisse, that night. It was a loving letter, full of tender solicitude. He told her not to hurry back, but if she and the babies liked it at Biloxi, to stay a month longer. He was getting along nicely; and though he missed them, he was willing to bear the separation a while longer—realizing that their health and pleasure were the first things to be considered.

V

As for Clarisse, she was charmed upon receiving her husband's letter. She and the babies were doing well. The society was agreeable; many of her old friends and acquaintances were at the bay. And the first free breath since her marriage seemed to restore the pleasant liberty of her maiden days. Devoted as she was to her husband, their conjugal life was something which she was more than willing to forego for a while.

So the storm passed and everyone was happy.

EXAMPLE FOR ANALYSIS
Love in L.A.
Dagoberto Gilb

Dagoberto Gilb's mother was an illegal immigrant from Mexico. She settled in Los Angeles, where she and his father, an ex-Marine sergeant of German ancestry, started a relationship that ended quickly. Born in 1950, Gilb grew up in Los Angeles, attended college, and worked for many years as a carpenter, which gave him time to write. He now teaches at University of Houston-Victoria and has published novels and collections of short stories and essays.

A student's analysis of "Love in L.A." follows the story.

Return to these questions after you have finished reading.

Analyzing the Reading

1. From whose point of view is the story told? Do you think the narrator is a neutral observer?

2. Does Jake act responsibly after the accident? What other choices did he consider? What does his response tell you about his character?

3. What do we learn about Mariana from her response, her car, and her mention of her parents? Do you find her behavior credible and realistic? Support your response with evidence from the text.

4. How does the setting on a freeway shape how we understand the two characters? Imagine the story told in a rural setting. Do you think the main characters would behave differently?

5. Put forth an argument about whether the title is appropriate for the story. Use details from the story to support your position.

6. Gilb often writes about lives of working-class Latinos. Do you think Gilb is sympathetic to Jake's behavior? Explain.

Exploring Ideas and Issues

Gilb's story narrates the accidental meeting of two young people in a large, sprawling metropolis. The author keeps the action straightforward and confines it to one location and a limited time period. Yet, though the story seems simple, it raises many issues of character, societal interaction, and even fate.

1. Mariana and Jake seem to come from different worlds. What might we assume about their backgrounds and positions in society? What assumptions do they seem to make about each other? Is it likely that the two characters would have met under any other circumstances? Are they attracted to one another? Write a short essay in which you answer these questions. Give quotations from the story to support your answers.

2. Think of Jake's conversation with the girl as a rhetorical act, and write a short analysis. Make sure you address the following questions: What is his purpose? What strategies does he use? How does he adjust his presentation to his audience? Is his presentation effective? Why or why not? Give examples from the story to illustrate your answers.

3. The story starts and ends with Jake sitting in "this '58 Buick he drove," fantasizing about a better life. What effect does the car accident have on his sense of himself and of his future? Does Jake have the capacity to "change his whole style"? Why or why not? Write an essay examining what you think the story says about people's ability to change in general. Remember to include quotations from the story to support your views.

Love in L.A.

Jake slouched in a clot of near motionless traffic, in the peculiar gray of concrete, smog, and early morning beneath the overpass of the Hollywood Freeway on Alvarado Street. He didn't really mind because he knew how much worse it could be trying to make a left onto the onramp. He certainly didn't do that everyday of his life, and he'd assure anyone who'd ask that he never would either. A steady occupation had its advantages and he couldn't deny thinking about that too. He needed an FM radio in something better than this '58 Buick he drove. It would have crushed velvet interior with electric controls for the LA summer, a nice warm heater and defroster for the winter drives at the beach, a cruise control for those longer trips, mellow speakers front and rear of course, windows that hum closed, snuffing out that nasty exterior noise of freeways. The fact was that he'd probably have to change his whole style. Exotic colognes, plush, dark nightclubs, maitais and daquiris, necklaced ladies in satin gowns, misty and sexy like in a tequila ad. Jake could imagine lots of possibilities when he let himself, but none that ended up with him pressed onto a stalled freeway.

Jake was thinking about this freedom of his so much that when he glimpsed its green light he just went ahead and stared bye bye to the steadily employed. When he turned his head the same direction his windshield faced, it was maybe one second too late. He pounced the brake pedal and steered the front wheels away from the tiny brakelights but the smack was unavoidable. Just one second sooner and it would only have been close. One second more and he'd be crawling up the Toyota's trunk. As it was, it seemed like only a harmless smack, much less solid than the one against his back bumper.

Jake considered driving past the Toyota but was afraid the traffic ahead would make it too difficult. As he pulled up against the curb a few carlengths ahead, it occurred to him that the traffic might have helped him get away too. He slammed the car door twice to make sure it was closed fully and to give himself another second more, then toured front and rear of his Buick for damage on or near the bumpers. Not an impressionable scratch even in the chrome. He perked up. Though the car's beauty was secondary to its ability to start and

253

move, the body and paint were clean except for a few minor dings. This stood out as one of his few clearcut accomplishments over the years.

Before he spoke to the driver of the Toyota, whose looks he could see might present him with an added complication, he signaled to the driver of the car that hit him, still in his car and stopped behind the Toyota, and waved his hands and shook his head to let the man know there was no problem as far as he was concerned. The driver waved back and started his engine.

"It didn't even scratch my paint," Jake told her in that way of his. "So how you doin? Any damage to the car? I'm kinda hoping so, just so it takes a little more time and we can talk some. Or else you can give me your phone number now and I won't have to lay my regular b.s. on you to get it later."

He took her smile as a good sign and relaxed. He inhaled her scent like it was clean air and straightened out his less than new but not unhip clothes.

"You've got Florida plates. You look like you must be Cuban."

"My parents are from Venezuela."

"My name's Jake." He held out his hand.

"Mariana."

They shook hands like she'd never done it before in her life.

"I really am sorry about hitting you like that." He sounded genuine. He fondled the wide dimple near the cracked taillight. "It's amazing how easy it is to put a dent in these new cars. They're so soft they might replace waterbeds soon." Jake was confused about how to proceed with this. So much seemed so unlikely, but there was always a possibility. "So maybe we should go out to breakfast somewhere and talk it over."

"I don't eat breakfast."

"Some coffee then."

"Thanks, but I really can't."

"You're not married, are you? Not that that would matter that much to me, I'm an openminded kinda guy."

She was smiling. "I have to get to work."

"That sounds boring."

"I better get your driver's license," she said.

Jake nodded, disappointed. "One little problem," he said. "I didn't bring it. I just forgot it this morning. I'm a musician," he exaggerated greatly, "and, well, I dunno, I left my wallet in the pants I was wearing last night. If you have some paper and a pen I'll give you my address and all that."

He followed her to the glove compartment side of her car.

"What if we don't report it to the insurance companies? I'll just get it fixed for you."

"I don't think my dad would let me do that."

"Your dad? It's not your car?"

"He bought it for me. And I live at home."

"Right." She was slipping away from him. He went back around to the back of her new Toyota and looked over the damage again. There was the trunk lid, the bumper, a rear panel, a taillight.

"You do have insurance?" she asked, suspicious, as she came around the back of the car.

"Oh yeah," he lied.

"I guess you better write the name of that down too."

He made up a last name and address and wrote down the name of an insurance company an old girlfriend once belonged to. He considered giving a real phone number but went against that idea and made one up.

"I act too," he lied to enhance the effect more. "Been in a couple of movies."

She smiled like a fan.

"So how about your phone number?" He was rebounding maturely.

She gave it to him.

"Mariana, you are beautiful," he said in his most sincere voice.

"Call me," she said timidly.

Jake beamed. "We'll see you, Mariana," he said holding out his hand. Her hand felt so warm and soft he felt like he'd been kissed.

Back in his car he took a moment or two to feel both proud and sad about his performance. Then he watched the rear view mirror as Mariana pulled up behind him. She was writing down the license plate numbers on his Buick, ones that he'd taken off a junk because the ones that belonged to his had expired so long ago. He turned the ignition key and revved the big engine and clicked into drive. His sense of freedom swelled as he drove into the now moving street traffic, though he couldn't stop the thought about that FM stereo radio and crushed velvet interior and the new car smell that would even make it better.

Quandre Brown

Professor Okafor

English 102

6 October 2011

Fender-bender Romance in Dagoberto Gilb's "Love in L.A."

The title of the story "Love in L.A." serves as metaphor for the nature of love and relationships in Los Angeles, and Hollywood in particular, has a reputation for being superficial. The setting in L.A. means everything; it is an L.A. story, not a New York City story, and certainly not a small town story. Everything is artifice and acting. The story "Love in L.A." describes a brief encounter following a fender-bender between a young man, Jake, and a young woman, Mariana. Jake and Mariana seem to be interested in each other, but we as the audience watching the scene unfold know that they are unlikely to ever see each other again. In fact, most of entire exchange between them was a lie—a big act. The two meet, flirt, lie, and then leave. Is this what love in L.A. is like?

The uninvolved narrator reveals that Jake is, at his core, a liar. In fact, he even lies to himself. Before the accident, the unemployed Jake is stuck in a traffic jam, daydreaming about owning a nicer car than his '58 Buick and living a finer lifestyle. As he watches the cars go up the onramp (on to steady jobs presumably in L.A.), Jake muses how much better it is not to have to do that, "He certainly didn't do that everyday of his life, and he'd assure anyone who'd ask that he never would either" (253). But while Jake may *tell* anyone who asked that he prefers his freedom, that doesn't necessarily mean he feels that way himself. Jake is really trying to convince himself that he has it better than the alternative. The fact that much of his daydream involves things that a steady job could provide—a nicer car, nightclubs, well-dressed women—reveals that he really wishes his life were different. The onramp represents an impediment to Jake's freedom (he is pleased that he doesn't have to cut across traffic to reach it) but it also represents the lifestyle a steady job can provide.

After the accident, we learn more about how far Jake's lying will go. In an honest moment, Jake sees the driver of the car he hit and admits to himself that her "looks might present him with an added complication" (254). The driver of the car is pretty, and *perhaps* this makes him more genuinely sorry he is about to lie through his teeth to her. The audience can't really tell, because the narrator leaves us wondering. " 'I really am sorry about hitting you like that.' He sounded genuine" (254). *Sounding* genuine is not necessarily *being* genuine, and it is interesting that the narrator uses this word to describe Jake's comment. Later in the story, when Jake tells Mariana that she is beautiful, the narrator relates that he says this "in his most sincere voice" (255). Another interesting word choice that leaves the audience to make up its own mind about the honesty of Jake's feelings. The fact that the accident happens just past the underpass of the Hollywood Freeway is significant. The setting is vital to the message the story is trying to convey. Love in L.A., it seems, is more about sounding the part, acting it out and delivering your lines the right way. Typical Hollywood.

Jake lies about not having his license with him, and makes up a false address with false auto insurance information, all the while trying to still pick Mariana up. Mariana flirts back with him, and does give him her phone number asking him to give her a call. But of course, we cannot be certain that the number she gave him was a real one. The narrator doesn't let us know what Mariana is thinking. For example, Mariana says she lives at home, but her car, however, has Florida license plates. While she may be a student home for summer break, she also may be lying to Jake about where she is from. Because the narrator does not tell us what Mariana is thinking, we have no way of knowing how truthful she is being. Before leaving, Mariana takes down Jake's license plate numbers, a clear indication that she really doesn't believe him.

Accidental meetings, superficial exchanges, a whole lot of acting, and two people going their separate ways sums up the nature of romance in a place like L.A. As he drives off, pleased with his performance, Jake resumes his daydream where he left off. Mariana will resume her trek to work. Cue the next act.

Work Cited

Gilb, Dagoberto. "Love in L.A." *Writing: A Guide for College and Beyond.* Ed. Lester
    Faigley. 3rd. ed. New York: Longman, 2012. 253–255. Print.

How to Write a Rhetorical Analysis

These steps for the process of writing a rhetorical analysis may not progress as neatly as this chart might suggest. Writing is not an assembly-line process.

As you write, be open to new insights about the subject you are analyzing. Writing often generates new ideas that you can use to strengthen your analysis.

1 SELECT A TEXT TO ANALYZE

- Examine the assignment.
- Find a text.
- Read the text carefully.
- Research the context.
- Research the author and audience.

2 ANALYZE CONTEXT AND TEXT

- Consider the medium and genre.
- Identify the main claim or claims
- Consider the evidence.
- Analyze the appeals. How does the author establish credibility? How logical are the arguments? What values does the author appeal to?
- Situate the text in its context. Where do you find evidence that the text was responding to other texts and events?
- Consider the style and tone.
- Make an analytical claim.

3
WRITE A DRAFT

- Decide on an organization. Make a working outline before you start writing.

- Write an introduction that describes briefly the text you are analyzing and gives information about the medium, the genre, when and where the text first appeared, and the author.

- State your thesis. Make sure your thesis is not an over-generalization and can be supported by textual and contextual evidence.

- Analyze the text. Discuss elements that show a pattern or illustrate specific techniques that you want to talk about. Build a critical mass of evidence with examples and quotations.

- Analyze the context. Connect the text to events and discussions that were going on at the time it was composed. Explain how the text took part in a larger conversation.

- Build a strong conclusion. Your conclusion is a good place to draw implications about larger issues.

- Write a descriptive title.

4
REVISE, REVISE, REVISE

- Check that your paper or project fulfills the assignment.

- Make sure your analysis has a clear focus and claim.

- Check that each point of your analysis is supported with evidence.

- Make sure your voice and tone will engage readers.

- Examine your organization and think of possible better ways to organize.

5
SUBMITTED VERSION

- Make sure your finished writing meets all formatting requirements.

1: Select a Text to Analyze

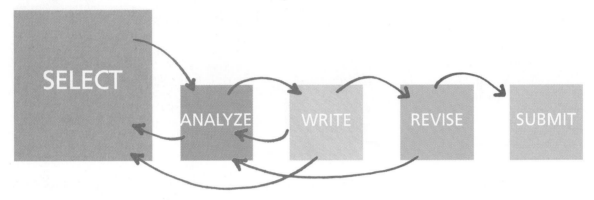

Examine the assignment

Read your assignment slowly and carefully. Look for words like *analyze or critique,* which tell that you are writing an analysis. Highlight any information about the length specified, date due, formatting, and other requirements. You can attend to this information later. At this point you want to zero in on the subject of your analysis.

Find a text to analyze

Choose a text that will be engaging for you and your readers. Your assignment may indicate what kind of text to analyze. Newspaper editorials, activist Web sites, speeches, proposals, and visual arguments are all good sources of texts for analysis. Look for a text that does something interesting, such as Tim Collins's comparison of his own battlefield speech with Marie Fatayi-Williams's emotional speech on the loss of her son.

Read the text carefully

In your first and second readings, your goal is to make sure you understand the text fully. Look up any names or events you don't know.

Research the context

What else was being written and said about this subject at the time the text was written? What events were taking place that might have influenced the author?

Research the author and the audience

Who is the author? What else has he or she said on this subject? What motivated him or her to produce this text? Who is the audience? Where did the text first appear (or, why was this image made or created)? Why did it appear at that particular moment?

WRITE NOW

Find a verbal text to analyze

Find at least three examples of verbal texts that intend to persuade you in some way. They may ask you to do something specific such as buy a product or vote for a candidate, or else they may aim at changing your attitude. Note what makes each text interesting and make a tentative claim.

Text	Deadspin.com blog
What makes it interesting	Takes a humorous look at sports, exposing the pretensions and lack of honesty among sports figures.
Claim	Deadspin.com represents the spirit of many blogs in going for the truth underneath layers of hype and having fun along the way.

WRITE NOW

Find a visual text to analyze

Identify at least three visual texts for possible analysis. Look for a visual text that in some way attempts to influence the viewer—an advertisement, a public building, a statue, a controversial work of art, a dramatic photograph, a television commercial, a corporate logo, and so on. Note what makes it interesting and make a tentative claim.

Text	Logos of competing political candidates
What makes it interesting	Candidate X's logo appears much better than candidate Y's logo among people I have asked, but they cannot explain why.
Claim	Candidate X has a better logo than candidate Y because the typeface and colors of X's logo express strength, energy, and movement while those on Y's logo suggest indecision and weakness.

Writer at work

Kelsey Turner was asked to write a rhetorical analysis for her composition class. She made the following notes and observations on her assignment sheet:

English 1010:
Introduction to Writing
Rhetorical Analysis of an Argument

Time, Newsweek, L.A. Times, Washington Post, NYT

Choose an editorial from a popular newspaper or magazine and analyze the techniques it uses to persuade its audience. You will want to focus on how the author employs logos, ethos, and pathos to persuade readers. Take a stand (make an argument of your own) as to how well these appeals work.

For example: It will work very well with certain audience; it would work better if...

Important dates:
September 8: Bring your editorial to class for discussion.
September 15: Draft due
September 22: Draft returned with comments
September 29: Final draft due

Our Essay Evaluation Form states that we will evaluate this paper by looking at the following four categories. As a class, we will go through these categories and articulate our understanding of good performance in each, for this paper:

Logic and organization (25%)
Evidence and development (25%)
Style (25%)
Grammar and mechanics (25%)

Could structure around the three types of appeals

Use actual words from the editorial as evidence

Kelsey found a *Washington Post* opinion piece on food banks and poverty that interested her (see pages 270–273 to read the full essay). She began by asking the questions she would need to answer to write a good rhetorical analysis (see page 224). Here are the questions and her responses:

<u>What is the author's purpose?</u>
—To make readers re-think their "generous" donations to food banks, and look at causes of hunger.

<u>Who is the audience?</u>
— Readers of Washington Post (nationwide distribution). People concerned with hunger and poverty. People who usually make gestures rather than really working for change?

<u>Who is the author?</u>
— He worked at a food bank, was very successful, became disillusioned. He understands the problem better than most people.

<u>What is the background?</u>
— It was published right before Thanksgiving, when people are thinking about having enough food as an American tradition.

<u>Which rhetorical appeals are used?</u>
— All three:

- Pathos—Appeals to readers' sympathy for those who are hungry. Describes fatigue of donors and volunteers with current system. Makes volunteering and donating seem foolish and possibly harmful.

- Ethos—His background. He assumes readers will agree that it is better to empower people and that we shouldn't patronize them just to make ourselves feel generous.

- Logos—Paints the bigger picture of poverty, of which hunger is just one part. But he goes back and forth between saying maybe food is given to people who don't need it, and then saying the more food we give, the more people need it. It seems like the meaning of "need" changes.

The pathos appeals are the strongest and most noticeable, but the ethos of the author probably works the best to persuade people.

<u>How does the language and style contribute to the purpose?</u>
— Words like "play," and "pep rally," are associated with frivolous activities. They belittle the actions of food pantry workers and donors. Author makes food-givers feel kind of stupid or self-interested and short-sighted. Like they are making the problem worse. Blaming them, almost.

2: Analyze Context and Text

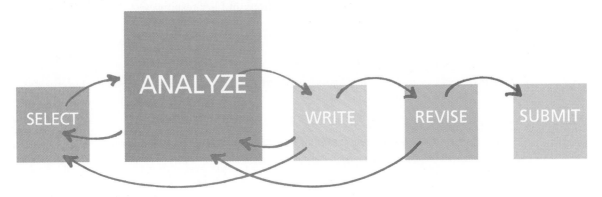

Consider the medium and genre

What is the medium: print, Web, video, or other? What is the genre? Is it an editorial? a proposal? a speech? a documentary film?

Consider the main claim or claims

Summarize the claim or describe the subject.

Consider the evidence

Note all the reasons and evidence given to support the claim.

Analyze the appeals

- **Ethos:** How trustworthy is the author? Does the author give you evidence to think he or she is knowledgeable or fair?
- **Pathos:** What emotions or values does the author appeal to?
- **Logos:** Where does the writer use facts and reasoning to support the claims?

Situate the text in its context

Where do you find evidence that this text was responding to other texts and events? How does the author contribute to the ongoing conversation of which this text is a part?

Consider the style and tone

How would you characterize the style? Is the style formal? informal? academic? How would you characterize the tone? Does the writer or speaker use humor or satire? How is language used to influence the audience? What metaphors are used?

Make an analytical claim

Your claim will be the focus of your analysis. Think about the evidence your will need to support your claim. It may come from the text itself or from your research into the context.

EXAMPLE ANALYTICAL CLAIM: Sojourner Truth's famous "Ain't I a Woman?" speech, made to an all-white and mostly male audience, uses powerful emotional and logical appeals to connect women's rights with the abolition of slavery.

Writer at work

Kelsey Turner read her chosen editorial carefully several times, making notes in the margins about the rhetorical appeals she saw being used.

Establishes his experiences early.

How can anyone not get caught up in the annual Thanksgiving turkey frenzy? At the food bank I co-founded in Hartford, Conn., November always meant cheering the caravans of fowl-laden trucks that roared into our parking lot. They came on the heels of the public appeals for "A bird in every pot," "No family left without a turkey" and our bank's own version -- "A turkey and a 20 [dollar bill]."

Language makes us think of high school kids having fun rather than serious problem solving.

Manipulating donors (Instead of giving them the truth?)

Like pompom girls leading a high school pep rally, we revved up the community's charitable impulse to a fever pitch with radio interviews, newspaper stories and dramatic television footage to extract the last gobbler from the stingiest citizen. After all, our nation's one great day of social equity was upon us. In skid row soup kitchens and the gated communities of hedge-fund billionaires alike, everyone was entitled, indeed expected, to sit down to a meal of turkey with all the fixings.

Food banks are not a real solution to hunger-they just pretend to be.

And here we are, putting on the same play again this year. But come Friday, as most of us stuff more leftovers into our bulging refrigerators, 35 million Americans will take their place in line again at soup kitchens, food banks and food stamp offices nationwide.

Exact figure?

Finally, Kelsey developed a position that could serve as a working thesis for her paper:

Mark Winne's essay gives good reasons for readers to stop supporting the food banking industry, but the belittling tone he uses to describe food bank donors and workers may insult or offend readers, making them less likely to agree with him.

3: Write a Draft

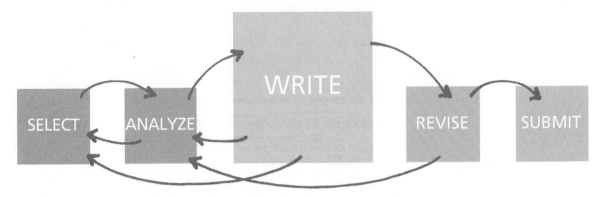

Decide on an organization

Make a working outline before you start writing.

- One method of organization is to introduce the text, state your thesis, and then give your analysis that supports your thesis.

- A second method is to introduce your text, then analyze the text section by section in order. In your conclusion you will need to come to a summary judgment.

Write a descriptive title

Don't settle for "An Analysis of ____." Give your readers a taste of what's to come.

Write an introduction

Describe briefly the text you are analyzing. Identify the medium and genre and when and where the text first appeared. Name the author and give any details about the author that are relevant. At the end of the introductory section, state your thesis. Make sure your thesis is not an overgeneralization and can be supported by textual and contextual evidence.

Analyze the text

Select the most important parts of the text to focus on.

- Choose elements that will show a pattern or illustrate specific techniques that you want to talk about.

- Build a critical mass of evidence with examples and quotations.

- Make the larger patterns or contrasts visible for your readers. For example, an author might appeal to two different audiences in the same editorial.

Analyze the context

Connect the text to events and discussions that were going on at the time it was composed. Explain how the text took part in a larger conversation.

Build a strong conclusion

Don't merely summarize what you have said. Your conclusion is a good place to draw implications about larger issues.

Writer at work

Kelsey used note cards to determine the best structure for her paper. She grouped them in different categories and changed their order until she was satisfied with the basic structure for her first draft.

INTRODUCTION
Context of essay: Printed just before Thanksgiving, when people are thinking about food and American tradition.

WINNE'S CLAIM:
Giving food to food banks doesn't end hunger. To end hunger, people should work to end poverty.
- Use proverb: "Give a man a fish, and you feed him for a day. Teach a man to fish, and you feed him for a lifetime."

MY CLAIM:
Winne's argument makes sense, but some of his appeals will probably do more to alienate readers than convince them.

ETHOS APPEAL:
Co-founded a food bank (shows he has experience, compassion)

ETHOS APPEAL:
makes readers feel suspicious about the motives of food banks. The system's "co-dependency" is "frankly troubling." Food banks "must curry favor . . ." They "carefully nurture [d] the belief" of "doing good"— sounds like they are lying to people.

PATHOS APPEAL:
describes the distribution of turkeys at his food bank as a "high school pep rally," and a "play," making them seem frivolous

PATHOS APPEAL:
volunteers giving out food "seemed even happier" than the recipients . . ." Volunteers are "trapped in . . . gratification." Makes them seem delusional and selfish.

LOGOS APPEAL:
Hunger is caused by poverty. Ending poverty will end hunger. Feeding the hungry without addressing poverty will never end hunger. "Give a man a fish . . .

LOGOS APPEAL:
In fact, Winne claims, if we only feed the hungry, we may make the problem of poverty even worse.

LOGOS APPEAL:
"more than 275,000 Connecticut residents—slightly less than 8.6 percent of the state's residents—remain hungry or what we call 'food insecure.'"

CONCLUDES WITH PATHOS APPEAL:
tries to motivate readers to really make a difference. Volunteers and donors could make a real difference if they forced government to make laws that would reduce poverty.

MY CONCLUSION: MAYBE HE IS TOO OPTIMISTIC?

LOGICAL FLAW:
If people take free food they don't really need, have the really become less "independent"? If they didn't need the food in the first place then they already are independent.

4: Revise, Revise, Revise

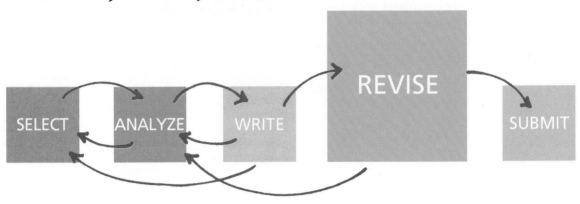

Skilled writers know that the secret to writing well is rewriting. Leave correcting errors for last.

Does your paper or project meet the assignment?	• Look again at your assignment. Does your paper or project do what the assignment asks? • Check the assignment for specific guidelines, including length, format, and amount of research. Does your work meet these guidelines?
Does your analysis have a clear purpose?	• Does it tell readers something they would not have otherwise noticed? • Do you make some kind of claim about the work you are analyzing? Is it a debatable claim?
Do you support your analysis with evidence?	• Do you provide a background about the author, intended audience, and the larger conversation surrounding the text you are analyzing? • Can you provide additional analysis to support your claims?
Is your organization effective?	• Is the order of your main points clear to your reader? • Are there any places where you find abrupt shifts or gaps? • Are there sections or paragraphs that could be rearranged to make your draft more effective?
Is the writing project visually effective?	• Is the font attractive and readable? • Are the headings and visuals effective?
Save the editing for last.	• When you have finished revising, edit and proofread carefully.

A peer review guide is on page 54.

Writer at work

Kelsey Turner received comments from her instructor on her draft. She used these comments to revise her draft.

Kelsey's instructor encouraged her to use Winne's own words instead of summarizing them.

> Winne casts doubt on the motives of food banks and their supporters. He makes the system sound unhealthy and dishonest. Food banks have to act grateful to big food companies even when they receive inedible food. He describes some business owners who wanted to sell horse meat to his food bank. This business's desire to work with the food bank was self-interested: if the food bank agreed to make poor people eat horse meat, maybe more people in America would decide it is acceptable to eat. Then these entrepreneurs would make more money.
>
> Food banks also have to lie to their own volunteers and reassure them they are doing a good thing. This picture of the food bank system makes it look very hypocritical. If food banks have gotten so good at acting grateful and pretending to end hunger, it's no wonder they don't question whether they are really succeeding.

Give us some of his language here—what words does he use that "sound unhealthy"?

Kelsey found several points in her paper where she had included information that did not directly advance her argument. Some of these points could be moved to other sections of the paper where they fit better; others she removed entirely.

How did Winne respond? Does he tell us? How does this fit with your point for the paragraph?

Kelsey received specific feedback on an important aspect of her analysis: the shifts back and forth between her voice and Winne's. To see how she distinguished her ideas from Winne's, see her submitted draft on page 230.

Is this your conclusion or Winne's?

5: Submitted Version

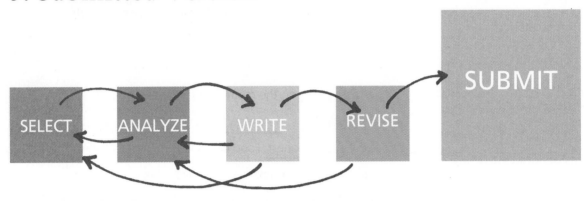

Turner 1

Kelsey Turner

Professor Perez

English 1010

29 September 2011

Biting the Hands that Feed America

Mark Winne's Thanksgiving 2007 article in the *Washington Post*, "When Handouts Keep Coming, the Food Line Never Ends," makes readers re-think their "generous" donations to food banks and pantries. Winne calls our attention instead to poverty, which causes hunger, and challenges us to end hunger by ending poverty. This challenge makes sense. After all, most of us have heard the proverb, "Give a man a fish, and you feed him for a day. Teach a man to fish, and you feed him for a lifetime." However, Winne's tone in his essay works against the logic of his argument. Even though he is a compassionate person who has spent much of his life working to feed the poor, the language he uses belittles the people who want to help. He tries to motivate readers, but he does this partly by making them feel ashamed of themselves. His frustration with the food bank system is understandable, but taking it out on casual readers diminishes sympathy for him and his cause.

Winne begins by mentioning that he co-founded a food bank in Hartford, Connecticut, which establishes a strong ethos for his argument, letting his readers know that Winne has experience with the system he is going to criticize. If anyone should know what works and doesn't work in food banking, it is the people who structure and run the food banks. He also establishes his compassion for the plight of the poor and hungry. Furthermore, Winne says he wants to empower the poor, not just feed them. Because America has a long tradition of self-reliant citizens who can take care of themselves, promoting self-reliance should sound like a worthy goal to most readers. Because we are a democracy, we want our citizens to be strong and self-supporting, not just well fed.

Winne makes a simple, logical argument: Hunger is caused by poverty. Ending poverty will end hunger. Feeding the hungry without addressing poverty will never end hunger. In fact, Winne claims, if we only feed the hungry, we may make the problem of poverty even worse.

Winne uses statistics to support his case. Despite his best efforts, and those of other food bank workers, he tells us, "more than 275,000 Connecticut residents— slightly less than 8.6 percent of the state's residents—remain hungry or what we call 'food insecure.'" After Thanksgiving, "35 million Americans will take their place in line again at soup kitchens, food banks and food stamp offices nationwide." We learn that families on food stamps only receive three dollars per person per day. These numbers make a compelling appeal to our sense of logic and reason. The problem is not going away. The government's response to hunger is inadequate. Anyone who can read the *Washington Post* is smart enough to know that a three-dollar food budget might buy enough French fries to keep you alive, but it wouldn't keep you healthy for very long.

A flaw undercuts his argument, however, when he describes a scene which made him realize the "futility" of food banks: "No one made any attempt to determine whether the recipients actually needed the food, nor to encourage the recipients to seek other forms of assistance, such as food stamps." Winne implies that some of the people taking the food didn't really need it, but just took it because it was free. The lines of people grew longer, leading Winne to observe, "It may have been that a donor-recipient co-dependency had developed. Both parties were trapped in an ever-expanding web of immediate gratification that offered the recipients no long-term hope of eventually achieving independence and self-reliance." If people take free food even though they don't need it, have they really become less "independent"? The fact that they didn't need the food in they first place means they already are independent.

Most people accept free things from time to time, but doing so doesn't automatically make us less self-reliant. Winne explains what he sees as a cause-and-effect problem—too much free food causing people to depend upon more free food—by quoting another food bank director: "The more you provide, the more demand there is." However, demand isn't the same thing as need. People may want free food, and take it when it is offered. They may even "demand" more of it when they don't get what they are expecting. But that's not the same as really needing it. Winne uses "demand" and "need" interchangeably, but he doesn't explain how people go from accepting free food they don't need, to needing free food. Do they get so used to receiving free food that they quit their jobs on the assumption that they don't need to earn money for food? Does free food make them eat more? Maybe there is some way free food can cause dependence, but Winne doesn't explain this process, and it's clearly not logical to assume that free food always makes people less self-reliant.

Winne's article was published on the Sunday before Thanksgiving when readers would be reminded of the American tradition of plentiful food. Likely many would feel sympathy for the hungry and possibly want to do something to help; however, Winne belittles and insults the generous impulses of donors and volunteers. He describes the distribution of turkeys at his food bank as a "high school pep rally" and a "play," making them seem like frivolous activities that make no real difference. This language is sure to make readers think twice before they give a turkey to their local food bank. Winne even makes them feel selfish for wanting to help. He says the volunteers giving out food "seemed even happier" than the recipients. He describes their charity as an "act of faith," and says they are "fortified by the belief that their act of benevolence was at least mildly appreciated." Like the recipients of the food,

Winne says, the volunteers are "trapped in an ever-expanding web of immediate gratification." Winne makes feeding the hungry seem like a selfish act rather than an act of charity.

Winne attempts to make readers suspicious about the motives of food banks and their supporters. He says the system's "co-dependency" is "frankly troubling." Food banks "must curry favor with the nation's food industry, which often regards food banks as a waste-management tool." Food banks keep their own volunteers "dependent on carefully nurtured belief that they are 'doing good' by 'feeding the hungry.'" This assertion renders volunteers as dupes for large corporations who have their own motives for supporting food banks. The hypocrisy of the food bank system is what prevents people who want to help from asking "if this is the best way to end hunger, food insecurity and their root cause, poverty."

Winne concludes by trying to motivate readers to really make a difference. All the energy poured into food banks by volunteers and donors could make a real difference, he feels, if it were used to force government to make policies that would reduce poverty. One the one hand, Winne's call to action appears unrealistic given that politicians largely ignore poverty because it is not an issue that stirs voters. On the other hand, Winne does effectively contrast the power of volunteers, who could "dismantle the Connecticut state capitol brick by brick" with his earlier descriptions of the fatigue and frustration of the current system. He at least gets us to think about food banks in a way other than a feel-good story on the evening news at Thanksgiving.

Work Cited

Winne, Mark. "When Handouts Keep Coming, the Food Line Never Ends."
    Washington Post. Washington Post, 8 Nov. 2007. Web. 8 Sept. 2011.

Projects

Analyzing is valuable for clarifying and developing your own thinking as well as for giving your readers a broader understanding.

Visual analysis

Find a visual text to analyze. You might analyze a popular consumer product, a public building, advertising, art, or a map.

▼

Make a claim about the visual text. Support your claim with close analysis. Describe key features.

▼

Analyze the context. Where and when was the visual created? What was the purpose? Who created it? What can you infer about the intended audience?

▼

Analyze the visual text. What kind of visual is it? What is the medium? How is it arranged? How would you characterize the style? Are any words connected?

Rhetorical analysis

Select a text to analyze—a speech, a sermon, an editorial, a persuasive letter, an essay, a Web site, a pamphlet, a brochure, or another kind of text.

▼

Explain briefly what kind of text it is, when and where it was first published or spoken, and its main argument.

▼

Make a claim about the text, which you support with close analysis.

▼

Analyze the context. Is the text part of a larger debate? What other texts or events does it respond to? Who is the author? What motivated the author to write this text? What can you infer about the intended audience?

▼

Analyze the appeals. What appeals to values and emotions are used? What appeals to logic are used? Do you find any logical fallacies (see pages 24–25)? Do you trust the writer?

▼

Analyze the organization and style. What are the major parts and how are they arranged? Is the style formal, informal, satirical, or something else? Are any metaphors used?

Critical literary analysis

Read carefully a short story or other literary text. Map out the plot. What is the conflict and how is it resolved?

▼

Examine the characterization, including the major and minor characters. Characters are not real people, but instead they are constructed for a purpose. What role does each character perform? The setting, too, is a character. What role does the setting play in the story?

▼

Consider the point of view. Does a character tell the story? Or is the narrator an all-knowing observer? Describe the language, style, and tone of the story. Identify any important images, symbols, and metaphors.

▼

Identify the story's central theme. How does the title of the story relate to the theme?

▼

Write an arguable thesis that connects one or more elements—characters, setting, language, metaphors, and so on—to the overall theme. A paper that begins with an engaging thesis arouses the reader's interest. Support your thesis with evidence from the text. A successful paper shares a discovery with the reader.

Analytical presentation

Choose a subject to analyze. Just as for rhetorical, visual, and literary analyses, an interesting text will help you to produce a presentation that will interest your audience. You will also need to do the same kind of close analysis of the text and research about the context (see page 223).

▼

Plan your presentation. Just as for a written analysis, you will need to write a working thesis to make a working outline. Make a list of key points and think about the best order to present them. Plan your introduction to gain the attention of the audience and to introduce your topic. End by giving the audience something to take away—a compelling example or an idea that gives the gist of your presentation.

▼

Create visuals that will help keep you and your audience oriented. Keep the visuals simple with one point per slide. Don't force your audience to read your presentation on the screen (see page 546).

▼

Deliver your presentation. Practice in advance so you don't have to fumble with your notes. Avoid the temptation to read to your audience. The best presentations make the audience feel like they have been in a conversation with the speaker. Invite response from your audience during and after your presentation (see page 547).

For support in learning this chapter's content, follow this path in **mycomplab:**

► **Resources** ► **Writing** ► **Writing Purposes** ► **Writing to Analyze**

Review the Instruction and Multimedia resources, then complete the **Exercises** and click on **Gradebook** to measure your progress.

10 Causal Arguments

An effective causal argument moves beyond the obvious to examine complex underlying causes.

Chapter Overview

Writing Causal Arguments

Have you ever wondered why your car is hard to start on a cold morning? Why all the shoppers in the supermarket seem to converge on the checkout stands at the same time? Why a company's stock price rises when it announces hundreds of layoffs?

Questions of causation confront us all the time.

Causal investigation also drives scientists, as they search for cures to diseases, to try to explain certain behaviors in people and animals, and attempt to predict the weather.

Answering these kinds of questions requires a causal analysis, which typically takes the form "SOMETHING causes (or does not cause) SOMETHING ELSE."

Keys to causal arguments

Causal arguments take three basic forms.

1. One cause leads to one or more effects.

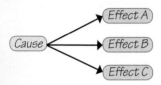

The invention of the telegraph led to the commodities market, the establishment of standard time zones, and news reporting as we know it today.

2. One effect has several causes.

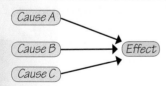

Hurricanes are becoming more financially destructive to the United States because of the greater intensity of recent storms, an increase in the commercial and residential development of coastal areas, and a reluctance to enforce certain construction standards in coastal residential areas.

3. A series of events form a chain, where one event causes another, which then causes a third, and so on.

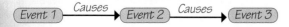

Making the HPV vaccination mandatory for adolescent girls will make unprotected sex seem safer, leading to greater promiscuity, ultimately resulting in more teenage pregnancies.

277

What Makes a Good Causal Argument?

1

Identify what is at stake

Because a strong causal claim may inspire people to change policies or behaviors or take other action, some readers may reject your claim. For example, although the causal link between cigarette smoke and cancer was widely accepted in scientific circles for many years, tobacco companies argued vociferously that no such link existed.

2

Move beyond the obvious to identify underlying causes

When people are involved, you can expect causes to be complex. Perhaps the cause you are seeking to link to an effect is only one of several causes. A well-thought-out causal analysis will trace multiple causes and consider their cumulative effect.

3

Avoid mistaking correlation for causations

A common pitfall of causal analysis is confusing causation with correlation. Events can be correlated, or mutually related in some way, without one being the cause of the other. Deaths by drowning and baseball games are correlated. But does one cause the other? Or is it because both occur most frequently in the summer? (See page 337.)

4

Pay attention to effects

It's not enough to simply identify causes. In order for a causal analysis to matter, you must make clear why the effects are important. Otherwise, readers are apt to ask, "So what?" We often look for causes so that we can prevent something bad from happening or facilitate something good.

5

Acknowledge other possible causes and make counterarguments

When causes are uncertain, disagreements often arise when various causes are proposed. Acknowledge possible causes that you think are flawed and explain why they are unlikely.

While people in Toulouse—the fattened force-fed duck-liver-eating area of France—do indeed have one of the lowest rates of heart disease in the developed world, they actually only eat the delicacy about six times a year. And they're a lot more likely to die of stroke than we are anyway.

    —Laura Fraser (see page 282)

6

Support your causal claims with evidence

Do research to find evidence to back up your claims.

Just to be born, the scavenger girl in Delhi had to overcome Indian parents' entrenched bias against girls—which has led to widespread abortions of female fetuses. The Indian census of 2001 recorded 927 girls aged six or less per 1,000 boys. This compares to 1,026 girls per thousand boys in Brazil and 1,029 in the United States.

    —Eduardo Porter (see page 324)

7

Conclude with strength

Simply repeating your claim often isn't the best way to end. Leave your readers with a memorable image, point, or implication.

Shirky ends the story of the lost Sidekick by asking, portentously, "What happens next?"—no doubt imagining future waves of digital protesters. But he has already answered the question. What happens next is more of the same. A networked, weak-tie world is good at things like helping Wall Streeters get phones back from teen-age girls. *Viva la revolución.*

    —Malcolm Gladwell (see page 308)

  Watch the Animation on Closings to Avoid at mycomplab.com

Visual causal arguments

Causal arguments can be made in charts.

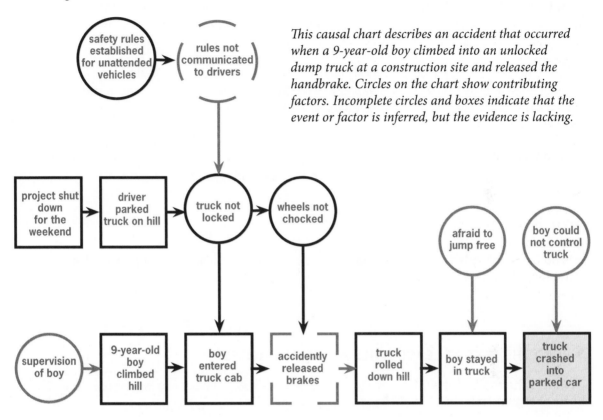

This causal chart describes an accident that occurred when a 9-year-old boy climbed into an unlocked dump truck at a construction site and released the handbrake. Circles on the chart show contributing factors. Incomplete circles and boxes indicate that the event or factor is inferred, but the evidence is lacking.

WRITE NOW

Find topics for causal arguments

Select a general database on your library's Web site such as *LexisNexis Academic, Academic Search Complete, Article First, ProQuest*, and so on (see page 570). Enter current trends as one search term and a topic that is in the news for the other such as the following: *cybersecurity, consumer debt, nuclear energy, food safety, the local food movement, Alzheimer's disease, concealed weapons*, and others.

Read a few of the articles that your search turns up and identify the particular trends they report. Think about possible causes for the trend. For three trends, write a causal claim in this form: "SOMETHING causes (or does not cause) SOMETHING ELSE."

How to Read Causal Arguments

▼ **BEFORE YOU BEGIN READING**   These notes are in response to "The French Paradox"; the reading begins on page 282.

What kind of text is it?	*Fraser's essay is a causal argument about habits of eating. It was published in 2000 in* **Salon,** *an online magazine that covers trends, technology, music, film reviews, and other current topics.*
Who wrote it?	*Laura Fraser is a journalist who has written extensively on food and relationship issues.*
Who is the intended audience?	**Salon** *appeals to a general audience interested in current American culture.*

▼ **READ THE TEXT AT LEAST TWICE AND MAKE NOTES**

What is the topic of the causal argument?	*Fraser states the topic in the first paragraph: Why do the French eat three times as much saturated fat as Americans do and suffer a third fewer heart attacks?*
What is the central causal claim?	*Fraser rejects various claims that the French are healthier because of what they eat and argues instead that the cause is how they eat with more structure and in smaller portions.*
What evidence does the writer use to support the causal claim?	*Fraser uses both anecdotal evidence and the results of a study to support her main claim.*
How would you characterize the style?	*Fraser writes in a neutral, journalistic style. She stays in the background and doesn't discuss her own issues with food.*

How is it organized?

This map shows the organization of "The French Paradox," which begins on the following page.

Beginning paragraph Paragraph 1	Fraser announces her subject—that French people have a low rate of heart disease while consuming a high-fat diet.
Rejection of first alternative cause Paragraph 2	High consumption of wine doesn't account for fewer heart attacks.
Rejection of alternative proposed cause Paragraph 3–6	Consumption of particular foods doesn't explain why French people are healthier than Americans.
Rejection of alternative proposed cause Paragraphs 7–10	Fraser rejects the "time lag" hypothesis that the French will eventually become as unhealthy as Americans.
Introduction of proposed cause Paragraphs 11–14	The French are healthier not because of what they eat but because of how they eat.
Evidence for causal claim Paragraphs 15–17	Researchers have found that Americans worry about what they eat while French people find pleasure in eating.
Conclusion Paragraphs 18–19	Fraser makes an additional point about the psychological effects of eating slowly.

The French Paradox
Laura Fraser

Laura Fraser started counting calories in kindergarten when she was a slightly plump child. Her parents' obsession with her weight drove her to bulimia, which she describes in her 1997 book *Losing It: America's Obsession with Weight and the Industry That Feeds on It.* She comes to the conclusion that diets don't work. In the "The French Paradox," published in the online magazine *Salon* in 2000, Fraser examines why the French can eat a high-fat, high-calorie diet and be far healthier than Americans.

1　For much of the past decade, American and British scientists have been annoyed by the phenomenon known as the French Paradox. Nutritionally speaking, the French have been getting away with murder: They eat all the butter, cream, foie gras, pastry and cheese that their hearts desire, and yet their rates of obesity and heart disease are much lower than ours. The French eat three times as much saturated animal fat as Americans do, and only a third as many die of heart attacks. It's maddening. ◀

Introduction:
Fraser starts fast, setting out the central questions: Why are the French healthier than Americans considering their respective diets?

2　Baffled, scientists struggled to come up with a few hypotheses: Maybe it was something in the red wine, they said. But while winemakers worldwide celebrated that news, more sober research has suggested that any alcohol—whether Lafite Rothschild, a banana daiquiri or a cold Bud—pretty much has the same nice, relaxing effect. So while a little wine is apt to do you good, the French aren't so special in having a drink now and then (though the fact that they drink wine moderately and slowly with meals, instead of downing shots at the bar, could make a difference). ◀

First rejected cause:
Wine consumption isn't the answer.

3　After the wine argument, scientists ventured that it must be the olive oil that keeps the French healthy. But this doesn't explain the butter or brie. Then, voilà, French scientist Serge Renaud (made famous on *60 Minutes* as an expert on the French Paradox) said it's the foie gras that melts away cholesterol. This, too, is dicey: While people in Toulouse—the fattened force-fed duck-liver-eating area of France—do indeed have one of the lowest rates of heart disease in the developed world, they actually only eat the delicacy about six times a year. And they're a lot more likely to die of stroke than we are anyway.

4   Other researchers, perhaps sponsored by the garlic and onion industry, suggested that the French Paradox effect is due to garlic and onions. Claude Fischler, a nutritional sociologist at INSERM, the French equivalent of America's National Institutes of Health, says all these single hypotheses are more wishful thinking than science. ◄────────────────────────────────

Second rejected cause: Particular foods don't explain why the French are healthier.

5   "The government loves the French Paradox because it sells red wine—Bordeaux wine in particular—it sells French lifestyle and a number of other French products," he tells me over dinner at an outdoor Paris bistro. "It's something in the cheese! Something from the fat from ducks! It's butter! Really, we're a long way from science here."

6   More than anything, Fischler thinks the French Paradox is a kind of cultural Rorschach test. "Americans think it's unfair, and Francophiles think it's wonderful."

7   Last May, researchers writing in the British Medical Journal came up with the least cheerful hypothesis of all. They argued that it's just a matter of time before the French—who are in fact eating more hamburgers and french fries these days—catch up with Americans, and begin suffering the same high rates of cardiovascular disease.

8   These researchers, Malcolm Law and Nicholas Wald (who must have thought up their hypothesis over dry kidney pie, while dreaming of the kind of duck in red wine and honey sauce I had with Claude Fischler), call this the "time lag explanation" for the French Paradox. As far as they are concerned, the McDonaldization (this is a French catch-all term for the importation of fast food and other American cultural horrors) of France will continue at a frantic pace, and it is as inevitable that French men will start keeling over of heart attacks as it is that French women will eventually wear jean shorts and marshmallow tennis shoes on the streets of Paris.

9   Nutritionists on this side of the Atlantic are just as dour in their predictions. Marion Nestle, chair of New York University's department of nutrition, says that the wonderful food she found on every street corner in Paris when she lived there in 1983 has changed. "Then you could go into some local bar, and you would be given a little tart, a little salad and a little quiche that would knock your socks off," she says wistfully. But now, she says, the quality of ingredients, the concern about flavor and the freshness of the food has declined. "Last time I was in Paris, everything seemed bigger, softer and more commercially prepared. If you wanted really high quality food, you had to pay for it." When she looked at food data in France, she saw that indeed the amount of fat has risen, and the French are snacking more, eating fewer long meals and visiting McDonald's more often on the sly. She, like Law and Wald, says, "Just wait."

10   The French, however, disagree about this time lag hypothesis. Nor do they believe that Parisian women will start wearing Nikes with skirts to work anytime soon. "It's hilarious!" says Fischler, finishing a fresh ricotta-stuffed tortellini appetizer. "The American attitude is always to look for a silver bullet—it's the wine, the cheese—or else it has to be nothing, we'll get worse, we haven't had time to get the terrible consequences of modern eating." Instead, says Fischler, the deeply rooted French traditions of eating not only explain the French Paradox, but will insure that it continues, even if it decreases somewhat.   ◄

Third rejected cause: Fraser refutes that the French will become as unhealthy with an American diet.

11   Americans, he says, are always painting the picture in extremes. The French, he continues over a piece of grilled fish, pouring me another glass of that medicinal red wine, have a long-evolved culture of eating that emphasizes pleasure—and order. The French eat *comme il faut*, "the way it should be done." They may eat whatever they want, but they eat by strict rules: no snacking, no seconds, no skipping meals, no bolting down food, no heading straight for dessert before first filling up on vegetables, salad and meat. They savor their food and eat smaller portions than Americans do.   ◄

Actual cause: The difference between the French and Americans is not what they eat but how they eat.

12   They also eat a greater diversity of food, which could have something to do with their health, too. And while traditions are loosening in France—more women are working, and so people are more apt to grab a sandwich at lunch—a recent survey Fischler took showed that while more people will skip the cheese course or the first course once or twice a week, they still don't skip meals. The French sit down at the table for well-prepared meals, with high-quality foods, and between times they don't eat. Period.

13   "In France, we eat in a socially controlled and regulated way, but it's pleasant," says Fischler. "Structure is something that constrains you but also supports you." Fischler and a food-loving University of Pennsylvania psychologist, Paul Rozin, say the fact that the French have lower rates of coronary artery disease and are skinnier than Americans doesn't have so much to do with what they eat, but how they eat—especially their positive attitudes about food. Talk to a French woman about whether she ever feels guilty about what she eats and she will tell you, as one impossibly young-looking 46-year-old dancer told me, "Absolutely not—I eat exactly what I please."

14   Then try to find a woman in the U.S. who will answer the same way. There's no magic ingredient that keeps French arteries clear, but instead a whole system of eating that allows them to indulge without overdoing it, and without feeling guilty. Fischler and Rozin say that the biggest predictor of health may not be the content of someone's diet, but how stressed out they are about food, and how relaxed they are about eating. In other words, the more pleasurable it is to eat, the healthier it is for you.

15   In a study published in the October issue of the journal *Appetite*, Fischler and Rozin surveyed 1,281 French, American, Japanese and Flemish people about their attitudes toward food. Participants were asked how much they worried about food and the healthiness of their diet, whether they bought low-fat and other diet foods and how much importance they placed on food as a positive force in life. Americans, it turned out, were much more likely than the French to worry about what they eat, buy

diet foods and still think of themselves as unhealthy eaters. The French and Belgians were at the other extreme, thinking about food as mainly a great pleasure, and feeling fine about how healthy their diet was. In word association tests, given "chocolate cake," the French would say "celebration," and Americans, "guilt." Given "heavy cream," the French said "whipped," while the Americans responded "unhealthy." Says Rozin, "The French are more inclined to think of food as something you eat and experience, and the Americans are thinking about some sort of chemicals that are getting into your body." ◄───────

Evidence for claim:
Fraser summarizes a study that supports the anecdotal evidence she has given.

16   Americans have the worst of both worlds, Rozin says – they have greater concerns about their diets, and they are much more dissatisfied with what they eat. And that sort of stress, he says, can result in a lot of poor eating habits for Americans—extreme dieting, bingeing, overeating and constantly obsessing about food—which are ultimately unhealthy. The real paradox, Rozin says, isn't that the French enjoy food and remain thin and heart disease-free. It's that Americans worry so much about food, do so much more to control their weight and end up so much more dissatisfied with their meals.   ◄───────

Conclusion:
Fraser reverses the paradox: Americans worry more about food than the French yet are fatter and less healthy.

17   American researchers are tentative about Fischler and Rozin's pleasure hypothesis. Eric Rimm, a nutritional epidemiologist at Harvard, says a pleasurable way of eating may be part of the puzzle. "There is something to eating patterns that makes a difference to overall health," he says. "It can't just be the total calories you get at the end of the day."

Eating slowly, he points out, may make a difference. And then there are psychosocial effects. "In France they eat with large families and social networks, which may be important to peace of mind, which has been linked to coronary disease." He hesitates. "Maybe there are psychological effects to the way they eat in France, too." ◄───────

Conclusion:
Fraser offers an additional point for her readers to think about.

18   As the French would say, with just a hint of derision, "*Mais oui—but of course.*" And then, like Claude Fischler and me, they would finish off a long, perfect meal with a couple little spoonfuls of intensely rich chocolate soufflé.

Why Should I Be Nice to You? Coffee Shops and the Politics of Good Service

Emily Raine

Emily Raine recently received a Master's degree in Communication Studies at McGill University in Montreal. She also writes about graffiti and street art. This essay appeared in the online journal *Bad Subjects* in 2005.

Return to these questions after you have finished reading.

Analyzing the Reading

1. What exactly is Raine's causal argument about why work in coffee chains is worse than in other kinds of service jobs?

2. Raine mixes technical terms with informal language. For example, she says, "Café labor is heavily grounded in the rationalism of Fordist manufacturing principles," which uses the technical term for the method of assembly line production developed by Henry Ford. But she also says she "felt like an aproned Coke machine." Look for other examples of technical and informal language. Why does she mix them?

3. Why is it important that coffee shop employees not act like individuals, from the employer's perspective?

4. Have you ever worked in a restaurant, coffee shop, retail store, or another service industry? If so, how was your experience similar to or different from Raine's? If not, think about your experiences as a customer in coffee shops and similar businesses. How did the employees behave?

5. Look at the last paragraph. Raine makes a new claim that rudeness allows workers to retain their individuality. Why does she put this claim in the conclusion? Does it lead to a strong conclusion?

Exploring Ideas and Issues

Raine presents a sophisticated analysis, explaining both employers' requirements and employees' responses. She uses expert opinion, historical facts, and personal experience to support her contention that the very way in which coffee bars are organized works against employers' demand that employees provide "good service."

1. Think about the causal argument that Raine presents and your own experiences as an employee or as a customer at a coffee shop, restaurant, store, or other service-oriented establishment. Do you agree with Raine's explanation of rudeness? Has she overlooked other possible causes of this behavior? Write a short rebuttal to Raine's argument, discussing at least one factor that Raine has overlooked.

2. Raine contends that uniforms obscure workers' individuality. However, people in many occupations—for example, police, military, medical personnel—must wear uniforms or adhere to specific grooming regimens. Write a short essay in which you discuss the effects that various kinds of uniforms can have. Is making practioners themselves seem "uniform" something that all have in common? Draw on examples from your personal experience to support your ideas.

287

Bad Subjects

home   about   articles   authors   books   contact us   **editorials**   links   news   reviews

Why Should I Be Nice To You?
Coffee Shops and the Politics of Good Service

"There is no more precious commodity than the relationship of trust and confidence a company has with its employees."

–STARBUCKS COFFEE COMPANY CHAIRMAN HOWARD SCHULTZ

I actually like to serve. I'm not sure if this comes from some innate inclination to mother and fuss over strangers, or if it's because the movement and sociability of service work provides a much-needed antidote to the solitude of academic research, but I've always found something about service industry work satisfying. I've done the gamut of service jobs, from fine dining to cocktail waitressing to hip euro-bistro counter work, and the only job where I've ever felt truly whipped was working as a barista at one of the now-ubiquitous specialty coffee chains, those bastions of jazz and public solitude that have spread through urban landscapes over the last ten years or so. The pay was poor, the shifts long and oddly dispersed, the work boring and monotonous, the managers demanding, and the customers regularly displayed that unique spleen that emerges in even the most pleasant people before they've had the morning's first coffee. I often felt like an aproned Coke machine, such was the effect my sparkling personality had on the clientele. And yet, some combination of service professionalism, fear of termination and an imperative to be "nice" allowed me to suck it up, smile and continue to provide that intangible trait that the industry holds above all else, good service.

Bad Subjects

Good service in coffee shops doesn't amount to much. Unlike table service, where interaction with customers spans a minimum of half an hour, the average contact with a café customer lasts less than ten seconds. Consider how specialty cafés are laid out: the customer service counter is arranged in a long line that clients move along to "use" the café. The linear coffee bar resembles an assembly line, and indeed, café labor is heavily grounded in the rationalism of Fordist manufacturing principles, which had already been tested for use in hospitality services by fast food chains. Each of the café workers is assigned a specific stage in the service process to perform exclusively, such as taking orders, using the cash registers, or handing clients cups of brewed coffee.

The specialization of tasks increases the speed of transactions and limits the duration of any one employee's interaction with the clientele. This means that in a given visit a customer might order from one worker, receive food from the next, then brewed coffee or tea from yet another, then pay a cashier before proceeding down the line of the counter, finishing the trip at the espresso machine which is always situated at its end. Ultimately, each of the café's products is processed and served by a different employee, who repeats the same preparation task for hours and attends to each customer only as they receive that one product.

Needless to say, the productive work in cafés is dreary and repetitive. Further, this style of service severely curtails interaction with the clientele, and the very brevity of each transaction precludes much chance for authentic friendliness or conversation—even asking about someone's day would slow the entire operation. The one aspect of service work that can be unpredictable—people—becomes redundant, and interaction with customers is reduced to a fatiguing eight-hour-long smile and the repetition of sentiments that allude to good service, such as injunctions to enjoy their purchases or to have a nice day. Rather than friendly exchanges with customers, barista workers' good service is reduced to a quick rictus in the customer's direction between a great deal of friendly interaction with the espresso machine.

eserver » bad home » bad editorials » 2006 » raza/race: why support immigrants?

Bad Subjects

home   about   articles   authors   books   contact us   **editorials**   links   news   reviews

As the hospitality industry really took off in the sixties, good service became one of the trademarks of its advertising claims, a way for brands to distinguish themselves from the rest of the pack. One needn't think too hard to come up with a litany of service slogans that holler the good graces of their personnel—at Starbucks where the baristas make the magic, at PSA where smiles aren't just painted on, or at McDonald's where smiles are free. Employee friendliness emerged as one of the chief distinguishing brand features of personal services, which means that the workers themselves become an aspect of the product for sale.

Our notions of good service revolve around a series of platitudes about professionalism—we're at your service, with a smile, where the customer's always right—each bragging the centrality of the customer to everything "we" do. Such claims imply an easy and equal exchange between two parties: the "we" that gladly serves and the "you" that happily receives. There is, however, always a third party involved in the service exchange, and that's whoever has hired the server, the body that ultimately decides just what the dimensions of good service will be.

Like most employees, a service worker sells labor to an employer at a set rate, often minimum wage, and the employer sells the product of that labor, the service itself, at market values. In many hospitality services, where gratuities make up the majority of employment revenue, the worker directly benefits from giving good service, which of course translates to good tips. But for the vast majority of service staff, and particularly those employed in venues yielding little or no gratuities—fast food outlets, café chains, cleaning and maintenance operations—this promises many workers little more than a unilateral imperative to be perpetually bright and amenable.

The vast majority of service personnel do not spontaneously produce an unaffected display of cheer and good will continuously for the duration of a shift. When a company markets its products on servers' friendliness, they must

Bad Subjects

home   about   articles   authors   books   contact us   **editorials**   links   news   reviews

then monitor and control employees' friendliness, so good service is defined and enforced from above. Particularly in chains, which are premised upon their consistent reproduction of the same experience in numerous locations, organizations are obliged to impose systems to manage employees' interaction with their customers. In some chains, namely the fast food giants such as McDonald's and Burger King, employee banter is scripted into cash registers, so that as soon as a customer orders, workers are cued to offer, "would you like a dessert with that?" (an offer of dubious benefit to the customer) and to wish them a nice day. Ultimately, this has allowed corporations to be able to assimilate "good service"—or, friendly workers—into their overall brand image.

While cafés genuflect toward the notion of good service, their layouts and management styles preclude much possibility of creating the warmth that this would entail. Good service is, of course, important, but not if it interferes with throughput. What's more, these cafés have been at the forefront of a new wave of organizations that not only market themselves on service quality but also describe employees' job satisfaction as the seed from which this flowers.

Perhaps the most glaring example of this is Starbucks, where cheerful young workers are displayed behind elevated counters as they banter back and forth, calling out fancy Italian drink names and creating theatre out of their productive labor. Starbucks' corporate literature gushes not only about the good service its customers will receive, but about the great joy that its "partners" take in providing it, given the company's unique ability to "provide a great work environment and treat each other with respect and dignity," and where its partners are "emotionally and intellectually committed to Starbucks success." In the epigraph to this essay, Starbucks' chairman even describes the company's relationship with its workers as a commodity. Not only does Starbucks offer good service, but it attempts to guarantee something even better: good service provided by employees that are genuinely happy to give it.

Bad Subjects

home   about   articles   authors   books   contact us   **editorials**   links   news   reviews

Starbucks has branded a new kind of worker, the happy, wholesome, perfume-free barista. The company offers unusual benefits for service workers, including stock options, health insurance, dental plans and other perks such as product discounts and giveaways. Further, they do so very, very publicly, and the company's promotional materials are filled with moving accounts of workers who never dreamed that corporate America could care so much. With the other hand, though, the company has smashed unionization drives in New York, Vancouver and at its Seattle roaster; it schedules workers at oddly timed shifts that never quite add up to full-time hours; the company pays only nominally more than minimum wage, and their staffs are still unable to subsist schlepping lattes alone.

Starbucks is not alone in marketing itself as an enlightened employer. When General Motors introduced its Saturn line, the new brand was promoted almost entirely on the company's good relations with its staff. The company's advertising spots often featured pictures of and quotes from the union contract, describing their unique partnership between manufacturer, workers and union, which allowed blue-collar personnel to have a say in everything from automobile designs to what would be served for lunch. The company rightly guessed that this strategy would go over well with liberal consumers concerned about the ethics of their purchases. Better yet, Saturn could market its cars based on workers' happiness whether personnel were satisfied or not, because very few consumers would ever have the chance to interact with them.

At the specialty coffee chains, however, consumers have to talk to employees, yet nobody ever really asks. The café service counter runs like a smooth piece of machinery, and I found that most people preferred to pretend that they were interacting with an appliance. In such short transactions, it is exceedingly difficult for customers to remember the humanity of each of the four to seven people they might interact with to get their coffees. Even fast food counters have one server who processes each customer's order, yet in cafés the workers just become another gadget in the well-oiled café machine. This is a definite downside for the

Bad **Subjects**

home   about   articles   authors   books   contact us   **editorials**   links   news   reviews

employees—clients are much ruder to café staff than in any other sector of the industry I ever worked in. I found that people were more likely to be annoyed than touched by any reference to my having a personality, and it took no small amount of thought on my part to realize why.

Barista workers are hired to represent an abstract category of worker, not to act as individuals. Because of the service system marked by short customer interaction periods and a homogenous staff, the services rendered are linked in the consumer imagination to the company and not to any one individual worker. Workers' assimilation into the company image makes employees in chain service as branded as the products they serve. The chain gang, the workers who hold these eminently collegiate after-school jobs, are proscribed sales scripts and drilled on customer service scenarios to standardize interactions with customers. The company issues protocols for hair length, color and maintenance, visible piercings and tattoos as well as personal hygiene and acceptable odorific products. Workers are made more interchangeable by the use of uniforms, which, of course, serve to make the staff just that. The organization is a constant intermediary in every transaction, interjecting its presence in every detail of the service experience, and this standardization amounts to an absorption of individuals' personalities into the corporate image.

Many of the measures that chains take to secure the homogeneity of their employees do not strike us as particularly alarming, likely because similar restrictions have been in place for several hundred years. Good service today has inherited many of the trappings of the good servant of yore, including prohibitions against eating, drinking, sitting or relaxing in front the served, entering and exiting through back doors and wearing uniforms to visually mark workers' status. These measures almost completely efface the social identities of staff during work hours, providing few clues to workers' status in their free time. Contact between service workers and their customers is thus limited to purely functional relations, so that the public only see them as workers, as makers of quality coffee, and never as possible peers.

Bad Subjects

home   about   articles   authors   books   contact us   **editorials**   links   news   reviews

Maintaining such divisions is integral to good service because this display of class distinctions ultimately underlies our notions of service quality. Good service means not only serving well, but also allowing customers to feel justified in issuing orders, to feel okay about being served—which, in turn, requires demonstrations of class difference and the smiles that suggest servers' comfort with having a subordinate role in the service exchange.

Unlike the penguin-suited household servant staffs whose class status was clearly defined, service industry workers today often have much more in common from a class perspective with those that they serve. This not only creates an imperative for them to wear their class otherness on their sleeves, as it were, but also to accept their subordinate role to those they serve by being unshakably tractable and polite.

Faith Popcorn has rather famously referred to the four-dollar latte as a "small indulgence," noting that while this is a lot to pay for a glass of hot milk, it is quite inexpensive for the feeling of luxury that can accompany it. In this service climate, the class status of the server and the served—anyone who can justify spending this much on a coffee—is blurry, indeed. Coffee shops that market themselves on employee satisfaction assert the same happy servant that allows politically conscientious consumers who are in many cases the workers' own age and class peers, to feel justified in receiving good service. Good service—as both an apparent affirmation of subordinate classes' desire to serve and as an enforced one-sided politeness—reproduces the class distinctions that have historically characterized servant-served relationships so that these are perpetuated within the contemporary service market.

The specialty coffee companies are large corporations, and for the twenty-somethings who stock their counters, barista work is too temporary to bother fighting the system. Mostly, people simply quit. Dissatisfied workers are stuck with

Bad Subjects

home   about   articles   authors   books   contact us   **editorials**   links   news   reviews

engaging in tactics that will change nothing but allow them to make the best of their lot. These include minor infractions such as taking liberties with the uniforms or grabbing little bits of company time for their own pleasure, what Michel de Certeau calls *la perruque* and the companies themselves call "time theft." As my time in the chain gang wore on, I developed my own tactic, the only one I found that jostled the customers out of their complacency and allowed me to be a barista and a person.

There is no easy way to serve without being a servant, and I have always found that the best way to do so is to show my actual emotions rather than affecting a smooth display of interminable patience and good will. For café customers, bettering baristas' lots can be as simple as asking about their day, addressing them by name—any little gesture to show that you noticed the person behind the service that they can provide. My tactic as a worker is equally simple, but it is simultaneously an assertion of individual identity at work, a refusal of the class distinctions that characterize the service environment and a rebuttal to the companies that would promote my satisfaction with their system: be rude. Not arbitrarily rude, of course—customers are people, too, and nobody gains anything by spreading bad will. But on those occasions when customer or management behavior warranted a zinging comeback, I would give it.

Rudeness, when it is demanded, undermines companies' claims on workers' personal warmth and allows them to retain their individuality by expressing genuine rather than affected feelings in at-work interpersonal exchanges. It is a refusal of the class distinctions that underlie consumers' unilateral prerogative of rudeness and servers' unilateral imperative to be nice. It runs contrary to everything that we have been taught, not only about service but about interrelating with others. But this seems to be the only method of asserting one's person-hood in the service environment, where workers' personalities are all too easily reduced to a space-time, conflated with the drinks they serve. Baristas of the world, if you want to avoid becoming a green-aproned coffee dispensary, you're just going to have to tell people off about it.

The New Girl Order
Kay S. Hymowitz

Kay S. Hymowitz is a contributing editor of *City Journal* and the William E. Simon Fellow at the Manhattan Institute. She writes about childhood and education in the United States as well as the breakdown of marriage and how it threatens the nation's future. She has published four books, including *Marriage and Caste in America: Separate and Unequal Families in a Post-Marital Age* (2006), which is a compilation of some of her previously published *City Journal* essays. Her most recent book is *Manning Up How the Rise of Women is Turning Men into Boys* (2011).

Return to these questions after you have finished reading.

Analyzing the Reading

1. The title of Hymowitz's essay is a play on the phrase "New World Order." Why do you think that she chose this phrase? What does this phrase mean to you? What is the history of this phrase?

2. The author suggests that the SYF lifestyle is spreading worldwide. What three factors does she say contribute to this growth?

3. What exactly is the SYF lifestyle, and why is it so attractive to women, according to Hymowitz?

4. What does Hymowitz see as the societal costs of the "New Girl Order"?

Exploring Ideas and Issues

Women's status has changed dramatically over the past century. It's as recently as 1920 that women's right to vote was recognized in the United States by the adoption of the Nineteenth Amendment. Some changes, such as the right to vote, have been enshrined in law; others, such as those described in Hymowitz's essay, are the result of personal decisions and societal forces.

1. Hymowitz does not directly discuss the role that changes in sexual mores may have played in the development of the SYF lifestyle. Think about your generation's attitude toward sex before marriage and children born out of wedlock. Compare that attitude with your parents' or your grandparents' view of the same issues. Write a short essay in which you analyze the differences and similarities.

2. The essay says, "It's a man's world. ... But if these trends continue, not so much." We can infer from this statement that the author thinks men will lose out in this "New Girl Order." Write an essay in which you either affirm or refute this idea. Give at least three examples to support your thesis.

3. The author ends her essay with dire predictions about the effects of the "New Girl Order" on society. Research at least two other views of demographic change that have predicted desperate outcomes. How often have these predictions come to pass? Write an essay in which you explore these ideas.

The New Girl Order

AFTER MY LOT AIRLINES FLIGHT from New York touched down at Warsaw's Frédéric Chopin Airport a few months back, I watched a middle-aged passenger rush to embrace a waiting younger woman—clearly her daughter. Like many people on the plane, the older woman wore drab clothing and had the short, square physique of someone familiar with too many potatoes and too much manual labor. Her Poland-based daughter, by contrast, was tall and smartly outfitted in pointy-toed pumps, slim-cut jeans, a cropped jacket revealing a toned midriff (Yoga? Pilates? Or just a low-carb diet?), and a large, brass-studded leather bag, into which she dropped a silver cell phone.

Yes: Carrie Bradshaw is alive and well and living in Warsaw. Well, not just Warsaw. Conceived and raised in the United States, Carrie may still see New York as a spiritual home. But today you can find her in cities across Europe, Asia, and North America. Seek out the trendy shoe stores in Shanghai, Berlin, Singapore, Seoul, and Dublin, and you'll see crowds of single young females (SYFs) in their twenties and thirties, who spend their hours working their abs and their careers, sipping cocktails, dancing at clubs, and (yawn) talking about relationships. *Sex and the City* has gone global; the SYF world is now flat.

Is this just the latest example of American cultural imperialism? Or is it the triumph of planetary feminism? Neither. The globalization of the SYF reflects a series of stunning demographic and economic shifts that are pointing much of the world—with important exceptions, including Africa and most of the Middle East—toward a New Girl Order. It's a man's world, James Brown always reminded us. But if these trends continue, not so much.

Three demographic facts are at the core of the New Girl Order. First, women—especially, but not only, in the developed world—are getting married and having kids considerably later than ever before. According to the UN's *World Fertility Report*, the worldwide median age of marriage for women is up two years, from 21.2 in the 1970s to 23.2 today. In the developed countries, the rise has been considerably steeper—from 22.0 to 26.1.

Demographers get really excited about shifts like these, but in case you don't get what the big deal is, consider: in 1960, 70 percent of American 25-year-old women were married with children; in 2000, only 25 percent of them were. In 1970, just 7.4 percent of all American 30- to 34-year-olds were unmarried; today, the number is 22 percent. That change took about

a generation to unfold, but in Asia and Eastern Europe the transformation
has been much more abrupt. In today's Hungary, for instance, 30 percent
of women in their early thirties are single, compared with 6 percent of their
mothers' generation at the same age. In South Korea, 40 percent of 30-year-
olds are single, compared with 14 percent only 20 years ago.

Nothing-new-under-the-sun skeptics point out, correctly, that
marrying at 27 or 28 was once commonplace for women, at least in the
United States and parts of northern Europe. The cultural anomaly was the
1950s and 60s, when the average age of marriage for women dipped to 20—
probably because of post-Depression and postwar cocooning. But today's
single 27-year-old has gone global—and even in the West, she differs from
her late-marrying great-grandma in fundamental ways that bring us to the
second piece of the demographic story. Today's aspiring middle-class women
are gearing up to be part of the paid labor market for most of their adult
lives; unlike their ancestral singles, they're looking for careers, not jobs. And
that means they need lots of schooling.

In the newly global economy, good jobs go to those with degrees,
and all over the world, young people, particularly women, are enrolling in
colleges and universities at unprecedented rates. Between 1960 and 2000,
the percentages of 20-, 25-, and 30-year-olds enrolled in school more than
doubled in the U.S., and enrollment in higher education doubled throughout
Europe. And the fairer sex makes up an increasing part of the total. The
majority of college students are female in the U.S., the U.K., France,
Germany, Norway, and Australia, to name only a few of many places, and
the gender gap is quickly narrowing in more traditional countries like China,
Japan, and South Korea. In a number of European countries, including
Denmark, Finland, and France, over half of all women between 20 and 24
are in school. The number of countries where women constitute the majority
of graduate students is also growing rapidly.

That educated women are staying single is unsurprising; degreed
women have always been more likely to marry late, if they marry at all. But
what has demographers taking notice is the sheer transnational numbers
of women postponing marriage while they get diplomas and start careers.
In the U.K., close to a third of 30-year-old college-educated women are
unmarried; some demographers predict that 30 percent of women with
university degrees there will remain forever childless. In Spain—not so
long ago a culturally Catholic country where a girl's family would jealously
chaperone her until handing her over to a husband at 21 or so—women now

constitute 54 percent of college students, up from 26 percent in 1970, and the average age of first birth has risen to nearly 30, which appears to be a world record.

Adding to the contemporary SYF's novelty is the third demographic shift: urbanization. American and northern European women in the nineteenth and early twentieth centuries might have married at 26, but after a long day in the dairy barn or cotton mill, they didn't hang out at Studio 54 while looking for Mr. Right (or, as the joke has it, Mr. Right for Now). In the past, women who delayed marriage generally lived with their parents; they also remained part of the family economy, laboring in their parents' shops or farms, or at the very least, contributing to the family kitty. A lot of today's bachelorettes, on the other hand, move from their native village or town to Boston or Berlin or Seoul because that's where the jobs, boys, and bars are—and they spend their earnings on themselves.

By the mid-1990s, in countries as diverse as Canada, France, Hungary, Ireland, Portugal, and Russia, women were out-urbanizing men, who still tended to hang around the home village. When they can afford to, these women live alone or with roommates. The Netherlands, for instance, is flush with public housing, some of it reserved for young students and workers, including lots of women. In the United States, the proportion of unmarried twentysomethings living with their parents has declined steadily over the last 100 years, despite sky-high rents and apartment prices. Even in countries where SYFs can't afford to move out of their parents' homes, the anonymity and diversity of city life tend to heighten their autonomy. Belgians, notes University of Maryland professor Jeffrey Jensen Arnett, have coined a term—"hotel families"—to describe the arrangement.

Combine these trends—delayed marriage, expanded higher education and labor-force participation, urbanization—add a global media and some disposable income, and voilà: an international lifestyle is born. One of its defining characteristics is long hours of office work, often in quasi-creative fields like media, fashion, communications, and design—areas in which the number of careers has exploded in the global economy over the past few decades. The lifestyle also means whole new realms of leisure and consumption, often enjoyed with a group of close girlfriends: trendy cafés and bars serving sweetish coffee concoctions and cocktails; fancy boutiques, malls, and emporiums hawking cosmetics, handbags, shoes, and $100-plus buttock-hugging jeans; gyms for toning and male-watching; ski resorts and beach hotels; and, everywhere, the frustrating hunt for a boyfriend and, though it's an ever more vexing subject, a husband.

The SYF lifestyle first appeared in primitive form in the U.S. during the seventies, after young women started moving into higher education, looking for meaningful work, and delaying marriage. Think of ur-SYF Mary Richards, the pre-Jordache career girl played by Mary Tyler Moore, whose dates dropped her off—that same evening, of course—at her apartment door. By the mid-nineties, such propriety was completely passé. Mary had become the vocationally and sexually assertive Carrie Bradshaw, and cities like New York had magically transformed into the young person's pleasure palace evoked by the hugely popular TV show *Sex and the City*. At around the same time, women in Asia and in post-Communist Europe began to join the SYF demographic, too. Not surprisingly, they also loved watching themselves, or at least Hollywood versions of themselves, on television. *Friends*, *Ally McBeal*, and *Sex and the City* became global favorites. In repressive places like Singapore and China, which banned SATC, women passed around pirated DVDs.

By the late 1990s, the SYF lifestyle was fully globalized. Indeed, you might think of SYFs as a sociological Starbucks: no matter how exotic the location, there they are, looking and behaving just like the American prototype. They shop for shoes in Kyoto, purses in Shanghai, jeans in Prague, and lip gloss in Singapore; they sip lattes in Dublin, drink cocktails in Chicago, and read lifestyle magazines in Kraków; they go to wine tastings in Boston, speed-dating events in Amsterdam, yoga classes in Paris, and ski resorts outside Tokyo. "At the fashionable Da Capo Café on bustling Kolonaki Square in downtown Athens, Greek professionals in their 30s and early 40s luxuriate over their iced cappuccinos," a *Newsweek International* article began last year. "Their favorite topic of conversation is, of course, relationships: men's reluctance to commit, women's independence, and when to have children." Thirty-seven-year-old Eirini Perpovlov, an administrative assistant at Associated Press, "loves her work and gets her social sustenance from her *parea*, or close-knit group of like-minded friends."

Sure sounds similar to this July's *Time* story about Vicky, "a purposeful, 29-year-old actuary who . . . loves nothing better than a party. She and her friends meet so regularly for dinner and at bars that she says she never eats at home anymore. As the pictures on her blog attest, they also throw regular theme parties to mark holidays like Halloween and Christmas, and last year took a holiday to Egypt." At the restaurant where the reporter interviews them, Vicky's friends gab about snowboarding, iPods, credit-card rates, and a popular resort off the coast of Thailand. Vicky, whose motto is "work hard, play harder," is not from New York, London, or even Athens; she's from the SYF delegation in Beijing, China, a country that appears to be racing from rice paddies to sushi bars in less than a generation—at least for a privileged minority.

With no children or parents to support, and with serious financial hardship a bedtime story told by aging grandparents, SYFs have ignited what *The Economist* calls the "Bridget Jones economy"—named, of course, after the book and movie heroine who is perhaps the most famous SYF of all. Bridget Jonesers, the magazine says, spend their disposable income "on whatever is fashionable, frivolous, and fun," manufactured by a bevy of new companies that cater to young women. In 2000, Marian Salzman—then the president of the London-based Intelligence Factory, an arm of Young & Rubicam—said that by the 1990s, "women living alone had come to comprise the strongest consumer bloc in much the same way that yuppies did in the 1980s."

SYFs drive the growth of apparel stores devoted to stylish career wear like Ann Taylor, which now has more than 800 shops in the United States, and the international Zara, with more than 1,000 in 54 countries. They also spend paychecks at the Paris-based Sephora, Europe's largest retailer of perfumes and cosmetics, which targets younger women in 14 countries, including such formerly sober redoubts as Poland and the Czech Republic. The chain plans to expand to China soon. According to *Forbes*, the Chinese cosmetics market, largely an urban phenomenon, was up 17 percent in 2006, and experts predict a growth rate of between 15 and 20 percent in upcoming years. Zara already has three stores there.

The power of the SYF's designer purse is also at work in the entertainment industry. By the mid-1990s, "chick lit," a contemporary urban version of the Harlequin romance with the SYF as heroine, was topping bestseller lists in England and the United States. Now chick lit has spread all over the world. The books of the Irish writer Marian Keyes, one of the first and most successful chick-litterateurs, appear in 29 languages. *The Devil Wears Prada* was an international hit as both a book (by Lauren Weisberger) and a movie (starring Meryl Streep). Meantime, the television industry is seeking to satisfy the SYF's appetite for single heroines with *Sex and the City* clones like *The Marrying Type* in South Korea and *The Balzac Age* in Russia.

Bridget Jonesers are also remaking the travel industry, especially in Asia. A 2005 report from MasterCard finds that women take four out of every ten trips in the Asia-Pacific region—up from one in ten back in the mid-1970s. While American women think about nature, adventure, or culture when choosing their travel destinations, says MasterCard, Asian women look for shopping, resorts, and, most of all, spas. Female travelers have led to what the report calls the "spa-ification of the Asian hotel industry." That industry is growing at a spectacular rate—200 percent annually.

And now the maturing Bridget Jones economy has begun to feature big-ticket items. In 2003, the Diamond Trading Company introduced the "right-hand ring," a diamond for women with no marital prospects but longing for a rock. ("Your left hand is your heart; your right hand is your voice," one ad explains.) In some SYF capitals, women are moving into the real-estate market. Canadian single women are buying homes at twice the rate of single men. The National Association of Realtors reports that in the U.S. last year, single women made up 22 percent of the real-estate market, compared with a paltry 9 percent for single men. The median age for first-time female buyers: 32. The real-estate firm Coldwell Banker is making eyes at these young buyers with a new motto, "Your perfect partner since 1906," while Lowe's, the home-renovation giant, is offering classes especially for them. SYFs are also looking for wheels, and manufacturers are designing autos and accessories with them in mind. In Japan, Nissan has introduced the Pino, which has seat covers festooned with stars and a red CD player shaped like a pair of lips. It comes in one of two colors: "milk tea beige" and pink.

Japan presents a striking example of the sudden rise of the New Girl Order outside the U.S. and Western Europe. As recently as the nation's boom years in the 1980s, the dominant image of the Japanese woman was of the housewife, or *sengyoshufu*, who doted on her young children, intently prepared older ones for the world economy, and waited on the man of the house after his 16-hour day at the office. She still exists, of course, but about a decade ago she met her nemesis: the Japanese SYF. Between 1994 and 2004, the number of Japanese women between 25 and 29 who were unmarried soared from 40 to 54 percent; even more remarkable was the number of 30- to 34-year-old females who were unmarried, which rocketed from 14 to 27 percent. Because of Tokyo's expensive real-estate market, a good many of these young single women have shacked up with their parents, leading a prominent sociologist to brand them "parasite singles." The derogatory term took off, but the girls weren't disturbed; according to *USA Today*, many proudly printed up business cards bearing their new title.

The New Girl Order may represent a disruptive transformation for a deeply traditional society, but Japanese women sure seem to be enjoying the single life. Older singles who can afford it have even been buying their own apartments. One of them, 37-year-old Junko Sakai, wrote a best-selling plaint called *The Howl of the Loser Dogs,* a title that co-opts the term *makeinu*— "loser"—once commonly used to describe husbandless 30-year-olds. "Society may call us dogs," she writes, "but we are happy and independent." Today's Japanese SYFs are world-class shoppers, and though they must still fight workplace discrimination and have limited career tracks—particularly if they aren't working for Westernized companies—they're somehow managing to earn enough yen to keep the country's many Vuitton, Burberry, and Issey Miyake boutiques buzzing. Not so long ago, Japanese hotels wouldn't serve women traveling alone, in part because they suspected that the guests might be spinsters intent on hurling themselves off balconies to end their desperate solitude. Today, the losers are happily checking in at Japanese mountain lodges, not to mention Australian spas, Vietnamese hotels, and Hawaiian beach resorts.

And unlike their foreign counterparts in the New Girl Order, Japanese singles don't seem to be worrying much about finding Mr. Right. A majority of Japanese single women between 25 and 54 say that they'd be just as happy never to marry. Peggy Orenstein, writing in the *New York Times Magazine* in 2001, noted that Japanese women find American-style sentimentality about marriage puzzling. Yoko Harruka, a television personality and author of a book called *I Won't Get Married*—written after she realized that her then-fiancé expected her to quit her career and serve him tea—says that her countrymen propose with lines like, "I want you to cook miso soup for me for the rest of my life." Japanese SYFs complain that men don't show affection and expect women to cook dinner obediently while they sit on their duffs reading the paper. Is it any wonder that the women prefer Burberry?

Post-Communist Europe is also going through the shock of the New Girl Order. Under Communist rule, women tended to marry and have kids early. In the late eighties, the mean age of first birth in East Germany, for instance, was 24.7, far lower than the West German average of 28.3. According to Tomáš Sobotka of the Vienna Institute of Demography, young people had plenty of reasons to schedule an early wedding day. Tying the knot was the only way to gain independence from parents, since married couples could get an apartment, while singles could not. Furthermore, access to modern contraception, which the state proved either unable or unwilling to produce at affordable prices, was limited. Marriages frequently began as the result of unplanned pregnancies.

And then the Wall came down. The free market launched shiny new job opportunities, making higher education more valuable than under Communist regimes, which had apportioned jobs and degrees. Suddenly, a young Polish or Hungarian woman might imagine having a career, and some fun at the same time. In cities like Warsaw and Budapest, young adults can find pleasures completely unknown to previous generations of singles. In one respect, Eastern European and Russian SYFs were better equipped than Japanese ones for the new order. The strong single woman, an invisible figure in Japan, has long been a prominent character in the social landscape of Eastern Europe and Russia, a legacy, doubtless, of the Communist-era emphasis on egalitarianism (however inconsistently applied) and the massive male casualties of World War II.

Not that the post-Communist SYF is any happier with the husband material than her Japanese counterpart is. Eastern European gals complain about men overindulged by widowed mothers and unable to adapt to the new economy. According to *The Economist*, many towns in what used to be East Germany now face *Frauenmangel*—a lack of women—as SYFs who excelled in school have moved west for jobs, leaving the poorly performing men behind. In some towns, the ratio is just 40 women to 100 men. Women constitute the majority of both high school and college graduates in Poland. Though Russian women haven't joined the new order to the same extent, they're also grumbling about the men. In Russian TV's *The Balzac Age*, which chronicles the adventures of four single thirtysomething women, Alla, a high-achieving yuppie attorney, calls a handyman for help in her apartment. The two—to their mutual horror—recognize each other as former high school sweethearts, now moving in utterly different social universes.

There's much to admire in the New Girl Order—and not just the previously hidden cleavage. Consider the lives most likely led by the mothers, grandmothers, great-grandmothers, and so on of the fashionista at the Warsaw airport or of the hard-partying Beijing actuary. Those women reached adulthood, which usually meant 18 or even younger; married guys from their village, or, if they were particularly daring, from the village across the river; and then had kids—end of story, except for maybe some goat milking, rice planting, or, in urban areas, shop tending. The New Girl Order means good-bye to such limitations. It means the possibility of more varied lives, of more expansively nourished aspirations. It also means a richer world. SYFs bring ambition, energy, and innovation to the economy, both local and global; they simultaneously promote and enjoy what author Brink Lindsey calls "the age of abundance." The SYF, in sum, represents a dramatic advance in personal freedom and wealth.

But as with any momentous social change, the New Girl Order comes with costs—in this case, profound ones. The globalized SYF upends centuries of cultural traditions. However limiting, those traditions shaped how families formed and the next generation grew up. So it makes sense that the SYF is partly to blame for a worldwide drop in fertility rates. To keep a population stable, or at its "replacement level," women must have an average of at least 2.1 children. Under the New Girl Order, though, women delay marriage and childbearing, which itself tends to reduce the number of kids, and sometimes—because the opportunity costs of children are much higher for educated women—they forgo them altogether. Save Albania, no European country stood at or above replacement levels in 2000. Three-quarters of Europeans now live in countries with fertility rates below 1.5, and even that number is inflated by a disproportionately high fertility rate among Muslim immigrants. Oddly, the most Catholic European countries— Italy, Spain, and Poland—have the lowest fertility rates, under 1.3. Much of Asia looks similar. In Japan, fertility rates are about 1.3. Hong Kong, according to the CIA's *World Factbook*, at 0.98 has broken the barrier of one child per woman.

For many, fertility decline seems to be one more reason to celebrate the New Girl Order. Fewer people means fewer carbon footprints, after all, and thus potential environmental relief. But while we're waiting for the temperature to drop a bit, economies will plunge in ways that will be extremely difficult to manage—and that, ironically, will likely spell the SYF lifestyle's demise. As Philip Longman explains in his important book *The Empty Cradle*, dramatic declines in fertility rates equal aging and eventually shriveling populations. Japan now has one of the oldest populations in the world—one-third of its population, demographers predict, will be over 60 within a decade. True, fertility decline often spurs a temporary economic boost, as more women enter the workforce and increase income and spending, as was the case in 1980s Japan. In time, though, those women— and their male peers—will get old and need pensions and more health care.

And who will pay for that? With fewer children, the labor force shrinks, and so do tax receipts. Europe today has 35 pensioners for every 100 workers, Longman points out. By 2050, those 100 will be responsible for 75 pensioners; in Spain and Italy, the ratio of workers to pensioners will be a disastrous *one-to-one*. Adding to the economic threat, seniors with few or no children are more likely to look to the state for support than are elderly people with more children. The final irony is that the ambitious, hardworking SYF will have created a world where her children, should she have them, will need to work even harder in order to support her in her golden years.

Aging populations present other problems. For one thing, innovation and technological breakthroughs tend to be a young person's game — think of the young Turks of the information technology revolution. Fewer young workers and higher tax burdens don't make a good recipe for innovation and growth. Also, having fewer people leads to declining markets, and thus less business investment and formation. Where would you want to expand your cosmetics business: Ireland, where the population continues to renew itself, or Japan, where it is imploding?

And finally, the New Girl Order has given birth to a worrying ambivalence toward domestic life and the men who would help create it. Many analysts argue that today's women of childbearing age would have more kids if only their countries provided generous benefits for working mothers, as they do in Sweden and France. And it's true that those two countries have seen fertility rates inch up toward replacement levels in recent years. But in countries newly entering the New Girl Order, what SYFs complain about isn't so much a gap between work and family life as a chasm between their own aspirations and those of the men who'd be their husbands (remember those Japanese women skeptical of a future cooking miso soup). Adding to the SYF's alienation from domesticity is another glaring fact usually ignored by demographers: the New Girl Order is fun. Why get married when you can party on?

That raises an interesting question: Why are SYFs in the United States — the Rome of the New Girl Order — still so interested in marriage? By large margins, surveys suggest, American women want to marry and have kids. Indeed, our fertility rates, though lower than replacement level among college-educated women, are still healthier than those in most SYF countries (including Sweden and France). The answer may be that the family has always been essential ballast to the individualism, diversity, mobility, and sheer giddiness of American life.

It helps that the U.S., like northwestern Europe, has a long tradition of "companionate marriage"—that is, marriage based not on strict roles but on common interests and mutual affection. Companionate marriage always rested on the assumption of female equality. Yet countries like Japan are joining the new order with no history of companionate relations, and when it comes to adapting to the new order, the cultural cupboard is bare. A number of analysts, including demographer Nicholas Eberstadt, have also argued that it is America's religiousness that explains our relatively robust fertility, though the Polish fertility decline raises questions about that explanation.

It's by no means certain that Americans will remain exceptional in this regard. The most recent census data show a "sharp increase," over just the past six years, in the percentage of Americans in their twenties who have never married. Every year sees more books celebrating the SYF life, boasting titles like *Singular Existence* and *Living Alone and Loving It*. And SYFs will increasingly find themselves in a disappointing marriage pool. The *New York Times* excited considerable discussion this summer with a front-page article announcing that young women working full-time in several cities were now outearning their male counterparts. A historically unprecedented trend like this is bound to have a further impact on relations between the sexes and on marriage and childbearing rates.

Still, for now, women don't seem too worried about the New Girl Order's downside. On the contrary. The order marches on, as one domino after another falls to its pleasures and aspirations. Now, the *Singapore Times* tells us, young women in Vietnam are suddenly putting off marriage because they "want to have some fun"—and fertility rates have plummeted from 3.8 children in 1998 to 2.1 in 2006.

And then there's India. "The Gen Now bachelorette brigade is in no hurry to tie the knot," reports the *India Tribune.* "They're single, independent, and happy." Young urbanites are pushing up sales of branded apparel; Indian chick lit, along with *Cosmopolitan* and *Vogue*, flies out of shops in Delhi and Mumbai. Amazingly enough, fertility rates have dropped below replacement level in several of India's major cities, thanks in part to aspirant fashionistas. If in India—*India!*—the New Girl Order can reduce population growth, then perhaps nothing is beyond its powers. At the very least, the Indian experiment gives new meaning to the phrase "shop till you drop."

Small Change
Malcolm Gladwell

Writer Malcolm Gladwell has written for *The New Yorker* since 1996. He is best known for his books *The Tipping Point* (2000), *Outliers* (2008), and *What the Dog Saw* (2009). Gladwell often address the surprising and unexpected results of research and its impact on people and societies. Drawing from academic research, he frequently uses historical data to explore social and cultural trends. This essay appeared in the October 4, 2010 issue of *The New Yorker*.

Return to these questions after you have finished reading.

Analyzing the Reading

1. Gladwell recounts the story of the Woolworth lunch counter sit-in that began on February 1, 1960. Why does he use this particular story to frame his argument?

2. In paragraph 5, Gladwell observes that social media advocates are quick to cite Twitter's role in spurring social change. Why does he think their claims are so much "grandiosity"?

3. Gladwell states "Innovators tend to be solipsists." What is a solipsist? Why does Gladwell believe that advocates for social media such as Twitter tend to be solipsists?

4. Why does Gladwell think that Aaker and Smith (paragraphs 17–19) have Facebook's role in activism backward?

Exploring Ideas and Issues

Activism involves intentional action to bring about social, cultural, political, economic, or environmental change. It usually occurs when a group of people believe that a fundamental injustice is at work. Activism may assume many forms—from the sit-ins described by Gladwell in Greensboro, South Carolina—to letter writing campaigns, boycotts, rallies, marches, and even hunger strikes. More recently, people have created activism pages for causes on Facebook, such as the ones Gladwell cites for Darfur.

1. Grassroots activism occurs when like-minded people join together to advance their cause. As Gladwell notes, the most successful campaigns have a hierarchal organization, in which activists hold meetings, strategize activities, and plan tactics to advance their cause. According to Gladwell, what are the elements of activism? What encourages activists to remain committed in the face of personal danger and hardship? Write a short essay outlining the elements of activism, and what cause, if any, you would face personal danger for.

2. What is the difference between grassroots activism and social media activism? What factors differentiate them? Based on what you have read in Gladwell's essay, as well as outside research, do you think that causes such as Civil Rights and the Women's Rights movement could have had successful outcomes if activists had used Twitter or Facebook? Write an essay exploring this idea.

3. Research some political or social causes on Facebook. Write an essay in which you either support or challenge the idea that activism can be profoundly advanced online through Facebook networking.

4. Research how Twitter has been used in some recent crisis, such as Iran, Japan, or Egypt. Write an essay on the role Twitter played in the crisis, including our perception of that role as reported in the media. Then explain why you agree or disagree with Gladwell's statement that "the revolution will not be Tweeted."

SMALL CHANGE

At four-thirty in the afternoon on Monday, February 1, 1960, four college students sat down at the lunch counter at the Woolworth's in downtown Greensboro, North Carolina. They were freshmen at North Carolina A. & T., a black college a mile or so away.

"I'd like a cup of coffee, please," one of the four, Ezell Blair, said to the waitress.

"We don't serve Negroes here," she replied.

The Woolworth's lunch counter was a long L-shaped bar that could seat sixty-six people, with a standup snack bar at one end. The seats were for whites. The snack bar was for blacks. Another employee, a black woman who worked at the steam table, approached the students and tried to warn them away. "You're acting stupid, ignorant!" she said. They didn't move. Around five-thirty, the front doors to the store were locked. The four still didn't move. Finally, they left by a side door. Outside, a small crowd had gathered, including a photographer from the Greensboro Record. "I'll be back tomorrow with A. & T. College," one of the students said.

By next morning, the protest had grown to twenty-seven men and four women, most from the same dormitory as the original four. The men were dressed in suits and ties. The students had brought their schoolwork, and studied as they sat at the counter. On Wednesday, students from Greensboro's "Negro" secondary school, Dudley High, joined in, and the number of protesters swelled to eighty. By Thursday, the protesters numbered three hundred, including three white women, from the Greensboro campus of the University of North Carolina. By Saturday, the sit-in had reached six hundred. People spilled out onto the street. White teen-agers waved Confederate flags. Someone threw a firecracker. At noon, the A. & T. football team arrived. "Here comes the wrecking crew," one of the white students shouted.

By the following Monday, sit-ins had spread to Winston-Salem, twenty-five miles away, and Durham, fifty miles away. The day after that, students at Fayetteville State Teachers College and at Johnson C. Smith College, in Charlotte, joined in, followed on Wednesday by students at St. Augustine's College and Shaw University, in Raleigh. On Thursday and Friday, the protest crossed state lines, surfacing in Hampton and Portsmouth, Virginia, in Rock Hill, South Carolina, and in Chattanooga, Tennessee. By the end of the month, there were sit-ins throughout the South, as far west as Texas. "I asked every student I met what the first day of the sitdowns had been like on his campus," the political theorist Michael Walzer wrote in Dissent. "The answer was always the same: 'It was like a fever. Everyone wanted to go.' " Some seventy thousand students eventually took part. Thousands were arrested and untold thousands more radicalized. These events in the early sixties became a civil-rights war that engulfed the South for the rest of the decade—and it happened without e-mail, texting, Facebook, or Twitter.

The world, we are told, is in the midst of a revolution. The new tools of social media have reinvented social activism. With Facebook and Twitter and the like, the traditional relationship between political authority and popular will has been upended, making it easier for the powerless to collaborate, coördinate, and give voice to their concerns. When ten thousand protesters took to the streets in Moldova in the spring of 2009 to protest against their country's Communist government, the action was dubbed the Twitter Revolution, because of the means by which the demonstrators had been brought together. A few months after that, when student protests rocked Tehran, the State Department took the unusual step of asking Twitter to suspend scheduled maintenance of its Web site, because the Administration didn't want such a critical organizing tool out of service at the height of the demonstrations. "Without Twitter the people of Iran would not have felt empowered and confident to stand up for freedom and democracy," Mark Pfeifle, a former national-security adviser, later wrote, calling for Twitter to be nominated for the Nobel Peace Prize. Where activists were once defined by their causes, they are now defined by their tools. Facebook warriors go online to push for change. "You are the best hope for us all," James K. Glassman, a former senior State Department official, told a crowd of cyber activists at a recent conference sponsored by Facebook, A. T. & T., Howcast, MTV, and Google. Sites like Facebook, Glassman said, "give the U.S. a significant competitive advantage over terrorists. Some time ago, I said that Al Qaeda was 'eating our lunch on the Internet.' That is no longer the case. Al Qaeda is stuck in Web 1.0. The Internet is now about interactivity and conversation."

These are strong, and puzzling, claims. Why does it matter who is eating whose lunch on the Internet? Are people who log on to their Facebook page really the best hope for us all? As for Moldova's so-called Twitter Revolution, Evgeny Morozov, a scholar at Stanford who has been the most persistent of digital evangelism's critics, points out that Twitter had scant internal significance in Moldova, a country where very few Twitter accounts exist. Nor does it seem to have been a revolution, not least because the protests—as Anne Applebaum suggested in the Washington Post— may well have been a bit of stagecraft cooked up by the government. (In a country paranoid about Romanian revanchism, the protesters flew a Romanian flag over the Parliament building.) In the Iranian case, meanwhile, the people tweeting about the demonstrations were almost all in the West. "It is time to get Twitter's role in the events in Iran right," Golnaz Esfandiari wrote, this past summer, in Foreign Policy. "Simply put: There was no Twitter Revolution inside Iran." The cadre of prominent bloggers, like Andrew Sullivan, who championed the role of social media in Iran, Esfandiari continued, misunderstood the situation. "Western journalists who couldn't reach—or didn't bother reaching?—people on the ground in Iran simply scrolled through the English-language tweets post with tag #iranelection," she wrote. "Through it all, no one seemed to wonder why people trying to coordinate protests in Iran would be writing in any language other than Farsi."

Some of this grandiosity is to be expected. Innovators tend to be solipsists. They often want to cram every stray fact and experience into their new model. As the historian Robert Darnton has written, "The marvels of communication technology in the present have produced a false consciousness about the past—even a sense that communication has no history, or had nothing of importance to consider before the days of television and the Internet." But there is something else at work here, in the outsized enthusiasm for social media. Fifty years after one of the most extraordinary episodes of social upheaval in American history, we seem to have forgotten what activism is.

Greensboro in the early nineteen-sixties was the kind of place where racial insubordination was routinely met with violence. The four students who first sat down at the lunch counter were terrified. "I suppose if anyone had come up behind me and yelled 'Boo,' I think I would have fallen off my seat," one of them said later. On the first day, the store manager notified the police chief, who immediately sent two officers to the store. On the third day, a gang of white toughs showed up at the lunch counter and stood ostentatiously behind the protesters, ominously muttering epithets such as "burr-head nigger." A local Ku Klux Klan leader made an appearance. On Saturday, as tensions grew, someone called in a bomb threat, and the entire store had to be evacuated.

The dangers were even clearer in the Mississippi Freedom Summer Project of 1964, another of the sentinel campaigns of the civil-rights movement. The Student Nonviolent Coordinating Committee recruited hundreds of Northern, largely white unpaid volunteers to run Freedom Schools, register black voters, and raise civil-rights awareness in the Deep South. "No one should go anywhere alone, but certainly not in an automobile and certainly not at night," they were instructed. Within days of arriving in Mississippi, three volunteers—Michael Schwerner, James Chaney, and Andrew Goodman—were kidnapped and killed, and, during the rest of the summer, thirty-seven black churches were set on fire and dozens of safe houses were bombed; volunteers were beaten, shot at, arrested, and trailed by pickup trucks full of armed men. A quarter of those in the program dropped out. Activism that challenges the status quo—that attacks deeply rooted problems—is not for the faint of heart.

What makes people capable of this kind of activism? The Stanford sociologist Doug McAdam compared the Freedom Summer dropouts with the participants who stayed, and discovered that the key difference wasn't, as might be expected, ideological fervor. "All of the applicants—participants and withdrawals alike—emerge as highly committed, articulate supporters of the goals and values of the summer program," he concluded. What mattered more was an applicant's degree of personal connection to the civil-rights movement. All the volunteers were required to provide a list of personal contacts—the people they wanted kept apprised of their activities—and participants were far more likely than dropouts to have close friends who were also going to Mississippi. High-risk activism, McAdam concluded, is a "strong-tie" phenomenon.

This pattern shows up again and again. One study of the Red Brigades, the Italian terrorist group of the nineteen-seventies, found that seventy per cent of recruits had at least one good friend already in the organization. The same is true of the men who joined the mujahideen in Afghanistan. Even revolutionary actions that look spontaneous, like the demonstrations in East Germany that led to the fall of the Berlin Wall, are, at core, strong-tie phenomena. The opposition movement in East Germany consisted of several hundred groups, each with roughly a dozen members. Each group was in limited contact with the others: at the time, only thirteen per cent of East Germans even had a phone. All they knew was that on Monday nights, outside St. Nicholas Church in downtown Leipzig, people gathered to voice their anger at the state. And the primary determinant of who showed up was "critical friends"—the more friends you had who were critical of the regime the more likely you were to join the protest.

So one crucial fact about the four freshmen at the Greensboro lunch counter—David Richmond, Franklin McCain, Ezell Blair, and Joseph McNeil—was their relationship with one another. McNeil was a roommate of Blair's in A. & T.'s Scott Hall dormitory. Richmond roomed with McCain one floor up, and Blair, Richmond, and McCain had all gone to Dudley High School. The four would smuggle beer into the dorm and talk late into the night in Blair and McNeil's room. They would all have remembered the murder of Emmett Till in 1955, the Montgomery bus boycott that same year, and the showdown in Little Rock in 1957. It was McNeil who brought up the idea of a sit-in at Woolworth's. They'd discussed it for nearly a month. Then McNeil came into the dorm room and asked the others if they were ready. There was a pause, and McCain said, in a way that works only with people who talk late into the night with one another, "Are you guys chicken or not?" Ezell Blair worked up the courage the next day to ask for a cup of coffee because he was flanked by his roommate and two good friends from high school.

The kind of activism associated with social media isn't like this at all. The platforms of social media are built around weak ties. Twitter is a way of following (or being followed by) people you may never have met. Facebook is a tool for efficiently managing your acquaintances, for keeping up with the people you would not otherwise be able to stay in touch with. That's why you can have a thousand "friends" on Facebook, as you never could in real life.

This is in many ways a wonderful thing. There is strength in weak ties, as the sociologist Mark Granovetter has observed. Our acquaintances—not our friends—are our greatest source of new ideas and information. The Internet lets us exploit the power of these kinds of distant connections with marvellous efficiency. It's terrific at the diffusion of innovation, interdisciplinary collaboration, seamlessly matching up buyers and sellers, and the logistical functions of the dating world. But weak ties seldom lead to high-risk activism.

In a new book called "The Dragonfly Effect: Quick, Effective, and Powerful Ways to Use Social Media to Drive Social Change," the business consultant Andy Smith and the Stanford Business School professor Jennifer Aaker tell the story of Sameer Bhatia, a young Silicon Valley entrepreneur who came down with acute myelogenous leukemia. It's a perfect illustration of social media's strengths. Bhatia needed a bone-marrow transplant, but he could not find a match among his relatives and friends. The odds were best with a donor of his ethnicity, and there were few South Asians in the national bone-marrow database. So Bhatia's business partner sent out an e-mail explaining Bhatia's plight to more than four hundred of their acquaintances, who forwarded the e-mail to their personal contacts; Facebook pages and YouTube videos were devoted to the Help Sameer campaign. Eventually, nearly twenty-five thousand new people were registered in the bone-marrow database, and Bhatia found a match.

But how did the campaign get so many people to sign up? By not asking too much of them. That's the only way you can get someone you don't really know to do something on your behalf. You can get thousands of people to sign up for a donor registry, because doing so is pretty easy. You have to send in a cheek swab and—in the highly unlikely event that your bone marrow is a good match for someone in need—spend a few hours at the hospital. Donating bone marrow isn't a trivial matter. But it doesn't involve financial or personal risk; it doesn't mean spending a summer being chased by armed men in pickup trucks. It doesn't require that you confront socially entrenched norms and practices. In fact, it's the kind of commitment that will bring only social acknowledgment and praise.

The evangelists of social media don't understand this distinction; they seem to believe that a Facebook friend is the same as a real friend and that signing up for a donor registry in Silicon Valley today is activism in the same sense as sitting at a segregated lunch counter in Greensboro in 1960. "Social networks are particularly effective at increasing motivation," Aaker and Smith write. But that's not true. Social networks are effective at increasing participation—by lessening the level of motivation that participation requires. The Facebook page of the Save Darfur Coalition has 1,282,339 members, who have donated an average of nine cents apiece. The next biggest Darfur charity on Facebook has 22,073 members, who have donated an average of thirty-five cents. Help Save Darfur has 2,797 members, who have given, on average, fifteen cents. A spokesperson for the Save Darfur Coalition told Newsweek, "We wouldn't necessarily gauge someone's value to the advocacy movement based on what they've given. This is a powerful mechanism to engage this critical population. They inform their community, attend events, volunteer. It's not something you can measure by looking at a ledger." In other words, Facebook activism succeeds not by motivating people to make a real sacrifice but by motivating them to do the things that people do when they are not motivated enough to make a real sacrifice. We are a long way from the lunch counters of Greensboro.

The students who joined the sit-ins across the South during the winter of 1960 described the movement as a "fever." But the civil-rights movement was more like a military campaign than like a contagion. In the late nineteen-fifties, there had been sixteen sit-ins in various cities throughout the South, fifteen of which were formally organized by civil-rights organizations like the N.A.A.C.P. and CORE. Possible locations for activism were scouted. Plans were drawn up. Movement activists held training sessions and retreats for would-be protesters. The Greensboro Four were a product of this groundwork: all were members of the N.A.A.C.P. Youth Council. They had close ties with the head of the local N.A.A.C.P. chapter. They had been briefed on the earlier wave of sit-ins in Durham, and had been part of a series of movement meetings in activist churches. When the sit-in movement spread from Greensboro throughout the South, it did not spread indiscriminately. It spread to those cities which had preëxisting "movement centers"—a core of dedicated and trained activists ready to turn the "fever" into action.

The civil-rights movement was high-risk activism. It was also, crucially, strategic activism: a challenge to the establishment mounted with precision and discipline. The N.A.A.C.P. was a centralized organization, run from New York according to highly formalized operating procedures. At the Southern Christian Leadership Conference, Martin Luther King, Jr., was the unquestioned authority. At the center of the movement was the black church, which had, as Aldon D. Morris points out in his superb 1984 study, "The Origins of the Civil Rights Movement," a carefully demarcated division of labor, with various standing committees and disciplined groups. "Each group was task-oriented and coordinated its activities through authority structures," Morris writes. "Individuals were held accountable for their assigned duties, and important conflicts were resolved by the minister, who usually exercised ultimate authority over the congregation."

This is the second crucial distinction between traditional activism and its online variant: social media are not about this kind of hierarchical organization. Facebook and the like are tools for building networks, which are the opposite, in structure and character, of hierarchies. Unlike hierarchies, with their rules and procedures, networks aren't controlled by a single central authority. Decisions are made through consensus, and the ties that bind people to the group are loose.

This structure makes networks enormously resilient and adaptable in low-risk situations. Wikipedia is a perfect example. It doesn't have an editor, sitting in New York, who directs and corrects each entry. The effort of putting together each entry is self-organized. If every entry in Wikipedia were to be erased tomorrow, the content would swiftly be restored, because that's what happens when a network of thousands spontaneously devote their time to a task.

There are many things, though, that networks don't do well. Car companies sensibly use a network to organize their hundreds of suppliers, but not to design their cars. No one believes that the articulation of a coherent design philosophy is best handled by a sprawling, leaderless organizational system. Because networks don't have a centralized leadership structure and clear lines of authority, they have real difficulty reaching consensus and setting goals. They can't think strategically; they are chronically prone to conflict and error. How do you make difficult choices about tactics or strategy or philosophical direction when everyone has an equal say?

The Palestine Liberation Organization originated as a network, and the international-relations scholars Mette Eilstrup-Sangiovanni and Calvert Jones argue in a recent essay in International Security that this is why it ran into such trouble as it grew: "Structural features typical of networks—the absence of central authority, the unchecked autonomy of rival groups, and the inability to arbitrate quarrels through formal mechanisms—made the P.L.O. excessively vulnerable to outside manipulation and internal strife."

In Germany in the nineteen-seventies, they go on, "the far more unified and successful left-wing terrorists tended to organize hierarchically, with professional management and clear divisions of labor. They were concentrated geographically in universities, where they could establish central leadership, trust, and camaraderie through regular, face-to-face meetings." They seldom betrayed their comrades in arms during police interrogations. Their counterparts on the right were organized as decentralized networks, and had no such discipline. These groups were regularly infiltrated, and members, once arrested, easily gave up their comrades. Similarly, Al Qaeda was most dangerous when it was a unified hierarchy. Now that it has dissipated into a network, it has proved far less effective.

The drawbacks of networks scarcely matter if the network isn't interested in systemic change—if it just wants to frighten or humiliate or make a splash—or if it doesn't need to think strategically. But if you're taking on a powerful and organized establishment you have to be a hierarchy. The Montgomery bus boycott required the participation of tens of thousands of people who depended on public transit to get to and from work each day. It lasted a year. In order to persuade those people to stay true to the cause, the boycott's organizers tasked each local black church with maintaining morale, and put together a free alternative private carpool service, with forty-eight dispatchers and forty-two pickup stations. Even the White Citizens Council, King later said, conceded that the carpool system moved with "military precision." By the time King came to Birmingham, for the climactic showdown with Police Commissioner Eugene (Bull) Connor, he had a budget of a million dollars, and a hundred full-time staff members on the ground, divided into operational units. The operation itself was divided into steadily escalating phases, mapped out in advance. Support was maintained through consecutive mass meetings rotating from church to church around the city.

Boycotts and sit-ins and nonviolent confrontations—which were the weapons of choice for the civil-rights movement—are high-risk strategies. They leave little room for conflict and error. The moment even one protester deviates from the script and responds to provocation, the moral legitimacy of the entire protest is compromised. Enthusiasts for social media would no doubt have us believe that King's task in Birmingham would have been made infinitely easier had he been able to communicate with his followers through Facebook, and contented himself with tweets from a Birmingham jail. But networks are messy: think of the ceaseless pattern of correction and revision, amendment and debate, that characterizes Wikipedia. If Martin Luther King, Jr., had tried to do a wiki-boycott in Montgomery, he would have been steamrollered by the white power structure. And of what use would a digital communication tool be in a town where ninety-eight per cent of the black community could be reached every Sunday morning at church? The things that King needed in Birmingham—discipline and strategy—were things that online social media cannot provide.

The bible of the social-media movement is Clay Shirky's "Here Comes Everybody." Shirky, who teaches at New York University, sets out to demonstrate the organizing power of the Internet, and he begins with the story of Evan, who worked on Wall Street, and his friend Ivanna, after she left her smart phone, an expensive Sidekick, on the back seat of a New York City taxicab. The telephone company transferred the data on Ivanna's lost phone to a new phone, whereupon she and Evan discovered that the Sidekick was now in the hands of a teen-ager from Queens, who was using it to take photographs of herself and her friends.

When Evan e-mailed the teen-ager, Sasha, asking for the phone back, she replied that his "white ass" didn't deserve to have it back. Miffed, he set up a Web page with her picture and a description of what had happened. He forwarded the link to his friends, and they forwarded it to their friends. Someone found the MySpace page of Sasha's boyfriend, and a link to it found its way onto the site. Someone found her address online and took a video of her home while driving by; Evan posted the video on the site. The story was picked up by the news filter Digg. Evan was now up to ten e-mails a minute. He created a bulletin board for his readers to share their stories, but it crashed under the weight of responses. Evan and Ivanna went to the police, but the police filed the report under "lost," rather than "stolen," which essentially closed the case. "By this point millions of readers were watching," Shirky writes, "and dozens of mainstream news outlets had covered the story." Bowing to the pressure, the N.Y.P.D. reclassified the item as "stolen." Sasha was arrested, and Evan got his friend's Sidekick back.

Shirky's argument is that this is the kind of thing that could never have happened in the pre-Internet age—and he's right. Evan could never have tracked down Sasha. The story of the Sidekick would never have been publicized. An army of people could never have been assembled to wage this fight. The police wouldn't have bowed to the pressure of a lone person who had misplaced something as trivial as a cell phone. The story, to Shirky, illustrates "the ease and speed with which a group can be mobilized for the right kind of cause" in the Internet age.

Shirky considers this model of activism an upgrade. But it is simply a form of organizing which favors the weak-tie connections that give us access to information over the strong-tie connections that help us persevere in the face of danger. It shifts our energies from organizations that promote strategic and disciplined activity and toward those which promote resilience and adaptability. It makes it easier for activists to express themselves, and harder for that expression to have any impact. The instruments of social media are well suited to making the existing social order more efficient. They are not a natural enemy of the status quo. If you are of the opinion that all the world needs is a little buffing around the edges, this should not trouble you. But if you think that there are still lunch counters out there that need integrating it ought to give you pause.

Shirky ends the story of the lost Sidekick by asking, portentously, "What happens next?"—no doubt imagining future waves of digital protesters. But he has already answered the question. What happens next is more of the same. A networked, weak-tie world is good at things like helping Wall Streeters get phones back from teen-age girls. Viva la revolución.

Gin, Television, and Social Surplus
Clay Shirky

Clay Shirky teaches at New York University. His articles and interviews have been appeared in many publications, including Business *2.0*, the *Wall Street Journal*, and *Wired*. He is the author of *Cognitive Surplus: Creativity and Generosity in a Connected Age* (2010). An expert on the economic and social effects of Internet technology, he delivered this speech on April 26, 2008 at the Web 2.0 Conference.

Return to these questions after you have finished reading.

Analyzing the Reading

1. Shirky proposes some surprising "technology" that marked social transformations. What technology does he cite for the 19th and 20th centuries, and how was it connected to the social changes of each era?

2. What opinion does Shirky have of television and its influence? Of the Internet? Of the intrinsic value of each? Cite examples in his speech.

3. Why does Shriky "snap" at the interviewer? Why is he irritated with her line of questioning and understanding of his points?

4. How old do you think Shirky is? What clues does he give in his speech? Does knowing his approximate age lend legitimacy to his perspective and argument? Explain with examples.

Exploring Ideas and Issues

In April 2011, Facebook reported that it had more than 500 million active users, 50% of whom were logged on at some point every day. It also noted that users were spending over 700 billion minutes per month on Facebook, with almost 70% of users located outside the United States. On *Wikipedia*, there are nearly four million articles in the English version alone, representing over 100 million hours of human labor.

   Shirky points out that projects like *Wikipedia* represent "an architecture of participation" due to a surplus of time we now have on our hands. "As we expand our participation, people start experimenting with it, in order for the surplus to get integrated, and the course of the integration can transform society." View Shirky's expanded explanation of cognitive surplus on BigThink.com (http://bigthink.com/ideas/20746) and why he feels it will change the world.

1. What are the possible benefits of cognitive surplus? How could it transform society for the better? Write an essay in which you explore how the world might change as a result of participation online in projects that benefit from cognitive surplus.

2. In his video, Shirky asks "What do we as a society want to get out of this resource [cognitive surplus]?" Answer his question in a short essay with your own viewpoint.

3. In his essay, Shirky becomes irritated with a television interviewer's question "Where do people find the time?" Over the course of several days, carefully record what you spend your time doing. Write a personal narrative exploring how you spend your time and why.

4. Shirky shares that he loves the Wiki Map app tracking crime in Brazil. What apps do you think hold the most potential to transform society? Write a short essay that explores how the app might change the world.

Gin, Television, and Social Surplus

I was recently reminded of some reading I did in college, way back in the last century, by a British historian arguing that the critical technology, for the early phase of the industrial revolution, was gin. The transformation from rural to urban life was so sudden, and so wrenching, that the only thing society could do to manage was to drink itself into a stupor for a generation. The stories from that era are amazing—there were gin pushcarts working their way through the streets of London.

And it wasn't until society woke up from that collective bender that we actually started to get the institutional structures that we associate with the industrial revolution today. Things like public libraries and museums, increasingly broad education for children, elected leaders—a lot of things we like—didn't happen until having all of those people together stopped seeming like a crisis and started seeming like an asset. It wasn't until people started thinking of this as a vast civic surplus, one they could design for rather than just dissipate, that we started to get what we think of now as an industrial society.

If I had to pick the critical technology for the 20th century, the bit of social lubricant without which the wheels would've come off the whole enterprise, I'd say it was the sitcom. Starting with the Second World War a whole series of things happened—rising GDP per capita, rising educational attainment, rising life expectancy and, critically, a rising number of people who were working five-day work weeks. For the first time, society forced onto an enormous number of its citizens the requirement to manage something they had never had to manage before—free time.

And what did we do with that free time? Well, mostly we spent it watching TV.

We did that for decades. We watched "I Love Lucy." We watched "Gilligan's Island." We watch "Malcolm in the Middle." We watch "Desperate Housewives." "Desperate Housewives" essentially functioned as a kind of cognitive heat sink, dissipating thinking that might otherwise have built up and caused society to overheat. And it's only now, as we're waking up from that collective bender, that we're starting to see the cognitive surplus as an asset rather than as a crisis. We're seeing things being designed to take advantage of that surplus, to deploy it in ways more engaging than just having a TV in everybody's basement.

This hit me in a conversation I had about two months ago. I've finished a book called Here Comes Everybody, which has recently come out, and this recognition came out of a conversation I had about the book. I was being interviewed by a TV producer to see whether I should be on their show, and she asked me, "What are you seeing out there that's interesting?" I started telling her about the Wikipedia article on Pluto. You may remember that Pluto got kicked out of the planet club a couple of years ago, so all of a sudden there was all of this activity on Wikipedia. The talk pages light up, people are editing the article like mad, and the whole community is in an ruckus—"How should we characterize this change in Pluto's status?" And a little bit at a time they move the article—fighting offstage all the while—from, "Pluto is the ninth planet," to "Pluto is an odd-shaped rock with an odd-shaped orbit at the edge of the solar system."

So I tell her all this stuff, and I think, "Okay, we're going to have a conversation about authority or social construction or whatever." That wasn't her question. She heard this story and she shook her head and said, "Where do people find the time?" That was her question. And I just kind of snapped. And I said, "No one who works in TV gets to ask that question. You know where the time comes from. It comes from the cognitive surplus you've been masking for 50 years."

So how big is that surplus? If you take Wikipedia as a kind of unit, all of Wikipedia, the whole project—every page, every edit, every talk page, every line of code, in every language that Wikipedia exists in—that represents something like the cumulation of 100 million hours of human thought. I worked this out with Martin Wattenberg at IBM; it's a back-of-the-envelope calculation, but it's the right order of magnitude, about 100 million hours of thought.

And television watching? Two hundred billion hours, in the U.S. alone, every year. Put another way, now that we have a unit, that's 2,000 Wikipedia projects a year spent watching television. Or put still another way, in the U.S., we spend 100 million hours every weekend, just watching the ads. This is a pretty big surplus. People asking, "Where do they find the time?" when they're looking at things like Wikipedia don't understand how tiny that entire project is, as a carve-out of this asset that's finally being dragged into what Tim calls an architecture of participation.

Now, the interesting thing about a surplus like that is that society doesn't know what to do with it at first—hence the gin, hence the sitcoms. Because if people knew what to do with a surplus with reference to the existing social institutions, then it wouldn't be a surplus, would it? It's precisely when no one has any idea how to deploy something that people have to start experimenting with it, in order for the surplus to get integrated, and the course of that integration can transform society.

The early phase for taking advantage of this cognitive surplus, the phase I think we're still in, is all special cases. The physics of participation is much more like the physics of weather than it is like the physics of gravity. We know all the forces that combine to make these kinds of things work: there's an interesting community over here, there's an interesting sharing model over there, those people are collaborating on open source software. But despite knowing the inputs, we can't predict the outputs yet because there's so much complexity. The way you explore complex ecosystems is you just try lots and lots and lots of things, and you hope that everybody who fails fails informatively so that you can at least find a skull on a pikestaff near where you're going. That's the phase we're in now.

Just to pick one example, one I'm in love with, but it's tiny. A couple of weeks one of my students forwarded me a project started by a professor in Brazil, in Fortaleza, named Vasco Furtado. It's a Wiki Map for crime in Brazil. If there's an assault, if there's a burglary, if there's a mugging, a robbery, a rape, a murder, you can go and put a push-pin on a Google Map, and you can characterize the assault, and you start to see a map of where these crimes are occurring.

Now, this already exists as tacit information. Anybody who knows a town has some sense of, "Don't go there. That street corner is dangerous. Don't go in this neighborhood. Be careful there after dark." But it's something society knows without society really knowing it, which is to say there's no public source where you can take advantage of it. And the cops, if they have that information, they're certainly not sharing. In fact, one of the things Furtado says in starting the Wiki crime map was, "This information may or may not exist some place in society, but it's actually easier for me to try to rebuild it from scratch than to try and get it from the authorities who might have it now."

Maybe this will succeed or maybe it will fail. The normal case of social software is still failure; most of these experiments don't pan out. But the ones that do are quite incredible, and I hope that this one succeeds, obviously. But even if it doesn't, it's illustrated the point already, which is that someone working alone, with really cheap tools, has a reasonable hope of carving out enough of the cognitive surplus, enough of the desire to participate, enough of the collective goodwill of the citizens, to create a resource you couldn't have imagined existing even five years ago.

So that's the answer to the question, "Where do they find the time?" Or, rather, that's the numerical answer. But beneath that question was another thought, this one not a question but an observation. In this same conversation with the TV producer I was talking about World of Warcraft guilds, and as I was talking, I could sort of see what she was thinking: "Losers. Grown men sitting in their basement pretending to be elves."

At least they're doing something.

Did you ever see that episode of "Gilligan's Island" where they almost get off the island and then Gilligan messes up and then they don't? I saw that one. I saw that one a lot when I was growing up. And every half-hour that I watched that was a half an hour I wasn't posting at my blog or editing Wikipedia or contributing to a mailing list. Now I had an ironclad excuse for not doing those things, which is that none of those things existed then. I was forced into the channel of media the way it was because it was the only option. Now it's not, and that's the big surprise. However lousy it is to sit in your basement and pretend to be an elf, I can tell you from personal experience it's worse to sit in your basement and try to figure if Ginger or Mary Ann is cuter.

And I'm willing to raise that to a general principle. It's better to do something than to do nothing. Even lolcats, even cute pictures of kittens made even cuter with the addition of cute captions, hold out an invitation to participation. When you see a lolcat, one of the things it says to the viewer is, "If you have some sans-serif fonts on your computer, you can play this game, too." And that's message—I can do that, too—is a big change.

This is something that people in the media world don't understand. Media in the 20th century was run as a single race—consumption. How much can we produce? How much can you consume? Can we produce more and you'll consume more? And the answer to that question has generally been yes. But media is actually a triathlon, it's three different events. People like to consume, but they also like to produce, and they like to share. And what's astonished people who were committed to the structure of the previous society, prior to trying to take this surplus and do something interesting, is that they're discovering that when you offer people the opportunity to produce and to share, they'll take you up on that offer. It doesn't mean that we'll never sit around mindlessly watching "Scrubs" on the couch. It just means we'll do it less.

And this is the other thing about the size of the cognitive surplus we're talking about. It's so large that even a small change could have huge ramifications. Let's say that everything stays 99 percent the same, that people watch 99 percent as much television as they used to, but 1 percent of that is carved out for producing and for sharing. The Internet-connected population watches roughly a trillion hours of TV a year. That's about five times the size of the annual U.S. consumption. One per cent of that is 100 Wikipedia projects per year worth of participation.

I think that's going to be a big deal. Don't you?

Well, the TV producer did not think this was going to be a big deal; she was not digging this line of thought. And her final question to me was essentially, "Isn't this all just a fad?" You know, sort of the flagpole-sitting of the early early 21st century? It's fun to go out and produce and share a little bit, but then people are going to eventually realize, "This isn't as good as doing what I was doing before, and settle down. And I made a spirited argument that no, this wasn't the case, that this was in fact a big one-time shift, more analogous to the industrial revolution than to flagpole-sitting. I was arguing that this isn't the sort of thing society grows out of. It's the sort of thing that society grows into. But I'm not sure she believed me, in part because she didn't want to believe me, but also in part because I didn't have the right story yet. And now I do.

I was having dinner with a group of friends about a month ago, and one of them was talking about sitting with his four-year-old daughter watching a DVD. And in the middle of the movie, apropos nothing, she jumps up off the couch and runs around behind the screen. That seems like a cute moment. Maybe she's going back there to see if Dora is really back there or whatever. But that wasn't what she was doing. She started rooting around in the cables. And her dad said, "What you doing?" And she stuck her head out from behind the screen and said, "Looking for the mouse."

Here's something four-year-olds know: A screen that ships without a mouse ships broken. Here's something four-year-olds know: Media that's targeted at you but doesn't include you may not be worth sitting still for. Those are things that make me believe that this is a one-way change. Because four-year-olds, the people who are soaking most deeply in the current environment, who won't have to go through the trauma that I have to go through of trying to unlearn a childhood spent watching "Gilligan's Island," they just assume that media includes consuming, producing and sharing.

It's also become my motto, when people ask me what we're doing—and when I say "we" I mean the larger society trying to figure out how to deploy this cognitive surplus, but I also mean we, especially, the people who are working hammer and tongs at figuring out the next good idea. From now on, that's what I'm going to tell them: We're looking for the mouse. We're going to look at every place that a reader or a listener or a viewer or a user has been locked out, has been served up passive or a fixed or a canned experience, and ask ourselves, "If we carve out a little bit of the cognitive surplus and deploy it here, could we make a good thing happen?" And I'm betting the answer is yes.

Thank you very much.

The Price of Crossing Borders
Eduardo Porter

Eduardo Porter writes about business and economics. He is currently on the staff of the New York Times. He has also worked as a journalist in Mexico City, Tokyo, London, São Paulo, and Los Angeles. He was the editor of *América Economía*, a business and economics magazine based in Sao Paulo. He is the author of *The Price of Everything: Solving the Mystery of Why We Pay What We Do* (2011), from which this next reading is excerpted.

Return to these questions after you have finished reading.

Analyzing the Reading

1. Porter observes that every decision we make "amounts to a choice among options to which we assign different values." How can being mindful of the "price" of the decisions we make help us understand ourselves better? Explain.

2. What is the price of crossing the border into the United States from Mexico? Consider in your answer the financial costs as well as the human ones.

3. Porter notes that the debate over illegal immigration is deeply connected to the price Americans believe they pay. What are the perceived costs of illegal immigration?

4. Did this essay encourage you to think differently about the meaning of the word "price" and the value of your personal decisions? Why or why not?

Exploring Ideas and Issues

In New Delhi, India, boys are generally valued more than girls, primarily because they do not require a bridal payment (dowry) and have potential to bring in income. In 2008, the Delhi government launched the "Laadli scheme" by which the state government promised to deposit 100,000 rupees (about $2250) in the account of every girl born to poor parents by her 18th birthday. The funds can be used for the girl's dowry upon marriage or for higher education. The plan was conceived due to the disturbing increase in the abortion rate of female fetuses, creating a distressing gender ration gap in that region of India. In 2011, the Delhi government observed that the gender ratio gap in that region had continued to widen, despite the new incentive carry female fetuses to term, but that it was still too soon to determine the impact of the plan.

1. Research the Laadli scheme and find out more about cultural influences responsible for the gender ratio gap in India. Based on what you learn, is the Laadli scheme likely to improve the problem? Write a short essay arguing either that the program is likely to succeed or likely to fail in the long run.

2. In Delhi, poor parents must decide whether to incur the cost of having a female child. In the U.S., illegal immigrant parents must decide how and whether to bring their children across the border. Write an essay that examines in what ways are the situations faced by both parents similar, and in what ways are they different?

3. Porter notes that we organize our lives by evaluating the "opportunity cost" of the decisions we make. Write a short essay about the opportunity cost of the decision you made to pursue higher education. What have you given up, and what do you expect to get as a result of your decision?

The Price of Crossing Borders

MOST OF US think of prices in the context of shopping expeditions. In the marketplace, prices ration what we consume, guiding how we allocate resources among our many wants. They prompt us to set priorities within the limits of our budgets. Just as prices steer our purchasing patterns, they steer the decisions of the companies that make what we buy, enabling them to meet our demand with their supply. That's how markets organize a capitalist economy.

But prices are all over the place, not only attached to things we buy in a store. At every crossroads, prices nudge us to take one course of action or another. In a way, this is obvious: every decision amounts to a choice among options to which we assign different values. But identifying these prices allows us to understand more fully our decisions. They can be measured in money, cash, or credit. But costs and benefits can also be set in love, toil, or time. Our most important currency is, in fact, opportunity. The cost of taking any action or embracing any path consists of the alternatives that were available to us at the time. The price of a five-dollar slice of pizza is all the other things we could have done with the five dollars. The price of marriage includes all the things we would have done had we remained single. One day we succumb to the allure of love and companionship. Years later we wonder what happened to the freedom we traded away at the altar. Economists call this the "opportunity cost." By evaluating opportunity costs, we organize our lives.

Just to be born, the scavenger girl in Delhi had to overcome Indian parents' entrenched bias against girls—which has led to widespread abortions of female fetuses. The Indian census of 2001 recorded 927 girls aged six or less per 1,000 boys. This compares to 1,026 girls per thousand boys in Brazil and 1,029 in the United States. This bias is due to a deeply unfavourable cost-benefit analysis: while boys are meant to take over the family property and care for their parents in old age, daughters must be married off, which requires an onerous dowry. To redress the balance of incentives, regional governments across India have been experimenting with antipoverty programs aimed at increasing parents' appetite for girls. In 2008, Delhi launched a program to deposit 10,000 rupees into the account of newly born girls in poor families—making subsequent deposits as they progress in school. The objective is to build a cushion of resources for them to marry or pursue higher education. A social insurance program launched in 2006 in Haryana pays parents who only have daughters 500 rupees a month between the age of forty-five and the age of sixty, when it is replaced by the general public pension.

I remember a conversation I had a few years ago with an illegal immigrant in Stockton, California. I worked at the Wall Street Journal writing about the Hispanic population of the United States. The immigrant was educating me about the relative merits of having his two young children smuggled from Mexico por el monte— a gruelling hike across the desert— or por la linea, across a regular checkpoint using forged documents. The choice was hard. He couldn't have made more than $8 or $9 an hour, picking asparagus, cherries, and everything else that grew in California's San Joaquin Valley. He would have to pay about $1,500 each for a "coyote" to guide his kids across the desert. Yet he figured that getting a smuggler with fake documents to bring them across a border checkpoint would put him back about $5,000 per child. The conversation laid in stark relief the type of bare-knuckle cost-benefit analyses that steer people's lives.

Over the last decade and a half, the Border Patrol's budget has grown roughly fivefold. Average coyote fees increased accordingly, to about $2,600 in 2008. Yet the price that rose most sharply is measured in the odds of dying on the way, as border crossing that used to take less than a day around San Diego became a three- to four-day trek through the Arizona desert, evading thieves and the Border Patrol, lugging jugs of water. In 1994, 24 migrants died trying to cross the border. By 2008, the death toll was 725. The calculation of the immigrant I spoke to was straightforward enough. To bring his children into the United States through a checkpoint, he would have to work longer to earn the price of passage. But it would lower the risk that his children would perish along the way.

The debate among Americans about illegal immigration is itself a discussion about prices. Critics charge that illegal immigrants lower the price of natives' labor by offering to do the job for less. They argue that immigrants impose a burden on natives when they consume public services, like education for their children and emergency medical care.

These arguments are weaker than they seem. Most illegal immigrants work on the books using false IDs, and have taxes withheld from their paychecks like any other worker. They can't draw benefits from most government programs. And there is scant evidence that immigrants lower the wages of American workers. Some industries only exist because of cheap immigrant labor—California's agricultural industry comes to mind. Absent the immigrants, the farm jobs would disappear too, along with an array of jobs from the fields to the packing plant. We would import the asparagus and the strawberries instead.

Illegal immigrants do affect prices in the United States. One study calculated that the surge in immigration experienced between 1980 and 2000 reduced the average price of services such as housekeeping or gardening by more than 9 percent, mainly by undercutting wages. Still, it had a negligible impact on natives' wages because poor illegal immigrants compete in the job market with other poor illegal immigrants.

Immigration policy has always been determined by who bears its costs and who draws its benefits. Illegal immigrants are tolerated by the political system because their cheap labor is useful for agribusiness and other industries. It provides affordable nannies to middleclass Americans. This suggests that despite presidential lip service to the need to reform immigration law, nothing much is likely to be done. Creating a legal path for illegal immigrants to work in the United States would be politically risky and could provide a big incentive for more illegal flows. By contrast, cutting illegal immigration entirely would be prohibitively costly. The status quo is too comfortable to bear tinkering like that.

The ebb and flow of immigration will continue to be determined by potential immigrants' measuring the prospect of a minimum-wage job—perhaps a first step up the ladder of prosperity— against the costs imposed by the harsh border. The price may occasionally be too high. As joblessness soared following the financial crisis of 2008, many potential immigrants decided to stay at home. The Department of Homeland Security estimates the illegal immigrant population dropped by 1 million from its peak in 2007 to 10.8 million in 2009. But this will prove to be no more than a blip in the broad historical trend.

How to Write a Causal Argument

These steps for the process of writing a causal argument may not progress as neatly as this chart might suggest. Writing is not an assembly-line process. As you write, you are constantly reading what you have written and rethinking.

Continue thinking about causation as you write and revise. The process of writing may lead you to additional causal relationships.

1 MAKE A CAUSAL CLAIM

- Examine a social trend, law, or policy.

- Analyze problems in your neighborhood or at your school.

- Investigate natural phenomena.

- Investigate the impact of human activity on the environment.

- Think about what is at stake. What could or should change if the cause were known?

- Put your claim in the form "_____ causes (or does not cause) _____."

2 THINK ABOUT POSSIBLE CAUSES AND EFFECTS

- What are the obvious causes or effects?

- What are the underlying causes?

- What causes or effects might be hidden?

- What are the causes or effects that most people have not recognized before?

- Who is affected by what you are investigating? Do your readers have a stake in what you are analyzing?

- Look for disagreement among your sources. If they all agree on the cause, probably you won't have much to add.

3
WRITE A DRAFT

- Describe the trend, event, or phenomenon.
- Give the background your readers will need.
- If the trend or event you are analyzing is unfamiliar to your readers, explain the cause or the chain of causation.
- Another way to organize the body of your analysis is to set out the causes that have already been offered and reject them one by one. Then you can present the cause or causes that you think are the right ones.
- A third method is to look at a series of causes one by one, analyzing the importance of each.
- Do more than simply summarize in your conclusion. You might consider additional effects beyond those you have previously noted, or explain to readers any action you think should be taken based on your conclusions.
- Choose a title that will interest readers in your essay.
- Include any necessary images or tables.

4
REVISE, REVISE, REVISE

- Check that your causal analysis fulfills the assignment.
- Make sure that your claim is clear and that you have sufficient evidence to convince readers.
- Look at additional potential causes, if necessary.
- Reconsider how multiple causes might interact.
- Go further back in the causal chain, if necessary, showing how the causes you examine have their roots in other events.
- Examine the organization of your analysis and think of possible better ways to organize.
- Review the visual presentation of your analysis for readability and maximum impact.
- Proofread carefully.

5
SUBMITTED VERSION

- Make sure your finished writing meets all formatting requirements.

1: Make a Causal Claim

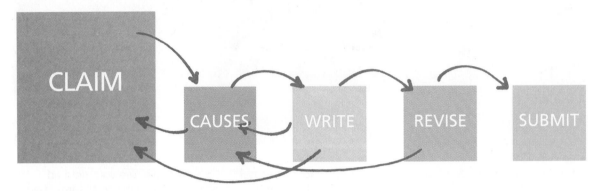

Analyze the assignment

Read your assignment slowly and carefully. Look for words like *causes*, *effect*, *result*, *impact*, and *why*, which signal that you are writing a causal argument. Highlight any information about the length specified, date due, formatting, and other requirements. You can attend to this information later. At this point you want to give your attention to the topic and criteria you will use in your argument.

Explore possible topics

- Make a list of fashion trends including cars, clothing, hairstyles, food, tattoos, and piercing. Look at your list and think about where and why a particular trend originates.

- Make a list of social trends including music, television shows, movies, sports, exercising, childrearing, and leisure. Look at your list and think about where and why a particular trend originates.

- Make a list of important historical events or discoveries that changed the course of civilization. Make notes about what led to these events or discoveries and how people's lives were changed.

- Identify two or three possibilities for a causal argument.

Make an initial causal claim

Select one of your possibilities and make a causal claim. Use the form: "SOMETHING causes (or does not cause) SOMETHING ELSE."

Think about what's at stake

Remember that people often have a stake in the outcome of a causal argument. Ask: Who will agree with me? Who will disagree, and why? If people accept your causal argument, will anything change?

Watch the Animation on Types of Claims at mycomplab.com

Make a claim that matters

MAKE AN ARGUABLE CLAIM

Easy answers generally make bad arguments. If all the sources you consult agree about the cause of the effect you are interested in, there is probably no need for you to make another argument saying the same thing. Look for a phenomenon that hasn't been explained to everyone's satisfaction.

OFF TRACK
Cigarette smoke is a leading cause of lung cancer.
ON TRACK
New research indicates that childhood asthma may be linked to exposure to cockroaches.

EXPLAIN WHY IT MATTERS

Readers need to know why this cause-and-effect relationship is important. If we determine the cause of this phenomenon, what will change? What can we do? What might happen?

OFF TRACK
This paper will investigate the most common causes of foundation failure in U.S. residential housing.
ON TRACK
Foundation failure, especially cracked slabs, can cost anywhere from a few thousand to tens of thousands of dollars to repair. Determining the primary causes of foundation failure can help homeowners and insurers protect themselves against economic loss and inconvenience.

WRITE NOW

Think about causal factors

1. Consider trends or problems you are familiar with—in your daily life, or in the larger world.
2. List these trends and problems on the right side of a piece of paper. On the left side, write down what you think some of the causes of the problems might be. Underline the causes that you are confident about.
3. Look over your two lists. Which topics seem most interesting to you? If an entry has many underlined causes or effects, it may be too obvious to write about.

Writer at work

Armadi Tansal was asked to write a paper analyzing the effects of a current trend in popular culture for his Social Trends and Problems course. He made the following notes on his assignment sheet while his class was discussing the assignment.

Sociology 032
Social Trends and Problems

Macro and micro effects

Identify a trend in American popular culture that interests you, and analyze its impact—postive or negative—on society. Some topics we have discussed in class that might make good papers include the rising number of unwed teenage mothers who keep their babies; the popularity of video games; people ignoring social protocol while talking on cell phones; and the growth of pet ownership over the past fifteen years. Look for large-scale social consequences as well as the effects on individuals for which this trend might be responsible.

Use outside sources to help make your claims, and find authoritative opinions on the topic whenever possible. It usually isn't possible to definitively identify the effects of a social trend, so beware of making a claim that is too sweeping. Social science often relies on probability and plausibility rather than absolute certainty.

Look for causation – not just correlation

Length and deadlines
You should be able to complete this assignment in about four double-spaced, typed pages. Papers are due on October 28, and I will return them to you one week later with a grade. If you then wish to rewrite your paper, you will have one week to do so. I will average the rewrite grade with your first grade to give you your final grade.

I encourage you to share your papers with your discussion groups as you draft them. You should also plan to take your paper to the writing center. This is not required, but it is highly recommended.

Evaluation
Papers will be evaluated according to how well they use logic and evidence to show causation. In addition, I will consider how well you contextualize your analysis for readers (Why does it matter? Who is affected? And so on).

Read the assignment closely

Armadi Tansal began by circling the words and phrases that indicated his analytical task. Then he highlighted information about dates and processes for the project.

Choose a topic

Armadi Tansal made a list of trends he might write about. After each item on his list, he made notes about why the topic would matter, and to whom. He also made preliminary observations about where he might find "authoritative opinions" on each topic, wrote down any possible causes that occurred to him at the time, and noted any other observations or questions he had about that topic. Finally, he chose one trend for further research.

POPULARITY OF ANIME

- Is it more popular with certain age groups or other demographic groups?
- Is there any scholarly/authoritative research on it? Maybe in Art History?
- I've seen tons of magazines devoted to it at the bookstore.
- Could interview Sarah about the collection she has.

POPULARITY OF VIDEO GAMES   **** Best research possibilities****

- What types of games are most popular?
- How much time do people spend gaming instead of doing something else? Consequences?
- Effect on friendships/relationships?
- What's the effect of gaming on the brain?
- What about violence in games? Does it affect behavior?
- Is there any scholarly/authoritative research on it?
- Could interview a friend (anonymously).

SUV SALES

- Why do people want to drive "off-roading" cars to work every day?
- What does this do to the environment?
- Are sales declining with rising gas prices?
- Is this even a trend any more? People are buying VWs and Mini Coopers now.

"ILLEGAL" FILE SHARING

- Why do so many people do it if it is "illegal"? (Because you get something for free.)
- Impact on morals—plagiarism?
- What are the arguments saying that it is or isn't illegal?
- Easy answer: people are willing to "steal" in this case because there is still significant disagreement over whether it is really stealing.

2: Think about possible causes and effects

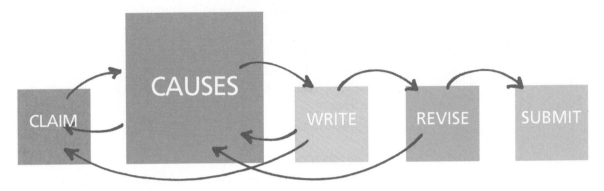

Find the obvious causes and effects, and then dig deeper

- **What factors might be hidden from the general observer, and why?** Use your imagination; hidden causes and subtle effects require new thinking if they are to be uncovered.
- **How do various causal factors interact?** Several causes together might contribute to an effect, rather than any single cause being the determining factor.
- **What "causes the cause" that you have identified?** What prior conditions does each cause arise from? If poor attendance is a factor in dropout rates, what causes some students to have poor attendance in the first place?

Think about common threads

Sometimes causes can be identified because two or more similar events share a common factor. The common factor may be the cause. For example, a mysterious outbreak of deadly *E. coli* bacteria in Germany in 2011 was traced to eating organic bean sprouts.

Think about relevant differences

Relevant difference reasoning attempts to identify causes that produce different effects. For example, studies of identical twins raised apart from each other rule out genetic influences. Differences between the twins in physical characteristics, intelligence, and behavior are determined by environmental factors.

Research your analysis

- **Look for some disagreement among your sources.** If they all agree, your analysis won't matter much.
- **When your sources disagree, ask why.** Does one give more weight to some pieces of evidence than to others? Do they draw different conclusions from the same evidence?
- **Be on the lookout for new potential causes or unexpected effects, or new findings that could help you rule out potential causes and effects.**

Writer at work

Armadi Tansal began his analysis by brainstorming for all the possible effects he could think of. Then, he researched the topic to find information on the effects he had listed and also to learn about other potential effects that had been put forward.

Tansal thought about his own experience with the trend to help define his audience. Finally, Tansal identified what he thought were the most likely effects of playing violent video games.

POSSIBLE EFFECTS OF PLAYING VIOLENT VIDEO GAMES:

- Time spent gaming instead of on other activities: school, sports, friends, family, exercising? Does gaming lead gamers to be unsociable? - Any physical effects? increased heart rate? weight gain?
- Aggressive behavior: Anderson talks about "delinquency, fighting at school and during free play periods, and violent criminal behavior."
- Violent thoughts and feelings: Anderson says there's a link here.
- Players rewarded for being violent: Anderson mentions the active role in video games as opposed to passive experience of violence on TV and in movies. So violent games are a stronger influence than violent shows.

**I've played violent video games. What about "John"? He does a lot of gaming, and he's not a criminal!

**Talk about causation vs. correlation: Is the link between playing violent video games and behaving aggressively just coincidental? See Ferguson and Kilburn on this.

**Also, a main factor vs. a contributing factor: Does playing violent video games lead to criminal behavior in a healthy person? Think about Mill's idea of concomitant variation.

**Effect on individuals vs. effect on society: Gaming might not have much of an impact on most people, but what about its impact on the small number of people who are already prone to be aggressive?

Most important effects to talk about: link to aggressive or criminal behavior; individuals lose out socially; mass effect on society.

3: Write a Draft

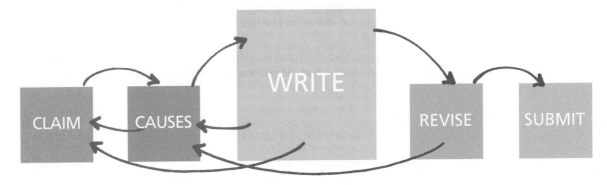

Introduce the subject of your argument

Describe the trend, event, or phenomenon you will be analyzing. Give your readers any background information they will need. Explain why it is important to determine the causes or effects of this phenomenon (you can save this for the conclusion if you wish).

Describe the causal relationship

- Explain how the chain of causation works to produce the effect in question. Break down each step so readers can follow the process.
- Alternatively, set out the causes or effects offered by other people and show how they can be ruled out. Then, introduce your own claim and demonstrate why it is superior to others'.
- A third method is to look at a series of possible causes or effects one at a time. Analyze each cause and make a claim about its relative impact on a phenomenon, or analyze each effect and make a claim about the likelihood that it is a consequence of the phenomenon.

Anticipate and address opposing viewpoints

Acknowledge other stakeholders in the analysis and consider their claims. Demonstrate why your claim is preferable.

Conclude by doing more than summarizing

Spell out the importance of the analysis, if you haven't already done so. Consider additional causes or effects you haven't previously discussed. Explain any action you think needs to be taken on the basis of your conclusion.

STAYING ON TRACK
Look at the big picture

DON'T CONFUSE CORRELATION WITH CAUSATION

Remember that the relationship of separate events is causal only when all other variables are accounted for.

OFF TRACK

The drop in the number of Americans living in poverty during the Clinton administration was due to a number of factors.

ON TRACK

The lower number of Americans living in poverty during the Clinton administration was due to a number of factors. How much did the Welfare Reform Act contribute to this trend? The general economic prosperity experienced by the entire country during that time probably had a greater impact. Statistics show that the primary effect of the Welfare Reform Act was to simply remove people from welfare rolls, not actually lift them out of poverty.

IDENTIFY THE STAKEHOLDERS IN YOUR ANALYSIS

Be especially alert for opinions about your topic from people who would be adversely affected by a different causal outcome.

OFF TRACK

Can megadoses of vitamin C prevent colds, flu, and other illnesses? Good health is important to everyone, so we should all be interested in the news that vitamin C has many important health benefits.

ON TRACK

Can megadoses of vitamin C prevent colds, flu, and other illnesses? The supplements industry has spent millions of dollars to convince consumers that this is the case. The industry stands to make hundreds of millions more if people believe them. But evidence from independent researchers casts some doubt on the effectiveness of megadoses of vitamin C in preventing illness.

Writer at work

Armadi Tansal tested three organizational patterns for his analysis. First he looked at how describing a chain of causation could illuminate his analysis. Next, he considered examining effects one by one and eliminating them before describing the effects he thought most likely and most important. Finally, he structured his analysis as an examination of possible effects, one by one, with accompanying discussion of how likely each effect is to be true. This method seemed to be the best for making his analysis, so he used it to write his draft.

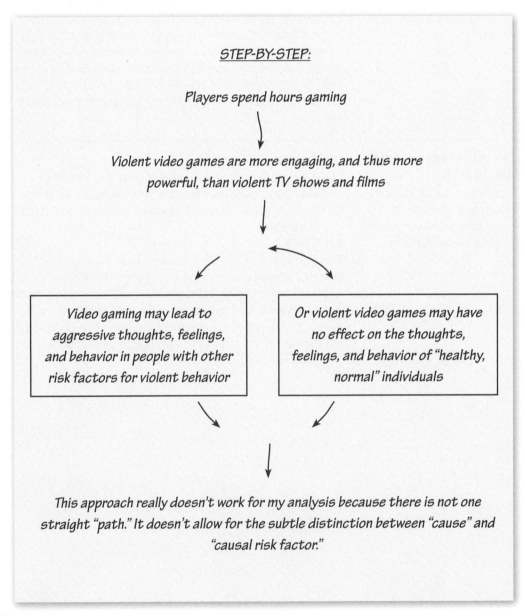

STEP-BY-STEP:

Players spend hours gaming

Violent video games are more engaging, and thus more powerful, than violent TV shows and films

Video gaming may lead to aggressive thoughts, feelings, and behavior in people with other risk factors for violent behavior

Or violent video games may have no effect on the thoughts, feelings, and behavior of "healthy, normal" individuals

This approach really doesn't work for my analysis because there is not one straight "path." It doesn't allow for the subtle distinction between "cause" and "causal risk factor."

<u>*DISPROVING ALTERNATE EFFECTS:*</u>

Playing violent video games <u>always</u> leads to violent behavior.
  - Experts agree there's no definitive proof that this is so.

Playing violent video games has no impact on the behavior of "healthy, normal" individuals.
  - Experts seem to concede that this is likely.

Playing violent video games promotes aggressive behavior in individuals already at risk for violent behavior.
  - Researchers don't dispute this, but some say the impact of this effect on society is minimal.

<u>*ONE EFFECT AT A TIME:*</u>

Anderson thinks video game violence is more influential than TV and movie violence because of the gamer's active role. (Web article)
  - Gaming is a common activity with little discernible effect anecdotally. (Interview with "John"; my own experience)

Minimally, violent video games are a "causal risk factor" (Anderson) especially when other risk factors are present (Anderson et al.)
  - Though the influence on most gamers is probably minor, the impact on society as a whole, even if only a few become more violent, can be great.

This strategy is the best approach because it lets me look at all the possible effects in detail and finish with a meaningful conclusion .

4: Revise, revise, revise

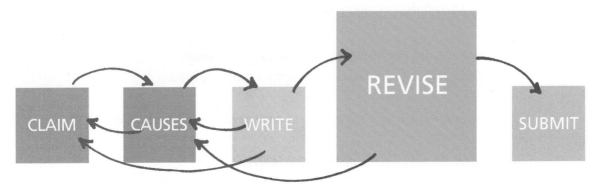

Skilled writers know that the secret to writing well is rewriting. You must have effective strategies for revising if you're going to be successful. The biggest trap you can fall into is starting off with the little stuff first. Leave the small stuff for last.

Does your paper or project meet the assignment?	• Look again at your assignment. Does your paper or project do what the assignment asks? • Look again at the assignment for specific guidelines, including length, format, and amount of research. Does your work meet these guidelines?
Is your causal claim arguable?	• Do enough people disagree with you to make the evaluation worthwhile? • Who cares about this topic? Do you explain to readers why it is important?
Is your evidence authoritative and convincing?	• Have you found the most accurate available information about your topic? • Have you carefully examined the analysis and conclusions of people who have already expressed an opinion on this topic?
Save the editing for last.	When you have finished revising, edit and proofread carefully.

A peer review guide is on page 54.

Writer at work

Armadi Tansal talked with his peer group about his analysis, and he took his draft to the writing center for a consultation. He wrote notes on the draft to help him revise, and then he made some changes to the draft. His peers particularly urged him to cite more research and explain what "violent" means. Here is part of Armadi Tansal's original draft, with notes he made, and the same section as he revised it for his final draft.

Give more details about games so readers can see what "violent" means.

Cite some specific research—not my own opinion. Maybe add a quote?

I've never seen John act violently, and he's never been in trouble with the law. But (new research) on violent video games suggests that John's gaming habit puts him at risk for violent or aggressive behavior. (I agree) that when people play these games a lot, they get used to being rewarded for violent behavior. For example, the multiplayer version of *Modern Warfare 2* and games like *Left 4 Dead*, *Halo*, and *Grand Theft Auto* (are all violent.) To do well in all of these games, you have to commit acts of violence. But does acting violently in games make you more violent in real life?

I've never seen John act violently, and he's never been in trouble with the law. But new research on violent video games suggests that John's gaming habit puts him at risk for violent or aggressive behavior. Dr. Craig Anderson, a psychologist at the University of Iowa, says "the active role required by video games . . . may make violent video games even more hazardous than violent television or cinema." When people like John play these games, they get used to being rewarded for violent behavior. For example, in the multiplayer version of *Modern Warfare 2*, if the player gets a five-kill streak, he can call in a Predator missile strike. If you kill twenty-five people in a row, you can call in a tactical nuclear strike. Missile strikes help you advance toward the mission goals more quickly, so the more people you kill, the faster you'll win.

Along with *Modern Warfare 2*, John plays games like *Left 4 Dead*, *Halo*, and *Grand Theft Auto*. All these games are rated *M* for "Mature," which according to the Entertainment Software Rating Board means they "may contain intense violence, blood and gore, sexual content and/or strong language." Some M-rated games, like *Grand Theft Auto*, feature random violence, where players can run amok in a city, beat up and kill people, and smash stuff for no reason. In others, like *Modern Warfare 2*, the violence takes place in the context of military action. To do well in all of these games, you have to commit acts of violence. But does acting violently in games make you more violent in real life?

5: Submitted version

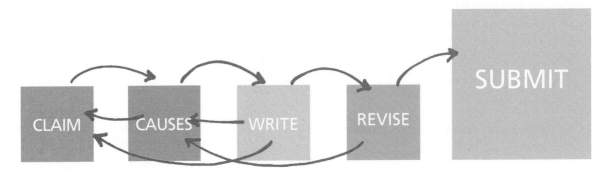

Tansal 1

Armadi Tansal

Professor Stewart

English 115

28 October 2011

Modern Warfare: Video Games' Link to Real-World Violence

"John" is a nineteen-year-old college student who gets decent grades. He comes from a typical upper-middle-class family and plans to get his MBA after he graduates. John is also my friend, which is why I'm not using his real name.

John has been playing moderately violent video games since he was nine years old. I started playing video and console games around that age too, and I played a lot in junior high, but John plays more than anyone I know. John says that over the past year he has played video games at least four hours every day, and "sometimes all day and night on the weekends." I have personally witnessed John play *Call of Duty: Modern Warfare 2* for six hours straight, with breaks only to use the bathroom or eat something.

I've never seen John act violently, and he's never been in trouble with the law. But new research on violent video games suggests that John's gaming habit puts him at risk for violent or aggressive behavior. Dr. Craig Anderson, a psychologist at the University of Iowa, says "the active role required by video games . . . may make violent video games even more hazardous than violent television or cinema" (Anderson). When people like John play these games, they get used to being rewarded for violent behavior. For example, in the multiplayer version of *Modern Warfare 2*, if the player gets a five-kill streak, he can call in a Predator missile strike. If you kill twenty-five people in a row, you can call in a tactical nuclear strike. Missile strikes help you advance toward the mission goals more quickly, so the more people you kill, the faster you'll win.

Along with *Modern Warfare 2*, John plays games like *Left 4 Dead*, *Halo*, and *Grand Theft Auto*. All these games are rated M for Mature, which according to the Entertainment Software Rating Board means they "may contain intense violence, blood and gore, sexual content and/or strong language." Some M-rated games, like *Grand Theft Auto*, feature random violence, where players can run amok in a city, beat up and kill people, and smash stuff for no reason. In others, like *Modern Warfare 2*, the violence takes place in the context of military action. To do well in all of these games, you have to commit acts of violence. But does acting violently in games make you more violent in real life?

Anderson says studies show that "violent video games are significantly associated with: increased aggressive behavior, thoughts, and affect [feelings]; increased physiological arousal; and decreased prosocial (helping) behavior" (Anderson). He also claims that "high levels of violent video game exposure have been linked to delinquency, fighting at school and during free play periods, and violent criminal behavior (e.g., self-reported assault, robbery)."

Being "associated with" and "linked to" violent behavior doesn't necessarily mean video games cause such behavior. Many people have argued that the links Anderson sees are coincidental, or that any effects video games might have on behavior are so slight that we shouldn't worry about them. Christopher Ferguson and John Kilburn, professors of criminal justice at Texas A&M International University, feel that the existing research does not support Anderson's claims. In a report published in the *Journal of Pediatrics*, they point out that in past studies, "the closer aggression measures got to actual violent behavior, the weaker the effects seen."

From what I can tell, John doesn't have any more violent thoughts and feelings than most men his age. When I asked him if he thought the games had made him more violent or aggressive in real life, he said, "I'm actually less violent now. When we were kids we used to play 'war' with fake guns and sticks, chasing each other around the neighborhood and fighting commando-style. We didn't really fight but sometimes kids got banged up. No one ever gets hurt playing a video game."

Anderson admits that "a healthy, normal, nonviolent child or adolescent who has no other risk factors for high aggression or violence is not going to become a school shooter simply because they play five hours or 10 hours a week of these violent video games" (qtd. in St. George). But just because violent video games don't turn all players into mass murderers, that doesn't mean they have no effect on a player's behavior and personality. For example, my friend John doesn't get into fights or rob people, but he doesn't display a lot of prosocial "helping" behaviors either. He spends most of his free time gaming, so he doesn't get out of his apartment much. Also, the friends he does have mostly play video games with him.

Even though the games restrict his interactions with other humans and condition him to behave violently onscreen, John is probably not at high risk of becoming violent in real life. But according to researchers, this low risk of becoming violent is because none of the dozens of other risk factors associated with violent behavior are present in his life (Anderson et al. 160). If John were a high school dropout, came from a broken home, or abused alcohol and other drugs, his game playing might be more likely to contribute to violent behavior.

Anderson contends that violent video games are a "causal risk factor" for violence and aggression—not that they alone cause violent aggression. In other words, the games are a small piece of a much larger problem. People like my friend John are not likely to become violent because of the video games they play. But Anderson's research indicates that some people do. Although there is no simple way to tell who those people are, we should include video games as a possible risk factor when we think about who is likely to become violent.

Even if the risk contributed by violent video games is slight for each individual, the total impact of the games on violence in society could be huge. *Call of Duty: Modern Warfare 2* is the third-best-selling video game in the United States (Orry). Its creator, Activision Blizzard, had $1.3 billion in sales in the just first three months of 2010 (Pham). Millions of people play this game and games like it, and they aren't all as well-adjusted as John. If video games contribute to violent tendencies in only a small fraction of players, they could still have a terrible impact.

Tansal 4

Works Cited

Anderson, Craig. "Violent Video Games: Myths, Facts, and Unanswered Questions."
Psychological Science Agenda 16.5 (2003): n. pag. Web. 6 Oct. 2011.

Anderson, Craig, et al. "Violent Video Game Effects on Aggression, Empathy, and Prosocial
Behavior in Eastern and Western Countries." _Psychological Bulletin_ 136.2 (2010):
151–73. Print.

Entertainment Software Rating Board. _Game Ratings and Descriptor Guide._ Entertainment
Software Association, n.d. Web. 7 Oct. 2011.

Ferguson, Christopher J., and John Kilburn. "The Public Health Risks of Media Violence:
A Meta-Analytic Review." _Journal of Pediatrics_ 154.5 (2009): 759–63. Print.

John (pseudonym). Personal interview. 4 Oct. 2011.

Orry, James. "Modern Warfare 2 the 3rd Best-Selling Game in the US." _Videogamer.com._
Pro-G Media Ltd., 12 Mar. 2010. Web. 6 Oct. 2011.

Pham, Alex. "Call of Duty: Modern Warfare 2 Propels Revenue, Profit for Activision
Blizzard." _Los Angeles Times._ Los Angeles Times, 6 May 2010. Web. 7 Oct. 2011.

St. George, Donna. "Study Links Violent Video Games, Hostility." _Washington Post._
Washington Post, 3 Nov. 2008. Web. 5 Oct. 2011.

Projects

A causal argument answers the question: How did something get that way?

Analyzing claims and stakeholders

 Identify a causal relationship that is now generally accepted but was once in doubt, such as Galileo's explanation of the phases of the moon, the link between DDT and the decline of bald eagle populations, or the effects of vitamin B12 on developing fetuses.

Research the arguments that were made for and against these causal relationships. Who initially proposed the cause? What was the reaction? Who argued against them, and why? How did the causal relationship come to be accepted as real? Write a short essay outlining the stakeholders in the issue you have chosen.

 Explain the arguments made for and against the now-accepted cause, and the evidence presented. Why were the arguments of the now-accepted cause more effective?

Causal analysis of a trend

Identify a significant change in human behavior over a period of months or years. Why have mega-churches grown rapidly? Why has reality television become popular? Why have the wealthiest one percent of Americans grown significantly richer over the past twenty years? Why have homicide rates dropped to levels not seen since the 1960s? Why are children increasingly obese?

 Determine the time span of the trend. When did it start? When did it stop? Is it still going on? You likely will need to do research.

 Analyze the possible causes of the trend, arguing for the ones you think are most likely the true causes. Look for underlying and hidden causes.

 Remember that providing facts is not the same thing as establishing causes, even though facts can help support your causal analysis.

 **mycomplab**

For support in learning this chapter's content, follow this path in **mycomplab:**

▶ **Resources** ▶ **Writing** ▶ **Writing Purposes** ▶ **Writing to Argue or Persuade**

Review the Instruction and Multimedia resources, then complete the **Exercises** and click on **Gradebook** to measure your progress.

Causal analysis of a human-influenced natural phenomenon

Find a natural phenomenon or trend that is (or may be) the result of human activity. Is the growing hole in the Earth's ozone layer the result of human-produced chemicals in the atmosphere? Why have populations of American alligators rebounded in the southern United States? Are sinkholes in a Kentucky town the result of new mining activity in the area? Why are more and more bacteria developing resistance to antibiotics? Choose a topic that interests you and that you feel is important. If you think the topic is important, it will be easier to convince your audience that your analysis is important.

Research the possible causes of the phenomenon, focusing on the ones you think are most likely the true causes. Remember to look at underlying and hidden causes.

Think about possible alternative causes. Do you need to incorporate them? If you don't think they are valid causes, then you need to refute them.

Recognize that causal relationships between humans and the natural world are so complex and large in scale that it is often difficult to prove them definitively. Don't oversimplify or make sweeping claims that can't be proven.

Causal argument Web site

Choose a topic for a causal argument (see page 330). You will need to identify your thesis and outline your argument, just as you would for a paper. Decide if you are going to argue for a chain of causes, the effects of a particular cause, or that alternative causes that have been proposed are flawed and the cause you are proposing is the deciding cause.

Divide the elements of your argument into separate Web pages. Give the main argument on the home page and offer evidence and other background on other pages.

Find Web-editing software on your campus if you do not have it on your computer. Campus labs will have programs like Dreamweaver that can produce a handsome site.

Create user-friendly pages with headings and subheadings, a navigation menu with links to move among pages, and visual elements such as graphics and photographs. Avoid large blocks of unbroken text.

Make sure your links work, and proofread carefully before posting your site.

11 Evaluation Arguments

Convincing evaluations rely on selecting criteria and supporting a claim with reasons and evidence.

Chapter Overview

Writing Evaluation Arguments

People make evaluation arguments constantly. You choose a favorite band, a favorite sports team, a favorite mobile device, a favorite ring tone, and so on. Newspapers, magazines, and Web sites feature "best of" polls that let people vote for their favorite restaurants, coffeehouses, neighborhood parks, places to get married, and so on. And the introduction of the "like" button on *Facebook* in 2009 changed the way people communicate and has spread to many thousands of other Web sites.

Evaluation arguments differ from "best of" polls and the like button by setting out clearly defined criteria to make a value judgment. Sometimes it will be necessary to argue for the criteria that you think your readers should consider. If your readers accept your criteria, it's likely they will agree with your conclusions.

Evaluation arguments in the world

Reviews offer opinions about many products, services, and forms of entertainment  like movies and concerts. Reviews often don't announce the criteria but rather include the criteria in the discussion of their subjects.

Other genres of evaluation arguments

- **Policy evaluations** argue what particular policies and laws are good or bad.
- **Evaluations of colleges and universities** use both reputation and statistical criteria such as graduation rates and student selectivity.
- **Evaluations of culture** make judgments about how we eat, work, travel, live in communities, and entertain ourselves.

Keys to evaluation arguments

Evaluation arguments often argue for specific criteria and then judge something to be good or bad (or better, or best) according to those criteria.

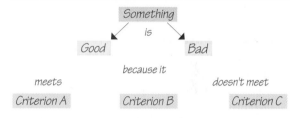

Evaluative claims argue that SOMETHING is a GOOD (or BAD)——because it meets certain criteria.

Something is Good Bad because it meets Criterion A, Criterion B, doesn't meet Criterion C

Google maps is the best mapping program because it is easy to use, it is accurate, and it provides entertaining and educational features such as Google Earth.

Goals of evaluation

When you write an evaluation, your goal is usually to convince readers to agree with your judgment. Convincing other people that your judgment is sound depends on the validity of the criteria you will use to make your evaluation. You may think a movie is good because it has exceptional cinematography, but an action-movie fan is less likely to go see a movie just because it is visually beautiful. Sometimes you must argue for the validity of your criteria before readers will accept them.

Criteria for evaluation

Things are usually judged to be good (or bad) either because they work well (**practical criteria**), because they are beautiful or ugly (**aesthetic criteria**), or because they are or are not fair or just (**ethical criteria**). An evaluative argument may use any or all of these types of criteria, and can emphasize them in different ways. For example, if you want to convince your penny-pinching roommate to go to an expensive restaurant, you would probably emphasize the aesthetic experience and downplay the cost.

349

What Makes a Good Evaluation Argument?

1

Find an interesting topic

A controversial policy, law, or social practice is often is a good subject for an evaluation argument (see page 360). There are many possibilities for reviews, including services like Craigslist (see page 373).

2

Consider your readers

How interesting will your topic be to your readers? Which criteria will be most convincing to them? Consider other views opposed to yours. Which criteria do they use?

3

Describe your subject of your evaluation

Because your readers may be unfamiliar with what you are evaluating, describe what you are evaluating. In some cases you may need to provide background information.

4

Choose the appropriate criteria

- **Practical criteria** will demand that the thing being evaluated work efficiently or lead to good outcomes (improved conditions, lower costs, and so on).
- **Aesthetic criteria** hinge on the importance and value of beauty, image, or tradition.
- **Ethical criteria** are used to evaluate whether something is morally right, consistent with the law, and upholds fairness.

Industrial livestock production is essentially indefensible—ethically, ecologically, and otherwise.
  —Bill McKibben (see page 363)

5

Explain your criteria

The importance of many criteria may not be evident to your readers. You may need to state explicitly each criterion you use and explain why it is relevant.

First and foremost, we crave satisfying work, every single day. The exact nature of this "satisfying work" is different from person to person, but for everyone it means being immersed in clearly defined, demanding activities that allow us to see the direct impact of our efforts.
  —Jane McGonigal (see page 367)

6

Be fair

Be honest about the strengths and weaknesses of what you are evaluating. Rarely is anything perfectly good or absolutely bad. Your credibility will increase if you give a balanced view.

7

Support your judgments with evidence

Back up your claims with specific evidence. If you write that a restaurant serves inedible food, describe examples in detail.

In some parts of the country Craigslist housing postings are an essential part of the real estate biosphere. New York is by far the leader in this regard (it had some 180,245 housing listings last Thursday).
  —Stephanie Rosenbloom (see page 373)

8

Conclude with strength

If you have not announced your stance, then you can make your summary evaluation. If your readers know where you stand, you might end with a compelling example.

Visual evaluations

Among the first photographs published in newspapers were Jacob Riis's images of slums in New York City in the 1880s, intended to convince readers that living conditions for the poor were intolerable. Beginning in 1908, Lewis Hine worked for a decade photographing child laborers in the United States. Hine's photographs help to mobilize support for state-level child labor laws and later the passage of a federal law to abolish child labor.

Riis's and Hine's photographs were powerful because they provided evidence for larger social movements to improve living conditions in New York City and to end most child labor.

Lewis Hine. *Addie Card, twelve-year-old-spinner (1910).*

WRITE NOW

What makes an effective review?

1. Look at a several amateur online reviews of a particular film, restaurant, book, or a consumer product. You can find movie reviews on imdb.com and consumer reviews of thousands of books and products on Amazon.com, Epionions.com, and other sites.

2. Select several examples of reviews that you think are persuasive and several that are not (see if you can find some persuasive reviews that you don't necessarily agree with).

3. Analyze the criteria the reviewers use to evaluate. What types of criteria do the persuasive reviewers use? What types do the less persuasive reviews use? Do you see any patterns that make reviews effective?

How to Read Evaluation Arguments

▼ BEFORE YOU BEGIN READING

These notes are in response to *"The End of the Affair"*; the reading begins on page 354

What kind of text is it?	··········▶	*O'Rourke's essay is both a causal and an evaluation argument, but it turns quickly to the question of how Americans value cars. It was published in May 2009 in the* Wall Street Journal, *the largest newspaper in the United States by circulation.*

Who wrote it?	··········▶	*P.J. O'Rourke is a humorist and satirist who writes from a libertarian point of view.*

Who is the intended audience?	··········▶	The Wall Street Journal *primary focus is on business. The editorial pages take a politically conservative stance, but the paper also reports on culture. Many of the Journal's readers at the time were no doubt sympathetic to O'Rourke's jabs at government regulation.*

▼ READ THE TEXT AT LEAST TWICE AND MAKE NOTES

What is the topic of the evaluation argument?	··········▶	*The first two paragraphs give the argument in a nutshell: the problems of the American auto industry come from how Americans value cars.*

What kinds of criteria does the writer use?	··········▶	*O'Rourke announces early that he will use aesthetic criteria, and he blames practical criteria for causing the downturn in the American automobile industry.*

What evidence does the writer use to support the evaluation?	··········▶	*Most of the evidence is anecdotal, drawn from memories of O'Rourke's childhood and life as a young man.*

How would you characterize the style?	··········▶	*The style is informal and humorous. O'Rourke inserts colorful metaphors for how cars turned awkward young men (he uses the Yiddish slang term "schlub") into knights of the Round Table.*

How is it organized?

This map shows the organization of "The End of the Affair," which begins on the following page.

Beginning paragraph: Paragraph 1	O'Rourke identifies his subject—the American auto industry which was on the verge of bankruptcy in 2009 and indicates his stance.
Introduction of aesthetic criteria: Paragraphs 2–4	In paragraph 2, O'Rourke dismisses the usual causes given for the problems of the auto industry and argues that cars can best be understood as love affairs. He turns a causal argument into an evaluation argument.
Arguments for aesthetic criteria: Paragraphs 5–10	Beginning in paragraph 5, O'Rourke observes how cars once conferred status and were "cool." Young boys dreamed of the day when they could drive.
Arguments against practical criteria: Paragraphs 11–18	Cars became judged by practical criteria. O'Rourke accuses them of being reduced to motorized cup holders.
Conclusion: Paragraphs 19–22	O'Rourke is nostalgic for the romantic individualism of the early car makers. He says only a small segment of young people haven't lost their love for their cars and that their creative energy is likely to fade.

The End of the Affair

P. J. O'Rourke

P. J. O'Rourke is a humorist and an author of sixteen books, including *Driving Like Crazy* (2009). He follows in the tradition of the New Journalism where there is no pretense of objectivity and the biases of the writer are in the foreground. Even those who don't agree with his libertarian conservative political views still find him funny, like Bill Maher, who invites O'Rourke on his HBO show. O'Rourke's humor is infused with outrage over the influence of government in ordinary life, which you will find in this evaluation argument.

1   The phrase "bankrupt General Motors," which we expect to hear uttered on Monday, leaves Americans my age in economic shock. The words are as melodramatic as "Mom's nude photos." And, indeed, if we want to understand what doomed the American automobile, we should give up on economics and turn to melodrama.

2   Politicians, journalists, financial analysts and other purveyors of banality have been looking at cars as if a convertible were a business. Fire the MBAs and hire a poet. The fate of Detroit isn't a matter of financial crisis, foreign competition, corporate greed, union intransigence, energy costs or measuring the shoe size of the footprints in the carbon. It's a tragic romance—unleashed passions, titanic clashes, lost love and wild horses. Foremost are the horses. Cars can't be comprehended without them. A hundred and some years ago Rudyard Kipling wrote "The Ballad of the King's Jest," in which an Afghan tribesman avers: Four things greater than all things are—Women and Horses and Power and War.

3   Insert another "power" after the horse and the verse was as true in the suburbs of my 1950s boyhood as it was in the Khyber Pass.

4   Horsepower is not a quaint leftover of linguistics or a vague metaphoric anachronism. James Watt, father of the steam engine and progenitor of the industrial revolution, lacked a measurement for the movement of weight over distance in time—what we call energy. (What we call energy wasn't even an intellectual concept in the late 18th century—in case you think the recent collapse of

Beginning paragraph: O'Rourke begins by announcing his topic and that he is from an older generation.

Introduction of aesthetic criteria: O'Rourke's favored criteria—romance, passion, horses—have to do with aesthetics, not practical issues like safety or environmental impact.

global capitalism was history's most transformative moment.) Mr. Watt did research using draft animals and found that, under optimal conditions, a dray horse could lift 33,000 pounds one foot off the ground in one minute. Mr. Watt—the eponymous watt not yet existing—called this unit of energy "1 horse-power."

5   In 1970 a Pontiac GTO (may the brand name rest in peace) had horsepower to the number of 370. In the time of one minute, for the space of one foot, it could move 12,210,000 pounds. And it could move those pounds down every foot of every mile of all the roads to the ends of the earth for every minute of every hour until the driver nodded off at the wheel. Forty years ago the pimply kid down the block, using $3,500 in saved-up soda-jerking money, procured might and main beyond the wildest dreams of Genghis Khan, whose hordes went forth to pillage mounted upon less oomph than is in a modern ← leaf blower.

Aesthetic criteria: Status and being cool have nothing to do with practicality and everything to do with aesthetics.

6   Horses and horsepower alike are about status and being cool. A knight in ancient Rome was bluntly called "guy on horseback," Equesitis. Chevalier means the same, as does Cavalier. Lose the capitalization and the dictionary says, "insouciant and debonair; marked by a lofty disregard of others' interests, rights, or feelings; high-handed and arrogant and supercilious." How cool is that? Then there are cowboys—always cool—and the U.S. cavalry that coolly comes to their rescue plus the proverbially cool-handed "Man on Horseback" to whom we turn in troubled times.

7   Early witnesses to the automobile urged motorists to get a horse. But that, in effect, was what the automobile would do—get a horse for everybody. Once the Model T was introduced in 1908 we all became Sir Lancelot, gained a seat at the Round Table and were privileged to joust for the favors of fair maidens (at drive-in movies). The pride and prestige of a noble mount was vouchsafed to the common man. And woman, too. No one ever tried to persuade ladies to drive sidesaddle with both legs hanging out the car door.

8   For the purpose of ennobling us schlubs, the car is better than the
horse in every way. Even more advantageous than cost, convenience
and not getting kicked and smelly is how much easier it is to drive
than to ride. I speak with feeling on this subject, having taken up
riding when I was nearly 60 and having begun to drive when I was so
small that my cousin Tommy had to lie on the transmission hump and
operate the accelerator and the brake with his hands.

9   After the grown-ups had gone to bed, Tommy and I shifted the
Buick into neutral, pushed it down the driveway and out of earshot,
started the engine and toured the neighborhood. The sheer difficulty
of horsemanship can be illustrated by what happened to Tommy and
me next. Nothing. We maneuvered the car home, turned it off and
rolled it back up the driveway. (We were raised in the blessedly flat
Midwest.) During our foray the Buick's speedometer reached 30. But
30 miles per hour is a full gallop on a horse. Delete what you've seen
of horse riding in movies. Possibly a kid who'd never been on a horse
could ride at a gallop without killing himself. Possibly one of the
Jonas Brothers could land an F-14 on a carrier deck.

10   Thus cars usurped the place of horses in our hearts. Once we'd
caught a glimpse of a well-turned Goodyear, checked out the curves
of the bodywork and gaped at that swell pair of headlights, well, the
old gray mare was not what she used to be. We embarked upon life in
the fast lane with our new paramour. It was a great love story of man
and machine. The road to the future was paved with bliss.

11   Then we got married and moved to the suburbs. Being away
from central cities meant Americans had to spend more of their time
driving. Over the years away got farther away. Eventually this meant
that Americans had to spend all of their time driving. The play date
was 40 miles from the Chuck E. Cheese. The swim meet was 40 miles
from the cello lesson. The Montessori was 40 miles from the math
coach. Mom's job was 40 miles from Dad's job and the three-car
garage was 40 miles from both.

Style:
Schlub is a Yiddish term for an unattractive person. Why does O'Rourke use it?

Aesthetic criteria:
Cars in the 1950s and 1960s represented the triumph of aesthetics over practical issues like gas mileage.

Practical criteria:
Practicality gained the upper hand over aesthetics.

12   The car ceased to be object of desire and equipment for adventure and turned into office, rec room, communications hub, breakfast nook and recycling bin—a motorized cup holder. Americans, the richest people on Earth, were stuck in the confines of their crossover SUVs, squeezed into less space than tech-support call-center employees in a Mumbai cubicle farm. Never mind the six-bedroom, eight-bath, pseudo-Tudor with cathedral-ceilinged great room and 1,000-bottle controlled-climate wine cellar. That was a day's walk away.

Style:
O'Rourke mocks practicality that has reduced cars to motorized cup holders.

13   We became sick and tired of our cars and even angry at them. Pointy-headed busybodies of the environmentalist, new urbanist, utopian communitarian ilk blamed the victim. They claimed the car had forced us to live in widely scattered settlements in the great wasteland of big-box stores and the Olive Garden. If we would all just get on our Schwinns or hop a trolley, they said, America could become an archipelago of cozy gulags on the Portland, Ore., model with everyone nestled together in the most sustainably carbon-neutral, diverse and ecologically unimpactful way.

14   But cars didn't shape our existence; cars let us escape with our lives. We're way the heck out here in Valley Bottom Heights and Trout Antler Estates because we were at war with the cities. We fought rotten public schools, idiot municipal bureaucracies, corrupt political machines, rampant criminality and the pointy-headed busybodies. Cars gave us our dragoons and hussars, lent us speed and mobility, let us scout the terrain and probe the enemy's lines. And thanks to our cars, when we lost the cities we weren't forced to surrender, we were able to retreat.

Style:
O'Rourke reverses the usual positive meaning of the metaphor of turning swords into plowshares.

15   But our poor cars paid the price. They were flashing swords beaten into dull plowshares. Cars became appliances. Or worse. Nobody's ticked off at the dryer or the dishwasher, much less the fridge. We recognize these as labor-saving devices. The car, on the other hand, seems to create labor. We hold the car responsible for all the dreary errands to which it needs to be steered. Hell, a golf cart's

more fun. You can ride around in a golf cart with a six-pack, safe from breathalyzers, chasing Canada geese on the fairways and taking swings at gophers with a mashie.

16   We've lost our love for cars and forgotten our debt to them and meanwhile the pointy-headed busybodies have been exacting their revenge. We escaped the poke of their noses once, when we lived downtown, but we won't be able to peel out so fast the next time. In the name of safety, emissions control and fuel economy, the simple mechanical elegance of the automobile has been rendered ponderous, cumbersome and incomprehensible. One might as well pry the back off an iPod as pop the hood on a contemporary motor vehicle. An aging shade-tree mechanic like myself stares aghast and sits back down in the shade. Or would if the car weren't squawking at me like a rehearsal for divorce. You left the key in. You left the door open. You left the lights on. You left your dirty socks in the middle of the bedroom floor.

Practical criteria: O'Rourke accuses practical criteria of ruining the experience of cars.

17   I don't believe the pointy-heads give a damn about climate change or gas mileage, much less about whether I survive a head-on with one of their tax-sucking mass-transit projects. All they want to is to make me hate my car. How proud and handsome would Bucephalas look, or Traveler or Rachel Alexandra, with seat and shoulder belts, air bags, 5-mph bumpers and a maze of pollution-control equipment under the tail?

18   And there's the end of the American automobile industry. When it comes to dull, practical, ugly things that bore and annoy me, Japanese things cost less and the cup holders are more conveniently located.

19   The American automobile is—that is, was—never a product of Japanese-style industrialism. America's steel, coal, beer, beaver pelts and PCs may have come from our business plutocracy, but American cars have been manufactured mostly by romantic fools. David Buick, Ransom E. Olds, Louis Chevrolet, Robert and Louis Hupp of the

Hupmobile, the Dodge brothers, the Studebaker brothers, the Packard brothers, the Duesenberg brothers, Charles W. Nash, E. L. Cord, John North Willys, Preston Tucker and William H. Murphy, whose Cadillac cars were designed by the young Henry Ford, all went broke making cars. The man who founded General Motors in 1908, William Crapo (really) Durant, went broke twice. Henry Ford, of course, did not go broke, nor was he a romantic, but judging by his opinions he certainly was a fool.

Conclusion:
O'Rourke is nostalgic for the days when car makers were romantic individualists.

20   America's romantic foolishness with cars is finished, however, or nearly so. In the far boondocks a few good old boys haven't got the memo and still tear up the back roads. Doubtless the Obama administration's Department of Transportation is even now calculating a way to tap federal stimulus funds for mandatory OnStar installations to locate and subdue these reprobates.

21   Among certain youths—often first-generation Americans— there remains a vestigial fondness for Chevelle low-riders or Honda "tuners." The pointy-headed busybodies have yet to enfold these youngsters in the iron-clad conformity of cultural diversity's embrace. Soon the kids will be expressing their creative energy in a more constructive way, planting bok choy in community gardens and decorating homeless shelters with murals of Che.

22   I myself have something old-school under a tarp in the basement garage. I bet when my will has been probated, some child of mine will yank the dust cover and use the proceeds of the eBay sale to buy a mountain bike. Four things greater than all things are, and I'm pretty sure one of them isn't bicycles. There are those of us who have had the good fortune to meet with strength and beauty, with majestic force in which we were willing to trust our lives. Then a day comes, that strength and beauty fails, and a man does what a man has to do. I'm going downstairs to put a bullet in a V-8.

The Worst Policy on Campus
Badger Herald Editorial Board

The *Badger Herald*, the student newspaper of the University of Wisconsin-Madison, is the largest fully independent daily campus newspaper in the nation. In December 2010, the Wisconsin football team was invited to play in the 2011 Rose Bowl, and the 5,800 student tickets available for the game were sold out within 20 minutes. On December 5, 2010, the *Badger Herald* ran an angry editorial titled "The Worst People on Campus" and listed the names of 36 students who had put their Rose Bowl tickets up for sale on Facebook Marketplace. Editor-in-Chief Kevin Bargnes noted that "Face value was $150. Some were trying to get the tickets for more than $400 a pop." Bargnes then added, "Truly, there is a special place in Hell for [students] who buy Rose Bowl tickets with the sole intention of profiting from them. It is entirely unfair to those who actually love this football team and were counting on a cheap face value ticket in order to make the trip to Pasadena an economic reality."

On December 8, 2010, the *Badger Herald* ran a second editorial reprinted on the next page.

Return to these questions after you have finished reading.

Analyzing the Reading

1. The students who advertised their tickets for sale engaged in a practice known as "scalping." Tickets for major concerts and sporting events are routinely resold for profit by companies like Ticketmaster, and individuals resell tickets on StubHub, eBay, Craigslist, and other sites. Why was the *Badger Herald* editorial staff so outraged when students attempted to sell tickets they knew were valuable?

2. This editorial is a response to another editorial that ran three days earlier. Why did the *Badger Herald* feel it necessary to publish a second editorial?

3. What is the goal of this editorial? Why was it written?

4. Is this issue specific to the 2011 Rose Bowl or does it have a larger significance? Why or why not?

Exploring Ideas and Issues

The editorial makes a strong evaluation argument, claiming that students who resold their tickets for profit deserve "a special place in Hell." By publishing the students' names, the *Badger Herald* editorial staff wanted to inflict public disgrace. But in fact, everyone else was allowed to profit from the game without condemnation. The coaches received large bonuses; the sports administrators enjoyed lavish accommodations, meals, and other benefits; the players received gifts that are ordinarily not allowed; and the television network, the University of Wisconsin, and the Big Ten Conference all received millions of dollars. Yet the students who tried to do a little free enterprise, according to the *Badger Herald,* were despicable people.

1. Write an essay in which you argue whether it is ethical or not ethical for students to resell tickets. Spell out in explicit terms the criteria for your position. You may have to argue that your criteria are valid for this case.

2. Write an editorial from the perspective of a University of Wisconsin-Madison student who decided to sell his or her tickets on Facebook Marketplace. If you wish, you could include the broader issue of having your name published for the entire university to see in the *Badger Herald*.

3. How might the problem of the ticket resale have been avoided? Based on what you know about the incident, propose a solution for future ticket sales that should be adopted by the athletic department. If you wish, you may argue that no action is necessary in a free-market economy.

The Worst Policy on Campus

Monday's list titled "The Worst Policy on Campus," that ran on this opinion page has garnered a tremendous amount of buzz, not only on this campus but across the nation.

Feedback has been divided between support and derision for the choice to run this article naming students who immediately posted their coveted Rose Bowl tickets online to turn a profit.

It should be said the original article was written and published by Editor-in-Chief Kevin Bargnes. He did not consult the rest of this board before doing so.

We retrospectively stand by the main points made in the article however.

While we may debate the appropriateness of running the list of names, that act generated an enormous amount of attention for an issue people obviously care passionately about.

It is not fair for students who were counting on a cheap ticket to get to Pasadena to be cheated out of it by their profit-driven classmates. We hope they recognize the community outrage caused by their actions and immediately desist from profiting at the expense of their peers, school and team.

What we don't encourage is harassment of these individuals. Several of the students named in the opinion piece Monday were contacted by people they didn't know who felt like giving them a hard time — at least one even received a death threat.

We regret the pain this has caused. While we maintain that it's wrong for students to scalp their tickets for a profit, the fact that this ridicule reached such extreme levels is unfortunate.

Looking forward, we believe it is time to refocus the discussion. There is a second culprit in this ordeal that cannot be overlooked. One who is, in many ways, far more worthy of passionate derision than the students listed in the original article.

The perpetrating students are enabled by extremely poor policy on the part of the Athletic Department.

The current practice of distributing tickets on campus and essentially allowing a lottery system to determine who is lucky enough to get them not only enables the deplorable practice of hawking them for a profit, but also implicitly encourages it.

The last time the Badgers played in the Rose Bowl, students had to pick up the tickets in Pasadena. When Auburn plays Oregon for the BCS National Championship next month, students at that university won't be able to pick up their tickets until they get to Glendale, Ariz., for the game.

While this may not be a perfect system, it would undoubtedly solve the present problem that has incited the level of outrage surrounding the initial post.

We ask that the UW Athletic Department move distribution of the tickets to Pasadena, on Dec. 30, Dec. 31, and the day of the game, Jan. 1. You can offer students who won't be going out there — the scalpers — the opportunity to refund their tickets, then resell the returned tickets back to the UW student body.

By allowing students the opportunity to succumb to the obvious financial incentives of scalping, the Athletic Department is in a sense hurting itself the most. In addition to fostering resentment toward the department itself, potentially diluting the already small student section with less passionate fans that are able to afford exorbitant prices hurts the team and their chances for success.

We hope the Athletic Department recognizes the outrage this controversy has made apparent and takes the simple action to right the injustice they enable. We further encourage those taking advantage of the Athletic Department's failings to rethink the true meaning of their actions and resist the temptation to profit at the expense of their fellow Badgers.

The Only Way to Have a Cow

Bill McKibben

Bill McKibben is an American environmentalist and author who frequently writes about climate change. He is the author of many books, including *The End of Nature* (1989), *The Age of Missing Information* (1992), and most recently, *Earth: Making a Life on a Tough New Planet* (2010). This essay appeared in the March/April 2010 issue of *Orion* magazine.

Return to these questions after you have finished reading.

Analyzing the Reading

1. On what grounds does McKibben claim that industrial livestock production is "essentially indefensible"? Summarize his evidence and explain why you agree or disagree with his argument.

2. McKibben begins his essay by taking a "defensive" stance. Why is he defensive? How does his position contribute to the points he makes regarding industrial meat production?

3. Why does McKibben make an effort to establish that he "does not have a cow in this fight"? Would it matter if he did (or did not)?

4. In his conclusion, why does McKibben think that both McDonald's and Paul McCarthy wouldn't agree with his position? Explain.

Exploring Ideas and Issues

Bill McKibben founded 350.org, a global grassroots movement that works to address the climate crisis. 350 parts per million is what many scientists and climate experts believe is the safe upper limit for CO_2 in the atmosphere. Accelerating arctic warming and other early climate impacts have led scientists to conclude that we are already above the safe zone at our current 388 ppm, and that unless we are able to rapidly return to below 350 ppm this century, we risk reaching tipping points and irreversible impacts such as the melting of the Greenland ice sheet and major methane releases from increased permafrost melt.

1. Visit 350.org and learn more about what this number means and about CO_2 levels in the Earth's atmosphere. What factors are contributing to CO_2 levels? What steps need to happen to reduce them? The 350.org Web site provides suggestions for reducing carbon emissions. Pick one and write an essay that examines how feasible it would be to implement in your community or school.

2. McKibben notes that he is married to someone whose "dietary scruples" preclude her from eating meat. Try following a vegetarian lifestyle for a week and write about your experience from both a physical and ethical viewpoint. If you are already a vegetarian or vegan, write an essay explaining why you made this choice or why someone else should follow your example.

3. Using the information McKibben provides in his essay, as well as information from 350.org, design a plan to reduce the use of industrially produced beef at your school. How would you "sell" the idea to students and administrators? What obstacles would you face?

THE ONLY WAY TO HAVE A COW

May I say—somewhat defensively—that I haven't cooked red meat in many years? That I haven't visited a McDonald's since college? That if you asked me how I like my steak, I'd say I don't really remember? I'm not a moral abstainer—I'll eat meat when poor people in distant places offer it to me, especially when they're proud to do so and I'd be an ass to say no. But in everyday life, for a series of reasons that began with the dietary scruples of the woman I chose to marry, hamburgers just don't come into play.

I begin this way because I plan to wade into one of the most impassioned fracases now underway on the planet—to meat or not to meat—and I want to establish that I Do Not Have A Cow In This Fight. In recent years vegetarians and vegans have upped their attack on the consumption of animal flesh, pointing out not only that it's disgusting (read Jonathan Safran Foer's new book) but also a major cause of climate change. The numbers range from 18 percent of the world's greenhouse gas emissions to—in one recent study that was quickly discredited—51 percent. Whatever the exact figure, suffice it to say it's high: there's the carbon that comes from cutting down the forest to start the farm, and from the fertilizer and diesel fuel it takes to grow the corn, there's the truck exhaust from shipping cows hither and yon, and most of all the methane that emanates from the cows themselves (95 percent of it from the front end, not the hind, and these millions of feedlot cows would prefer if you used the word eructate in place of belch). This news has led to an almost endless series of statistical calculations: going vegan is 50 percent more effective in reducing greenhouse gas emissions than switching to a hybrid car, according to a University of Chicago study; the UN Food and Agriculture Organization finds that a half pound of ground beef has the same effect on climate change as driving an SUV ten miles. It has led to a lot of political statements: the British health secretary last fall called on Englishmen to cut their beefeating by dropping at least a sausage a week from their diets, and Paul McCartney has declared that "the biggest change anyone could make in their own lifestyle to help the environment would be to become vegetarian." It has even led to the marketing of a men's flip-flop called the Stop Global Warming Toepeeka that's made along entirely vegan lines.

Industrial livestock production is essentially indefensible—ethically, ecologically, and otherwise. We now use an enormous percentage of our arable land to grow corn that we feed to cows who stand in feedlots and eructate until they are slaughtered in a variety of gross ways and lodge in our ever-larger abdomens. And the fact that the product of this exercise "tastes good" sounds pretty lame as an excuse. There are technofixes—engineering the corn feed so it produces less methane, or giving the cows shots so they eructate less violently. But this type of tailpipe fix only works around the edges, and with the planet warming fast that's not enough. We should simply stop eating factory-farmed meat, and the effects on climate change would be but one of the many benefits.

Still, even once you've made that commitment, there's a nagging ecological question that's just now being raised. It goes like this: long before humans had figured out the whole cow thing, nature had its own herds of hoofed ungulates. Big herds of big animals—perhaps 60 million bison ranging across North America, and maybe 100 million antelope. That's considerably more than the number of cows now resident in these United States. These were noble creatures, but uncouth—eructate hadn't been coined yet. They really did just belch. So why weren't they filling the atmosphere with methane? Why wasn't their manure giving off great quantities of atmosphere-altering gas?

The answer, so far as we can tell, is both interesting and potentially radical in its implications. These old-school ungulates weren't all that different in their plumbing—they were methane factories with legs too. But they used those legs for something. They didn't stand still in feedlots waiting for corn, and they didn't stand still in big western federal allotments overgrazing the same tender grass. They didn't stand still at all. Maybe they would have enjoyed stationary life, but like teenagers in a small town, they were continually moved along by their own version of the police: wolves. And big cats. And eventually Indians. By predators.

As they moved, they kept eating grass and dropping manure. Or, as soil scientists would put it, they grazed the same perennials once or twice a year to "convert aboveground biomass to dung and urine." Then dung beetles buried the results in the soil, nurturing the grass to grow back. These grasslands covered places that don't get much rain—the Southwest and the Plains, Australia, Africa, much of Asia. And all that grass-land sequestered stupendous amounts of carbon and methane from out of the atmosphere—recent preliminary research indicates that methane-loving bacteria in healthy soils will sequester more of the gas in a day than cows supported by the same area will emit in a year.

We're flat out of predators in most parts of the world, and it's hard to imagine, in the short time that we have to deal with climate change, ending the eating of meat and returning the herds of buffalo and packs of wolves to all the necessary spots. It's marginally easier to imagine mimicking those systems with cows. The key technology here is the single-strand electric fence—you move your herd or your flock once or twice a day from one small pasture to the next, forcing them to eat everything that's growing there but moving them along before they graze all the good stuff down to bare ground. Now their manure isn't a problem that fills a cesspool, but a key part of making the system work. Done right, some studies suggest, this method of raising cattle could put much of the atmosphere's oversupply of greenhouse gases back in the soil inside half a century. That means shifting from feedlot farming to rotational grazing is one of the few changes we could make that's on the same scale as the problem of global warming. It won't do away with the need for radically cutting emissions, but it could help get the car exhaust you emitted back in high school out of the atmosphere.

Oh, and grass-fed beef is apparently much better for you—full of Omega 3s, like sardines that moo. Better yet, it's going to be more expensive, because you can't automate the process the same way you can feedlot agriculture. You need the guy to move the fence every afternoon. (That's why about a billion of our fellow humans currently make their livings as herders of one kind or another—some of them use slingshots, or dogs, or shepherd's crooks, or horses instead of electric fence, but the principle is the same.) More expensive, in this case, as in many others, is good; we'd end up eating meat the way most of the world does— as a condiment, a flavor, an ingredient, not an entrée.

I doubt McDonald's will be in favor. I doubt Paul McCartney will be in favor. It doesn't get rid of the essential dilemma of killing something and then putting it in your mouth. But it's possible that the atmosphere would be in favor, and that's worth putting down your fork and thinking about.

Reality Is Broken

Jane McGonigal

Jane McGonigal is a game designer, researcher, and author who specializes in understanding the way multiplayer reality games can generate "collective intelligence" and how such gaming experiences can improve human life. She is the Director of Game Research & Development at Institute for the Future, a Palo Alto, California–based think tank. Her first book, *Reality Is Broken: Why Games Make Us Better and How They Can Change the World* (2011), from which this next essay is excerpted, explores how games contribute to happiness and motivation.

Return to these questions after you have finished reading.

Analyzing the Reading

1. According to McGonigal, what are the four secrets to making our own happiness? Evaluate each one and determine for yourself if you agree with her. Is there anything in your view that seems to be missing?

2. What is "hedonic adaptation"? How can it undermine our happiness? Explain.

3. Sonja Lyubomirsky says "We've been sold the American Dream." What is the American Dream and why does she feel it the wrong path to true happiness?

4. We have been conditioned to believe that the easier life is, the happier we will be. Explore this idea. Why, according to McGonigal, is it untrue? What do you think?

Exploring Ideas and Issues

1. Drawing from the information provided in McGonigal's essay, and your own personal reflection, consider your own "set-point" and what influences it. Write an essay in which you explore your personal state of happiness, what elevates it, and what depletes it. Finally, consider what steps, if any, you might wish to take to make lasting changes to improve your personal happiness.

2. Many people fantasize about winning the lottery, believing that they will achieve true and lasting happiness if they could live the carefree life of a multimillionaire. Research, however, reports that many people who win the lottery soon lose their "winner's high." Write an essay in which you explore the reasons why winning the lottery does not bring lasting happiness. What problems do people believe a lottery win would solve? What new issues might result?

3. Building upon the concepts raised in question 2, write a personal narrative in which you explore how winning $5 million dollars would, or would not, make you happier overall than you are now.

THE FOUR SECRETS TO MAKING OUR OWN HAPPINESS

Many different competing theories of happiness have emerged from the field of positive psychology, but if there's one thing virtually all positive psychologists agree on, it's this: there are many ways to be happy, but we cannot find happiness. No object, no event, no outcome or life circumstance can deliver real happiness to us. We have to *make our own* happiness—by working hard at activities that provide their own reward.

When we try to find happiness outside of ourselves, we're focused on what positive psychologists call "extrinsic" rewards—money, material goods, status, or praise. When we get what we want, we feel good. Unfortunately, the pleasures of found happiness don't last very long. We build up a tolerance for our favorite things and start to want more. It takes bigger and better rewards just to trigger the same level of satisfaction and pleasure. The more we try to "find" happiness, the harder it gets. Positive psychologists call this process "hedonic adaptation," and it's one of the biggest hindrances to long-term life satisfaction. The more we consume, acquire, and elevate our status, the harder it is to stay happy. Whether it's money, grades, promotions, popularity, attention, or just plain material things we want, scientists agree: seeking out external rewards is a sure path to sabotaging our own happiness.

On the other hand, when we set out to make our own happiness, we're focused on activity that generates *intrinsic* rewards—the positive emotions, personal strengths, and social connections that we build by engaging intensely with the world around us. We're not looking for praise or payouts. The very act of what we're doing, the enjoyment of being fully engaged, is enough.

The scientific term for this kind of self-motivated, self-rewarding activity is *autotelic* (from the Greek words for "self," *auto*, and "goal," *telos*). We do autotelic work because it engages us completely, and because intense engagement is the most pleasurable, satisfying, and meaningful emotional state we can experience.

As long as we are regularly immersed in self-rewarding hard work, we will be happy more often than not—no matter what else is going on in our lives. This is one of the earliest hypotheses of positive psychology, and a fairly radical idea. It contradicts what so many of us have been taught to believe—that we need life to be a certain way in order for us to be happy, and that the easier life is the happier we are. But the relationship between hard work, intrinsic reward, and lasting happiness has been verified and confirmed through hundreds of studies and experiments.

One well-known study conducted at the University of Rochester, published in 2009, neatly upturns one of the most common assumptions about how happiness works. Researchers tracked 150 recent college graduates for two years, monitoring their goals and reported happiness levels. They compared the rates at which the graduates achieved both extrinsic and intrinsic rewards, with self-reported levels of well-being and life satisfaction. The researchers' unequivocal conclusion: "The attainment of extrinsic, or 'American Dream,' goals—money, fame, and being considered physically attractive by others—*does not contribute to happiness at all.*" In fact, they reported, far from creating well-being, achieving extrinsic rewards "actually does contribute to some ill-being." If we let our desire for more and more extrinsic rewards monopolize our time and attention, it prevents us from engaging in autotelic activities that would actually increase our happiness.

On the other hand, in the same study the University of Rochester researchers found that individuals who focused on intrinsically rewarding activity, working hard to develop their personal strengths and build social relationships, for example, were measurably happier over the entire two-year period *completely regardless of external life circumstances* like salary or social status.

This research confirms what dozens of other major studies have found: happiness derived from intrinsic reward is incredibly resilient. Every time we engage in autotelic activities, the very opposite of hedonic adaptation occurs. We wean ourselves off consumption and acquisition as sources of pleasure and develop our *hedonic resilience.* As research psychologist Sonja Lyubomirsky, a leading expert on intrinsic reward, explains: "One of the chief reasons for the durability of happiness activities is that . . . they are hard won. You've devoted time and effort. . . . You have made these practices happen, and you have the ability to make them happen again. This sense of capability and responsibility is a powerful boost in and of itself." In other words, we become better able to protect and strengthen our quality of life, regardless of external circumstances. We rely less and less on unreliable and short-lived external rewards and take control of our own happiness. "When the source of positive emotion is yourself . . . , it can continue to yield pleasure and make you happy. When the source of positive emotion is yourself, it is *renewable.*

The prevailing positive-psychology theory that we are the one and only source of our own happiness isn't just a metaphor. It's a biological fact. Our brains and bodies produce neurochemicals and physiological sensations that we experience, in different quantities and combinations, as pleasure, enjoyment, satisfaction, ecstasy, contentment, love, and every other kind of happiness. And positive psychologists have shown that we don't need to wait for life to trigger these chemicals and sensations for us. We can trigger them ourselves through scientifically measurable autotelic activities.

In fact, from a neurological and physiological point of view, "intrinsic reward" is really just another way of describing the emotional payoffs we get by stimulating our internal happiness systems.

By undertaking a difficult challenge, such as trying to finish a task in a shorter time than usual, we can produce in our own bodies a rush of adrenaline, the excitement hormone that makes us feel confident, energetic, and highly motivated.

By accomplishing something that is very hard for us, like solving a puzzle or finishing a race, our brains release a potent cocktail of norepinephrine, epinephrine, and dopamine. These three neurochemicals in combination make us feel satisfied, proud, and highly aroused.

When we make someone else laugh or smile, our brain is flooded with dopamine, the neurotransmitter associated with pleasure and reward. If we laugh or smile, too, the effect is even more pronounced.

Every time we coordinate or synchronize our physical movements with others, such as in dance or sports, we release oxytocin into our bloodstream, a neurochemical that makes us feel blissed out and ecstatic.

When we seek out what we might describe as "powerful" and "moving" stories, media, or live performances, we're actually triggering our vagus nerve, which makes us feel emotionally "choked up" in our chests and throats, or we're firing up our nervous system's pilomotor reflex, which gives us pleasurable chills and goose bumps.

And if we provoke our curiosity by exposing ourselves to ambiguous visual stimulus, like a wrapped present or a door that is just barely ajar, we experience a rush of "interest" biochemicals also known as "internal opiates." These include endorphins, which make us feel powerful and in control, and betaendorphin, a "well-being" neurotransmitter that is eighty times more powerful than morphine.

Few of us set out intentionally to trigger these systems. We don't think of happiness as a process of tapping strategically into our neurochemistry. We just know what feels good and meaningful and satisfying, and that's the kind of activity we'll do for its own sake.

Of course, we've also developed many external shortcuts to triggering our hardwired happiness systems: addictive drugs and alcohol, rich but unhealthy food, and chronic shopping, to name a few. But none of these methods are sustainable or effective in the long term. As scientists have shown, hedonic adaptation to extrinsic reward will cause our shortcut happiness behaviors to spiral out of control until they no longer work or we can no longer afford them, or even until they kill us.

Fortunately, we don't have to fight this losing battle. As long as we're focused on intrinsic and not extrinsic reward, we never run out of the raw materials for making our own happiness. We're hardwired with neurochemical systems to make all the happiness we need. We just have to work hard at things that activate us and immerse ourselves in challenging activities we enjoy for their own sake.

Writer and self-described happiness explorer Elizabeth Gilbert puts it best: "Happiness is the consequence of personal effort. . . . You have to participate relentlessly in the manifestations of your own blessings." We have the biological capability to create our happiness through hard work. And the harder we work to experience intrinsic rewards, the stronger our internal happiness-making capabilities become.

So which intrinsic rewards, exactly, are most essential to our happiness? There's no definitive list, but a few key ideas and examples appear over and over again in the scientific literature. My analysis of significant positive-psychology findings from the past decade suggests that intrinsic rewards fall into four major categories.

First and foremost, we crave **satisfying work**, every single day. The exact nature of this "satisfying work" is different from person to person, but for everyone it means being immersed in clearly defined, demanding activities that allow us to see the direct impact of our efforts.

Second we crave **the experience, or at least the hope, of being successful.** We want to feel powerful in our own lives and show off to others what we're good at. We want to be optimistic about our own chances for success, to aspire to something, and to feel like we're getting better over time.

Third, we crave **social connection**. Humans are extremely social creatures, and even the most introverted among us derive a large percentage of our happiness from spending time with the people we care about. We want to share experiences and build bonds, and we most often accomplish that by doing things that matter together.

Fourth, and finally, we crave **meaning**, or the chance to be a part of something larger than ourselves. We want to feel curiosity, awe and wonder about things that unfold on epic scales. And most importantly, we want to belong to and contribute to something that has lasting significance beyond our own individual lives.

These four kinds of intrinsic rewards are the foundation for optimal human experience. They're the most powerful motivations we have other than our basic survival needs (food, safety, and sex). And what these rewards all have in common is that they're all ways of engaging deeply with the world around us—with our environment, with other people, and with causes and projects bigger than ourselves.

If intrinsic reward is so much more satisfying and effective in boosting our happiness than extrinsic reward, then shouldn't we all naturally spend most of our time tackling unnecessary obstacles and engaging in autotelic activity?

Unfortunately, as Sonja Lyubomirsky eloquently explains: "We have been conditioned to believe that the wrong things will make us lastingly happy." We've been sold the American dream. And increasingly, it's not just Americans who are giving up real happiness in favor of the pursuit of wealth, fame, and beauty. Thanks to the globalization of consumer and popular culture, everyone on the planet is being sold the same dream of extrinsic reward. This is especially true in emerging economies like China, India, and Brazil, where more and more people are being ushered onto the global hedonic treadmill, encouraged to consume more and to compete for limited natural resources as a way to increase their quality of life.

But there is cause for hope. One group is opting out of this soul-deadening, planet-exhausting hedonic grind, and in larger and larger numbers: hard-core gamers.

Games, after all, are the quintessential autotelic activity. We only ever play because we want to. Games don't fuel our appetite for extrinsic reward: they don't pay us, they don't advance our careers, and they don't help us accumulate luxury goods. Instead, games enrich us with intrinsic rewards. They actively engage us in satisfying work that we have the chance to be successful at. They give us a highly structured way to spend time and build bonds with people we like. And if we play a game long enough, with a big enough network of players, we feel a part of something bigger than ourselves—part of an epic story, an important project, or a global community.

Good games help us experience the four things we crave most—and they do it safely, cheaply, and reliably.

Good games *are* productive. They're producing a higher quality of life.

When we realize that this *reorientation toward intrinsic reward* is what's really behind the 3 billion hours a week we spend gaming globally, the mass exodus to game worlds is neither surprising nor particularly alarming. Instead, it's overwhelming confirmation of what positive psychologists have found in their scientific research: self-motivated, self-rewarding activity really does make us happier. More importantly, it's evidence that gamers aren't escaping their real lives by playing games.

They're actively making their real lives more rewarding.

The Nitpicking Nation
Stephanie Rosenbloom

A 1997 Colgate University graduate, Stephanie Rosenbloom became a frequent contributor to the *New York Times* in 2000. As a business reporter for the paper, she covered companies such as Walmart, Saks, and Macy's. She was also a reporter for the Sunday Real Estate section. Currently a staff reporter for the Style section, she writes extensively about social trends. "The Nitpicking Nation" appeared in the *New York Times* in May 2006.

Return to these questions after you have finished reading.

Analyzing the Reading

1. What are the criteria that, according to Rosenbloom, have led to the emergence of Craigslist as the "gold standard" of online roommate-matching services?

2. The article details criteria people use to evaluate potential roommates. List at least three of these criteria. Do there seem to be agreed-upon preferences for an ideal roommate?

3. Does the author explicitly recommend the use of Craigslist? What pros and cons about the site emerge from the article?

4. How would you characterize the author's tone? Give at least three examples from the article that illustrate its tone. Do you think the tone is suitable for the article's subject? Why or why not?

Exploring Ideas and Issues

The Internet has revolutionized the ways in which people handle day-to-day activities such as banking and shopping, as well as how they find romantic partners, roommates, and like-minded friends. Has the Internet also changed the criteria by which we evaluate what we find, as well as the methods we use?

1. What criteria do you use to evaluate roommates? What makes an ideal roommate in your view? Write a short essay in which you list at least three of your criteria for a roommate. Use examples from your personal experience and the experiences of your friends to support your ideas.

2. Rosenbloom cites Craig Newmark's belief that Craigslist operates in a "culture of trust," inspiring users to be honest. How does this culture work? Does it always work? Write an essay explaining how and why this culture of trust works (or doesn't). Use your own or others' experiences with listing sites such as Craigslist, eBay, and others to provide support for your explanation.

3. Think of a product that you already own or would like to own. Enter the name of the product, followed by the word *review*, into a search engine such as Google. If you don't find many reviews, try consumersearch.com. Read several reviews and make a list of the most frequent criteria used to evaluate the product. Write a short essay based on your assessment.

The Nitpicking Nation

THEY ARE SINGLE, GAY, straight, biracial, conservative, liberal and tattooed—and they have as many preferences for a potential roommate as an online dater has for a potential lover. They are bankers, fetishists, self-declared nerds and drug users. They have old wounds and new hopes, and are willing to barter their cooking and sexual expertise for free or discounted rent.

They are all seeking and selling housing on Craigslist.org, the electronic listing service with sites in all 50 states and more than 200 worldwide. And because users pay nothing (for now) and are able to go on at length about who they are and what they want, their postings provide a sociological window into housing trends and desires across the country, from the neon cityscape of the Las Vegas Strip to the wheat fields of Wichita, Kan.

Myriad other sites provide roommate-matching services, but in the last decade Craigslist has emerged as the gold standard. It is easy to navigate, has an extensive number of listings and does not require people to complete an online sign-up sheet to view postings in their entirety. And the intimate and sometimes politically incorrect nature of Craigslist postings can make them fun to read—amusing, frank and even kinky.

Perhaps the most eyebrow-raising thing about the housing listings is the abundance of users—even young, savvy residents of anything-goes metropolises like Los Angeles and Miami—who want mellow, nonpartying roommates. Las Vegas sounds more like Snore City if you judge it by its housing listings. And New Yorkers can come off sounding square. "No parties" and "no drama" are common refrains.

There are exceptions, but even club-hopping Paris Hilton hopefuls seem to have their limits. As four women (ages 19 to 22) seeking a fifth roommate in Boston wrote, "We want a partier, not a puker."

People in their 20's often list their alma maters and request a roommate in their own age group. Cleanliness is a must, or at least "clean-ish," "decently clean" or "clean in public spaces." And spending life with a "professional" appears to be just as important to users of Craigslist's housing listings as it is to users of Match.com.

Some listings have stirred up trouble, however, and the Chicago Lawyers' Committee for Civil Rights Under Law, a nonprofit group, has filed a lawsuit in federal court against Craigslist for "publishing housing advertisements which exclude prospective tenants on the basis of race, gender, family status, marital status, national origin and religion."

A news release issued by the organization said that the Craigslist postings contained such language as "no minorities," "African-Americans and Arabians tend to clash with me so that won't work out," "ladies, please rent from me," "requirements: clean godly Christian male," "will allow only single occupancy," and "no children."

The suit is addressed on Craigslist: "Although in all likelihood this suit will be dismissed on the grounds that Internet sites cannot legally be held liable for content posted by users, Craigslist has no need to hide behind this well-established immunity."

The statement also says that Craigslist respects constitutionally protected free speech rights and that "discriminatory postings are exceedingly uncommon, and those few that do reach the site are typically removed quickly by our users through the flagging system that accompanies each ad."

Craig Newmark, the founder of Craigslist, said that its "culture of trust" inspires users to be straightforward. In fact, some users do not even feel compelled to embellish the descriptions of their spaces, as housing advertisements commonly do. Rather, they take a certain pride in the gritty crudeness of their offerings. A small room for rent in the East Village is described as "definitely a young person's

apartment" with "two small junky TV's that we have cheap antennas on, but we get the normal channels, and that is enough for us."

"There is no window," the listing says, "but you have a full-sized door."

And where else do you find housing listings that include candid photographs of the owner or leaseholder instead of the property they are advertising? (A man in Fort Lauderdale, Fla., compromised and included images of his bare room and his bare chest.)

Indeed, Craigslist is where sex and real estate can truly merge. Near Dallas, a married couple are looking for a female roommate "with benefits." A listing for Astoria, Queens, reads: "I am offering a free room for up to three months for any females who are ticklish." A single man in Los Angeles is offering foot massages and free rent to women with comely feet.

Those are some of the tamer overtures, though the majority of roommate listings are not suggestive.

But just who are the most desirable roommates?

Many people prefer women to men. There are women who feel more comfortable sharing a home with someone of the same sex, men who say they get along better with female housemates, and a few cyberspace Casanovas who want to take a shot at turning a roommate into a bedmate. Interns are also desirable, apparently because they are thought to be hard-working, responsible and willing to pay good money for cramped rooms.

But couples are sometimes lumped into a list of the unacceptable, like cigarette smoking. Over all, Democrats are more vocal than Republicans in expressing a desire not to live with the opposing party, though two "hip professional guys" found elusive harmony on Capitol Hill: "One guy is straight, and one is gay. One is a Republican, and the other is a Democrat," they wrote in a listing for a third roommate. "We appreciate and welcome diversity."

Users in the San Francisco Bay Area appear to be among the least interested in rooming with a pet. This area had the highest percentage of "no pets" listings during a key-word search last Thursday (slightly more than 16 percent of 32,295 housing listings). In Boston, about 14 percent of 45,880 listings said "no pets."

Dallas, Wyoming and Birmingham, Ala., seemed quite pet-friendly by comparison: only about 1 percent of the housing listings in each location said "no pets." But Wichita, Kan., emerged as one of the most accepting places, with less than 1 percent of the listings snubbing pets.

In some parts of the country Craigslist housing postings are an essential part of the real estate biosphere. New York is by far the leader in this regard (it had some 180,245 housing listings last Thursday).

Mr. Newmark said there were two reasons for that. "New York real estate is kind of a blood sport," he said, "and also, because our site is free, brokers tend to post a lot of redundant ads."

He said he hoped to address that problem in a matter of weeks by beginning to charge a fee.

Although Mr. Newmark has not studied how the number of housing listings fluctuates day to day, he believes they remain fairly steady on weekdays and drop off on weekends.

Boston had 45,880 housing listings last Thursday, and the San Francisco Bay Area had 32,295. In other places like Montana and Louisville, Ky., there were just a few hundred postings, and North Dakota had fewer than 100.

The New York listings include some of the most expensive, precarious sleeping arrangements in the country. A sofa bed in the living room/kitchen of a one-bedroom apartment on 55th Street between Eighth and Ninth Avenues is $683 a month. You could get a 780-square-foot one-bedroom cottage in Savannah, Ga., for $665 a month. A couch on the West Coast, in a Los

Angeles apartment belonging to three actors, is merely $400 a month and includes utilities, cable, Netflix membership, Starbucks wireless membership and wireless Internet, as well as household staples like toothpaste and shampoo.

New Yorkers are also adept at constructing what the military calls a zone of separation. A woman with an apartment at Union Square posted a photograph, not of the bedroom she wanted to rent out for $1,150 a month, but of a large divider she planned to use to create the bedroom from part of her living room.

Near Columbus Circle, a "very small, but cozy space enclosed by tall bookshelves and bamboo screens" is listed for $1,700 a month. Potential occupants are advised that they must be older than 30 and cannot wear shoes inside the apartment, smoke, consume alcohol, invite guests over or have "sleepovers."

A plethora of "no smokers" statements in the New York housing listings make it appear that the public smoking ban has infiltrated private spaces, too.

But while cigarettes are a deal breaker for some, a number of Craigslist users across the country (Denver and Boulder, Colo.; San Francisco; Boston; and Portland, Ore.,

to name but a few) say that they are "420 friendly," slang for marijuana use. References to 420 were nonexistent in other cities, including Little Rock, Ark.; Santa Fe, N.M.; and Boise, Idaho.

There are also myriad references to amenities, everything from the use of old record collections and video games to a trapeze suspended in a Brooklyn loft. A posting for a room for rent in Detroit lacks images of the property, though there is a photograph of the L.C.D. television.

And if nothing else, Craigslist housing postings in the United States confirm the zaniness of the hunt and provide a taste of the free-spirited, random connections that have always been part of the experience.

A posting in Asheville, N.C., says that two 21-year-old women are planning to drive almost 20 hours to Austin, Tex., this summer, where they will rent a two-bedroom apartment for $550 a month. "We are looking for one or two (yeah, you can bring a buddy) cool people to ride out there and split an apartment with us," the listing reads. "Are you up for being spontaneous?"

Would-be Jack Kerouacs, take note: they hit the road at the end of the month.

How to Write an Evaluation Argument

These steps for the process of writing an evaluation may not progress as neatly as this chart might suggest. Writing is not an assembly-line process.

As you write and revise, think about how you might sharpen your criteria and better explain how they apply to what you are evaluating. Your instructor and fellow students may give you comments that help you to rethink your argument from the beginning.

1 CHOOSE A SUBJECT

- Analyze the assignment.

- Explore possible subjects by making lists. Consider which items on your list you might evaluate.

- Analyze a subject by thinking about other things like it.

- Make an evaluative claim that something is good, bad, best, or worst if measured by certain criteria.

- Think about what's at stake. If nearly everyone agrees with you, your claim probably isn't important. Why would some people disagree with you?

2 THINK ABOUT YOUR CRITERIA

- List the criteria that makes something good or bad.

- Which criteria are the most important?

- Which criteria are fairly obvious, and which will you have to argue for?

- How familiar will your readers be with what you are evaluating?

- Which criteria will they accept with little explanation, and which will they possibly disagree with?

- Research your argument by finding evidence and reliable sources.

3
WRITE A DRAFT

- Introduce the issue and give the necesary background.

- Describe each criterion and then analyze how well what you are evaluating meets that criterion.

- If you are making an evaluation according to the effects of something, describe those effects in detail.

- Anticipate where readers might question your criteria and address possible objections.

- Anticipate and address opposing viewpoints by acknowledging how others' evaluations might differ.

- Conclude with either your position, a compelling example, or what is at stake.

- Choose a title that will interest readers in your essay.

4
REVISE, REVISE, REVISE

- Check that your paper or project fulfills the assignment.

- Is your evaluative claim arguable?

- Are your criteria reasonable, and will your audience accept them?

- Is your evidence convincing and sufficient?

- Do you address opposing views?

- Review the visual presentation of your paper or project.

- Proofread carefully.

5
SUBMITTED VERSION

- Make sure your finished writing meets all formatting requirements.

1: Explore the Writing Task

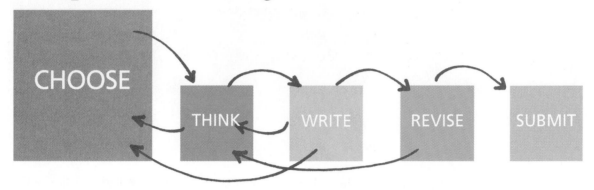

Analyze the assignment

Read your assignment slowly and carefully. Look for key words like *evaluate, rank,* or *review,* which signal an evaluation argument. Identify any information about the length specified, date due, formatting, and other requirements. You can attend to this information later. At this point you want to give your attention to your topic of your evaluation.

Explore possible topics

- **Make a list** of goods and services you consume; sports, entertainment, or hobbies you enjoy; books you have read recently; films you have seen; or policies and laws that affect or concern you.
- **Consider** which items are interesting to you. Which ones also might interest your readers?
- **Choose** something to evaluate that is potentially controversial. You will engage your readers successfully if you can get them to think more about the subject of your evaluation.

Analyze your subject

What does your subject attempt to achieve? What do other similar subjects attempt to achieve? How much do you know about your subject? If it isn't familiar, what research will you need to do?

Analyze your potential readers

What do your readers likely know about your subject? If your readers are knowledgeable, you can introduce technical concepts without much explanation. The more general your audience, the more you will have to define key terms and provide background information. For example, most general readers probably don't know why the practice of breeding dogs for confirmation showing is controversial. If you decide to argue that dog shows that award best in breed are good or bad, you will need to discuss the health issues affecting pedigree dogs.

Think about what is at stake

Why does your evaluation matter? In some cases the stakes are relatively low, such as which food trailer serves the best Thai food. Others, like Bill McKibben's evaluation (see page 363), take on global issues of food production.

STAYING ON TRACK

Make an arguable claim

A claim that is too obvious or too general will not produce an interesting evaluation.
Don't waste your time—or your readers'.

OFF TRACK
Michael Jordan was a great basketball player.
ON TRACK
Bill Russell was the best clutch player in the history of professional basketball.

OFF TRACK
Running is great exercise and a great way to lose weight.
ON TRACK
If you start running to lose weight, be aware of the risks: your body running exerts eight times its weight on your feet, ankles, legs, hips, and lower back, often causing injury to your joints. Swimming, biking, or exercise machines might be the better choice.

WRITE NOW

Finding a subject to evaluate

1. Make a list of possible subjects to evaluate, and select the one that appears most promising.

2. Write nonstop for five minutes about what you like and dislike about this particular subject.

3. Write nonstop for five minutes about what you like and dislike about things in the same category (Mexican restaurants, world leaders, horror movies, mountain bikes, and so on).

4. Write nonstop for five minutes about what people in general like and dislike about things in this category.

5. Underline the likes and dislikes in all three freewrites. You should gain a sense of how your evaluation stacks up against those of others. You may discover a way you can write against the grain, showing others a good or bad aspect of this subject that they may not have observed.

Writer at work

Jenna Picchi began by underlining the words and phrases that indicated her evaluative task and highlighting information about dates and processes for the project. She then made notes and a list of possible subjects. She selected the policy of producing organic foods on a massive, industrial scale, which she knew about firsthand as a consumer.

**English 1302
Evaluating Policy and Law**

Write an essay that <u>evaluates</u> a government or corporate policy, or a law. Explain the policy in some detail, <u>and assess it in terms of its impact.</u> Write with the goal of persuading an <u>informed but uncommitted</u> audience to share your opinion. Your paper should be about 4-6 pages long.

Some factors you may want to consider in your assessment are: the people directly affected by the policy; the people indirectly affected; the cost of the policy; the impact of the policy on national security, the environment, international relations, or other sectors of society; and the policy's original purpose. Do not base your assessment solely on practical criteria. Remember that law and policy are intended to effect some good, whether for the public at large, for the benefit of shareholders–for someone.

Remember to look for <u>all</u> types of criteria.

Think about who will be interested in your topic. <u>Who are you talking to?</u> <u>Who has a stake in this issue?</u> How do you need to tailor your argument to reach your <u>audience</u>?

AUDIENCE

Peer review
You will discuss drafts of your essay in your peer groups during class two weeks from today. Final drafts will be due the following week.

Grading Criteria
I will grade your essay according to how well it does the following:
- Accurately describes the policy or law under consideration.
- Presents persuasive criteria and evidence.
- Appeals to its intended audience.

CLAIMS COULD BE:

1. The prosecution of WikiLeaks founder Julian Assange is not an effective way to address the damage published leaks do to American foreign policy.
2. The campus-wide smoking ban is a policy that protects the health of students, faculty, and staff.
3. <u>The policy of producing organic foods on a massive scale is not as good for the environment or consumers as producing and selling organic foods on a smaller scale.</u>
4. The university's policy of diverting food waste to the composting program is one of the best of its kind.
5. The current policy regarding blood doping and other drug use in professional cycling does not effectively deter drug use.

FREEWRITE:

Many people buy organic foods in the belief that these foods and products are free of pesticides, additives, and other harmful chemicals. A visit to a Whole Foods or even the organic section in an average supermarket is like a trip to a food museum that sets idyllic goods on display. The labels seem to certify that the foods are more wholesome and more humanely raised and harvested than the other choices in the supermarket. Although the marketing message of organic foods seems to be one of purity and natural, simple goodness, the big business that is involved in bringing these foods to consumers is anything but simple. When we imagine organic foods being healthier and grown with traditional methods that are better for the environment, we picture exactly what these marketing messages would prefer. In fact, the companies and farms bringing these foods to us are the same ones producing the cheaper, mass-produced goods from industrial farms.

People have to assert the right to know where their food comes from. The marketing and sales of organic foods tap into consumer desire to have natural, honest food choices. But when giant manufacturers and chains increasingly sell organic products in supermarkets, it is more likely that without scrutiny these organic standards are not being met. Private label organic brands—those sold at a particular chain of stores—allow consumers to get organic goods at lower prices. But when Aurora Dairy, the supplier for many in-house brands of organic milk, was discovered to have broken fourteen of the organic standards in 2007, it took a federal investigation to bring that information to light. Even then Aurora continued to operate without penalty. We can't trust that factory-farming operations are going to follow organic farming principles; they must be required to follow organic certification. If consumers can't trust that organic certification is valid, then the organic label will cease to be meaningful, hurting small family farmers even further. Many who operate smaller, organic family farms are concerned that if the image of organic foods erodes from scandals and exploitation by industrial farms, they will be the ones who suffer the most, even being put out of business.

Even though the goal of "eat local" may not be attainable everywhere for practical reasons, buying local and sensibly traded foods that are sustainably produced is important for the environment and our planet's quickly expanding population.

2: Focus Your Topic and Write a Thesis

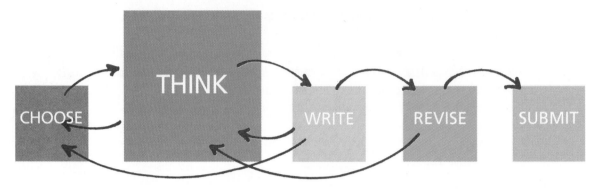

Find the obvious criteria and then dig deeper

Write down the criteria you know you will use in your evaluation. Then think about other criteria that might apply to your evaluation. Think about whether these criteria are practical, aesthetic, or ethical. You may risk losing your readers if you use only one type of criteria, such as aesthetics, and neglect others, like practicality. A beautiful chair that hurts your back isn't a good chair.

Make comparisons based on criteria

Evaluation arguments can look at just one case in isolation, but often they make comparisons. You could construct an argument to preserve the oldest commercial building in your city and turn it into a museum rather than tearing it down as part of a downtown revitalization plan. You might argue that the museum will have economic benefits (a practical criterion), that the carved stone facade is an important example of architecture (an aesthetic criterion), and that the oldest houses have historic preservation status (an ethical criterion of fairness).

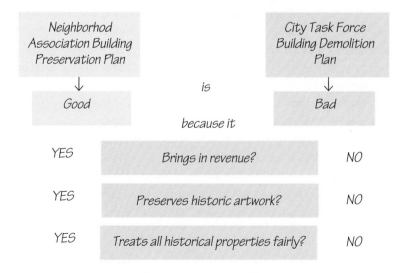

Specify and argue for your criteria

Specify your criteria
Show exactly how your criteria apply to what you are evaluating.

OFF TRACK
Border collies make the best pets because they are smart, friendly, and easy to train. *[Vague; many pets are smart, friendly, and easy to train]*

ON TRACK
Border collies are ideal family pets because their intelligence and trainability enable them to fit into almost any household, no matter how crowded.

Support your criteria
Give evidence to demonstrate why your criteria are valid.

OFF TRACK
Swimming is better exercise than running because you get a better workout. *[How so?]*

ON TRACK
Health professionals maintain that for those who have access to pools or lakes, swimming is the best workout because it exercises all major muscle groups and it's not prone to causing injuries.

Don't assume your audience shares your criteria
It's easy to forget that other people have different concerns and priorities. Your challenge as a writer is finding common ground with people who think differently.

OFF TRACK
Coach X is a bad coach who should be fired because he has lost to our rival school three years in a row. *[For some fans beating the big rival is the only criterion, but not all fans.]*

ON TRACK
While coach X hasn't beaten our big rival in three years, he has succeeded in increasing attendance by 50%, adding a new sports complex built by donations, and raising the players' graduation rate to 80%.

Writer at work

Jenna Picchi made the following notes about her evaluative claim.

TOPIC

The policy of producing and selling organic foods on a massive, industrial scale is not as good for the environment or consumers as producing and selling organic foods on a smaller scale. Although organic foods produced on an industrial scale are less expensive and more convenient, all industrial foods require massive use of fossil fuels to bring them to consumers and may be less sustainably produced.

WHAT ARE INDUSTRIALLY PRODUCED ORGANIC FOODS?

Organic foods are increasingly grown on a mass scale by centralized businesses that run industrial farm operations. These companies replicate many of the practices of mainstream factory farms to keep prices low and maximize profits.

WHO IS AFFECTED?

- Consumers who are looking to organic foods for health and aesthetic reasons
- Those interested in responsible agriculture as a way to protect the environment
- Local organic farmers

MY EXPERIENCE

- Organic options at campus markets are limited to national brands.
- Farmer's markets that offer locally grown produce in our community are not easily accessible to students and have limited hours.

CRITERIA

Practical

- Big organic food producers bring organic options at lower cost to more people.
- Organics cost more and bring in high profits. But big corporate producers of organic goods drive down prices for local farmers, making it harder for traditional, local organic farmers to compete.

Ethical

- Big industrial organic companies produce things that are not consistent with organic principles that encourage eating more whole foods (rather than processed ones) that are sustainably grown.
- Instances where larger corporations have cut corners. Industrial scale food producers have been caught stretching or breaking organic guidelines and were cited by the federal government.

Aesthetic
- Marketing for organic foods uses images of traditional, idyllic farms, equating organic with naturalness and purity. But the reality of factory-scaled farms is quite different and these images are inaccurate.

AUDIENCE

Who has a stake in this issue? What do they know about it? How should I appeal to them?

Consumers of organic foods
- Consumers want to purchase the healthiest, most environmentally sustainable choices and are often fairly well informed about the issue.
- Organic shoppers often have a strong sense of the ethical importance of sustainable, safely produced foods. They are likely to feel upset if they find that the organic industry is misrepresenting itself.

Local farmers
- Farmers feel direct effect in prices and regulations.

All citizens
- Citizens feel a sense of empathy for the farmers who produce our food.
- All taxpayers benefit when citizens eat whole and organic foods that keep them healthier and reduce disease.

BACKGROUND

Many people know about the benefits of organic foods but may not know how the spread of low-cost, industrially produced organic options involves compromises to organic ideals.

TO RESEARCH
- Need to get info on how organic industry evolved and grew, and what impact this growth had.
- Find anecdotes on the threat to standards posed by the industrial organic industry.
- Find evidence of the effects of eating locally.

3: Write a Draft

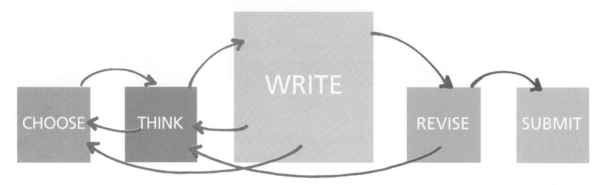

Introduce the issue

Give your readers any background information they will need. State your stance up front, if you wish. Some evaluations work better if the writer's judgment is issued at the beginning; sometimes, it is more effective to build up a mass of evidence and then issue your verdict at the end.

Describe your criteria and offer evidence

Organize the criteria to be as effective as possible. Identify your strongest criterion, and think about if you want to lead with it or save it for the last. Explain each criterion and give reasons why it applies if it isn't obvious. Provide specific examples of how well your subject meets or does not meet each criterion.

Anticipate and address opposing viewpoints

Acknowledge why others may have a different opinion than you do. Demonstrate why your evaluation is better by pointing out either why your criteria are better or why you have better evidence and reasons.

Conclude with strength

State your summary evaluation if you have not done so already. Offer a compelling example or analogy to end your essay. State explicitly what is at stake in your evaluation, especially if you are evaluating a policy or issue that affects many people.

Choose a title that will interest your readers

A bland, generic title like "An Evaluation of X" gives little incentive to want to read the essay.

Writer at work

Based on her lists of criteria, her conclusions about her audience, and her research, Jenna Picchi sketched out a rough outline for her essay.

1. Opening personal anecdote about trying to shop organic near campus. End with claim.

2. Specific example about issues related to industrial organic farming: the image of natural, healthy foods produced with traditional methods vs. reality of factory farms

3. Look at industrial organic food industry
   a. What is it
   b. Why is it growing
   c. What are its origins (the move from small organic to Big Organic)

4. First criterion: good organic food policy should produce healthy foods that are sustainably produced
   a. Better for the environment
   b. Better for individuals and for public health
   c. Better for taxpayers

5. Second criterion: good policy should protect consumers and guarantee valid organic certifications
   a. Organic standards hard to police
   b. Federal investigations into major organic milk producers breaking rules
   c. If organic label isn't protected consumers won't trust it

6. Third criterion: good policy avoids negative impacts on small farms
   a. Industrial organic companies help define organic standards
   b. Industrial organic companies involved in setting prices
   c. Local farms can be held accountable about standards and sustainability, earn consumer trust

7. Conclusion and perspective

4: Revise, Revise, Revise

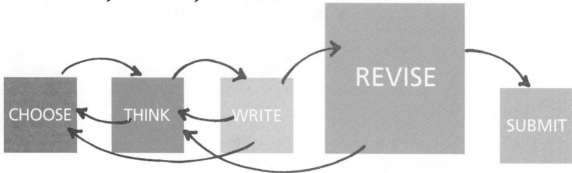

Skilled writers know that the secret to writing well is rewriting. Leave correcting errors for last.

Does your paper or project meet the assignment?	• Look again at your assignment. Does your paper or project do what the assignment asks? • Look again at the assignment for specific guidelines, including length, format, and amount of research. Does your work meet these guidelines?
Is your evaluative claim arguable?	• Do enough people disagree with you to make the evaluation worthwhile? • Does anyone but you care about this topic?
Are your criteria reasonable, and will your audience accept them?	• Do you provide compelling reasons for readers to accept your criteria for evaluation, if they weren't predisposed to do so? • Do you weight criteria appropriately, balancing aesthetic, ethical, and practical considerations?
Is your evidence convincing and sufficient?	• Will readers believe what you say about the thing you are evaluating? What proof do you offer that it does or doesn't meet your criteria?
Do you address opposing views?	• Have you acknowledged the opinions of people who disagree with you? • Where do you show why your evaluation is better?
Is the writing project visually effective?	• Is the font attractive and readable? • Are the headings and visuals effective? • If you use images or tables as part of your evaluation, are they legible and appropriately placed?
Save the editing for last.	• See guidelines for editing and proofreading on page 55.

A peer review guide is on page 54.

Watch the Animation on How to Edit at mycomplab.com

Writer at work

Working with a group of her fellow students, Jenna Picchi noted their suggestions on her rough draft, and she used them to help produce a final draft.

This starts to sound like conspiracy or rumors—find some quotes or anecdotes to illustrate it so people believe it really happens, and that it really affects consumers.

Organic foods that are industrially produced may mislead consumers into thinking they are more natural and wholesome than they really are. For the most part, government agencies carefully regulate and define the meanings of the words on food labels. Consumers should be able to expect that foods with the organic label are healthy food choices that are sustainably produced. Organic foods are marketed as more wholesome or more humanely raised and harvested than other foods in the store. Packaging suggests organic foods are pure, natural, and simply better. But in reality, many of these organic products are grown by big, industrial companies that produce foods in a way that are not consistent with organic principles. The reality of the organic foods we find at Walmart, Target, and other major retail chains is that they are produced on a mass scale—the same industrial-sized operations that bring us cheap, "regular" products. These industrial "Big Organic" producers are stretching organic standards to become more vaguely worded and harder to enforce. Organic standards are not being met.

The "us" versus "them" tone will alienate people who feel differently about convenience foods. Many people are busy and want food that is convenient and also healthy and sustainably produced.

If the goal is to offer healthy choices to consumers who are trained to expect cheap, convenient options, industrial producers of organic foods have made significant contributions. They have put organic foods within reach for average consumers, not just affluent ones. But the growth of the organic food industry has come at a great price. Early on, the organic movement encouraged people to choose more whole foods rather than processed ones. Now all kinds of processed convenience foods containing synthetic additives carry the organic label. Although industrially produced organic foods are convenient, they present a natural, earth-friendly image that is often not the reality. The organic ideal has been polluted when it is applied to processed foods that include corn syrup along with other confusing additives. The marketing message and the reality of what is in many processed foods with the organic label do not match. Small, local organic farmers are well positioned to deliver on the organic movement's original ideals and give consumers foods grown using meaningful organic standards. It is worth questioning whether organic standards mean what they seem and worth it to seek out the local, organic farmers who are able to show their commitment to sustainably produced organic foods. Labeling foods organic cannot be just a marketing ploy, and the organic industry will continue to grow if it can ensure this label has real meaning.

Giving too much weight to ethics, not enough to practicality. What option would be better than supporting and buying only a watered-down definition of organic food, but still practical?

5: Submitted Version

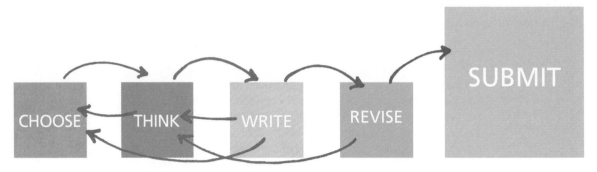

Picchi 1

Jenna Picchi
Professor Alameno
English 101
2 December 2010

Organic Foods Should Come Clean

As a kid growing up not far from rural communities, I took for granted the access to local produce and the farm stands and my family frequented. When I moved to a college town, I assumed I would have access to an even wider variety of foods and better choices. I wanted to continue eating organic as I had at home, even though it would be more work than a campus-dining plan. I learned quickly that even in a large college town, it takes determined searching in most supermarkets to find the organic produce, bread, meat, and dairy products that are scattered in less-trafficked corners of the store. Instead of shopping at the farmer's market (which keeps hours I cannot attend), I choose these supermarket fruits and vegetables from the lackluster and small display of things shipped in from California and Central America. Taking a recent look at these organic departments, I noticed that almost all the products are store or national brands. It never occurred to me that living in the middle of an agricultural state my choices would be so limited. After spending much time and energy seeking out organic products in stores all around town, I wondered whether the effort is worth it. How healthy are these foods in the local supermarket? And are these national brands as good for the environment as they seem?

Many people shop for organic foods in the belief that they are free of pesticides, additives, and other chemicals that can harm people and the environment over time. Visit an average supermarket's organic department and you will see signs and labels confirming this idea. Organic foods are marketed as more wholesome or more humanely raised and harvested than other foods in the store. Packaging suggests organic foods are pure, natural, and simply better. But the big businesses that bring these products to consumers are anything but simple. The reality of the organic foods we find at Walmart, Target, and other major retail chains is that they are produced on a mass scale—the same industrial-sized operations that bring us cheap, "regular" products. And it may be that the policy of producing and selling organic foods on a massive, industrial scale is not as good for the environment or consumers as producing and selling organic foods on a smaller scale. Although industrially produced organic foods are convenient, they present a natural, earth-friendly image that is often not the reality. The industrial organic food industry makes many claims that deserve a closer look.

Consumers willing to pay more for organic foods might be surprised to learn that mass-produced organic foods come from farms that barely resemble the old-fashioned images on their milk carton. The majority of organic food sales come via a very large industry, not an idealistic or environmentalist movement. In fact, organic foods are the fastest-growing category in the food industry, now worth about $11 billion (Pollan 136). The way food is produced has been changing more over the past fifty years than in the previous 10,000 years (Kenner). Many organic foods are grown by big, industrial producers. These companies—often owned by large corporations—use many of the same practices as mainstream factory farms to keep costs low. They can distribute and market their products nationally, and while organic foods cost more overall, these corporations succeed because they have made organic food available to average customers (not just affluent ones). If the goal is to offer healthy choices to consumers who are trained to expect cheap, convenient options, industrial producers of organic foods have made significant contributions. The organic label works wonders in marketing—and the big corporations who produce and deliver the foods in our supermarkets are taking advantage of it.

The history of the organic food movement was originally small, locally based, and in response to the industrialization of food. The evolution away from an organic movement toward an organic food industry is fairly recent. The organic pioneers of the 1970s had "a vision small farms, whole food, and local distribution" (Fromartz 194). They hoped to help people eat fewer processed foods, produced organically and distributed from local sources. But for some farmers the allure of reaching more consumers and national sales lead to compromises. In *Omnivore's Dilemma,* Michael Pollan traces the pressure some farmers felt in the early 1990s to "sell out" and work with agribusiness (153). Farmers like Gene Kahn, the founder of Cascadian Farm (now owned by food giant General Mills), saw that he could change and redefine the way food is grown and still reach a mass market. Even though this meant giving up on two ideals of the organic movement—local distribution and eating more whole foods—organic foods were becoming a large-scale business, bringing more naturally produced choices to more and more consumers.

One concern for Pollan and others is that the organic label is being used by companies who are not invested in organic principles. In fact, chemical farming and big agribusiness had once been the enemy of the organic movement. But then agribusiness got into the organic market (Fromartz 194). The worry is, as industrial organic operations grow and adopt more and more big agribusiness methods, whether the term organic is becoming just another marketing gimmick.

As organic foods become increasingly industrial, it important for consumers to be able to verify whether the products they buy are defined and produced using truly organic standards. Organic standards have evolved in recent years and now regulate not just small farms but also large-scale industrial operations. But even as the standards are changing, they must at a minimum guarantee healthy foods that are sustainably produced. Organic agriculture is valuable for the way it protects the environment. Marion Nestle, a scholar on food and public health, describes research that organic farming uses less energy and leaves soils in better condition than traditional farms (213). In addition to protecting lands from excessive chemical use, another possible benefit of organic, local farming is that it can require less use of fossil fuels. Fossil fuels are spent whenever farm supplies must be shipped or when foods are sent for processing. Foods travel long distances across the country and foods are shipped from across the world, draining fossil fuels. But Pollan states that organic food can be produced with about one-third less fossil fuel than conventional food (183). Using fewer fossil fuels and chemicals should be a goal for any organic farmer or consumer concerned with pollution and creating a more sustainable food industry.

Less research is available to prove that organic foods are better nutritionally. Officially, Pollan says, the government takes the position that "organic food is no better than conventional food" (178). But he believes current research reveals organic foods grown in more naturally fertile soil to be more nutritious. And Nestle believes organic foods may be safer than conventional foods because people who eat them will have fewer synthetic pesticides and chemicals in their bodies (213). If consumers can rely on organic foods for their health benefits, a larger good would be granted in overall public health. As a society we all benefit when people eat whole foods and organic foods as part of diets that maintain a health and fight weight-related disease. Foods with an organic label should be able to guarantee these benefits to individuals and to public health.

Another benefit to taxpayers is that organic farms are far less subsidized and in particular do not receive direct government payments (Pollan 182). Many organic farms do not participate in the complicated system of paying farmers directly that mainstream farmers participate in, though Pollan points out that many industrial organic farms do benefit from less direct subsidies. For example, many states subsidize access to cheaper water and electricity to power farms. However, supporting the less subsidized farmers may bring savings taxpayers in the end.

Organic labels and standards are difficult but crucial to police and enforce. Consumers who are willing to pay extra for natural food choices will lose faith if it turns out the organic labels are not honest. Organic farmers traditionally set themselves up as an alternative to big agribusiness. But as Pollan explains, as giant manufacturers and chains sell more and more of the organic foods in supermarkets, organic agriculture has become more and more like the industrial food system it was supposed to challenge (151). As a result, it is more likely that without scrutiny organic standards are not being met.

Organic milk offers one example of a product where organic standards have recently been an issue. A handful of very large companies produce most of the organic milk we buy. Many chain stores have begun successfully competing, selling their own private label organic milk. These huge private label organic brands allow consumers to get organic goods at even lower prices. But one recent case of possible organic fraud involves Aurora Dairy, the supplier for many in-house brands of organic milk for stores such as Walmart and Costco. Aurora was discovered to have broken fourteen of the organic standards in 2007. The USDA cited them because their herds included cows that were fed inappropriate feed and because some cows had no access to pastures. It took a federal investigation to bring information about these violations to light and yet even then they continued to operate without penalty (Gunther). But when organic standards are vaguely worded and unenforceable or go unmonitored at factory dairy farms, violations of organic principles are bound to happen.

The overwhelming pressure for access to foods that are cheap and convenient is something all consumers feel. But most people interested in buying organic foods do so because they believe they're doing something positive for their health, for the health of their community, and in the best interests of the environment. Often these consumers have a strong sense of the ethical importance of sustainable produced food. Because of this interest in doing what is right, these consumers are likely to be especially upset by news that the goods they're paying extra for are being misrepresented. These consumers expect and welcome organic standards that are meaningfully set and policed. Good organic agriculture policy would help ensure strong standards; without them consumers will become jaded and not trust the organic label.

Consumers interested in the monitoring of these standards might be concerned to see how standards in the past decade have changed. In crafting these rules, the government consults with some of the biggest businesses involved in organic food production. Many long-time organic farmers believe that the role of these corporations has watered down organic standards. The farmers themselves are voicing concerns that regulations should be tougher. Elizabeth Henderson, an organic farmer and member of the large organic co-op, Organic Valley, spoke out in 2004 about the huge growth of organic food as coming "at an awful price, compromising standards, undercutting small farms, diluting healthy food, ignoring social justice—polluting the very ideals embodied in the word *organic*" (qtd in Fromartz 190).

In one recent example, Horizon Organic, the giant milk producer, fought for the development of USDA rules that ensure its factory farms in Idaho would not be required to give all cows a specific amount of time to graze on pasture (Pollan 157). The watered down USDA standard Horizon helped to craft instead is very vague. The image most consumers have of organic milk coming from cows grazing in pasture is an ideal that many mainstream organic milk producers don't even approach. Many small dairy farmers follow older organic practices on their own, but current "organic" labels do not guarantee this.

Another challenge for consumers looking for sustainably produced organic products is that the industrial-sized producers are more efficient, making it hard for smaller farmers to compete. Local small farms, like personal gardens, are both "more expensive but also less efficient than larger operations in terms of transportation, labor, and materials required" (Dubner). Big organic companies can set lower prices, ship foods long distances quickly, and make distribution simpler for the supermarkets (Pollan 168). The growth of industrially produced organic foods has helped bring prices down overall. The competition is good in theory, allowing more people access to organic choices. But faced with these competing choices, perhaps only very informed consumers of organic foods may sympathize with and support their local organic farmers.

Good organic agriculture policy would ideally avoid having a negative impact on small, local producers. I would acknowledge that locally produced food is not necessarily more sustainable or by definition produced with less energy or better for the environment (McWilliams 22). The smaller-scale farm also has to be committed to sustainable practices. Local farms can be held accountable for whether they are meeting organic standards and following sustainable farming practices. A dairy farmer you can talk to at a local farmer's market can, in theory, earn trust and be held accountable to customers.

Small, local organic farmers are well positioned to deliver on the organic movement's original ideals of sustainably produced foods. Consumers should have a right to know where their food comes from and how organic standards are defined. In fact, as organic foods become more widely available to most consumers—even college students—it is worth questioning whether organic standards mean what they seem. Labeling foods organic cannot be just a marketing ploy, and the organic industry will continue to reach and inform more consumers if it can ensure this label has real meaning.

Works Cited

Dubner, Stephen J. "Do We Really Need a Few Billion Locavores?" *New York Times*. New York Times, 9 June 2008. Web. 30 Nov. 2010.

Fromartz, Samuel. *Organic, Inc.: Natural Foods and How They Grew*. New York: Houghton, 2006. Print.

Gunther, Marc. "An Organic Milk War Turns Sour." *Cornucopia Institute*. 3 Oct. 2007. Web. 30 Nov. 2010.

Kenner, Robert, dir. *Food Inc*. 2009. Magnolia Pictures. Film.

McWilliams, James E. *Just Food: Where Locavores Get It Wrong and How We Can Truly Eat Responsibly*. New York: Little, 2009. Print.

Nestle, Marion. "Eating Made Simple." *Food Inc.: How Industrial Food Is Making Us Sicker, Fatter, and Poorer—and What You Can Do About It*. Ed. Karl Weber. New York: PublicAffairs, 2009. 209-18. Print.

Pollan, Michael. *Omnivore's Dilemma: A Natural History of Four Meals*. New York: Penguin, 2006. Print.

Projects

Effective evaluation arguments depend on finding the right criteria and convincing your readers that these criteria are the best ones to use.

Film review

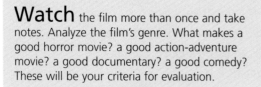

Select a film to review. Choose a specific magazine, newspaper, or online publication as the place where you would publish the review.

Watch the film more than once and take notes. Analyze the film's genre. What makes a good horror movie? a good action-adventure movie? a good documentary? a good comedy? These will be your criteria for evaluation.

Find information on the film. The Internet Movie Database (**www.imdb.com**) is a good place to start.

Write a thesis that makes an evaluative claim: the film is a successful or unsuccessful example of its genre. Use evidence from the film to support your claim.

Evaluate a controversial subject

Think of controversial subjects on your campus or in your community for which you can find recent articles in your campus or local newspaper. For example, is your mayor or city manager an effective leader? Is your campus recreational sports facility adequate? Is a new condominium complex built on city land that was used as a park good or bad?

Identify what is at stake in the evaluation. Who thinks it is good or effective? Who thinks it is bad or ineffective? Why does it matter?

List the criteria that make something or someone good or bad. Which criteria are the most important? Which will you have to argue for?

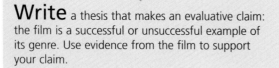

Analyze your potential readers. How familiar will they be with what you are evaluating? Which criteria will they likely accept and which might they disagree with?

Write a draft. Introduce your subject, and give the necessary background. Make your evaluative claim either at the beginning or as your conclusion. Describe each criterion and evaluate your subject on each criterion. Be sure to address opposing viewpoints by acknowledging how their evaluations might be different.

Evaluate a campus policy

Identify a policy on your campus that affects you. Examples include the way your school schedules classes and has students register, the way parking spaces are allotted on campus, the library's late fee and returns policy, housing or admissions policies, or rules regulating student organizations.

Consider your target audience as the readers of your campus newspaper. Who else besides you does this issue affect? What office or division of the school is responsible for the program? Who implemented it in the first place? Keep in mind that your school's administration is part of your audience.

Determine the criteria for your evaluation. Which criteria will be most important for other students? for the faculty and staff? for the administration?

Take a clear position about the policy. If you think the policy is unfair or ineffective, acknowledge why it was put into place. Sometimes good intentions lead to bad results. If you think the policy is fair or effective, explain why according to the criteria you set out. In either case, give reasons and examples to support your judgment.

Video evaluation

Find a subject to evaluate by making a video. You might evaluate something you own, such as your phone, your television, or your bicycle. Or you might evaluate something on your campus, such as the student union, a campus gym, or a campus event.

Plan your content. In much the same way you write an evaluation essay, you will need to identify criteria and gather evidence. Think about whether you will need to interview anyone. Draft a storyboard, which is a shot-by-shot representation of your project, which will help you arrange your schedule.

Arrange for your equipment and compose your video. If you don't own a video camera, find out if you can get one from a campus lab. Quality video takes many hours to shoot and edit. Visit all locations in advance to take into account issues such as lighting and noise.

Edit your video. Editing software allows you to combine video clips and edit audio. Your multimedia lab may have instructions or consultants for using video editing software. Allow ample time for editing.

For support in learning this chapter's content, follow this path in **mycomplab:**

▶ **Resources** ▶ **Writing** ▶ **Writing Purposes** ▶ **Writing to Evaluate**

Review the Instruction and Multimedia resources, then complete the **Exercises** and click on **Gradebook** to measure your progress.

 Apply the Concept of Evaluation Arguments at mycomplab.com

12 Position Arguments

Position arguments aim to change readers' attitudes and beliefs. César Chávez spent his adult life arguing for civil rights for farm workers.

Chapter Overview

▶ **Writing position arguments**
(see p. 403)

▶ **What makes a good position argument?**
(see p. 404)

▶ **How to read position arguments**
(see p. 406)

▶ **How to write a position argument**
(see p. 442)

▶ **Projects**
(see p. 460)

Writing Position Arguments

In college it is not sufficient simply to write that "I believe this" or "It's just my opinion." Readers in college assume that if you make a claim in writing, you believe that claim. More important, a claim is rarely only your opinion. Because most beliefs and assumptions are shared by many people, responsible readers will consider your position seriously.

Keys to position arguments

In a position argument you make a claim about a controversial issue. Position arguments often take two forms—definition arguments and rebuttal arguments.

Definition arguments set out criteria and then argue that whatever is being defined meets or does not meet those criteria.

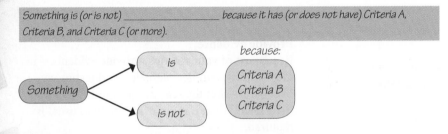

Something is (or is not) _____ because it has (or does not have) Criteria A, Criteria B, and Criteria C (or more).

Graffiti is art because it is a means of self-expression. it shows an understanding of design principles, and it simulates both the senses and the mind.

Rebuttal arguments take the opposite position. They challenge either the criteria a writer uses to define something or the evidence that supports the claim.

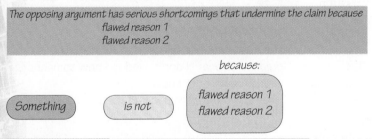

The opposing argument has serious shortcomings that undermine the claim because flawed reason 1 flawed reason 2

The great white shark gained a false reputation as a "man eater" from the 1975 movie Jaws, but in fact attacks on humans are rare and most bites have been "test bites," which is a common shark behavior with unfamiliar objects.

Position arguments in the world

Position arguments are at the heart of much political and public discourse. People in business and organizations also write position papers frequently to argue for or against a particular strategy or practice.

Watch the Animation on **Commentaries** on mycomplab.com

What Makes a Good Position Argument?

1

Define the issue

Your subject should be clear to your readers. If readers are unfamiliar with the issue, you should give enough examples so they understand the issue in concrete terms.

The US spends almost $50 billion each year on education, so why aren't kids learning?
— James Paul Gee (see page 436)

2

Identify the stakeholders

Who is immediately affected by this issue? Who is affected indirectly?

The rich inheritance of justice, liberty, prosperity, and independence, bequeathed by your fathers, is shared by you, not me.
— Frederick Douglass (see page 412)

3

Read about the issue

Every significant issue has an extensive history of discussion involving many people and various points of view. Before you formulate a claim about an issue, become familiar with the conversation about that issue by reading.

4

State your position

You may want to state your thesis in the opening paragraph to let readers know your position immediately. If your issue is unfamiliar, you may want to find out more before you state your position. In any case, you should take a definite position on the issue.

Ordinary food is still out there, however, still being grown and even occasionally sold in the supermarket, and this ordinary food is what we should eat.
— Michael Pollan (see page 425)

5

Find reasons

List as many reasons as you can think of. Develop the ones that are most convincing.

The risk is that the multibillion-dollar system of food banking has become such a pervasive force in the anti-hunger world, and so tied to its donors and its volunteers, that it cannot step back and ask if this is the best way to end hunger, food insecurity and their root cause, poverty.
— Mark Winne (see page 420)

6

Provide evidence

In support of your reasons, provide evidence—in the form of examples, statistics, and testimony of experts—that the reasons are valid. When the issue is unfamiliar, more evidence than usual is required.

7

Acknowledge opposing views

Anticipate what objections might be made to your position. You can answer possible objections in two ways: that the objections are not valid or that the objections have some validity but your argument is stronger.

The most frequent objection to Twitter is a predictable one: "I don't need to know someone is eating a donut right now."
— David Carr (see page 432)

Visual position arguments

Images don't speak for themselves but they can combine with words to make powerful arguments. One type of visual argument is visual metaphor, which is used frequently in advertising. As people have become more familiar with visual metaphors, the amount of text has decreased and viewers are expected to infer the argument.

On World Water Day, March 22, 2007, UNICEF launched their Tap project, in which diners at restaurants in select cities could donate $1 for every glass of tap water they order. The advertising campaign began with the striking visual metaphor of a boy pointing a water pistol at his head followed by other powerful images. Since its inception, the Tap Project has raised $2.5 million in the United States to provide clean drinking water for children in more than 100 countries.

The caption says, "Bad water kills more children than war."

WRITE NOW

Identify reasons that support conflicting claims

Select a controversial issue for which there are multiple points of view.
You can find a list of issues at **www.dir.yahoo.com/Society_and_Culture/Issues_and_Causes/.**

Explore the links for one of the issues to get a sense of the range of opinion.
Analyze two Web sites. Write down the following for each site.

- What is the main claim of the Web site?
- What reason or reasons are given?
- What evidence (facts, examples, statistics, and the testimony of authorities) is offered?

Write a one-page analysis that addresses these questions. How do the reasons differ for opposing claims? What assumptions underlie the reasons? How does the evidence differ?

How to Read Position Arguments

▼ BEFORE YOU BEGIN READING

These notes are in response to "Take My Privacy, Please!"; the reading begins on page 408.

What kind of text is it?	*"Take My Privacy, Please!" is an opinion essay published on the editorial pages of the New York Times.*
Who wrote it?	*For 25 years Ted Koppel was the anchor of the news program Nightline. Since retiring in 2005 he has worked as a news analyst for National Public Radio and BBC World News America.*
Who is the intended audience?	*The New York Times has a national and international readership. Its Web site is the most popular American online newspaper Web site, and the print edition remains the leader in metropolitan circulation.*

▼ READ THE TEXT AT LEAST TWICE AND MAKE NOTES

What is the writer's thesis or main idea?	*Koppel introduces his issue and his stance in the first two paragraphs, but he waits until the last paragraph to offer his thesis as a conclusion.*
What reasons are offered in support the position?	*The main reason is that people have given up privacy for convenience, putting their personal information at great risk.*
What kinds of evidence are introduced?	*Koppel offers two kinds of evidence: several kinds of collection of personal information and examples of security breaches that exposed personal information.*
How would you characterize the style?	*The style is informal and journalistic. At times Koppel uses satire to make his points.*

How is it organized?

This map shows the organization of "Take My Privacy, Please!" which begins on the following page.

Introduction Paragraphs 1–2	Koppel identifies his subject as threats to individual and collective privacy.
Reasons Paragraph 3	Koppel gives his main reason: we willingly give up privacy if technology promises to make our lives easier and comes in a nonthreatening package. He offers an OnStar commercial as his first example.
Reasons Paragraphs 4–5	Koppel asks if it is good that OnStar always knows where we are driving, and he observes that people would not otherwise make their location available to everyone.
Evidence Paragraphs 6–13	Several examples of passive data collection and breaches of security are cited.
Conclusion Paragraph 14	Koppel gives his thesis as the conclusion: we should be informed about what data is being gathered about us.

Take My Privacy, Please!
Ted Koppel

Ted Koppel joined ABC News in 1963 and served from 1980 until 2005 as the anchor and managing editor of *Nightline*, the first late-night network news program. He has had a major reporting role in every presidential campaign since 1964. "Take My Privacy, Please!" which appeared in June 2005 in the *New York Times*, is an example of a position argument that doesn't begin with a thesis but first gives a series of examples.

Take My Privacy, Please!

1   THE PATRIOT ACT—brilliant! Its critics would have preferred a less stirring title, perhaps something along the lines of the Enhanced Snooping, Library and Hospital Database Seizure Act. But then who, even right after 9/11, would have voted for that?

2   Precisely. He who names it and frames it, claims it. The Patriot Act, however, may turn out to be among the lesser threats to our individual and collective privacy.

3   There is no end to what we will endure, support, pay for and promote if only it makes our lives easier, promises to save us money, appears to enhance our security and comes to us in a warm, cuddly and altogether nonthreatening package. To wit: OnStar, the subscription vehicle tracking and assistance system. Part of its mission statement, as found on the OnStar Web site, is the creation of "safety, security and peace of mind for drivers and passengers with thoughtful wireless services that are always there, always ready." You've surely seen or heard their commercials, one of which goes like this:

ANNOUNCER -- The following is an OnStar conversation. (Ring)

ONSTAR -- OnStar emergency, this is Dwight.

DRIVER -- (crying) Yes, yes??!

Introduction:
Koppel announces his stance and his subject in the first two paragraphs. He questions the Patriot Act and then suggests that there may be bigger threats to privacy.

Evidence:
The OnStar commercial is described in detail as the first example.

ONSTAR -- Are there any injuries, ma'am?

DRIVER -- My leg hurts, my arm hurts.

ONSTAR -- O.K. I do understand. I will be contacting emergency services.

ANNOUNCER -- If your airbags deploy, OnStar receives a signal and calls to check on you. (Ring)

EMERGENCY SERVICES -- Police.

ONSTAR -- This is Dwight with OnStar. I'd like to report a vehicle crash with airbag deployment on West 106th Street.

EMERGENCY SERVICES -- We'll send police and E.M.S. out there. ◄

DRIVER -- (crying) I'm so scared!

ONSTAR -- O.K., I'm here with you, ma'am; you needn't be scared.

4 Well, maybe just a little scared. Tell us again how Dwight knows just ◄ where the accident took place. Oh, right! It's those thoughtful wireless services that are always there. Always, as in any time a driver gets into an OnStar-equipped vehicle. OnStar insists that it would disclose the whereabouts of a subscriber's vehicle only after being presented with a criminal court order or after the vehicle has been reported stolen. That's ◄ certainly a relief. I wouldn't want to think that anyone but Dwight knows where I am whenever I'm traveling in my car.

5 Of course, E-ZPass and most other toll-collecting systems already know whenever a customer passes through one of their scanners. That's because of radio frequency identification technology. In return for the convenience of zipping through toll booths, you need to have in your car a wireless device. This tag contains information about your account, permitting E-ZPass to deduct the necessary toll—and to note when your ◄ car whisked through that particular toll booth. They wouldn't share that information with anyone, either; that is, unless they had to.

Evidence:
In the ad, OnStar is portrayed as a technology that can save lives.

Style:
The language is conversational and often satirical.

Reasons:
Koppel uses critical thinking to question the main assumption of the ad: Is it necessarily good that OnStar always knows where you are while driving?

Reasons:
Convenient technologies also keep track of our movements. Koppel gets his readers to think about what happens to personal information that is passively collected.

6 Radio frequency identification technology has been used for about 15 years now to reunite lost pets with their owners. Applied Digital Solutions, for example, manufactures the VeriChip, a tiny, implantable device that holds a small amount of data. Animal shelters can scan the chip for the name and phone number of the lost pet's owner. The product is now referred to as the HomeAgain Microchip Identification System.

7 Useful? Sure. Indeed, it's not much of a leap to suggest that one day, the VeriChip might be routinely implanted under the skin of, let's say, an Alzheimer's patient. The Food and Drug Administration approved the VeriChip for use in people last October. An Applied Digital Solutions spokesman estimates that about 1,000 people have already had a VeriChip implanted, usually in the right triceps. At the moment, it doesn't carry much information, just an identification number that health care providers can use to tap into a patient's medical history. A Barcelona nightclub also uses it to admit customers with a qualifying code to enter a V.I.P. room where drinks are automatically put on their bill. Possible variations on the theme are staggering.

Evidence: Technologies used to track pets can also track people.

8 And how about all the information collected by popular devices like TiVo, the digital video recorder that enables you to watch and store an entire season's worth of favorite programs at your own convenience? It also lets you electronically mark the programs you favor, allowing TiVo to suggest similar programs for your viewing pleasure. In February, TiVo announced the most frequently played and replayed commercial moment during the Super Bowl (it involves a wardrobe malfunction, but believe me, you don't want to know), drawing on aggregated data from a sample of 10,000 anonymous TiVo households. No one is suggesting that TiVo tracks what each subscriber records and replays. But could they, if they needed to? That's unclear, although TiVo does have a privacy policy. "Your privacy," it says in part, "is very important to us. Due to factors beyond our control, however, we cannot fully ensure that your user information will not be disclosed to third parties."

Evidence: The popular TiVo service admits that it does not fully protect the privacy of its subscribers.

9 Unexpected and unfortunate things happen, of course, even to the most reputable and best-run organizations. Only last February, the Bank of America Corporation notified federal investigators that it had lost computer backup tapes containing personal information about 1.2 million

federal government employees, including some senators. In April, LexisNexis unintentionally gave outsiders access to the personal files (addresses, Social Security numbers, drivers license information) of as many as 310,000 people. In May, Time Warner revealed that an outside storage company had misplaced data stored on computer backup tapes on 600,000 current and former employees. That same month, United Parcel Service picked up a box of computer tapes in New Jersey from CitiFinancial, the consumer finance subsidiary of Citigroup, that contained the names, addresses, Social Security numbers, account numbers, payment histories and other details on small personal loans made to an estimated 3.9 million customers. The box is still missing.

Evidence:
Numerous accidents and data thefts have given private information to unauthorized people.

10   Whoops!

11   CitiFinancial correctly informed its own customers and, inevitably, the rest of the world about the security breach. Would they have done so entirely on their own? That is less clear. In July 2003, California started requiring companies to inform customers living in the state of any breach in security that compromises personally identifiable information. Six other states have passed similar legislation.

12   No such legislation exists on the federal stage, however—only discretionary guidelines for financial institutions about whether and how they should inform their customers with respect to breaches in the security of their personal information.

Conclusion:
Koppel hopes by this point he has raised concerns about privacy for his readers. He now gives his thesis: The public has the right to know what is being done with private information they give to companies and services.

13   Both the House and Senate are now considering federal legislation similar to the California law. It's a start but not nearly enough. We need mandatory clarity and transparency; not just with regard to the services that these miracles of microchip and satellite technology offer but also the degree to which companies share and exchange their harvest of private data.

14   We cannot even begin to control the growing army of businesses and industries that monitor what we buy, what we watch on television, where we drive, the debts we pay or fail to pay, our marriages and divorces, our litigations, our health and tax records and all else that may or may not yet exist on some computer tape, if we don't fully understand everything we're signing up for when we avail ourselves of one of these services.

What to the Slave Is the Fourth of July?

Frederick Douglass

On the fifth of July in 1852, former slave Frederick Douglass spoke at a meeting of the Ladies' Anti-Slavery Society in Rochester, New York. In this series of excerpts from his lengthy oration (published shortly thereafter as a pamphlet), Douglass reminds his audience of the irony of celebrating freedom and liberty in a land where much of the population was enslaved.

Return to these questions after you have finished reading.

Analyzing the Reading

1. Douglass spends considerable time telling his audience what points do not need to be argued: that a slave is human, that man is entitled to liberty, and so on. If in fact these points are agreed upon by all, why do you think Douglass spends so much time talking about them?

2. Douglass was speaking in the last few years before the American Civil War (1861–1865). How is the vivid imagery in this speech likely to have affected listeners? Read carefully through Douglass's descriptions of the slave trade and its impact on individuals and families. What values is he appealing to?

3. What impact does Douglass's personal history have on his credibility? Would the argument in this speech have been as compelling if it had been made by someone who had never experienced slavery firsthand?

4. What words would you use to describe the overall tone of Douglass's speech? Is it angry? threatening? hopeful? pessimistic? Why do you think Douglass chose the tone he used in this argument?

Exploring Ideas and Issues

Douglass was renowned as both an orator and a writer. His first autobiography, *Narrative of the Life of Frederick Douglass, an American Slave,* remains a major historical American document. In addition to working for the abolition of slavery, Douglass was also a passionate advocate for women's suffrage.

1. Douglass appeals to both reason and emotion in the speech he gives. What additional kinds of evidence might he have used? What kinds of evidence do you think an audience can absorb more easily through reading than through listening, and vice versa? Write a short essay in which you identify two additional kinds of evidence and explain why you believe they would be more suitable in a written than in a spoken argument.

2. Does society have an obligation to redress the injustices of the past? For example, is affirmative action in favor of minorities and women in college applications and hiring necessary or fair? Is the payment of slave reparations appropriate? What about prohibiting same-sex schools? Write an essay in which you argue for or against such measures. Include appeals to logic and emotion. If possible, do some research on the subject and include evidence from your research.

3. Some groups have advocated extending certain rights to nonhumans. Using Douglass's basic train of logic—that a slave is a man and therefore entitled to the same rights as nonslaves—construct an argument in favor of or against recognizing animals' rights. Write an essay in which you support your argument with appeals to emotion and examples of expert testimony, as well.

What to the Slave is the Fourth of July?

Fellow-citizens, pardon me, allow me to ask, why am I called upon to speak here to-day? What have I, or those I represent, to do with your national independence? Are the great principles of political freedom and of natural justice, embodied in that Declaration of Independence, extended to us? And am I, therefore, called upon to bring our humble offering to the national altar, and to confess the benefits and express devout gratitude for the blessings resulting from your independence to us?

But, such is not the state of the case. I say it with a sad sense of the disparity between us. I am not included within the pale of this glorious anniversary! Your high independence only reveals the immeasurable distance between us. The blessings in which you, this day, rejoice, are not enjoyed in common. The rich inheritance of justice, liberty, prosperity, and independence, bequeathed by your fathers, is shared by you, not by me. The sunlight that brought life and healing to you has brought stripes and death to me. This Fourth [of] July is yours, not mine. You may rejoice, I must mourn. To drag a man in fetters into the grand illuminated temple of liberty, and call upon him to join you in joyous anthems is inhuman mockery and sacrilegious irony. Do you mean, citizens, to mock me, by asking me to speak to-day?

Fellow-citizens, above your national, tumultuous joy, I hear the mournful wail of millions whose chains, heavy and grievous yesterday, are, to-day, rendered more intolerable by the jubilee shouts that reach them. To forget them, to pass lightly over their wrongs, and to chime in with the popular theme, would be treason most scandalous and shocking, and would make me a reproach before God and the world. My subject, then fellow citizens, is AMERICAN

SLAVERY. I shall see, this day, and its popular characteristics, from the slave's point of view. Standing, there, identified with the American bondman, making his wrongs mine, I do not hesitate to declare, with all my soul, that the character and conduct of this nation never looked blacker to me than on this 4th of July! Whether we turn to the declarations of the past, or to the professions of the present, the conduct of the nation seems equally hideous and revolting. America is false to the past, false to the present, and solemnly binds herself to be false to the future. Standing with God and the crushed and bleeding slave on this occasion, I will, in the name of humanity which is outraged, in the name of liberty which is fettered, in the name of the constitution and the Bible, which are disregarded and trampled upon, dare to call in question and to denounce, with all the emphasis I can command, everything that serves to perpetuate slavery—the great sin and shame of America! "I will not equivocate; I will not excuse"; I will use the severest language I can command; and yet not one word shall escape me that any man, whose judgment is not blinded by prejudice, or who is not at heart a slaveholder, shall not confess to be right and just.

But I fancy I hear some one of my audience say, it is just in this circumstance that you and your brother abolitionists fail to make a favorable impression on the public mind. Would you argue more, and denounce less, would you persuade more, and rebuke less, your cause would be much more likely to succeed. But, I submit, where all is plain there is nothing to be argued. What point in the anti-slavery creed would you have me argue? On what branch of the subject do the people of this country need light? Must I undertake to prove that the slave is a man? That point is conceded already. Nobody doubts it. The slaveholders themselves acknowledge it in the enactment of laws for their government. They acknowledge it when they punish disobedience on the part of the slave. There are seventy-two crimes in the State of Virginia, which, if committed by a black man, (no matter how ignorant he be), subject him to the punishment of death; while only two of the same crimes will subject a white man to the like punishment. What is this but the acknowledgement that the slave is a moral, intellectual and responsible being? The manhood of the slave is conceded. It is admitted in the fact that Southern statute books are covered with enactments forbidding, under severe fines and penalties, the teaching of the slave to read or to write. When you can point to any such laws, in reference to the beasts of the field, then I may consent to argue the manhood of the slave. When the dogs in your streets, when the fowls of the air, when the cattle on your hills, when the fish of the sea, and the reptiles that crawl, shall be unable to distinguish the slave from a brute, there will I argue with you that the slave is a man!

For the present, it is enough to affirm the equal manhood of the negro race. Is it not astonishing that, while we are ploughing, planting and reaping, using all kinds of mechanical tools, erecting houses, constructing bridges, building ships, working in metals of brass, iron, copper, silver and gold; that, while we are reading, writing and ciphering, acting as clerks, merchants and secretaries, having among us lawyers, doctors, ministers, poets, authors, editors, orators and teachers; that, while we are engaged in all manner of enterprises common to other men, digging gold in California, capturing the whale in the Pacific, feeding sheep and cattle on the hillside, living, moving, acting, thinking, planning, living in families as husbands, wives and children, and, above all, confessing and worshipping the Christian's God, and looking hopefully for life and immortality beyond the grave, we are called upon to prove that we are men!

Would you have me argue that man is entitled to liberty? That he is the rightful owner of his own body? You have already declared it. Must I argue the wrongfulness of slavery? Is it to be settled by the rules of logic and argumentation, as a matter beset with great difficulty, involving a doubtful application of the principle of justice, hard to be understood? How should I look to-day, in the presence of Americans, dividing, and subdividing a discourse, to show that men have a natural right to freedom? speaking of it relatively, and positively, negatively, and affirmatively. To do so would be to make myself ridiculous and offer an insult to your understanding. There is not a man beneath the canopy of heaven that does not know that slavery is wrong for him.

What, am I to argue that it is wrong to make men brutes, to rob them of their liberty, to work them without wages, to keep them ignorant of their relations to their fellow men, to beat them with sticks, to flay their flesh with the lash, to load their limbs with irons, to hunt them with dogs, to sell them at auction, to sunder their families, to knock out their teeth, to burn their flesh, to starve them into obedience and submission to their masters? Must I argue that a system thus marked with blood, and stained with pollution, is wrong? No! I will not. I have better employments for my time and strength, than such arguments would imply.

What, then, remains to be argued? Is it that slavery is not divine; that God did not establish it; that our doctors of divinity are mistaken? There is blasphemy in the thought. That which is inhuman, cannot be divine! Who can reason on such a proposition? They that can, may; I cannot. The time for such argument is past.

What, to the American slave, is your 4th of July? I answer: a day that reveals to him, more than all other days in the year, the gross injustice and cruelty to which he is the constant victim. To him, your celebration is a sham; your boasted liberty, an unholy license; your national greatness, swelling vanity; your sounds of rejoicing are empty and heartless; your denunciations of tyrants, brass fronted impudence; your shouts of liberty and equality, hollow mockery; your prayers and hymns, your sermons and thanksgivings, with all your religious parade, and solemnity, are, to him, mere bombast, fraud, deception, impiety, and hypocrisy—a thin veil to cover up crimes which would disgrace a nation of savages. There is not a nation on the earth guilty of practices, more shocking and bloody, than are the people of these United States, at this very hour.

Go where you may, search where you will, roam through all the monarchies and despotisms of the old world, travel through South America, search out every abuse, and when you have found the last, lay your facts by the side of the everyday practices of this nation, and you will say with me, that, for revolting barbarity and shameless hypocrisy, America reigns without a rival. Take the American slave-trade, which we are told by the papers, is especially prosperous just now. Ex-Senator Benton tells us that the price of men was never higher than now. He mentions the fact to show that slavery is in no danger. This trade is one of the peculiarities of American institutions. It is carried on in all the large towns and cities in one-half of this confederacy; and millions are pocketed every year, by dealers in this horrid traffic. In several states, this trade is a chief source of wealth. It is called (in contradistinction to the foreign slave-trade) "the internal slave trade." It is, probably, called so, too, in order to divert from it the horror with which the foreign slave-trade is contemplated. That trade has long since been denounced by this government, as piracy. It has been denounced with burning words, from the high places of the nation, as an execrable traffic. To arrest it, to put an end to it, this nation keeps a squadron, at immense cost, on the coast of Africa. Everywhere, in this country, it is safe to speak of this foreign slave-trade, as a most inhuman traffic, opposed alike to the laws of God and of man. The duty to extirpate and destroy it is admitted even by our DOCTORS OF DIVINITY. In order to put an end to it, some of these last have consented that their colored brethren (nominally free) should leave this country, and establish themselves on the western coast of Africa! It is, however, a notable fact that, while so much execration is poured out by Americans upon those engaged in the foreign slave-trade, the men engaged in the slave-trade between the states pass without condemnation, and their business is deemed honorable.

Behold the practical operation of this internal slave-trade, the American slave-trade, sustained by American politics and American religion. Here you will see men and women reared like swine for the market. You know what is a swine-drover? I will show you a man-drover. They inhabit all our Southern States. They perambulate the country and crowd the highways of the nation, with droves of human stock. You will see one of these human flesh-jobbers, armed with pistol, whip and Bowie-knife, driving a company of a hundred men, women, and children from the Potomac to the slave market at New

Orleans. These wretched people are to be sold singly, or in lots, to suit purchasers. They are food for the cotton-field, and the deadly sugar-mill. Mark the sad procession, as it moves wearily along, and the inhuman wretch who drives them. Hear his savage yells and his blood-chilling oaths, as he hurries on his affrighted captives! There, see the old man, with locks thinned and gray. Cast one glance, if you please, upon that young mother, whose shoulders are bare to the scorching sun, her briny tears falling on the brow of the babe in her arms. See, too, that girl of thirteen, weeping, yes! weeping, as she thinks of the mother from whom she has been torn! The drove moves tardily. Heat and sorrow have nearly consumed their strength; suddenly you hear a quick snap, like the discharge of a rifle; the fetters clank, and the chain rattles simultaneously; your ears are saluted with a scream, that seems to have torn its way to the centre of your soul! The crack you heard, was the sound of the slave-whip; the scream you heard, was from the woman you saw with the babe. Her speed had faltered under the weight of her child and her chains! that gash on her shoulder tells her to move on. Follow this drove to New Orleans. Attend the auction; see men examined like horses; see the forms of women rudely and brutally exposed to the shocking gaze of American slave-buyers. See this drove sold and separated forever; and never forget the deep, sad sobs that arose from that scattered multitude. Tell me citizens, WHERE, under the sun, you can witness a spectacle more fiendish and shocking. Yet this is but a glance at the American slave-trade, as it exists, at this moment, in the ruling part of the United States.

I was born amid such sights and scenes. To me the American slave-trade is a terrible reality. When a child, my soul was often pierced with a sense of its horrors. I lived on Philpot Street, Fell's Point, Baltimore, and have watched from the wharves, the slave ships in the Basin, anchored from the shore, with their cargoes of human flesh, waiting for favorable winds to waft them down the Chesapeake. There was, at that time, a grand slave mart kept at the head of Pratt Street, by Austin Woldfolk. His agents were sent into every town and county in Maryland, announcing their arrival, through the papers, and on flaming "hand-bills," headed CASH FOR NEGROES. These men were generally well dressed men, and very captivating in their manners. Ever ready to drink, to treat, and to gamble. The fate of many a slave has depended upon the turn of a single card; and many a child has been snatched from the arms of its mother by bargains arranged in a state of brutal drunkenness.

Allow me to say, in conclusion, notwithstanding the dark picture I have this day presented of the state of the nation, I do not despair of this country. There are forces in operation, which must inevitably work the downfall of slavery. "The arm of the Lord is not shortened," and the doom of slavery is certain. I, therefore, leave off where I began, with hope. While drawing encouragement from the Declaration of Independence, the great principles it contains, and the genius of American Institutions, my spirit is also cheered by the obvious tendencies of the age. Nations do not now stand in the same relation to each other that they did ages ago. No nation can now shut itself up from the surrounding world, and trot round in the same old path of its fathers without interference. The time was when such could be done. Long established customs of hurtful character could formerly fence themselves in, and do their evil work with social impunity. Knowledge was then confined and enjoyed by the privileged few, and the multitude walked on in mental darkness. But a change has now come over the affairs of mankind. Walled cities and empires have become unfashionable. The arm of commerce has borne away the gates of the strong city. Intelligence is penetrating the darkest corners of the globe. It makes its pathway over and under the sea, as well as on the earth. Wind, steam, and lightning are its chartered agents. Oceans no longer divide, but link nations together. From Boston to London is now a holiday excursion. Space is comparatively annihilated. Thoughts expressed on one side of the Atlantic are distinctly heard on the other. The far off and almost fabulous Pacific rolls in grandeur at our feet. The Celestial Empire, the mystery of ages, is being solved. The fiat of the Almighty, "Let there be Light," has not yet spent its force. No abuse, no outrage whether in taste, sport or avarice, can now hide itself from the all-pervading light.

When Handouts Keep Coming, the Food Line Never Ends

Mark Winne

Mark Winne was the director of Connecticut's Hartford Food System from 1979 to 2003. He is the author of *Closing the Food Gap: Resetting the Table in the Land of Plenty* (2008), which examines how people from all classes obtain food: from lower-income people at food pantries and convenience stores to more affluent people who tend to seek out organic and local products. Instead of the term *hunger,* Winne uses the phrase *food insecure,* which refers to a lack of access at all times to enough food for an active, healthy life. According to the USDA, 10.9% of households in the United States were food insecure at least some time during 2006. "When Handouts Keep Coming, the Food Line Never Ends" was published in the *Washington Post* on November 18, 2007.

Return to these questions after you have finished reading.

Analyzing the Reading

1. Winne begins his article by talking about the flurry of giving that occurs during Thanksgiving. Why do you think people are more likely to make donations and volunteer during the holiday season?

2. In this article, Winne explains his position on the government's methods of dealing with poverty. In doing so, he sets up several causal relationships, the most clearly stated of which is this: "We know hunger's cause—poverty. We know its solution—end poverty." What are the others?

3. Winne is making a controversial claim—that we need to rethink our devotion to food donation. What is at stake in this claim for donors, food banks, and the poor? What is at stake for Winne in making this argument?

4. The article provides many details—some of them potentially surprising—about the operations of food banks and of public food services. Why do you think Winne does this? How do these details affect his argument? his credibility?

Exploring Ideas and Issues

As Winne points out, certain kinds of philanthropy continue—even though a change in policy might be more effective—because donors, whether corporations, organizations, or individuals, gain some benefit such as good public relations or even just the opportunity to feel good.

1. Have you ever had an experience of volunteering, even if it was only an act of helping a stranger? Were you motivated by the idea of "doing good," as Winne suggests? What other motivations might people have for volunteering? Write a short essay in which you argue that volunteerism has, or does not have, valuable benefits for individuals and society. Give examples from your own experience or the experiences of people you know.

2. Winne's article implies that food pantries are inadequate partly because they do not supply nutritionally sound food, they perpetuate recipients' dependency, and they have unstable and insecure financing. Write a short essay in which you make a proposal that addresses *one* of these inadequacies. Remember to add enough detail to make your idea clear and convincing.

3. Winne argues that the institution of charitable food banks "distract[s] the public and policymakers from the task of harnessing the political will needed to end hunger in the United States." Write an essay in which you argue for or against the idea that it's the responsibility of government, not of private or religious charities, to alleviate poverty and hunger. Give reasons for your position, and use facts from Winn's essay, or from your own research, to support your points.

WHEN HANDOUTS KEEP COMING, THE FOOD LINE NEVER ENDS

How can anyone not get caught up in the annual Thanksgiving turkey frenzy? At the food bank I co-founded in Hartford, Conn., November always meant cheering the caravans of fowl-laden trucks that roared into our parking lot. They came on the heels of the public appeals for "A bird in every pot," "No family left without a turkey" and our bank's own version—"A turkey and a 20 [dollar bill]."

Like pompom girls leading a high school pep rally, we revved up the community's charitable impulse to a fever pitch with radio interviews, newspaper stories and dramatic television footage to extract the last gobbler from the stingiest citizen. After all, our nation's one great day of social equity was upon us. In skid row soup kitchens and the gated communities of hedge-fund billionaires alike, everyone was entitled, indeed expected, to sit down to a meal of turkey with all the fixings.

And here we are, putting on the same play again this year. But come Friday, as most of us stuff more leftovers into our bulging refrigerators, 35 million Americans will take their place in line again at soup kitchens, food banks and food stamp offices nationwide. The good souls who staff America's tens of thousands of emergency food sites will renew their pleas to donors fatigued by their burst of holiday philanthropy. Food stamp workers will return to their desks and try to convince mothers that they can feed their families on the $3 per person per day that the government allots them. The cycle of need—always present, rarely sated, never resolved—will continue.

Unless we rethink our devotion to food donation.

America's far-flung network of emergency food programs—from Second Harvest to tens of thousands of neighborhood food pantries—constitutes one of the largest charitable institutions in the nation. Its vast base of volunteers and donors and its ever-expanding distribution infrastructure have made it a powerful force in shaping popular perceptions of domestic hunger and other forms of need. But in the end, one of its most lasting effects has been to sidetrack efforts to eradicate hunger and its root cause, poverty.

As sociologist Janet Poppendieck made clear in her book Sweet Charity, there is something in the food-banking culture and its relationship with donors that dampens the desire to empower the poor and take a more muscular, public stand against hunger.

It used to be my job to scour every nook and cranny of Hartford for food resources, and I've known the desperation of workers who saw the lines of the poor grow longer while the food bank's inventory shrank. The cutback in federal support for social welfare programs triggered by the Reagan administration in the 1980s unleashed a wave of charitable innovation and growth not seen since the Great Depression. As demand for food rose unabated—as it does to this day—our food bank's staff became increasingly adept at securing sustenance from previously unimaginable sources.

No food donation was too small, too strange or too nutritionally unsound to be refused.

I remember the load of nearly rotten potatoes that we "gratefully" accepted at the warehouse loading dock and then promptly shoveled into the dumpster once the donor was safely out of sight. One of our early food bank meetings included a cooking demonstration by a group of local entrepreneurs who were trying to develop a market for horse meat. The product's name was Cheva-lean, taken from "cheval," the French word for horse. The promoters reminded us that the French, the world's leading authorities on food, ate horse meat, implying that therefore our poor clients could certainly do the same. The only thing that topped that was when we had to secure recipes from the University of Maine to help us use the moose parts proudly presented by representatives of the Connecticut Fish and Game Division who'd been forced to put down the disoriented Bullwinkle found wandering through suburban back yards.

We did our job well, and everything grew: Over 25 years, the food bank leapfrogged five times from warehouse to ever-vaster warehouse, finally landing in a state-of-the-art facility that's the equal of most commercial food distribution centers in the country. The volunteers multiplied to 3,000 because the donations of food, much of it unfit for human consumption, required many hands for sorting and discarding. The number of food distribution sites skyrocketed from five in 1982 to 360 today.

But in spite of all the outward signs of progress, more than 275,000 Connecticut residents—slightly less than 8.6 percent of the state's residents—remain hungry or what we call "food insecure." The Department of Agriculture puts 11 percent of the U.S. population in this category. (The department also provides state-by-state breakdowns.)

The overall futility of the effort became evident to me one summer day in 2003 when I observed a food bank truck pull up to a low-income housing project in Hartford. The residents had known when and where the truck would arrive, and they were already lined up at the edge of the parking lot to receive handouts. Staff members and volunteers set up folding tables and proceeded to stack them with produce, boxed cereal and other food items. People stood quietly in line until it was their turn to receive a bag of pre-selected food.

No one made any attempt to determine whether the recipients actually needed the food, nor to encourage the recipients to seek other forms of assistance, such as food stamps. The food distribution was an unequivocal act of faith based on generally accepted knowledge that this was a known area of need. The recipients seemed reasonably grateful, but the staff members and volunteers seemed even happier, having been fortified by the belief that their act of benevolence was at least mildly appreciated.

As word spread, the lines got longer until finally the truck was empty. The following week, it returned at the same time, and once again the people were waiting. Only this time there were more of them. It may have been that a donor-recipient co-dependency had developed. Both parties were trapped in an ever-expanding web of immediate gratification that offered the recipients no long-term hope of eventually achieving independence and self-reliance. As the food bank's director told me later, "The more you provide, the more demand there is."

My experience of 25 years in food banking has led me to conclude that co-dependency within the system is multifaceted and frankly troubling. As a system that depends on donated goods, it must curry favor with the nation's food industry, which often regards food banks as a waste-management tool. As an operation that must sort through billions of pounds of damaged and partially salvageable food, it requires an army of volunteers who themselves are dependent on the carefully nurtured belief that they are "doing good" by "feeding the hungry." And as a charity that lives from one multimillion-dollar capital campaign to the next (most recently, the Hartford food bank raised $4.5 million), it must maintain a ready supply of well-heeled philanthropists and captains of industry to raise the dollars and public awareness necessary to make the next warehouse expansion possible.

Food banks are a dominant institution in this country, and they assert their power at the local and state levels by commanding the attention of people of good will who want to address hunger. Their ability to attract volunteers and to raise money approaches that of major hospitals and universities. While none of this is inherently wrong, it does distract the public and policymakers from the task of harnessing the political will needed to end hunger in the United States.

The risk is that the multibillion-dollar system of food banking has become such a pervasive force in the anti-hunger world, and so tied to its donors and its volunteers, that it cannot step back and ask if this is the best way to end hunger, food insecurity and their root cause, poverty.

During my tenure in Hartford, I often wondered what would happen if the collective energy that went into soliciting and distributing food were put into ending hunger and poverty instead. Surely it would have a sizable impact if 3,000 Hartford-area volunteers, led by some of Connecticut's most privileged and respected citizens, showed up one day at the state legislature, demanding enough resources to end hunger and poverty. Multiply those volunteers by three or four—the number of volunteers in the state's other food banks and hundreds of emergency food sites—and you would have enough people to dismantle the Connecticut state capitol brick by brick. Put all the emergency food volunteers and staff and board members from across the country on buses to Washington, to tell Congress to mandate a living wage, health care for all and adequate employment and child-care programs, and you would have a convoy that might stretch from New York City to our nation's capital.

But what we have done instead is to continue down a road that never comes to an end. Like transportation planners who add more lanes to already clogged highways, we add more space to our food banks in the futile hope of relieving the congestion.

We know hunger's cause—poverty. We know its solution—end poverty. Let this Thanksgiving remind us of that task.

Eat Food: Food Defined
Michael Pollan

Author Michael Pollan is a "foodie intellectual" who achieved notable fame through two of his best-selling books, *The Omnivore's Dilemma* (2005) and *In Defense of Food* (2008). The first book follows the four basic ways human societies obtain food (industrialize systems; organic operations, self-sufficient farming; and hunting/gathering). The second book explores how Western diets, which have been "intellectualized" by deconstructing foods into individual nutrients, is in fact very unhealthy. The following essay in an excerpt from this latter book, in which he urges readers to follow three simple dietary rules: "Eat food. Not too much. Mostly plants."

Return to these questions after you have finished reading.

Analyzing the Reading

1. According to Pollan, what is "real food"? What has replaced real food on our supermarket shelves?

2. Pollan makes a distinction between "ordinary food" and "foodlike substitutes." Based on what you have read, what "food" do you usually eat? How would he categorize your breakfast, lunch, dinner and snack choices? Explain.

3. According to Pollan, what problems arise when we deconstruct whole foods into individual nutrients? Why isn't it enough to add nutrients to processed foods? Explain.

4. Pollan makes five suggestions for a better diet. Summarize each one and note how difficult or easy it would be to follow his recommendations.

Exploring Ideas and Issues

In his book, *In Defense of Food,* Pollan recommends that consumers "shop the parameter" of supermarkets where foods your great-grandmother would have recognized are most likely to be found—fresh, whole, and unprocessed foods. In 2007, University of Washington researchers Adam Drwnowksi and Pablo Monsivais checked the prices of fresh fruits and vegetables, whole grains, fish, and lean meats at numerous stores in the Seattle area. They discovered that prices for healthy foods had risen nearly 20% compared to an overall 5% inflation rate in food prices. Moreover, prices for processed foods remained about the same, and in some cases had dropped.

1. Pollan advocates that people eat "real food." In a down-economy, can people afford to eat in the way he suggests? Why or why not?

2. Check the prices for food in your local supermarket. Compare the prices of unprocessed foods to those of processed ones offering a similar level of nutrition. Write a short essay on the economic challenges for a healthy diet.

3. According to the U.S. Department of Agriculture, Americans spend just under 6% of their income on food. As a comparison, people in Denmark spend almost 11%, and in Indonesia and Azerbaijan people spend around 50%. Write an editorial in which you explain why Americans should spend more, rather than less, of their income on food.

4. What steps would you need to take in order to eat healthier? Would you have to give up something in order to afford it? Would you have to travel far out of your daily sphere to have access to "real food"? What other challenges, if any, would you face?

Eat Food: Food Defined

The first time I heard the advice to "just eat food" it was in a speech by Joan Gussow, and it completely baffled me. Of course you should eat food—what else is there to eat? But Gussow, who grows much of her own food on a flood-prone finger of land jutting into the Hudson River, refuses to dignify most of the products for sale in the supermarket with that title. "In the thirty-four years I've been in the field of nutrition," she said in the same speech, "I have watched real food disappear from large areas of the supermarket and from much of the rest of the eating world." Taking food's place on the shelves has been an unending stream of foodlike substitutes, some seventeen thousand new ones every year—"products constructed largely around commerce and hope, supported by frighteningly little actual knowledge." Ordinary food is still out there, however, still being grown and even occasionally sold in the supermarket, and this ordinary food is what we should eat.

But given our current state of confusion and given the thousands of products calling themselves food, this is more easily said than done. So consider these related rules of thumb. Each proposes a different sort of map to the contemporary food landscape, but all should take you to more or less the same place.

DON'T EAT ANYTHING YOUR GREAT GRANDMOTHER WOULDN'T RECOGNIZE AS FOOD. Why your great grandmother? Because at this point your mother and possibly even your grandmother is as confused as the rest of us; to be safe we need to go back at least a couple generations, to a time before the advent of most modern foods. So depending on your age (and your grandmother), you may need to go back to your great- or even great-great grandmother. Some nutritionists recommend going back even further. John Yudkin, a British nutritionist whose early alarms about the dangers of refined carbohydrates were overlooked in the 1960s and 1970s, once advised, "Just don't eat anything your Neolithic ancestors wouldn't have recognized and you'll be ok."

What would shopping this way mean in the supermarket? Well imagine your great grandmother at your side as you roll down the aisles. You're standing together in front of the dairy case. She picks up a package of Go-Gurt Portable Yogurt tubes—and has no idea what this could possibly be. Is it a food or a toothpaste? And how, exactly, do you introduce it into your body? You could tell her it's just yogurt in a squirtable form, yet if she read the ingredients label she would have every reason to doubt that that was in fact the case. Sure, there's some yoghurt in there, but there are also a dozen other things that aren't remotely yoghurtlike, ingredients she would probably fail to recognize as foods of any kind, including high-fructose corn syrup, modified corn starch, kosher gelatin, carrageenan, tricalcium phosphate, natural and artificial flavours, vitamins, and so forth. (And there's a whole other list of ingredients for the "berry bubblegum bash" flavoring, containing everything but berries or bubblegum.) How did yoghurt, which in your great grandmother's day consisted of simply milk inoculated with a bacterial culture, ever get to be so complicated? Is a product like Go-Gurt Portable Yogurt still a whole food? A food of any kind? Or is it just a food product?

There are in fact hundreds of foodish products in the supermarket that your ancestors simply wouldn't recognize as food: breakfast cereal bars transacted by bright white veins representing, but in reality having nothing to do with, milk; "protein waters" and "non-dairy creamer"; cheeselike foodstuffs equally innocent of any bovine contribution; cakelike cylinders (with creamlike fillings) called Twinkles that never grow stale, *Don't eat anything incapable of rotting* is another personal policy you might consider adopting.

There are many reasons to avoid eating such complicated food products beyond the various chemical additives and corn and soy derivatives they contain. One of the problems with products of food science is that, as Joan Gussow has pointed out, they lie to your body; their artificial colors and flavours and synthetic sweeteners and novel fats confound the senses we rely on to assess new foods and prepare our bodies to deal with them. Foods that lie leave us with little choice but eat by numbers, consulting labels rather than our senses.

It's true that foods have long been processed in order to preserve them, as when we pickle or ferment or smoke, but industrial processing aims to do much more than extend shelf life. Today foods are processed in ways specifically designed to sell us more food by pushing our evolutionary buttons—our inborn preferences for sweetness and fat and salt. These qualities are difficult to find in nature but cheap and easy for the food scientist to deploy, with the result that processing induces us to consume much more of these ecological rarities than is good for us. "Tastes great, less filling!" could be the motto for most processed foods, which are far more energy dense than most whole foods: They contain much less water, fiber, and micronutrients, and generally much more sugar and fat, making them at the same time, to coin a marketing slogan, "More fattening, less nutritious!"

The great grandma rule will help keep many of these products out of your cart. But not all of them. Because thanks to the FDA's willingness, post-1973, to let food makers freely alter the identity of "traditional foods that everyone knows" without having to call them imitations, your great grandmother could easily be fooled into thinking that that loaf of bread or wedge of cheese is in fact a loaf of bread or a wedge of cheese. This is why we need slightly more detailed personal policy to capture these imitation foods; to wit:

AVOID FOOD PRODUCTS CONTAINING INGREDIENTS THAT ARE A) UNFAMILIAR, B) UNPRONOUNCEABLE, C) MORE THAN FIVE IN NUMBER, OR THAT INCLUDE D) HIGH-FRUCTOSE CORN SYRUP. None of these characteristics, not even the last one, is necessarily harmful in and of itself, but all of them are reliable markers for foods that have been highly processed to the points where they may no longer be what they purport to be. They have crossed over from foods to food products.

Consider a loaf of bread, one of the "traditional foods that everyone knows" specifically singled out for protection in the 1938 imitation rule. As your grandmother could tell you, bread is traditionally made using a remarkably small number of familiar ingredients: flour, yeast, water, and a pinch of salt will do it. But industrial bread—even industrial whole-grain bread—has become a far more complicated product of modern food science (not to mention commerce and hope). Here's the complete ingredients list for Sara Lee's Soft & Smooth Whole Grain White Bread. (Wait a minute—isn't "Whole Grain White Bread" a contradiction in terms? Evidently not any more.)

> Enriched bleached flour [wheat flour, malted barley flour, niacin, iron, thiamine mononitrate (vitamin B_1), riboflavin (vitamin B_2), folic acid], water, whole grains [whole wheat flour, brown rice flour (rice flour, rice bran)], high fructose corn syrup [hello], whey, wheat gluten, yeast, cellulose. Contains 2% or less of each of the following: honey, calcium sulfate, vegetable oil (soybean and/or cottonseed oils), salt, butter (cream, salt), dough conditioners (may contain one or more of the following; mono- and diglycerides, ethoxylated mono- and diglycerides, ascorbic acid, enzymes, azodicarbonamide), guar gum, calcium propionate (preservative), distilled vinegar, yeast nutrients (monocalcium phosphate, calcium sulfate, ammonium sulfate), corn starch, natural flavor, betacarontene (color), vitamin D_3, soy lecithin, soy flour.

There are many things you could say about this intricate loaf of "bread," but note first that even if it managed to slip by your great grandmother (because it is a loaf of bread, or at least is called one and strongly resembles one), the product fails every test proposed under rule number two: It's got unfamiliar ingredients (monoglycerides I've heard of before, but ethoxylated monoglycerides?); unpronounceable ingredients (try "azodicarbonamide"); it exceeds the maximum of five ingredients (by roughly thirty-six); and it contains high-fructose corn syrup. Sorry, Sara Lee, but your Soft & Smooth Whole Grain White Bread is not food and if not for the indulgence of the FDA could not even be labelled "bread."

Sara Lee's Soft & Smooth Whole Grain White Bread could serve as a monument to the age of nutritionism. It embodies the latest nutritional wisdom from science and government (which in its most recent food pyramid recommends that at least half our consumption of grain come from whole grains) but leavens that wisdom with the commercial recognition that American eaters (and American children in particular) have come to prefer their wheat highly refined—which is to say, cottonly soft, snowy white, and exceptionally sweet on the tongue. In its marketing materials, Sara Lee treats this clash of interests as some sort of Gordian knot— it speaks in terms of an ambitious quest to build a "no compromise" loaf—which only the most sophisticated food science could possibly cut.

And so it has, with the invention of whole-grain white bread. Because the small percentage of whole grains in the bread would render it that much less sweet than, say, all-white Wonder Bread—which scarcely waits to be chewed before transforming itself into glucose—the food scientists have added high-fructose corn syrup and honey to make up the difference; to overcome the problematic heft and toothsomeness of a real whole grain bread, they've deployed "dough conditioner," including guar gum and the aforementioned azodicarbonamide, to simulate the texture of supermarket white bread. By incorporating certain varieties of albino wheat, they've managed to maintain that deathly appealing Wonder Bread pallor.

Who would have thought Wonder Bread would ever become an ideal of aesthetic and gustatory perfection to which bakers would actually aspire—Sara Lee's Mona Lisa?

Very often food science's efforts to make traditional foods more nutritious make them much more complicated, but not necessarily any better for you. To make dairy products low fat, it's not enough to remove the fat. You then have to go to great lengths to preserve the body or creamy texture by working in all kinds of food additives. In the case of low-fat or skim milk, that usually means adding powdered milk. But powdered milk contains oxidized cholesterol, which scientists believe is much worse for your arteries than ordinary cholestrol, so food makers sometimes compensate by adding antioxidants, further complicating what had been a simple one-ingredient whole food. Also, removing the fat makes it that much harder for your body to absorb the fat-soluble vitamins that are one of the reasons to drink milk in the first place.

All this heroic and occasionally counterproductive food science has been undertaken in the name of our health—so that Sara Lee can add to its plastic wrapper the magic words "good source of whole grain" or a food company can ballyhoo the even more magic words "low fat." Which brings us to a related food policy that may at first sound counterproductive to a health-conscious eater:

AVOID FOOD PRODUCTS THAT MAKE HEALTH CLAIMS. For a food product to make health claims on its package it must first have a package, so right off the bat it's more likely to be a processed than a whole food. Generally speaking, it is only the big food companies that have the wherewithal to secure FDA-approved health claims for their products and then trumpet them to the world. Recently, however, some of the tonier fruits and nuts have begun boasting about their health-enhancing properties, and there will surely be more as each crop council scrounges together the money to commission its own scientific study. Because all plants contain antioxidants, all these studies are guaranteed to find something on which to base a health oriented marketing campaign.

But for the most part it is the products of food science that make the boldest health claims, and these are often founded on incomplete and often erroneous science—the dubious fruits of nutritionism. Don't forget that trans-fat-rich margarine, one of the first industrial foods to claim it was healthier than the traditional food it replaced, turned out to give people heart attacks. Since that debacle, the FDA, under tremendous pressure from industry , has made it only easier for food companies to make increasingly doubtful health claims, such as the one Frito-Lay now puts on some of its chips—that eating them is somehow good for your heart. If you bother to read the health claims closely (as food marketers make sure consumers seldom do), you will find that there is often considerably less to them than meets the eye.

Consider a recent "qualified" health claim approved by the FDA for (don't laugh) corn oil. ("Qualified" is a whole new category of health claim, introduced in 2002 at the behest of industry.) Corn oil, you may recall, is particularly high in the omega-6 fatty acids we're already consuming far too many of.

> Very limited and preliminary scientific evidence suggests that eating about one tablespoon (16 grams) of corn oil daily may reduce the risk of heart disease due to the unsaturated fat content in corn oil.

The tablespoon is a particularly rich touch, conjuring images of moms administering medicine, or perhaps cod-liver oil, to their children. But what the FDA gives with one hand, it takes away with the other. Here's the small-print "qualification" of this already notably diffident health claim:

> [The] FDA concludes that there is little scientific evidence supporting this claim.

And then to make matters still more perplexing:

> To achieve this possible health benefit, corn oil is to replace a similar amount of saturated fat and not increase the total number of calories you eat in a day.

This little masterpiece of pseudoscientific bureaucratese was extracted from the FDA by the manufacturer of Mazola corn oil. It would appear that "qualified" is an official FDA euphemism for "all but meaningless." Though someone might have let the consumer in on this game: The FDA's own research indicates that consumers have no idea what to make of qualified health claims (how would they?), and its rules allow companies to promote the claims pretty much any way they want—they can use really big type for the claim, for example, and then print the disclaimers in teeny-tiny type. No doubt we can look forward to a qualified health claim for high-fructose corn syrup, a tablespoon of which probably does contribute to your health—as long as it replaces a comparable amount of, say, poison in your diet and doesn't increase the total number of calories you eat in a day.

When corn oil and chips and sugary breakfast cereals can all boast being good for your heart, health claims have become hopelessly corrupt. The American Heart Association currently bestows (for a fee) its heart-healthy seal of approval on Lucky Charms, Cocoa Puffs, and Trix cereals, Yoo-hoo lite chocolate drink, and Healthy Choice's Premium Caramel Swirl Ice Cream Sandwich—this at a time when scientists are coming to recognize that dietary sugar probably plays a more important role in heart disease than dietary fat. Meanwhile, the genuinely heart-healthy whole foods in the produce section, lacking the financial and political clout of the packaged goods a few sales aisles over, are mute. But don't take the silence of the yams as a sign that they have nothing valuable to say about health.

Why Twitter Will Endure
David Carr

The journalist David Carr, who joined the *New York Times* in 2002, writes "The Media Equation," a column that covers the business aspect of media industries, and works as a general assignment reporter covering popular culture. His writing has also appeared in the *Atlantic Monthly* and *New York Magazine*. The following *Times* article was published on January 3, 2010.

Return to these questions after you have finished reading.

Analyzing the Reading

1. The author initially thought Twitter would not last. What reasons does he give for that belief?

2. Why did the author change his mind? What does he see as the specific value of Twitter?

3. What obstacles did the author need to overcome in his use of Twitter in order to get value from it?

4. How would you characterize the author's tone? Find examples in the selection that illustrate it. Is the tone effective? Why or why not?

Exploring Ideas and Issues

1. Think about your own encounters with new media technology—for example, smartphones, texting, digital cameras, or even Twitter. What was your initial response? Were you excited to try it? Or did you think the technology was a waste of time? Did your attitude change as you used the technology more and more? In what ways? Write a short essay in which you argue for the usefulness, or uselessness, of the specific technology you experienced.

2. Carr says that Twitter has changed his life in several ways. If you already have a smartphone, speculate on how your life would change if you were to give it up. Using the smartphone as an example, write a short essay on the impact that technology has on a person's life. Your tone can be light and humorous, or serious.

3. Some people argue that technological advances are not always good. They contend, for example, that e-readers will make books obsolete, or that surrogate mothering is unnatural. Should science and technology be allowed to proceed on their own, or should society exercise stronger oversight? Write an essay in which you argue for more or less societal (or governmental) intervention in areas of innovation.

WHY TWITTER WILL ENDURE

I can remember when I first thought seriously about Twitter. Last March, I was at the SXSW conference, a conclave in Austin, Tex., where technology, media, and music are mashed up and re-imagined, and, not so coincidentally, where Twitter first rolled out in 2007. As someone who was oversubscribed on Facebook, overwhelmed by the computer-generated RSS feeds of news that came flying at me, and swamped by incoming e-mail messages, the last thing I wanted was one more Web-borne intrusion into my life.

And then there was the name. Twitter. In the pantheon of digital nomenclature—brands within a sector of the economy that grew so fast that all the sensible names were quickly taken—it would be hard to come up with a noun more trite than Twitter. It impugns itself, promising something slight and inconsequential, yet another way to make hours disappear and have nothing to show for it. And just in case the noun is not sufficiently indicting, the verb "to tweet" is even more embarrassing.

Beyond the dippy lingo, the idea that something intelligent, something worthy of mindshare, might occur in the space of 140 characters—Twitter's parameters were set by what would fit in a text message on a phone—seems unlikely.

But it was clear that at the conference, the primary news platform was Twitter, with real-time annotation of the panels on stage and critical updates about what was happening elsewhere at a very hectic convention. At 52, I succumbed, partly out of professional necessity.

And now, nearly a year later, has Twitter turned my brain to mush? No, I'm in narrative on more things in a given moment than I ever thought possible, and instead of spending a half-hour surfing in search of illumination, I get a sense of the day's news and how people are reacting to it in the time that it takes to wait for coffee at Starbucks. Yes, I worry about my ability to think long thoughts—where was I, anyway?—but the tradeoff has been worth it.

Some time soon, the company won't say when, the 100-millionth person will have signed on to Twitter to follow and be followed by friends and strangers. That may sound like a MySpace waiting to happen—remember MySpace?—but I'm convinced Twitter is here to stay.

And I'm not alone. "The history of the Internet suggests that there have been cool Web sites that go in and out of fashion and then there have been open standards that become plumbing," said Steven Johnson, the author and technology observer who wrote a seminal piece about Twitter for *Time* last June. "Twitter is looking more and more like plumbing, and plumbing is eternal."

Really? What could anyone possibly find useful in this cacophony of short-burst communication? Well, that depends on whom you ask, but more importantly whom you follow. On Twitter, anyone may follow anyone, but there is very little expectation of reciprocity. By carefully curating the people you follow, Twitter becomes an always-on data stream from really bright people in their respective fields, whose tweets are often full of links to incredibly vital, timely information.

The most frequent objection to Twitter is a predictable one: "I don't need to know someone is eating a donut right now." But if that someone is a serious user of Twitter, she or he might actually be eating the curmudgeon's lunch, racing ahead with a clear, up-to-the-second picture of an increasingly connected, busy world. The service has obvious utility for a journalist, but no matter what business you are in, imagine knowing what the thought leaders in your industry were reading and considering. And beyond following specific individuals, Twitter hash tags allow you to go deep into interests and obsessions: #rollerderby, #physics, #puppets and #Avatar, to name just a few of manythousands.

The act of publishing on Twitter is so friction-free—a few keystrokes and hit send— that you can forget that others are out there listening. I was on a Virgin America cross-country flight, and used its wireless connection to tweet about the fact that the guy next to me seemed to be the leader of a cult involving Axe body spray. A half-hour later, a steward approached me and said he wondered if I would be more comfortable with a seat in the bulkhead. (He turned out to be a great guy, but I was doing a story involving another part of the company, so I had to decline the offer. @VirginAmerica, its corporate Twitter account, sent me a message afterward saying perhaps it should develop a screening process for Axe. It was creepy and comforting all at once.)

Like many newbies on Twitter, I vastly overestimated the importance of broadcasting on Twitter; and after a while, I realized that I was not Moses and neither Twitter nor its users were wondering what I thought. Nearly a year in, I've come to understand that the real value of the service is listening to a wired collective voice.

Not that long ago, I was at a conference at Yale and looked at the sea of open laptops in the seats in front of me. So why wasn't my laptop open? Because I follow people on Twitter who serve as my Web-crawling proxies, each of them tweeting links that I could examine and read on a Blackberry. Regardless of where I am, I surf far less than I used to.

At first, Twitter can be overwhelming, but think of it as a river of data rushing past that I dip a cup into every once in a while. Much of what I need to know is in that cup: if it looks like Apple is going to demo its new tablet, or Amazon sold more Kindles than actual books at Christmas, or the final vote in the Senate gets locked in on health care, I almost always learn about it first on Twitter.

The expressive limits of a kind of narrative developed from text messages, with less space to digress or explain than this sentence, has significant upsides. The best people on Twitter communicate with economy and precision, with each element—links, hash tags and comments—freighted with meaning. Professional acquaintances whom I find insufferable on every other platform suddenly become interesting within the confines of Twitter.

Twitter is incredibly customizable, with little of the social expectations that go with Facebook. Depending on whom you follow, Twitter can reveal a nation riveted by the last episode of "Jersey Shore" or a short-form conclave of brilliance. There is plenty of nonsense—#Tiger had quite a run—but there are rich threads on the day's news and bravura solo performances from learned autodidacts. And the ethos of Twitter, which is based on self-defining groups, is far more well-mannered than many parts of the Web—more Toastmasters than mosh pit. On Twitter, you are your avatar and your avatar is you, so best not to act like a lout and when people want to flame you for something you said, they are responding to their own followers, not yours, so trolls quickly lose interest.

"Anything that is useful to both dissidents in Iran and Martha Stewart has a lot going for it; Twitter has more raw capability for users than anything since e-mail," said Clay Shirky, who wrote "Here Comes Everybody," a book about social media. "It will be hard to wait out Twitter because it is lightweight, endlessly useful and gets better as more people use it. Brands are using it, institutions are using it, and it is becoming a place where a lot of important conversations are being held." Twitter helps define what is important by what Mr. Shirky has called "algorithmic authority," meaning that if all kinds of people are pointing at the same thing at the same instant, it must be a pretty big deal.

Beyond the throbbing networked intelligence, there is the possibility of practical magic. Twitter can tell you what kind of netbook you should buy for your wife for Christmas— thanks Twitter!—or call you out when you complain about the long lines it took to buy it, as a tweeter on behalf of the electronics store B & H did when I shared the experience on my Blackberry while in line. I have found transcendent tacos at a car wash in San Antonio, rediscovered a brand of reporter's notepad I adore, uncovered sources for stories, all just by typing a query into Twitter.

All those riches do not come at zero cost: If you think e-mail and surfing can make time disappear, wait until you get ahold of Twitter, or more likely, it gets ahold of you. There is always something more interesting on Twitter than whatever you happen to be working on.

But in the right circumstance, Twitter can flex some big muscles. Think of last weekend, a heavy travel period marked by a terrorist incident on Friday. As news outlets were scrambling to understand the implications for travelers on Saturday morning, Twitter began lighting up with reports of new security initiatives, including one from @CharleneLi, a consultant who tweeted from the Montreal airport at about 7:30 A.M.: "New security rules for int'l flights into US. 1 bag, no electronics the ENTIRE flight, no getting up last hour of flight." It was far from the whole story and getting ahead of the news by some hours would seem like no big deal, but imagine you or someone you loved was flying later that same day: Twitter might seem very useful.

Twitter's growing informational hegemony is not assured. There have been serious outages in recent weeks, leading many business and government users to wonder about the stability of the platform. And this being the Web, many smart folks are plotting ways to turn Twitter into so much pixilated mist. But I don't think so. I can go anywhere I want on the Web, but there is no guarantee that my Twitter gang will come with me. I may have quite a few followers, but that doesn't make me Moses.

Games, Not Schools, Are Teaching Kids to Think

James Paul Gee

As Mary Lou Fulton Presidential Professor of Literacy Studies at Arizona State University, James Paul Gee has published widely in the fields of linguistics and education. His book *Sociolinguistics and Literacies* (1990) helped establish the area of New Literacy Studies, an interdisciplinary field that combines language, learning, and literacy studies. Gee's most recent books deal with video games, language, and learning. He has published widely in academic journals as well as consumer publications. The following article appeared in the May 2003 issue of *Wired* magazine.

Return to these questions after you have finished reading.

Analyzing the Reading

1. The article opens with the question "why aren't kids learning?" What does the author say that schools are actually teaching kids? What is the author's definition of real learning?

2. In paragraph 3, the author praises five specific video games. What are they? What kinds of skills does he say the games teach?

3. What two characteristics of a successful video game's "underlying architecture" make it a "teaching machine"? How do schools exemplify, or not exemplify those characteristics, according to Gee?

4. What evidence does the article give that successful video games are the result of "free-market economics"?

Exploring Ideas and Issues

What's your experience with video games? Is playing video games an "educational" experience, purely an entertaining activity, or a waste of time?

1. One widespread understanding of games is that they are all learning experiences—helping to prepare children for adult activities. For example, when children play "house," they experiment with being parents and running a household. Think of other positive purposes that games might have for children. Write a short essay in which you explore three such purposes. Draw on examples from your own experience and the experiences of people you know to show how specific games fulfill these purposes.

2. Gee says, "Learning isn't about memorizing isolated facts." But is there a role for memorization in education? For example, do children gain anything by memorizing the capitals of states, the multiplication tables, or the words to a poem? Write a short essay in which you agree or disagree with Gee's statement. Be sure to include examples to support your ideas.

3. Gee says that schools are responding, ineffectually, "with more tests, more drills, and more rigidity" to the crisis in education demonstrated by studies that compare students in the United States with students in other countries. Do some research on suggested causes for this crisis—for example, lack of money, poor teacher training, and low parental involvement. What proposals are being put forth to address these issues? Do these proposals make sense to you? Write an essay in which you identify one possible cause of the education crisis and evaluate the recommendations advanced for remedying this problem.

Games, Not Schools,
Are Teaching Kids to Think

The US spends almost $50 billion each year on education, so why aren't kids learning? Forty percent of students lack basic reading skills, and their academic performance is dismal compared with that of their foreign counterparts. In response to this crisis, schools are skilling-and-drilling their way "back to basics," moving toward mechanical instruction methods that rely on line-by-line scripting for teachers and endless multiple-choice testing. Consequently, kids aren't learning how to think anymore—they're learning how to memorize. This might be an ideal recipe for the future Babbitts of the world, but it won't produce the kind of agile, analytical minds that will lead the high tech global age. Fortunately, we've got *Grand Theft Auto: Vice City* and *Deus X* for that.

After school, kids are devouring new information, concepts, and skills every day, and, like it or not, they're doing it controller in hand, plastered to the TV. The fact is, when kids play videogames they can experience a much more powerful form of learning than when they're in the classroom. Learning isn't about memorizing isolated facts. It's about connecting and manipulating them. Doubt it? Just ask anyone who's beaten *Legend of Zelda* or solved *Morrowind*.

The phenomenon of the videogame as an agent of mental training is largely unstudied; more often, games are denigrated for being violent or they're just plain ignored. They shouldn't be. Young gamers today aren't training to be gun-toting carjackers. They're learning how to learn. In *Pikmin*, children manage an army of plantlike aliens and strategize to solve problems. In *Metal Gear Solid 2*, players move stealthily through virtual environments and carry out intricate missions. Even in the notorious *Vice City*, players craft a persona, build a history, and shape a virtual world. In strategy games like *WarCraft III* and *Age of Mythology*, they learn to micromanage an array of elements while simultaneously balancing short- and long-term goals. That sounds like something for their resumes.

The secret of a videogame as a teaching machine isn't its immersive 3-D graphics but its underlying architecture. Each level dances around the outer limits of the player's abilities, seeking at every point to be hard enough to be just doable. In cognitive science, this is referred to as the "regime of competence principle," which results in a feeling of simultaneous pleasure and frustration—a sensation as familiar to gamers as sore thumbs. Cognitive scientist Andy diSessa has argued that the best instruction hovers at the boundary of a student's competence. Most schools, however, seek to avoid invoking feelings of both pleasure and frustration, blind to the fact that these emotions can be extremely useful when it comes to teaching kids.

Also, good videogames incorporate the principle of expertise. They tend to encourage players to achieve total mastery of one level, only to challenge and undo that mastery in the next, forcing kids to adapt and evolve. This carefully choreographed dialectic has been identified by learning theorists as the best way to achieve expertise in any field. This doesn't happen much in our routine-driven schools, where "good" students are often just good at "doing school."

How did videogames become such successful models of effective learning? Game coders aren't trained as cognitive scientists. It's a simple case of free-market economics: If a title doesn't teach players how to play it well, it won't sell well. Game companies don't rake in $6.9 billion a year by dumbing down the material—aficionados condemn short and easy games like *Half Life: Blue Shift* and *Devil May Cry 2*. Designers respond by making harder and more complex games that require mastery of sophisticated worlds and as many as 50 to 100 hours to complete. Schools, meanwhile, respond with more tests, more drills, and more rigidity. They're in the cognitive-science dark ages.

We don't often think about videogames as relevant to education reform, but maybe we should. Game designers don't often think of themselves as learning theorists. Maybe they should. Kids often say it doesn't feel like learning when they're gaming— they're much too focused on playing. If kids were to say that about a science lesson, our country's education problems would be solved.

"Buff Daddy"
"Food Cops Bust Cookie Monster"

"Buff Daddy" was created by the Ad Council (**www.adcouncil.org**) as part of its public service campaign to fight obesity. Supported by corporations, foundations, and individuals, the Ad Council has a goal of advertising in the public interest. Its campaigns are produced without charge by advertising agencies.

The Center for Consumer Freedom (**www.ConsumerFreedom.com**), an organization sponsored by restaurants and food companies, has produced a series of ads taking a different position on obesity, including "Food Cops Bust Cookie Monster." These ads defend what the organization describes as "the right of adults and parents to choose what they eat, drink, and how to enjoy themselves."

Return to these questions after you have finished reading.

Analyzing the Reading

1. Both of these ads make visual arguments. What are those arguments? Why do you think the producers of each ad chose the image they did? How effective is each visual in communicating the ad's central message?

2. The ads both use humor. Who or what is the target of the humor in each ad? What is the tone of the humor in the ads? How successful do you think the humor is in convincing each audience that the ad's claims are valid?

3. The ConsumerFreedom.com ad refers to "Food Cops" and "nutrition nags." Why did the creators of this ad choose these terms? What audience are they trying to appeal to with these kinds of labels? How effective are the labels in supporting the ad's message?

4. The Ad Council image invites viewers to make a direct connection between actions ("Started shooting hoops with son") and physical changes in the person acting. How would this argument sound if it were stated as a simple claim plus reasons? Would the ad be more or less effective in nonvisual form? Why?

Exploring Ideas and Issues

Despite the enduring prevalence of advertising, little is actually definitively known about whether, when, or how ads work. With their strong visual appeal, ads can make compelling arguments, but to what extent do the ads actually influence behavior?

1. How important are ads in your life? Do you use ads as sources of information, for example, or do ads cause you to *avoid* certain products? Write a short essay in which you suggest that consumers take a particular approach to advertisements. Use examples from your own experience to support your ideas.

2. Think about other public service ads (PSAs) you have seen—in magazines, on billboards, on the Internet, or on television. Choose one that you feel is particularly *ineffective* and write a short essay describing the ad and explaining why you think it fails to get its message across to its audience.

3. In his 2004 article in *The Journal of the Royal Society of Medicine* about the relationship between advertising and obesity in children, Dr. David Ashton concludes, "For every complex problem there is a simple solution—and it is always wrong. The claim that food advertising is a major contributor to children's food choices and the rising tide of childhood obesity has obvious appeal, but as an argument it does not stand up to scrutiny." Do some research on this issue. What evidence do you find that causes you to agree or disagree with Ashton? Write an essay giving your point of view.

439

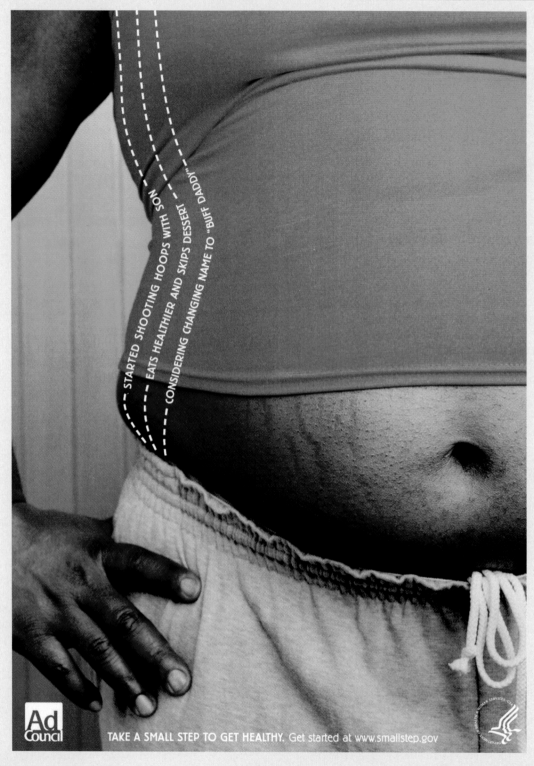

ConsumerFreedom.com Editorial Infographic

Food Cops Bust Cookie Monster

Farce again became reality as the children's TV show *Sesame Street* has bowed to obesity hysteria from nutrition nags. In a nod to calorie killjoys, Cookie Monster will tout health foods, and his famous song, "C is For Cookie, That's Good Enough For Me," will be replaced with "A Cookie Is a Sometimes Food." This U-Turn may not be the last. Predictions:

C is for Cookie

Big Bird becomes Svelte Bird

Miss Piggy becomes Miss Moderation

Mayor McCheese voted out of office and replaced with Mayor McSoy-Slice

Keebler elves to make only unflavored rice cakes

Cap'n Crunch forced to sail in only skim milk

Count Chocula stabbed through heart with a carrot stick

Fat Albert becomes "Weight Watchers patient #00873-Albert"

© 2005 The Center For Consumer Freedom

441

How to Write a Position Argument

These steps for the process of writing a position argument may not progress as neatly as this chart might suggest. Writing is not an assembly-line process.

As you write and revise you may think of additional reasons to support your position. Your instructor and fellow students may give you comments that help you to rethink your argument. Use their comments to work through your paper or project again, strengthening your content and making your writing better organized and more readable.

1 FIND AN ISSUE

- Read your assignment slowly and carefully. Note key words like *argue for* and *take a stand* that indicate the assignment requires a position argument.

- Make a list of possible issues.

- Select a possible issue.

- Read about your issue.

- Analyze your potential readers. What do your readers likely know about the issue? Where are they most likely to disagree with you?

2 DEVELOP REASONS AND A THESIS

- Take a definite position.

- Develop reasons by considering whether you can argue from a definition, compare or contrast, consider good and bad effects, or refute objections.

- Support your reasons by making observations and finding facts, statistics, and statements from authorities.

- Write a working thesis.

3
WRITE A DRAFT

- Introduce the issue and give the necessary background. Explain why the issue is important.

- Think about how readers will view you, the writer.

- If you argue from a definition, set out the criteria.

- Avoid fallacies.

- Provide evidence to support your main points.

- Address opposing views. Summarize opposing positions and explain why your position is preferable.

- Make counterarguments if necessary. Examine the facts and assumptions on which competing claims are based.

- Conclude with strength. Avoid merely summarizing. Emphasize the importance of your argument and possibly make an additional point or draw implications.

- Choose a title that will interest readers.

4
REVISE, REVISE, REVISE

- Check that your position argument fulfills the assignment.

- Make sure that your claim is arguable and focused.

- Check your reasons and add more if you can.

- Add additional evidence where reasons need more support.

- Examine the organization.

- Review the visual presentation.

- Proofread carefully.

5
SUBMITTED VERSION

- Make sure your finished writing meets all formatting requirements.

1: Find an Issue

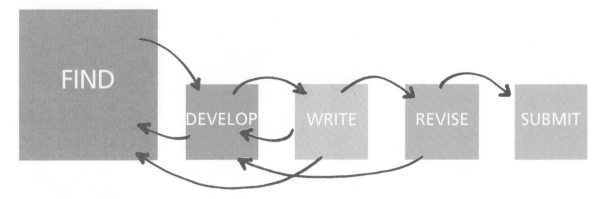

Analyze the assignment

Read your assignment slowly and carefully. Look for words like *argue for, take a stand,* or *write on a controversial issue,* which signal that you are writing a position argument. Highlight any information about the length specified, date due, formatting, and other requirements. You can attend to this information later. At this point you want to give your attention to finding an issue if one is not specified.

Make a list of possible campus issues

Think about issues that are debated on your campus such as these.

- Should smoking be banned on campus?
- Should varsity athletes get paid for playing sports that bring in revenue?
- Should admissions decisions be based exclusively on academic achievement?
- Should colleges offer financial incentives for students to graduate in three years rather than four?

Make a list of possible community issues

Think about issues that are debated in your community such as these.

- Should more tax dollars be shifted from building highways to public transportation?
- Should sex education be increased in schools to reduce teenage pregnancy?
- Should talking on phones and texting while driving be banned?
- Should bike lanes be designated on streets to encourage more people to ride bicycles?

Make a list of possible national and international issues

Think about national and international issues such as these.

- Should advertising be banned on television shows aimed at preschool children?
- Should people who are terminally ill be allowed to end their lives?
- Should animals be used for scientific research?
- Should any citizen who does not have a criminal record be permitted to carry a concealed handgun?

Select an issue and take stock of what you know

Freewrite (see page 42) or make a list of everything you know about the issue. Why are you interested in this issue? What is your stance on the issue? What do you need to know more about?

Read about your issue

Read broadly about your issue. You'll find that writers respond to the opinions and ideas of other writers. Major issues are the sites of ongoing conversations. By mapping the conversation, you may see an opportunity to enter the larger conversation (see pages 28–31).

Analyze the stakeholders

For whom does this issue matter? Whose interests are at stake? Who stands to win and lose?

Analyze your potential readers

How familiar are your potential readers with your issue? What background will you need to supply? What attitudes and beliefs will your readers likely have about this issue? Where will you likely find common ground with your readers? Where will your readers most likely disagree with you?

WRITE NOW

Choose an issue that you care about

1. Make a list of issues that fulfill your assignment.

2. Put a checkmark beside the issues that look most interesting to write about or the ones that mean the most to you.

3. Put a question mark beside the issues that you don't know very much about. If you choose one of these issues, you will probably have to do in-depth research—by talking to people, by using the Internet, or by going to the library.

4. Select a possible issue. What is your stand on this issue? Write nonstop for five minutes about why this issue is important and how it affects you.

Writer at work

Patrice Conley received an assignment to write a position argument. She made notes on and highlighted important parts of her assignment sheet.

English 101
Position Argument Assignment

Choose a current controversial issue that interests you. If no issue comes to mind immediately, visit these library databases: *Opposing Views in Context, Issue Tracker* (on *CQ Researcher*), and *Times Topics* (from the *New York Times*).

Gain an overview of the issue by reading several articles and possibly books. You will need to cite at least five sources in your paper.

Take a position on the issue. You will need to provide reasons and evidence in support of your position, and you will need to acknowledge and discuss opposing viewpoints. Also, most controversial issues have long histories, which you should summarize briefly.

**HEART OF THE PAPER
Give reasons and evidence for position and acknowledge opposing views.*

Submitting a draft on April 14
For the workshop draft, submit two copies
  • A paper copy for your in-class editor (print in advance of class)
  • A digital copy to the Discussion Board

*Paper and digital copies required

So that everyone in class will have easy access to your drafts, you will post them electronically via the Discussion Board. Simply locate the appropriate forum, type in a brief introduction to the paper, and then upload the paper as an attachment to your message. In your introduction, discuss your writing process and what you hoped to achieve by the draft.

Format
Use MLA format in both the draft and final versions. The format is explained in Chapter 23 of the *Brief Penguin Handbook,* 4th ed. Pay particular attention to pages 267 and 281, which give checklists of formatting features. Note that MLA does not require a title page but does have a standard format for headings. Note too that MLA double-spaces everything.

*Get the little things right

Length: 1200–1500 words (approximately 4-5 double-spaced pages)
Due dates:
April 14: Draft due
April 28: Final version due

Read the assignment closely

Patrice Conley began by marking information about the due dates and requirements.

Choose a topic

Patrice enjoys playing and watching sports, so she started by making a list of current controversial issues in college sports.

Explore the issue

Patrice made her initial search on Google, using the search terms "student athlete salaries," which turned up many articles She also searched library databases and the library catalog. In addition, she watched "Money & March Madness" on the PBS series *Frontline*. People interviewed on the program gave arguments against the NCAA's policy of not paying players. The President of the NCAA, Mark Emmert, defended the NCAA's definition of amateurism.

College sports controversies

1. *Equal opportunities for women athletes*

2. *Big-time sports overshadow education*

3. *Financing college sports*

4. *Paying student-athletes in big-time college sports*

5. *Ethics: win-at-all-costs philosophy*

6. *The BCS championship system in big-time college football*

NOTES

College sports is big business. NYT estimates NCAA's licensing deals at $4 billion in 2010.

Coaches receive outlandish salaries while players are paid nothing. John Calipari at Kentucky gets $4 million a year.

Univ. of North Carolina College Sports Research Inst. 2010 study: 54.8% of major college football players at 117 schools graduated within six years, compared to 73.7% of other full-time students. Gap greater in basketball, with 44.6 percent of athletes graduating compared to 75.7% of the general student body.

Tim Tebow autographed Florida jerseys sell for $349.99 but Tebow gets nothing.

Student musicians can get paid; school even helps them find jobs. What's the difference between student musicians and student athletes?

Olympic Games dropped the professional-amateur distinction in 1988.

History: professional-amateur distinction arose in Britain in the 1800s when middle-class and upper-class students didn't want to play against working-class sportsmen, who had to be paid for time taken off work.

2: Develop Reasons and a Thesis

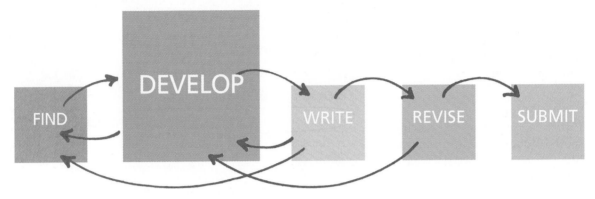

Take an arguable position

A position argument requires that you make a claim that a reasonable person could disagree with and support that claim with one or more reasons. Statements of facts that can be verified by doing research are not arguable. Likewise, claims of personal taste (e.g., your favorite food) and of faith are not arguable.

Write a working thesis

Is your thesis arguable? Statements of fact are not arguable unless the facts are disputed.

NOT ARGUABLE: The population of the United States grew faster in the 1990s than in any previous decade because Congress increased the level of legal immigration and the government stopped enforcing most laws against illegal immigration in the interior of the country.

ARGUABLE: Allowing a high rate of immigration helps the United States deal with the problems of an increasingly aging society and helps provide funding for millions of Social Security recipients.

ARGUABLE: The increase in the number of visas to foreign workers in technology industries is the major cause of unemployment in those industries.

Develop reasons

- Can you argue from a definition? Is _____ a _____? What criteria are necessary for _____ to be a _____? If you want to argue, for example, that zoos are guilty of cruelty to animals, you will have to argue for a definition of cruelty based on criteria, then assert that those criteria apply to zoos.

- Can you write a rebuttal to another position argument? There are two basic strategies for writing a rebuttal. In a **refutation**, you can demonstrate the shortcoming of an argument you wish to discredit. In a **counterargument**, you emphasize the strengths of the position you support in contrast to the argument you are opposing.

- Can you compare and contrast? Is _____ like or unlike _____? For example, should health care in the United States be more like the health care in Canada?

Support your reasons

Search for facts, statistics, statements from authorities, and textual evidence to support your reasons. If you are writing about a campus or community issue, you may also need to visit the site and make observations.

Writer at work

Patrice Conley decided to make a map in order to find a center for her broad topic of whether student athletes in big-time college sports should be paid.

She started with her general topic, stating it in a few words and drawing a box around it.

Next Patrice asked additional questions:
- What is the current situation?
- Who is involved?
- How long has it been going on?
- What else is like it?
- What exactly is the problem?
- What possible solutions are there for the problem?

She thought of some general categories for her topic in response to those questions and drew boxes for each.

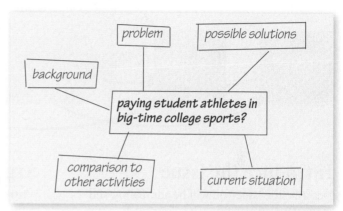

She then looked at her notes from what she had read. She began to generate ideas for each of the subcategories and put them on her map.

When she finished she took stock of her map. She picked up a marker and drew a box around a possible central idea for her project.

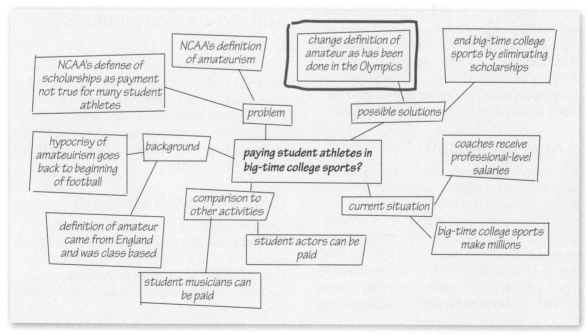

She succeeded in narrowing her general topic to the more specific topic of changing the definition of amateur as it applies to student athletes.

👁 Watch the Animation on Mapping (Clustering) at mycomplab.com   **449**

3: Write a Draft

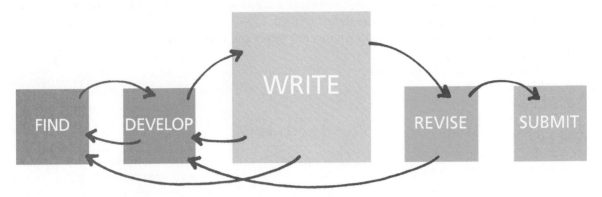

Introduce the issue

Describe the issue you will be addressing and make your claim early. Give your readers any background information they will need.

Think about your credibility

Think about how you can connect with your readers as you write by appealing to their sense of fairness, their core beliefs, and their sense of logic. Readers tend to trust writers who have done their homework, and they appreciate a writer's ability to see a subject from multiple perspectives. Nothing impresses readers more than graceful, fluent writing that is clear, direct, and forceful.

Argue responsibly

When you begin an argument by saying "In my opinion," you are evading responsibility. Readers assume that what you write is your opinion. The more important point is that the claim is rarely only your opinion, and if it is, it can be easily dismissed. If your position is held by other people, your readers should take the position seriously. You argue responsibly when you set out reasons for making your claim and you provide evidence.

Argue respectfully

Written arguments almost never end by getting in the last word. Think of arguments as ongoing conversations. Your goal is to create a dialogue. Show that you understand and respect opposing positions, even if you think the position is ultimately wrong.

Make counterarguments if necessary

Examine the primary assumption of the claim you are rejecting. Is the assumption flawed? What other assumptions are involved? Examine the facts on which a competing claim is based. Are they accurate, current, and representative? Are the sources reliable? Are the sources treated fairly or taken out of context?

Conclude with strength

Avoid summarizing what you have just said. Emphasize the importance of your argument and consider making an additional point. Effective conclusions are interesting and provocative, leaving the reader with something to think about.

Writer at work

Patrice Conley prefers to write a "zero draft" to generate ideas before she plans her organization. She knows that nearly all of what she writes will not make it into the final draft, but she finds that writing as fast as she can frees up her thinking. (You can read Patrice's zero draft on page 42.)

When Patrice finished her zero draft, she let it sit for a day and then took stock of the key points that she had underlined. She rearranged these key points into a working outline.

PATRICE CREATES A WORKING OUTLINE FROM HER ZERO DRAFT

WORKING TITLE: *Should Student Athletes in Big-Time College Sports Be Paid?*

SECTION 1: *Student athletes in college sign away their rights for payment.*

SECTION 2: *College athletics are big business, and top coaches receive multimillion-dollar salaries.*

SECTION 3: *NCAA defends classifying student athletes as amateurs to protect them from exploitation.*

SECTION 4: *The history of amateurism arose in 19th c. Britain when middle- and upper-class sportsmen didn't want to play against working-class teams. The Olympics abandoned the distinction in 1988.*

SECTION 5: *Student musicians and student actors get paid when they perform professionally.*

SECTION 6: *Student athletes cannot be paid for use of their names and images even after they graduate.*

SECTION 7: *Defenders of the current system claim that student athletes are paid with scholarships, but in big-time sports many do not graduate.*

SECTION 8: *NCAA should adopt a different definition of amateur that allows athletes to be paid for what they earn for their schools.*

4: Revise, Revise, Revise

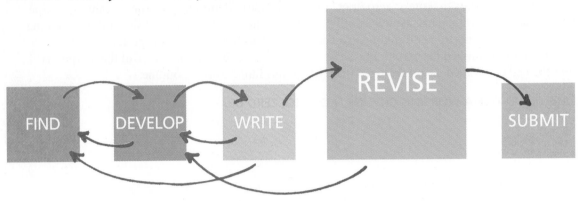

Skilled writers know that the secret to writing well is rewriting.

Does your position argument fulfill the assignment?	• Look again at your assignment. Does your paper or project do what the assignment asks? • Look again at the assignment for specific guidelines, including length, format, and amount of research. Does your work meet these guidelines?
Is your claim arguable and focused?	• Is your position arguable? Statements of fact and statements of religious belief are not arguable. • Can you make your claim more specific to avoid ambiguous language and situations where your claim may not apply?
Are your reasons adequate?	• Are your reasons clear to your readers? • Can you add additional reasons to strengthen your argument?? • Have you acknowledged the views of people who disagree with your position?
Are your reasons supported with evidence?	• Have you found the most accurate information available about your issue? • Can you find additional evidence in the form of examples, quotations from experts, statistics, and observations?
Save the editing for last	• When you have finished revising, edit and proofread carefully.

A peer review guide is on page 54.

Writer at work

Patrice Conley received both global and local comments from her instructor. Patrice first dealt with her instructor's global comments.

RETURNED DRAFT WITH COMMENTS

> College athletics are big business. The most visible college sports—big-time men's football and basketball—generate staggering sums of money. Even more money comes in from video games, clothing, and similar licenses.
>
> *Your major claims need to be supported with evidence. Give specific examples.*

Patrice did additional research to find examples to support her claim.

PATRICE'S REVISION

> Make no mistake: college athletics are big business. The most visible college sports—big-time men's football and basketball—generate staggering sums of money. For example, the twelve universities in the Southeastern Conference receive $205 million each year from CBS and ESPN for the right to broadcast its football games (Smith and Ourand). Even more money comes in from video games, clothing, and similar licenses. In 2010, the *New York Times* reported, "the NCAA's licensing deals are estimated at more than $4 billion" per year (Thamel). While the staggering executive pay at big corporations has brought public outrage, coaches' salaries are even more outlandish. Kentucky basketball coach, John Calipari, is paid over $4 million a year for a basketball program that makes about $35–40 million a year, more than 10% of the entire revenue.

Then she moved on to her instructor's local comments. Her instructor noted a transition is needed between two paragraphs, and Patrice added a sentence, highlighted in yellow below.

PATRICE'S REVISION

> The college sports empire in the United States run by the NCAA is the last bastion of amateurism for sports that draw audiences large enough to be televised. Colleges might be able to defend the policy of amateurism if they extended this definition to all students. A fair policy is one that treats all students the same. A fair policy doesn't result in some students getting paid for professional work, while other students do not.

You can read Patrice's completed paper on pages 454–459.

 Watch the Animation on *Peer Review for Global Issues* at mycomplab.com

Watch the Animation on *Peer Review for Local Issues* at mycomplab.com

5: Submitted Version

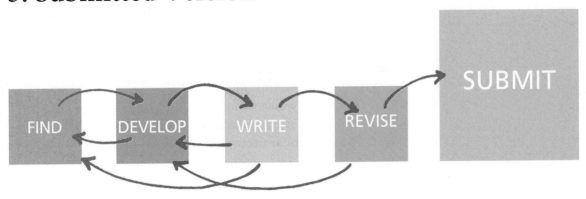

Conley 1

Patrice Conley
Professor Douglas
English 101
28 April 2011

Flagrant Foul: The NCAA's Definition of Student Athletes as Amateurs

Every year, thousands of student athletes across America sign the National Collegiate Athletic Association's Form 08-3a, the "Student-Athlete" form, waiving their right to receive payment for the use of their name and image (McCann). The form defines student athletes as amateurs, who cannot receive payment for playing their sports. While their schools and coaches may make millions of dollars in salaries and endorsement deals and are the highest-paid public employees in many states, student athletes can never earn a single penny from their college athletic careers. Former Nike executive Sonny Vacarro sums it up: "Everybody has a right except for the player. The player has no rights" ("Money").

Make no mistake: college athletics are big business. The most visible college sports—big-time men's football and basketball—generate staggering sums of money. For example, the twelve universities in the Southeastern Conference receive $205 million each year from CBS and ESPN for the right to broadcast its football games (Smith and Ourand). Even more money comes in from video games, clothing, and similar licenses. In 2010, the *New York Times* reported, "the NCAA's licensing deals are estimated at more than $4 billion" per year (Thamel). While the staggering executive pay at big corporations has brought public outrage, coaches' salaries are even more outlandish. Kentucky basketball coach, John Calipari, is paid over $4 million a year for a basketball program that makes about $35-40 million a year, more than 10% of the entire revenue. Tom Van Riper observes that no corporate CEO commands this large a share of the profits. He observes that if Steve Ballmer, the CEO at Microsoft, had Calipari's deal, Ballmer would make over $6 billion a year.

How can colleges allow advertisers, arena operators, concession owners, athletic gear manufacturers, retailers, game companies, and media moguls, along with coaches and university officials, to make millions and pay the stars of the show nothing? The answer is that colleges define athletes as amateurs. Not only are student athletes not paid for playing their sport, they cannot receive gifts and are not allowed to endorse products, which may be a violation of their right to free speech. The NCAA, an organization of colleges and schools, forces student athletes to sign away their rights because, it says, it is protecting the students. If student athletes could accept money from anyone, the NCAA argues, they might be exploited, cheated, or even bribed. Taking money out of the equation is supposed to let students focus on academics and preserve the amateur status of college sports.

The definition of amateur arose in the nineteenth century in Britain, when team sports became popular. Middle-class and upper-class students in college had ample time to play their sports while working-class athletes had only a half-day off (no sports were played on Sundays in that era). Teams began to pay top working-class sportsmen for the time they had to take off from work. Middle-class and upper-class sportsmen didn't want to play against the working-class teams, so they made the distinction between amateurs and professionals. The definition of amateur crossed the Atlantic to the United States, where college sports became popular in the 1880s. But it was not long until the hypocrisy of amateurism undermined the ideal. Top football programs like Yale had slush funds to pay athletes, and others used ringers—players who weren't students—and even players from other schools (Zimbalist 7).

The Olympic Games maintained the amateur-professional distinction until 1988, but it was long evident that Communist bloc nations were paying athletes to train full-time and Western nations were paying athletes through endorsement contracts. The only Olympic sport that now requires amateur status is boxing. The college sports empire in the United States run by the NCAA is the last bastion of amateurism for sports that draw audiences large enough to be televised.

Colleges might be able to defend the policy of amateurism if they extended this definition to all students. A fair policy is one that treats all students the same. A fair policy doesn't result in some students getting paid for professional work, while other students do not. Consider the students in the Butler School of Music at the University of Texas at Austin, for example. Many student musicians perform at the professional level. Does the school prevent them from earning money for their musical performances? No. In fact, the school runs a referral service that connects its students with people and businesses who want to hire professional musicians. The university even advises its students on how to negotiate a contract and get paid for their performance ("Welcome").

Likewise, why are student actors and actresses allowed to earn money from their work and images, while student athletes are not? Think about actress Emma Watson, who enrolled at Brown University in Rhode Island. Can you imagine the university officials at Brown telling Watson that she would have to make the next two Harry Potter films for free, instead of for the $5 million she has been offered? Can you imagine Brown University telling Watson that all the revenue from Harry Potter merchandise bearing her likeness would have to be paid directly to the university, for the rest of her life? They would if Watson were an athlete instead of an actress.

In fact, compared to musicians and actors, student athletes have an even greater need to earn money while they are still in college. Athletes' professional careers are likely to be much shorter than musicians' or actors'. College may be the only time some athletes have the opportunity to capitalize on their success.

(Indeed, rather than focusing student athletes on their academic careers, the NCAA policy sometimes forces students to leave college early, so they can earn a living before their peak playing years are over.) Student athletes often leave school with permanent injuries and no medical insurance or job prospects, whereas student musicians and actors rarely suffer career-ending injuries on the job.

Student athletes are prevented from profiting from their name and image. The NCAA says this rule preserves their standing as amateurs and protects them from the celebrity and media frenzy surrounding professional sports stars. Search for a "Tim Tebow Jersey" online, and you can buy officially branded Florida Gators shirts, ranging in price from $34.99 to $349.99 (autographed by Tebow). The NCAA, the University of Florida, Nike, and the other parties involved in the production and sale of these products get around the problem of using an amateur's name by using his team number instead. Tebow's name doesn't appear anywhere on the jerseys—just his number, fifteen. Yet all these jerseys are identified as "Official Tim Tebow Gators merchandise," and they are certainly bought by fans of Tebow rather than people who just happen to like the number fifteen. Nobody is saying how much money these jerseys have made for Nike, or for the University of Florida. What we do know for sure is the amount Tim Tebow has made off the jerseys: nothing.

Defenders of the current system argue that student athletes on scholarships are paid with free tuition, free room and board, free books, and tutoring help. The total package can be the equivalent of $120,000 over four years. For those student athletes who are motivated to take advantage of the opportunity, the lifetime benefits can be enormous. Unfortunately, too few student athletes do take advantage of the opportunity. Seldom does a major college football and men's basketball program have a graduation rate at or close to overall student body. A study by the University of North Carolina's College Sports Research Institute released in 2010 accuses the NCAA of playing fast and loose with graduation rates by counting part-time students in statistics for the general student body, which makes graduation rates for athletes look better in a comparison. Student athletes must be full-time students; thus they should be compared to other full-time students. The North Carolina Institute reports that 54.8% of major college

(Football Bowl Subdivision) football players at 117 schools graduated within six years, compared to 73.7% of other full-time students. The gap between basketball players was even greater, with 44.6% of athletes graduating compared to 75.7% of the general student body (Zaiger). For the handful of talented athletes who can play in the National Football League or the National Basketball Association, college sports provide training for their future lucrative, although short-lived, profession. But as the NCAA itself points out in its ads, the great majority of student athletes "go pro in something other than sports." For the 55% of college basketball players who fail to graduate, the supposed $120,000 package is an air ball.

The NCAA would be wise to return to the older definition of amateur, which comes from Latin through old French, meaning "lover of." It doesn't necessarily have to have anything to do with money. Whether it's a jazz performer or dancer or an athlete, an amateur ought to be considered someone in love with an activity—someone who cares deeply about the activity, studies the activity in depth, and practices in order to be highly proficient. NBA players, Olympians, college athletes, high school players, and even bird watchers, star gazers, and open-source programmers: they're all amateurs. If they are lucky enough to be paid, so be it.

Conley 6

Works Cited

McCann, Michael. "NCAA Faces Unspecified Damages, Changes in Latest Anti-Trust
Case." *SI.com*. Time, Inc., 21 July 2009. Web. 6 Apr. 2011.

"Money and March Madness." *Frontline*. PBS, 29 Mar. 2011. Web. 3 Apr. 2011.

National Collegiate Athletic Association. Advertisement. *NCAA.org*. NCAA, 13 Mar.
2007. Web. 3 Apr. 2011.

Smith, Michael, and John Ourand. "ESPN Pays $2.25B for SEC Rights." *SportsBusiness
Journal*. Smith and Street, 25 Aug. 2008. Web. 1 Apr. 2011.

Thamel, Pete. "N.C.A.A. Fails to Stop Licensing Lawsuit."
New York Times. New York Times, 8 Feb. 2010. Web. 1 Apr. 2011.

Van Riper, Thomas. "The Highest-Paid College Basketball Coaches." *Forbes.com*.
Forbes, 8 Mar. 2010. Web. 6 Apr. 2011.

"Welcome to the Music Referral Service." *Butler School of Music*.
Univ. of Texas at Austin, n.d. Web. 5 Apr. 2011.

Zaiger, Alan Scher. "Study: NCAA Graduation Rate Comparisons Flawed." *ABC News*.
ABC News, 20 Apr. 2010. Web. 1 Apr. 2011.

Zimbalist, Andrew. *Unpaid Professionals: Commercialism and Conflict in Big-Time
College Sports*. Princeton UP, 2001. Print.

Projects

Position arguments are not merely statements of opinion but are reasoned arguments backed by evidence that are intended to advance the discussion of an issue.

Position argument

Make a position claim on a controversial issue. See pages 444–445 for help on identifying an issue.

Identify the key term. Often position arguments depend on the definition of the key term. What criteria are necessary for something to meet this definition? How would others benefit from a different definition?

Analyze your potential readers. How does the claim you are making affect them? How familiar are they with the issue? How likely will they be to accept your claim or the definition that underlies your claim?

Write an essay on a controversial issue that takes a stand supported by developed reasons.

Rebuttal argument

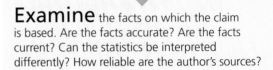

Identify a position argument to argue against. What is its main claim or claims? A fair summary of your opponent's position should be included in your finished rebuttal.

Examine the facts on which the claim is based. Are the facts accurate? Are the facts current? Can the statistics be interpreted differently? How reliable are the author's sources?

Analyze the assumptions on which the claim is based. What is the primary assumption of the claim you are rejecting? What are the secondary assumptions? How are these assumptions flawed? What fallacies does the author commit (see pages 24–25)?

Consider your readers. To what extent do your potential readers support the claim you are rejecting? If they strongly support that claim, then how do you get them to change their minds? What beliefs and assumptions do you share with them?

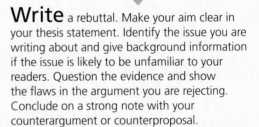

Write a rebuttal. Make your aim clear in your thesis statement. Identify the issue you are writing about and give background information if the issue is likely to be unfamiliar to your readers. Question the evidence and show the flaws in the argument you are rejecting. Conclude on a strong note with your counterargument or counterproposal.

460

Narrative position argument

Think about an experience you have had that makes an implicit causal argument. Have you ever experienced being stereotyped? Have you ever had to jump through many unnecessary bureaucratic hoops? Have you ever been treated differently because of your perceived level of income? Have you ever experienced unfair application of laws and law enforcement?

How common is your experience? If other people have similar experiences, probably what happened to you will ring true.

Describe the experience in detail. When did it happen? How old were you? Why were you there? Who else was there? Where did it happen? If the place is important, describe what it looked like.

Reflect on the significance of the event. How did you feel about the experience when it happened? How do you feel about the experience now? What long-term effects has it had on your life?

Write an essay. You might need to give some background, but if the story is compelling, often it is best to jump right in. Let the story do most of the work. Avoid drawing a simple moral lesson. Your readers should feel the same way you do if you tell your story well.

Position argument brochure

Brochures are used by many organizations to make position arguments. They are easy to make with software and inexpensive to print and distribute.

Select an issue for your brochure (see pages 444–445). Identify your target audience. Think about what background they may need about your issue, and what you want them to take away from your brochure.

Develop a layout. A typical brochure has six panels—three on the front and three on the back. Take two pieces of standard paper, place them together, and fold them in three sections. Then sketch what will go on each panel.

Open your software program, create two new pages, and change the page layout to horizontal. Create text boxes for each panel, three boxes on each page. Add your content and images inside the boxes.

Check the formatting. Print your draft pages, put them together, and fold them in the correct order. Inspect the alignment and the readability of your text. You may need to enlarge the type size or insert blank space to set apart key points. Edit and proofread carefully when you finish.

For support in learning this chapter's content, follow this path in **mycomplab:**

▶ **Resources** ▶ **Writing** ▶ **Writing Purposes** ▶ **Writing to Argue or Persuade**

Review the Instruction and Multimedia resources, then complete the **Exercises** and click on **Gradebook** to measure your progress.

13 Proposal Arguments

Proposal arguments aim to convince others to take action for change (or not to take action).

Chapter Overview

Writing Proposal Arguments

Proposal arguments make the case that someone should do something: "The federal government should raise grazing fees on public lands." "The student union should renovate the old swimming pool in Butler Gymnasium." "All parents should secure their children in booster seats when driving, even for short distances." Proposals can also argue that something should not be done, or that people should stop doing something: "The plan to extend Highway 45 is a waste of tax dollars and citizens should *not* vote for it." "Don't drink and drive."

The challenge for writers of proposal arguments is to convince readers to take action. It's easy for readers to agree that something should be done, as long as they don't have to do it. It's much harder to get readers involved with the situation or convince them to spend their time or money trying to carry out the proposal. A successful proposal argument conveys a sense of urgency to motivate readers and describes definite actions they should take.

Keys to proposal arguments

Successful proposals use good reasons to convince readers that if they act, something positive will happen (or something negative will be avoided). If your readers believe that taking action will benefit them, they are more likely to help bring about what you propose.

Proposal arguments take this form.

We should convert existing train tracks in the downtown area to a light-rail system and build a new freight track around the city because we need to relieve traffic and parking congestion downtown.

Proposal arguments in the world

Proposal essays make general readers aware of a specific problem and present a solution that ideally will get readers to act.

Other genres of proposal arguments

- **Grant proposals** often aim to gain support for nonprofit organizations.

- **Internal proposals** try to persuade those in charge to get something done within an organization such as initiating a new project or solving an existing problem.

- **Business proposals** seek funding from bankers and investors for a new business or a business expansion.

463

What Makes a Good Proposal Argument?

1

Identify and define the problem

Sometimes, your audience is already fully aware of the problem you want to solve. If your city frequently tears up streets and then leaves them for months without fixing them, you shouldn't have much trouble convincing citizens that streets should be repaired more quickly. But if you raise a problem unfamiliar to your readers, first you will have to convince them that the problem is real. Citizens will not see the need to replace miles of sewer lines running under the streets, for example, unless you convince them that the pipes are old and corroded and are a risk to everyone's safety. The clearer you are about what must be done, and by whom, the stronger your argument will be.

2

State a proposed solution

A strong proposal offers a clear, definite statement of exactly what you are proposing. Vague statements that "Something must be done!" may get readers stirred up about the issue but are unlikely to lead to constructive action. A detailed proposal also adds credibility to your argument, showing that you are concerned enough to think through the nuts and bolts of the changes to be made. You can state your proposed solution near the beginning of your argument or introduce it later—for example, after you have considered and rejected other possible solutions.

Connecting the City . . . envisions the year 2020 when 100 miles of crosstown bikeways will help a growing populations of San Francisco residents and visitors bike more often, relieving our crowded roadways and strained transit system.

—San Francisco Bicycle Coalition (see page 502)

3

Convince readers that the proposed solution is fair and will work

Once your readers agree that a problem exists and a solution should be found, you have to convince them that your solution is the best one. Perhaps you want your city to fire the planning committee members who are responsible for street repair. You will need to show that those officials are indeed responsible for the delays, and that, once they are fired, the city will be able to quickly hire new, more effective planners.

4

Consider other possible solutions

You may also have to show how your proposal is better than other possible actions that could be taken. Perhaps others believe your city should hire private contractors to repair the streets more quickly, or reward work crews who finish quickly with extra pay or days off. If there are multiple proposed solutions, all perceived as equally good, then there is no clear course of action for your audience to work for. Very often, that means nothing will happen.

5

Demonstrate that the solution is feasible

Your solution not only has to work; it must be feasible, or practical, to implement. You might be able to raise money for street repairs by billing property owners for repairs to the streets in front of their houses, but opposition to such a proposal would be fierce. Most Americans will object to making individuals responsible for road repair costs when roads are used by all drivers.

Visual Proposals

Many proposal arguments depend on presenting information visually, in multimedia, or in images, in addition to using written language.

NASA global climate computer model (GCM) calculates many factors, such as the temperature of air and water, how much sunlight is reflected and absorbed, and the distribution of clouds, rain, and snow. NASA has released an educational version that runs on a PC so teachers and students can conduct the same kinds of experiments that scientists are running to predict climate change.

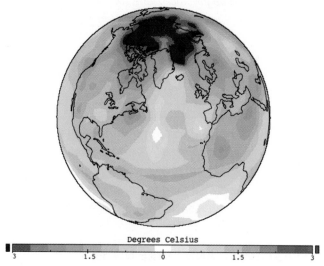

Surface air temperature increase by 2040. Source: NASA.

WRITE NOW

Make a list of campus and community problems to solve

First, make a list of all the problems you can think of on your campus: the library closes too early, shuttle buses run late, long waits at the heath center, food options too limited, and so on. Next make a list of problems in your community: too few bike lanes, traffic, downtown in decline, off-campus housing too expensive, and so on.

Share your lists in a group of three or four students or with the entire class. Record any problems that turn up on more than one list. Discuss the following:

- Which problems are the most important?

- Which are possible to solve?

- Which are the most interesting? Which are the least interesting?

Analyze the Interactive Visual Argument at mycomplab.com

How to Read Proposal Arguments

▼ **BEFORE YOU BEGIN READING**

These notes are in response to the *Declaration of Independence*; the reading begins on page 468.

What kind of text is it?	*The Declaration of Independence is a public statement adopted by the Continental Congress on July 4, 1776. It gives justifications for a proposal that the thirteen American colonies are now a nation independent from Great Britain.*
Who wrote it?	*Thomas Jefferson was the principal author with help from others.*
Who is the intended audience?	*The Declaration of Independence was printed immediately after approval. The document was read in public within a week, and it was widely printed in newspapers. Clearly it was intended for all citizens of the colonies and people sympathetic to American independence in other countries.*

▼ **READ THE TEXT AT LEAST TWICE AND MAKE NOTES**

What exactly is the problem, what causes it, and who is affected?	*Most of the Declaration of Independence is a description of the problem, which is caused by the unwillingness of King George III to grant autonomy to the colonists.*
What is the proposed solution?	*Separation from Britain is proposed in the first sentence. The proposal is reiterated in the concluding paragraph.*
What reasons are offered in support of the proposal?	*The famous second sentence declares that people have natural rights including "life, liberty, and the pursuit of happiness."*
How would you characterize the style?	*The style is formal. The Declaration of Independence draws on political philosophy of its time. Some sections read like a legal text, but lively and emotional metaphors are employed, such as when British administrators are described as swarms of insects.*

How is it organized?

This map shows the organization of the *Declaration of Independence*, which begins on the following page.

Beginning paragraph Paragraph 1	In the first sentence the *Declaration of Independence* announces the separation from Britain and uses the concept of natural law as the justification.
Reasons Paragraph 2	The lengthy second paragraph argues that people have certain natural rights, and when a government violates those rights, the government should be altered or abolished.
Problem Paragraph 3–30	Paragraph 3 begins a long list of accusations against King George III. Many colonists at the time still felt loyalty to the King, and the document attempted to convince them that the King no longer deserved their loyalty.
Ethos Paragraph 31	The document claims the colonists attempted peaceful solutions to problems only to be rebuffed by the British.
Conclusion Paragraph 32	The proposal for separations is asserted again.

The Declaration of Independence
Thomas Jefferson and others

The American Revolution had already begun with the battles of Lexington, Concord, and Bunker Hill, and George Washington had been named to head the colonial army by June 7, 1776, when the Continental Congress moved to draft a Declaration of Independence. Thomas Jefferson was given eighteen days to complete the task with the help of Benjamin Franklin and John Adams.

IN CONGRESS, JULY 4, 1776.

The unanimous Declaration of the thirteen united States of America

1   When, in the Course of human events, it becomes necessary for one people to dissolve the political bands which have connected them with another, and to assume among the powers of the earth, the separate and equal station to which the laws of nature and of nature's God entitle them, a decent respect to the opinions of mankind requires that they should declare the causes which impel them to the separation.

2   We hold these truths to be self-evident: That all men are created equal; that they are endowed by their Creator with certain unalienable rights; that among these are life, liberty and the pursuit of happiness. That, to secure these rights, governments are instituted among men, deriving their just powers from the consent of the governed; that, whenever any form of government becomes destructive of these ends, it is the right of the people to alter or to abolish it, and to institute new Government, laying its foundation on such principles, and organizing its powers in such form, as to them shall seem most likely to effect their safety and happiness. Prudence,

Proposal: Jefferson maintains that the drastic solution of declaring independence is justified if the problem is of great magnitude.

Reasons: The rationale for the proposal is a definition argument. According to Jefferson, the purpose of a government is to ensure the rights of the governed. When a government fails to achieve its defined purpose—to ensure the rights of the people—the people have the right to abolish it. The British used similar arguments to justify the revolution against King James II in 1688.

indeed, will dictate that governments long established should not be changed for light and transient causes; and accordingly all experience hath shown, that mankind are more disposed to suffer, while evils are sufferable, than to right themselves by abolishing the forms to which they are accustomed. But when a long train of abuses and usurpations, pursuing invariably the same object evinces a design to reduce them under absolute despotism, it is their right, it is their duty, to throw off such government and to provide new guards for their future security. Such has been the patient sufferance of these colonies, and such is now the necessity which constrains them to alter their former systems of government. The history of the present king of Great Britain is a history of repeated injuries and usurpations, all having in direct object the establishment of an absolute tyranny over these States. To prove this, let facts be submitted to a candid world.

3   He has refused his assent to laws, the most wholesome and necessary for the public good.

4   He has forbidden his governors to pass laws of immediate and pressing importance, unless suspended in their operation till his Assent should be obtained, and, when so suspended, he has utterly neglected to attend to them.

Problem: The burden for Jefferson is to convince others of the severity of the problem—that life is intolerable under the King. He goes on to detail a long list of complaints. His goal is to prove the need for change rather than to outline how the solution will work.

5   He has refused to pass other laws for the accommodation of large districts of people, unless those people would relinquish the right of representation in the legislature–a right inestimable to them and formidable to tyrants only.

6   He has called together legislative bodies at places unusual, uncomfortable, and distant from the depository of their public Records, for the sole purpose of fatiguing them into compliance with his measures.

7   He has dissolved representative houses repeatedly, for opposing with manly firmness his invasions on the rights of the people.

8   He has refused for a long time, after such dissolutions, to cause others to be elected; whereby the legislative powers, incapable of annihilation, have returned to the people at large for their exercise; the State remaining in the mean time exposed to all the dangers of invasion from without, and convulsions within.

9   He has endeavored to prevent the population of these states; for that purpose obstructing the laws for naturalization of foreigners; refusing to pass others to encourage their migrations hither, and raising the conditions of new appropriations of lands.

10   He has obstructed the administration of justice by refusing his assent to laws for establishing judiciary powers.

11   He has made judges dependent on his will alone, for the tenure of their offices, and the amount and payment of their salaries.

12   He has erected a multitude of new offices, and sent hither swarms of officers to harass our people, and eat out their substance.

Style: The legalistic list of charges is made more vivid by the use of metaphors such as "swarms of officers," which likens the British to a plague of insects.

13   He has kept among us, in times of peace, standing armies without the consent of our legislatures.

14   He has affected to render the military independent of and superior to the civil power.

15   He has combined with others to subject us to a jurisdiction foreign to our constitution, and unacknowledged by our laws; giving his assent to their acts of pretended legislation:

16   For quartering large bodies of armed troops among us;

17   For protecting them, by a mock trial, from punishment for any murders which they should commit on the inhabitants of these States;

18   For cutting off our trade with all parts of the world;

19   For imposing taxes on us without our consent;

20   For depriving us in many cases, of the benefits of trial by jury;

21   For transporting us beyond seas to be tried for pretended offences;

22   For abolishing the free system of English laws in a neighboring province, establishing therein an arbitrary government, and enlarging its boundaries so as to render it at once an example and fit instrument for introducing the same absolute rule into these colonies;

23   For taking away our charters, abolishing our most valuable laws, and altering fundamentally the forms of our governments;

24   For suspending our own legislatures, and declaring themselves invested with power to legislate for us in all cases whatsoever.

25   He has abdicated government here, by declaring us out of his protection and waging war against us.

26   He has plundered our seas, ravaged our coasts, burnt our towns, and destroyed the lives of our people.

27   He is at this time transporting large armies of foreign mercenaries to complete the works of death, desolation and tyranny, already begun with circumstances of cruelty and perfidy scarcely paralleled in the most barbarous ages, and totally unworthy the head of a civilized nation.

28   He has constrained our fellow citizens taken captive on the high seas to bear arms against their country, to become the executioners of their friends and brethren, or to fall themselves by their hands.

29   He has excited domestic insurrections amongst us, and has endeavored to bring on the inhabitants of our frontiers, the merciless Indian savages, whose known rule of warfare is an undistinguished destruction of all ages, sexes and conditions.

30   In every stage of these oppressions we have petitioned for redress in the most humble terms; our repeated petitions have been answered only by repeated injury. A prince,

Style: The strongest charges against the king are placed at the end of the list.

whose character is thus marked by every act which may define a tyrant, is unfit to be the ruler of a free people.

31   Nor have we been wanting in attentions to our British brethren. We have warned them from time to time of attempts by their legislature to extend an unwarrantable jurisdiction over us. We have reminded them of the circumstances of our emigration and settlement here. We have appealed to their native justice and magnanimity, and we have conjured them by the ties of our common kindred to disavow these usurpations, which would inevitably interrupt our connections and correspondence. They too have been deaf to the voice of justice and of consanguinity. We must, therefore, acquiesce in the necessity, which denounces our separation, and hold them, as we hold the rest of mankind, enemies in war, in peace, friends.

Ethos:
To build credibility Jefferson makes a case that the colonists' frustration with the British government is justified. He argues that the colonists have tried the peaceful approach only to be rebuffed.

32   We, therefore, the representatives of the United States of America, in general congress, assembled, appealing to the Supreme Judge of the world for the rectitude of our intentions, do, in the name, and by authority of the good people of these colonies, solemnly publish and declare, that these united colonies are, and of right ought to be free and independent states; that they are absolved from all allegiance to the British crown, and that all political connection between them and the state of Great Britain, is and ought to be totally dissolved; and that as free and independent states, they have full power to levy war, conclude peace, contract alliances, establish commerce, and to do all other acts and things which independent states may of right do. And for the support of this declaration, with a firm reliance on the protection of Divine Providence, we mutually pledge to each other our lives, our fortunes and our sacred honor.

Conclusion: The proposal is that the colonies no longer have any political connection to Great Britain and possess all the rights of an independent country.

Building the Interstate Highway System
Richard Nixon

In July 1954, President Dwight Eisenhower was scheduled to deliver a speech to the annual conference of United States Governors held at Lake George, New York, but was called away by a death in the family. Vice President Richard Nixon filled in for the president and, speaking from Eisenhower's notes, unveiled a startling plan: the federal government proposed to dedicate $50 billion—an enormous sum in 1954 ($3.65 trillion in today's dollars)—to create a system of interstate highways connecting the country from coast to coast, and from border to border. The proposal was electrifying news, and it led directly to the creation of the Interstate Highway System we use today.

Return to these questions after you have finished reading.

Analyzing the Reading

1. What evidence does the vice president present that the state of America's highways is indeed a problem? What are the specific problems this plan is intended to solve?

2. Traffic in many locations today is more congested than it was when Nixon delivered his speech in 1954. Some politicians today argue for building more roads. How are arguments for more roads today similar to and different from Nixon's arguments?

3. Nixon's speech was covered in the media for the general public, whose approval was needed in order for the proposal to pass through Congress into law. But the immediate audience for the speech consisted of forty-eight state governors. What gestures do you see in this speech that show the vice president and president wanted to appeal to them specifically and that they understood the governors' unique concerns?

4. Vice President Nixon delivered this speech on President Eisenhower's behalf, using Eisenhower's notes. Therefore, the occasion required Nixon both to present the president's ideas as worthy and to present himself as a credible substitute. How does he try to accomplish these goals? Is he effective? Why or why not?

Exploring Ideas and Issues

President Eisenhower's support for an interstate highway system was successful, and in 1956, he signed the Federal-Aid Highway Act. Although the idea of an interstate system was not new, the federal contribution to funding, which ultimately amounted to 90% of construction costs, helped make the idea a reality.

1. The Interstate Highway System can be see as an investment in the country's future. What kinds of investments do families and individuals make in their future? Write a short essay proposing a family "investment"—for example, sending a child to college. Give at least two reasons that such an investment would be valuable. Explain how you would finance the activity.

2. The Interstate Highway System addressed some issues, but it also created some problems. Identify one problem that the current system of highways has created or failed to address. Write an essay in which you propose a solution for this problem. If your solution involves expenditures, describe how you would finance it.

3. In his speech, Vice President Nixon identifies a number of transportation problems that he says will be solved by the construction of an interstate highway system. What transportation problems do you see in your own community that could be solved by government action? Write a short proposal, addressed to your local government, suggesting a specific course of action.

Building the Interstate Highway System

A Cabinet committee has just been established by the President to explore and to help formulate a comprehensive transportation policy for the Nation, taking into account the vital interests of carriers, shippers, the States and communities, the public at large. But more specifically, our highway net is inadequate locally, and obsolete as a national system.

To start to meet this problem at this session of the Congress, we have increased by approximately 500 million dollars the Federal monies available to the States for road development. This seems like a very substantial sum. But the experts say that 5 billion dollars a year for ten years, in addition to all current, normal expenditures, will pay off in economic growth; and when we have spent 50 billion dollars in the next ten years, we shall only have made a good start on the highways the country will need for a population of 200 million people.

A 50 billion dollar highway program in ten years is a goal toward which we can—and we should—look.

Now, let us look at the highway net of the United States as it is. What is wrong with it? It is obsolete because in large part it just happened. It was governed in the beginning by terrain, existing Indian trails, cattle trails, arbitrary section lines. It was designed largely for local movement at low speeds of one or two horsepower. It has been adjusted, it is true, at intervals to meet metropolitan traffic gluts, transcontinental movement, and increased horsepower. But it has never been completely overhauled or planned to satisfy the needs ten years ahead.

At this point in his notes, the President had a personal anecdote illustrating the problem. Thirty-five years ago this month, the Secretary of War initiated a transcontinental truck convoy to prove that the gas engine had displaced the mule, even on our relatively primitive roads. A Second Lieutenant named Dwight Eisenhower went along as an observer. All-weather roads in the United States at that time totaled 300,000 miles. The autos and trucks numbered 7.6 million. That truck convoy left Washington July the 7th. It arrived in San Francisco on September the 5th, sixty days and 6000 breakdowns later.

Today, all-weather mileage is approximately 1.8 million as compared with 300,000 miles. But autos and trucks number more than 56 million, as compared with 7.6 million.

It is obvious, then, that the increase in mileage has lagged behind the increase in vehicles. The road system, moreover, is fundamentally the same, either haphazard or completely arbitrary in its origin, designed for local movement, in an age of transcontinental travel.

Now, what are the penalties of this obsolete net which we have today? Our first most apparent [is] an annual death toll comparable to the casualties of a bloody war, beyond calculation in dollar terms. It approaches 40,000 killed and exceeds 1.3 million injured annually.

And second, the annual wastage of billions of hours in detours, traffic jams, and so on, measurable by any traffic engineer and amounting to billions of dollars in productive time.

Third, all the civil suits that clog up our courts. It has been estimated that more than half have their origins on highways, roads and streets.

Nullification of efficiency in the production of goods by inefficiency in the transport of goods is another result of this obsolete net that we have today.

And finally, the appalling inadequacies to meet the demands of catastrophe or defense, should an atomic war come.

These penalties warrant the expenditures of billions to correct them.

Now, let us look at the highway net as it should be. The President believes that the requirements are these: a grand plan for a properly articulated system that solves the problems of speedy, safe, transcontinental travel; intercity communication; access highways;

and farm-to-market movement; metropolitan area congestion; bottlenecks; and parking.

Second, a financing proposal based on self-liquidation of each project, wherever that is possible, through tolls or the assured increase in gas tax revenue, and on Federal help where the national interest demands it.

And third, and I would emphasize this, particularly at this Conference, because I know how deeply the President believes in this principle: a cooperative alliance between the Federal government and the states so that local government and the most efficient sort of government in the administration of funds, will be the manager of its own area.

And the fourth, very probably, a program initiated by the Federal government, with State cooperation, for the planning and construction of a modern State highway system, with the Federal government functions, for example, being to advance funds or guarantee the obligations of localities or States which undertake to construct new, or modernize existing highways.

And then I would like to read to you the last sentence from the President's notes, exactly as it appears in them, because it is an exhortation to the members of this Conference: "I hope that you will study the matter, and recommend to me the cooperative action you think the Federal government and the 48 States should take to meet these requirements, so that I can submit positive proposals to the next session of the Congress."

And I know that in making this request to the Governors Conference, that the President believes it is essential that we have cooperation in this field. He believes that only with cooperation, and with the maximum of State and local initiative and control can we make a program which will deal with the problem and deal with it effectively.

A Nation of Jailers

Glenn Loury

Glenn C. Loury, a prominent African American intellectual, holds the posts of Merton P. Stoltz Professor of the Social Sciences and Professor of Economics at Brown University. His areas of study include game theory, industrial organization, welfare economics, natural resource economics, and the economics of income distribution. He has also written and spoken extensively on racial issues, with his most recent book being *Ethnicity, Social Mobility, and Public Policy: Comparing the US and the UK* (2005). The following essay appeared in the March 11, 2009, issue of *Cato Unbound*, an online forum of The Cato Institute, which is a public policy think tank "dedicated to the principles of individual liberty, limited government, free markets and peace."

Return to these questions after you have finished reading.

Analyzing the Reading

1. Loury states his thesis at the beginning of the essay, calling it "a preeminent moral challenge for our time." Restate his thesis in your own words.

2. The essay offers statistical evidence for the "truly historic expansion" of the penal system in the United States. What is that evidence? How effectively does it support Loury's thesis?

3. What does Loury say is the current purpose of the penal system? What role does rehabilitation play?

4. Loury talks about a "them" versus "us" mentality. How, in his view, is this responsible for the state of the penal system? What does he say about individual responsibility and societal responsibility? What does he claim are the causes for what he calls the "racially disparate incidence of punishment" in our society?

Exploring Ideas and Issues

One argument against capital punishment is that blacks convicted of essentially the same crime as whites are disproportionately likely to receive the death penalty. Moreover, recently DNA evidence has actually exonerated individuals on death row. Consequently, some observers believe that in the past innocent people, including perhaps a disproportionate number of African Americans, are likely to have been convicted and executed in our legal system.

1. In your view, what should the purposes of incarceration be? List at least three purposes and rank them in order of their value to society, prisoners, prisoners' families, and victims and their families. Write a short essay in which you give reasons for how you prioritized these goals. Remember to include examples to support your choices.

2. According to the author, society has collectively created the conditions that keep African Americans isolated and marginalized. He argues that society bears some responsibility for the actions of African Americans who suffer from those conditions. Do you agree with Loury's assessment of societal versus individual responsibility? Why or why not? Write an essay arguing your view. Give at least two reasons for your thesis and support each reason with personal or researched examples.

3. Stressing statistics about high school dropouts, the article implies a strong connection between lack of education and incarceration: "Inmates in state institutions average fewer than eleven years of schooling." Do some research on the relationship between education and incarceration for a range of races and ethnicities (African Americans, Hispanics, Asians, Native Americans, and whites). How do the rates compare for high school, two-year college, four-year college, and graduate school? Write an essay about your findings. What conclusions can you draw?

A Nation of Jailers

The most challenging problems of social policy in the modern world are never merely technical. In order properly to decide how we should govern ourselves, we must take up questions of social ethics and human values. What manner of people are we Americans? What vision would we affirm, and what example would we set, before the rest of the world? What kind of society would we bequeath to our children? How shall we live? Inevitably, queries such as these lurk just beneath the surface of the great policy debates of the day. So, those who would enter into public argument about what ails our common life need make no apology for speaking in such terms.

It is precisely in these terms that I wish to discuss a preeminent moral challenge for our time—that imprisonment on a massive scale has become one of the central aspects of our nation's social policy toward the poor, powerfully impairing the lives of some of the most marginal of our fellow citizens, especially the poorly educated black and Hispanic men who reside in large numbers in our great urban centers.

The bare facts of this matter—concerning both the scale of incarceration and its racial disparity—have been much remarked upon of late. Simply put, we have become a nation of jailers and, arguably, racist jailers at that. The past four decades have witnessed a truly historic expansion, and transformation, of penal institutions in the United States—at every level of government, and in all regions of the country. We have, by any measure, become a vastly more punitive society. Measured in constant dollars and taking account of all levels of government, spending on corrections and law enforcement in the United States has more than quadrupled over the last quarter century. As a result, the American prison system has grown into a leviathan unmatched in human history. This development should be deeply troubling to anyone who professes to love liberty.

Here, as in other areas of social policy, the United States is a stark international outlier, sitting at the most rightward end of the political spectrum: We imprison at a far higher rate than the other industrial democracies—higher, indeed, than either Russia or China, and vastly higher than any of the countries of Western Europe. According to the International Centre for Prison Studies in London, there were in 2005 some 9 million prisoners in the world; more than 2 million were being held in the United States. With approximately one twentieth of the world's population, America had nearly one fourth of the world's inmates. At more than 700 per 100,000 residents, the U.S. incarceration rate was far greater than our nearest competitors (the Bahamas,

Belarus, and Russia, which each have a rate of about 500 per 100,000). Other industrial societies, some of them with big crime problems of their own, were less punitive than we by an order of magnitude: the United States incarcerated at 6.2 times the rate of Canada, 7.8 times the rate of France, and 12.3 times the rate of Japan.

The demographic profile of the inmate population has also been much discussed. In this, too, the U.S. is an international outlier. African Americans and Hispanics, who taken together are about one fourth of the population, account for about two thirds of state prison inmates. Roughly one third of state prisoners were locked up for committing violent offenses, with the remainder being property and drug offenders. Nine in ten are male, and most are impoverished. Inmates in state institutions average fewer than eleven years of schooling.

The extent of racial disparity in imprisonment rates exceeds that to be found in any other arena of American social life: at eight to one, the black to white ratio of male incarceration rates dwarfs the two to one ratio of unemployment rates, the three to one non-marital child bearing ratio, the two to one ratio of infant mortality rates and the one to five ratio of net worth. More black male high school dropouts are in prison than belong to unions or are enrolled in any state or federal social welfare programs. The brute fact of the matter is that the primary contact between black American young adult men and their government is via the police and the penal apparatus. Coercion is the most salient feature of their encounters with the state. According to estimates compiled by sociologist Bruce Western, nearly 60% of black male dropouts born between 1965 and 1969 had spent at least one year in prison before reaching the age of 35.

For these men, and the families and communities with which they are associated, the adverse effects of incarceration will extend beyond their stays behind bars. My point is that this is not merely law enforcement policy. It is social policy writ large. And no other country in the world does it quite like we do.

This is far more than a technical issue—entailing more, that is, than the task of finding the most efficient crime control policies. Consider, for instance, that it is not possible to conduct a cost-benefit analysis of our nation's world-historic prison buildup over the past 35 years without implicitly specifying how the costs imposed on the persons imprisoned, and their families, are to be reckoned. Of course, this has not stopped analysts from pronouncing on the purported net benefits to "society" of greater incarceration without addressing that question! Still, how—or, indeed, whether—to weigh the costs born by law-breakers—that is, how (or whether) to acknowledge their humanity—remains a fundamental and difficult question of social ethics. Political discourses in the United States have given insufficient weight to the collateral damage imposed by punishment policies on the offenders themselves, and on those who are knitted together with offenders in networks of social and psychic affiliation.

Whether or not one agrees, two things should be clear: social scientists can have no answers for the question of what weight to put on a "thug's," or his family's, well-being; and a morally defensible public policy to deal with criminal offenders cannot be promulgated without addressing that question. To know whether or not our criminal justice policies comport with our deepest values, we must ask how much additional cost borne by the offending class is justifiable per marginal unit of security, or of peace of mind, for the rest of us. This question is barely being asked, let alone answered, in the contemporary debate.

Nor is it merely the scope of the mass imprisonment state that has expanded so impressively in the United States. The ideas underlying the doing of criminal justice—the superstructure of justifications and rationalizations—have also undergone a sea change. Rehabilitation is a dead letter; retribution is the thing. The function of imprisonment is not to reform or redirect offenders. Rather, it is to keep them away from us. "The prison," writes sociologist David Garland, "is used today as a kind of reservation, a quarantine zone in which purportedly dangerous individuals are segregated in the name of public safety." We have elaborated what are, in effect, a "string of work camps and prisons strung across a vast country housing millions of people drawn mainly from classes and racial groups that are seen as politically and economically problematic." We have, in other words, marched quite a long way down the punitive road, in the name of securing public safety and meting out to criminals their just deserts.

And we should be ashamed of ourselves for having done so. Consider a striking feature of this policy development, one that is crucial to this moral assessment: the ways in which we now deal with criminal offenders in the United States have evolved in recent decades in order to serve expressive and not only instrumental ends. We have wanted to "send a message," and have done so with a vengeance. Yet in the process we have also, in effect, provided an answer for the question: who is to blame for the maladies that beset our troubled civilization? That is, we have constructed a narrative, created scapegoats, assuaged our fears, and indulged our need to feel virtuous about ourselves. We have met the enemy and the enemy, in the now familiar caricature, is them—a bunch of anomic, menacing, morally deviant "thugs." In the midst of this dramaturgy—unavoidably so in America—lurks a potent racial subplot.

This issue is personal for me. As a black American male, a baby-boomer born and raised on Chicago's South Side, I can identify with the plight of the urban poor because I have lived among them. I am related to them by the bonds of social and psychic affiliation. As it happens, I have myself passed through the courtroom, and the jailhouse, on my way along life's journey. I have sat in the visitor's room at a state prison; I have known, personally and intimately, men and women who lived their entire lives with one foot to either side of the law. Whenever I step to a lectern to speak about the growth of imprisonment in our society, I envision voiceless and despairing people who would have me speak on their behalf. Of course, personal biography can carry no authority to compel agreement about public policy. Still, I prefer candor to the false pretense of clinical detachment and scientific objectivity. I am not running for high office; I need not pretend to a cool neutrality that I do not possess. While I recognize that these revelations will discredit me in some quarters, this is a fate I can live with.

So, my racial identity is not irrelevant to my discussion of the subject at hand. But, then, neither is it irrelevant that among the millions now in custody and under state supervision are to be found a vastly disproportionate number of the black and the brown. There is no need to justify injecting race into this discourse, for prisons are the most race-conscious public institutions that we have. No big city police officer is "colorblind" nor, arguably, can any afford to be. Crime and punishment in America have a color—just turn on a television, or open a magazine, or listen carefully to the rhetoric of a political campaign—and you will see what I mean. The fact is that, in this society as in any other, order is maintained by the threat and the use of force. We enjoy our good lives because we are shielded by the forces of law and order upon which we rely to keep the unruly at bay. Yet, in this society to an extent unlike virtually any other, those bearing the heavy burden of order-enforcement belong, in numbers far exceeding their presence in the population at large, to racially defined and historically marginalized groups. Why should this be so? And how can those charged with the supervision of our penal apparatus sleep well at night knowing that it is so?

This punitive turn in the nation's social policy is intimately connected, I would maintain, with public rhetoric about responsibility, dependency, social hygiene, and the reclamation of public order. And such rhetoric, in turn, can be fully grasped only when viewed against the backdrop of America's often ugly and violent racial history: There is a reason why our inclination toward forgiveness and the extension of a second chance to those who have violated our behavioral strictures is so stunted, and why our mainstream political discourses are so bereft of self-examination and searching social criticism. An historical resonance between the stigma of race and the stigma of prison has served to keep alive in our public culture the subordinating social meanings that have always been associated with blackness. Many historians and political scientists—though, of course, not all—agree that the shifting character of race relations over the course of the nineteenth and twentieth centuries helps to explain why the United States is exceptional among democratic industrial societies in the severity of its punitive policy and the paucity of its social-welfare institutions. Put directly and without benefit of euphemism, the racially disparate incidence of punishment in the United States is a morally troubling residual effect of the nation's history of enslavement, disenfranchisement, segregation, and discrimination. It is not merely the accidental accretion of neutral state action, applied to a racially divergent social flux. It is an abhorrent expression of who we Americans are as a people, even now, at the dawn of the twenty-first century.

My recitation of the brutal facts about punishment in today's America may sound to some like a primal scream at this monstrous social machine that is grinding poor black communities to dust. And I confess that these facts do at times leave me inclined to cry out in despair. But my argument is intended to be moral, not existential, and its principal thesis is this: we law-abiding, middle-class Americans have made collective decisions on social and incarceration policy questions, and we benefit from those decisions. That is, we benefit from a system of suffering, rooted in state violence, meted out at our behest. Put differently our society—the society we together have made—first tolerates crime-promoting conditions in our sprawling urban ghettos, and then goes on to act out rituals of punishment against them as some awful form of human sacrifice.

It is a central reality of our time that a wide racial gap has opened up in cognitive skills, the extent of law-abidingness, stability of family relations, and attachment to the work force. This is the basis, many would hold, for the racial gap in imprisonment. Yet I maintain that this gap in human development is, as a historical matter, rooted in political, economic, social, and cultural factors peculiar to this society and reflective of its unlovely racial history. That is to say, it is a societal, not communal or personal, achievement. At the level of the individual case we must, of course, act as if this were not so. There could be no law, and so no civilization, absent the imputation to persons of responsibility for their wrongful acts. But the sum of a million cases, each one rightly judged fairly on its individual merits, may nevertheless constitute a great historic wrong. This is, in my view, now the case in regards to the race and social class disparities that characterize the very punitive policy that we have directed at lawbreakers. And yet, the state does not only deal with individual cases. It also makes policies in the aggregate, and the consequences of these policies are more or less knowable. It is in the making of such aggregate policy judgments that questions of social responsibility arise.

This situation raises a moral problem that we cannot avoid. We cannot pretend that there are more important problems in our society, or that this circumstance is the necessary solution to other, more pressing problems—unless we are also prepared to say that we have turned our backs on the ideal of equality for all citizens and abandoned the principles of justice. We ought to be asking ourselves two questions: Just what manner of people are we Americans? And in light of this, what are our obligations to our fellow citizens—even those who break our laws?

Without trying to make a full-fledged philosophical argument here, I nevertheless wish to gesture—in the spirit of the philosopher John Rawls—toward some answers to these questions. I will not set forth a policy manifesto at this time. What I aim to do is suggest, in a general way, how we ought to be thinking differently about this problem. Specifically, given our nation's history and political culture, I think that there are severe limits to the applicability in this circumstance of a pure ethic of personal responsibility, as the basis for distributing the negative good of punishment in contemporary America. I urge that we shift the boundary toward greater acknowledgment of social responsibility in our punishment policy discourse—even for wrongful acts freely chosen by individual persons. In suggesting this, I am not so much making a "root causes" argument—he did the crime, but only because he had no choice—as I am arguing that the society at large is implicated in his choices because we have acquiesced in structural arrangements which work to our benefit and his detriment, and yet which shape his consciousness and sense of identity in such a way that the choices he makes. We condemn those choices, but they are nevertheless compelling to him. I am interested in the moral implications of what the sociologist Loïc Wacquant has called the "double-sided production of urban marginality." I approach this problem of moral judgment by emphasizing that closed and bounded social structures—like racially homogeneous urban ghettos—create contexts where "pathological" and "dysfunctional" cultural forms emerge, but these forms are not intrinsic to the people caught in these structures. Neither are they independent of the behavior of the people who stand outside of them.

Several years ago, I took time to read some of the nonfiction writings of the great nineteenth century Russian novelist Leo Tolstoy. Toward the end of his life he had become an eccentric pacifist and radical Christian social critic. I was stunned at the force of his arguments. What struck me most was Tolstoy's provocative claim that the core of Christianity lies in Jesus' Sermon on the Mount: You see that fellow over there committing some terrible sin? Well, if you have ever lusted, or allowed jealousy, or envy or hatred to enter your own heart, then you are to be equally condemned! This, Tolstoy claims, is the central teaching of the Christian faith: we're all in the same fix.

Now, without invoking any religious authority, I nevertheless want to suggest that there is a grain of truth in this religious sentiment that is relevant to the problem at hand: That is, while the behavioral pathologies and cultural threats that we see in society— the moral erosions "out there"—the crime, drug addiction, sexually transmitted disease, idleness, violence and all manner of deviance—while these are worrisome, nevertheless, our moral crusade against these evils can take on a pathological dimension of its own. We can become self-righteous, legalistic, ungenerous, stiff-necked, and hypocritical. We can fail to see the beam in our own eye. We can neglect to raise questions of social justice. We can blind ourselves to the close relationship that actually exists between, on the one hand, behavioral pathology in the so-called urban underclass of our country and, on the other hand, society-wide factors—like our greed-driven economy, our worship of the self, our endemic culture of materialism, our vacuous political discourses, our declining civic engagement, and our aversion to sacrificing private gain on behalf of much needed social investments. We can fail to see, in other words, that the problems of the so-called underclass—to which we have reacted with a massive, coercive mobilization—are but an expression, at the bottom of the social hierarchy, of a more profound and widespread moral deviance—one involving all of us.

Taking this position does not make me a moral relativist. I merely hold that, when thinking about the lives of the disadvantaged in our society, the fundamental premise that should guide us is that we are all in this together. Those people languishing in the corners of our society are our people—they are us—whatever may be their race, creed, or country of origin, whether they be the crack-addicted, the HIV-infected, the mentally ill homeless, the juvenile drug sellers, or worse. Whatever the malady, and whatever the offense, we're all in the same fix. We're all in this thing together.

Just look at what we have wrought. We Americans have established what, to many an outside observer, looks like a system of racial caste in the center of our great cities. I refer here to millions of stigmatized, feared, and invisible people. The extent of disparity in the opportunity to achieve their full human potential, as between the children of the middle class and the children of the disadvantaged—a disparity that one takes for granted in America—is virtually unrivaled elsewhere in the industrial, advanced, civilized, free world.

Yet too many Americans have concluded, in effect, that those languishing at the margins of our society are simply reaping what they have sown. Their suffering is seen as having nothing to do with us—as not being evidence of systemic failures that can be corrected through collective action. Thus, as I noted, we have given up on the ideal of rehabilitating criminals, and have settled for simply warehousing them. Thus we accept—despite much rhetoric to the contrary—that it is virtually impossible effectively to educate the children of the poor. Despite the best efforts of good people and progressive institutions—despite the encouraging signs of moral engagement with these issues that I have seen in my students over the years, and that give me hope—despite these things, it remains the case that, speaking of the country as a whole, there is no broadly based demand for reform, no sense of moral outrage, no anguished self-criticism, no public reflection in the face of this massive, collective failure.

The core of the problem is that the socially marginal are not seen as belonging to the same general public body as the rest of us. It therefore becomes impossible to do just about anything with them. At least implicitly, our political community acts as though some are different from the rest and, because of their culture—because of their bad values, their self-destructive behavior, their malfeasance, their criminality, their lack of responsibility, their unwillingness to engage in hard work—they deserve their fate.

But this is quite wrongheaded. What we Americans fail to recognize—not merely as individuals, I stress, but as a political community—is that these ghetto enclaves and marginal spaces of our cities, which are the source of most prison inmates, are products of our own making: Precisely because we do not want those people near us, we have structured the space in our urban environment so as to keep them away from us. Then, when they fester in their isolation and their marginality, we hypocritically point a finger, saying in effect: "Look at those people. They threaten the civilized body. They must therefore be expelled, imprisoned, controlled." It is not we who must take social responsibility to reform our institutions but, rather, it is they who need to take personal responsibility for their wrongful acts. It is not we who must set our collective affairs aright, but they who must get their individual acts together. This posture, I suggest, is inconsistent with the attainment of a just distribution of benefits and burdens in society.

Civic inclusion has been the historical imperative in Western political life for 150 years. And yet—despite our self-declared status as a light unto the nations, as a beacon of hope to freedom-loving peoples everywhere—despite these lofty proclamations, which were belied by images from the rooftops in flooded New Orleans in September 2005, and are contradicted by our overcrowded prisons—the fact is that this historical project of civic inclusion is woefully incomplete in these United States.

At every step of the way, reactionary political forces have declared the futility of pursuing civic inclusion. Yet, in every instance, these forces have been proven wrong. At one time or another, they have derided the inclusion of women, landless peasants, former serfs and slaves, or immigrants more fully in the civic body. Extending to them the franchise, educating their children, providing health and social welfare to them has always been controversial. But this has been the direction in which the self-declared "civilized" and wealthy nations have been steadily moving since Bismarck, since the revolutions of 1848 and 1870, since the American Civil War with its Reconstruction Amendments, since the Progressive Era and through the New Deal on to the Great Society. This is why we have a progressive federal income tax and an estate tax in this country, why we feed, clothe and house the needy, why we (used to) worry about investing in our cities' infrastructure, and in the human capital of our people. What the brutal facts about punishment in today's America show is that this American project of civic inclusion remains incomplete. Nowhere is that incompleteness more evident than in the prisons and jails of America. And this as yet unfulfilled promise of American democracy reveals a yawning chasm between an ugly and uniquely American reality, and our nation's exalted image of herself.

Bound to Burn

Peter Huber

Peter Huber is a lawyer, an author, and senior fellow at the Manhattan Institute, a conservative "think tank." He is the author of many books, including *Hard Green: Saving the Environment from the Environmentalists* (2000), and *The Bottomless Well* (2010), coauthored with Mark Mills. Huber has also published articles in scholarly journals and magazines such as the *Harvard Law Review, Science, The Wall Street Journal, Reason*, and *National Review*. He has appeared on numerous television and radio programs, including *Face the Nation* and *The NewsHour with Jim Lehrer*.

Return to these questions after you have finished reading.

Analyzing the Reading

1. What is an "indulgence" (paragraph 1)? How does it connect to our need for forgiveness of "carbon sins"?

2. According to Huber, why is it impossible for the "rich" West to stop the carbon emissions coming from the world's five billion poor? Does he seem to think there is nothing we can do to stop global warming from carbon emissions?

3. Why are carbon-based fuels so much cheaper and easier to use than greener alternatives? What does the expense of green energy mean in our global effort to reduce carbon emissions?

4. What is Huber's view of "green" advocates and of the people who control most of the world's carbon-based fuels? Identify passages and words he uses that reveal his viewpoint.

Exploring Ideas and Issues

Huber makes several references to the Kyoto Protocol. The Kyoto Protocol, initially adopted in December 1997, is an international agreement linked to the United Nations Framework Convention on Climate Change. The major feature of the Kyoto Protocol is that it sets binding targets for industrialized countries and the European community for reducing greenhouse gas emissions. By 2010, 191 countries signed and ratified the protocol. Read more about the Kyoto Protocol at http://unfccc.int/kyoto_protocol/items/2830.php.

1. The United States is one of the few Western countries that did not ratify the treaty. After reading more about the Kyoto Protocol, write a short essay expression you own view on why the United States should or should not ratify it. You may wish to reference points Huber makes in his essay in your response.

2. In this essay, Huber notes that the Kyoto protocol has "hurt the anti-carbon mission far more than carbon zealots seem to grasp." How effective has the protocol been on reducing carbon emissions? Explain.

3. Huber observes that the United States was right to "steer clear" of unenforceable treaties like the Kyoto Protocol. Why is it unenforceable? Based on Huber's essay and what you research about the treaty, write an essay about the future of this treaty.

Bound to Burn

Humanity will keep spewing carbon into the atmosphere, but good policy can help sink it back into the earth.

Spring 2009

Like medieval priests, today's carbon brokers will sell you an indulgence that forgives your carbon sins. It will run you about $500 for 5 tons of forgiveness—about how much the typical American needs every year. Or about $2,000 a year for a typical four-person household. Your broker will spend the money on such things as reducing methane emissions from hog farms in Brazil.

But if you really want to make a difference, you must send a check large enough to forgive the carbon emitted by four poor Brazilian households, too—because they're not going to do it themselves. To cover all five households, then, send $4,000. And you probably forgot to send in a check last year, and you might forget again in the future, so you'd best make it an even $40,000, to take care of a decade right now. If you decline to write your own check while insisting that to save the world we must ditch the carbon, you are just burdening your already sooty soul with another ton of self-righteous hypocrisy. And you can't possibly afford what it will cost to forgive that.

If making carbon this personal seems rude, then think globally instead. During the presidential race, Barack Obama was heard to remark that he would bankrupt the coal industry. No one can doubt Washington's power to bankrupt almost anything—in the United States. But China is adding 100 gigawatts of coal-fired electrical capacity a year. That's another whole United States' worth of coal consumption added every three years, with no stopping point in sight. Much of the rest of the developing world is on a similar path.

Cut to the chase. We rich people can't stop the world's 5 billion poor people from burning the couple of trillion tons of cheap carbon that they have within easy reach. We can't even make any durable dent in global emissions—because emissions from the developing world are growing too fast, because the other 80 percent of humanity desperately needs cheap energy, and because we and they are now part of the same global economy. What we can do, if we're foolish enough, is let carbon worries send our jobs and industries to their shores, making them grow even faster, and their carbon emissions faster still.

We don't control the global supply of carbon.

Ten countries ruled by nasty people control 80 percent of the planet's oil reserves—about 1 trillion barrels, currently worth about $40 trillion. If $40 trillion worth of gold were located where most of the oil is, one could only scoff at any suggestion that we might somehow persuade the nasty people to leave the wealth buried. They can lift most of their oil at a cost well under $10 a barrel. They will drill. They will pump. And they will find buyers. Oil is all they've got.

Poor countries all around the planet are sitting on a second, even bigger source of carbon—almost a trillion tons of cheap, easily accessible coal. They also control most of the planet's third great carbon reservoir—the rain forests and soil. They will keep squeezing the carbon out of cheap coal, and cheap forest, and cheap soil, because that's all they've got. Unless they can find something even cheaper. But they won't—not any time in the foreseeable future.

We no longer control the demand for carbon, either. The 5 billion poor—the other 80 percent—are already the main problem, not us. Collectively, they emit 20 percent more greenhouse gas than we do. We burn a lot more carbon individually, but they have a lot more children. Their fecundity has eclipsed our gluttony, and the gap is now widening fast. China, not the United States, is now the planet's largest emitter. Brazil, India, Indonesia, South Africa, and others are in hot pursuit. And these countries have all made it clear that they aren't interested in spending what money they have on low-carb diets. It is idle to argue, as some have done, that global warming can be solved—decades hence—at a cost of 1 to 2 percent of the global economy. Eighty percent of the global population hasn't signed on to pay more than 0 percent.

Accepting this last, self-evident fact, the Kyoto Protocol divides the world into two groups. The roughly 1.2 billion citizens of industrialized countries are expected to reduce their emissions. The other 5 billion—including both China and India, each of which is about as populous as the entire Organisation for Economic Co-operation and Development—aren't. These numbers alone guarantee that humanity isn't going to reduce global emissions at any point in the foreseeable future—unless it does it the old-fashioned way, by getting poorer. But the current recession won't last forever, and the long-term trend is clear. Their populations and per-capita emissions are rising far faster than ours could fall under any remotely plausible carbon-reduction scheme.

Might we simply buy their cooperation? Various plans have circulated for having the rich pay the poor to stop burning down rain forests and to lower greenhouse-gas emissions from primitive agricultural practices. But taking control of what belongs to someone else ultimately means buying it. Over the long term, we would in effect have to buy up a large fraction of all the world's forests, soil, coal, and oil—and then post guards to make sure that poor people didn't sneak in and grab all the carbon anyway. Buying off people just doesn't fly when they outnumber you four to one.

Might we instead manage to give the world something cheaper than carbon? The moon-shot law of economics says yes, of course we can. If we just put our minds to it, it will happen. Atom bomb, moon landing, ultracheap energy—all it takes is a triumph of political will.

Really? For the very poorest, this would mean beating the price of the free rain forest that they burn down to clear land to plant a subsistence crop. For the slightly less poor, it would mean beating the price of coal used to generate electricity at under 3 cents per kilowatt-hour.

And with one important exception, which we will return to shortly, no carbon-free fuel or technology comes remotely close to being able to do that. Fossil fuels are extremely cheap because geological forces happen to have created large deposits of these dense forms of energy in accessible places. Find a mountain of coal, and you can just shovel gargantuan amounts of energy into the boxcars.

Shoveling wind and sun is much, much harder. Windmills are now 50-story skyscrapers. Yet one windmill generates a piddling 2 to 3 megawatts. A jumbo jet needs 100 megawatts to get off the ground; Google is building 100-megawatt server farms. Meeting New York City's total energy demand would require 13,000 of those skyscrapers spinning at top speed, which would require scattering about 50,000 of them across the state, to make sure that you always hit enough windy spots. To answer the howls of green protest that inevitably greet realistic engineering estimates like these, note that real-world systems must be able to meet peak, not average, demand; that reserve margins are essential; and that converting electric power into liquid or gaseous fuels to power the existing transportation and heating systems would entail substantial losses. What was Mayor Bloomberg thinking when he suggested that he might just tuck windmills into Manhattan? Such thoughts betray a deep ignorance about how difficult it is to get a lot of energy out of sources as thin and dilute as wind and sun.

It's often suggested that technology improvements and mass production will sharply lower the cost of wind and solar. But engineers have pursued these technologies for decades, and while costs of some components have fallen, there is no serious prospect of costs plummeting and performance soaring as they have in our laptops and cell phones. When you replace conventional with renewable energy, everything gets bigger, not smaller—and bigger costs more, not less. Even if solar cells themselves were free, solar power would remain very expensive because of the huge structures and support systems required to extract large amounts of electricity from a source so weak that it takes hours to deliver a tan.

This is why the (few) greens ready to accept engineering and economic reality have suddenly emerged as avid proponents of nuclear power. In the aftermath of the Three Mile Island accident—which didn't harm anyone, and wouldn't even have damaged the reactor core if the operators had simply kept their hands off the switches and let the automatic safety systems do their job—ostensibly green anti-nuclear activists unwittingly boosted U.S. coal consumption by about 400 million tons per year. The United States would be in compliance with the Kyoto Protocol today if we could simply undo their handiwork and conjure back into existence the nuclear plants that were in the pipeline in nuclear power's heyday. Nuclear power is fantastically compact, and—as America's nuclear navy, several commercial U.S. operators, France, Japan, and a handful of other countries have convincingly established—it's both safe and cheap wherever engineers are allowed to get on with it.

But getting on with it briskly is essential, because costs hinge on the huge, up-front capital investment in the power plant. Years of delay between the capital investment and when it starts earning a return are ruinous. Most of the developed world has made nuclear power unaffordable by surrounding it with a regulatory process so sluggish and unpredictable that no one will pour a couple of billion dollars into a new plant, for the good reason that no one knows when (or even if) the investment will be allowed to start making money.

And countries that don't trust nuclear power on their own soil must hesitate to share the technology with countries where you never know who will be in charge next year, or what he might decide to do with his nuclear toys. So much for the possibility that cheap nuclear power might replace carbon-spewing sources of energy in the developing world. Moreover, even India and China, which have mastered nuclear technologies, are deploying far more new coal capacity.

Remember, finally, that most of the cost of carbon-based energy resides not in the fuels but in the gigantic infrastructure of furnaces, turbines, and engines. Those costs are sunk, which means that carbon-free alternatives—with their own huge, attendant, front-end capital costs—must be cheap enough to beat carbon fuels that already have their infrastructure in place. That won't happen in our life-times.

Another argument commonly advanced is that getting over carbon will, nevertheless, be comparatively cheap, because it will get us over oil, too—which will impoverish our enemies and save us a bundle at the Pentagon and the Department of Homeland Security. But uranium aside, the most economical substitute for oil is, in fact, electricity generated with coal. Cheap coal-fired electricity has been, is, and will continue to be a substitute for oil, or a substitute for natural gas, which can in turn substitute for oil. By sharply boosting the cost of coal electricity, the war on carbon will make us more dependent on oil, not less.

The first place where coal displaces oil is in the electric power plant itself. When oil prices spiked in the early 1980s, U.S. utilities quickly switched to other fuels, with coal leading the pack; the coal-fired plants now being built in China, India, and other developing countries are displacing diesel generators. More power plants burning coal to produce cheap electricity can also mean less natural gas used to generate electricity. And less used for industrial, commercial, and residential heating, welding, and chemical processing, as these users switch to electrically powered alternatives. The gas that's freed up this way can then substitute for diesel fuel in heavy trucks, delivery vehicles, and buses. And coal-fired electricity will eventually begin displacing gasoline, too, as soon as plug-in hybrid cars start recharging their batteries directly from the grid.

To top it all, using electricity generated in large part by coal to power our passenger cars would lower carbon emissions—even in Indiana, which generates 75 percent of its electricity with coal. Big power plants are so much more efficient than the gasoline engines in our cars that a plug-in hybrid car running on electricity supplied by Indiana's current grid still ends up more carbon-frugal than comparable cars burning gasoline in a conventional engine under the hood. Old-guard energy types have been saying this for decades. In a major report released last March, the World Wildlife Fund finally concluded that they were right all along.

But true carbon zealots won't settle for modest reductions in carbon emissions when fat targets beckon. They see coal-fired electricity as the dragon to slay first. Huge, stationary sources can't run or hide, and the cost of doing without them doesn't get rung up in plain view at the gas pump. California, Pennsylvania, and other greener-than-thou states have made flatlining electricity consumption the linchpin of their war on carbon. That is the one certain way to halt the displacement of foreign oil by cheap, domestic electricity.

The oil-coal economics come down to this. Per unit of energy delivered, coal costs about one-fifth as much as oil—but contains one-third more carbon. High carbon taxes (or tradable permits, or any other economic equivalent) sharply narrow the price gap between oil and the one fuel that can displace it worldwide, here and now. The oil nasties will celebrate the green war on carbon as enthusiastically as the coal industry celebrated the green war on uranium 30 years ago.

The other 5 billion are too poor to deny these economic realities. For them, the price to beat is 3-cent coal-fired electricity. China and India won't trade 3-cent coal for 15-cent wind or 30-cent solar. As for us, if we embrace those economically frivolous alternatives on our own, we will certainly end up doing more harm than good.

By pouring money into anything-but-carbon fuels, we will lower demand for carbon, making it even cheaper for the rest of the world to buy and burn. The rest will use cheaper energy to accelerate their own economic growth. Jobs will go where energy is cheap, just as they go where labor is cheap. Manufacturing and heavy industry require a great deal of energy, and in a global economy, no competitor can survive while paying substantially more for an essential input. The carbon police acknowledge the problem and talk vaguely of using tariffs and such to address it. But carbon is far too deeply embedded in the global economy, and materials, goods, and services move and intermingle far too freely, for the customs agents to track.

Consider your next Google search. As noted in a recent article in *Harper's*, "Google . . . and its rivals now head abroad for cheaper, often dirtier power."

Google itself (the "don't be evil" company) is looking to set up one of its electrically voracious server farms at a site in Lithuania, "disingenuously described as being near a hydroelectric dam." But Lithuania's grid is 0.5 percent hydroelectric and 78 percent nuclear. Perhaps the company's next huge farm will be "near" the Three Gorges Dam in China, built to generate over three times as much power as our own Grand Coulee Dam in Washington State. China will be happy to play along, while it quietly plugs another coal plant into its grid a few pylons down the line. All the while, of course, Google will maintain its low-energy headquarters in California, a state that often boasts of the wise regulatory policies—centered, one is told, on efficiency and conservation—that have made it such a frugal energy user. But in fact, sky-high prices have played the key role, curbing internal demand and propelling the flight from California of power plants, heavy industries, chip fabs, server farms, and much else.

So the suggestion that we can lift ourselves out of the economic doldrums by spending lavishly on exceptionally expensive new sources of energy is absurd. "Green jobs" means Americans paying other Americans to chase carbon while the rest of the world builds new power plants and factories. And the environmental consequences of outsourcing jobs, industries, and carbon to developing countries are beyond dispute. They use energy far less efficiently than we do, and they remain almost completely oblivious to environmental impacts, just as we were in our own first century of industrialization. A massive transfer of carbon, industry, and jobs from us to them will raise carbon emissions, not lower them.

The grand theory for how the developed world can unilaterally save the planet seems to run like this. We buy time for the planet by rapidly slashing our own emissions. We do so by developing carbon-free alternatives even cheaper than carbon. The rest of the world will then quickly adopt these alternatives, leaving most of its trillion barrels of oil and trillion tons of coal safely buried, most of the rain forests standing, and most of the planet's carbon-rich soil undisturbed. From end to end, however, this vision strains credulity.

Perhaps it's the recognition of that inconvenient truth that has made the anti-carbon rhetoric increasingly apocalyptic. Coal trains have been analogized to box-cars headed for Auschwitz. There is talk of the extinction of all humanity. But then, we have heard such things before. It is indeed quite routine, in environmental discourse, to frame choices as involving potentially infinite costs on the green side of the ledger. If they really are infinite, no reasonable person can quibble about spending mere billions, or even trillions, on the dollar side, to dodge the apocalyptic bullet.

Thirty years ago, the case against nuclear power was framed as the "Zero-Infinity Dilemma." The risks of a meltdown might be vanishingly small, but if it happened, the costs would be infinitely large, so we should forget about uranium. Computer models demonstrated that meltdowns were highly unlikely and that the costs of a meltdown, should one occur, would be manageable—but greens scoffed: huge computer models couldn't be trusted. So we ended up burning much more coal. The software shoe is on the other foot now; the machines that said nukes wouldn't melt now say that the ice caps will. Warming skeptics scoff in turn, and can quite plausibly argue that a planet is harder to model than a nuclear reactor. But that's a detail. From a rhetorical perspective, any claim that the infinite, the apocalypse, or the Almighty supports your side of the argument shuts down all further discussion.

To judge by actions rather than words, however, few people and almost no national governments actually believe in the infinite rewards of exorcising carbon from economic life. Kyoto has hurt the anti-carbon mission far more than carbon zealots seem to grasp. It has proved only that with carbon, governments will say and sign anything—and then do less than nothing. The United States should steer well clear of such treaties because they are unenforceable, routinely ignored, and therefore worthless.

If we're truly worried about carbon, we must instead approach it as if the emissions originated in an annual eruption of Mount Krakatoa. Don't try to persuade the volcano to sign a treaty promising to stop. Focus instead on what might be done to protect and promote the planet's carbon sinks—the systems that suck carbon back out of the air and bury it. Green plants currently pump 15 to 20 times as much carbon out of the atmosphere as humanity releases into it—that's the pump that put all that carbon underground in the first place, millions of years ago. At present, almost all of that plant-captured carbon is released back into the atmosphere within a year or so by animal consumers. North America, however, is currently sinking almost two-thirds of its carbon emissions back into prairies and forests that were originally leveled in the 1800s but are now recovering. For the next 50 years or so, we should focus on promoting better land use and reforestation worldwide. Beyond that, weather and the oceans naturally sink about one-fifth of total fossil-fuel emissions. We should also investigate large-scale options for accelerating the process of ocean sequestration.

Carbon zealots despise carbon-sinking schemes because, they insist, nobody can be sure that the sunk carbon will stay sunk. Yet everything they propose hinges on the assumption that carbon already sunk by nature in what are now hugely valuable deposits of oil and coal can be kept sunk by treaty and imaginary cheaper-than-carbon alternatives. This, yet again, gets things backward. We certainly know how to improve agriculture to protect soil, and how to grow new trees, and how to maintain existing forests, and we can almost certainly learn how to mummify carbon and bury it back in the earth or the depths of the oceans, in ways that neither man nor nature will disturb. It's keeping nature's black gold sequestered from humanity that's impossible.

If we do need to do something serious about carbon, the sequestration of carbon after it's burned is the one approach that accepts the growth of carbon emissions as an inescapable fact of the twenty-first century. And it's the one approach that the rest of the world can embrace, too, here and now, because it begins with improving land use, which can lead directly and quickly to greater prosperity. If, on the other hand, we persist in building green bridges to nowhere, we will make things worse, not better. Good intentions aren't enough. Turned into ineffectual action, they can cost the earth and accelerate its ruin at the same time.

Should Pandas Be Left to Face Extinction?

Chris Packham and Mark Wright

In September 2009, the well-known British naturalist, photographer, and writer Chris Packham created an international furor when during a radio interview he proposed that giant pandas ought to be allowed to go extinct. A fierce advocate for nature and wildlife, he nevertheless contends that "T-shirt animals" like pandas get far too much attention and draw resources from far more critical environmental concerns. On September 23, 2009, the British newspaper The *Guardian* carried a debate between Packham and Mark Wright, a leading scientist for the World Wide Fund for Nature.

Return to these questions after you have finished reading.

Analyzing the Reading

1. Packham argues that we should simply allow pandas to become extinct. List at least three reasons he gives for his point of view.

2. Wright argues that we should do our best not to allow pandas to become extinct. List at least three reasons he gives for his point of view.

3. Both debaters acknowledge points made by the other person. What effect does this strategy have on the reader?

4. To what extent do each person's arguments rely on *logos*, *ethos*, and *pathos*? Explain.

Exploring Ideas and Issues

Conservation of wildlife and wild habitats is a major concern of our time. It has drawn together ecologists and other scientists, as well as hunters, sport fishermen, organic farmers, and recreational users of the natural world, in what can be seen as an unlikely alliance. Yet the issues remain complex and not easily resolved.

1. Whose arguments—Packham's or Wright's—do you find more convincing? Why? Write a short essay explaining your view. Include examples from both debaters.

2. Both debaters concede that the panda attracts attention and sympathy while other animals, such as the river dolphin, do not. How is using attractive animals like pandas and tigers to gain support similar, or not similar, to using celebrities to sell a product? Write a short essay in which you defend or criticize the practice of using animals in this way.

3. Packham says, "I'm not trying to play God; I'm playing God's accountant." Do we have an obligation to save the giant panda and other endangered wildlife at all costs? What is the nature of that obligation? Write a short essay in which you argue yes or no, giving at least three reasons for your point of view.

4. Do some research on conservation issues in the United States. Choose one issue; for example, the forestry and logging practice of clearcutting. Write an essay in which you compare viewpoints of at least two competing interests—commercial, environmentalist, agricultural, and so on. If possible, include a current proposal aimed at reconciling these viewpoints.

SHOULD PANDAS BE LEFT TO FACE EXTINCTION?

Yes, says Chris Packham

I don't want the panda to die out. I want species to stay alive—that's why I get up in the morning. I don't even kill mosquitoes or flies. So if pandas can survive, that would be great. But let's face it: conservation, both nationally and globally, has a limited amount of resources, and I think we're going to have to make some hard, pragmatic choices.

The truth is, pandas are extraordinarily expensive to keep going. We spend millions and millions of pounds on pretty much this one species, and a few others, when we know that the best thing we could do would be to look after the world's biodiversity hotspots with greater

A giant panda, an example of what Chris Packham calls "T-shirt animals"

care. Without habitat, you've got nothing. So maybe if we took all the cash we spend on pandas and just bought rainforest with it, we might be doing a better job.

Of course, it's easier to raise money for something fluffy. Charismatic megafauna like the panda do appeal to people's emotional side, and attract a lot of public attention. They are emblematic of what I would call single-species conservation: i.e., a focus on one animal. This approach began in the 1970s with Save the Tiger, Save the Panda, Save the Whale, and so on, and it is now out of date. I think pandas have had a valuable role in raising the profile of conservation, but perhaps "had" is the right word.

Panda conservationists may stand up and say, "It's a flagship species. We're also conserving Chinese forest, where there is a whole plethora of other things." And when that works, I'm not against it. But we have to accept that some species are stronger than others. The panda is a species of bear that has gone herbivorous, and that eats a type of food that isn't all that nutritious, and that dies out sporadically. It is susceptible to various diseases, and, up until recently, it has been almost impossible to breed in captivity. They've also got a very restricted range, which is ever decreasing, due to encroachment on their habitat by the Chinese population. Perhaps the panda was already destined to run out of time. Extinction is very much a part of life on earth. And we are going to have to get used to it in the next few years because climate change is going to result in all sorts of disappearances. The last large mammal extinction was another animal in China—the Yangtze river dolphin, which looked like a worn-out piece of pink soap with piggy eyes and was never going to make it on to anyone's T-shirt. If that had appeared beautiful to us, then I doubt very much that it would be extinct. But it vanished, because it was pig-ugly and swam around in a river where no one saw it. And now, sadly, it has gone for ever.

I'm not trying to play God; I'm playing God's accountant. I'm saying we won't be able to save it all, so let's do the best we can. And at the moment I don't think our strategies are best placed to do that. We should be focusing our conservation endeavours on biodiversity hotspots, spreading our net more widely and looking at good-quality habitat maintenance in order to preserve as much of the life as we possibly can, using hard science to make educated decisions as to which species are essential to a community's maintenance. It may well be that we can lose the cherries from the cake. But you don't want to lose the substance. Save the Rainforest, or Save the Kalahari: that would be better.

No, says Mark Wright

You are reading this because it is about giant pandas. We could have this argument about the frogs of the rainforest and the issues would be identical, but the ability to get people's attention would be far lower. So in that sense, yes, you could argue that conservationists capitalize on the panda's appeal.

And, to be fair, I can understand where Chris Packham is coming from. Everywhere you look on this planet there are issues to be addressed, and we have finite resources. So we do make really horrible choices. But nowadays, almost exclusively, when people work in conservation they focus on saving habitats.

Chris has talked about pandas being an evolutionary cul-de-sac, and it's certainly unusual for a carnivore to take up herbivory. But there are many, many other species that live in a narrowly defined habitat. When he says that if you leave them be, they will die out, that's simply not true. If we don't destroy their habitat they will just chunter along in the same way that they have for the thousands of years.

And besides, in terms of its biodiversity and the threats it faces, I think that the part of China where pandas live should be on the preservation list anyway. The giant panda shares its habitat with the red panda, golden monkeys, and various birds that are found nowhere else in the world. The giant panda's numbers are increasing in the wild, so I don't see them dying out, and I haven't heard anything to suggest that other biodiversity isn't thriving equally.

It is true, though, that there some cases where preserving an animal is not the best use of resources. If you asked 100 conservationists—even at the World Wide Fund—you would probably get 90 different answers, but look at what happened with the northern white rhino in Africa, which we're pretty sure has died out. We lament its loss. But at the same time it had gotten to the stage where the likelihood of success was at a critically low level. If you were doing a battlefield triage system, the rhino would probably have had to be a casualty.

Otherwise, charismatic megafauna can be extremely useful. Smaller creatures often don't need a big habitat to live in, so in conservation terms it's better to go for something further up the food chain, because then by definition you are protecting a much larger area, which in turn encompasses the smaller animals.

And of course they are an extraordinarily good vehicle for the messages we want to put out on habitat conservation. Look at Borneo, where you instantly think of the orangutans. In the southern oceans, you think of the blue whale. Then there are polar bears in the north. There are things you pull out from the picture because people can relate to them. And it does make a difference.

Connecting the City
San Francisco Bicycle Coalition

The San Francisco Bicycle Coalition (SFBC) is a nonprofit public organization that aims to "transform San Francisco's streets and neighborhoods into more livable and safe places by promoting the bicycle for everyday transportation." Currently, the SFBC's primary goal is creating a citywide network of bike lanes that connect every neighborhood in San Francisco. Many citizens of San Francisco have embraced the project, and the coalition claims over 12,000 dues-paying members.

Return to these questions after you have finished reading.

Analyzing the Reading

1. What reasons are given for creating more bikeways in San Francisco?

2. What action does the information sheet ask the viewer to do? Is it clear to the reader?

3. If you received this information sheet in your mailbox or saw it in a newspaper or magazine, how likely would you be to stop and read it? Where would you expect to see it? Explain.

4. Examine the way this information sheet is designed. Where does your eye look first? Second? Why do you think the sheet was designed this way?

Exploring and Writing

The Netherlands is one of the most bike-friendly countries in the world, with a majority of the population regularly using bicycles as their primary mode of transportation. The country is well equipped with a network of cycle paths that reaches all parts of the nation. These "cycleways" have their own sets of rules including traffic signals/lights, tunnels, and lanes. Children begin cycling to school around the age of 8 and grow up with an appreciation and understanding of the traffic rules that govern cycling. The sheer number of cyclists has created a social structure in which the needs of cyclists come before the needs of motorists. In fact, auto insurers consider the driver to always be at fault in a collision with a bicyclist, making drivers extra careful driving where cyclists are also present.

1. If you were given the option of cycling on safe bike paths in your city or town, would you use a bicycle as your primary means of transportation?

2. The Netherlands is a very old country, but it redesigned the streets of most of its towns and many of its highways to accommodate bicycles. Do you think your city or town could adopt a similar model? Why or why not?

3. Write an essay exploring the multiple benefits of incorporating cycling path networks in urban planning. Include the social, ecological, financial, and personal benefits in your evaluation. Conversely, you could write an essay exploring why incorporating a cycling path network would not benefit your city or town.

CONNECTING THE CITY
Crosstown Bikeways
for Everyone!

A Project of the
San Francisco
Bicycle Coalition

What is Connecting the City?

Connecting the City addresses the question of how to make San Francisco a city that is easy to shop, live, work and play in while also preserving our unique neighborhoods and commercial districts. By designing our city's bike network for everyone, from an eight-year-old child to an eighty-year-old grandmother, we can provide inviting and safe door-to-door access to shop, commute and play by bicycle. Already, seven in 10 San Franciscans rode a bike last year thanks to improvements like the Market Street separated bike lanes and events like Sunday Streets — it's clear that more San Franciscans want to get around by bike.

Connecting the City builds on this demand and envisions the year 2020 when 100 miles of crosstown bikeways will help a growing population of San Francisco residents and visitors bike more often, relieving our crowded roadways and strained transit system. Elegantly designed bikeways that are physically separated from vehicles will help everyone from your boss, your neighbor's child or your mother-in-law to feel comfortable and safe biking on San Francisco streets. We are already working towards our first ambitious goal, to complete the Bay to Beach bikeway route by 2012 to showcase the comfort, safety and freedom of *Connecting the City's* bikeways. Learn more about the bikeway routes.

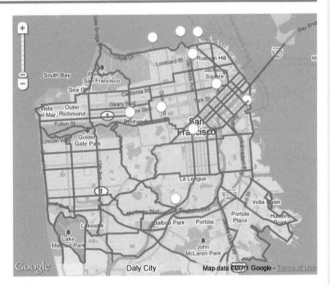

More Stories

Ask Mayor Lee for crosstown bikeways to connect the city

BAY TO BEACH   CONNECTING THE CITY

Goals

2011: Three continuous miles of bikeway

We will achieve this by getting 1.5 miles of separated bikeway on the Bay to Beach route on JFK Drive by May 2011, and connecting it with a bikeway on Fell and Oak streets and the traffic-calmed streets of the Wiggle route in the lower Haight by December 2011.

2011: Improvements to Market Street

We are already working to enhance our city's busiest bicycling street by: filling in the gaps in the bikeway between Octavia Boulevard and Eighth Street; enhancing the required right turn at Sixth Street by including right-turn arrows for drivers and a colored channel for people bicycling just south of the transit boarding island; trialing a "bike boardwalk" in the mid-Market area using Parklet technology to leverage the unused sidewalk edge and adding a new, flush surface to create a fully separated, continuous, raised green bikeway.

2012: First continuous, crosstown bikeway

A completed Bay to Beach route will give more people of all ages the confidence to bicycle more often and will be a great demonstration of a comfortable, safe and inviting bikeway.

2015: 25 miles of bikeway

The Bay to Beach, Bay Trail and North-South bikeways are complete making San Francisco an easier place to shop, work, live and play.

How to Write a Proposal Argument

These steps for the process of writing an argument for change may not progress as neatly as this chart might suggest. Writing is not an assembly-line process.

As you write and revise, imagine that you are in a conversation with an audience that contains people who both agree and disagree with you. Think about what you would say to both and speak to these diverse readers.

1 IDENTIFY THE PROBLEM

- Read your assignment carefully and note exactly what you are being asked to do.

- Identify the problem, what causes it, and whom it affects.

- Do background research on what has been written about the problem and what solutions have been attempted.

- Describe what has been done or not done to address the problem.

- Make a claim advocating a specific change or course of action. Put the claim in this form: "We should (or should not) do _____."

2 PROPOSE YOUR SOLUTION

- State your solution as specifically as you can.

- Consider other solutions and describe why your solution is better.

- Examine if the solution will have enough money and support to be implemented.

- Analyze your potential readers. How interested will your readers be in this problem? How would your solution benefit them directly and indirectly?

3 WRITE A DRAFT

- Define the problem. Give the background your readers will need.

- Discuss other possible solutions.

- Present your solution. Explain exactly how it will work, how it will be accomplished, and if anything like it has been tried elsewhere.

- Argue that your proposal will work. Address any possible arguments that your solution will not work.

- Describe the positive consequences of your solution and the negative consequences that can be avoided.

- Conclude with a call for action. Be specific about exactly what readers need to do.

- Write a title that will interest readers.

- Include any neccessary images, tables, or graphics.

4 REVISE, REVISE, REVISE

- Recheck that your proposal fulfills the assignment.

- Make sure that your proposal claim is clear and focused.

- Add detail or further explanation about the problem.

- Add detail or further explanation about how your solution addresses the problem.

- Make sure you have considered other solutions and explain why yours is better.

- Examine your organization and think of possible better ways to organize.

- Review the visual presentation of your report for readability and maximum impact.

- Proofread carefully.

5 SUBMITTED VERSION

- Make sure your finished writing meets all formatting requirements.

1: Identify the Problem

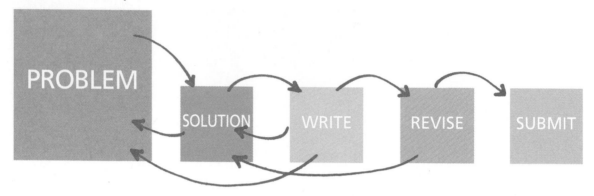

Analyze the assignment

Read your assignment slowly and carefully. Look for words like *propose*, *problem*, or *solution*, which signal that you are writing a proposal argument. Highlight any information about the length specified, date due, formatting, and other requirements. You can attend to this information later. At this point you want to zero in on your subject and your proposal claim.

Identify the problem

- What exactly is the problem?
- Who is most affected by the problem?
- What causes the problem?
- Has anyone tried to do anything about it? If so, why haven't they succeeded?
- What is likely to happen in the future if the problem isn't solved?

Do background research in online and print library sources and on the Web

- What has been written about the problem?
- What other solutions have been proposed?
- Where have other solutions been effective?
- Where have other solutions failed?
- Is there anyone involved with the problem whom you might interview?

Make a proposal claim

Proposal claims advocate a specific change or course of action. Put the claim in this form: "We should (or should not) do _____."

WRITE NOW

Make an idea map

When you have a number of ideas and facts about a topic, write them on sticky notes. Then post the sticky notes and move them around, so you can begin to see how they might fit together. When you find an organization that suits your subject, make a working outline from your sticky notes.

PROBLEM:
Citizens of the United States born in another country cannot run for president

EXCEPTION:
Foreign-born citizens whose parents are American citizens

REQUIRED:
2/3s majority of Congress and 2/3s of state legislatures must approve

SOLUTION:
Amend the U.S. Constitution to allow foreign-born American citizens to run for and serve as the president of the United States

HOW WOULD IT WORK?
Grassroots campaign

WHO WOULD SUPPORT?
Probably Asian Americans, Mexican Americans, and other recent immigrant groups

WHO WOULD OPPOSE?
1) politicians afraid of angering voters
2) Americans who are afraid of foreigners

HOW LONG WOULD IT TAKE?
Probably years because of the approval process

PRO ARGUMENTS
1) Fairness
2) America's image of itself as a land of opportunity

COUNTERARGUMENT
Point out that foreign born doesn't mean untrustworthy

Writer at work

Kim Lee was asked to write a proposal argument for her Rhetoric and Writing course. Upon receiving the assignment, she made the following notes and observations.

RHE 306 Rhetoric and Writing
Policy Proposal

Change an old policy or make a new one.

For this assignment, you will write a policy proposal argument. Propose a change to an existing policy or law, or propose a new law, that will correct a problem. This problem might be a revenue shortfall, an existing inequality, poor living or working conditions, a safety or law-enforcement threat, or something similar. Your paper should be about 5–7 pages long.

Remember, a policy proposal typically deals with a problem that affects a large number of people, and is often concerned with bettering society in some way. It will require practical steps to implement of course, and you will need to describe these steps in your essay. What would it take to change a particular law? Who would have to approve your new policy? How would it be funded? Your audience will need to know these things to decide if they agree with your proposal.

have to show practical steps. U.S. laws don't change unless people protest, write to Congress, etc.

Must inspire them to do something.

Also think about moving your audience to action. No matter how easy or hard your proposal would be to implement, you must persuade people to act upon it.

Timeline
We will review first drafts of your proposals in class one week from today. After this initial review, we will schedule one-on-one conferences during my office hours. Final versions will be due on May 10.

Ten days from review to final draft. Try to schedule conference early.

Evaluation
Grades for the final essay will break down as follows:

20%—description of problem
25%—description of solution (specifics, feasibility)
25%—persuasiveness/call to action
20%—overall support/citation of sources
10%—grammar and mechanics

Read the assignment closely

Kim Lee began by highlighting key words in the assignment and noting specifics about the length and due date.

Choose a topic

Kim listed possible topics and then considered the strengths and weaknesses of each. She chose one that could be developed adequately and could motivate her audience.

Plan research strategies

Kim made a list of possible sources of information to begin her research.

POSSIBLE TOPICS

— Create a standardized form of testing for steroid use in all American sports (professional, educational, recreational).

> Might be too broad. Also, the science involved might be hard to explain in 5–7 pages

— Move the U.S. capital to St. Louis.

> Too regional?

— Amend the Constitution to allow foreign-born American citizens (or naturalized citizens) to serve as president of the United States.

An issue of fair treatment.
Good for motivating audience.

— Revitalize Youngstown, Ohio, by building a tourist trade around its previous Mafioso reputation as "Little Chicago."

> Could give lots of specific steps (funding, building plans, tourist info).

— Reformulate the means by which the Corporation for Public Broadcasting receives federal funds.

> Would be very dry, though T.V. shows like Sesame Street could be used to provoke interest/make people want to act.

To Do:
— Search Web and library databases for current discussion on this topic. What kinds of sites are discussing the "natural-born" clause?
— Search periodicals for discussions of this topic.
— Search academic and law journals for more sophisticated discussions.
— Any books???
— What groups (political, ideological) are discussing this right now?

2: Propose Your Solution

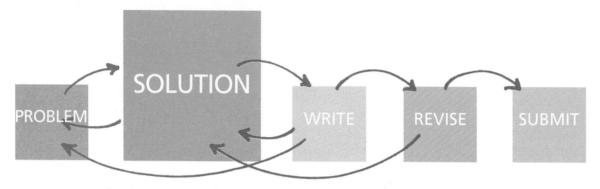

State your solution

Be as specific as possible.

- What exactly do you want to achieve?
- How exactly will your solution work?
- Can it be accomplished quickly, or will it have to be phased in over a few years?
- Has anything like it been tried elsewhere?
- Who will be involved?
- Is it possible that your solution might not work? Think of arguments against your solution and try to answer them.

Consider other solutions

What other solutions have been proposed for this problem, including doing nothing? What are the advantages and disadvantages of those solutions? You will need to acknowledge other solutions and argue for why your solution is better.

Examine the feasibility of your solution

- How easy is your solution to implement?
- Will people who are most affected go along with it? (For example, many people who support green energy still don't want wind farms in sight of their houses.)
- If it costs money, how do you propose paying for it?
- How can you best convince readers that your proposal can be achieved?

Analyze your potential readers

How interested will your readers be in this problem? Are they affected in any way by the problem? If they do not have an immediate stake in solving the problem, how can you gain their attention?

Acknowledging other points of view

Write for readers who may disagree with you

Proposal arguments that ignore other points of view and other possible solutions tend to convince only those who agree with you before you start writing. Your goal is to convince those who haven't thought about the problem and those who might disagree at the outset but can be persuaded. Think about why readers might disagree.

- Are they misinformed about the problem? If so, you will need to provide accurate information.
- Do they have different assumptions about the problem? If so, can you show them that your assumptions are better?
- Do they share your goals but think your solution is not the right one? If so, you will need to explain why your solution is better.

You might have to do some research to find out the views of others. If you are writing about a local problem, you may need to talk to people.

Deal fairly with other solutions and other points of view

OFF TRACK

Free tuition for all state high school graduates who attend state colleges is an idea too ridiculous to consider.
(No reason is given for rejecting an alternative solution, and those who propose it are insulted.)

ON TRACK

Free tuition for all state high school graduates is a desirable solution to get more students to attend college, but it is not likely to be implemented because of the cost. A merit-based solution similar to the HOPE scholarship program in Georgia, which is funded by state lottery money, could be implemented in our state.
(The author offers a reason for rejecting an alternative solution and proposes a solution that has some common ground with the alternative.)

Writer at work

Kim Lee began laying out her proposal by first stating her solution as specifically as possible. She used the following list of questions to guide her proposal argument.

PROPOSAL: Amend the U.S. Constitution to allow foreign-born American citizens to run for and serve as the president of the United States.

• How exactly will my solution work?

Through a nonpartisan grassroots campaign, we will work to pressure members of the U.S. Congress to propose the following amendment. Ultimately, this proposal is both for the people of the United States and the governmental body.

• Can it be accomplished quickly, or will it have to be phased in over a few years?

This is a tricky area. An amendment such as lowering the voting age to 18 during the Vietnam War did pass within four months. It often takes at least a couple years to work a proposed amendment through Congress.

• Who will be involved?

This will have to be a two-front battle. (1) the American people (specifically underrepresented voting blocks such as Asian Americans, Mexican Americans, and others, who are most directly affected by the limitations put forth by the current regulation). (2) the members of the United States Congress.

• Are any reasons why my solution might not work?

This has been brought up a number of times and never really gotten very far. It is a hot-button topic, especially as related to national security. Congressmen/women may not want to ruffle their constituents who may see this as a national threat and direct decrease in their own personal rights.

• How will I address those arguments?

Through pointing out the faulty logic that states foreign born=shifty and natural-born=patriotic.

• Can I think of any ways of strengthening my proposed solution in light of those possible criticisms?

I believe the strength in this is pointing to the (a) contradictions that exist between the rule and the governing notion of the United States as "melting pot," "land of freedom," and "a land where everyone can grow up to be president." The heart of this argument is to drive home its illogical nature, highlight contradictions in its logic, and include stipulations that ensure that the individual who is running for president is not merely a drop-in from another country.

OTHER SOLUTIONS
- *Solutions that have been discussed recently seem to differ in the length of required residence.*

Not necessarily disadvantages, but have been ineffective in achieving the goal. It comes from the people and not in support of one candidate, but an idea.

FEASIBILITY
- *How easy is my solution to implement?*

It all depends on the people's ability to move Congress to action.

- *Will the people who will be most affected be willing to go along with it?*

I believe the answer is yes.

- *How will we pay for it?*

Again, grassroots political fundraising. A major source may be ethnic/immigrant groups, etc.

- *Who is most likely to reject my proposal because it is not practical enough?*

Most likely (a) politicians who see support of the change as a threat to their positions (due to voter dissent) and (b) citizens who live in a state of fear.

- *How can I convince my readers that my proposal can be achieved?*

It must be proposed as being about the people and their ability to enact change. It is about empowerment.

POTENTIAL READERS
- *Whom am I writing for?*

American people (specifically the immigrant population).

- *How interested will my readers be in this problem?*

It is currently a hot topic, and hopefully making it more personally relevant will peak interest (not just about where President Obama was born).

- *How much does this problem affect them?*

Withholds a basic right for them and their children.

- *How would my solution benefit them directly and indirectly?*

Directly, it allows for naturalized citizens to run for president (or vice president). Indirectly, it fosters a sense of pride in one's ethnic identity and helps (through visibility and legislative legitimacy) to create an image of diversity and success.

3: Write a Draft

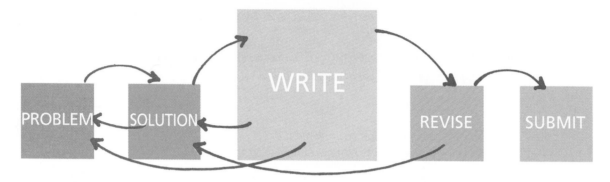

Define the problem

Set out the issue or problem. If the problem is local, you might begin by telling about your experience or the experience of someone you know.

Present your solution

- Describe other solutions that have been attempted and others that are possible. Explain why other solutions either don't solve the problem or are unrealistic.

- Make clear the goals of your solution. Many solutions cannot solve problems completely, but they can make things better.

- Describe in detail the steps in implementing your solution and how they will solve the problem you have identified. You can impress your readers by the care with which you have thought through this problem.

- Explain the positive consequences that will follow from your proposal. What good things will happen and what bad things will be avoided if your proposal is implemented?

Argue that your solution can be accomplished

Your proposal for solving the problem is a truly good idea only if it can be put into practice. If people have to change the ways they are doing things now, explain why they would want to change. If your proposal costs money, you need to identify exactly where the money would come from.

Conclude with a call for action

Make a call for action. Be direct that if your readers agree with you, they should be willing to take action. Restate and emphasize exactly what they need to do.

Writer at work

Here is the working outline upon which Kim Lee built the first draft of her proposal essay:

I. SET UP PROBLEM
    A. Story about son not being able to run
    B. Statistics
    C. Why it goes beyond just the hype

II. BACKGROUND
    A. Historical
        1. How this came about
        2. What is the historical logic behind it
    B. Current - Controversy over where Barack Obama was born

III. PROPOSAL
    A. Why
        1. Nation built on the melting pot
        2. Why is this issue important now?
        3. What have foreign-born Americans achieved?
        4. Who has it barred?
        5. Haven't we learned anything from past biases?
            a. Gitmo and Japanese American internment
            b. Natural-born traitors
        6. Tie to raising of voting age during Vietnam War
        7. Not a threat
    B. What
        1. Remove the "natural-born" clause
        2. Replace that clause with a different stipulation for president
            a. Must have been living in residence of the United States for at least 25 years
            b. Preserves the spirit of the clause
    C. How to do so in the most efficient and secure fashion
        1. Grassroots campaign to effect change with men and women of Congress
            a. We elect them
            b. Make this a major issue
            c. Use the minority voices who are often marginalized
        2. Ultimately it must be driven to Congress while keeping voices heard
    D. The actual governmental process

IV. CONCLUSION
    A. This will provide hope for the disenfranchised
    B. This will right an illogical wrong
    C. This will not place the country at risk
    D. This will create role models
    E. This will be one more step toward making this country what it professes to be

4: Revise, Revise, Revise

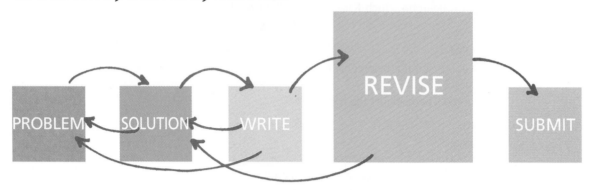

Take a break from your writing and come back to it with "fresh eyes." When you return, imagine you are someone who has never seen your proposal before. Read the proposal out loud. When you are done, ask yourself: Do I understand the problem? Does it really seem like a problem that must be dealt with? Is the solution clear? Does it seem like it is worth the trouble? Do I think it will really work? How much will it cost me, in money, effort, or inconvenience? The biggest trap you can fall into is starting off with the little stuff first. Leave the small stuff for last.

Does your paper or project meet the assignment?	• Look again at your assignment. Does your paper or project do what the assignment asks?
	• Look again at the assignment for specific guidelines, including length, format, and amount of research. Does your work meet these guidelines?
Is the proposal claim clear and focused?	• Does the proposal claim address the problem?
	• Does the proposal claim issue a clear call to action?
Do you identify the problem adequately?	• Do you need more evidence that the problem exists and is a serious concern?
	• Will your readers find credible any sources you include? Can you think of other sources that might be more persuasive?
Is it clear how your solution will address the problem?	• Can you find more evidence that your solution will resolve the problem?
	• Do you address potential objections to your solution?
	• Do you provide evidence that your solution is feasible? For example, if your solution requires money, where will the money come from?

Do you consider alternative solutions?	• Do you explain why your solution is better than the alternatives?
Is your organization effective?	• Is the order of your main points clear to your reader? • Are there any places where you find abrupt shifts or gaps? • Are there sections or paragraphs that could be rearranged to make your draft more effective?
Is your introduction effective?	• Can you get off to a faster start, perhaps with a striking example? • Can you think of a better way to engage your readers to be interested in the problem you identify? • Does your introduction give your readers a sense of why the problem is important?
Is your conclusion effective?	• Does your conclusion have a call for action? • Do you make it clear exactly what you want your readers to do?
Do you represent yourself effectively?	• To the extent you can, forget for a moment that you wrote what you are reading. What impression do you have of you, the writer? • Does "the writer" create an appropriate tone? • Has "the writer" done his or her homework?
Is the writing project visually effective?	• Is the font attractive and readable? • Is the overall layout attractive and readable? • If headings are used, do they make clear what comes under each of them? • Is each photograph, chart, graph, map, or table clearly labeled? Does each visual have a caption?
Save the editing for last	When you have finished revising, edit and proofread carefully.

A peer review guide is on page 54.

Writer at work

During peer review of her paper with fellow classmates, and in her meeting with her instructor, Kim Lee made notes on her rough draft. She used these comments to guide her revision of the essay.

The history of the United States of America is punctuated with rhetoric that positions the nation as one that embraces diversity and creates a land of equal opportunity for all of those who choose to live here. As the Statue of Liberty cries out "bring us your tired, your poor, your huddled masses yearning to breathe free," American politicians gleefully use such images to frame the United States a bastion for all things good, fair, and equal. As a proud American, however, I must nonetheless point out one of the cracks in this façade of equality ~~(and that is without even mentioning the repeated failed ratification of the women's Equal Rights Amendment). What flaw could this be?~~ Any foreign-born person with foreign parents is not eligible to be elected our president, even if that person became an American as a baby through adoption.

Opening sentence is too clunky. Need something more engaging.

Stay focused. Don't ask unnecessary questions. Give an example.

Think about the recent "birther" controversy about whether Barack Obama was born in Hawaii. The White House released the long-form birth certificate in April 2011. But does it really matter where Obama was born?

We as a nation must take this time to take a stand against this discriminatory and antiquated aspect of the Constitution.

Transition—the info on Schwrz. does not lead naturally into the renewed call for change. Need a link to show the relationship between this info and my proposal.

Watch the Animation on Revising and Editing Paragraphs at mycomplab.com

Look for ways to focus	Kim Lee responded to suggestions from her teacher and her peers to make her opening paragraph less wordy and better focused on her main point. She removed material that did not obviously inform readers about the problem she was interested in.
Check transitions	She also worked on strengthening transitions between paragraphs.
Read your paper aloud	Finally, Kim Lee read her essay aloud to check for misspelled words, awkward phrasing, and other mechanical problems.

STAYING ON TRACK
Reviewing your draft

Give yourself plenty of time for reviewing your draft. For detailed information on how to participate in a peer review, how to review it yourself, and how to respond to comments from your classmates, your instructor, or a campus writing consultant, see pages 52–56.

Some good questions to ask yourself when reviewing an argument for change

- Do you connect the problem to your readers? Even if the problem doesn't affect them directly, at the very least you should appeal to their sense of fairness.
- Can you explain more specifically how your solution will work?
- If resources including people and money are required for your solution, can you elaborate where these resources will come from?
- Do you include other possible solutions and discuss the advantages and disadvantages of each? Can you add to this discussion?
- Does your conclusion connect with the attitudes and values of your readers in addition to making clear what you want them to do? Can you add an additional point? Can you sharpen your call to action?

5: Submitted Version

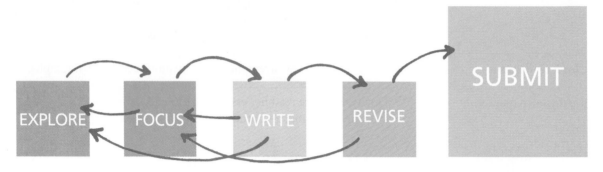

Lee 1

Kim Lee

Professor Patel

RHE 306

10 May 2011

Let's Make It a Real Melting Pot with Presidential Hopes for All

The image the United States likes to advertise is a country that embraces diversity and creates a land of equal opportunity for all. As the Statue of Liberty cries out, "give me your tired, your poor, your huddled masses yearning to breathe free," American politicians gleefully evoke such images to frame the United States as a bastion for all things good, fair, and equal. As a proud American, however, I must nonetheless highlight one of the cracks in this façade of equality. Imagine that a couple decides to adopt an orphaned child from China. They follow all of the legal processes deemed necessary by both countries. They fly abroad and bring home their (once parentless) six-month-old baby boy. They raise and nurture him, and while teaching him to embrace his ethnicity, they also teach him to love Captain Crunch, baseball, and

Lee 2

The Three Stooges. He grows and eventually attends an ethnically diverse American public school. One day his fifth-grade teacher tells the class that anyone can grow up to be president. To clarify her point, she turns to the boy, knowing his background, and states, "No, you could not be president, Stu, but you could still be a senator. That's something to aspire to!" How do Stu's parents explain this rule to this American-raised child? This scenario will become increasingly common, yet as the Constitution currently reads, only "natural-born" citizens may run for the offices of president and vice president. Neither these children nor the thousands of hardworking Americans who chose to make America their official homeland may aspire to the highest political position in the land. While the huddled masses may enter, it appears they must retain a second-class citizen ranking.

The issue arose most recently when bloggers, media personalities, and some elected officials alleged that Barack Obama was born in Kenya, not Hawaii, and that his birth certificate is a forgery. The release of a certified copy of Obama's Certificate of Live Birth (the "long form") and other evidence including birth announcements in two Hawaii newspapers in August 1961 answered Donald Trump and other prominent "birthers" (Shear). Lost in the controversy was the question: Should it matter where Obama or any other candidate was born? In a land where everyone but American Indians are immigrants or descendants of immigrants, why should being born in the United States be considered an essential qualification for election as President?

The provision arose from very different circumstances than those of today. The "natural-born" stipulation regarding the presidency stems from the self-same meeting of minds that brought the American people the Electoral

College. During the Constitutional Convention of 1787, the Congress

formulated the regulatory measures associated with the office of the president.

A letter sent from John Jay to George Washington during this period reads as

follows:

> "Permit me to hint," Jay wrote, "whether it would not be wise and
>
> seasonable to provide a strong check to the admission of foreigners into
>
> the administration of our national government; and to declare expressly
>
> that the Commander in Chief of the American army shall not be given to,
>
> nor devolve on, any but a natural-born citizen." (Mathews A1)

Shortly thereafter, Article II, Section I, Clause V, of the Constitution declared

that "No Person except a natural born Citizen, or a Citizen of the United States

at the time of the Adoption of this Constitution, shall be eligible to the Office of

President." Jill A. Pryor states in the *Yale Law Journal* that "some writers have

suggested that Jay was responding to rumors that foreign princes might be

asked to assume the presidency" (881). Many cite disastrous examples of

foreign rule in the eighteenth century as the impetus for the "natural-born"

clause. For example, in 1772—only 15 years prior to the adoption of the

statute—Poland had been divided up by Prussia, Russia, and Austria

(Kasindorf). Perhaps an element of self-preservation and not ethnocentrism led

to the questionable stipulation. Nonetheless, in the twenty-first century this

clause reeks of xenophobia.

The Fourteenth Amendment clarified the difference between "natural-

born" and "native-born" citizens by spelling out the citizenship status of children born to American parents outside of the United States (Ginsberg 929). This clause qualifies individuals such as Senator John McCain—born in Panama—for presidency. This change, however, is not adequate. I propose that the United States abolish the natural-born clause and replace it with a stipulation that allows naturalized citizens to run for president. This amendment would state that a candidate must have been naturalized and must have lived in residence in the United States for a period of at least twenty-five years. The present time is ideal for this change. This amendment could simultaneously honor the spirit of the Constitution, protect and ensure the interests of the United States, promote an international image of inclusiveness, and grant heretofore-withheld rights to thousands of legal and loyal United States citizens.

In our push for change, we must make clear the importance of this amendment. It would not provide special rights for would-be terrorists. To the contrary, it would fulfill the longtime promises of the nation. Naturalized citizens have been contributing to the United States for centuries. Many nameless Mexican, Irish, and Asian Americans sweated and toiled to build the American railroads. The public has welcomed naturalized Americans such as Bob Hope, Albert Pujols, and Peter Jennings into their hearts and living rooms. Individuals such as German-born Henry Kissinger and Czechoslovakian-born Madeleine Albright have held high posts in the American government and have served as respected aides to its presidents. The amendment must make clear that it is not about one man's celebrity. Approximately seven hundred foreign-born Americans have won the Medal of Honor, and over sixty thousand proudly serve in the United States military today (Siskind 5). The "natural-born" clause must be removed to provide each of these people—over half a million naturalized in 2003 alone—with equal footing to those who were born into citizenship rather than working for it (United States).

Since the passing of the Bill of Rights, only 17 amendments have been ratified. This process takes time and overwhelming congressional and statewide support. To alter the Constitution, a proposed amendment must pass with a two-thirds "supermajority" in both the House of Representatives and the Senate. In addition, the proposal must find favor in two-thirds (38) of state legislatures. In short, this task will not be easy. In order for this change to occur, a grassroots campaign must work to dispel misinformation regarding naturalized citizens and to force the hands of senators and representatives wishing to retain their congressional seats. We must take this proposal to ethnicity-specific political groups from both sides of the aisle, business organizations, and community activist groups. We must convince representatives that this issue matters. Only through raising voices and casting votes can the people enact change. Only then can every American child see the possibility for limitless achievement and equality. Only then can everyone find the same sense of pride in the possibility for true American diversity in the highest office in the land.

Works Cited

Epstein, Edward. "Doubt about a Foreign-Born President." *San Francisco Chronicle* 6 Oct. 2004: A5. *LexisNexis Academic*. Web. 16 Apr. 2011.

Ginsberg, Gordon. "Citizenship: Expatriation: Distinction between Naturalized and Natural Born Citizens." *Michigan Law Review* 50 (1952): 926–29. *JSTOR*. Web. 16 Apr. 2011.

Kasindorf, Martin. "Should the Constitution Be Amended for Arnold?" *USA Today* 2 Dec. 2004. *LexisNexis Academic*. Web. 18 Apr. 2011.

Mathews, Joe. "Maybe Anyone Can Be President." *Los Angeles Times* 2 Feb. 2005: A1. *LexisNexis Academic*. Web. 16 Apr. 2011.

Pryor, Jill A. "The Natural Born Citizen Clause and Presidential Eligibility: An Approach for Resolving Two Hundred Years of Uncertainty." *Yale Law Journal* 97.5 (1988): 881–99. Print.

Shear, Michael D. "With Document, Obama Seeks to End 'Birther' Issue." *New York Times*. New York Times, 27 Apr. 2011. Web. 28 Apr. 2011.

Siskind, Lawrence J. "Why Shouldn't Arnold Run?" *Recorder* 10 Dec. 2004: 5. *LexisNexis Academic*. Web. 10 Apr. 2011.

United States. Dept. of Commerce. Census Bureau. "The Fourth of July 2005." *Facts for Features*. US Dept. of Commerce, 27 June 2005. Web. 17 Apr. 2011.

Projects

If you want to persuade your readers to do something, you must convince them that a problem exists and that something needs to be done about it.

Teamwork: counterproposals

Find a proposal argument that you and three or four classmates are interested in. This might be a proposal to widen a road in your town, to pass a law making English the official language of your state government, or something similar.

Ask each person in the group to construct a one- or two-page counterproposal. Your counterproposals should address the same problem as the original proposal but should offer different solutions. Is there a way to solve the problem that is cheaper? less disruptive? more fair? less risky?

Present your counterproposals to the rest of your group, and discuss which is the most appealing. You may find that a combination of elements of the different proposals ends up being the best.

Proposal essay

Write a proposal of 1000–1250 words (about three to four double-spaced pages) that would solve a problem that you identify.

Choose a problem with which you have personal experience, but you should also think about how many other people this problem affects. Your proposal should take them into account as part of your audience.

Find out who would be in a position to enact your proposal. How can you make your solution seem like a good idea to these people?

Propose your solution as specifically as you can. What exactly do you want to achieve? How exactly will your solution work? Has anything like it been tried elsewhere? Who will be involved?

Consider other solutions that have been or might be proposed for this problem, including doing nothing. What are the advantages and disadvantages of those solutions? Why is your solution better?

Examine how easy your solution is to implement. Will the people most affected be willing to go along with it? Lots of things can be accomplished if enough people volunteer, but groups often have difficulty getting enough volunteers to work without pay. If it costs money, how do you propose paying for it?

For support in learning this chapter's content, follow this path in **mycomplab:**

► **Resources** ► **Writing** ► **Writing Purposes** ► **Writing to Argue or Persuade**

Review the Instruction and Multimedia resources, then complete the **Exercises** and click on **Gradebook** to measure your progress.

Reconstructing a proposal

You may not have a lot of experience writing proposals. Nevertheless, proposals have had a profound impact on your life. Almost every program, law, policy, or business that affects you had to be proposed before it became a reality.

Think of some things in your life that were proposed by people: the building where you attended high school, for example. At some point, that building was proposed as a way of solving a certain problem—perhaps your town had one old, overflowing high school, and your building was proposed to solve the overcrowding. Its location was probably chosen carefully, to avoid causing more problems with traffic, and to ensure that it was easy for students to reach.

Choose something you are familiar with that went through a proposal process. Try to reconstruct the four components of the original proposal. What problem do you think people were trying to solve? How did concerns about fairness and feasibility shape the program, building, or policy?

Outline your re-created proposal in a page or two.

Ask yourself if this policy, program, or business truly solved the problem it was intended to solve? Clearly, the proposal itself was successful, for the school was built, the law was passed, or the business was started. But how successful was the proposed solution in reality?

Nonprofit proposal

Nonprofit organizations depend to a large extent on external funding. Many rely on help from volunteers, including students, to write proposals. Find a nonprofit organization in your community that seeks funding. Select a project that the organization wishes to undertake and identify possible funding sources. You will need to write a proposal that includes the following elements.

Cover letters give a brief overview of the organization and the purpose and goals of the funding request. A title page and executive summary usually begin the proposal with a concise statement of the project, the purpose, the amount of money requested, and contact information.

Problem statements describe the need and the target population. This section is critical because the funding agency must be convinced that what you are proposing is important.

Goals and objectives are in a separate section that details what will be accomplished, how the community will benefit, and how success will be measured. Long-term strategies for maintaining the successes of the project should also be described. The budget delineates the costs and makes an argument for the feasibility of the proposal.

Organizational information explains the broad mission of the organization and its history.

 Apply the Concept of Proposal Arguments at mycomplab.com   527

Get info
Join the
snacks too!
(On-Campus
Post till 11/7
Thurs. Nov. 6th,
(1st Floor, Student

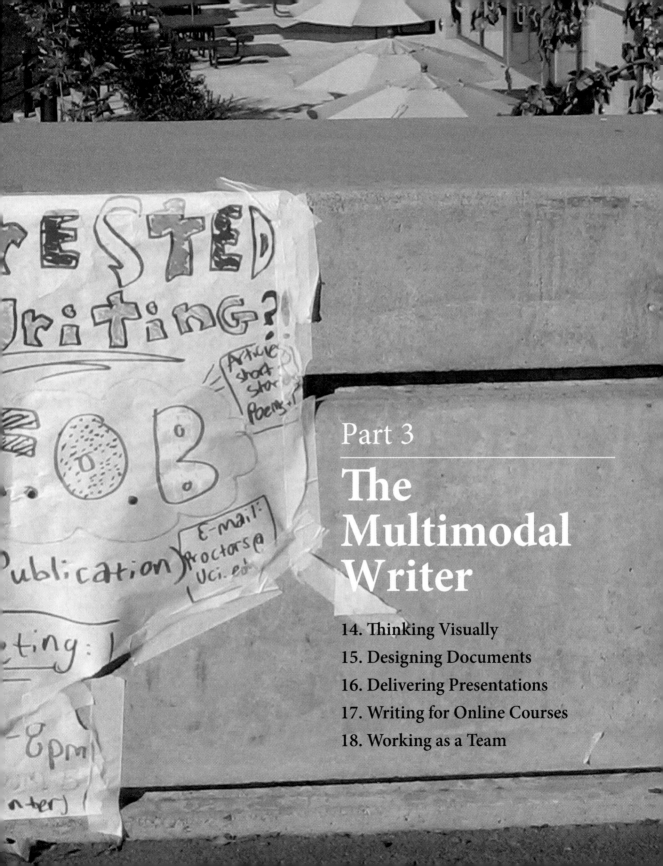

Part 3

The Multimodal Writer

14 Thinking Visually

The principles of good design, like those of good writing, begin with your audience and what you are trying to accomplish.

Chapter Overview

► Communicate with visuals and words
(see p. 531)

► Know when to use images and graphics
(see p. 532)

► Take pictures that aren't boring
(see p. 533)

► Compose images
(see p. 534)

► Create tables, charts, and graphs
(see p. 535)

Communicate with Visuals and Words

The word *writing* makes us think of words, yet in our daily experience reading newspapers, magazines, advertisements, Web sites, and signs, along with watching television, we find words combined with images and graphics. Understanding the relationships of words and visuals will make you a better writer.

What do visuals do best?

Visuals work well when they

- Deliver spatial information, especially through maps, floor plans, and other graphic representations of space
- Represent statistical relationships
- Produce a strong immediate impact, even shock value
- Emphasize a point made in words

What do words do best?

Words can do many things that images cannot. Written words work best when they

- Communicate abstract ideas
- Report information
- Persuade using elaborated reasoning
- Communicate online using minimal bandwidth

WRITE NOW

Photographs don't speak for themselves

The image that has come to represent the Great Depression of the 1930s and the suffering people endured during those years is Dorothea Lange's photograph of Florence Thomson with three of her children, a photograph that has come to be known as *Migrant Mother*. Lange's actual title for the photograph is *Destitute pea pickers in California. Mother of seven children. Age thirty-two. Nipomo, California.*

Change the meaning of this photograph by changing the words that surround it. Make a different argument using the photograph. You might create a political poster, a pamphlet, a sign, a Web site, or an advertisement (which has been done many times). Think of a new caption that conveys the new meaning you are giving to the photograph.

Know When to Use Images and Graphics

Computers, digital cameras, smart phones, printers, and the Web have made it easy to include images and graphics in what we write. But these technologies don't tell us when or how to use images and graphics.

- Think about your readers' expectations for the medium you are using. Most essays don't use images. Readers expect essays to use words primarily to convey ideas. Most Web sites and brochures do use images and graphics because readers expect to see their subjects in addition to reading about them.

- Think about the purpose of an image or graphic. Does it illustrate a concept? highlight an important point? show something that is hard to explain in words alone? If you don't know the purpose, you may not need the image.

- Think about the placement of an image or graphic in your text. It should be as close as possible to a relevant point in your text.

- Think about the focus of an image. Will readers see the part that matters? If not, you may need to crop the image.

- Provide informative captions for the images and graphics you use and refer to them in your text.

Uninformative caption:

Ghost town

Informative caption:

Following the discovery of quicksilver in the 1880s, Terlingua became a boom town, but the people left when the mines ceased production at the end of World War II.

• Analyze the Interactive **Visual Satellite Photo** at **mycomplab.com**

Take Pictures That Aren't Boring

No matter how easy it is now to take photographs, the great majority of pictures look the same. Why? It's because most people think pictures should look the same, taken at eye level with the subject in the center.

The result is boring, boring, boring.

This kind of picture has been taken many, many times. How else might you see this subject?

Squat

Change the angle

Lie down

Find a new eye level

Climb a tree

Kneel

Most people never stop to experience the visual richness of the world. Look for detail. Be open to what you see.

Compose Images

A common misperception is that a photograph is a direct representation of reality. Nothing could be further from the truth. A photograph shows not so much what the photographer sees but rather *how* the photographer sees. The key to becoming a good photographer is not to take pictures that show things exactly as they appear but to take pictures that convey meaning, organization, and an emotional response to the subject.

Eliminate nonessential elements
Most people include too much in their photographs. Decide what is essential and concentrate on getting those elements in the frame.

The mud on a tired horse after a race shows his exhaustion.

Framing

If you are taking a portrait, usually the closer you can get to your subject, the better. If your camera has a zoom, use it.

Decide what you want in a frame. If your goal is to show the habitat of pelicans, you'll need a wide shot.

But if you want a portrait of a pelican, get in tight.

● Analyze the Interactive Photo for Arrangement at mycomplab.com

Create Tables, Charts, and Graphs

Select the type of visual that best suits your purpose.

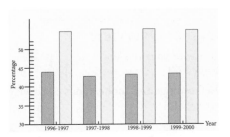

Table 25.1
Population Change for the Ten Largest U.S. Cities, 1990 to 200

City and State	Population April 1, 2000	April 1, 1990	Change, 1990 to 2000 Number	Percentage
New York, NY	8,008,278	7,322,564	685,714	9.4
Los Angeles, CA	3,694,820	3,485,398	209,422	6.0
Chicago, IL	2,896,016	2,783,726	112,290	4.0
Houston, TX	1,953,631	1,630,553	323,078	19.8
Philadelphia, PA	1,517,550	1,585,577	-68,027	-4.3
Phoenix, AZ	1,321,045	983,403	337,642	34.3
San Diego, CA	1,223,400	1,110,549	112,851	10.2
Dallas, TX	1,188,580	1,006,877	181,703	18.0
San Antonio, TX	1,144,646	935,933	208,713	22.3
Detroit, MI	951,270	1,027,974	-76,704	-7.5

Source: U.S. Cencus Bureau, Census 2000; 1990 Census, Population and Housing Unit Counts, United States (1990 CPH-2-1).

Tables

A table is used to display numerical data and similar types of information.

Bar Graphs

A bar graph compares the values of two or more items.

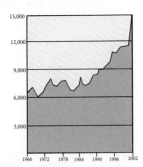

Line Graphs

A line graph shows change over time.

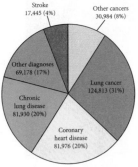

Pie Charts

A pie chart shows the parts making up a whole.

WRITE NOW

Create a Google Map

Google Maps are quickly becoming a new way of thinking about making connections between places and ideas in visually stimulating and interactive ways. Create a map about some aspect of your town or campus that not everyone knows about. Select your sites either by a specific area or a specific theme (e.g., best graffiti art, best food trailers, best places to watch sunset).

Your map should contain a minimum of five placemarks. Each placemark should have at least a paragraph of original text and a photograph taken at the site. You can make hyperlinks, but do not depend on links to do your work for you. Tell the story yourself. When you finish, submit the URL of your map to your instructor.

15 Designing Documents

Successful design should be both functional and handsome.

Chapter Overview

► **Start with your readers**
(*see p. 537*)

► **Use headings and subheadings effectively**
(*see p. 538*)

► **Design pages**
(*see p. 539*)

► **Understand typography**
(*see p. 540*)

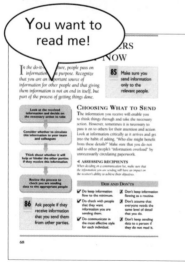

You know at a glance who is telling the truth.

Start with Your Readers

Imagine yourself in the shoes of your reader. Pretend for a moment that someone else has written about your subject. What do you, the reader, want from the writer?

Tell your reader what you are writing about

An accurate and informative title is critical for readers to decide if they want to read what you have written. Furthermore, the title is critical to allow the reader to return to something read earlier.

Some genres require **abstracts**, which are short summaries of a document. Abstracts are required for scholarly articles in the sciences and social sciences as well as dissertations. Business reports and other reports often have executive summaries, which are similar to abstracts but often briefer.

Make your organization visible to readers

Most longer texts and many shorter ones include headings, which give readers an at-a-glance overview and make the text easier to follow and remember. Headings visually indicate the major and subordinate sections of a text.

Some genres have specific formats for organization, such as the APA-style report of research that is divided into four parts: introduction, method, results, and discussion. If you are writing in a genre that requires a specific format, follow it. Readers will be irritated if you don't.

Help your reader to navigate your text

Do the little things that help readers. Remember to include page numbers, which word processing software can insert for you. Make cross references to other parts of your document when a subject is covered elsewhere. If you are citing sources, make sure they are all in your list of works cited.

Help your reader to understand the purposes of different parts of your text

Writers have traditionally relied on footnotes to add information that they did not want to interrupt the running text. Today writers often use boxes or sidebars to supply extra information. If you use boxes or sidebars, indicate them with a different design or a different color. The key is to make what is different look different.

You do research every day. If you compare prices online before you buy an airline ticket, or if you look up a detailed course description before registering for a class, you are doing research. If you want to settle an argument about the first African American to win an Olympic gold medal, you need to do research. In college, research means both investigating existing knowledge that is stored on computers and in libraries, and creating new knowledge through original analysis, surveys, experiments, and theorizing. When you start a research task in a college course, you need to understand the different kinds of possible research and to plan your strategy in advance.

If you have an assignment that requires research, look closely at what you are being asked to do.

The assignment may ask you to review, compare, survey, analyze, evaluate, or prove that something is true or untrue. You may be writing for experts, for students like yourself, or for the general public. The purpose of your research and your potential audience will help guide your strategies for research.

Pull quotes are often set off from the body text with a larger font and a different color.

Use Headings and Subheadings Effectively

Readers increasingly expect you to divide what you write into sections and label those sections with headings. A system of consistent headings should map the overall organization.

Determine levels of headings

Determine the level of importance of each heading by making an outline to see what fits under what. Then make the headings conform to the different levels by choosing a size and an effect such as boldfacing for each level. The type, the size, and the effect should signal the level of importance.

Phrase headings consistently

Headings should be similar in how they are worded. For example, if you are writing headings for an informative brochure about a service, you might use the most frequently asked questions as your headings.

TITLE

Saepe et multum hoc mecum cogitavi, bonine an mali plus attulerit hominibus et civitatibus copia dicendi ac summum eloquentiae studium.

Major Heading

Ac me quidem diu cogitantem ratio ipsa in hanc potissimum sententiam ducit, ut existimem sapientiam sine eloquentia parum prodesse civitatibus, eloquentiam vero sine sapientia nimium obesse plerumque, prodesse numquam.

Level 2 heading Ac si volumus huius rei, quae vocatur eloquentia, sive artis sive studii sive exercitationis cuiusdam sive facultatis ab natura profectae considerare principium, reperiemus id ex honestissimis causis natum atque optimis rationibus profectum.

Be a Quitter! Join Quitters

Why quit smoking?

- You'll lower your risk for heart attack, stroke, and cancer.
- You'll look, feel, and smell a whole lot better.
- You'll have extra money to spend on things other than cigarettes.

How will the Quitters class help me?

- You'll find out your individual level of nicotine-dependence.
- You'll utilize a brand-switching technique.
- You'll explore the use of nicotine replacement therapies.

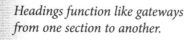

Headings function like gateways from one section to another.

Design Pages

Word processing programs design pages for you with their default settings for margins, paragraph indentations, and justification. Even if you use the default settings, you still have a range of options. Thinking about design will lead to better decisions.

Choose the orientation, size of your page, and columns

You can usually use the defaults on your word processing program for academic essays (remember to select double-spacing for line spacing if the default is single-spaced). For other kinds of texts you may want a horizontal rather than a vertical orientation, a size other than a standard sheet of paper, and two columns or more rather than one.

Divide your text into units

The paragraph is the basic unit of extended writing, but think also about when to use lists. This list is a bulleted list. You can also use a numbered list.

Use left aligned text with a ragged right margin

Fully and justified text aligns the right margin, which gives a more formal look but can also leave unsightly rivers of extra white space running through the middle of your text.

Giddens 3

stay in the military after their commitment ends. Congress first gave the military the authority to retain soldiers after the Vietnam War when new volunteers were too few to replace departing soldiers. In November 2002 the Pentagon gave stop-loss orders for Reserve and National Guard units activated to fight terrorism (Robertson).

- This policy is neither forthcoming, safe, nor compassionate toward those most directly impacted—the soldiers and their families.
- As the United States became more and more entrenched in the conflict in Iraq, the military was stretched thinner and thinner.
- By 2004, approximately 40% of those serving in Iraq and Afghanistan came from the ranks of the part-time soldiers: the Reserves and the National Guard (Gerard).

While these individuals did know that their countries could call if they enlisted, they continue to bear an inordinate burden of actual combat time, and this new policy continues to create situations further removed from the job for which they had enlisted. Recruiters often pitch the military—including the Reserves and the Guard–to young, impressionable, and often underprivileged kids.

The Pitch

I have experienced this pitch firsthand and seen the eyes of my classmates as the recruiter promised them a better and richer tomorrow. Seeing a golden opportunity for self-respect and achievement, young men and women sign on the dotted line. Today, other young men and women

---

Be conscious of white space

White space can make your text more readable and set off more important elements. Headings stand out more with white space surrounding them. Leave room around graphics. You don't want words to crowd too close to graphics because both the words and the visuals will become hard to read.

Be aware of MLA and APA design specifications

MLA and APA styles have specifications for margins, indentations, reference lists, and other things. See the sample papers in Chapters 24 and 25 if you are using MLA or APA style.

 Watch the Animation on Principles of Design at mycomplab.com   539

Understand Typography

Just as people communicate with body language, texts have a look and feel created by the layout, typefaces, type size, color, density, and other elements.

Typography is the designer's term for letters and symbols that make up the print on the page. You are already using important aspects of typography when you use capital letters, italics, boldface, or different sizes of type to signal a new sentence, identify the title of a book, or distinguish a heading from the body text.

Word processing programs and personal computers now enable you to use dozens of different typefaces (fonts), bold and italic versions of these fonts, and a range of font sizes. Fortunately, you can rely on some simple design principles to make good typographic choices for your documents.

Choosing a font

A font family consists of the font in different sizes as well as in its boldface and italic forms. Although computers now make hundreds of font styles and sizes available to writers, you should avoid confusing readers with too many typographical features. Limit the fonts in a document to one or two font families. A common practice is to choose one font family for all titles and headings and another for the body text.

A Font Family
Futura Light Condensed
Futura Light Condensed Italic
Futura Book
Futura Book Italic
Futura Heavy
Futura Heavy Italic
Futura Bold

The font family Futura, shown above in 14 point, is composed of style variations on the Futura design that include a variety of weights.

Serif and sans serif typefaces

Typefaces are normally divided into two groups—serif and sans serif. Serif typefaces include horizontal lines—or serifs—added to the major strokes of a letter or character such as a number. Sans serif typefaces, by contrast, do not have serifs. Notice the difference opposite.

The typical use and stylistic impact of the typefaces vary considerably. Serif typefaces are more traditional, conservative, and formal in appearance. By contrast, sans serif typefaces offer a more contemporary, progressive, and informal look. Serif is often used for longer pieces of writing, such as novels and textbooks. It is also the best bet for college papers.

The difference between serif and sans serif fonts

The horizontal lines make serif easier to read because they guide the eye from left to right across the page.

This **SERIF** font is called Garamond

This **SANS SERIF** font is called Helvetica

Think about font style

Not all fonts are suitable for extended pieces of writing. Sentences and paragraphs printed in fonts that imitate calligraphy or handwriting are difficult to read in long stretches. For most academic and business writing, you will probably want to choose a traditional font, such as Times Roman, that is easy to read and does not call attention to itself. This book is set in 10.5 point Minion.

Choosing the best font for the job

This piece of text is in a caligraphic font and may be right for some special situations, but there is no doubt that every single reader will be aware of the struggle to decipher it.

This font is **26 point Bickham Script**

This piece of text is in a handwriting font, and although easier to read than the above, it is still tedious.

This font is **17 point Tekton**

This is about as normal a font as you can find. It is called Times Roman, for the simple reason that it was designed for use in the *London Times* newspaper, and so had to be as readable as possible.

This font is **14 point Times New Roman**

```
This font is also very
readable and is very
common. It does, however,
require much more space
than other faces.
```

This font is **14 point Courier**

Think about font size

It's easy to change the size of a font when you write on a computer. For most types of writing in college, a 12-point font is the standard size for the main (body) text, with headings in a larger font.

Type sizes

8 point

12 point

18 point

36 point

48 point

Height can make a difference

To ensure that what you write can be read easily, you need to choose an appropriate size. Fonts differ by height, called the x-height, as well as point size. Fonts of the same point size can look different because of height. Effective size depends on the appearance of a font, not merely its point size.

To ensure that what you write can be read easily, you need to choose an appropriate size. Fonts differ by height, called the x-height, as well as point size. Fonts of the same point size can look different because of height. Effective size depends on the appearance of a font, not merely its point size.

Both texts are set the same "size" (12 point) but they appear different because of the x-heights. Bembo, left, looks much smaller and takes much less space than Glypha, right.

Type sizes for computer monitors

For Web pages, you should consider using a larger font to compensate for the added difficulty of reading from a computer monitor. For overhead transparencies and computer-projected displays, you should use an even larger size (such as 32 point) to ensure that the text can be read from a distance.

However, for Web pages, you consider using a larger font to sate for the added difficulty of from a computer monitor. For transparencies and computer displays, you should use an e size (such as 32 point) to ensure the text can be read from a d

Pixilation on the computer screen breaks up the font; thus the 12-point type in this example is too small.

ever, for Web pag u should consider us a larger font to com nsate for the added iculty of reading fron omputer monitor. F

You should consider enlarging to 18-point type as in this example.

Veb pages, ou should onsider usi

Or even 32 point if using an overhead projector or a computer-projected display.

Checklist for evaluating document design

1. Audience Who is the intended audience? Will the design be appealing to them? How does the design serve their needs?

2. Genre What is the genre? Does the design meet the requirements of the genre? For example, a brochure should fit in your pocket.

3. Organization Is the organization clear to readers? If headings are used, are they in the right places? If headings are used for more than one level, are these levels indicated consistently?

4. Readability Is the typeface attractive and readable? Are the margins sufficient? Is any contrasting text, such as boldface, italics, or all caps, brief enough to be legible? If color is used, does it direct emphasis to the right places?

5. Layout Can the basic layout be made more effective? Is there adequate white space around headings, images, and graphics?

WRITE NOW

Design a menu

Collect menus from a few restaurants, either in print or on the Web. Study the design of each menu.

Design a menu of your own. First, you have to decide what kind of food you will serve: burgers, Italian, Thai, seafood, and so on. Second, think about the clientele you want to attract: college students, families, office lunch crowd, or another demographic. Third, list a few food items for your menu. Fourth, name your restaurant and give it a theme.

Make a sketch of your menu. Decide what graphics, photographs, and backgrounds you want to use. Then create your menu.

16 Delivering Presentations

Effective presentations require putting the interests of the audience first.

Chapter Overview

► **Plan a presentation**
  (see p. 545)

► **Design effective visuals**
  (see p. 546)

► **Deliver a successful presentation**
  (see p. 547)

Plan a Presentation

A successful presentation, like a successful writing project, requires careful planning. Read your assignment carefully for guidance on how to plan your presentation.

FIND A TOPIC	Choosing and researching a topic for a presentation is similar to choosing and researching a topic for a writing assignment. Ask these questions: • Does the topic fit the assignment? • Will you enjoy speaking on this topic? • Do you know enough to speak on this topic? **→ See page 12**
IDENTIFY YOUR AUDIENCE	Who is your audience? How interested will they be in your topic? What will they likely know and believe about your topic? **→ See page 14**
IDENTIFY YOUR PURPOSE	Your assignment often specifies your purpose. **→ See page 9**
IDENTIFY YOUR CENTRAL IDEA	The central idea of a presentation is similar to a working thesis. It includes your purpose, your audience, and your objective. **Purpose:** To persuade **Audience:** my fellow students **Objective:** that they should volunteer at no-kill animal shelters. **→ See page 36**
DO THE NECESSARY RESEARCH	Find supporting material from sources. **→ See Chapters 20 and 21**
CREATE A WORKING OUTLINE	Make a list of key points and think about how best to order them. **→ See page 38**
PLAN YOUR INTRODUCTION	You must gain the attention of your audience, introduce your subject, indicate why it is important, and give a sense of where you are headed. **→ See page 46**
PLAN YOUR CONCLUSION	Give your audience something to take away—a compelling example or an idea that captures the gist of your presentation. **→ See page 48**

Design Effective Visuals

Less is more with slides. One text-filled slide after another is mind-numbingly dull. Create a presentation that engages your audience.

Keep it simple

Imagine you are making an argument that fewer animals would be euthanized at animal shelters if more people in your city knew that they could save a pet's life by adopting it. You could fill your slides with statistics alone. Or you tell your audience the facts while showing them slides that give emotional impact to your numbers,

Keep in mind these principles.
- One point per slide
- Very few fonts
- Quality photos, not clip art
- Less text, more images
- Easy on the special effects

But what if you have a lot of data to show? Make a handout that the audience can study later. They can take notes on your handout during your presentation. Keep your slides simple and emphasize the main points in the presentation.

Compare the following examples.

Pet Overpopulation in the United States

- Estimated number of animals that enter shelters each year: 6-8 million
- Estimated number of animals euthanized at shelters each year: 3-4 million
- Estimated number of animals adopted at shelters each year: 3-4 million

Source: "HSUS Pet Overpopulation Estimates." *Humane Society of the U.S.* Humane Society of the U.S., 9 Nov. 2009. 18 Oct. 2010.

Save a life. Adopt a pet.

Which slide makes the point most effectively?

Analyze the Interactive Presentation Slides at mycomplab.com

Deliver a Successful Presentation

If you are not passionate about your subject, you will never get your audience involved, no matter how good your slides are. Believe in what you say; enthusiasm is contagious.

It's all about you

The audience didn't come to see the back of your head in front of slides. Move away from the podium and connect with them. Make strong eye contact with individuals. You will make everyone feel like you were having a conversation instead of giving a speech.

Prepare in advance

Practice your presentation, even if you have to speak to a mirror. Check out the room and equipment in advance. If you are using your laptop with a projector installed in the room, make sure it connects. If the room has a computer connected to the projector, bring your presentation on a flash drive and download it to the computer.

Be professional

Pay attention to the little things.

- **Dress appropriately.** Think in advance about what your audience expects.

- **Invite response during your presentation.** Leave time for questions at the end.

- **Add a bit of humor.** Humor can be tricky, especially if you don't know your audience well. But if you can get your audience to laugh, they will be on your side. Remember to smile.

- **Slow down.** When you are nervous, you tend to go too fast. Stop and breathe. Let your audience take in what's on your slides.

- **Proofread carefully.** A glaring spelling error can destroy your credibility.

- **Be consistent.** If you randomly capitalize words or insert punctuation, your audience will be distracted.

- **Pay attention to the timing of your slides.** Stay in sync with your slides. Don't leave a slide up when you are talking about something else.

- **Finish on time or earlier.** Your audience will be grateful.

WRITE NOW

Moving across media

Convert a paper you have written into a presentation using visuals. Presentation software can help you create the visuals.

Think about your main points and how to support each point with facts, statistics, or other evidence. Think too about how to engage your audience at the beginning. Perhaps you will need to find a vivid example or anecdote to get your audience interested.

Avoid making the common mistake of putting too much text on your slides. Cutting and pasting from your written text often produces a dull, wordy presentation.

17 Writing for Online Courses

When you enroll in a course with an online component, your participation and engagement are the keys to your success.

Chapter Overview

▶ **Keep track of online coursework**
(see p. 549)

▶ **Participate in online discussions**
(see p. 550)

▶ **Manage online writing**
(see p. 551)

Keep Track of Online Coursework

You will excel in online courses if you communicate well, stay motivated, and produce outstanding work. If you miss assignments, you can fall behind in a hurry.

Use courseware

Many courses—not just those that meet only online—now offer online tools and content that are located within a course management system (such as Blackboard, Moodle, or Sakai). Whatever course management system your school uses, take advantage early in the semester of tutorials and help documents that guide you in how to e-mail, post to a discussion, or submit an assignment for your course.

Plan your time

Even more than in traditional face-to-face-classes, online courses require self-discipline and strong organization to keep your work on track. At the beginning of the term, use the course syllabus or online course schedule to create your own detailed schedule to be sure you keep up with reading and assignments.

Then stick to the schedule you have outlined. Know the course policy for late assignments, for written work, and other participation. The sooner you start the work for the course the better. As in any other class, keeping up with reading and due dates is essential.

WRITE NOW

Create a blog

Blogs assigned for courses sometimes allow students a great deal of freedom to select their subject matter and sometimes course blogs are on an assigned topic, such as responses to the readings. Your school may have a Web site where you can publish a blog, or you can use one of the many free sites such as these:

- Blogger: www.blogger.com
- edublogs: http://edublogs.org/
- WordPress: http://wordpress.org/

Great bloggers who attract many readers share four qualities. They write with a lively, personal voice. They are well informed. They are honest about what they know and don't know. And they write their blog entries to initiate conversations, not to have the last word on a subject. Keep these points in mind:

- Develop a personal voice that conveys your personality.
- Offer something new. If you don't have anything new, then point readers to the interesting writing of others.
- Do your homework. Let your readers know the sources of your information.
- Keep it short. If you have a lot to say about different subjects, write more than one entry.
- Provide relevant links.
- Remember that informal writing is not sloppy, error-filled writing.

Watch the Animation on Online Courses at mycomplab.com

Participate in Online Discussions

Discussion board posts are frequent assignments in writing classes. Usually they are short essays, no more than 300 words. Sources of any information still need to be cited.

When you are posting the first entry in a discussion thread, give your post a clear, specific subject line that lets readers know what you are writing before they open it. For new or response posts, offer the context (the assignment or reading name) and other background.

Discussion board posts are often similar to blogs, but they are typically written as a response to a question or posting by the instructor. The assignment for this post was to find and analyze an example of a visual metaphor.

Thread: "Use Only What You Need": The Denver Water Conservation Campaign
Author: Chrissy Yao
Posted Date: March 1, 2010 1:12 PM

In 2006, Denver Water, the city's oldest utility, launched a ten-year conservation plan based on using water efficiently ("Conservation"). Denver Water teamed up with the Sukle Advertising firm and produced the "Use Only What You Need Campaign" to help alleviate the water crisis that the city was enduring (Samuel). The campaign uses billboard advertising, magazine ads, and even stripped-down cars to impart messages of water conservation and efficiency.

Yao describes the ad campaign that uses the partial bus bench.

Clever visual metaphors are at the heart of the campaign. One example is a park bench with available seating only for one individual. The words, "USE ONLY WHAT YOU NEED," are stenciled in on the back of the bench. The bench, which can actually be used for sitting, conveys the idea that if only one person were using the bench, that person would only need a small area to sit on, not the whole thing. The bench makes concrete the concept of water conservation.

Yao analyzes the visual metaphor.

The innovative ad campaign that uses objects in addition to traditional advertising has proven successful. The simplicity and minimalist style of the ads made a convincing argument about using resources sparingly. The average water consumption of Denver dropped between 18% and 21% annually from 2006 to 2009.

Works Cited
"Conservation." *Denver Water*. Denver Water, 2010. Web. 23 Feb. 2010.

Samuel, Frederick. "Denver Water." *Ad Goodness*. N.p., 16 Nov. 2006.
    Web. 24 Feb. 2010.

Manage Online Writing

As in any course, be sure you back up files as a regular part of your routine to avoid losing your work.

Stay organized

In most online courses that you will be saving and then exchanging drafts with classmates. To avoid problems with lost drafts or confusing file names, develop a system for organizing drafts for each course. Set up a system of folders with one for your drafts, one for those from classmates and save files in these separate folders.

Give each of your drafts a name that includes specifics of the assignment and, if you plan to share it with others, your name (Sheri Harrison Reflection Draft 1). Your instructor may require or suggest a system for you. Including your name in the draft's file name helps your instructor and classmates keep track; also, put dates in the file names if you are writing multiple drafts.

Observe netiquette

In online courses your discussion posts, wiki entries, and other written work speak for and create an impression of you. Follow commonsense rules of netiquette.

- **Remember your classmates are people like you.** Address them by name if possible, and sign your post with your name. Don't say things online that you would not say to a classmate face-to-face.

- **Be aware of tone.** Often sarcasm and attempts at humor come off poorly when you are having a discussion online.

- **Be a forgiving reader.** You don't need to point out every minor error. If you feel strongly about a mistake, send the writer a private e-mail rather than addressing the entire class.

- **Keep the discussion civil.** Often a reply like "what a stupid idea" leads to a flame war with name calling, and the possibility of exploring an issue ends.

- **Don't spam your classmates.** Refrain from sending off-topic messages to everyone. Your classmates have enough to sort through without having to deal with frivolous messages.

- **Make yourself credible.** Check for punctuation, grammar, and spelling errors before you post.

WRITE NOW
Review drafts online

When you are reviewing drafts online, be sure you know what formats your instructor recommends and your classmates can read and open. After you comment on another student's draft, remember to change the file name.

See page 54 for a guide for responding to others' work.

18 Working as a Team

The better you understand how to write effectively with others, the more enjoyable and the more productive the process will be for you.

Chapter Overview

▶ **Organize a team**
(see p. 553)

▶ **Brainstorm as a team**
(see p. 554)

▶ **Work as a team**
(see p. 555)

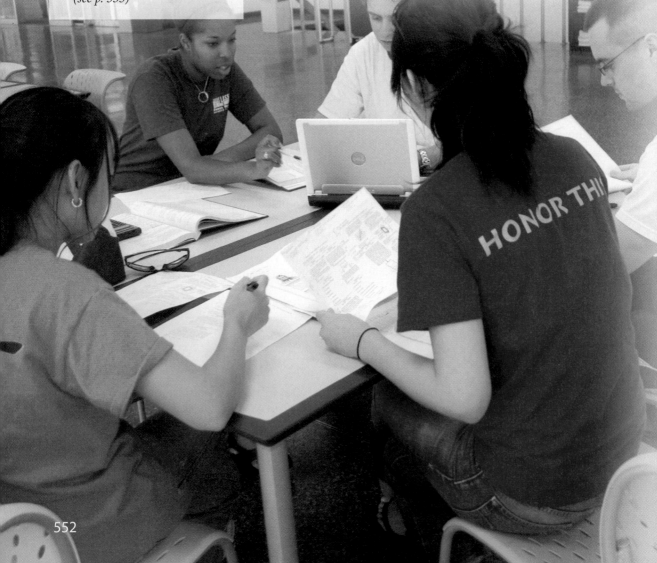

Organize a Team

Unlike sports teams where a coach is in charge, writing team members often have to organize themselves.

Analyze the assignment
- Identify what exactly you are being asked to do.
- Write down the goals as specifically as you can and discuss them as a team.
- Determine which tasks are required to meet those goals. Be as detailed as you can. Write down the tasks and arrange them in the order they need to be completed.

Make a work plan
- Make a time line. List the dates when specific tasks need to be completed and distribute it to all team members. Charts are useful tools for keeping track of progress.
- Assign tasks to all team members. Find out if anyone possesses additional skills that could be helpful to the team.

Keep goals in mind
- Revisit the team's goals often. To succeed, each team member must keep in mind what the team aims to accomplish.
- Communicate often. Most writing teams will not have an assigned leader. Each team member shares responsibility.

What makes a good team?

In sports, in the workplace, and in everyday life, successful teams have well-defined goals and work together to achieve these goals. Successful teams communicate well, make good decisions together, act quickly on their decisions, and continuously evaluate their progress. Successful teams achieve the right balance so that each team member can contribute.

WRITE NOW

Plan an oral presentation as a team

Much of the work in organizations, companies, and laboratories is done by teams of people. Frequently these teams give in-progress and summary oral presentations to report what they have accomplished.

- Determine the goals of the presentation and how long the presentation should last.
- Decide if visuals would be useful, especially if you are presenting statistical data.
- Assign each team member a role in the presentation.
- Find time to rehearse as a team to make sure the presentation meets the goals and time limit.

Brainstorm as a Team

Teams have the potential to generate many more ideas than individuals can, and teams bring the full experience of everyone to the issue or problem.

Online tools: Chat sessions, discussion boards, wikis, and collaborative documents all can be used for brainstorming. Online tools have the advantage of bringing together people who may not be able to meet in person.

Face-to-face tools: Team brainstorming sessions draw energy from the immediacy of the group. Simple tools like whiteboards, flipcharts, and sticky notes help team members to visualize problems and ideas.

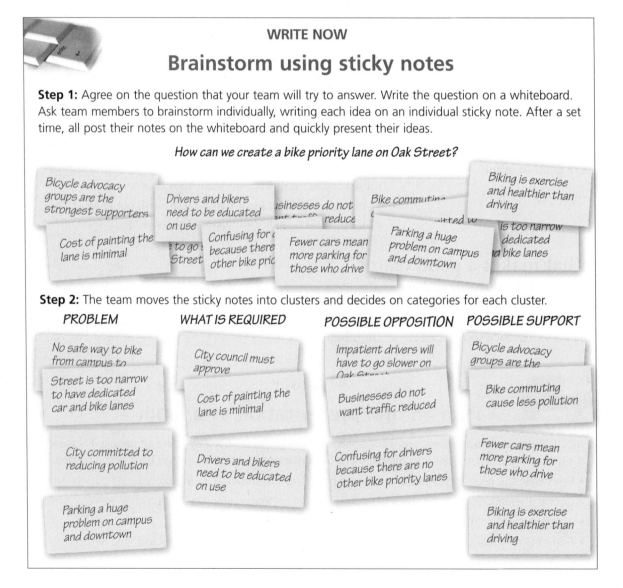

WRITE NOW

Brainstorm using sticky notes

Step 1: Agree on the question that your team will try to answer. Write the question on a whiteboard. Ask team members to brainstorm individually, writing each idea on an individual sticky note. After a set time, all post their notes on the whiteboard and quickly present their ideas.

How can we create a bike priority lane on Oak Street?

- Bicycle advocacy groups are the strongest supporters
- Drivers and bikers need to be educated on use
- ...sinesses do not ...nt traffic reduce
- Bike commuting ...
- Biking is exercise and healthier than driving
- Cost of painting the lane is minimal
- Confusing for ... because there ... other bike pric...
- Fewer cars mean more parking for those who drive
- Parking a huge problem on campus and downtown
- is too narrow dedicated a bike lanes

Step 2: The team moves the sticky notes into clusters and decides on categories for each cluster.

PROBLEM
- No safe way to bike from campus to
- Street is too narrow to have dedicated car and bike lanes
- City committed to reducing pollution
- Parking a huge problem on campus and downtown

WHAT IS REQUIRED
- City council must approve
- Cost of painting the lane is minimal
- Drivers and bikers need to be educated on use

POSSIBLE OPPOSITION
- Impatient drivers will have to go slower on Oak Street
- Businesses do not want traffic reduced
- Confusing for drivers because there are no other bike priority lanes

POSSIBLE SUPPORT
- Bicycle advocacy groups are the
- Bike commuting cause less pollution
- Fewer cars mean more parking for those who drive
- Biking is exercise and healthier than driving

Work as a Team

Work closely together in creating and revising content. You'll enjoy writing more and you'll have the benefit of more ideas.

Carry out the plan

- Decide on a process for monitoring progress. Set up specific dates for review and assign team members to be responsible for reviewing work that has been done.
- When you have a complete draft, each team member should evaluate it by providing written comments.
- Meet to compare evaluations and decide on a plan for revising and adding content.
- After revising, arrange for one or more persons to review the project. Meet again to determine if additional changes are needed.

Be aware of team dynamics

Teamwork requires some flexibility. Different people have different styles and contribute in different ways. Keep talking to each other along the way.

- Deal with problems when they come up.
- If a team member is not participating, find out why.
- If team members have different ideas about what needs to be done, find time to meet so that the team can reach an agreement.
- Get the team together if you are not meeting the deadlines you established in the work plan and, if necessary, devise a new plan.

WRITE NOW

What to do when problems arise

Working together in a team is most often a rewarding experience, but you need to know how to deal with problems when they arise. Generally it is better to make an effort to resolve problems within the team before asking your instructor to intervene. In a group of four or five students, discuss how you might respond as a group to a team member who

1. is "missing in action,"

2. doesn't come prepared,

3. doesn't answer e-mail,

4. is disrespectful to others,

5. refuses to allow anyone to critique or revise his or her work.

 Watch the Video on Group Dynamics at mycomplab.com **555**